EPISODE III

SCENE 2

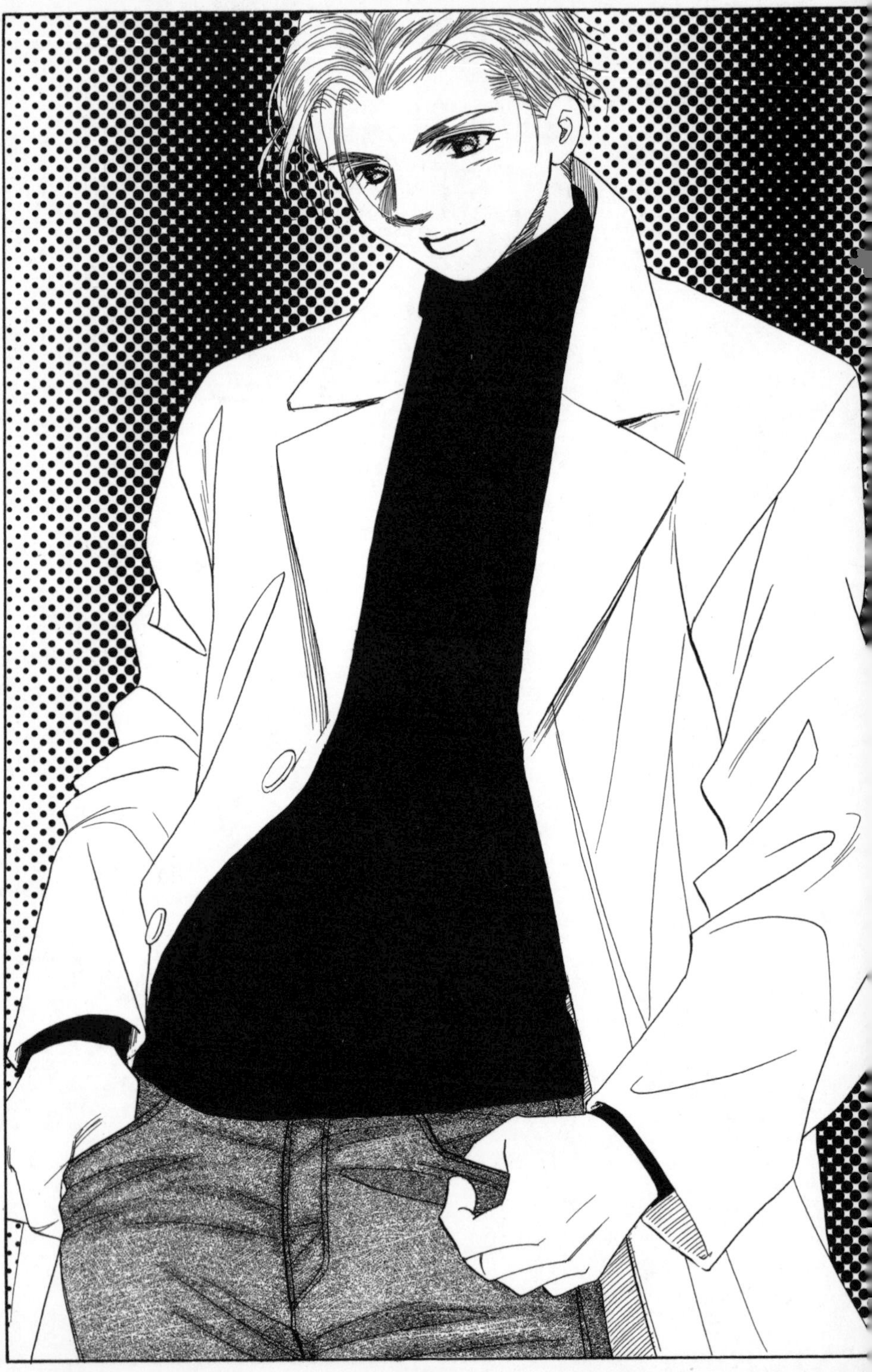

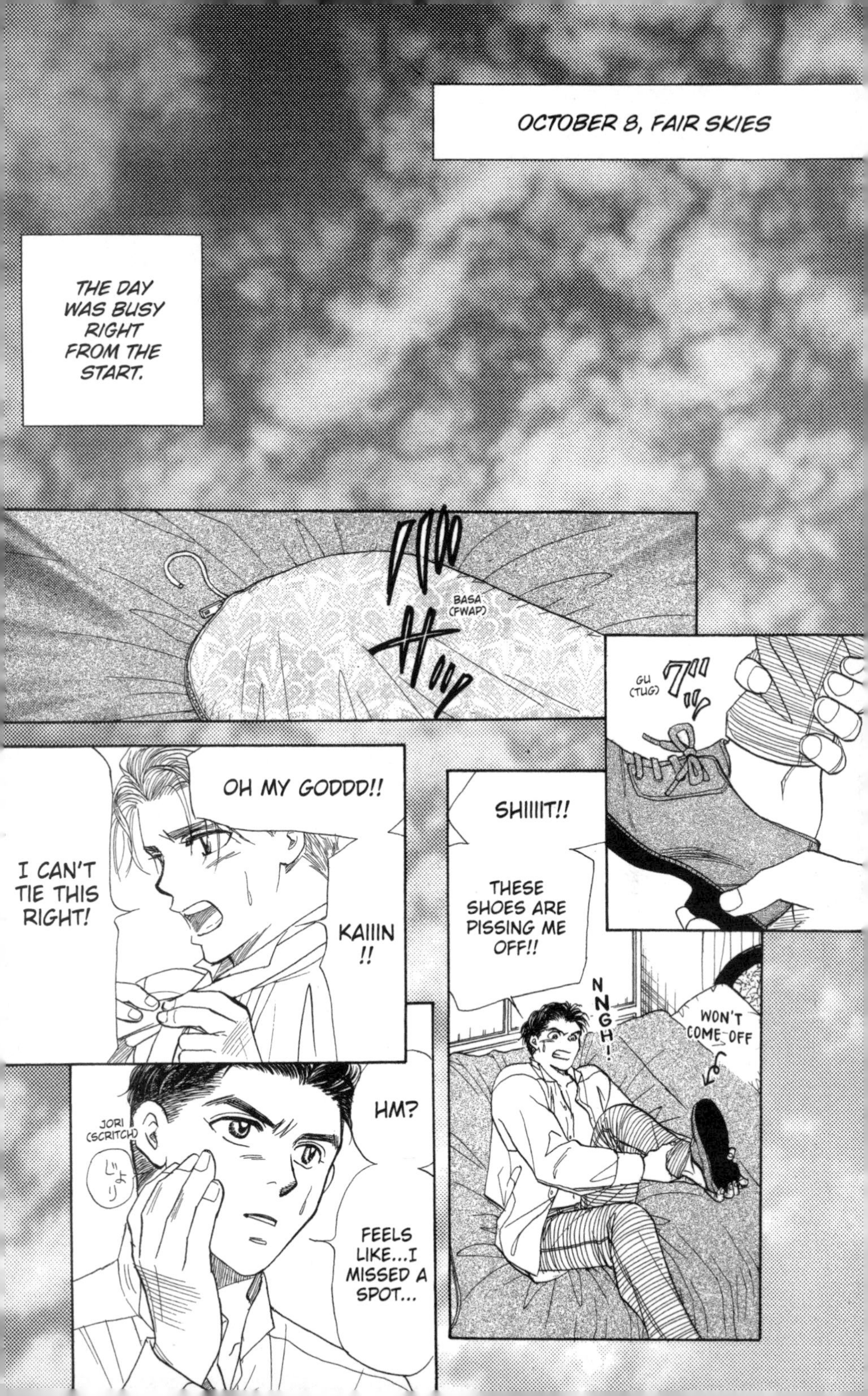
OCTOBER 8, FAIR SKIES
THE DAY WAS BUSY RIGHT FROM THE START.
BASA (PWAP)
GU (TUG)
SHIIIIT!!
THESE SHOES ARE PISSING ME OFF!!
NNGH!
WON'T COME OFF
OH MY GODDD!!
I CAN'T TIE THIS RIGHT!
KAIIIN!!
HM?
JORI (SCRITCH)
FEELS LIKE...I MISSED A SPOT...

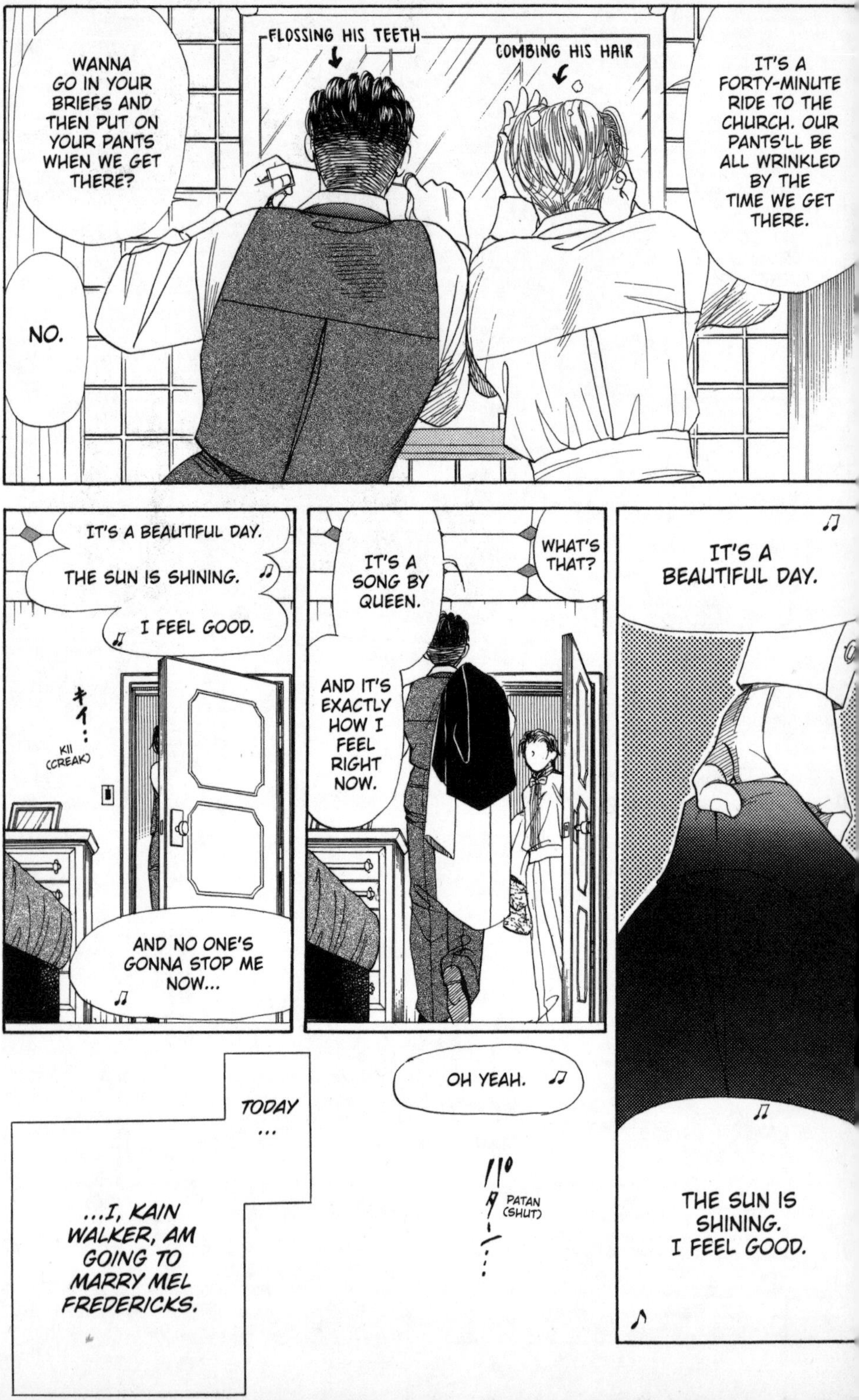

IT'S A FORTY-MINUTE RIDE TO THE CHURCH. OUR PANTS'LL BE ALL WRINKLED BY THE TIME WE GET THERE.
COMBING HIS HAIR
FLOSSING HIS TEETH
WANNA GO IN YOUR BRIEFS AND THEN PUT ON YOUR PANTS WHEN WE GET THERE?
NO.
IT'S A BEAUTIFUL DAY.
THE SUN IS SHINING. I FEEL GOOD.
WHAT'S THAT?
IT'S A SONG BY QUEEN.
AND IT'S EXACTLY HOW I FEEL RIGHT NOW.
IT'S A BEAUTIFUL DAY. THE SUN IS SHINING. I FEEL GOOD.
キイ…
KII (CREAK)
AND NO ONE'S GONNA STOP ME NOW...
OH YEAH.
パタン…
PATAN (SHUT)
TODAY...
...I, KAIN WALKER, AM GOING TO MARRY MEL FREDERICKS.

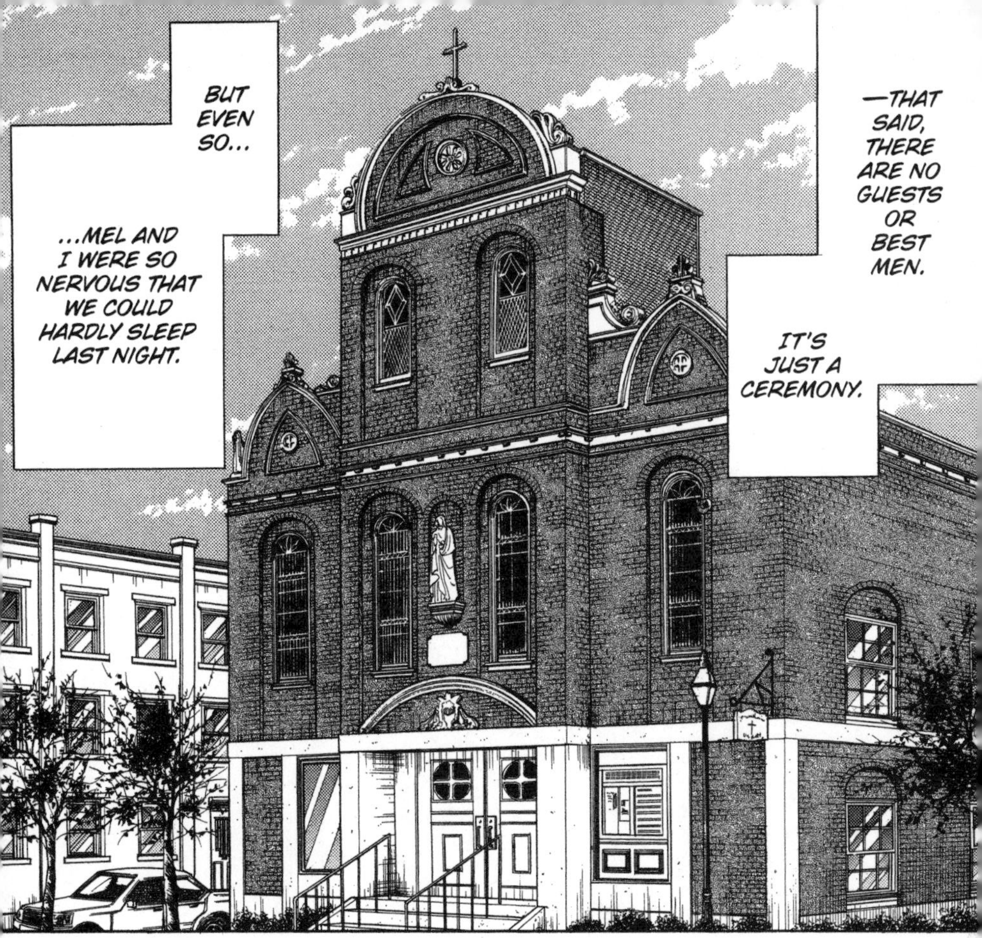
—THAT SAID, THERE ARE NO GUESTS OR BEST MEN.
IT'S JUST A CEREMONY.
BUT EVEN SO...
...MEL AND I WERE SO NERVOUS THAT WE COULD HARDLY SLEEP LAST NIGHT.

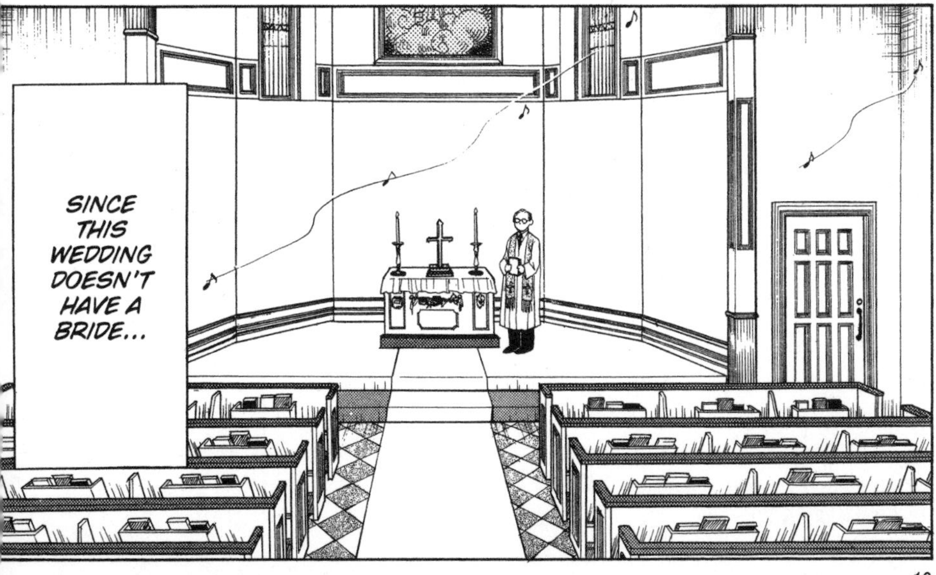
SINCE THIS WEDDING DOESN'T HAVE A BRIDE...

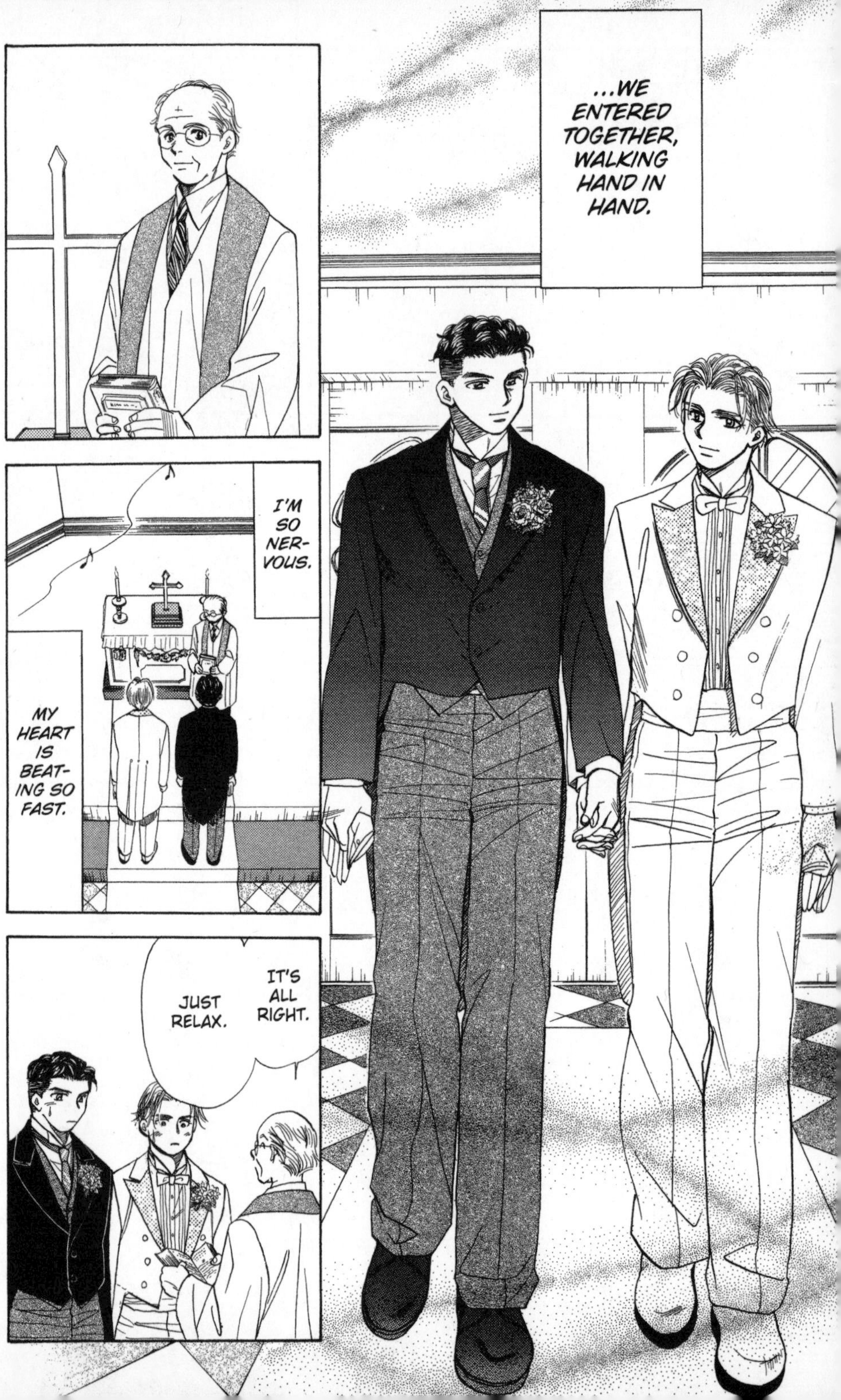
...WE ENTERED TOGETHER, WALKING HAND IN HAND.
I'M SO NER-VOUS.
MY HEART IS BEAT-ING SO FAST.
IT'S ALL RIGHT.
JUST RELAX.

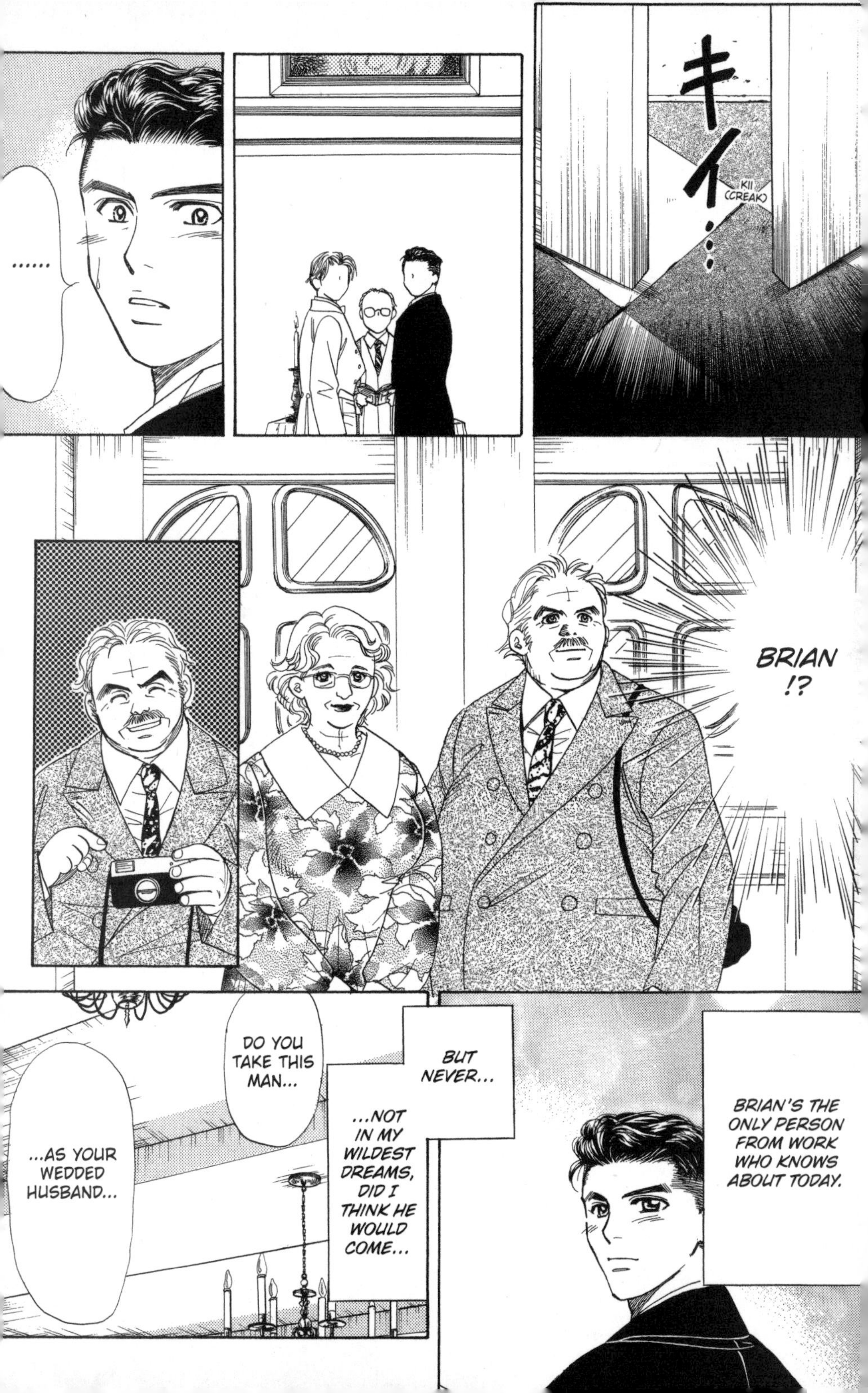
キイ…
KII (CREAK)
……
BRIAN !?
BRIAN'S THE ONLY PERSON FROM WORK WHO KNOWS ABOUT TODAY.
BUT NEVER…
DO YOU TAKE THIS MAN…
…NOT IN MY WILDEST DREAMS, DID I THINK HE WOULD COME…
…AS YOUR WEDDED HUSBAND…

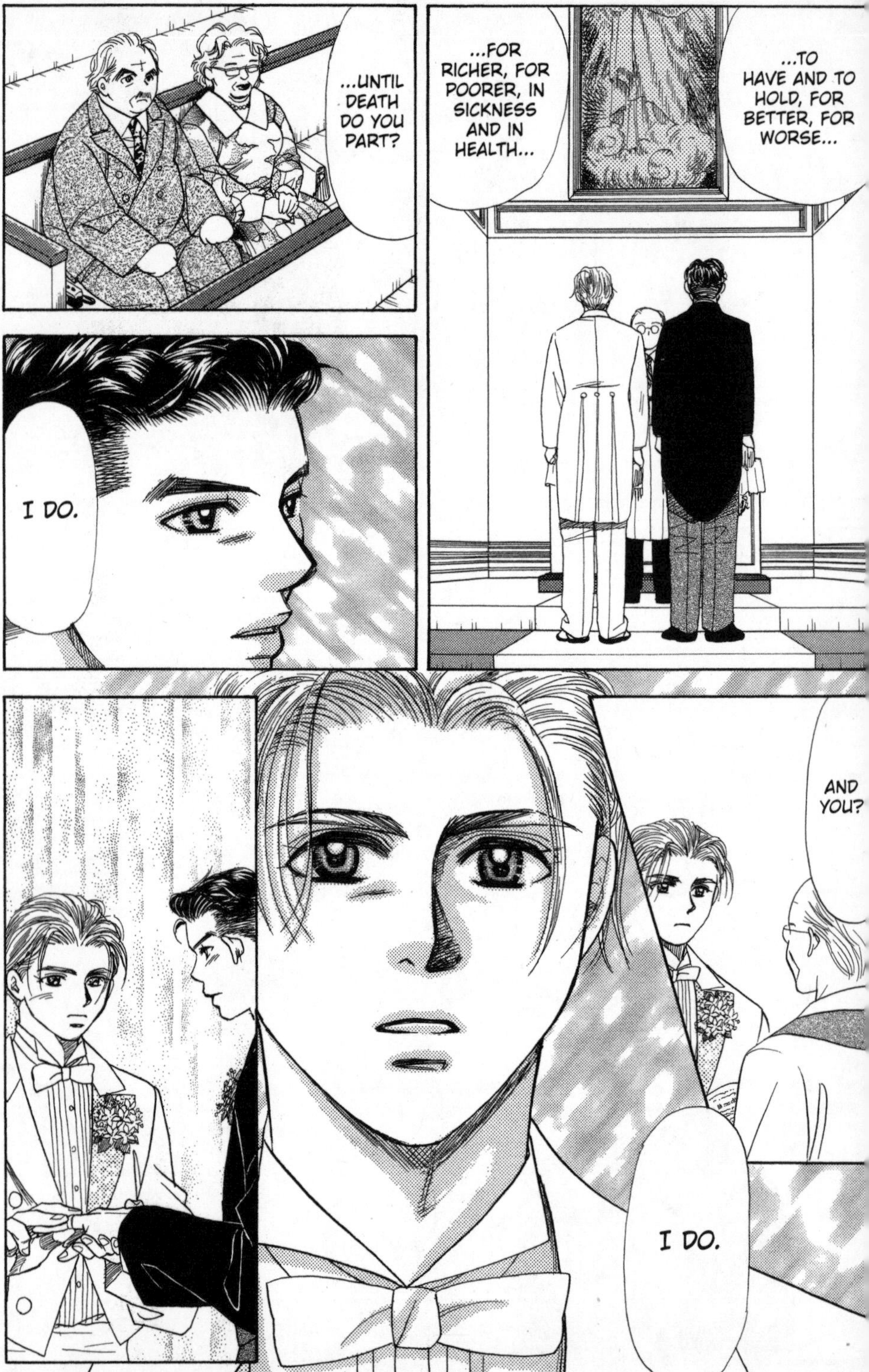
...TO HAVE AND TO HOLD, FOR BETTER, FOR WORSE...
...FOR RICHER, FOR POORER, IN SICKNESS AND IN HEALTH...
...UNTIL DEATH DO YOU PART?
I DO.
AND YOU?
I DO.

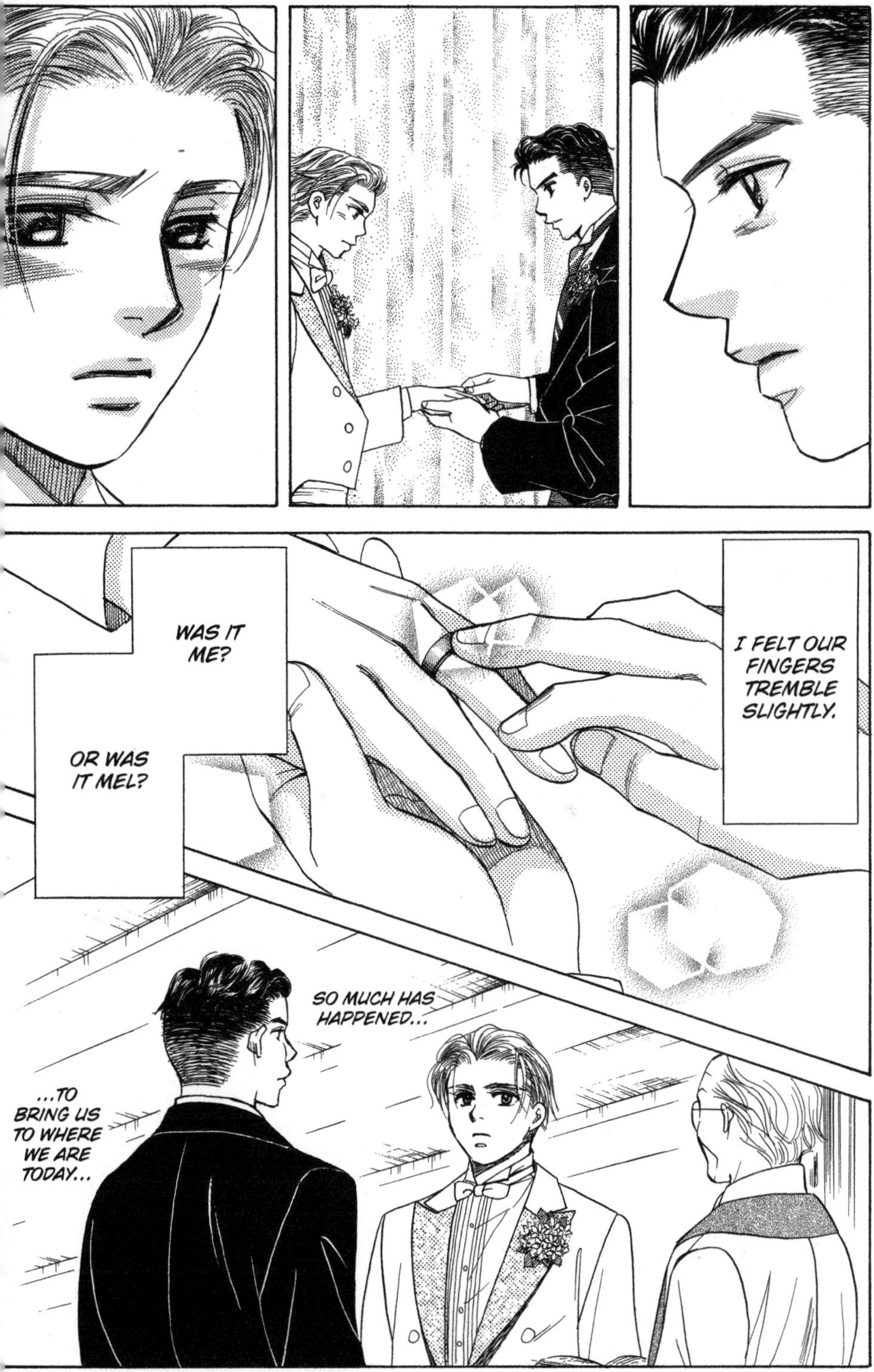
I FELT OUR FINGERS TREMBLE SLIGHTLY.
WAS IT ME?
OR WAS IT MEL?
SO MUCH HAS HAPPENED...
...TO BRING US TO WHERE WE ARE TODAY...

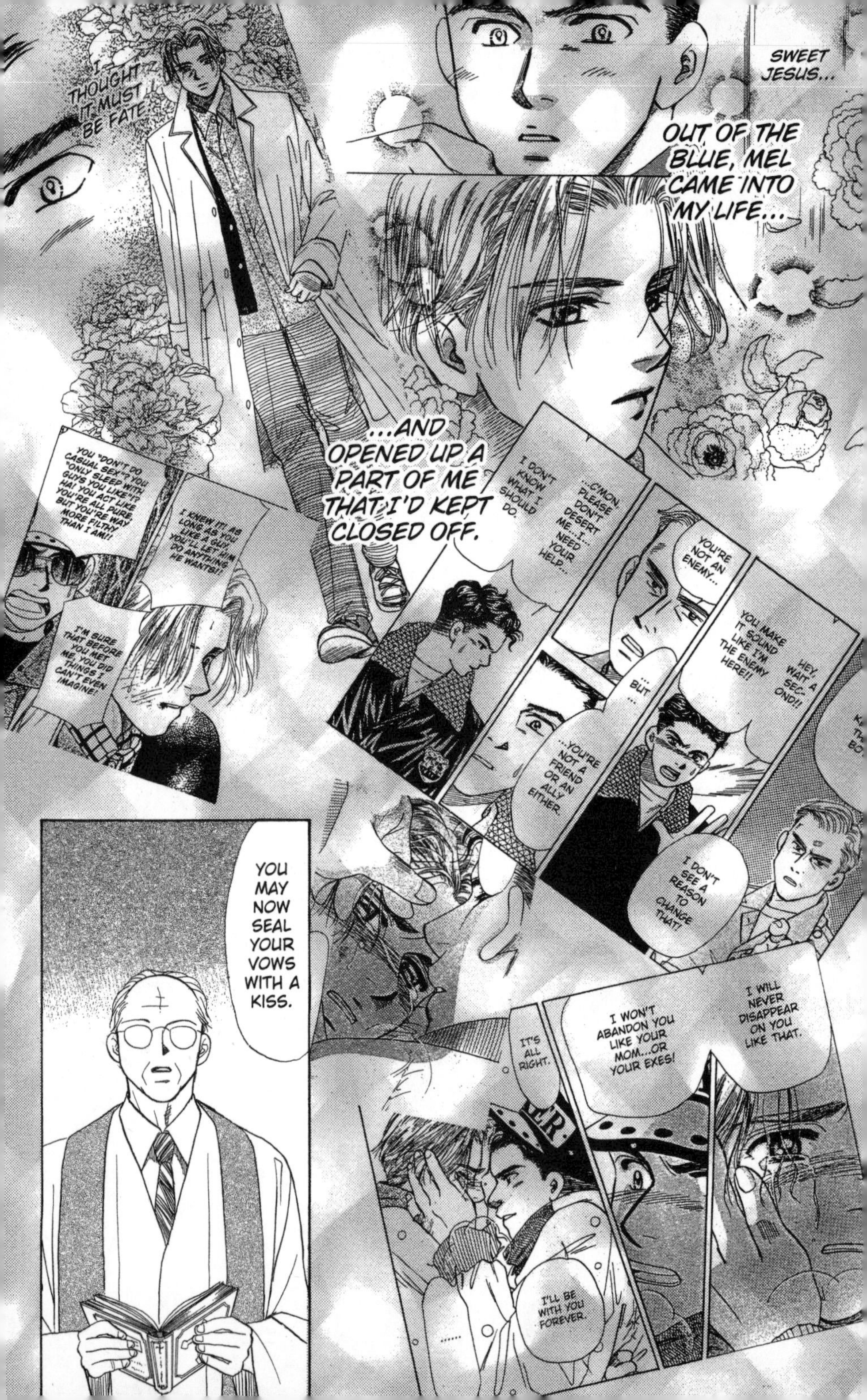
SWEET JESUS...
OUT OF THE BLUE, MEL CAME INTO MY LIFE...
I THOUGHT IT MUST BE FATE.
...AND OPENED UP A PART OF ME THAT I'D KEPT CLOSED OFF.
HEY, WAIT A SECOND!!
YOU MAKE IT SOUND LIKE I'M THE ENEMY HERE!!
YOU'RE NOT AN ENEMY...
...BUT...
...YOU'RE NOT A FRIEND OR AN ALLY EITHER.
I DON'T SEE A REASON TO CHANGE THAT!
...C'MON PLEASE DON'T DESERT ME...I NEED YOUR HELP...
I DON'T KNOW WHAT I SHOULD DO.
I KNEW IT AS LONG AS YOU LIKE A GUY, YOU'LL LET HIM DO ANYTHING HE WANTS!!
YOU "DON'T DO CASUAL SEX"? YOU "ONLY SLEEP WITH GUYS YOU LIKE"?! HA! YOU ACT LIKE YOU'RE ALL PURE, BUT YOU'RE WAY MORE FILTHY THAN I AM!!
I'M SURE THAT BEFORE YOU MET ME, YOU DID THINGS I CAN'T EVEN IMAGINE!
I WILL NEVER DISAPPEAR ON YOU LIKE THAT.
I WON'T ABANDON YOU LIKE YOUR MOM...OR YOUR EXES!
IT'S ALL RIGHT.
I'LL BE WITH YOU FOREVER.
......
YOU MAY NOW SEAL YOUR VOWS WITH A KISS.

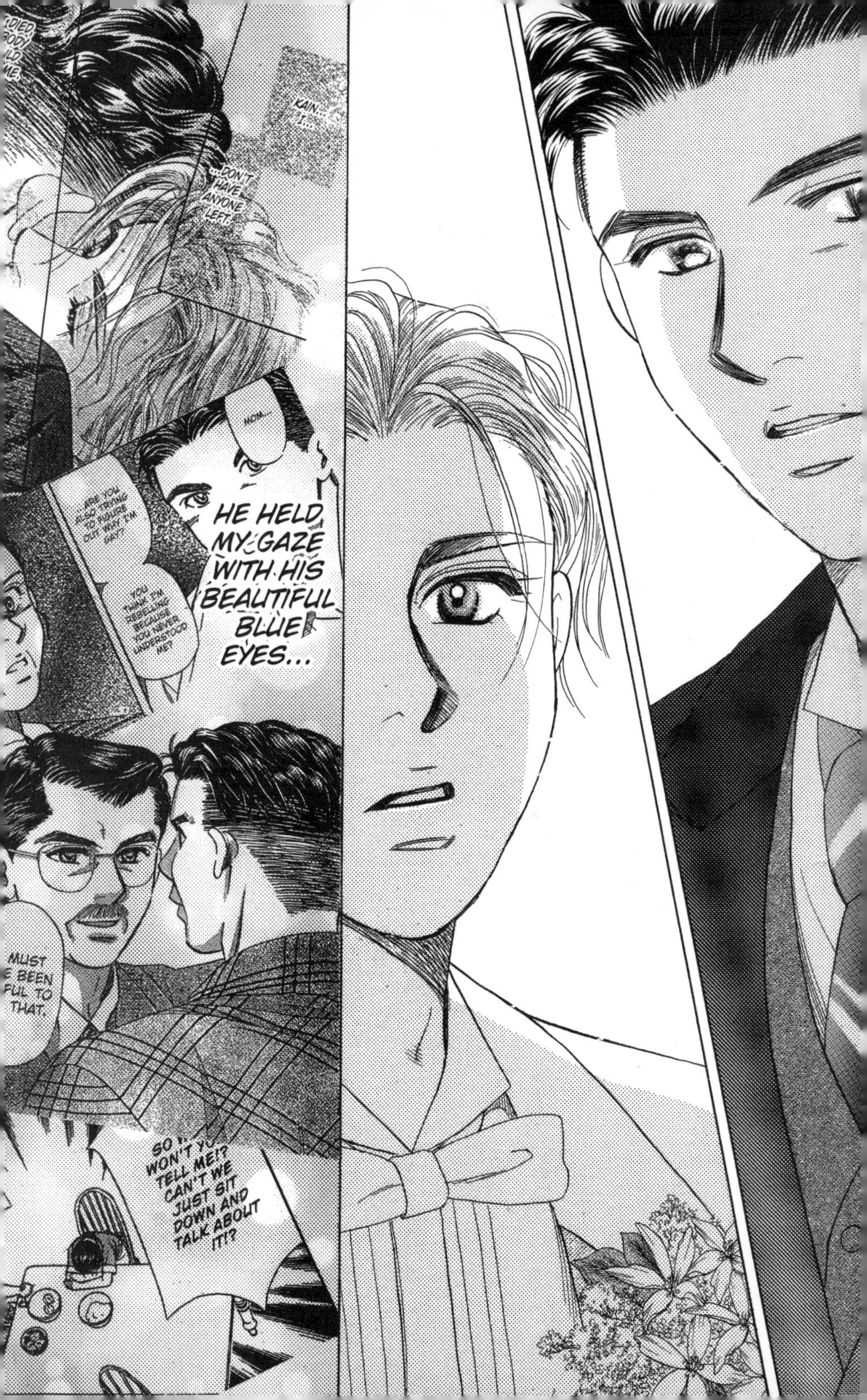
KAIN... I...
...DON'T HAVE ANYONE LEFT.
MOM...
...ARE YOU ALSO TRYING TO FIGURE OUT WHY I'M GAY?
YOU THINK I'M REBELLING BECAUSE YOU NEVER UNDERSTOOD ME?
HE HELD MY GAZE WITH HIS BEAUTIFUL BLUE EYES...
SO... WON'T YOU TELL ME!? CAN'T WE JUST SIT DOWN AND TALK ABOUT IT!?

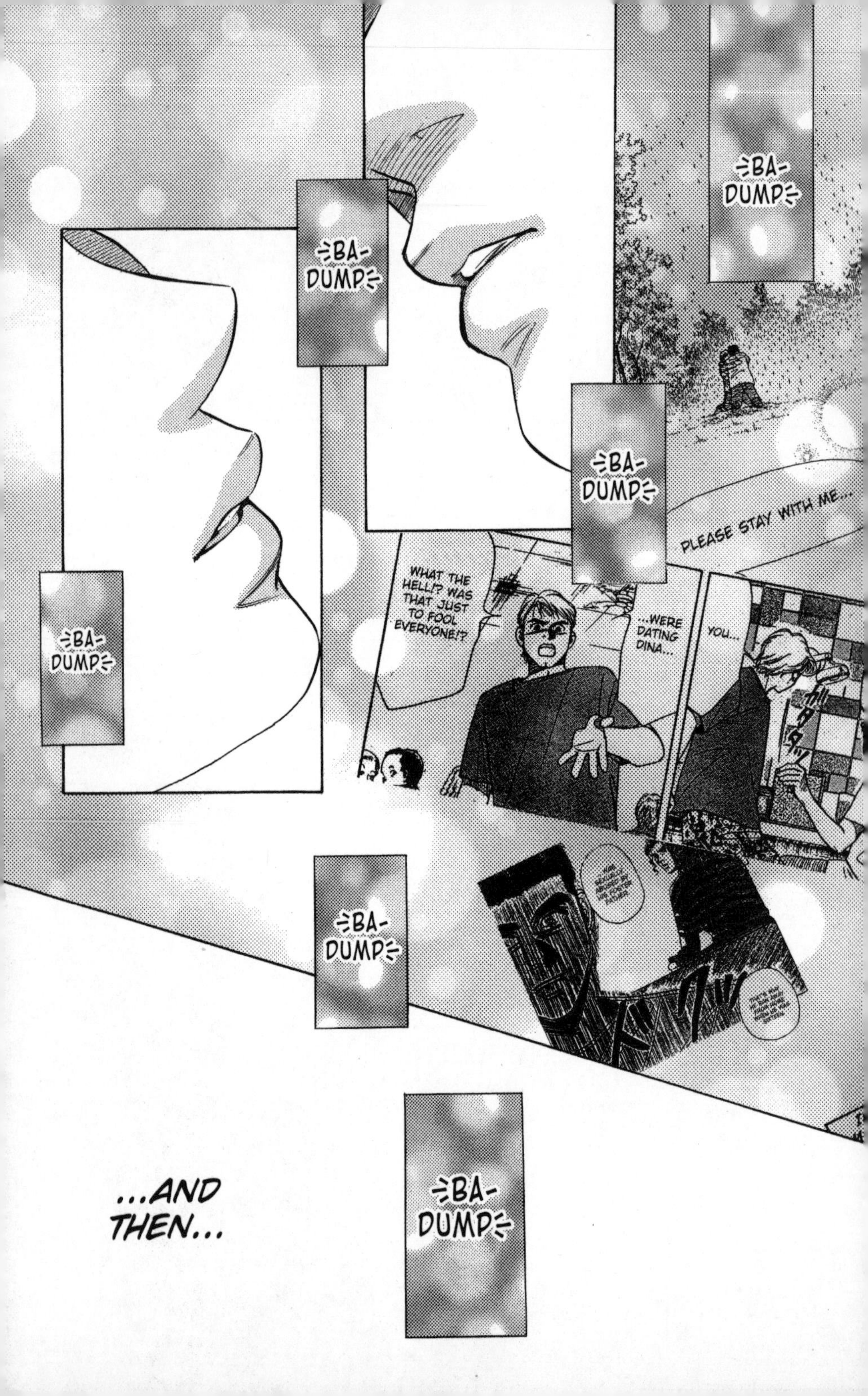
BA-DUMP
BA-DUMP
BA-DUMP
BA-DUMP
PLEASE STAY WITH ME...
YOU...
...WERE DATING DINA...
WHAT THE HELL!? WAS THAT JUST TO FOOL EVERYONE!?
...WAS SEXUALLY ABUSED BY HIS FOSTER FATHER
THAT'S WHY HE RAN AWAY FROM HOME WHEN HE WAS SIXTEEN
BA-DUMP
BA-DUMP
...AND THEN...

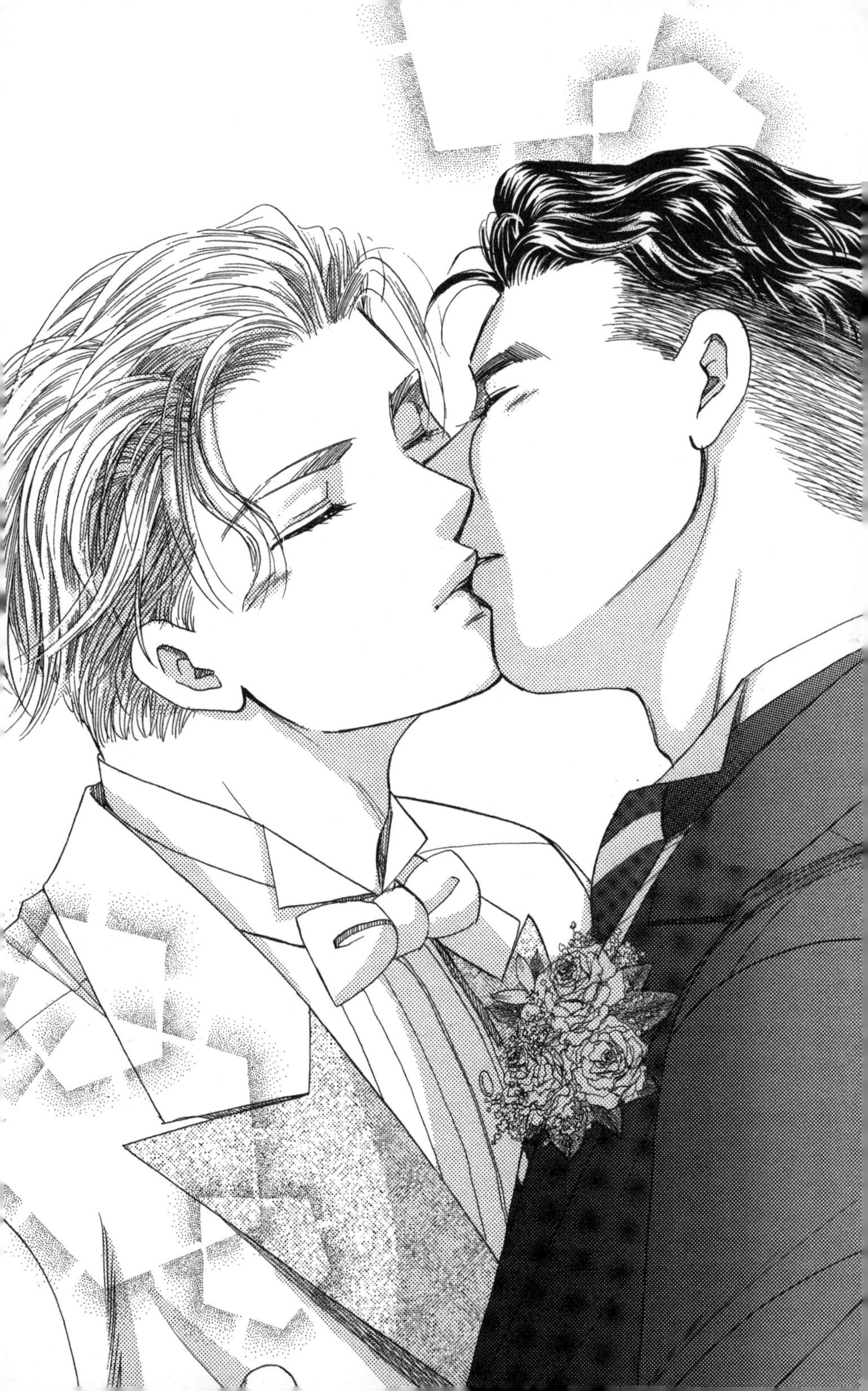

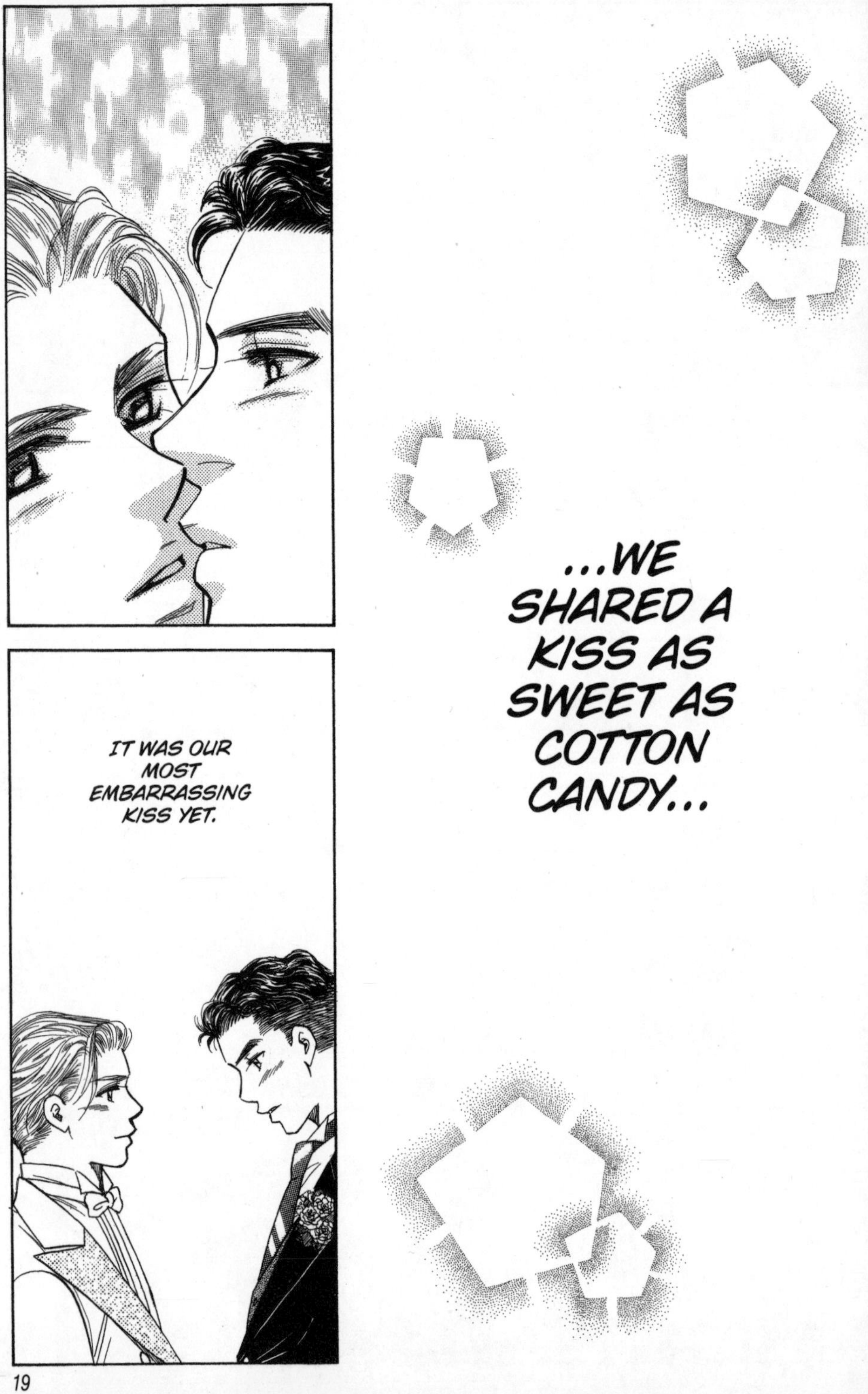
...WE SHARED A KISS AS SWEET AS COTTON CANDY...
IT WAS OUR MOST EMBARRASSING KISS YET.

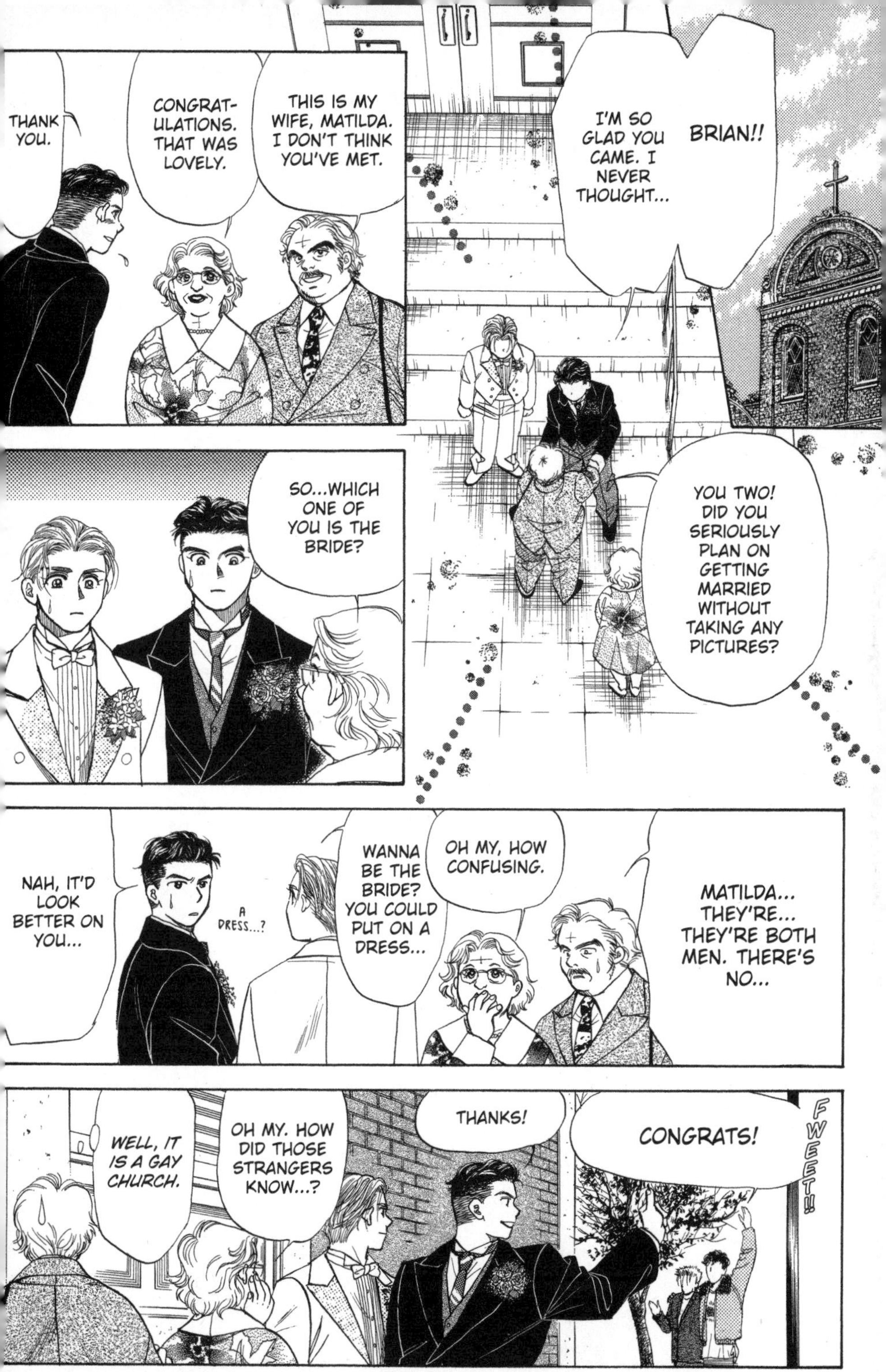
BRIAN!!
I'M SO GLAD YOU CAME. I NEVER THOUGHT...
YOU TWO! DID YOU SERIOUSLY PLAN ON GETTING MARRIED WITHOUT TAKING ANY PICTURES?
THIS IS MY WIFE, MATILDA. I DON'T THINK YOU'VE MET.
CONGRAT-ULATIONS. THAT WAS LOVELY.
THANK YOU.
SO...WHICH ONE OF YOU IS THE BRIDE?
MATILDA... THEY'RE... THEY'RE BOTH MEN. THERE'S NO...
OH MY, HOW CONFUSING.
WANNA BE THE BRIDE? YOU COULD PUT ON A DRESS...
A DRESS...?
NAH, IT'D LOOK BETTER ON YOU...
FWEET!!
CONGRATS!
THANKS!
OH MY. HOW DID THOSE STRANGERS KNOW...?
WELL, IT IS A GAY CHURCH.

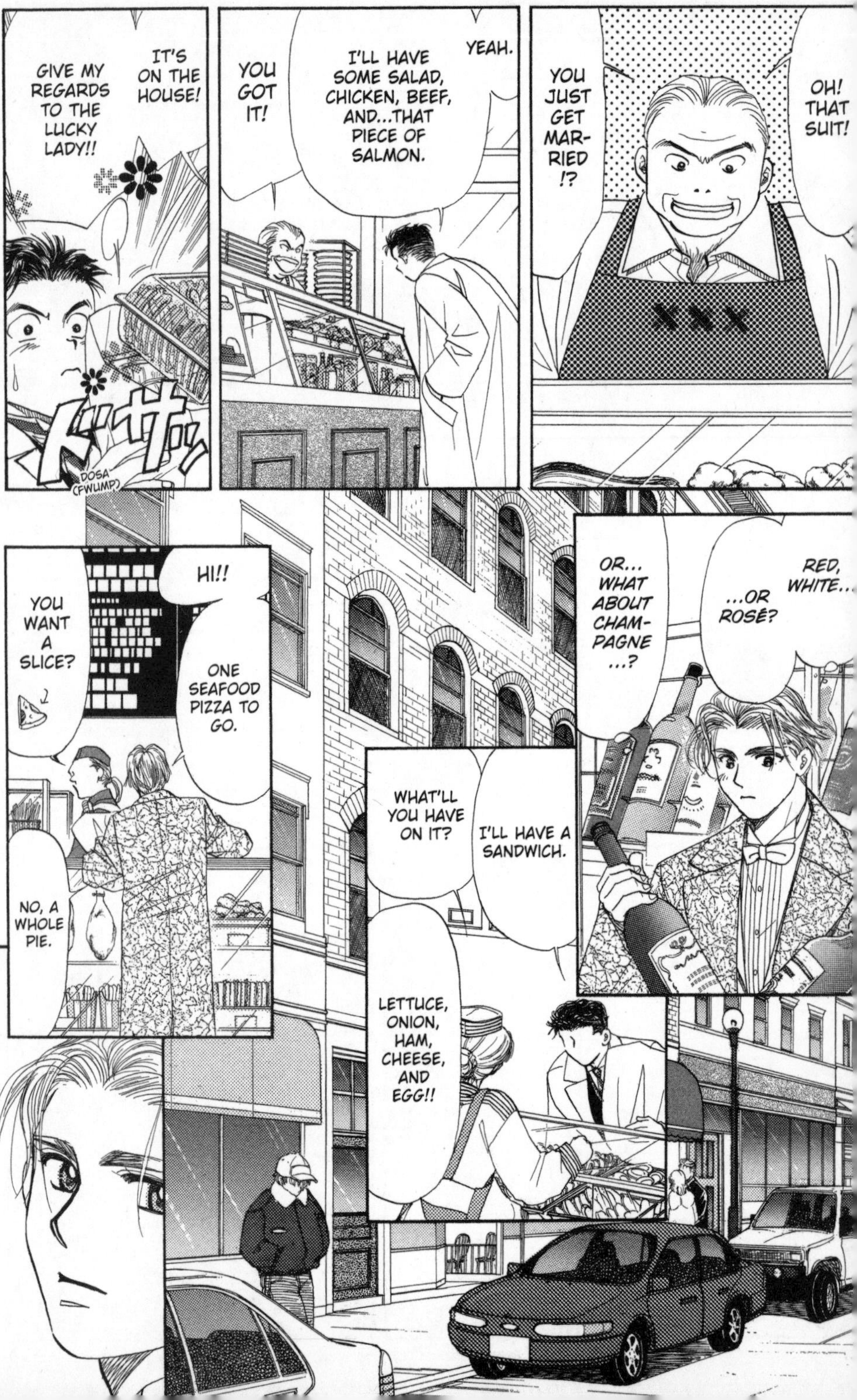
OH! THAT SUIT!
YOU JUST GET MAR-RIED!?
YEAH.
I'LL HAVE SOME SALAD, CHICKEN, BEEF, AND...THAT PIECE OF SALMON.
YOU GOT IT!
IT'S ON THE HOUSE!
GIVE MY REGARDS TO THE LUCKY LADY!!
DOSA (FWUMP)
RED, WHITE...
...OR ROSÉ?
OR... WHAT ABOUT CHAM-PAGNE...?
I'LL HAVE A SANDWICH.
WHAT'LL YOU HAVE ON IT?
LETTUCE, ONION, HAM, CHEESE, AND EGG!!
HI!!
ONE SEAFOOD PIZZA TO GO.
YOU WANT A SLICE?
NO, A WHOLE PIE.

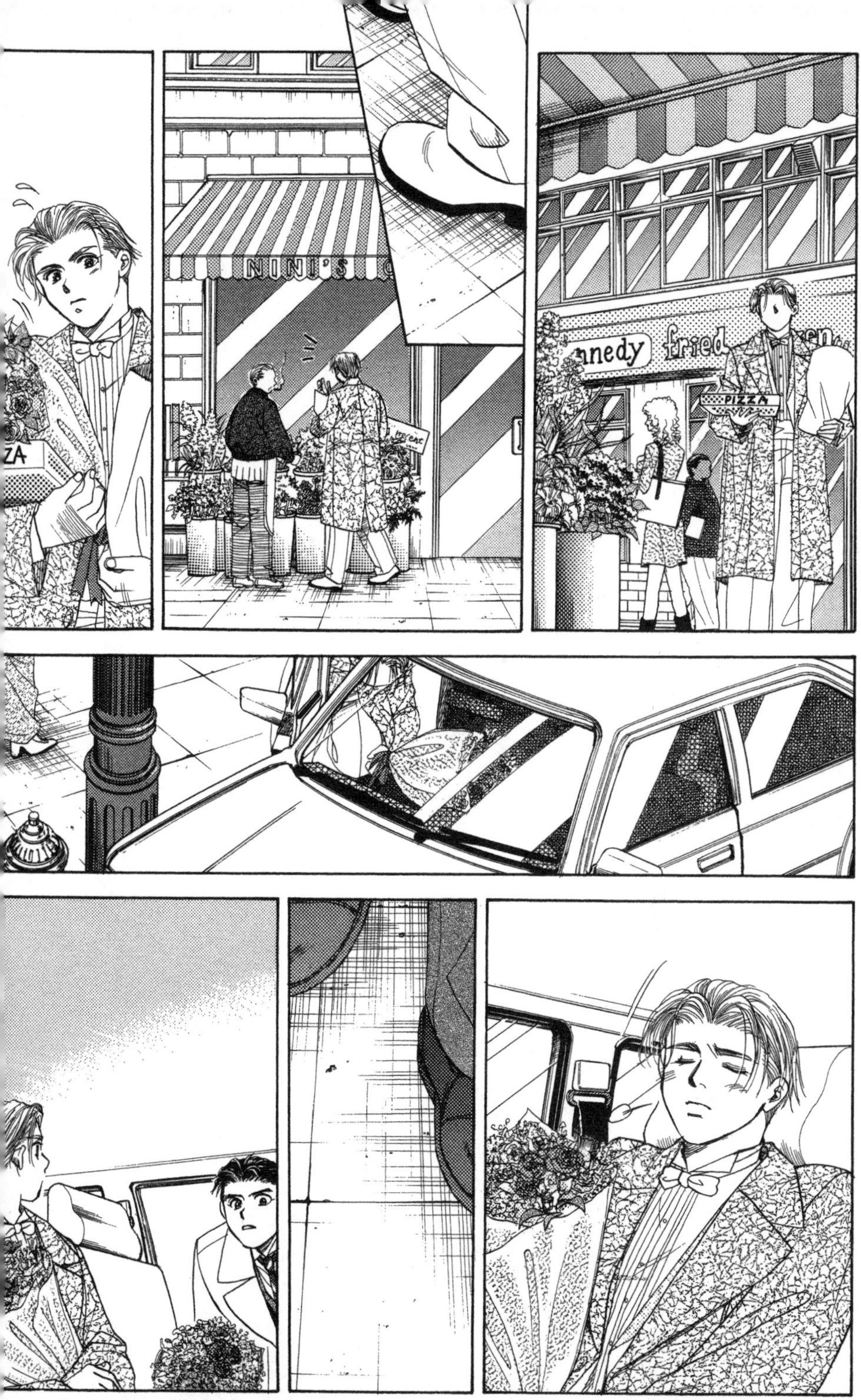
nnedy
fried
PIZZA
NINI'S
ZA

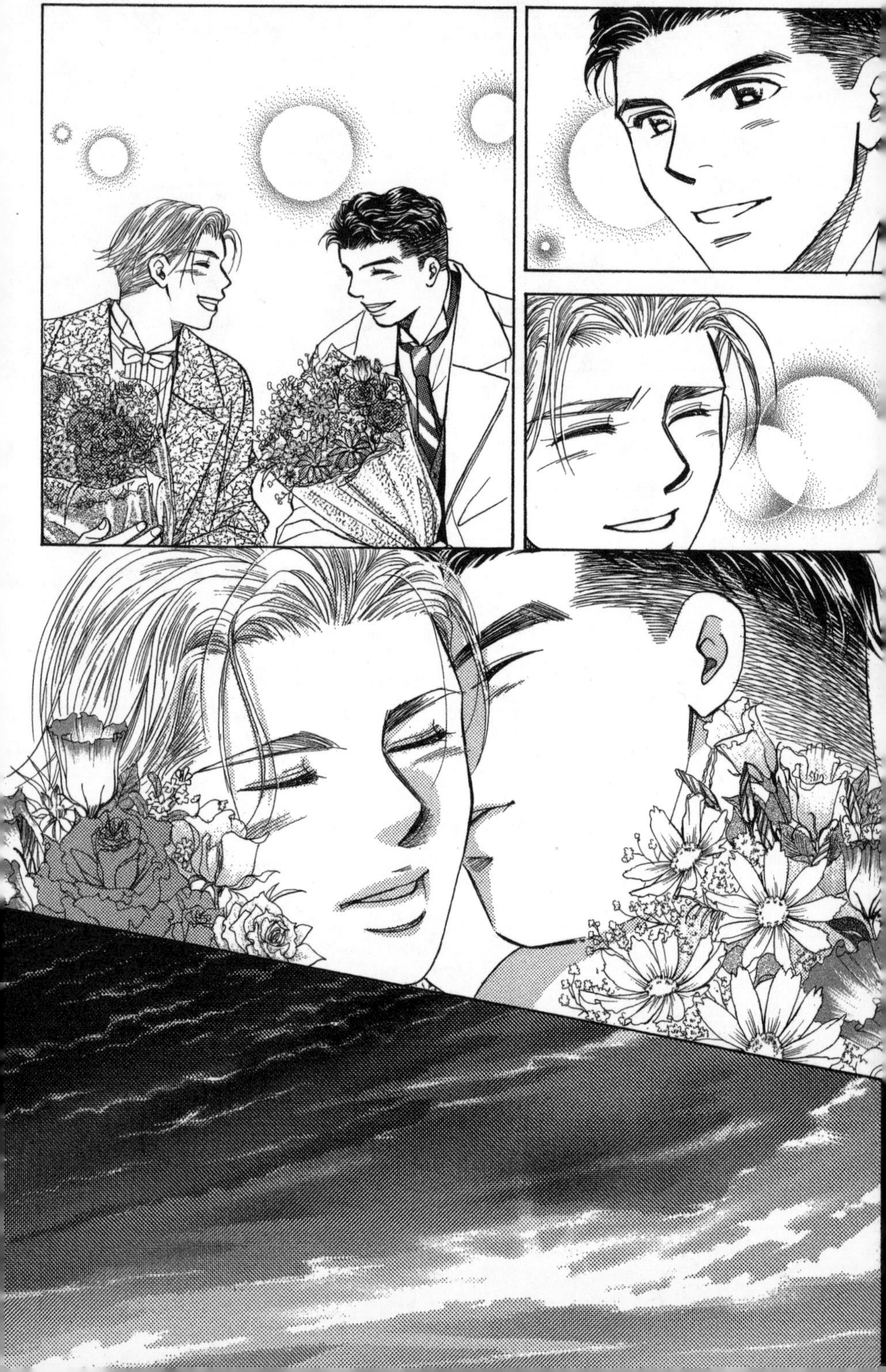

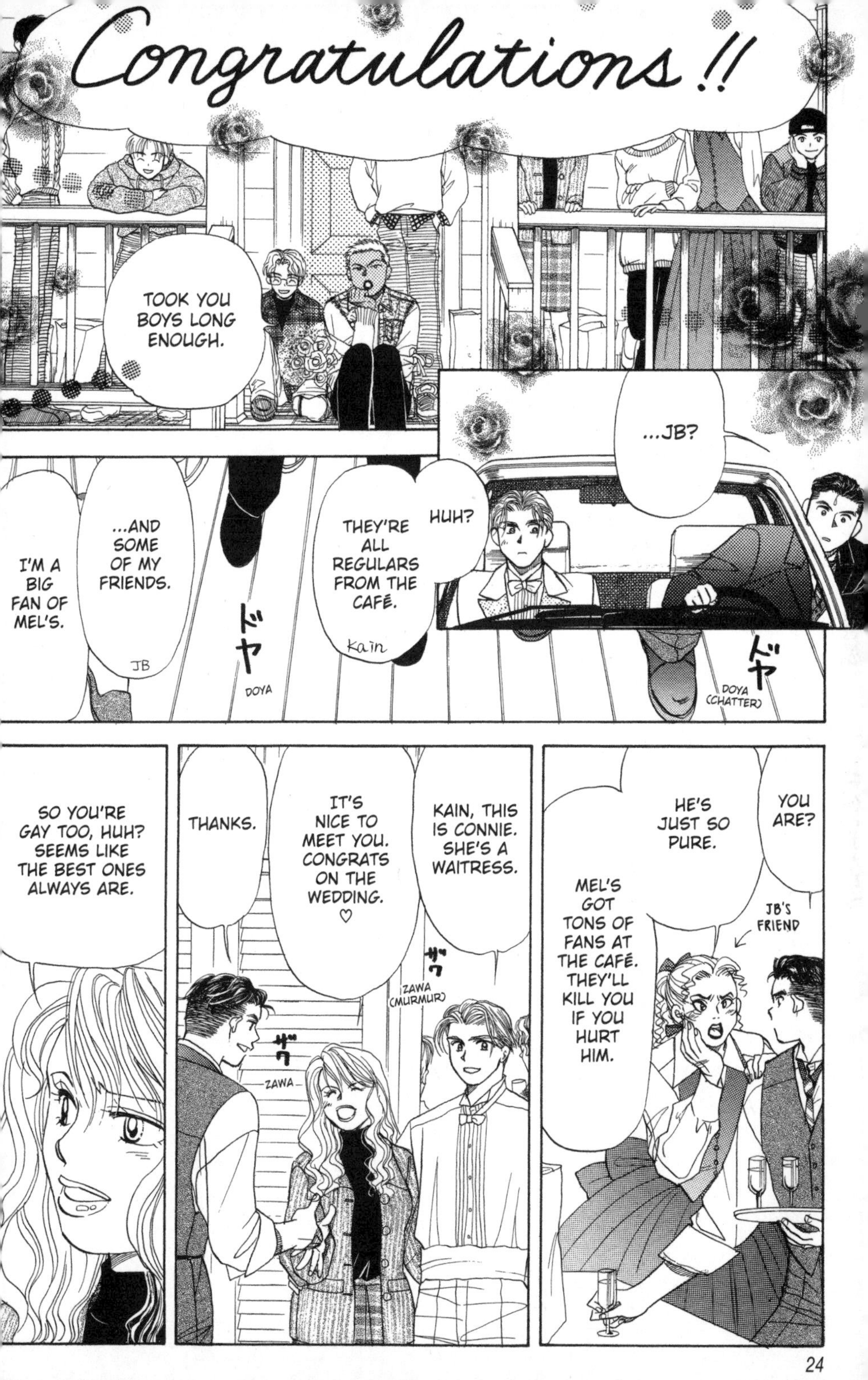
Congratulations!!
TOOK YOU BOYS LONG ENOUGH.
...JB?
HUH?
ドヤ
DOYA (CHATTER)
THEY'RE ALL REGULARS FROM THE CAFÉ.
Kain
...AND SOME OF MY FRIENDS.
JB
I'M A BIG FAN OF MEL'S.
ドヤ
DOYA
YOU ARE?
HE'S JUST SO PURE.
MEL'S GOT TONS OF FANS AT THE CAFÉ. THEY'LL KILL YOU IF YOU HURT HIM.
JB'S FRIEND
KAIN, THIS IS CONNIE. SHE'S A WAITRESS.
IT'S NICE TO MEET YOU. CONGRATS ON THE WEDDING. ♡
THANKS.
ザワ
ZAWA (MURMUR)
ザワ
ZAWA
SO YOU'RE GAY TOO, HUH? SEEMS LIKE THE BEST ONES ALWAYS ARE.

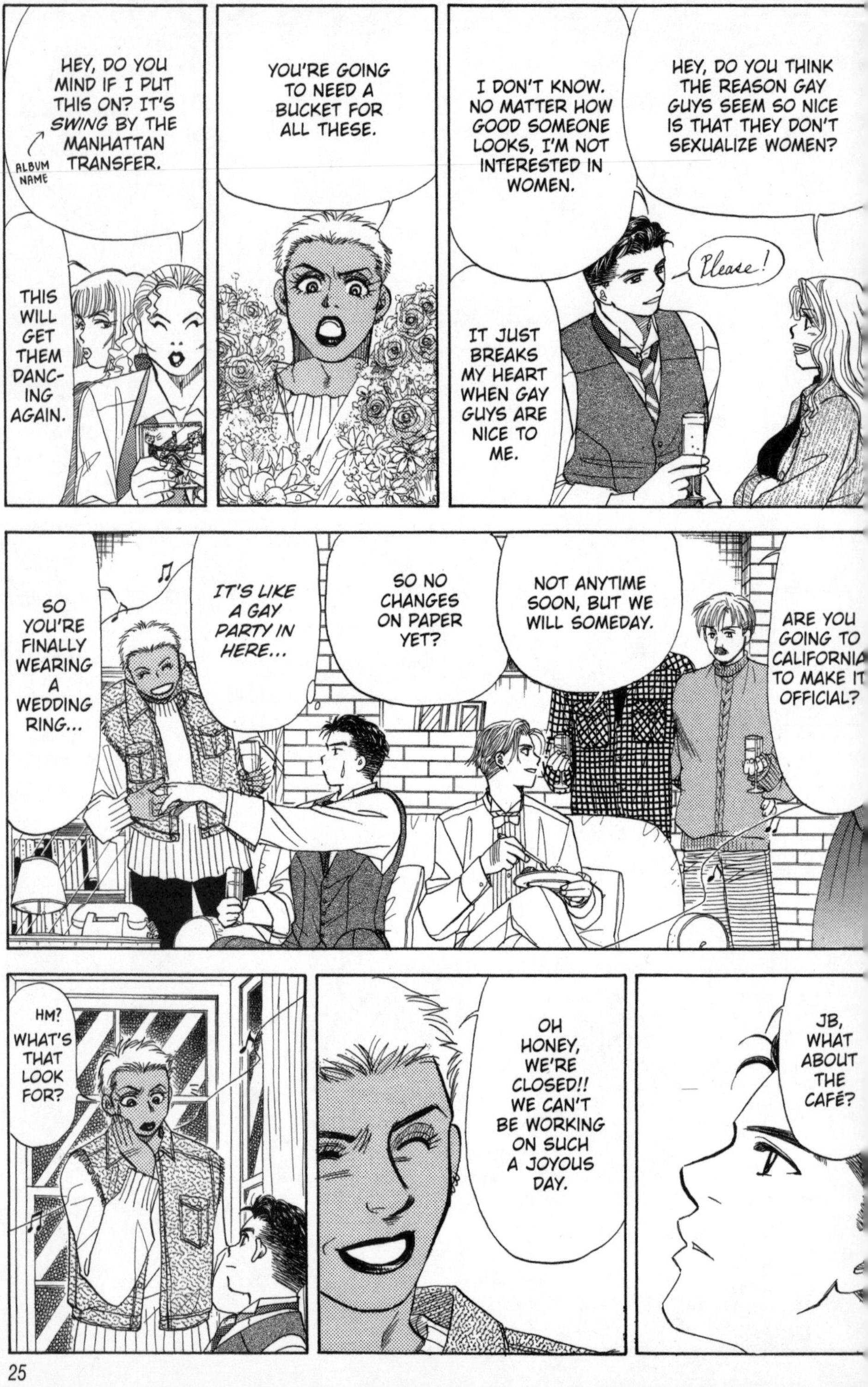
HEY, DO YOU THINK THE REASON GAY GUYS SEEM SO NICE IS THAT THEY DON'T SEXUALIZE WOMEN?
I DON'T KNOW. NO MATTER HOW GOOD SOMEONE LOOKS, I'M NOT INTERESTED IN WOMEN.
Please!
IT JUST BREAKS MY HEART WHEN GAY GUYS ARE NICE TO ME.
YOU'RE GOING TO NEED A BUCKET FOR ALL THESE.
HEY, DO YOU MIND IF I PUT THIS ON? IT'S *SWING* BY THE MANHATTAN TRANSFER.
ALBUM NAME
THIS WILL GET THEM DANC-ING AGAIN.
ARE YOU GOING TO CALIFORNIA TO MAKE IT OFFICIAL?
NOT ANYTIME SOON, BUT WE WILL SOMEDAY.
SO NO CHANGES ON PAPER YET?
IT'S LIKE A GAY PARTY IN HERE...
SO YOU'RE FINALLY WEARING A WEDDING RING...
JB, WHAT ABOUT THE CAFÉ?
OH HONEY, WE'RE CLOSED!! WE CAN'T BE WORKING ON SUCH A JOYOUS DAY.
HM? WHAT'S THAT LOOK FOR?

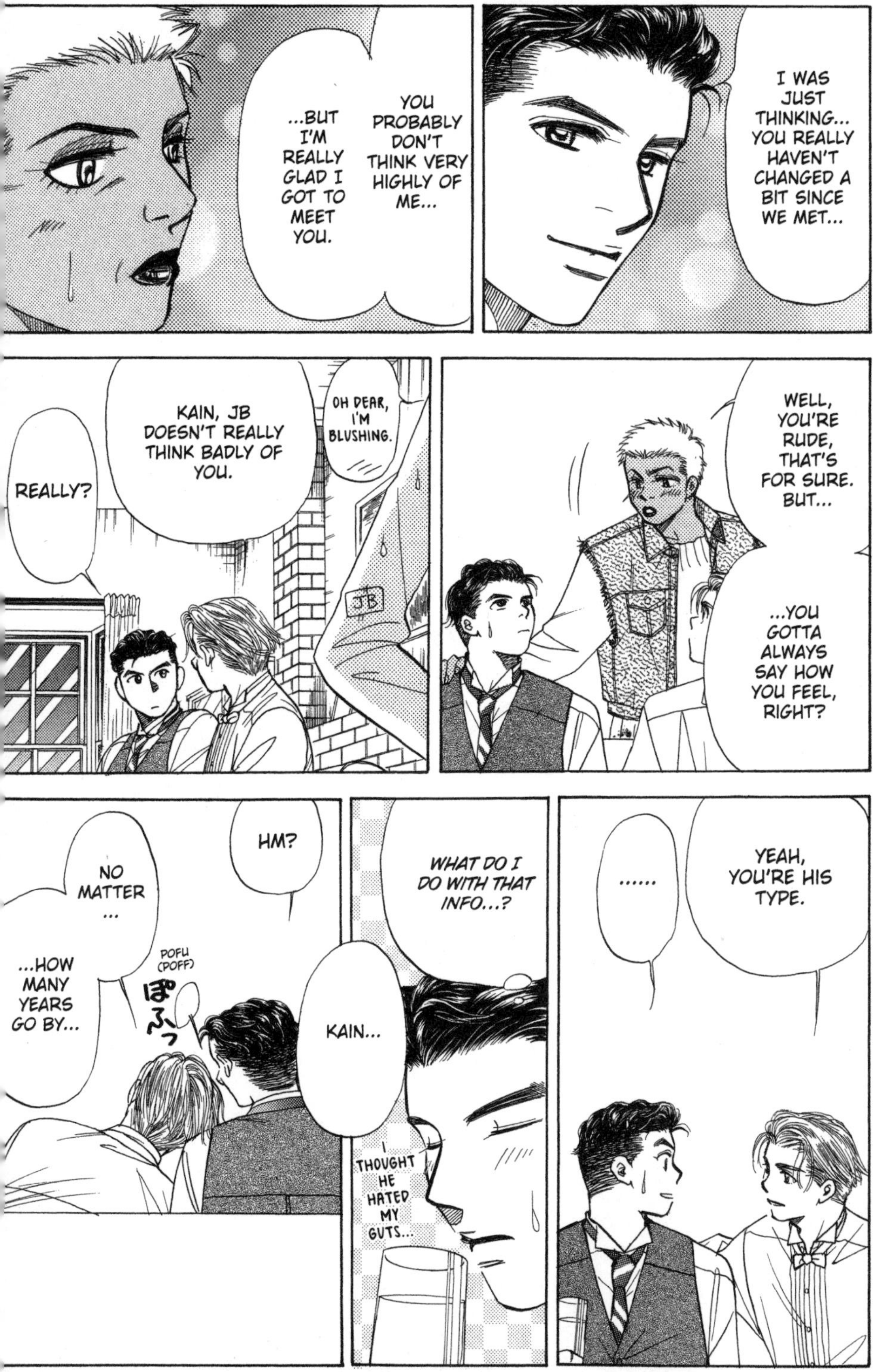
I WAS JUST THINKING... YOU REALLY HAVEN'T CHANGED A BIT SINCE WE MET...
YOU PROBABLY DON'T THINK VERY HIGHLY OF ME...
...BUT I'M REALLY GLAD I GOT TO MEET YOU.
WELL, YOU'RE RUDE, THAT'S FOR SURE. BUT...
...YOU GOTTA ALWAYS SAY HOW YOU FEEL, RIGHT?
OH DEAR, I'M BLUSHING.
KAIN, JB DOESN'T REALLY THINK BADLY OF YOU.
REALLY?
JB
YEAH, YOU'RE HIS TYPE.
......
WHAT DO I DO WITH THAT INFO...?
KAIN...
I THOUGHT HE HATED MY GUTS...
HM?
NO MATTER...
...HOW MANY YEARS GO BY...
POFU (POFF)
ぽふっ

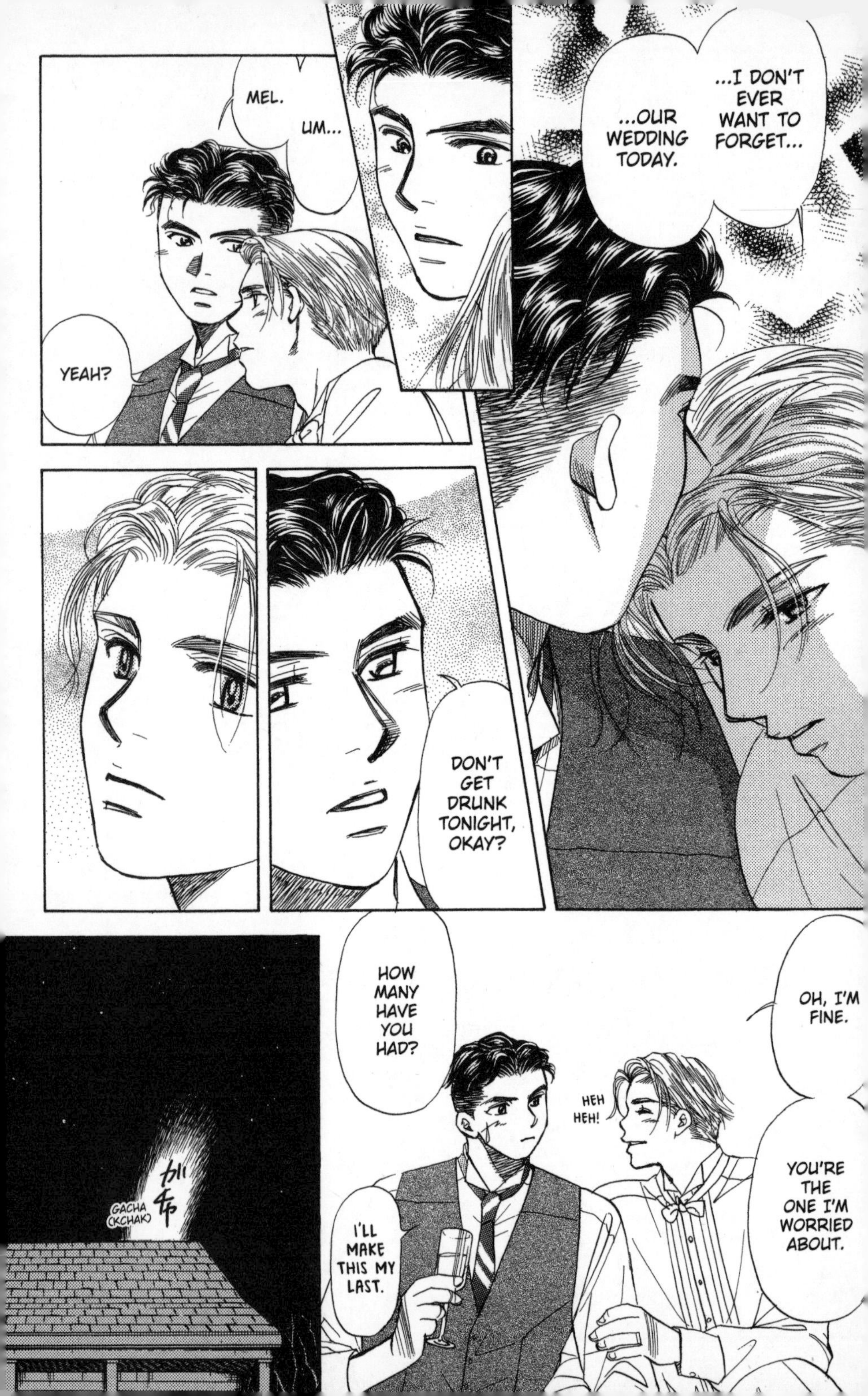
...I DON'T EVER WANT TO FORGET...
...OUR WEDDING TODAY.
MEL.
UM...
YEAH?
DON'T GET DRUNK TONIGHT, OKAY?
OH, I'M FINE.
YOU'RE THE ONE I'M WORRIED ABOUT.
HEH HEH!
HOW MANY HAVE YOU HAD?
I'LL MAKE THIS MY LAST.
カチャ
GACHA (KCHAK)

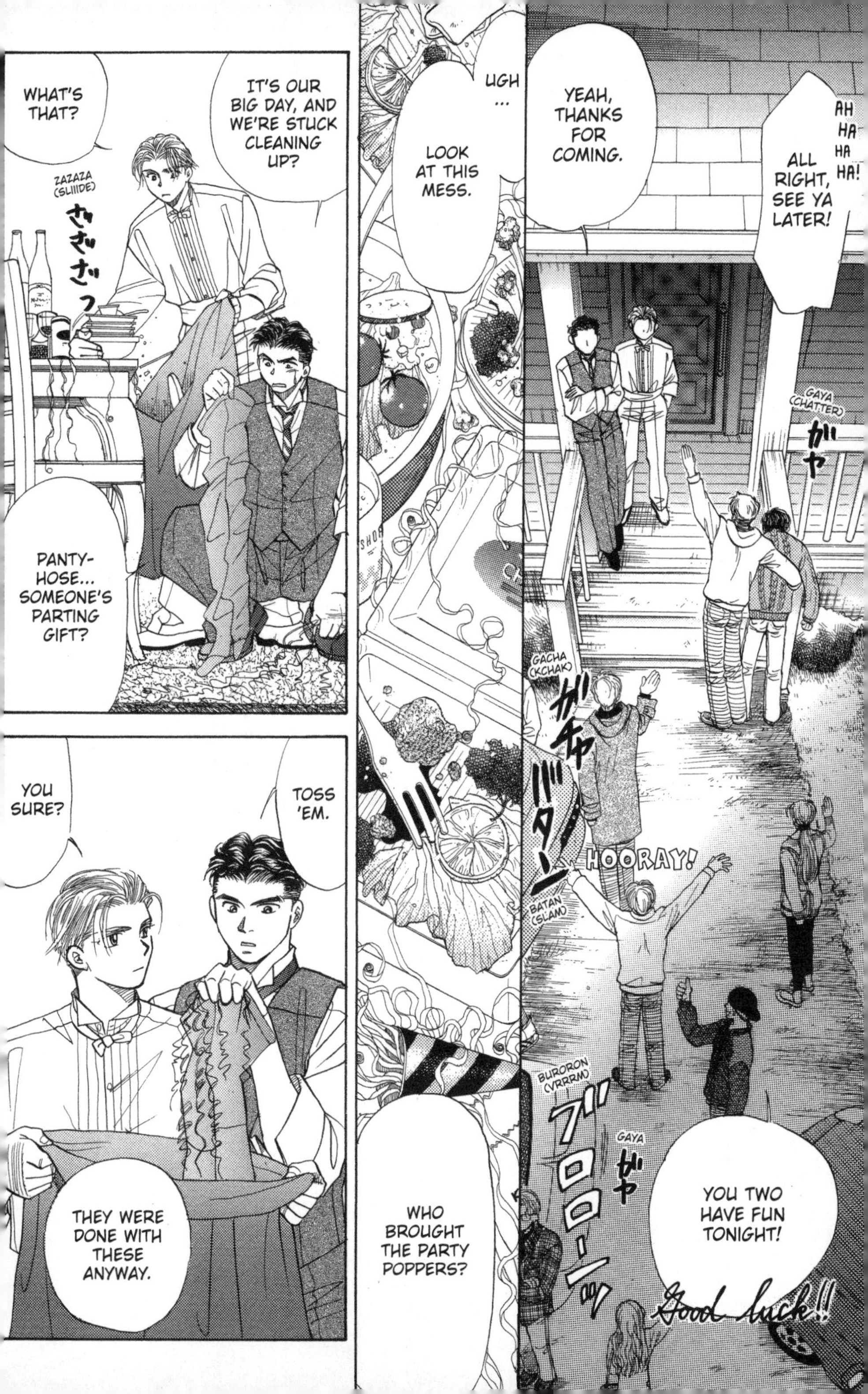
AH HA HA HA!
ALL RIGHT, SEE YA LATER!
YEAH, THANKS FOR COMING.
GAYA (CHATTER)
がや
GACHA (KCHAK)
ガチャ
バタン
BATAN (SLAM)
HOORAY!
BURORON (VRRRM)
ブロローン
GAYA
がや
YOU TWO HAVE FUN TONIGHT!
Good luck!!
UGH...
LOOK AT THIS MESS.
WHO BROUGHT THE PARTY POPPERS?
IT'S OUR BIG DAY, AND WE'RE STUCK CLEANING UP?
WHAT'S THAT?
ZAZAZA (SLIIIDE)
ざざざっ
PANTY-HOSE... SOMEONE'S PARTING GIFT?
TOSS 'EM.
YOU SURE?
THEY WERE DONE WITH THESE ANYWAY.

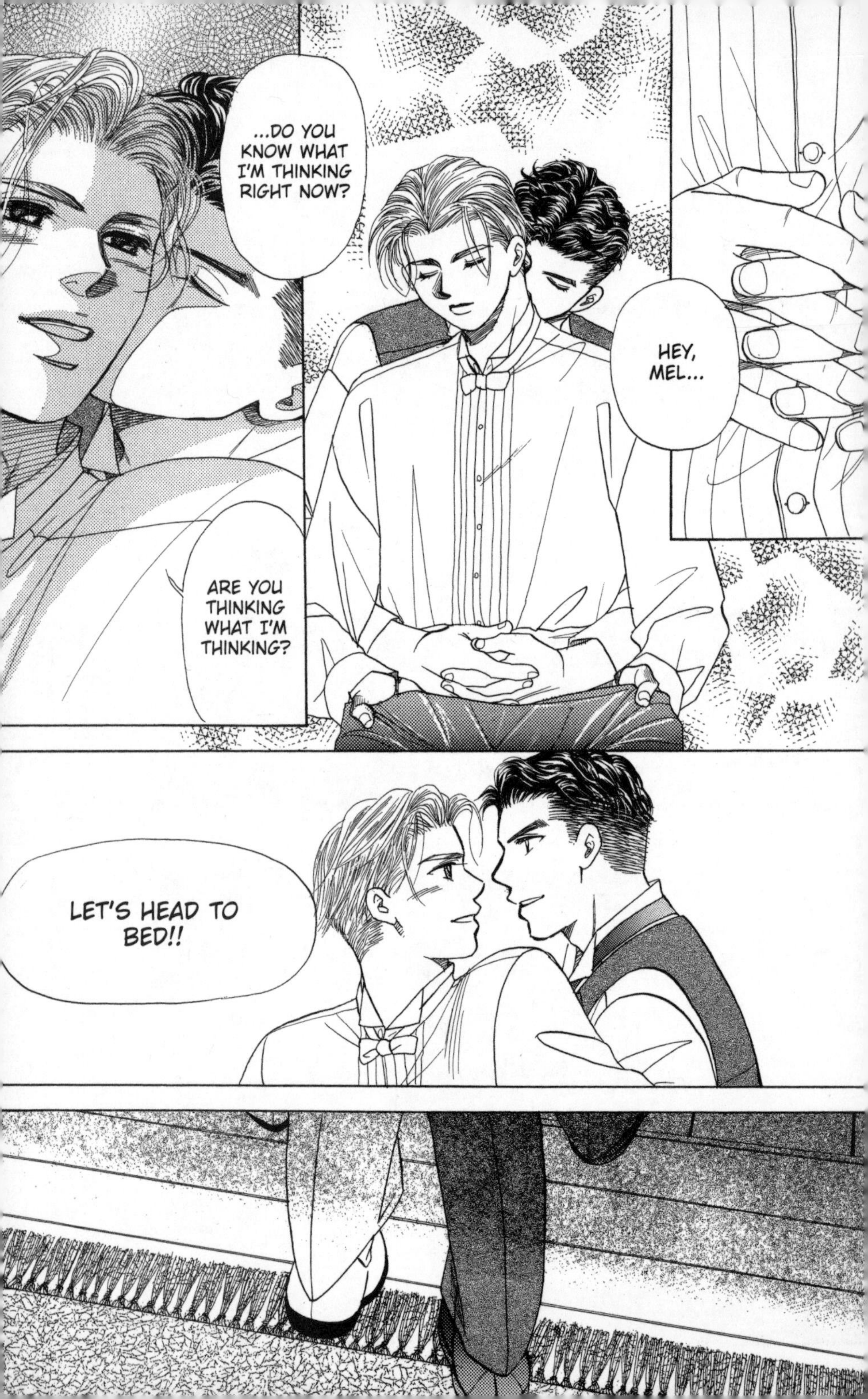
HEY, MEL...
...DO YOU KNOW WHAT I'M THINKING RIGHT NOW?
ARE YOU THINKING WHAT I'M THINKING?
LET'S HEAD TO BED!!

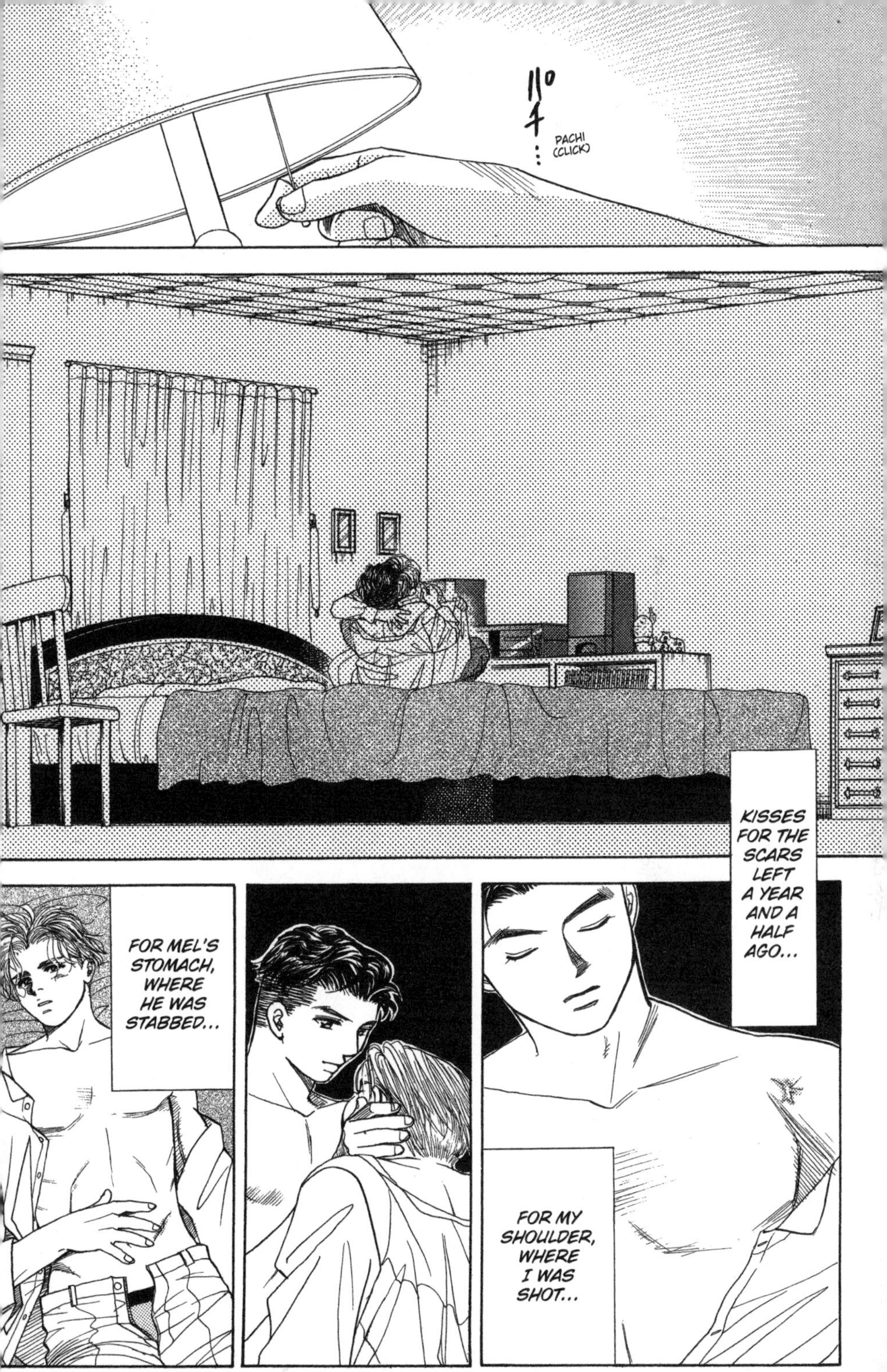

パチ…
PACHI (CLICK)
KISSES FOR THE SCARS LEFT A YEAR AND A HALF AGO...
FOR MY SHOULDER, WHERE I WAS SHOT...
FOR MEL'S STOMACH, WHERE HE WAS STABBED...

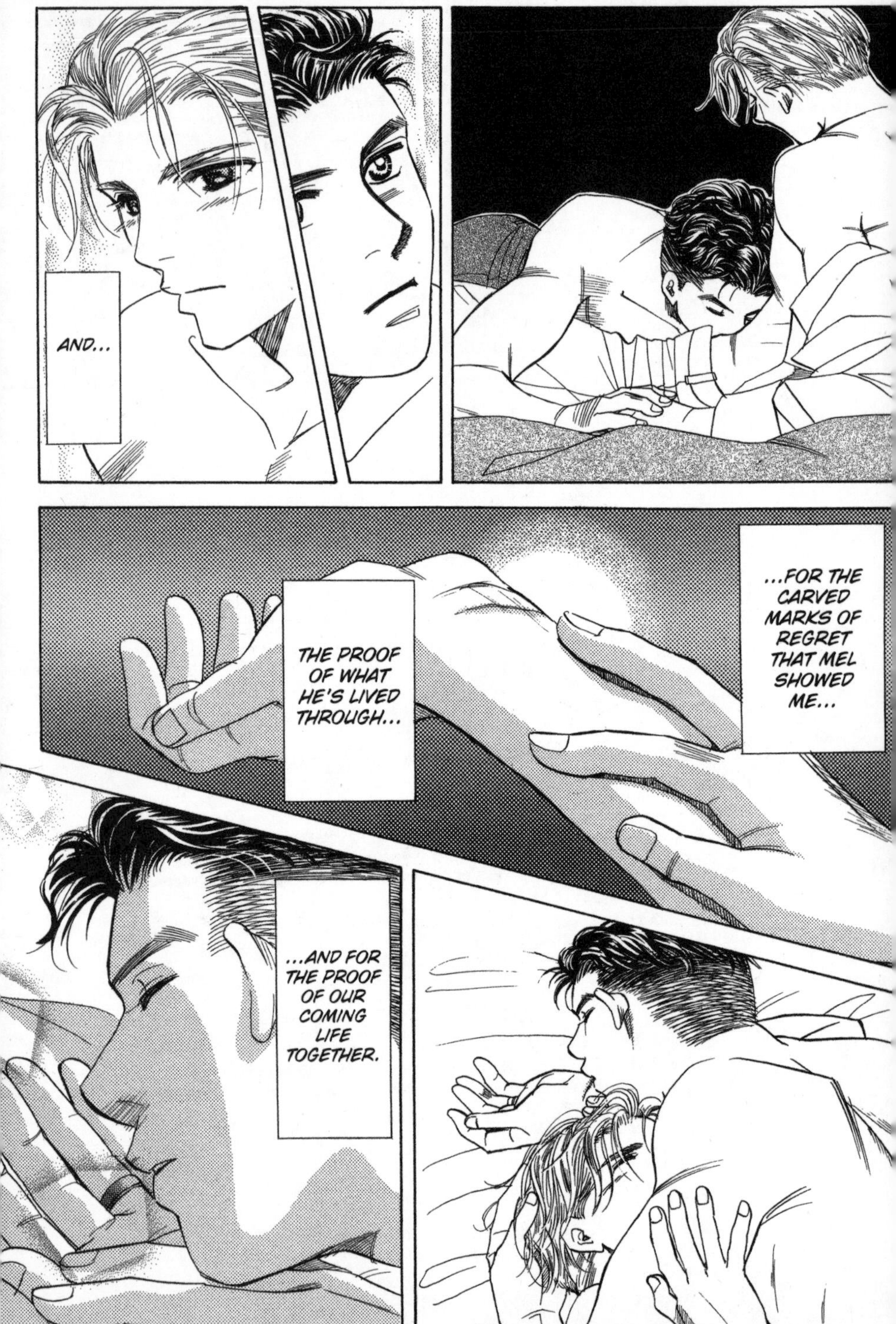
AND...
...FOR THE CARVED MARKS OF REGRET THAT MEL SHOWED ME...
THE PROOF OF WHAT HE'S LIVED THROUGH...
...AND FOR THE PROOF OF OUR COMING LIFE TOGETHER.

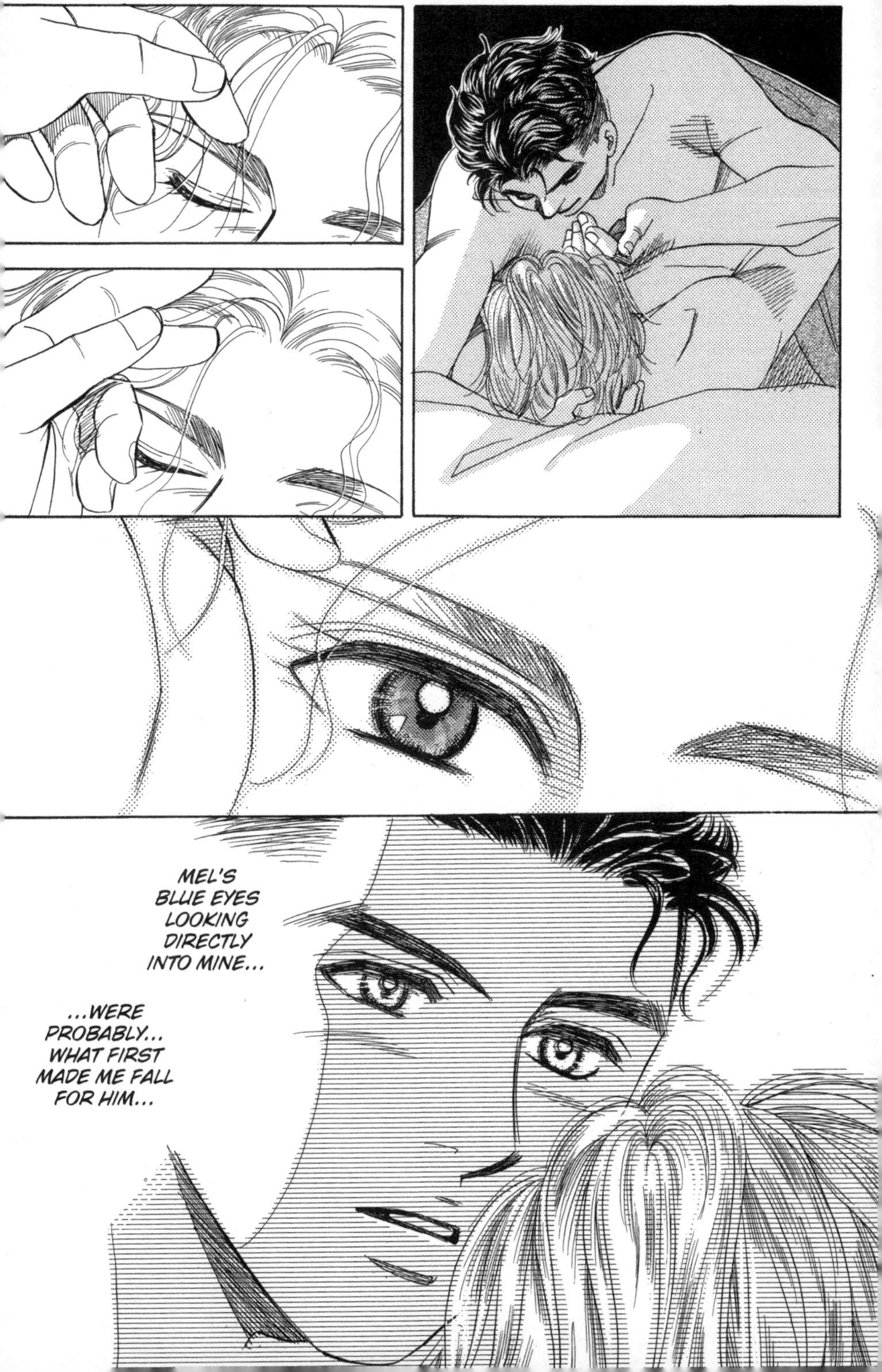
MEL'S BLUE EYES LOOKING DIRECTLY INTO MINE...
...WERE PROBABLY... WHAT FIRST MADE ME FALL FOR HIM...

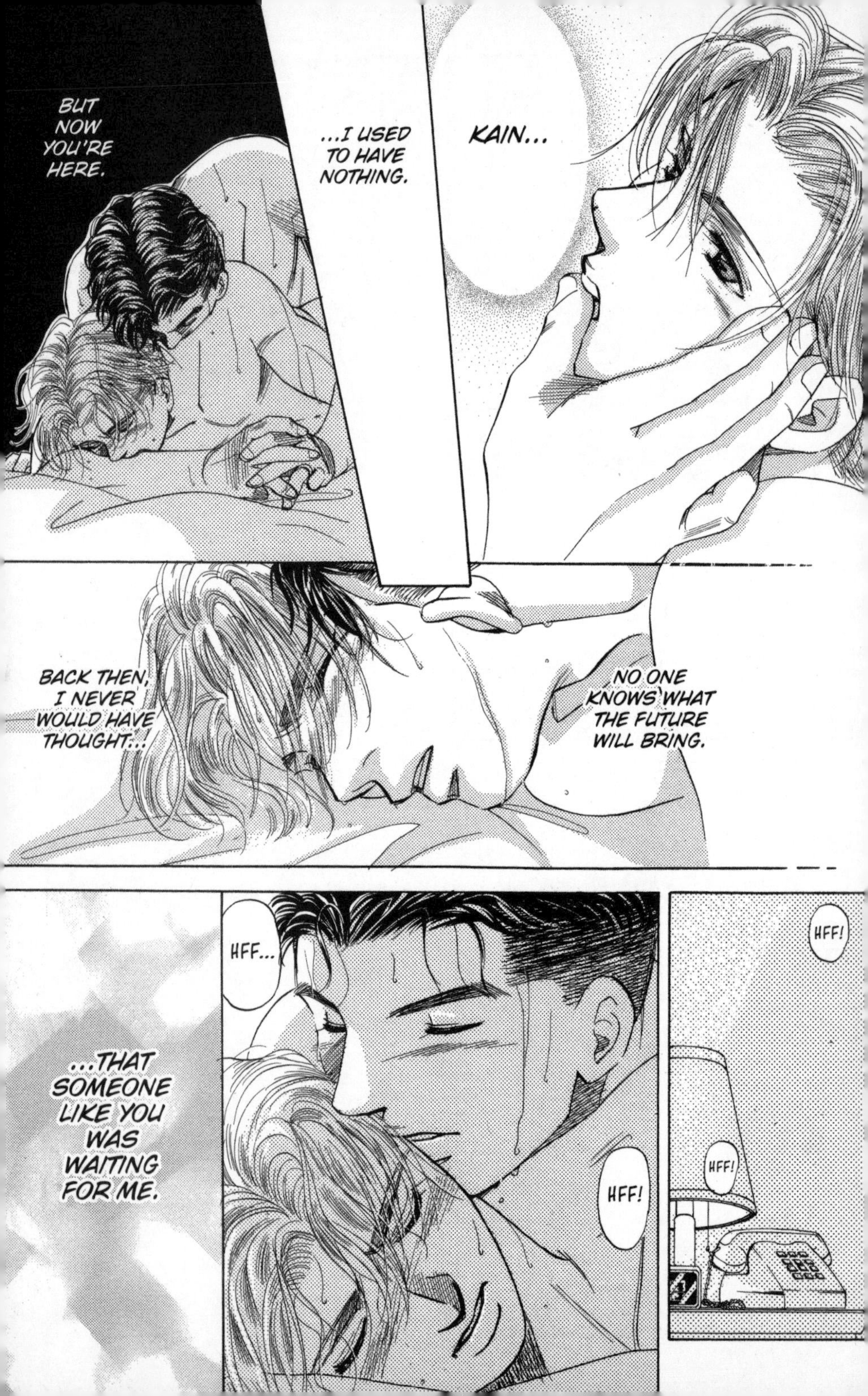
KAIN...
...I USED TO HAVE NOTHING.
BUT NOW YOU'RE HERE.
NO ONE KNOWS WHAT THE FUTURE WILL BRING.
BACK THEN, I NEVER WOULD HAVE THOUGHT...
HFF!
HFF!
HFF...
HFF!
...THAT SOMEONE LIKE YOU WAS WAITING FOR ME.

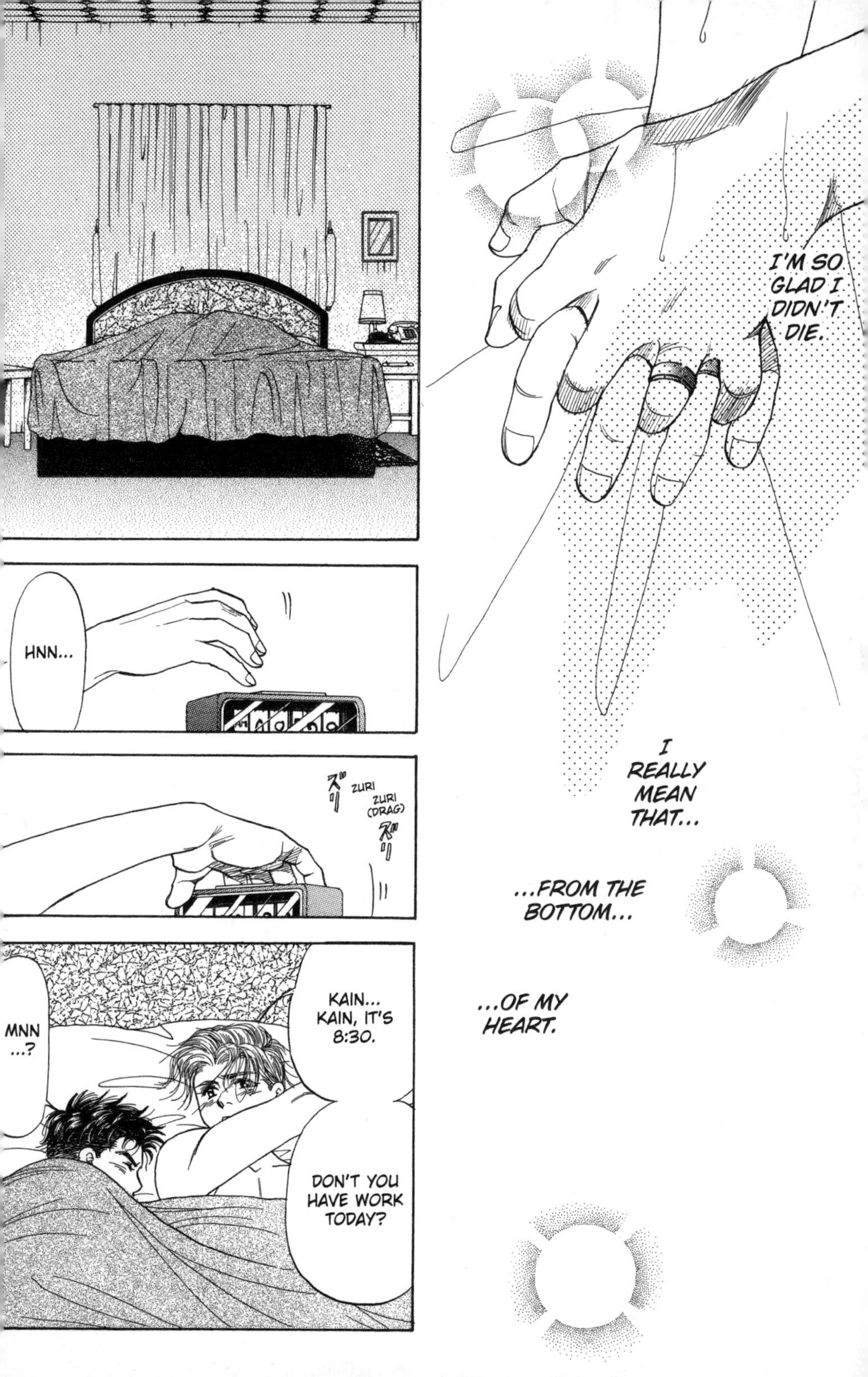
I'M SO GLAD I DIDN'T DIE.
I REALLY MEAN THAT...
...FROM THE BOTTOM...
...OF MY HEART.
HNN...
ZURI ZURI (DRAG)
KAIN... KAIN, IT'S 8:30.
DON'T YOU HAVE WORK TODAY?
MNN ...?

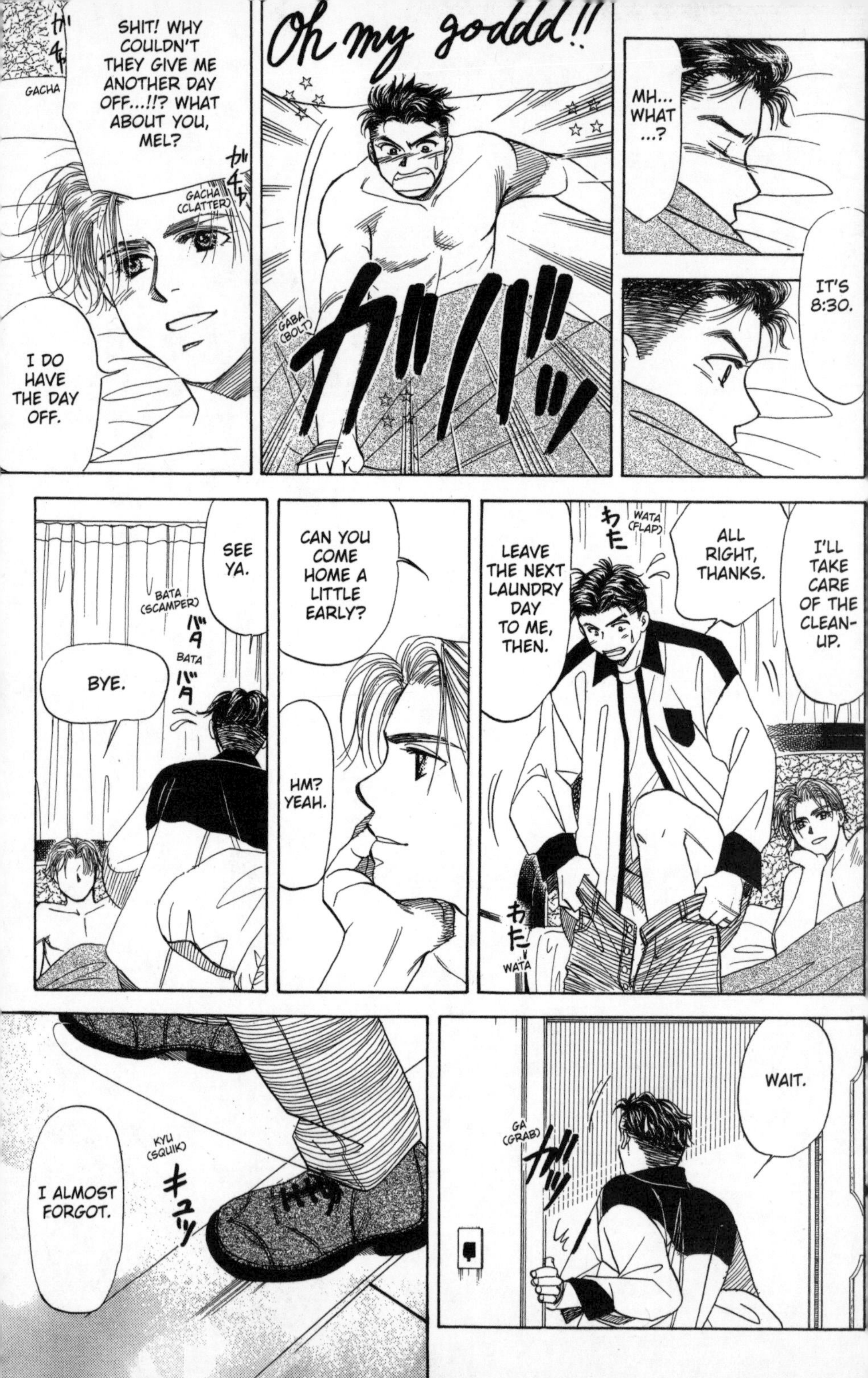
MH... WHAT ...?
IT'S 8:30.
Oh my goddd!!
GABA (BOLT)
GACHA
SHIT! WHY COULDN'T THEY GIVE ME ANOTHER DAY OFF...!!? WHAT ABOUT YOU, MEL?
GACHA (CLATTER)
I DO HAVE THE DAY OFF.
I'LL TAKE CARE OF THE CLEAN-UP.
ALL RIGHT, THANKS.
WATA (FLAP)
LEAVE THE NEXT LAUNDRY DAY TO ME, THEN.
WATA
CAN YOU COME HOME A LITTLE EARLY?
HM? YEAH.
SEE YA.
BATA (SCAMPER)
BATA
BYE.
WAIT.
GA (GRAB)
KYU (SQUIK)
I ALMOST FORGOT.

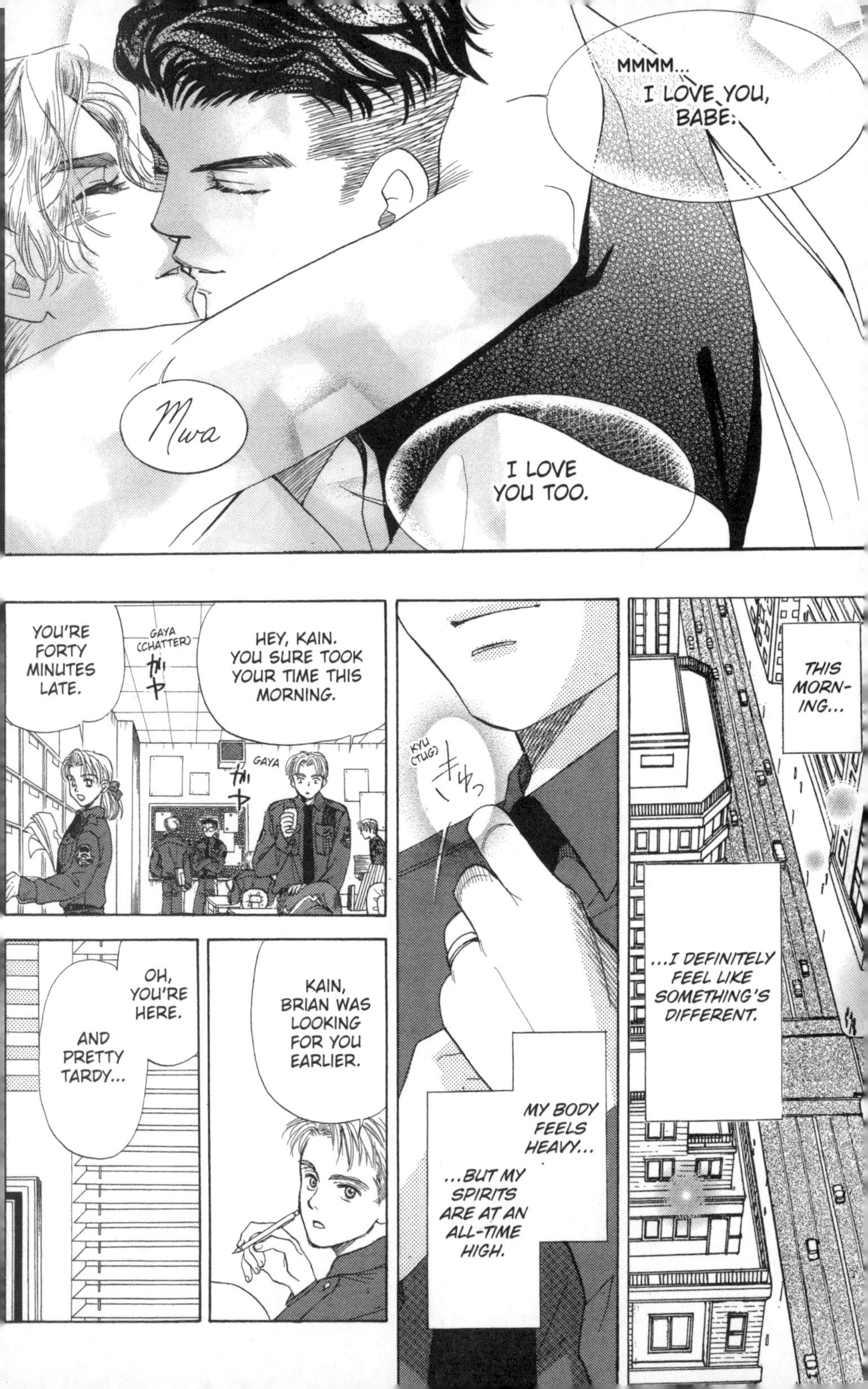
MMMM... I LOVE YOU, BABE.
Mwa
I LOVE YOU TOO.
THIS MORNING...
...I DEFINITELY FEEL LIKE SOMETHING'S DIFFERENT.
KYU (TUG)
きゅっ
MY BODY FEELS HEAVY...
...BUT MY SPIRITS ARE AT AN ALL-TIME HIGH.
HEY, KAIN. YOU SURE TOOK YOUR TIME THIS MORNING.
GAYA (CHATTER)
がや
YOU'RE FORTY MINUTES LATE.
GAYA
がや
KAIN, BRIAN WAS LOOKING FOR YOU EARLIER.
OH, YOU'RE HERE.
AND PRETTY TARDY...

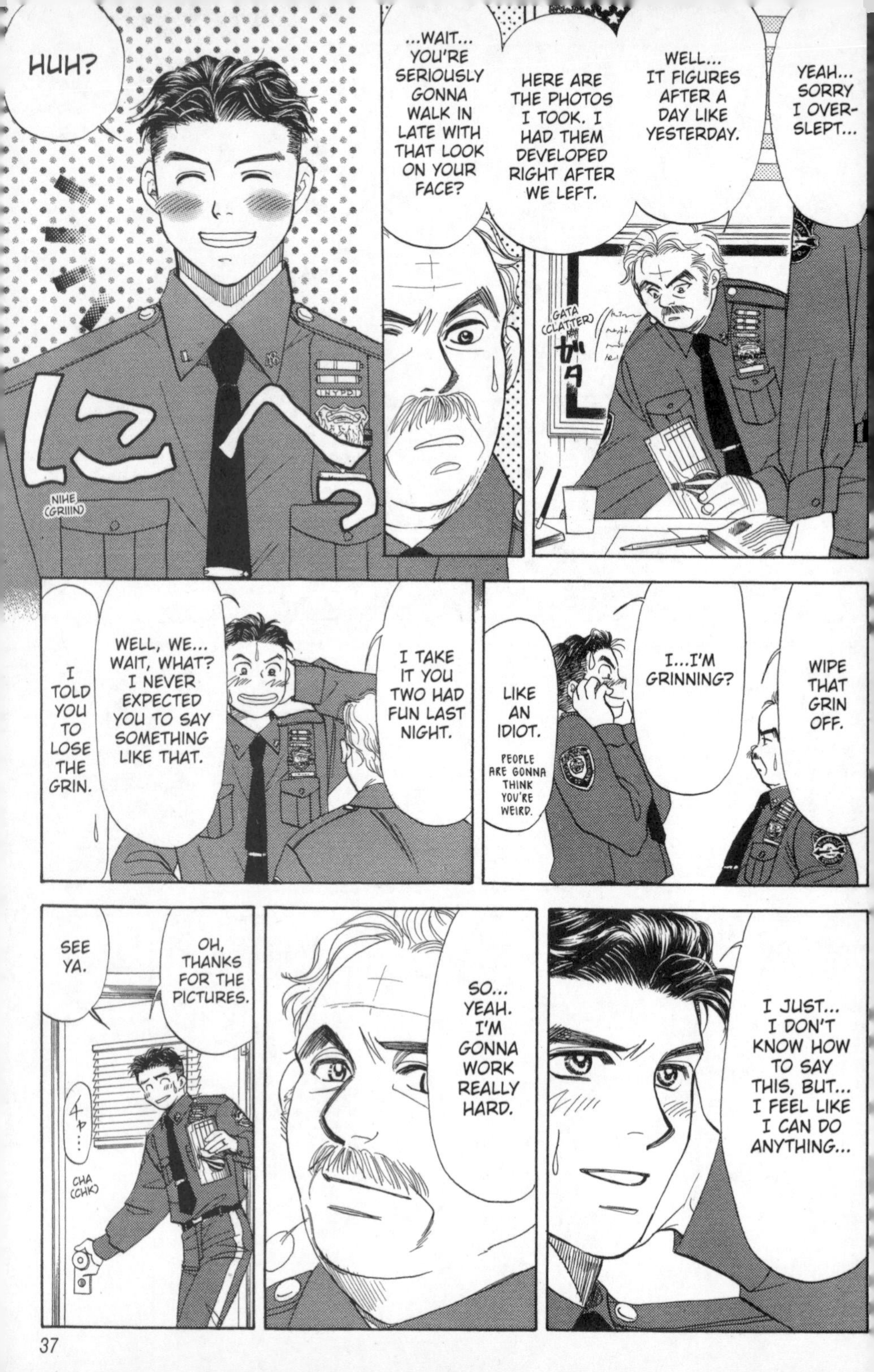
YEAH... SORRY I OVER-SLEPT...
WELL... IT FIGURES AFTER A DAY LIKE YESTERDAY.
HERE ARE THE PHOTOS I TOOK. I HAD THEM DEVELOPED RIGHT AFTER WE LEFT.
GATA (CLATTER)
...WAIT... YOU'RE SERIOUSLY GONNA WALK IN LATE WITH THAT LOOK ON YOUR FACE?
HUH?
NIHE (GRIIIN)
WIPE THAT GRIN OFF.
I...I'M GRINNING?
LIKE AN IDIOT.
PEOPLE ARE GONNA THINK YOU'RE WEIRD.
I TAKE IT YOU TWO HAD FUN LAST NIGHT.
WELL, WE... WAIT, WHAT? I NEVER EXPECTED YOU TO SAY SOMETHING LIKE THAT.
I TOLD YOU TO LOSE THE GRIN.
I JUST... I DON'T KNOW HOW TO SAY THIS, BUT... I FEEL LIKE I CAN DO ANYTHING...
SO... YEAH. I'M GONNA WORK REALLY HARD.
OH, THANKS FOR THE PICTURES.
SEE YA.
CHA (CHK)

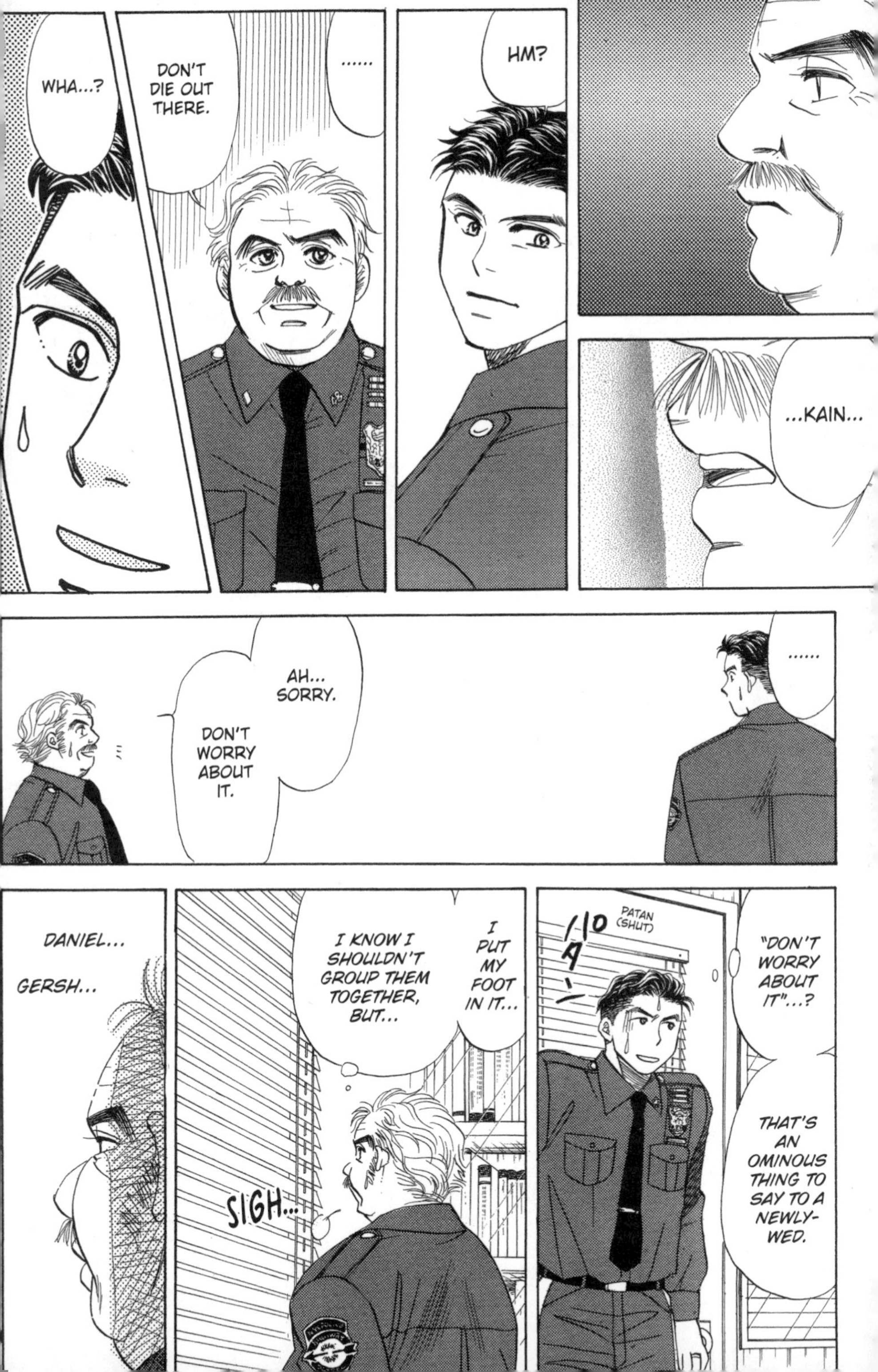

...KAIN...
HM?
......
DON'T DIE OUT THERE.
WHA...?
......
AH... SORRY.
DON'T WORRY ABOUT IT.
"DON'T WORRY ABOUT IT"...?
PATAN (SHUT)
THAT'S AN OMINOUS THING TO SAY TO A NEWLY-WED.
I PUT MY FOOT IN IT...
I KNOW I SHOULDN'T GROUP THEM TOGETHER, BUT...
SIGH...
DANIEL...
GERSH...

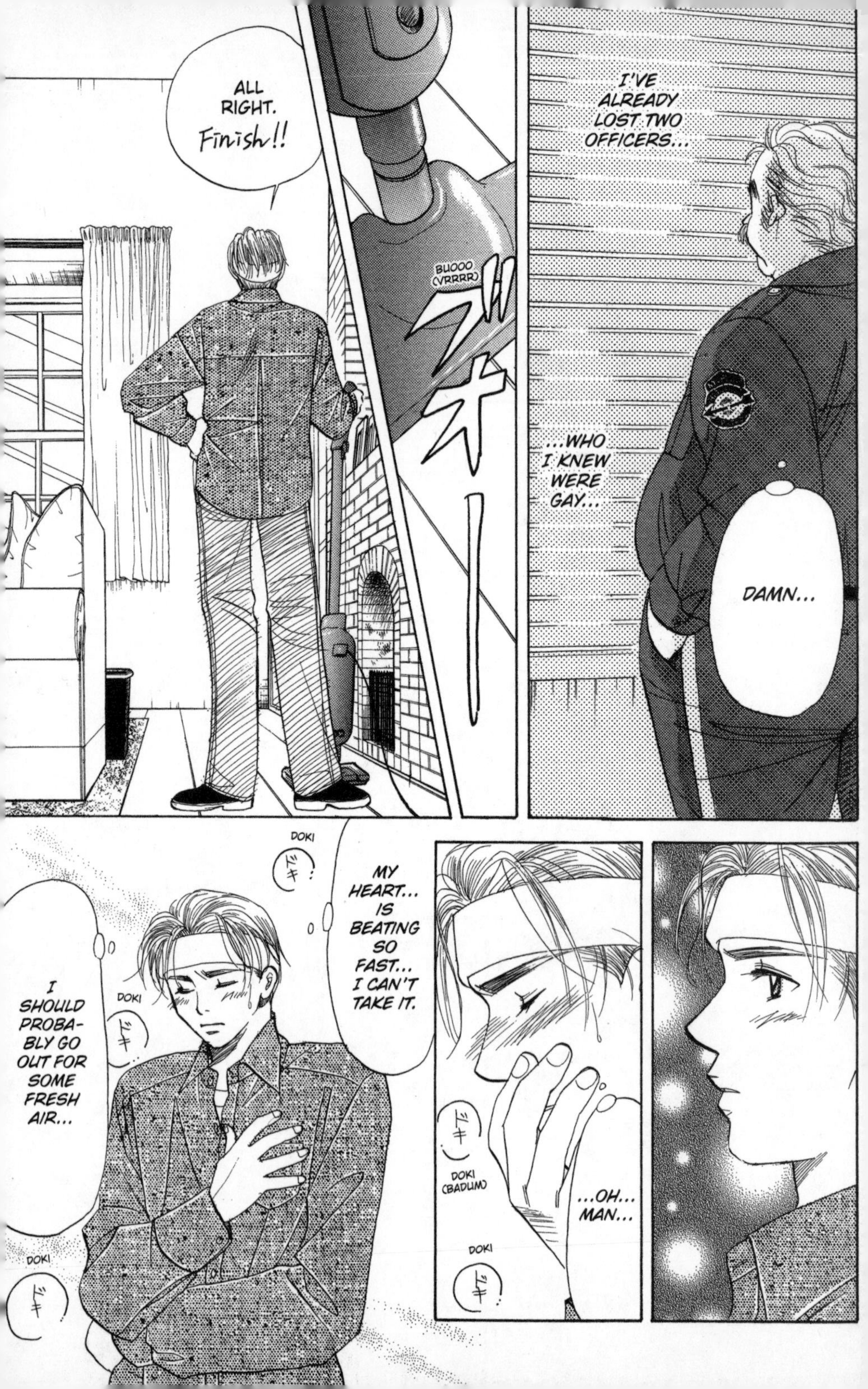
I'VE ALREADY LOST TWO OFFICERS...
...WHO I KNEW WERE GAY...
DAMN...
BUOOO (VRRRR)
ブォー
ALL RIGHT. Finish!!
DOKI (BADUM)
ドキ
...OH... MAN...
DOKI
ドキ
DOKI
ドキ
MY HEART... IS BEATING SO FAST... I CAN'T TAKE IT.
DOKI
ドキ
I SHOULD PROBA-BLY GO OUT FOR SOME FRESH AIR...
DOKI
ドキ

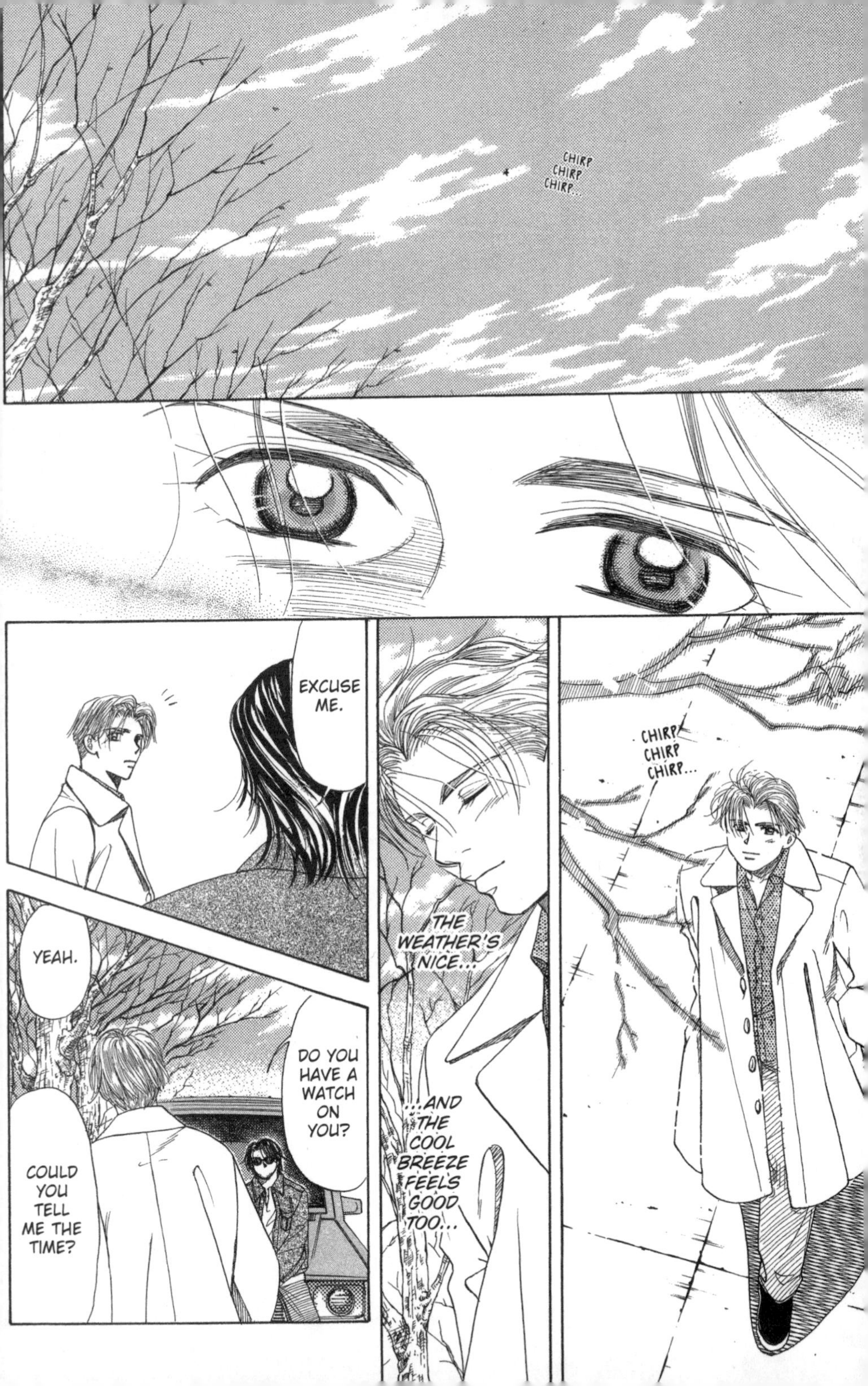
CHIRP
CHIRP
CHIRP...
CHIRP
CHIRP
CHIRP...
THE WEATHER'S NICE...
...AND THE COOL BREEZE FEELS GOOD TOO...
EXCUSE ME.
DO YOU HAVE A WATCH ON YOU?
YEAH.
COULD YOU TELL ME THE TIME?

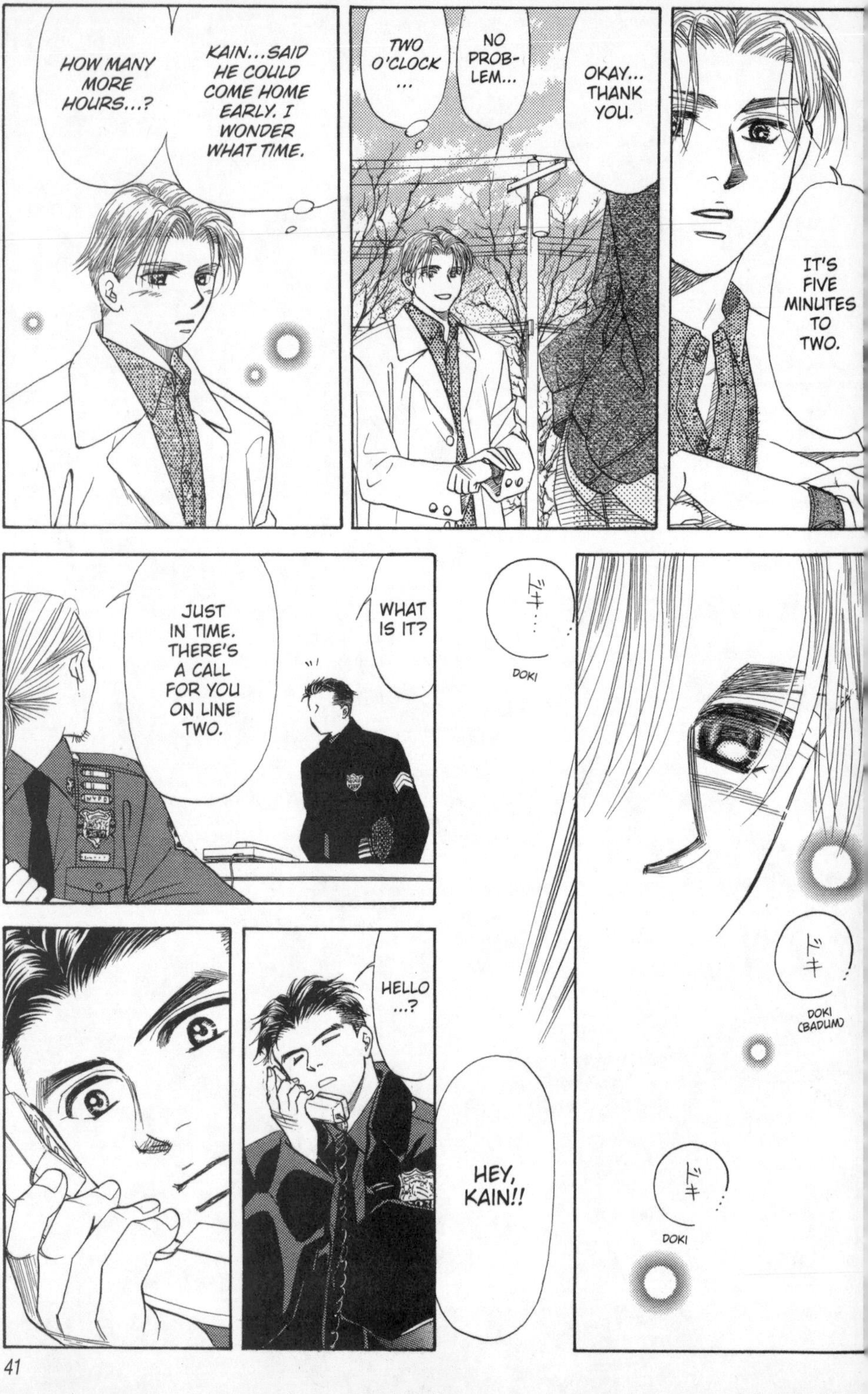
IT'S FIVE MINUTES TO TWO.
OKAY... THANK YOU.
NO PROB-LEM...
TWO O'CLOCK ...
KAIN...SAID HE COULD COME HOME EARLY. I WONDER WHAT TIME.
HOW MANY MORE HOURS...?
ドキ…
DOKI
ドキ
DOKI (BADUM)
ドキ…
DOKI
WHAT IS IT?
JUST IN TIME. THERE'S A CALL FOR YOU ON LINE TWO.
HELLO ...?
HEY, KAIN!!

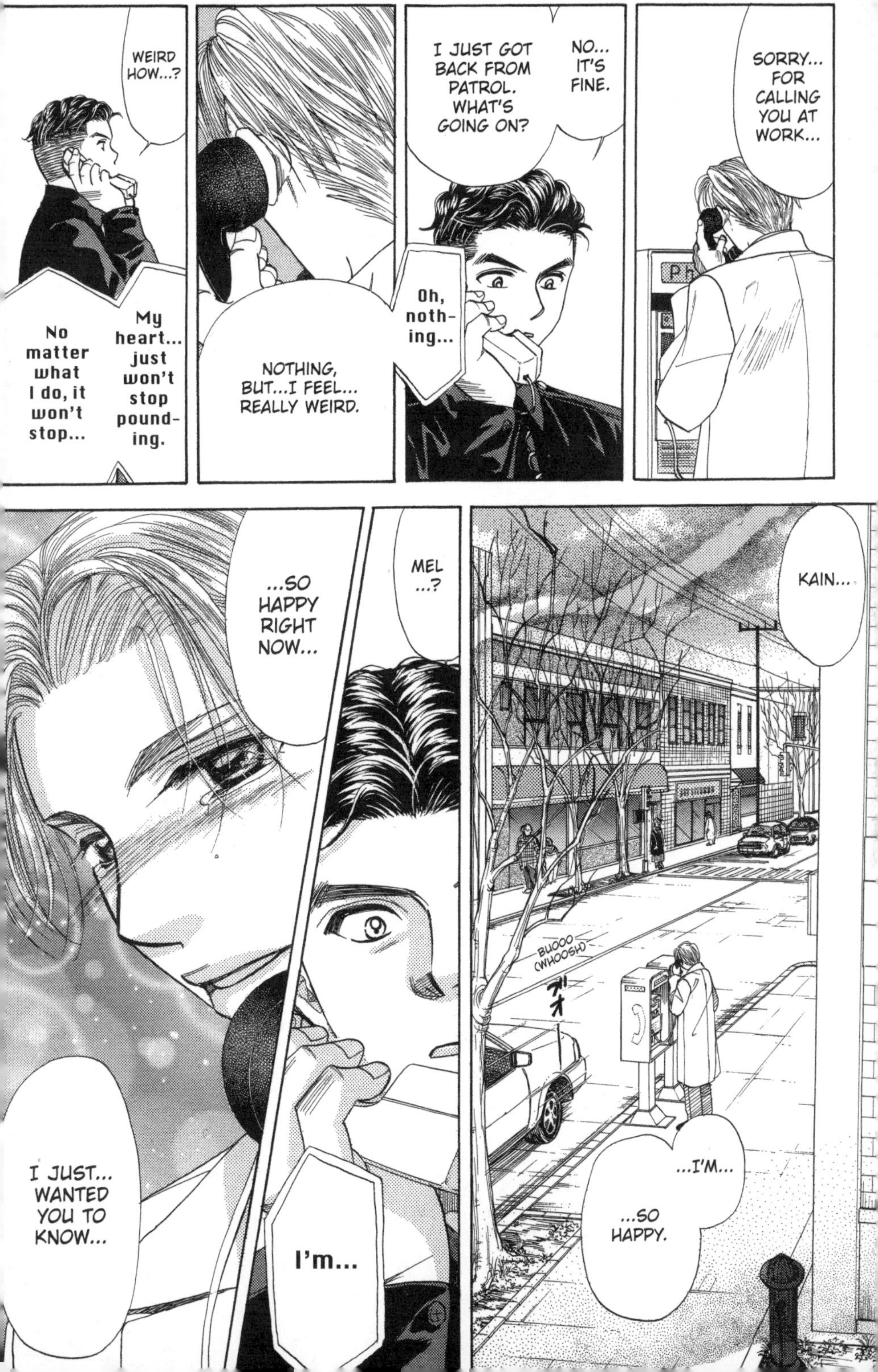
SORRY... FOR CALLING YOU AT WORK...
NO... IT'S FINE.
I JUST GOT BACK FROM PATROL. WHAT'S GOING ON?
Oh, nothing...
NOTHING, BUT...I FEEL... REALLY WEIRD.
WEIRD HOW...?
My heart... just won't stop pounding.
No matter what I do, it won't stop...
KAIN...
BUOOO (WHOOSH)
...I'M...
...SO HAPPY.
MEL ...?
I'm...
...SO HAPPY RIGHT NOW...
I JUST... WANTED YOU TO KNOW...

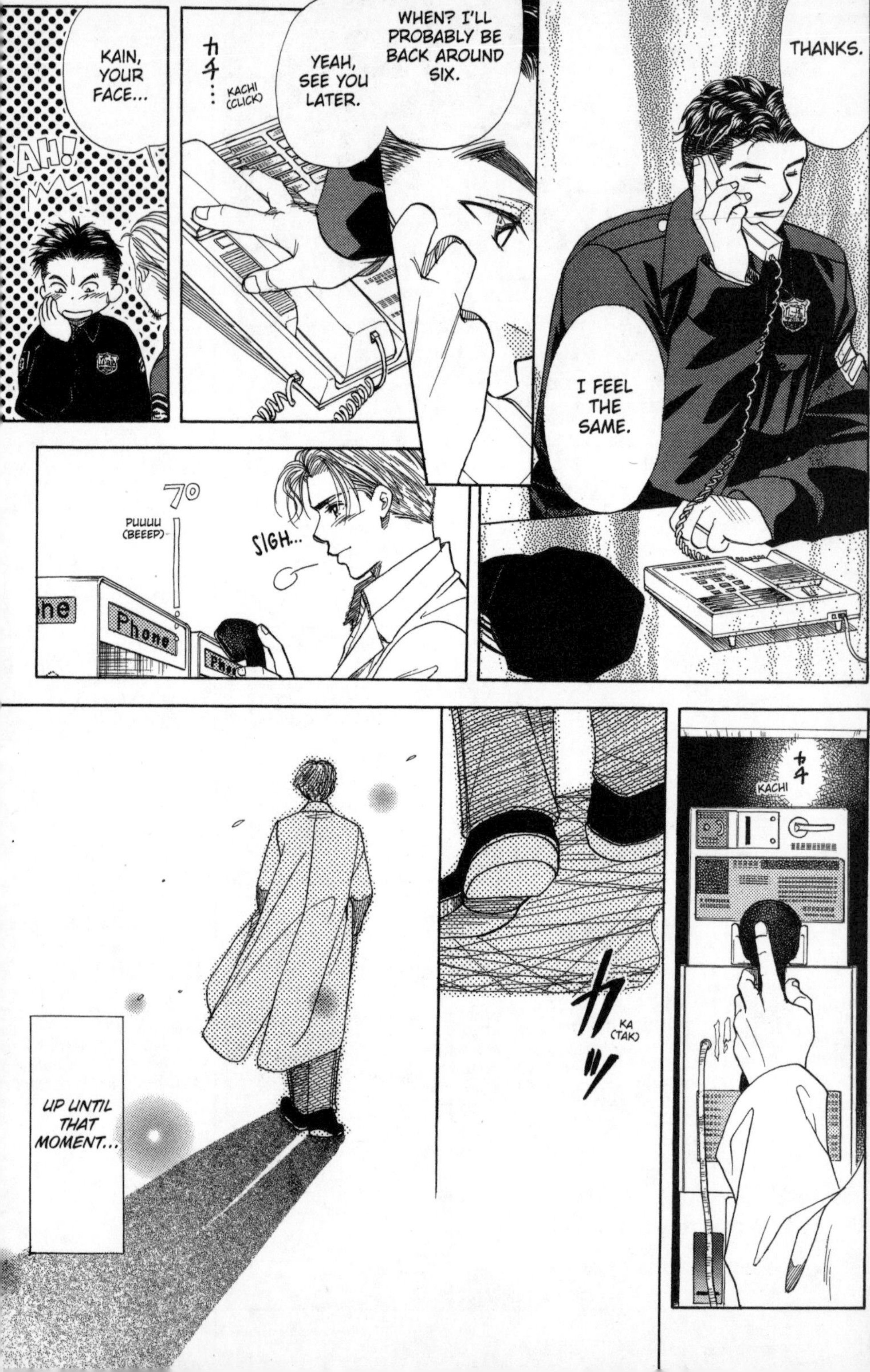
THANKS.
I FEEL THE SAME.
WHEN? I'LL PROBABLY BE BACK AROUND SIX.
YEAH, SEE YOU LATER.
カチ…
KACHI (CLICK)
KAIN, YOUR FACE...
AH!
PUUUU (BEEEP)
SIGH...
Phone
Phone
カチ
KACHI
カッ
KA (TAK)
UP UNTIL THAT MOMENT...

...WE WERE...

...TRULY HAPPY...

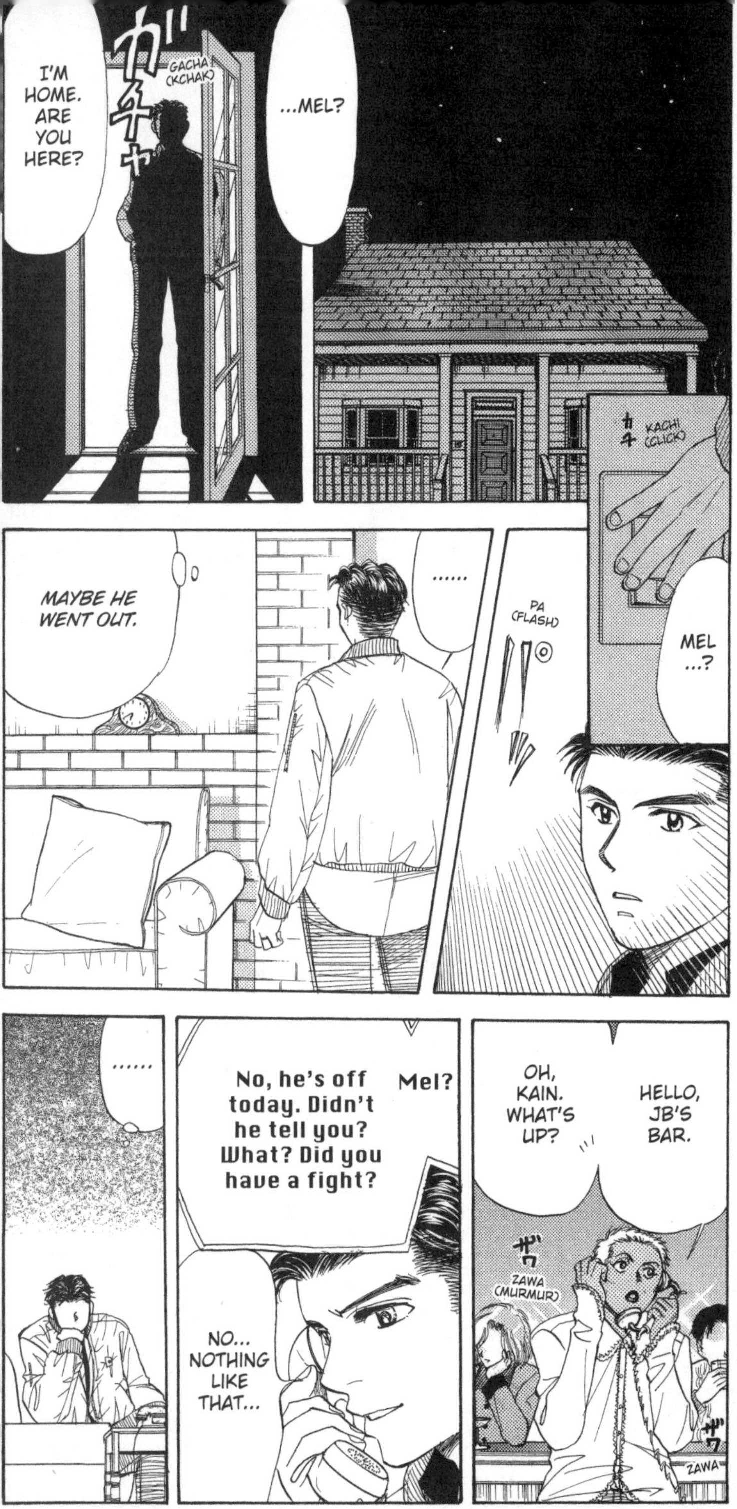

ガチャ
GACHA (KCHAK)
I'M HOME. ARE YOU HERE?
...MEL?
カチ
KACHI (CLICK)
PA (FLASH)
MEL ...?
......
MAYBE HE WENT OUT.
HELLO, JB'S BAR.
OH, KAIN. WHAT'S UP?
ザワ
ZAWA (MURMUR)
ザワ
ZAWA
Mel?
No, he's off today. Didn't he tell you? What? Did you have a fight?
NO... NOTHING LIKE THAT...
......

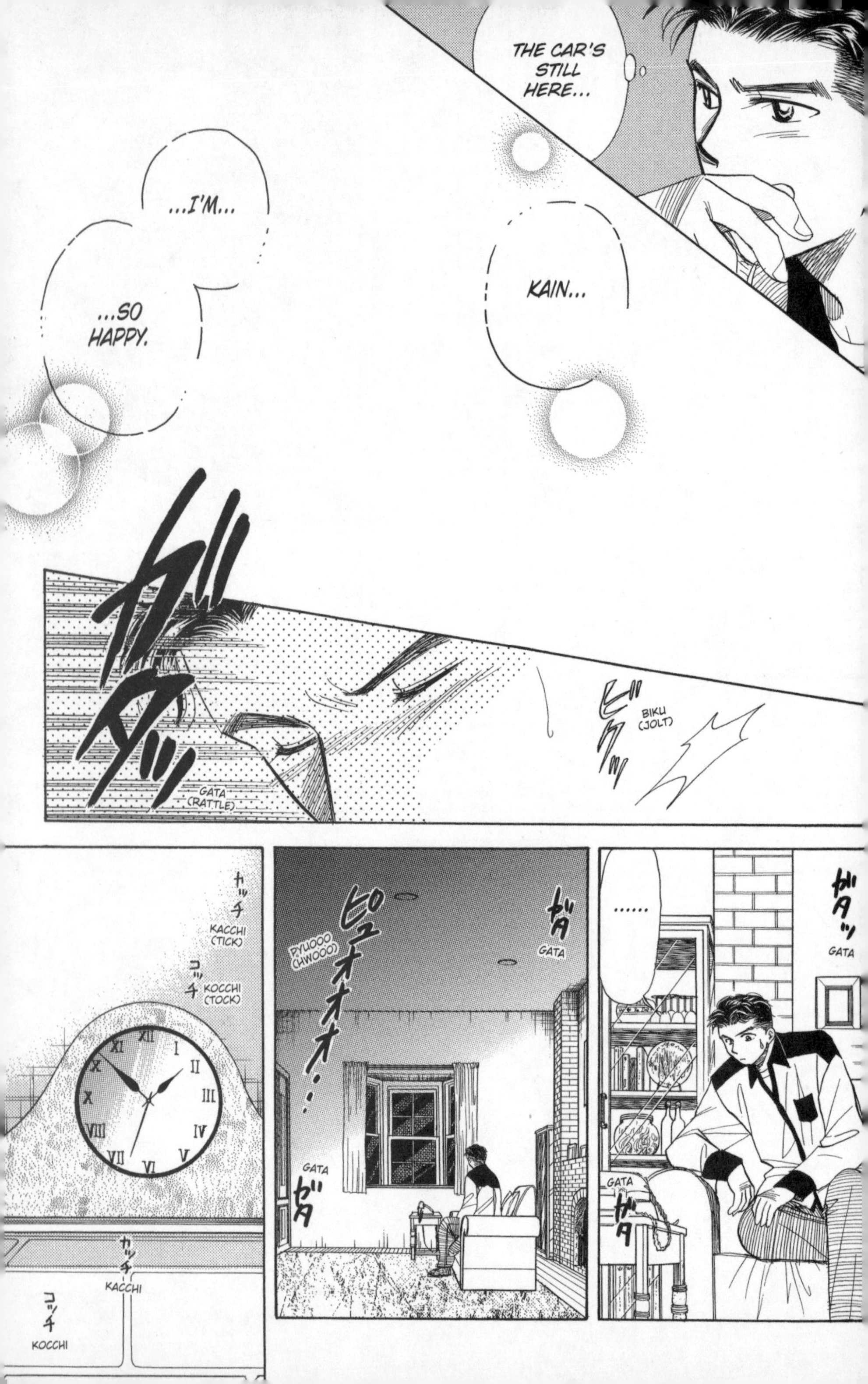
THE CAR'S STILL HERE...
KAIN...
...I'M...
...SO HAPPY.
ビクッ
BIKU (JOLT)
ガタッ
GATA (RATTLE)
ガタッ
GATA
......
GATA
ガタ
ガタ
GATA
ピュオオオ…
PYUOOO (HWOOO)
GATA
ガタ
カッチ
KACCHI (TICK)
コッチ
KOCCHI (TOCK)
カッチ
KACCHI
コッチ
KOCCHI

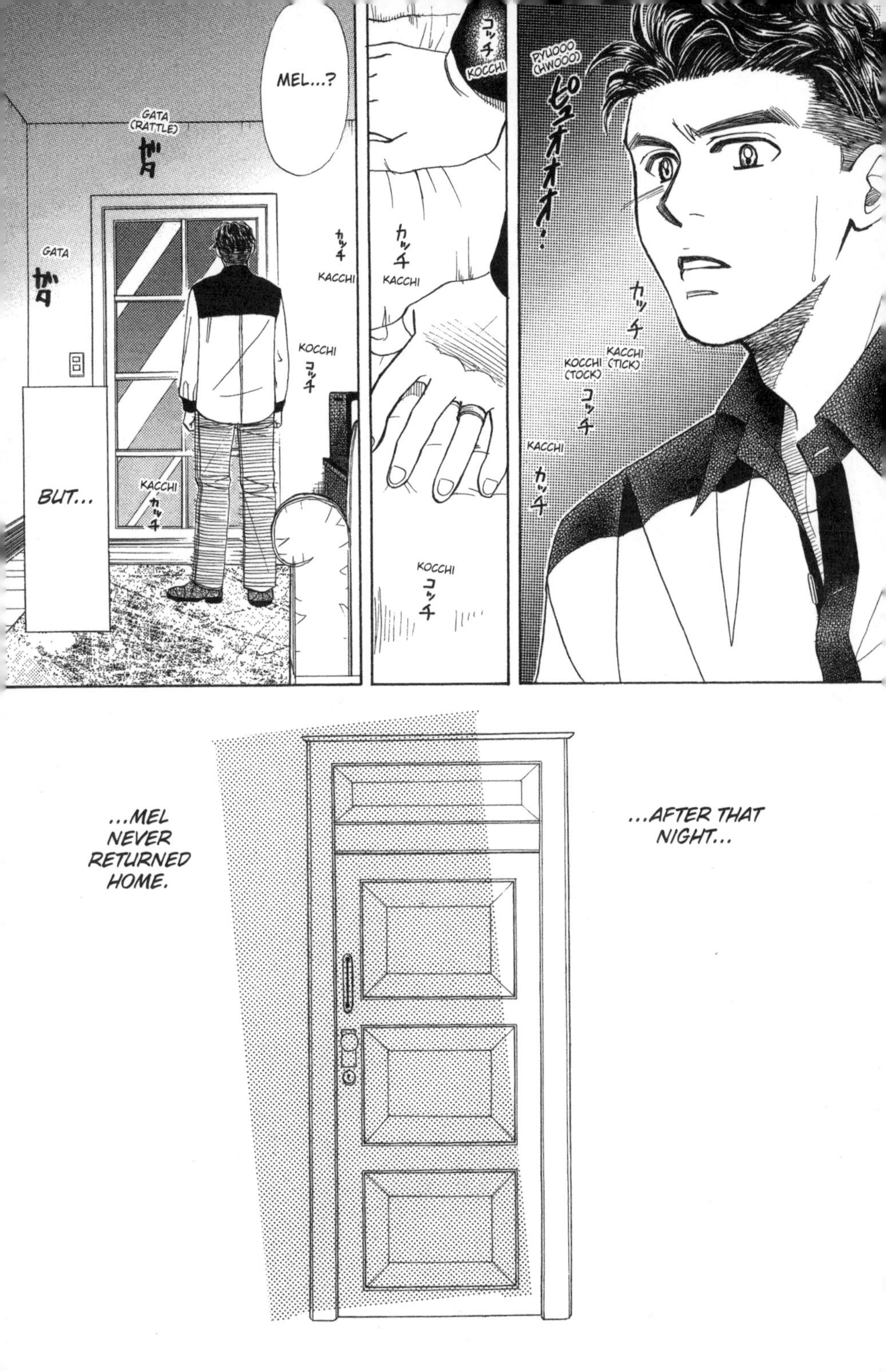
PYUOOO (HWOOO)
ピュオオオ…
カッチ
KACCHI (TICK)
KOCCHI (TOCK)
コッチ
KACCHI
カッチ
コッチ
KOCCHI
カッチ
KACCHI
KOCCHI
コッチ
MEL...?
GATA (RATTLE)
ガタ
GATA
ガタ
カッチ
KACCHI
KOCCHI
コッチ
KACCHI
カッチ
BUT...
...AFTER THAT NIGHT...
...MEL NEVER RETURNED HOME.

EPISODE IV

SCENE 1

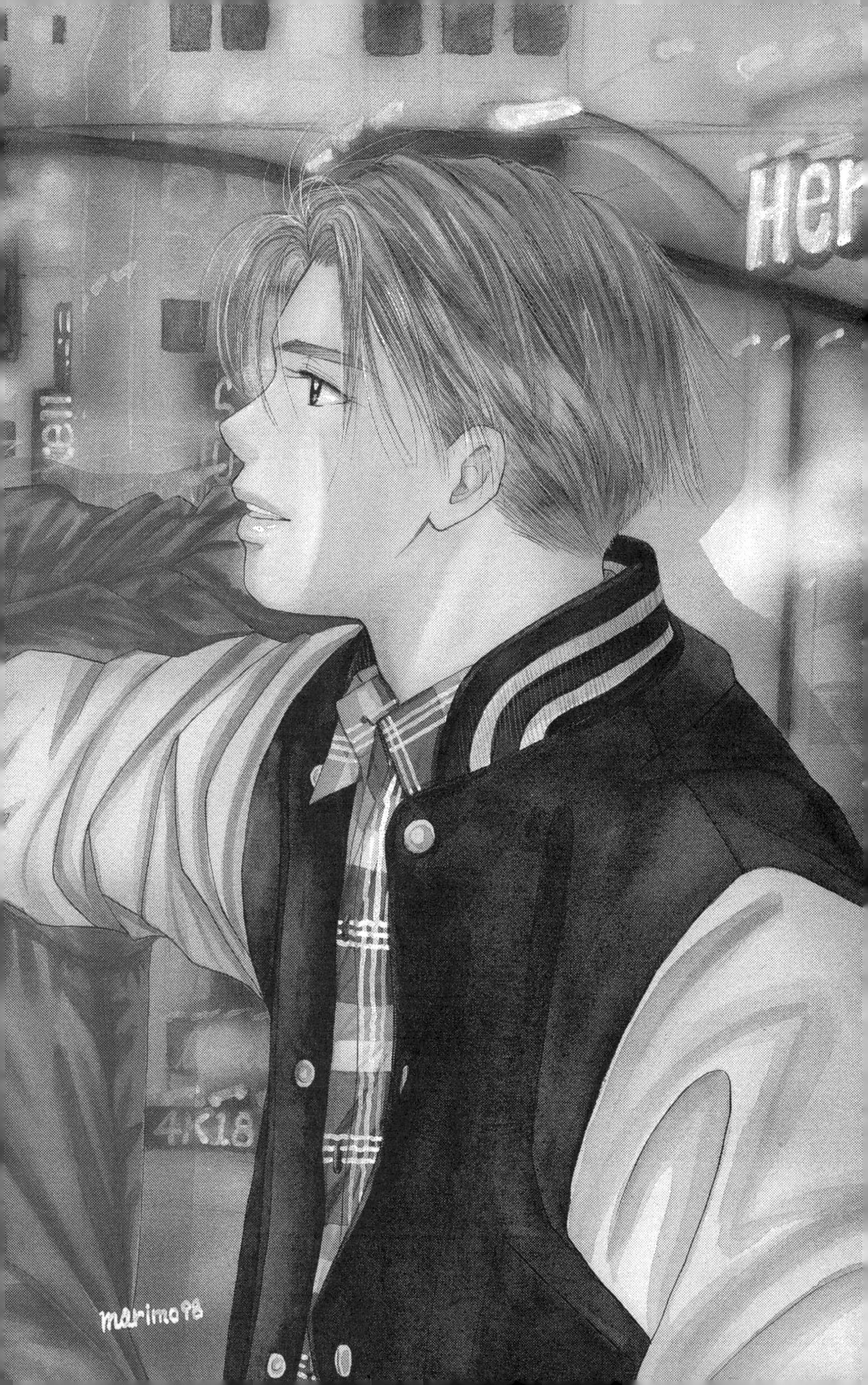
Her
4K18
marimo98

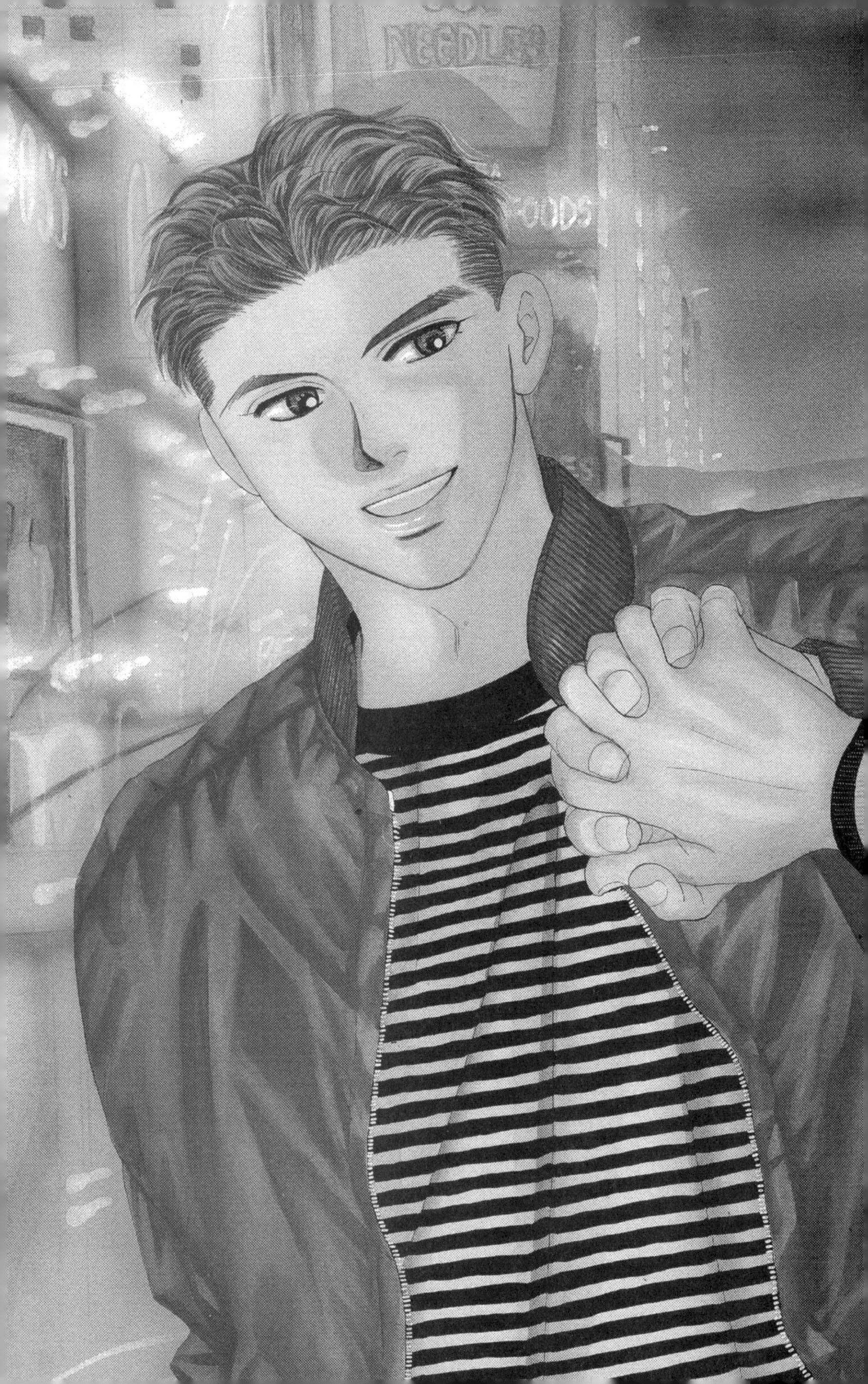
FOODS

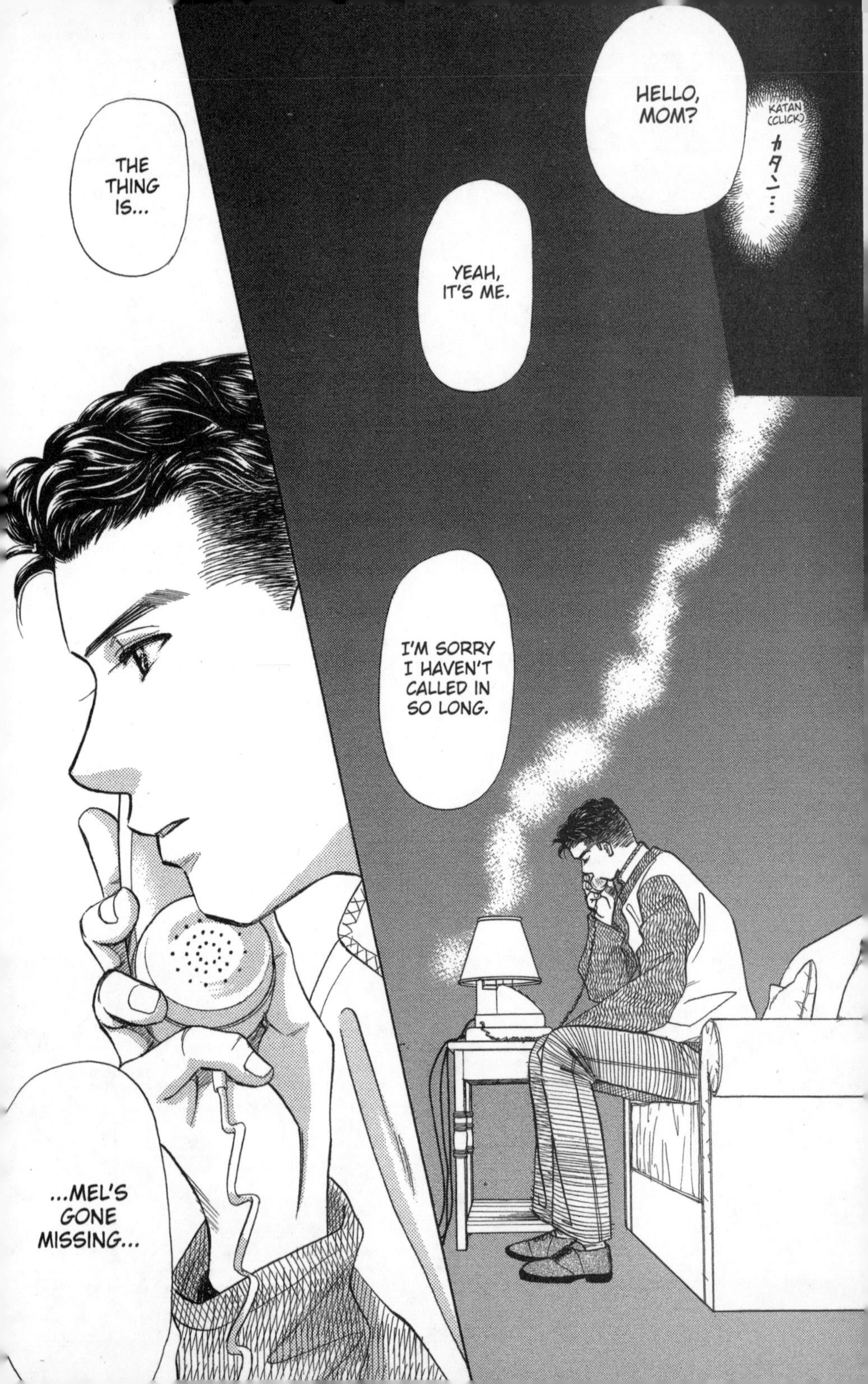
カタン…
KATAN (CLICK)
HELLO, MOM?
YEAH, IT'S ME.
I'M SORRY I HAVEN'T CALLED IN SO LONG.
THE THING IS...
...MEL'S GONE MISSING...

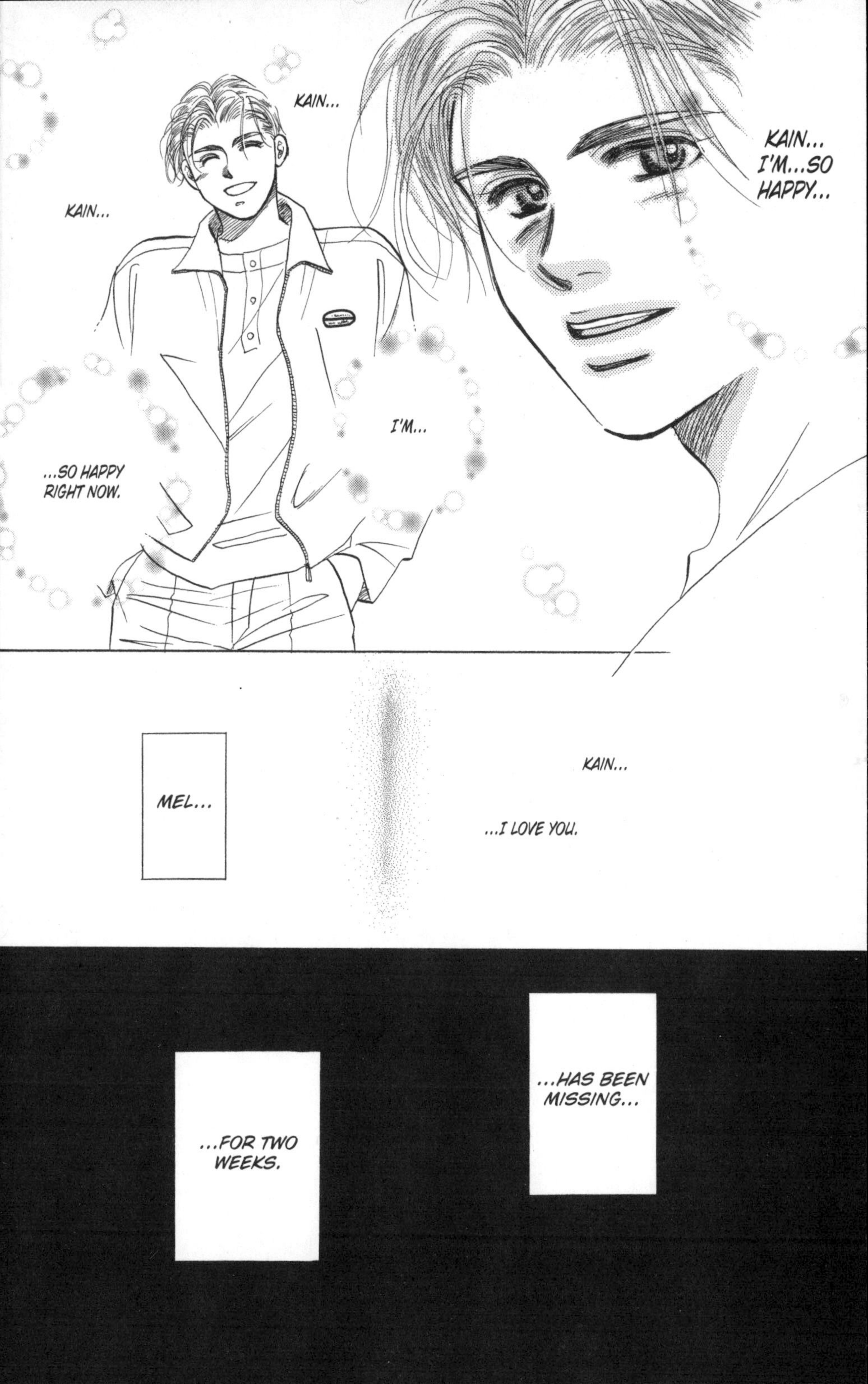
KAIN...
I'M...SO
HAPPY...
KAIN...
KAIN...
I'M...
...SO HAPPY
RIGHT NOW.
KAIN...
...I LOVE YOU.
MEL...
...HAS BEEN
MISSING...
...FOR TWO
WEEKS.

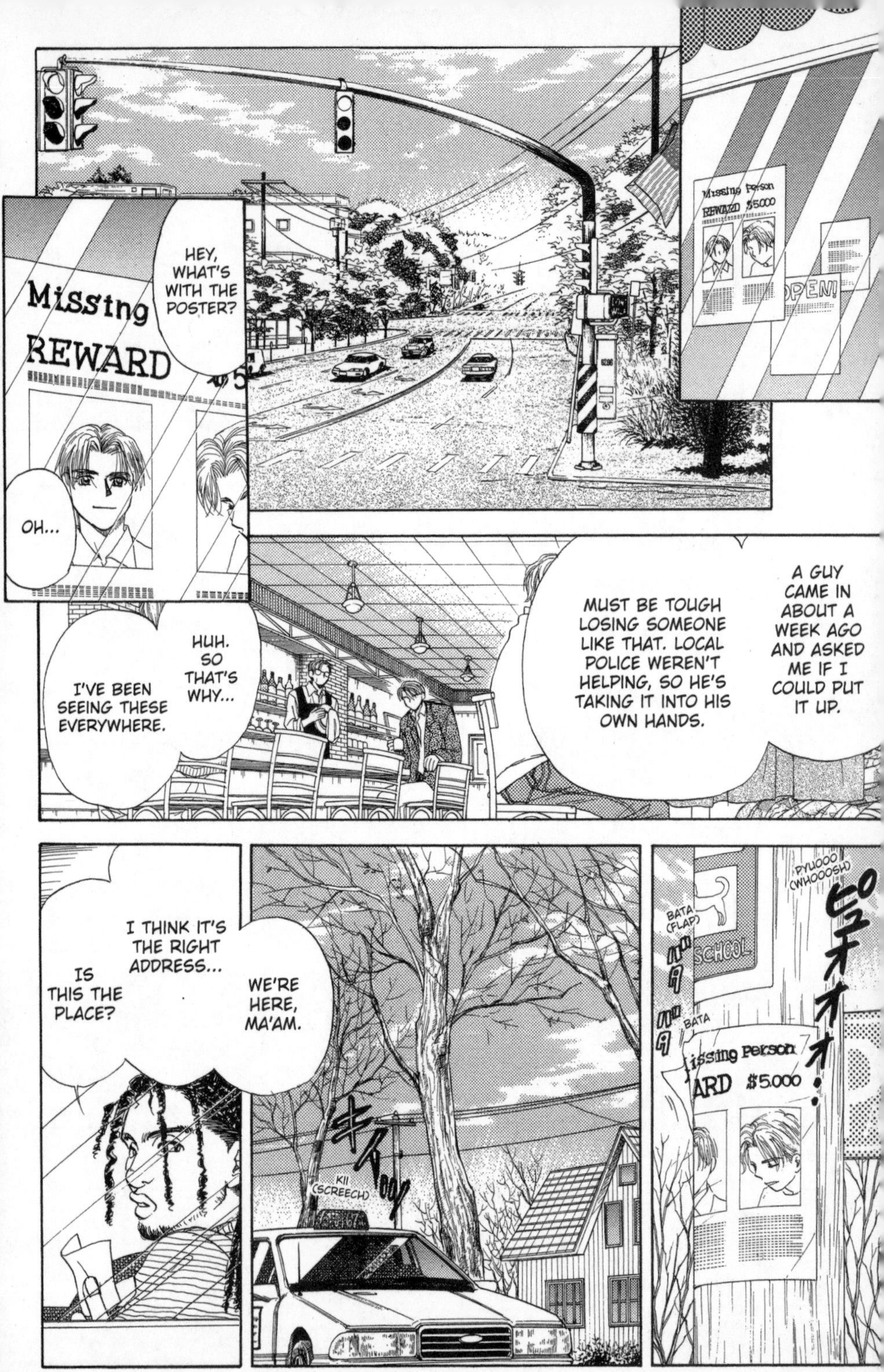
Missing Person
REWARD $5,000
OPEN!
HEY, WHAT'S WITH THE POSTER?
Missing
REWARD
OH...
A GUY CAME IN ABOUT A WEEK AGO AND ASKED ME IF I COULD PUT IT UP.
MUST BE TOUGH LOSING SOMEONE LIKE THAT. LOCAL POLICE WEREN'T HELPING, SO HE'S TAKING IT INTO HIS OWN HANDS.
HUH. SO THAT'S WHY...
I'VE BEEN SEEING THESE EVERYWHERE.
PYUOOO (WHOOOSH)
BATA (FLAP)
SCHOOL
BATA
issing Person
ARD $5,000
KII (SCREECH)
WE'RE HERE, MA'AM.
I THINK IT'S THE RIGHT ADDRESS...
IS THIS THE PLACE?

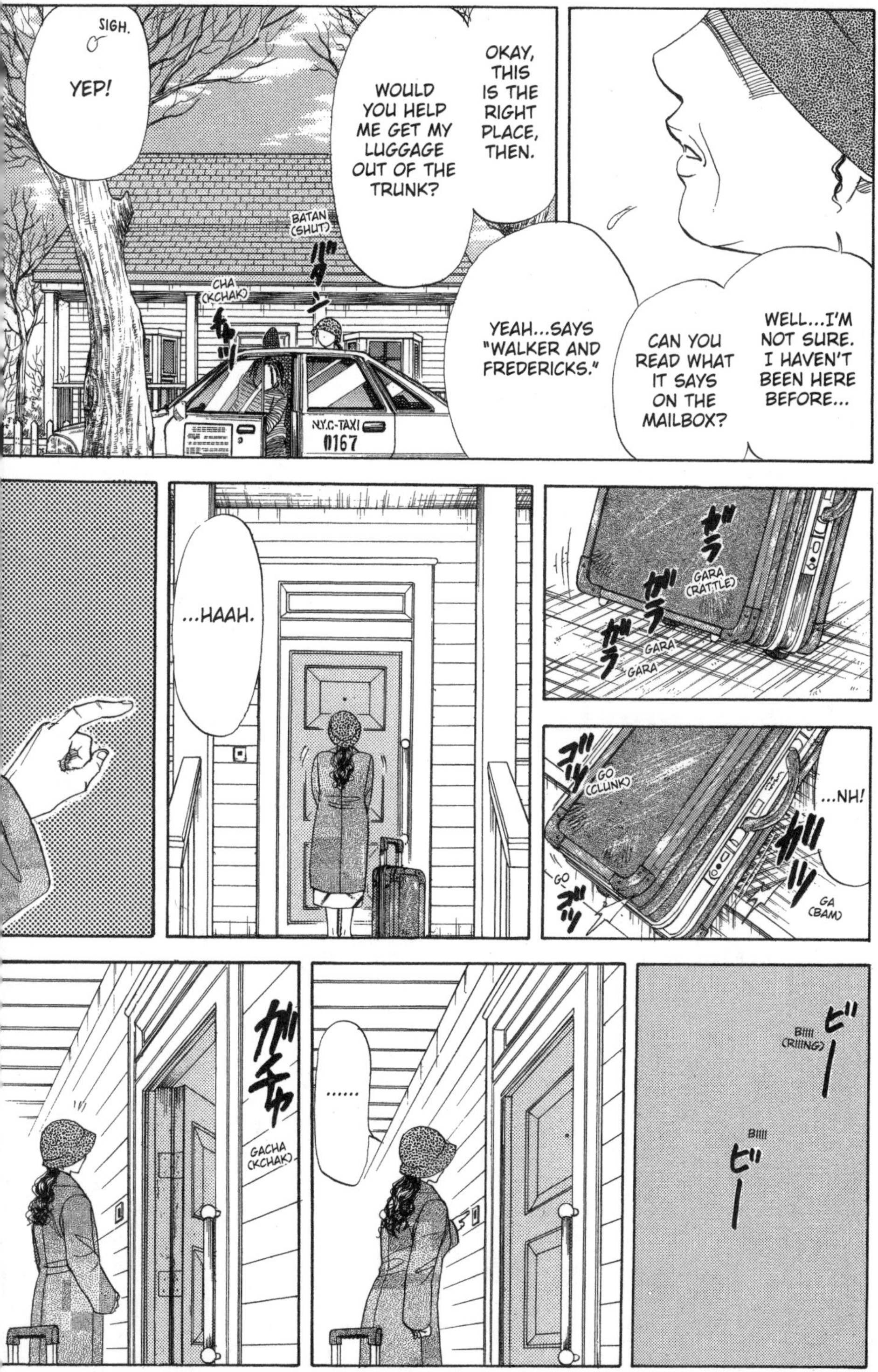
WELL...I'M NOT SURE. I HAVEN'T BEEN HERE BEFORE...
CAN YOU READ WHAT IT SAYS ON THE MAILBOX?
YEAH...SAYS "WALKER AND FREDERICKS."
OKAY, THIS IS THE RIGHT PLACE, THEN.
WOULD YOU HELP ME GET MY LUGGAGE OUT OF THE TRUNK?
BATAN (SHUT)
CHA (KCHAK)
SIGH.
YEP!
GARA (RATTLE)
GARA
GARA
...NH!
GO (CLUNK)
GA (BAM)
GO
...HAAH.
BIIII (RIIING)
BIIII
......
GACHA (KCHAK)

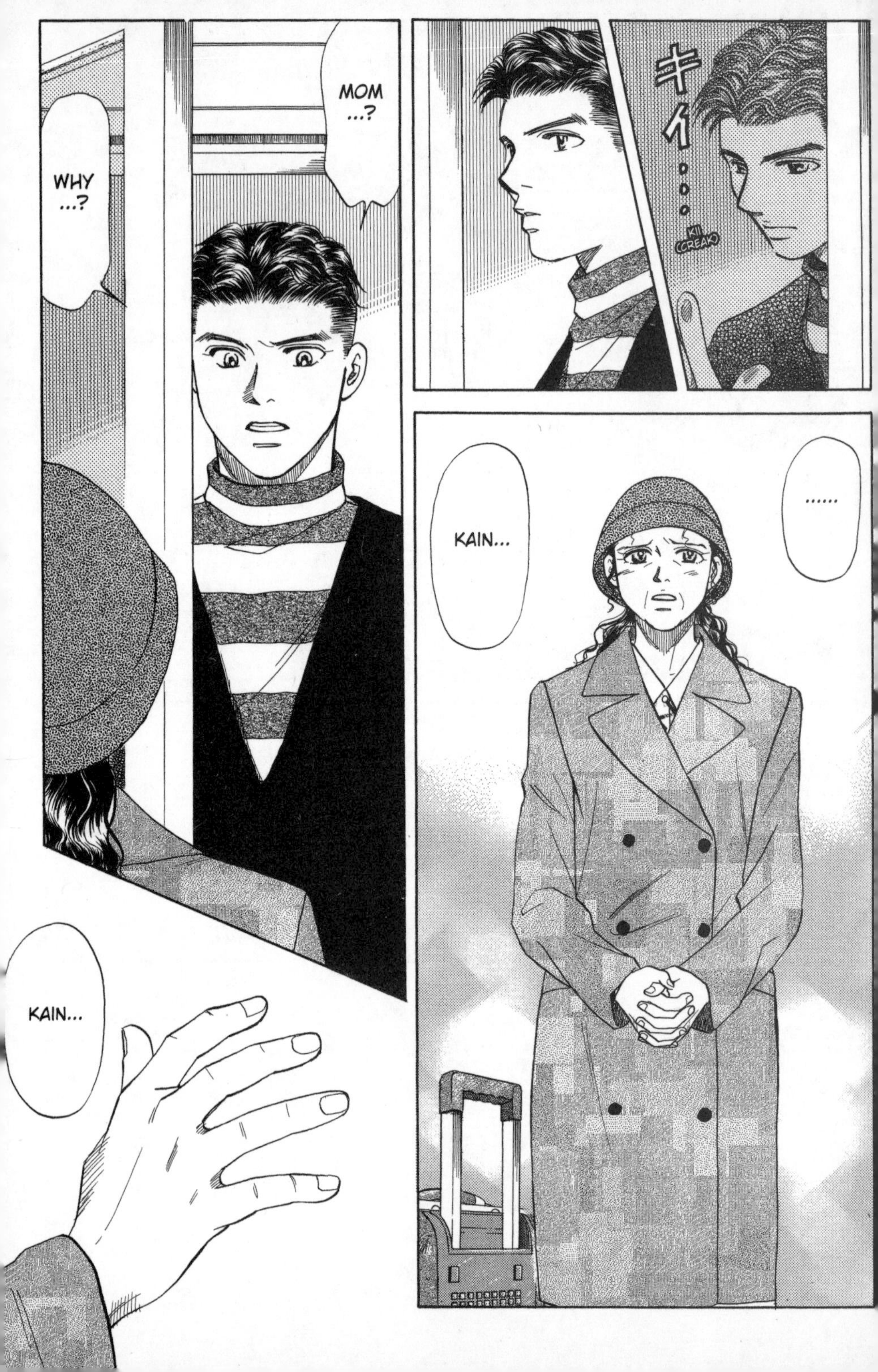
キィ...
KII (CREAK)
......
KAIN...
MOM ...?
WHY ...?
KAIN...

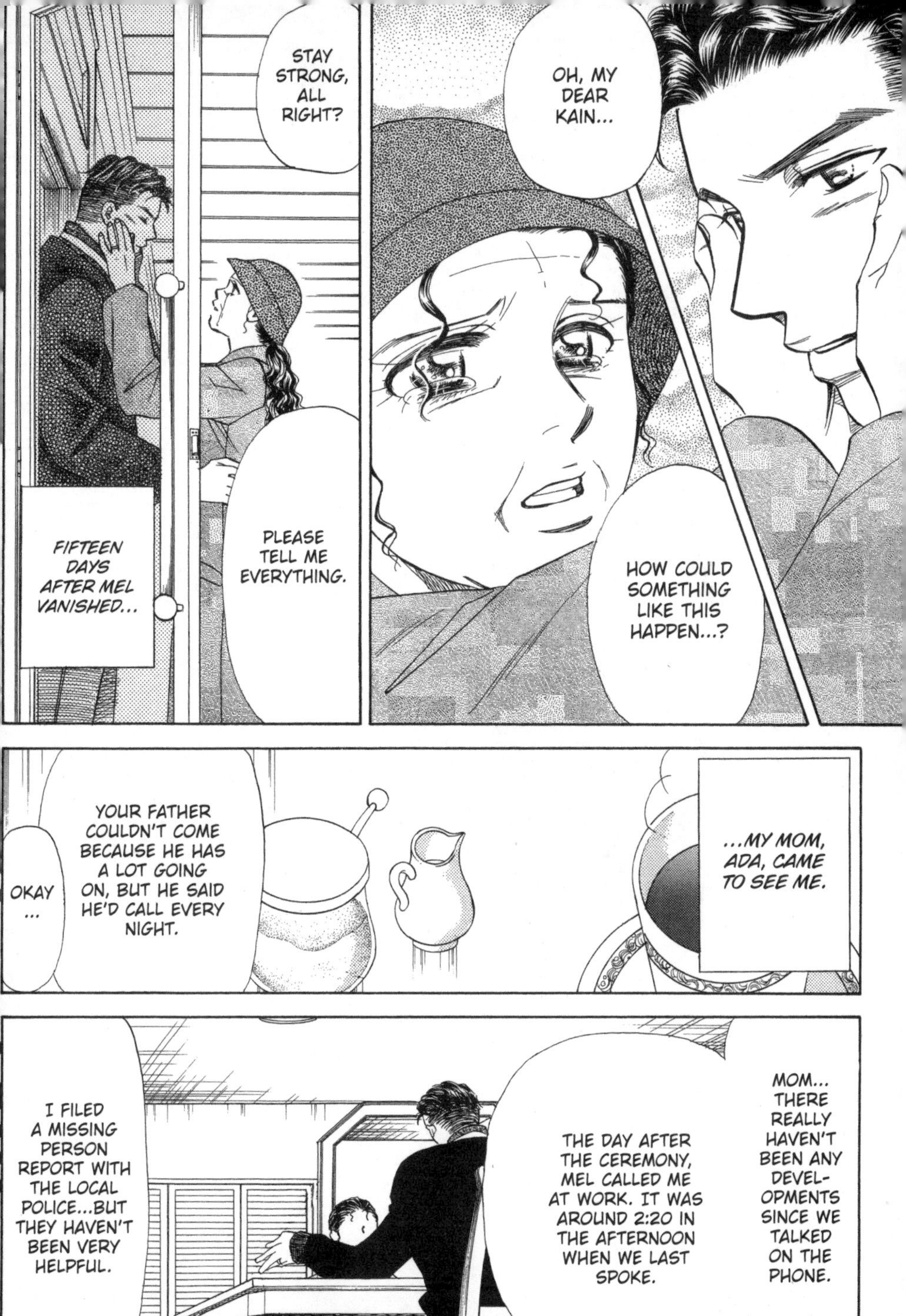
OH, MY DEAR KAIN...
HOW COULD SOMETHING LIKE THIS HAPPEN...?
STAY STRONG, ALL RIGHT?
PLEASE TELL ME EVERYTHING.
FIFTEEN DAYS AFTER MEL VANISHED...
...MY MOM, ADA, CAME TO SEE ME.
YOUR FATHER COULDN'T COME BECAUSE HE HAS A LOT GOING ON, BUT HE SAID HE'D CALL EVERY NIGHT.
OKAY ...
MOM... THERE REALLY HAVEN'T BEEN ANY DEVEL-OPMENTS SINCE WE TALKED ON THE PHONE.
THE DAY AFTER THE CEREMONY, MEL CALLED ME AT WORK. IT WAS AROUND 2:20 IN THE AFTERNOON WHEN WE LAST SPOKE.
I FILED A MISSING PERSON REPORT WITH THE LOCAL POLICE...BUT THEY HAVEN'T BEEN VERY HELPFUL.

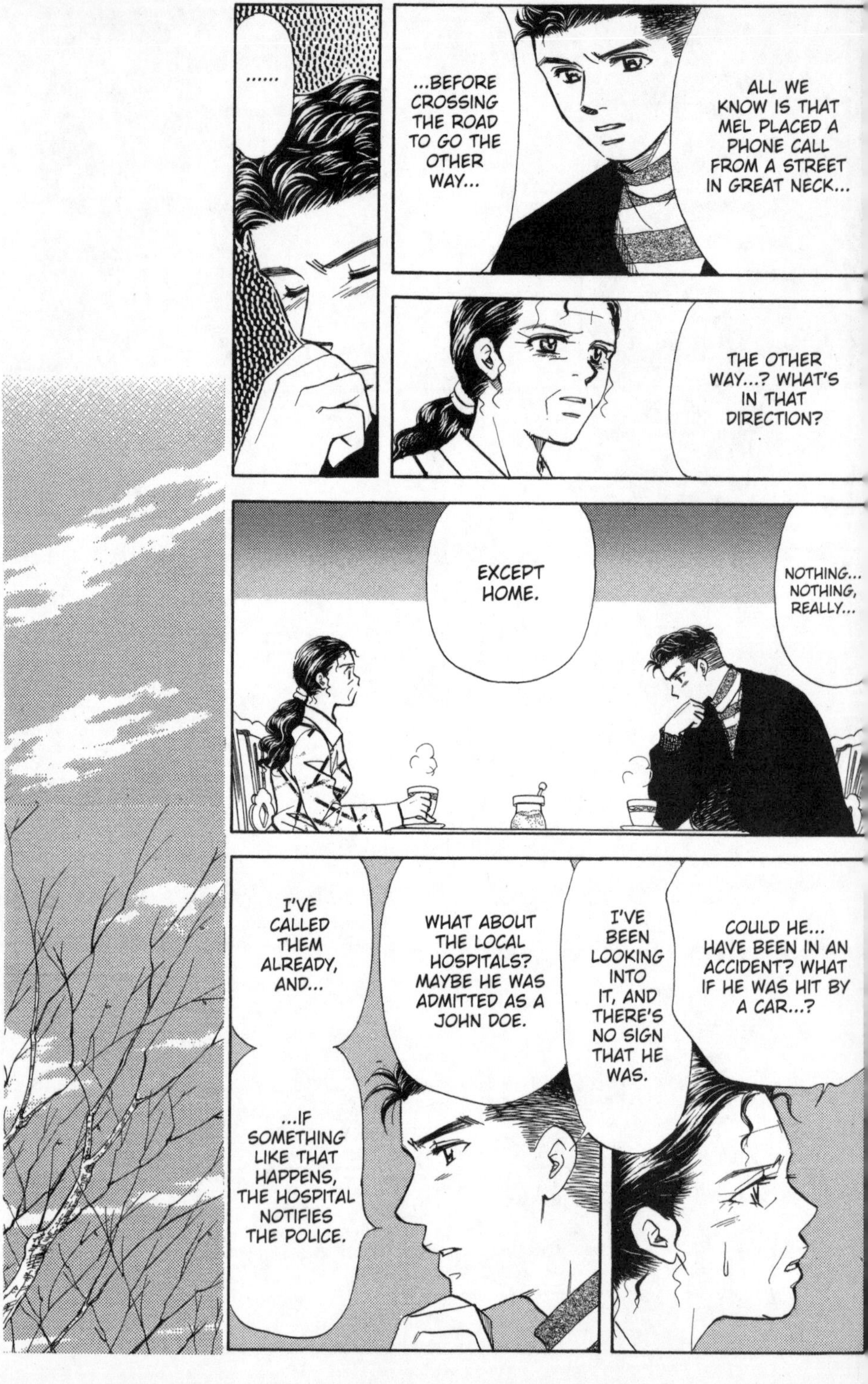
ALL WE KNOW IS THAT MEL PLACED A PHONE CALL FROM A STREET IN GREAT NECK...
...BEFORE CROSSING THE ROAD TO GO THE OTHER WAY...
THE OTHER WAY...? WHAT'S IN THAT DIRECTION?
......
NOTHING... NOTHING, REALLY...
EXCEPT HOME.
COULD HE... HAVE BEEN IN AN ACCIDENT? WHAT IF HE WAS HIT BY A CAR...?
I'VE BEEN LOOKING INTO IT, AND THERE'S NO SIGN THAT HE WAS.
WHAT ABOUT THE LOCAL HOSPITALS? MAYBE HE WAS ADMITTED AS A JOHN DOE.
I'VE CALLED THEM ALREADY, AND...
...IF SOMETHING LIKE THAT HAPPENS, THE HOSPITAL NOTIFIES THE POLICE.

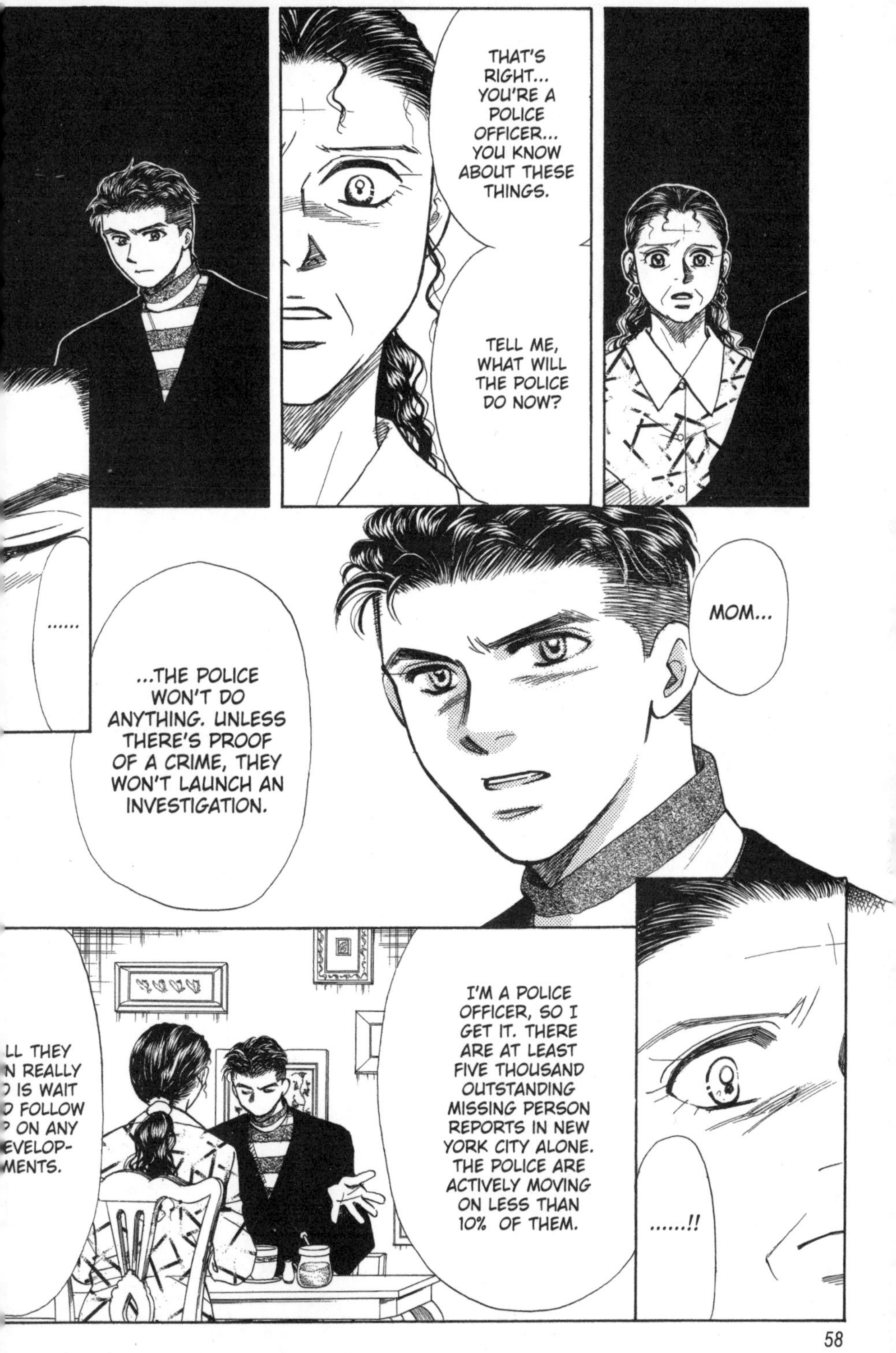
THAT'S RIGHT... YOU'RE A POLICE OFFICER... YOU KNOW ABOUT THESE THINGS.
TELL ME, WHAT WILL THE POLICE DO NOW?
MOM...
...THE POLICE WON'T DO ANYTHING. UNLESS THERE'S PROOF OF A CRIME, THEY WON'T LAUNCH AN INVESTIGATION.
......
......!!
I'M A POLICE OFFICER, SO I GET IT. THERE ARE AT LEAST FIVE THOUSAND OUTSTANDING MISSING PERSON REPORTS IN NEW YORK CITY ALONE. THE POLICE ARE ACTIVELY MOVING ON LESS THAN 10% OF THEM.
LL THEY N REALLY D IS WAIT D FOLLOW P ON ANY EVELOP-MENTS.

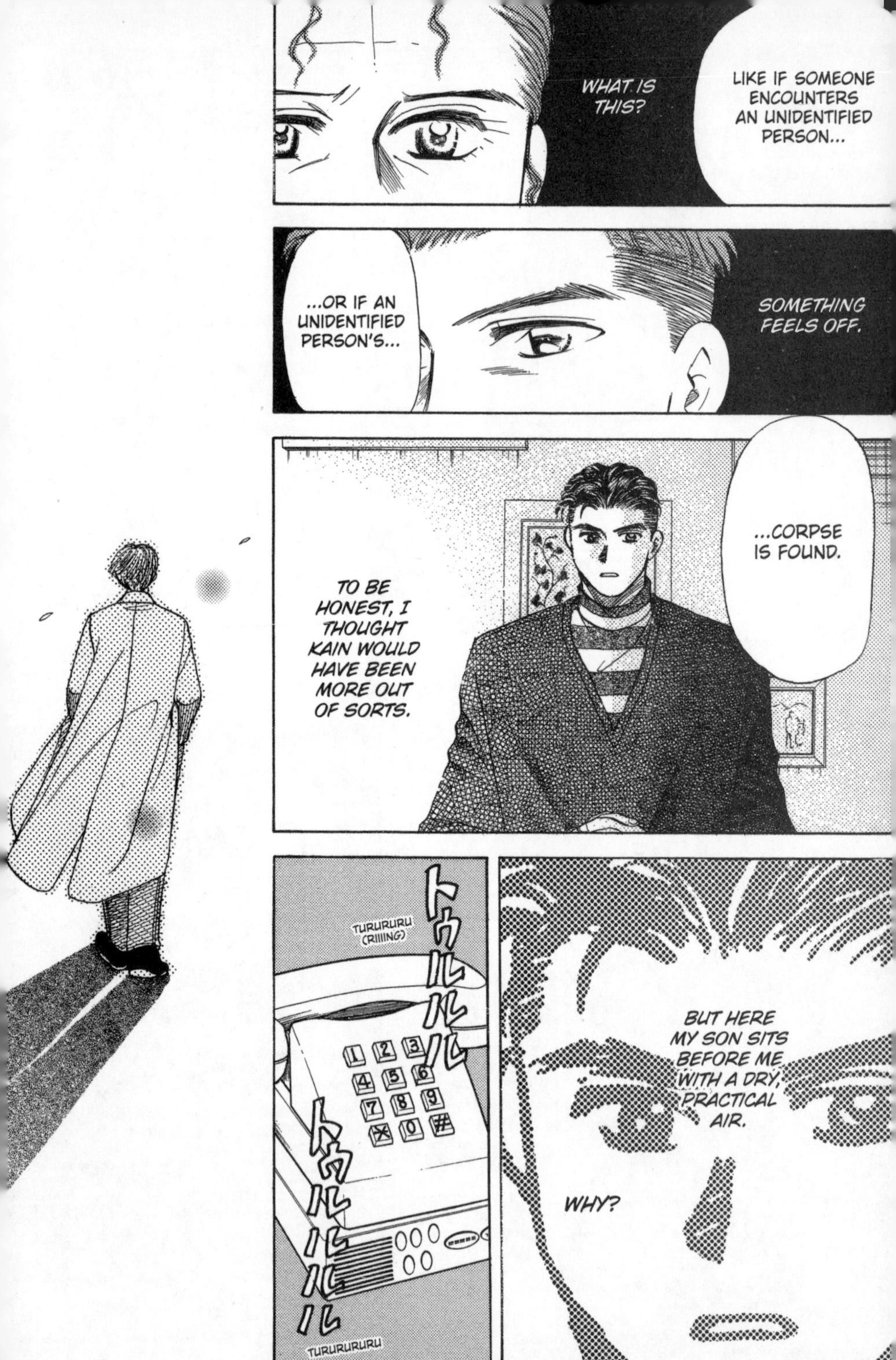
LIKE IF SOMEONE ENCOUNTERS AN UNIDENTIFIED PERSON...
WHAT IS THIS?
SOMETHING FEELS OFF.
...OR IF AN UNIDENTIFIED PERSON'S...
...CORPSE IS FOUND.
TO BE HONEST, I THOUGHT KAIN WOULD HAVE BEEN MORE OUT OF SORTS.
BUT HERE MY SON SITS BEFORE ME WITH A DRY, PRACTICAL AIR.
WHY?
トゥルルル
TURURURU (RIIIING)
トゥルルル
TURURURURU

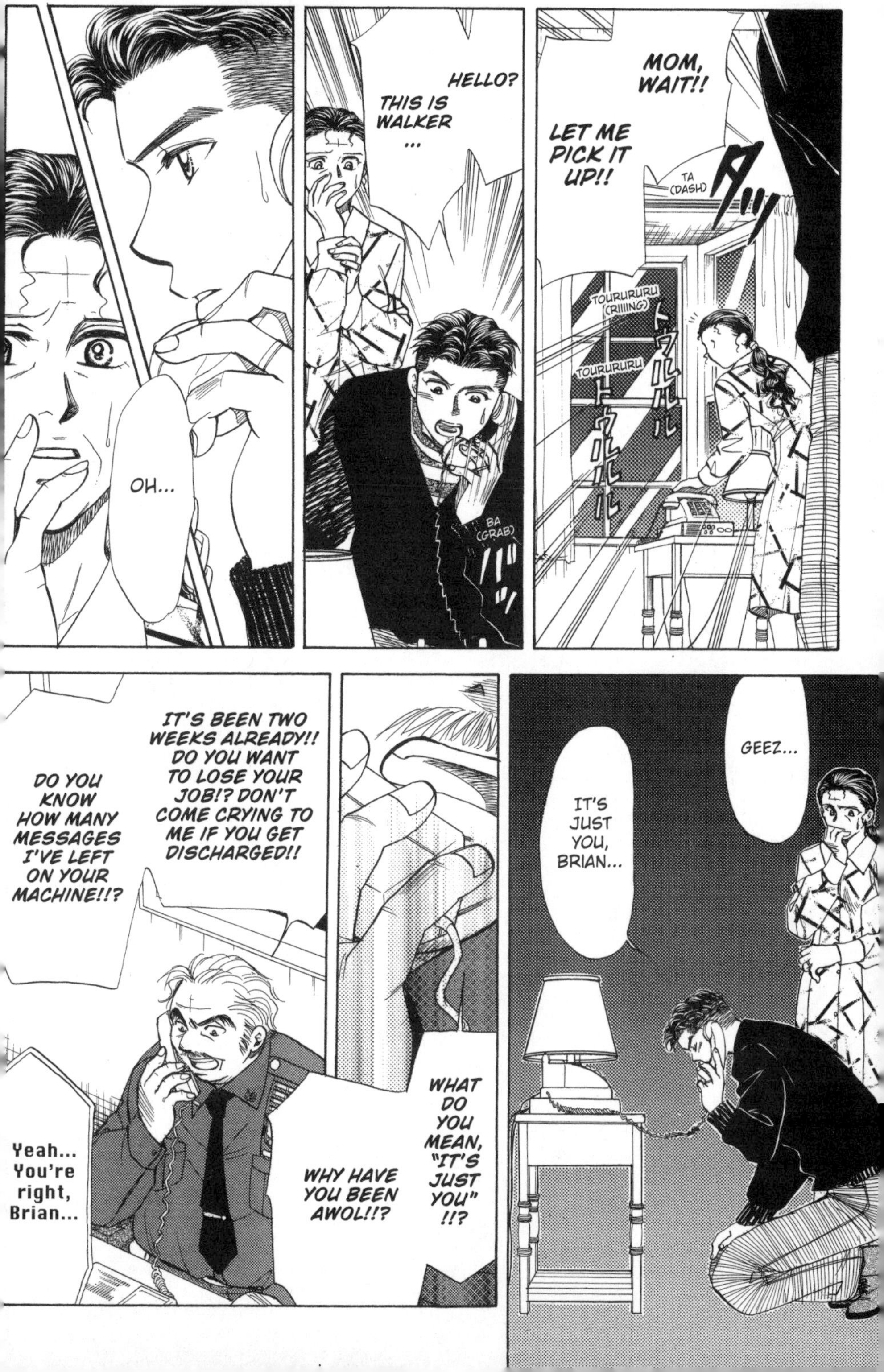
MOM, WAIT!!
LET ME PICK IT UP!!
TA (DASH)
ダッ
TOURURURU (RIIIING)
トゥルルル
TOURURURU
トゥルルル
HELLO?
THIS IS WALKER ...
BA (GRAB)
OH...
GEEZ...
IT'S JUST YOU, BRIAN...
WHAT DO YOU MEAN, "IT'S JUST YOU" !!?
WHY HAVE YOU BEEN AWOL!!?
IT'S BEEN TWO WEEKS ALREADY!! DO YOU WANT TO LOSE YOUR JOB!? DON'T COME CRYING TO ME IF YOU GET DISCHARGED!!
DO YOU KNOW HOW MANY MESSAGES I'VE LEFT ON YOUR MACHINE!!?
Yeah... You're right, Brian...

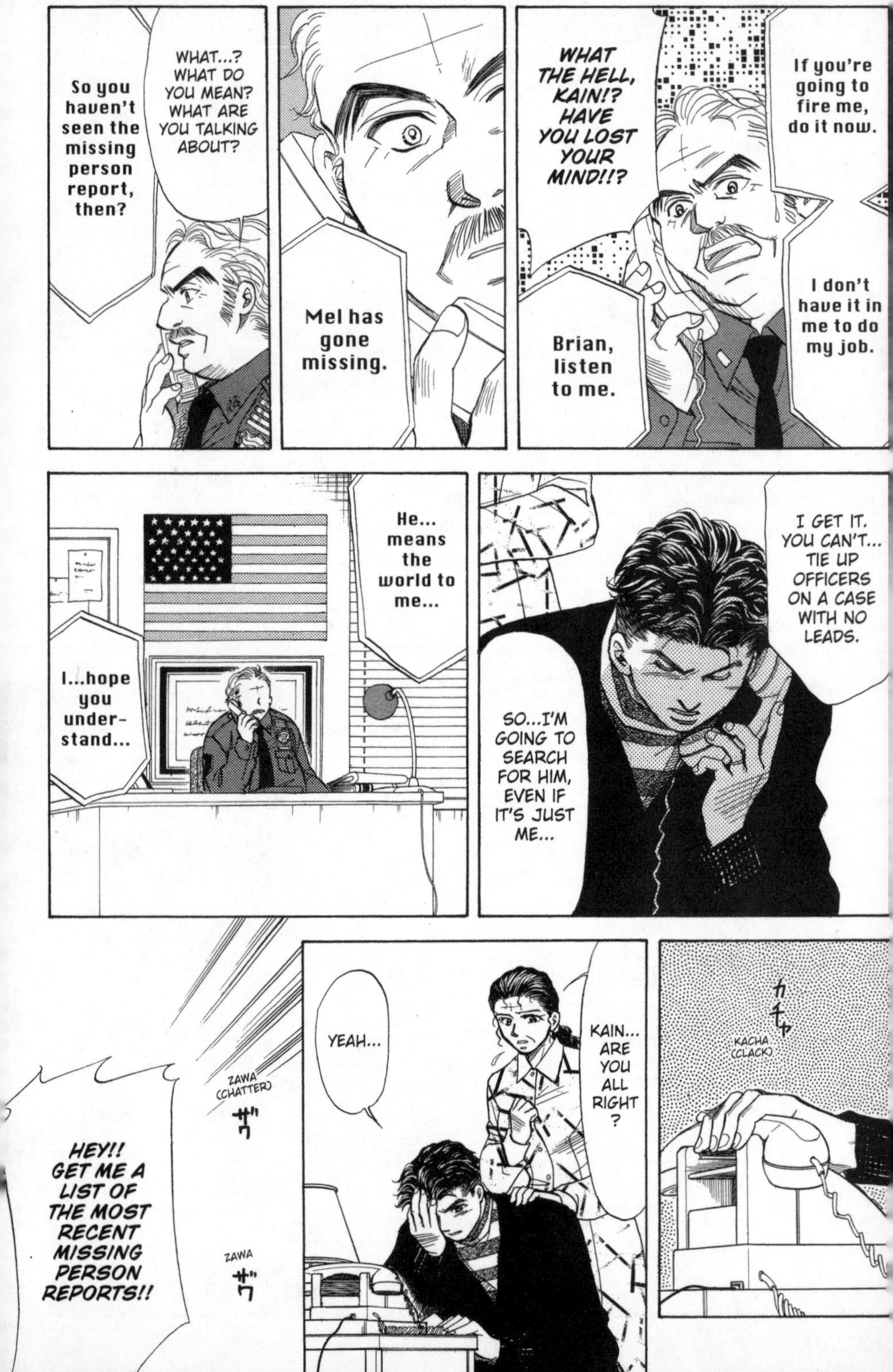
If you're going to fire me, do it now.
WHAT THE HELL, KAIN!? HAVE YOU LOST YOUR MIND!!?
I don't have it in me to do my job.
Brian, listen to me.
Mel has gone missing.
WHAT...? WHAT DO YOU MEAN? WHAT ARE YOU TALKING ABOUT?
So you haven't seen the missing person report, then?
I GET IT. YOU CAN'T... TIE UP OFFICERS ON A CASE WITH NO LEADS.
SO...I'M GOING TO SEARCH FOR HIM, EVEN IF IT'S JUST ME...
He... means the world to me...
I...hope you understand...
カチャ
KACHA (CLACK)
KAIN... ARE YOU ALL RIGHT?
YEAH...
ザワ
ZAWA (CHATTER)
ザワ
ZAWA
HEY!! GET ME A LIST OF THE MOST RECENT MISSING PERSON REPORTS!!

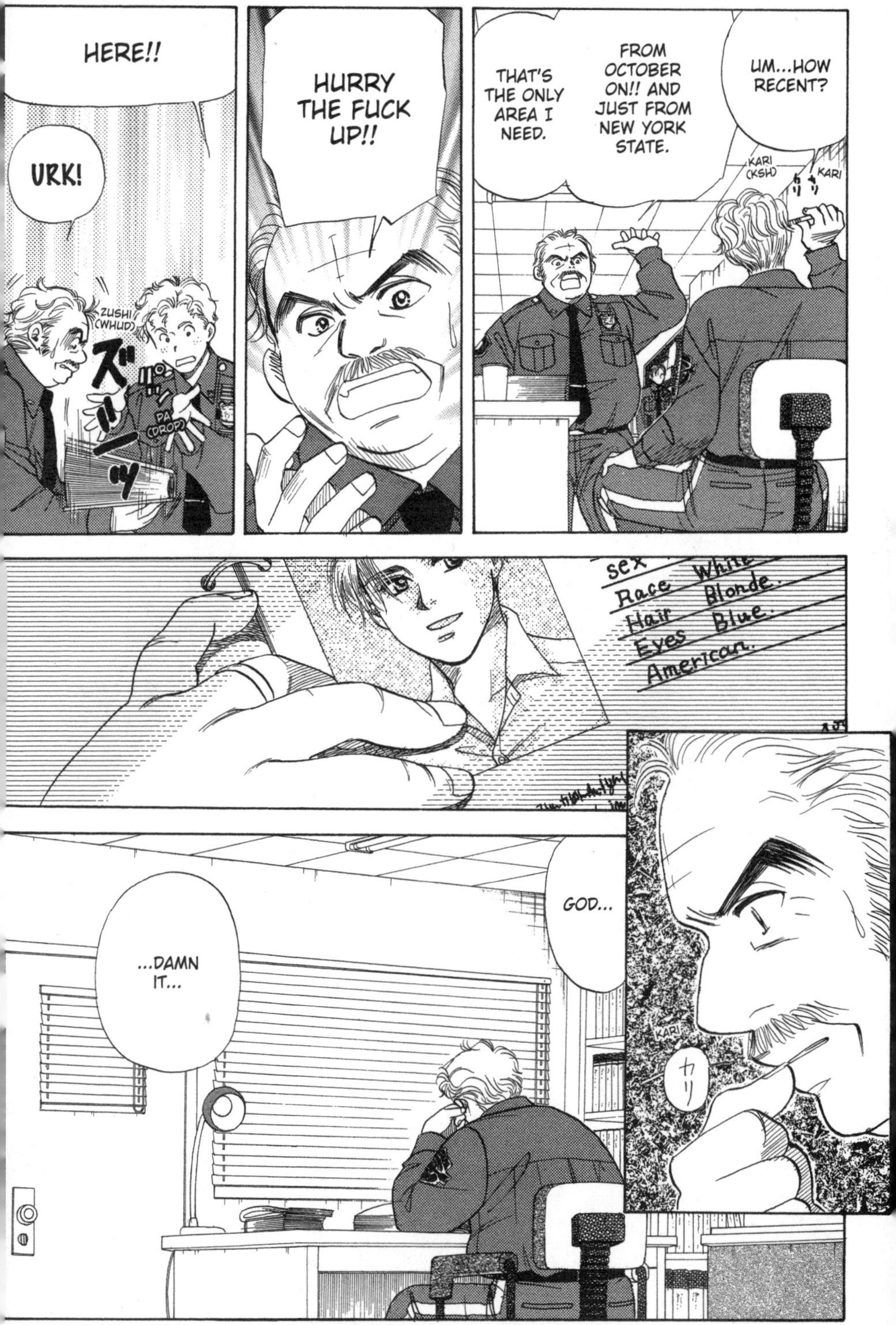
UM...HOW RECENT?
KARI
KARI (KSH)
FROM OCTOBER ON!! AND JUST FROM NEW YORK STATE.
THAT'S THE ONLY AREA I NEED.
HURRY THE FUCK UP!!
HERE!!
URK!
ZUSHI (WHUD)
PA (DROP)
sex
Race White
Hair Blonde.
Eyes Blue.
American.
GOD...
KARI
カリ
...DAMN IT...

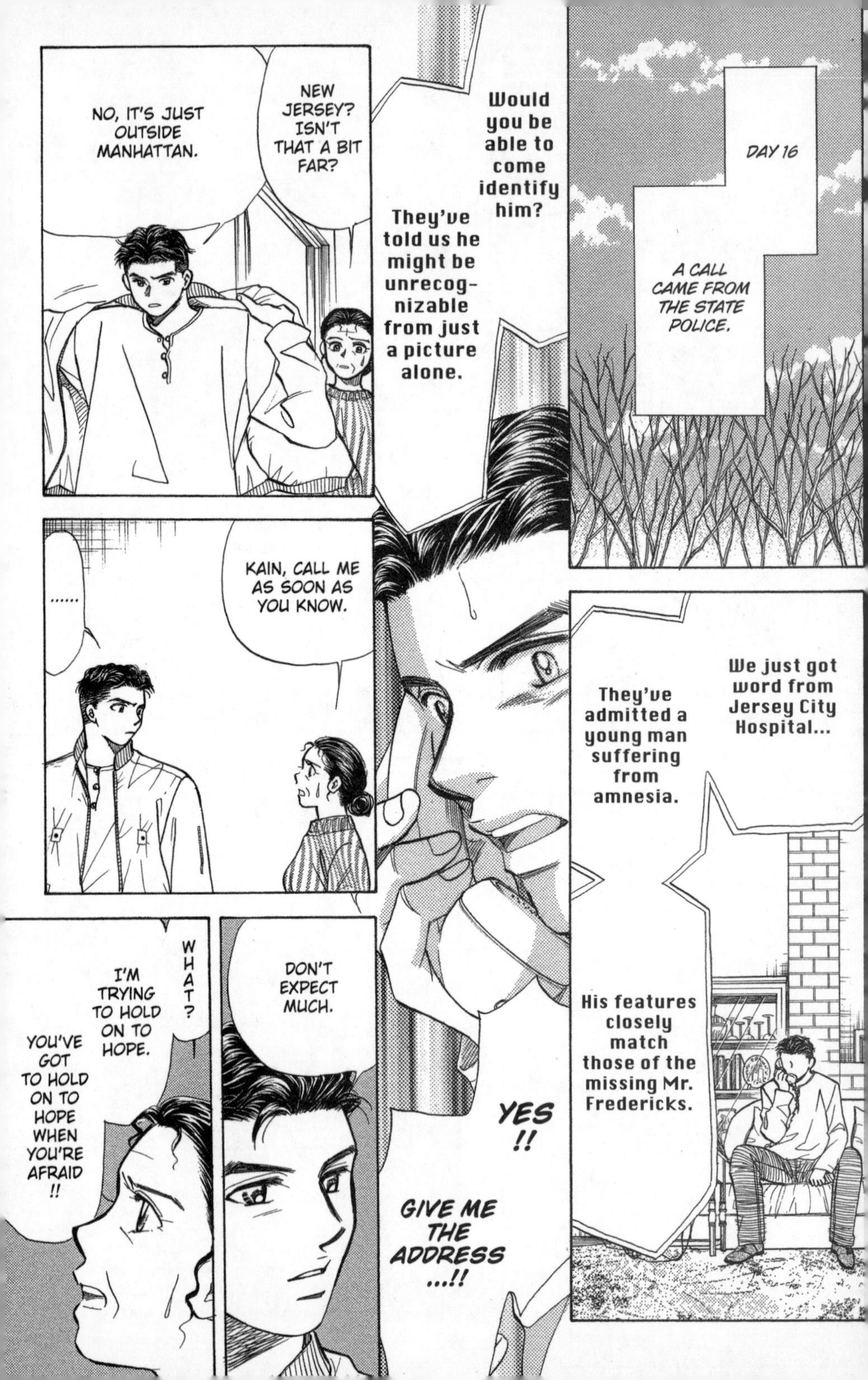
DAY 16
A CALL CAME FROM THE STATE POLICE.
We just got word from Jersey City Hospital...
They've admitted a young man suffering from amnesia.
His features closely match those of the missing Mr. Fredericks.
Would you be able to come identify him?
They've told us he might be unrecognizable from just a picture alone.
YES!!
GIVE ME THE ADDRESS ...!!
NEW JERSEY? ISN'T THAT A BIT FAR?
NO, IT'S JUST OUTSIDE MANHATTAN.
KAIN, CALL ME AS SOON AS YOU KNOW.
......
DON'T EXPECT MUCH.
WHAT?
I'M TRYING TO HOLD ON TO HOPE.
YOU'VE GOT TO HOLD ON TO HOPE WHEN YOU'RE AFRAID!!

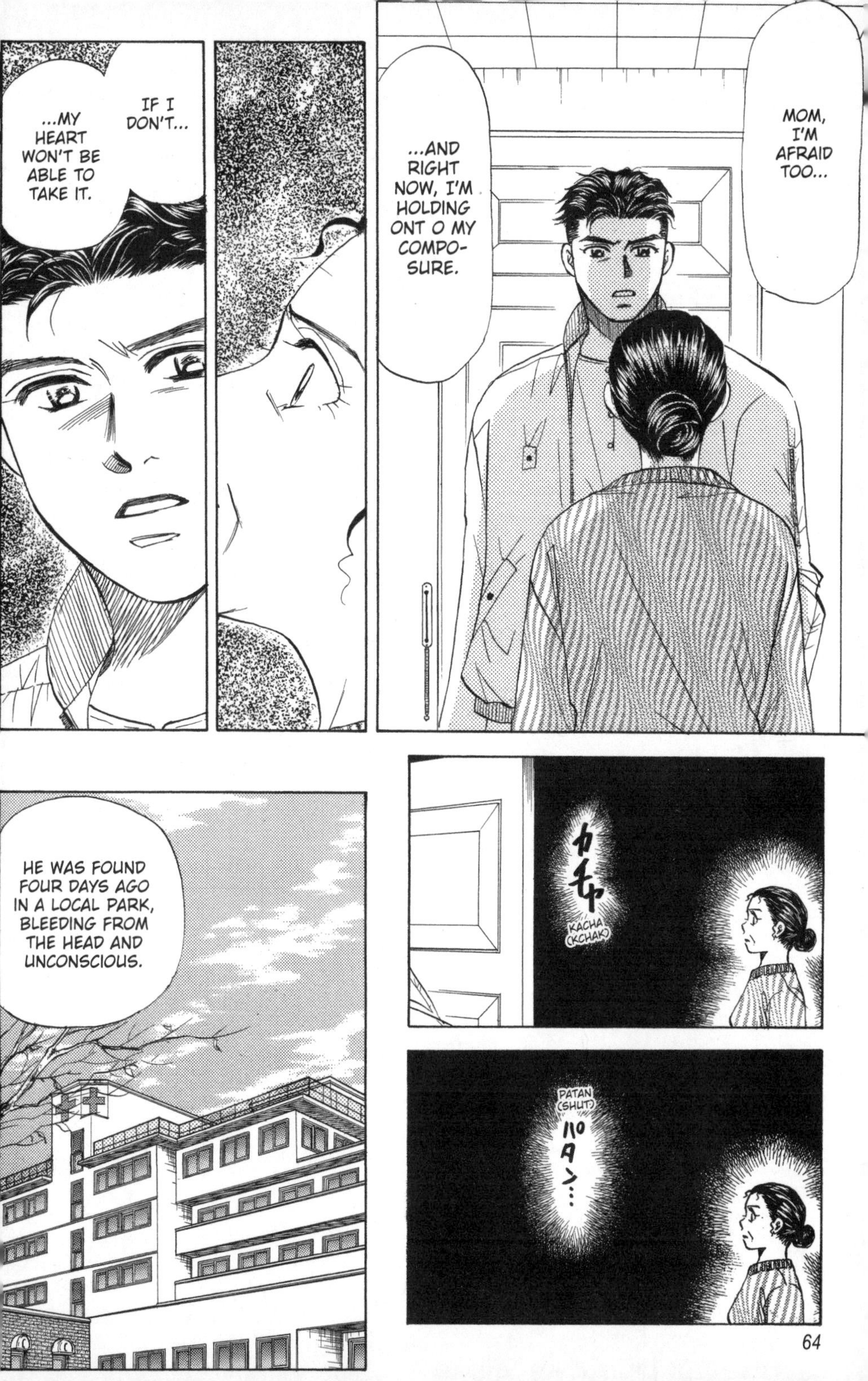
MOM, I'M AFRAID TOO...
...AND RIGHT NOW, I'M HOLDING ONT O MY COMPOSURE.
IF I DON'T...
...MY HEART WON'T BE ABLE TO TAKE IT.
カチャ
KACHA (KCHAK)
パタン…
PATAN (SHUT)
HE WAS FOUND FOUR DAYS AGO IN A LOCAL PARK, BLEEDING FROM THE HEAD AND UNCONSCIOUS.

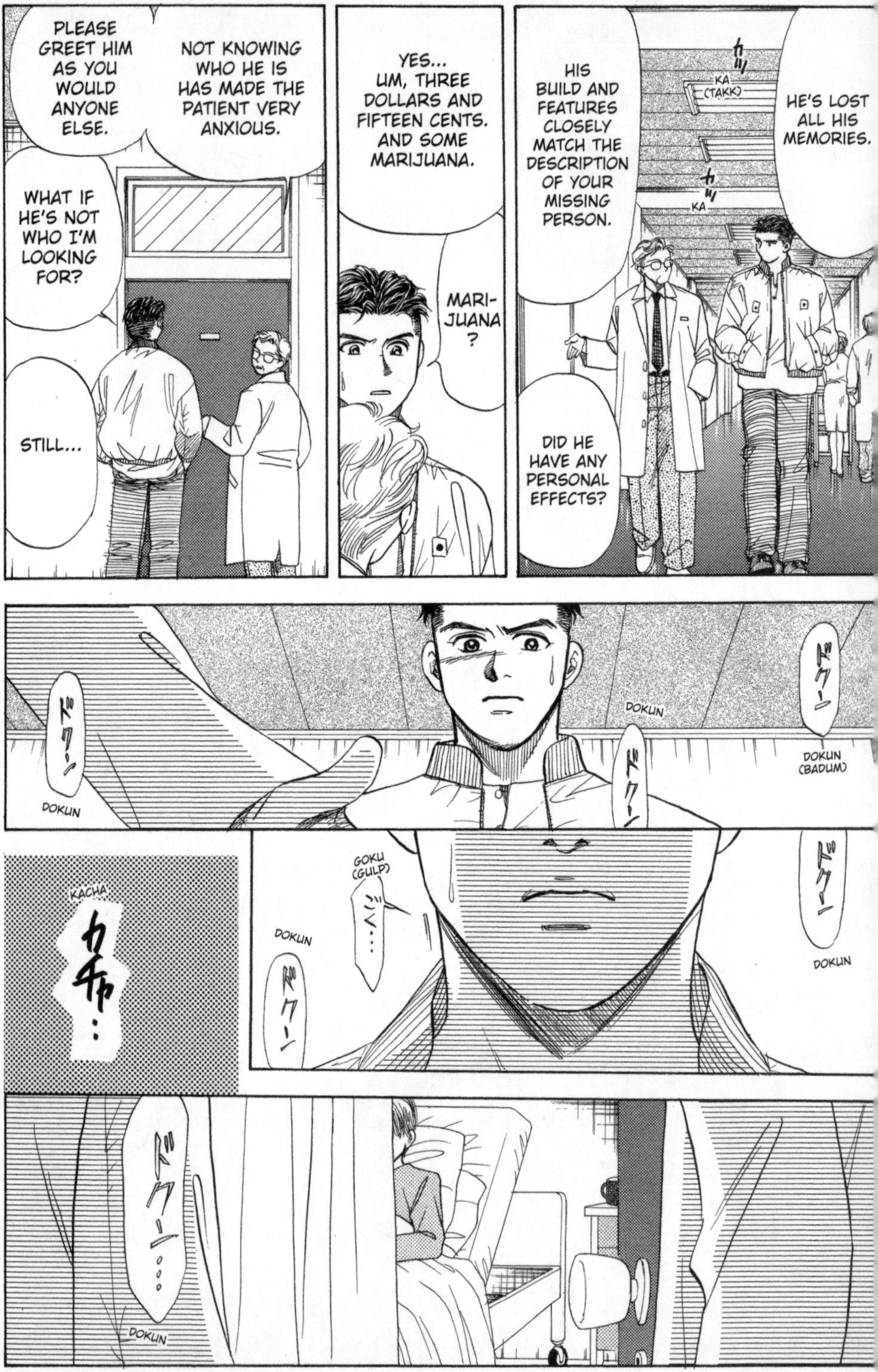

HE'S LOST ALL HIS MEMORIES.
KA (TAKK)
KA
HIS BUILD AND FEATURES CLOSELY MATCH THE DESCRIPTION OF YOUR MISSING PERSON.
DID HE HAVE ANY PERSONAL EFFECTS?
YES... UM, THREE DOLLARS AND FIFTEEN CENTS. AND SOME MARIJUANA.
MARIJUANA?
NOT KNOWING WHO HE IS HAS MADE THE PATIENT VERY ANXIOUS.
PLEASE GREET HIM AS YOU WOULD ANYONE ELSE.
WHAT IF HE'S NOT WHO I'M LOOKING FOR?
STILL...
DOKUN (BADUM)
DOKUN
DOKUN
DOKUN
GOKU (GULP)
DOKUN
KACHA
DOKUN

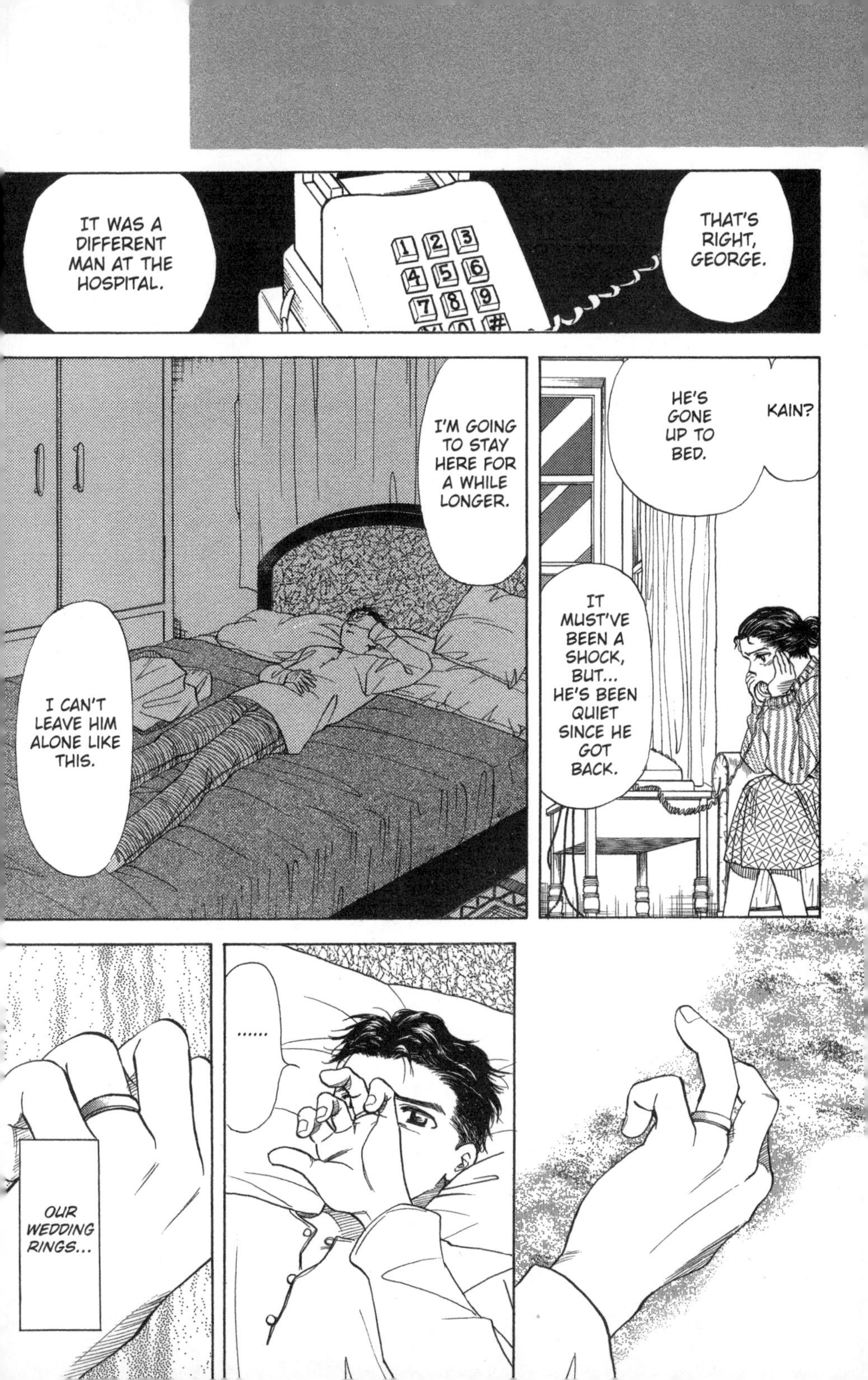
THAT'S RIGHT, GEORGE.
IT WAS A DIFFERENT MAN AT THE HOSPITAL.
KAIN?
HE'S GONE UP TO BED.
IT MUST'VE BEEN A SHOCK, BUT... HE'S BEEN QUIET SINCE HE GOT BACK.
I'M GOING TO STAY HERE FOR A WHILE LONGER.
I CAN'T LEAVE HIM ALONE LIKE THIS.
......
OUR WEDDING RINGS...

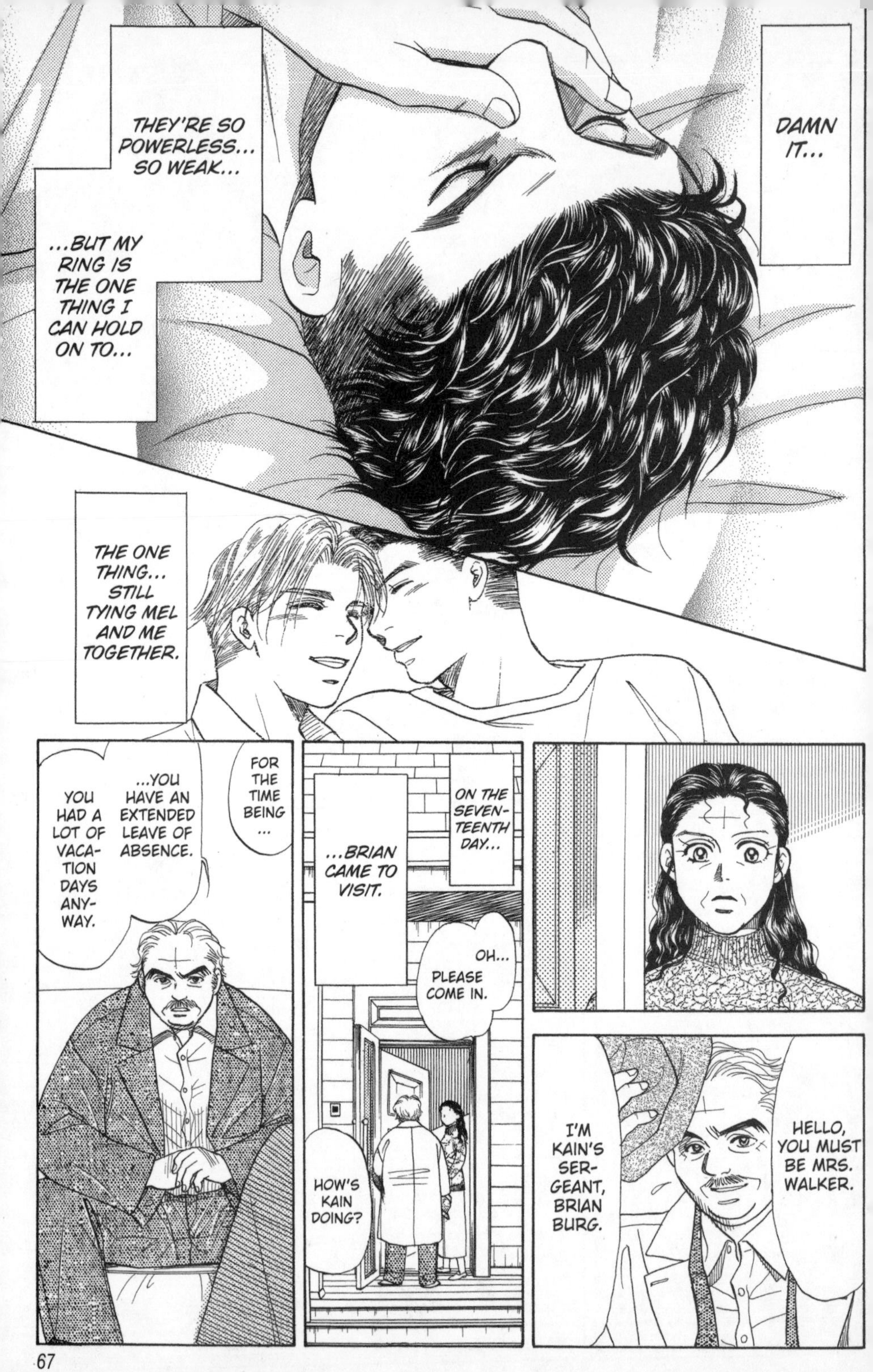
DAMN IT...
THEY'RE SO POWERLESS... SO WEAK...
...BUT MY RING IS THE ONE THING I CAN HOLD ON TO...
THE ONE THING... STILL TYING MEL AND ME TOGETHER.
HELLO, YOU MUST BE MRS. WALKER.
I'M KAIN'S SERGEANT, BRIAN BURG.
ON THE SEVENTEENTH DAY...
...BRIAN CAME TO VISIT.
OH... PLEASE COME IN.
HOW'S KAIN DOING?
FOR THE TIME BEING...
...YOU HAVE AN EXTENDED LEAVE OF ABSENCE.
YOU HAD A LOT OF VACATION DAYS ANYWAY.

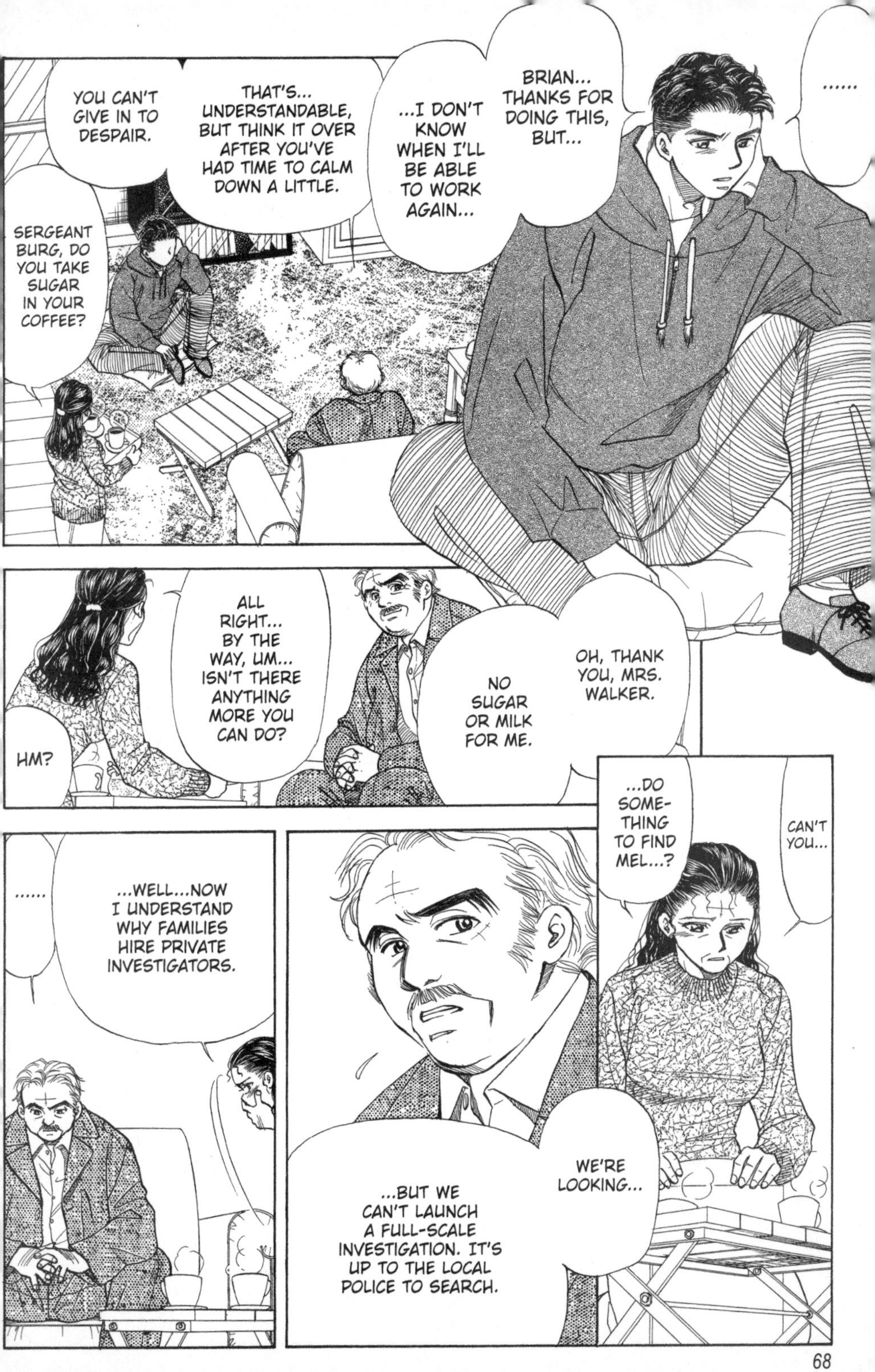
......
BRIAN... THANKS FOR DOING THIS, BUT...
...I DON'T KNOW WHEN I'LL BE ABLE TO WORK AGAIN...
THAT'S... UNDERSTANDABLE, BUT THINK IT OVER AFTER YOU'VE HAD TIME TO CALM DOWN A LITTLE.
YOU CAN'T GIVE IN TO DESPAIR.
SERGEANT BURG, DO YOU TAKE SUGAR IN YOUR COFFEE?
OH, THANK YOU, MRS. WALKER.
NO SUGAR OR MILK FOR ME.
ALL RIGHT... BY THE WAY, UM... ISN'T THERE ANYTHING MORE YOU CAN DO?
HM?
CAN'T YOU...
...DO SOME-THING TO FIND MEL...?
WE'RE LOOKING...
...BUT WE CAN'T LAUNCH A FULL-SCALE INVESTIGATION. IT'S UP TO THE LOCAL POLICE TO SEARCH.
......
...WELL...NOW I UNDERSTAND WHY FAMILIES HIRE PRIVATE INVESTIGATORS.

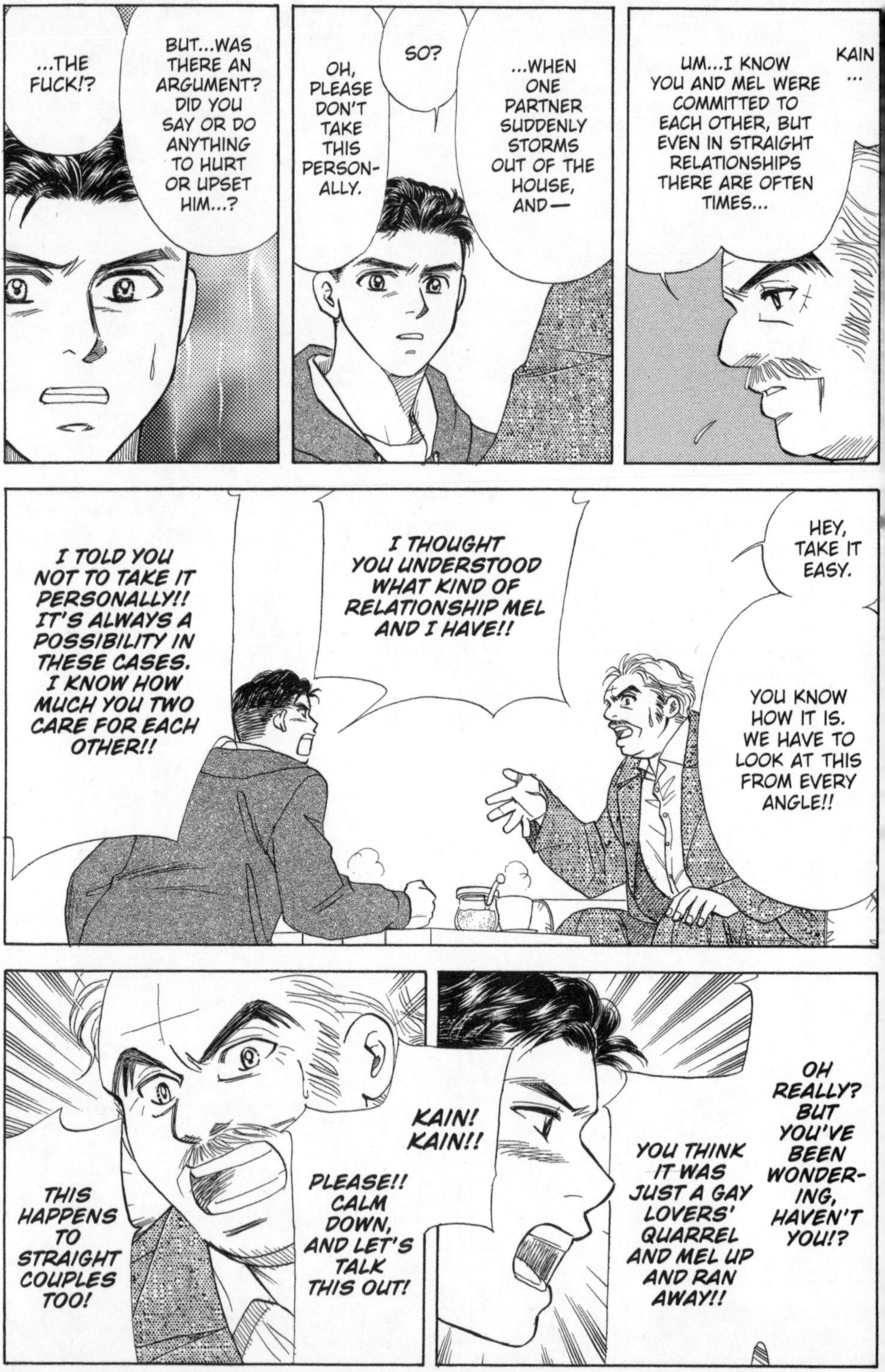
KAIN...
UM...I KNOW YOU AND MEL WERE COMMITTED TO EACH OTHER, BUT EVEN IN STRAIGHT RELATIONSHIPS THERE ARE OFTEN TIMES...
...WHEN ONE PARTNER SUDDENLY STORMS OUT OF THE HOUSE, AND—
SO?
OH, PLEASE DON'T TAKE THIS PERSON-ALLY.
BUT...WAS THERE AN ARGUMENT? DID YOU SAY OR DO ANYTHING TO HURT OR UPSET HIM...?
...THE FUCK!?
HEY, TAKE IT EASY.
YOU KNOW HOW IT IS. WE HAVE TO LOOK AT THIS FROM EVERY ANGLE!!
I THOUGHT YOU UNDERSTOOD WHAT KIND OF RELATIONSHIP MEL AND I HAVE!!
I TOLD YOU NOT TO TAKE IT PERSONALLY!! IT'S ALWAYS A POSSIBILITY IN THESE CASES. I KNOW HOW MUCH YOU TWO CARE FOR EACH OTHER!!
OH REALLY? BUT YOU'VE BEEN WONDER-ING, HAVEN'T YOU!?
YOU THINK IT WAS JUST A GAY LOVERS' QUARREL AND MEL UP AND RAN AWAY!!
KAIN! KAIN!!
PLEASE!! CALM DOWN, AND LET'S TALK THIS OUT!
THIS HAPPENS TO STRAIGHT COUPLES TOO!

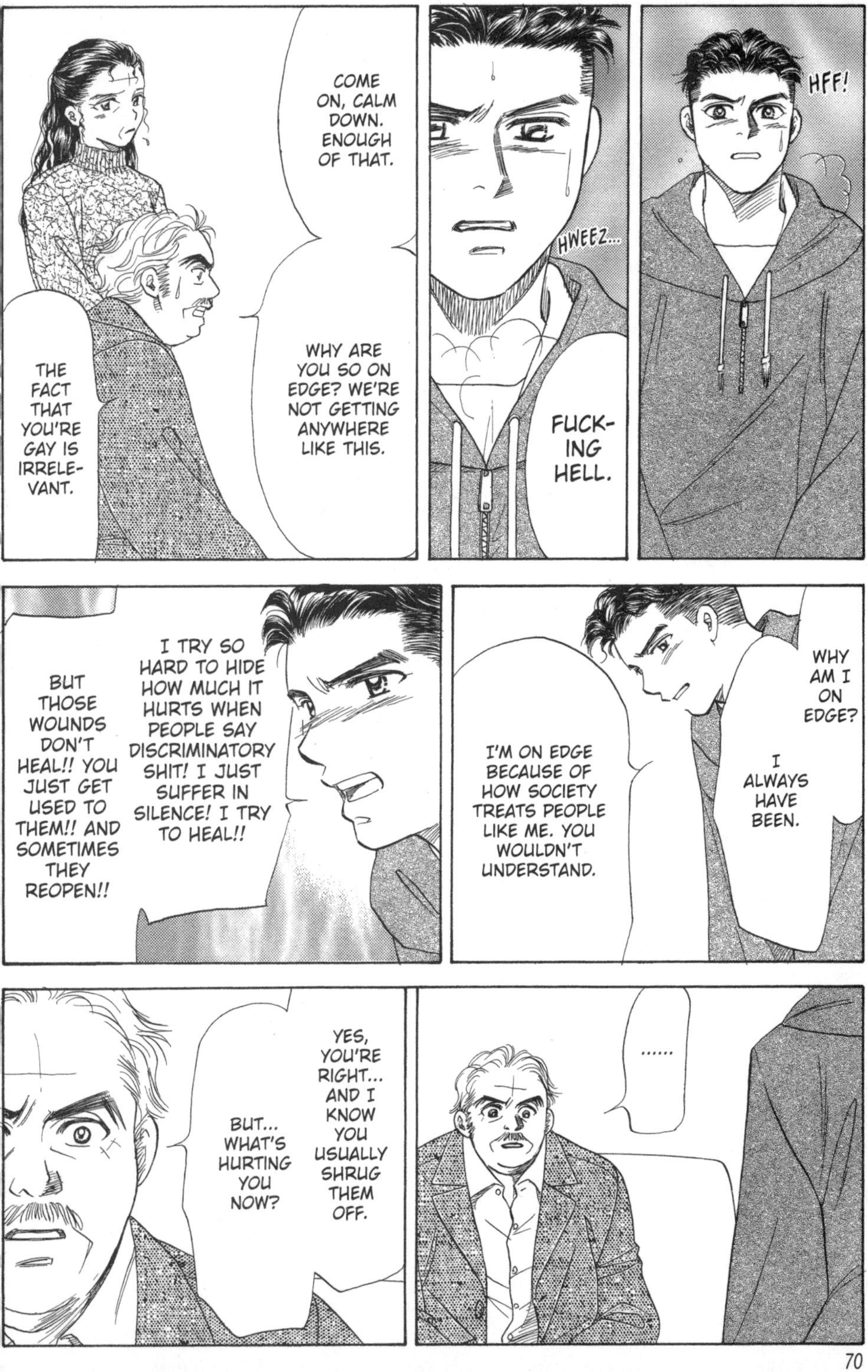
HFF!
HWEEZ...
FUCKING HELL.
COME ON, CALM DOWN. ENOUGH OF THAT.
WHY ARE YOU SO ON EDGE? WE'RE NOT GETTING ANYWHERE LIKE THIS.
THE FACT THAT YOU'RE GAY IS IRRELEVANT.
WHY AM I ON EDGE?
I ALWAYS HAVE BEEN.
I'M ON EDGE BECAUSE OF HOW SOCIETY TREATS PEOPLE LIKE ME. YOU WOULDN'T UNDERSTAND.
I TRY SO HARD TO HIDE HOW MUCH IT HURTS WHEN PEOPLE SAY DISCRIMINATORY SHIT! I JUST SUFFER IN SILENCE! I TRY TO HEAL!!
BUT THOSE WOUNDS DON'T HEAL!! YOU JUST GET USED TO THEM!! AND SOMETIMES THEY REOPEN!!
......
YES, YOU'RE RIGHT... AND I KNOW YOU USUALLY SHRUG THEM OFF.
BUT... WHAT'S HURTING YOU NOW?

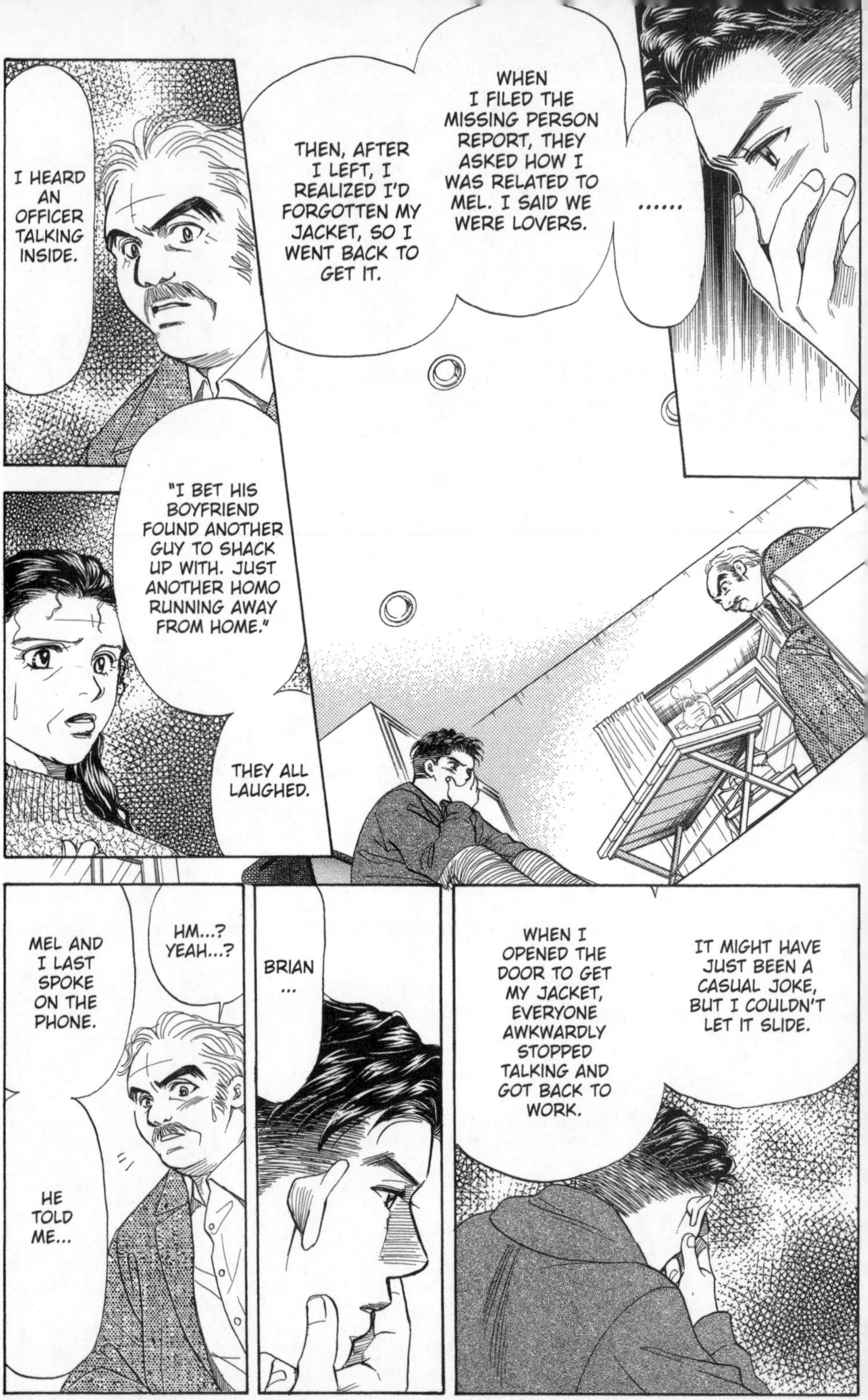
......
WHEN I FILED THE MISSING PERSON REPORT, THEY ASKED HOW I WAS RELATED TO MEL. I SAID WE WERE LOVERS.
THEN, AFTER I LEFT, I REALIZED I'D FORGOTTEN MY JACKET, SO I WENT BACK TO GET IT.
I HEARD AN OFFICER TALKING INSIDE.
"I BET HIS BOYFRIEND FOUND ANOTHER GUY TO SHACK UP WITH. JUST ANOTHER HOMO RUNNING AWAY FROM HOME."
THEY ALL LAUGHED.
IT MIGHT HAVE JUST BEEN A CASUAL JOKE, BUT I COULDN'T LET IT SLIDE.
WHEN I OPENED THE DOOR TO GET MY JACKET, EVERYONE AWKWARDLY STOPPED TALKING AND GOT BACK TO WORK.
BRIAN ...
HM...? YEAH...?
MEL AND I LAST SPOKE ON THE PHONE.
HE TOLD ME...

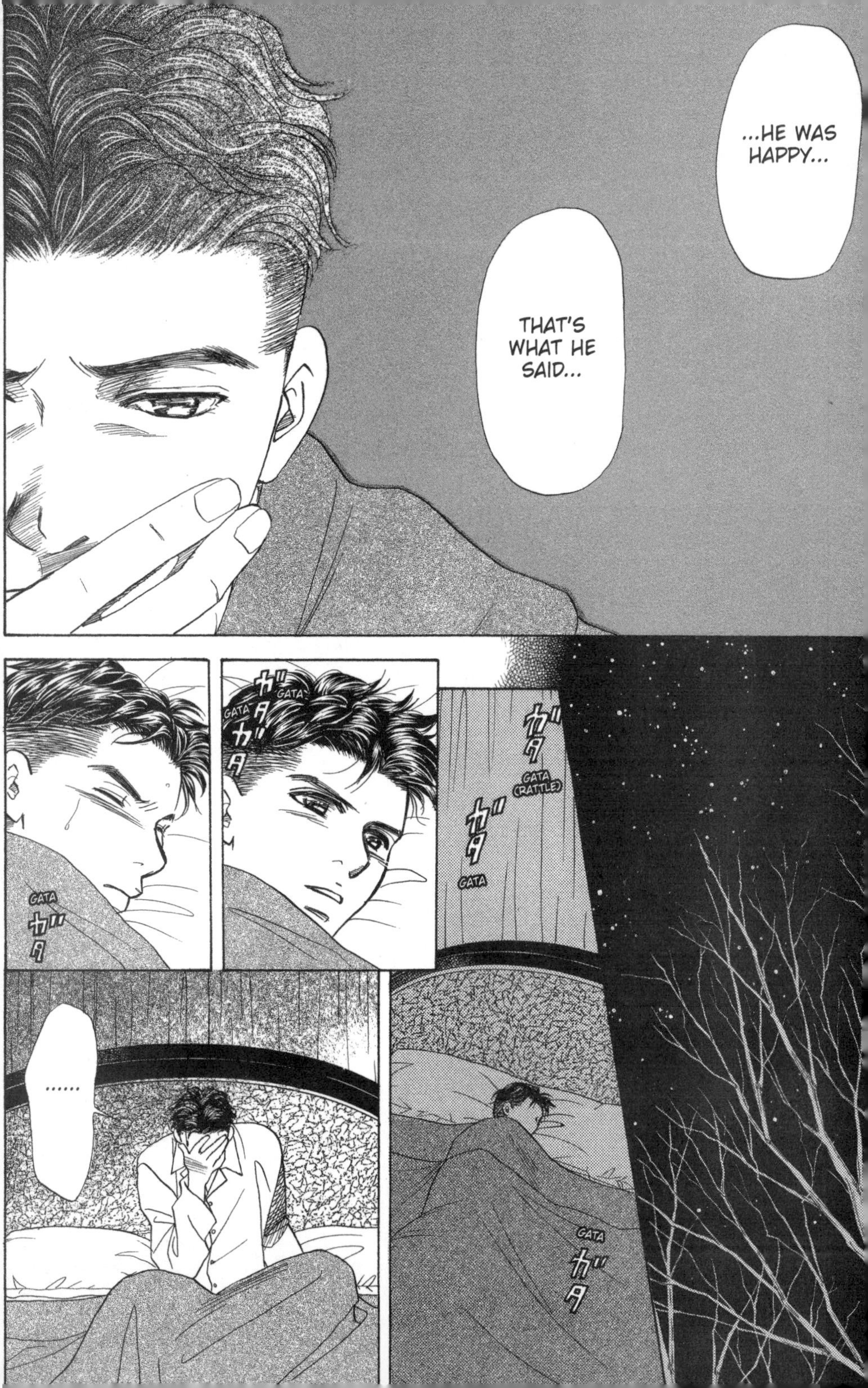
...HE WAS HAPPY...
THAT'S WHAT HE SAID...
GATA (RATTLE)
GATA
GATA
GATA
GATA
GATA
......

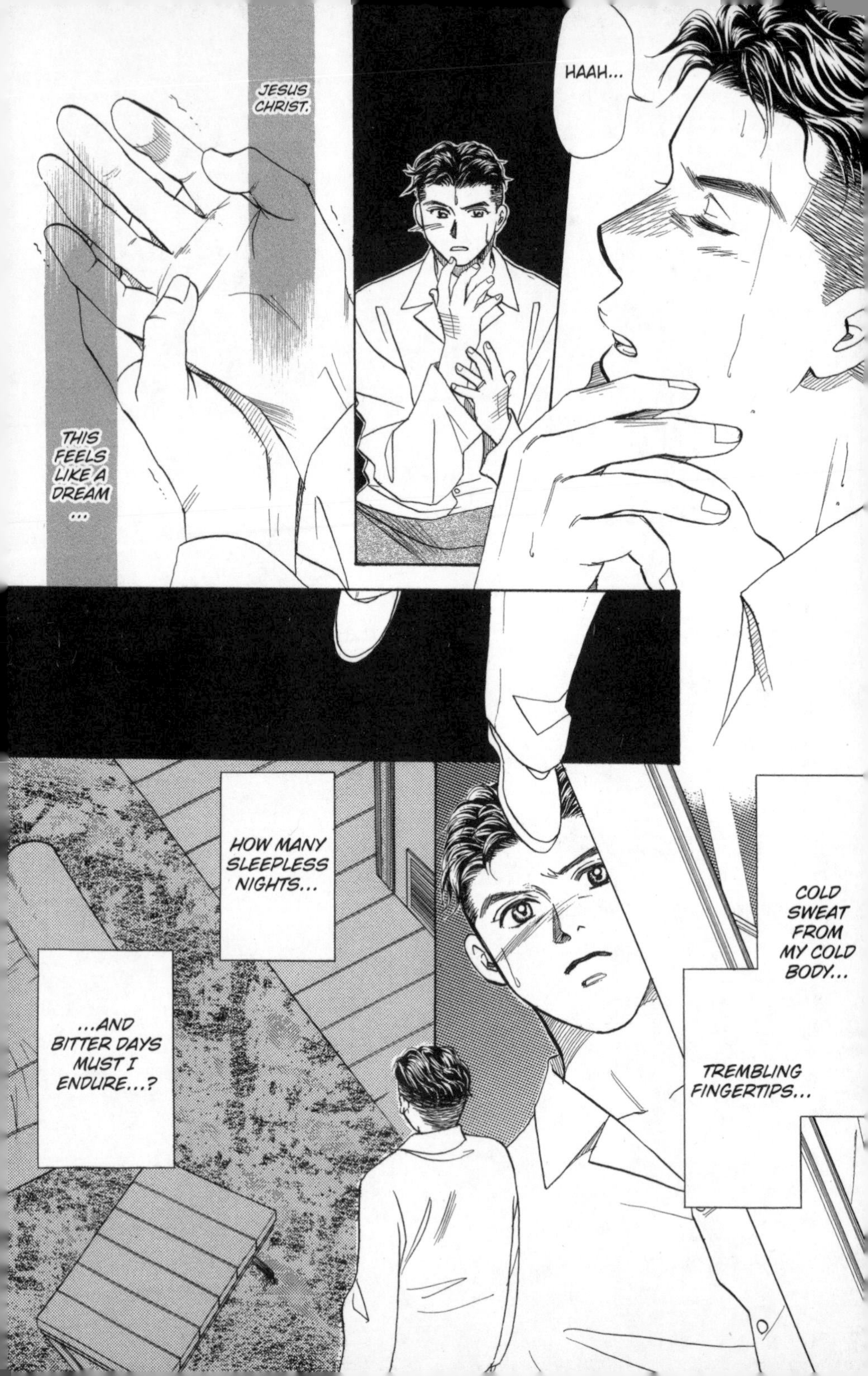
HAAH...
JESUS CHRIST.
THIS FEELS LIKE A DREAM...
COLD SWEAT FROM MY COLD BODY...
TREMBLING FINGERTIPS...
HOW MANY SLEEPLESS NIGHTS...
...AND BITTER DAYS MUST I ENDURE...?

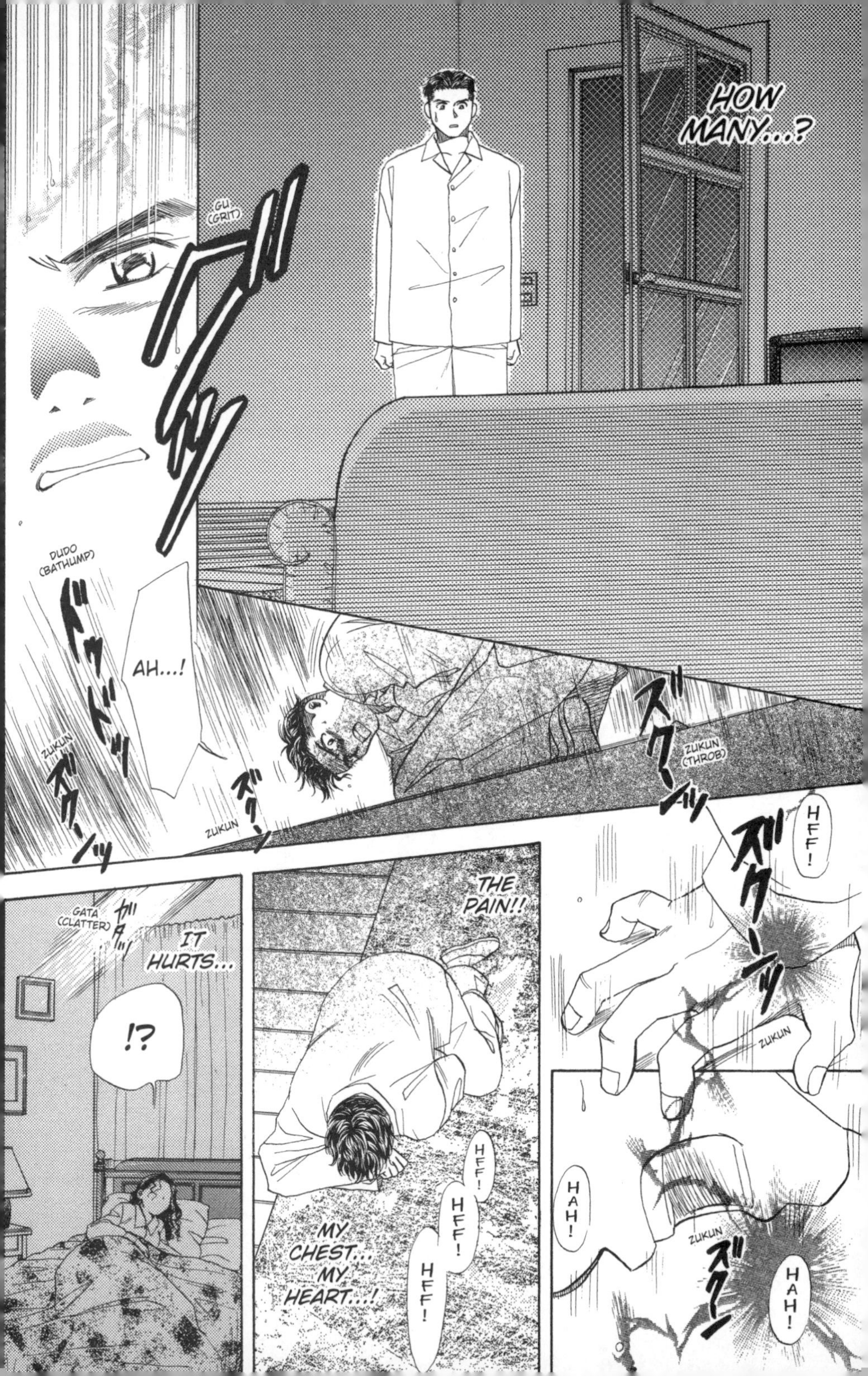
HOW MANY...?
GU (GRIT)
ZUKUN (THROB)
AH...!
DUDO (BATHUMP)
ZUKUN
ZUKUN
HFF!
ZUKUN
HAH!
ZUKUN
HAH!
THE PAIN!!
HFF!
HFF!
HFF!
MY CHEST... MY HEART...!
GATA (CLATTER)
IT HURTS...
!?

KII...
(CREAK)

CHI
(TICK)
CHI

CHI

IT'S 3:05...

CHI
CHI

KAIN!!

WHAT'S
GOING
ON!?

KAIN
!?

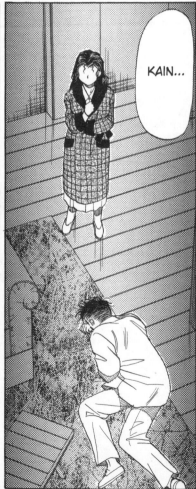

KAIN...

IG...
IGNORE...
ME.

MY
CHEST
HAS
BEEN
HURT-
ING...

...FOR
A
WHILE
NOW...

—ME...

75

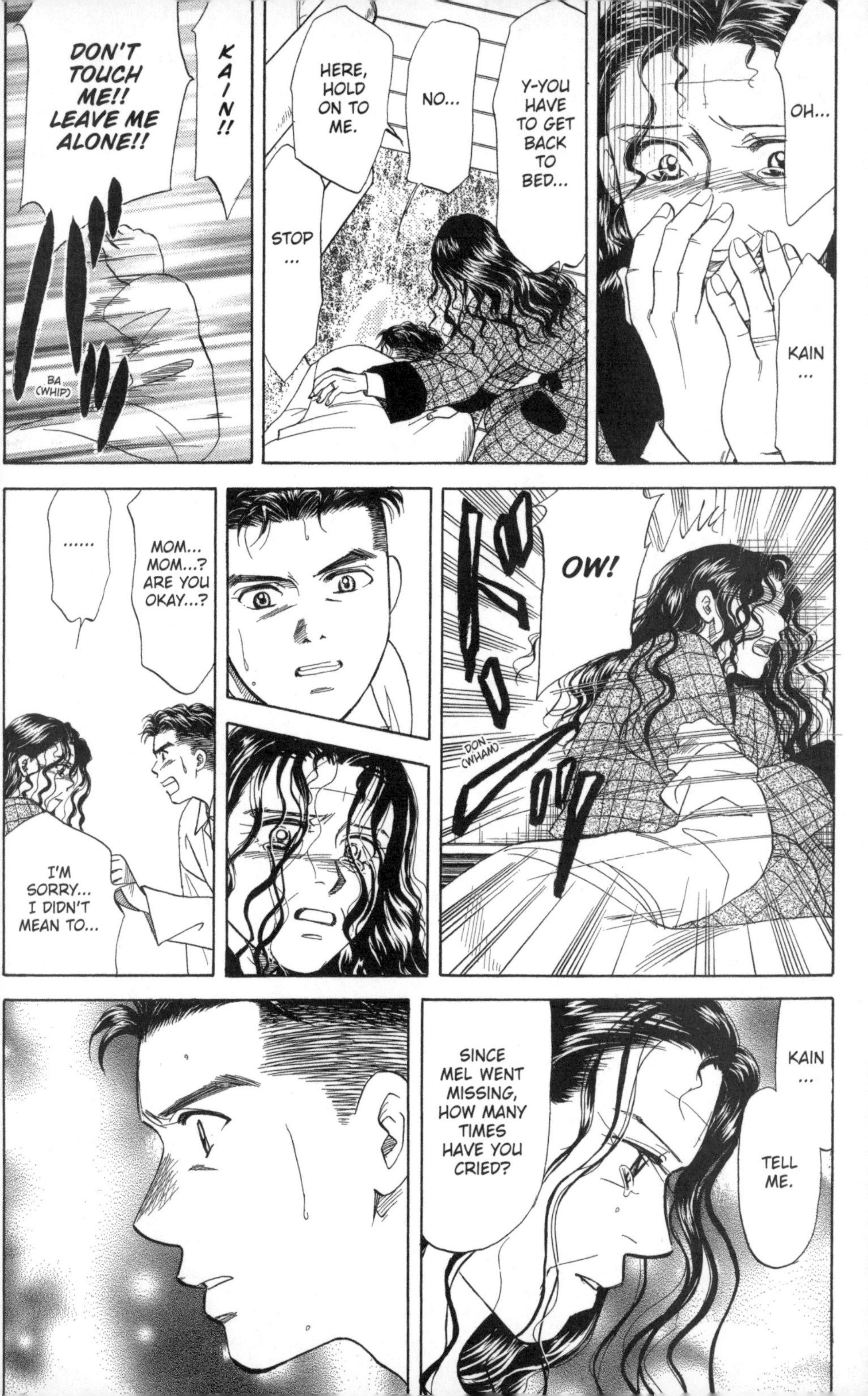
OH...
KAIN...
Y-YOU HAVE TO GET BACK TO BED...
NO...
HERE, HOLD ON TO ME.
STOP...
KAIN!!
DON'T TOUCH ME!! LEAVE ME ALONE!!
BA (WHIP)
OW!
DON (WHAM)
MOM... MOM...? ARE YOU OKAY...?
......
I'M SORRY... I DIDN'T MEAN TO...
KAIN...
TELL ME.
SINCE MEL WENT MISSING, HOW MANY TIMES HAVE YOU CRIED?

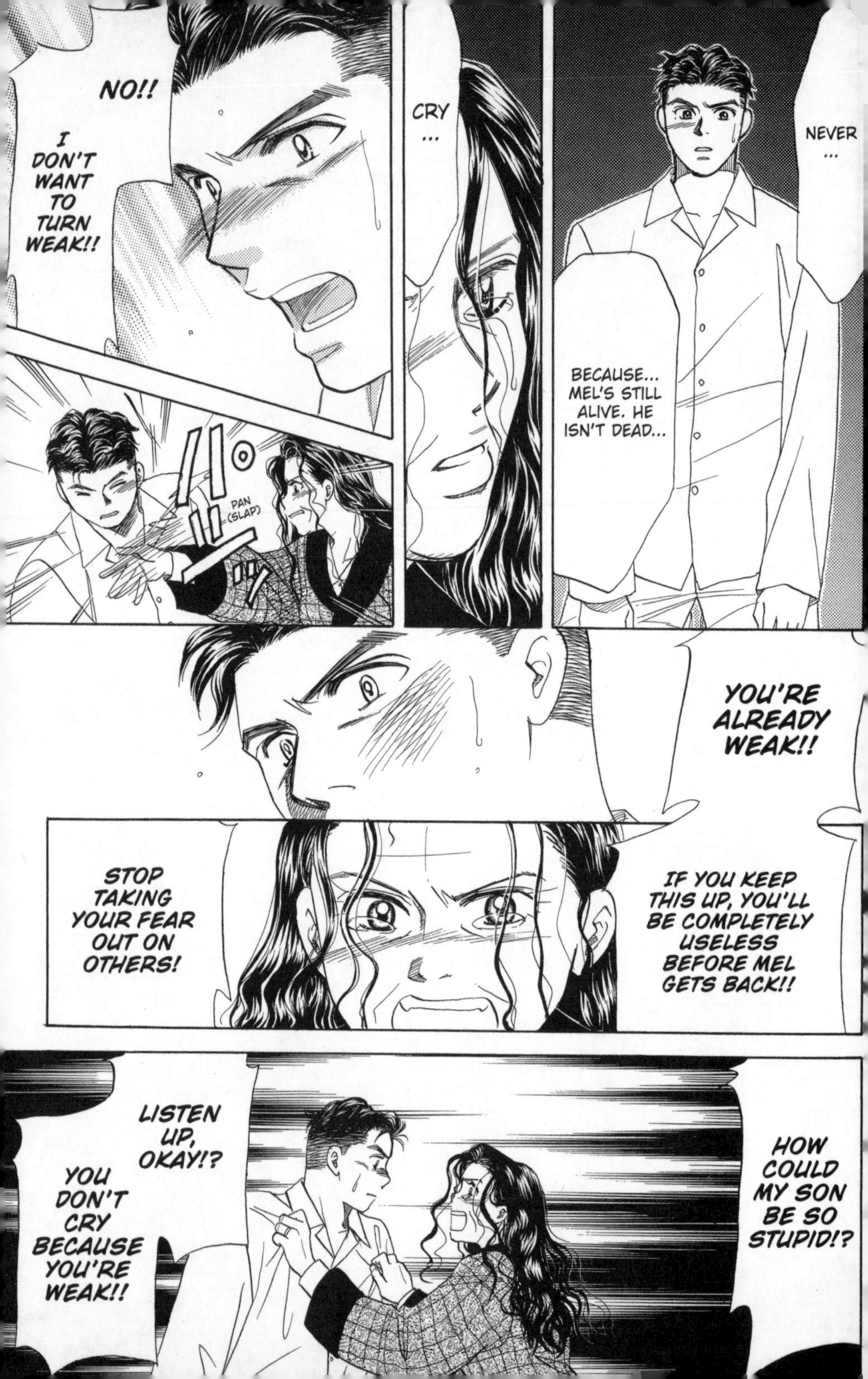
NEVER ...
BECAUSE... MEL'S STILL ALIVE. HE ISN'T DEAD...
CRY ...
NO!!
I DON'T WANT TO TURN WEAK!!
PAN (SLAP)
YOU'RE ALREADY WEAK!!
IF YOU KEEP THIS UP, YOU'LL BE COMPLETELY USELESS BEFORE MEL GETS BACK!!
STOP TAKING YOUR FEAR OUT ON OTHERS!
HOW COULD MY SON BE SO STUPID!?
LISTEN UP, OKAY!?
YOU DON'T CRY BECAUSE YOU'RE WEAK!!

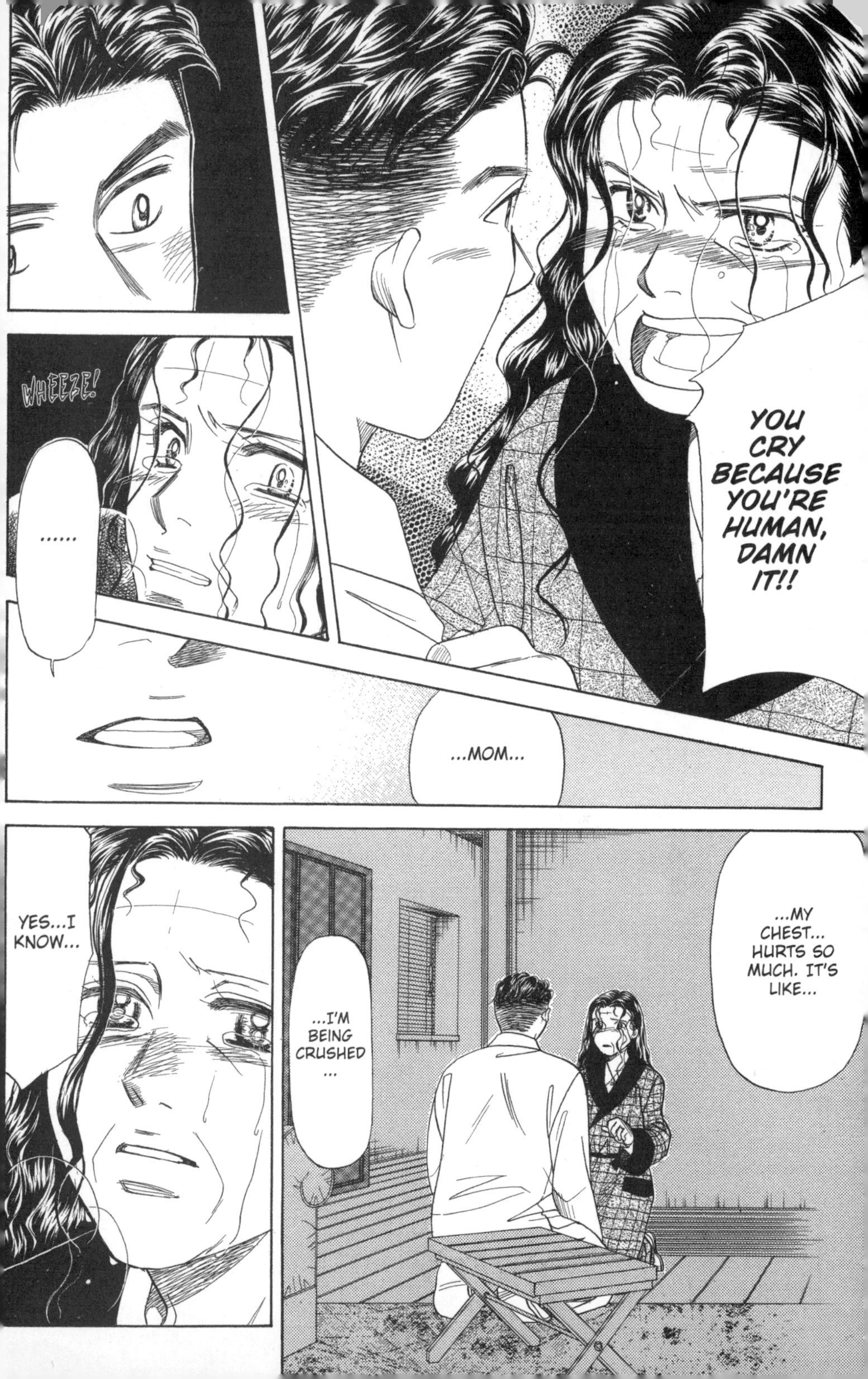
YOU CRY BECAUSE YOU'RE HUMAN, DAMN IT!!
WHEEZE!
......
...MOM...
...MY CHEST... HURTS SO MUCH. IT'S LIKE...
...I'M BEING CRUSHED ...
YES...I KNOW...

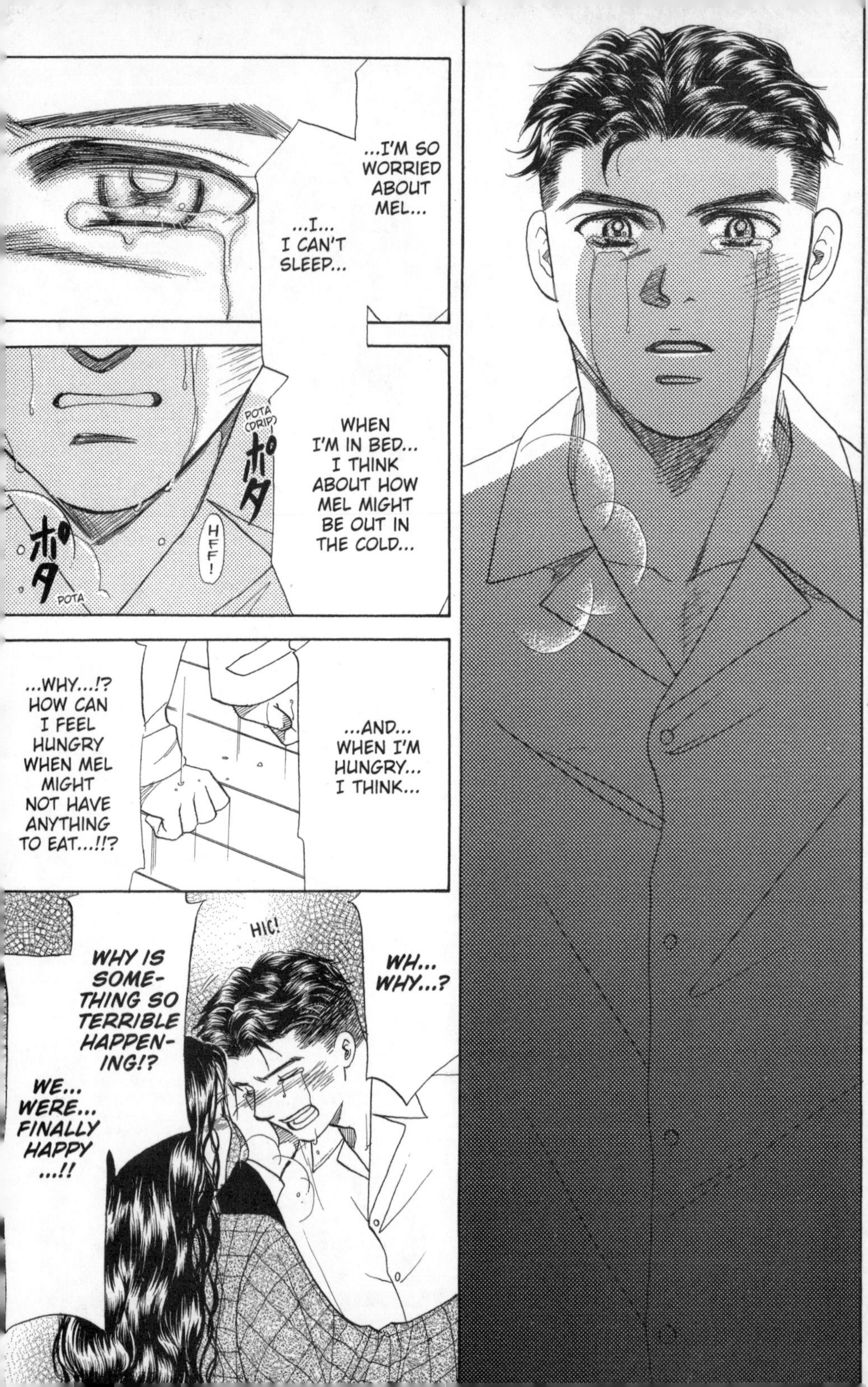
...I'M SO WORRIED ABOUT MEL...
...I... I CAN'T SLEEP...
WHEN I'M IN BED... I THINK ABOUT HOW MEL MIGHT BE OUT IN THE COLD...
POTA (DRIP)
ポタ
HFF!
ポタ
POTA
...AND... WHEN I'M HUNGRY... I THINK...
...WHY...!? HOW CAN I FEEL HUNGRY WHEN MEL MIGHT NOT HAVE ANYTHING TO EAT...!!?
HIC!
WH... WHY...?
WHY IS SOME-THING SO TERRIBLE HAPPEN-ING!?
WE... WERE... FINALLY HAPPY ...!!

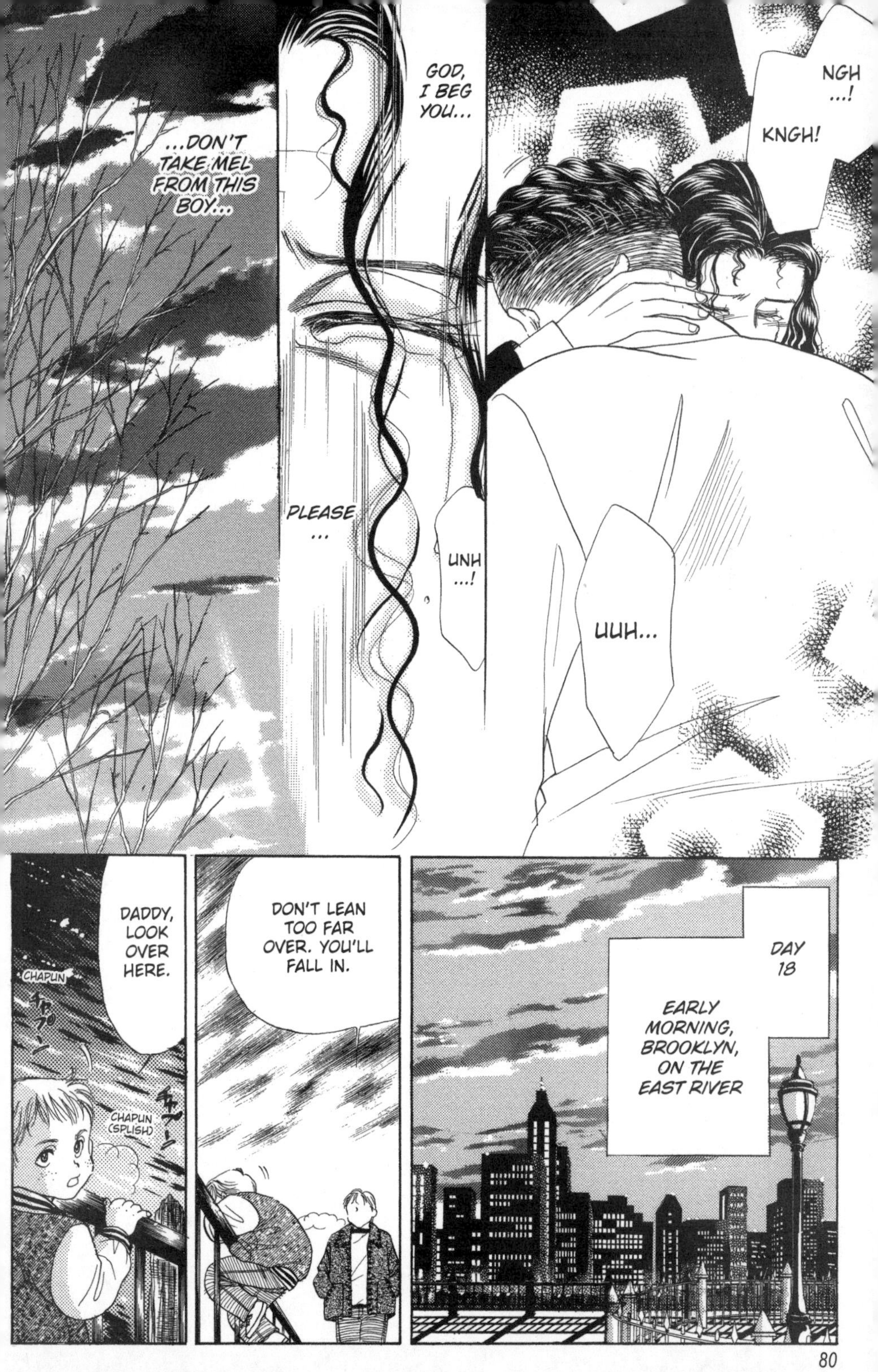
NGH ...!
KNGH!
UNH ...!
UUH...
GOD, I BEG YOU...
PLEASE ...
...DON'T TAKE MEL FROM THIS BOY...
DAY 18
EARLY MORNING, BROOKLYN, ON THE EAST RIVER
DON'T LEAN TOO FAR OVER. YOU'LL FALL IN.
DADDY, LOOK OVER HERE.
CHAPUN
CHAPUN (SPLISH)

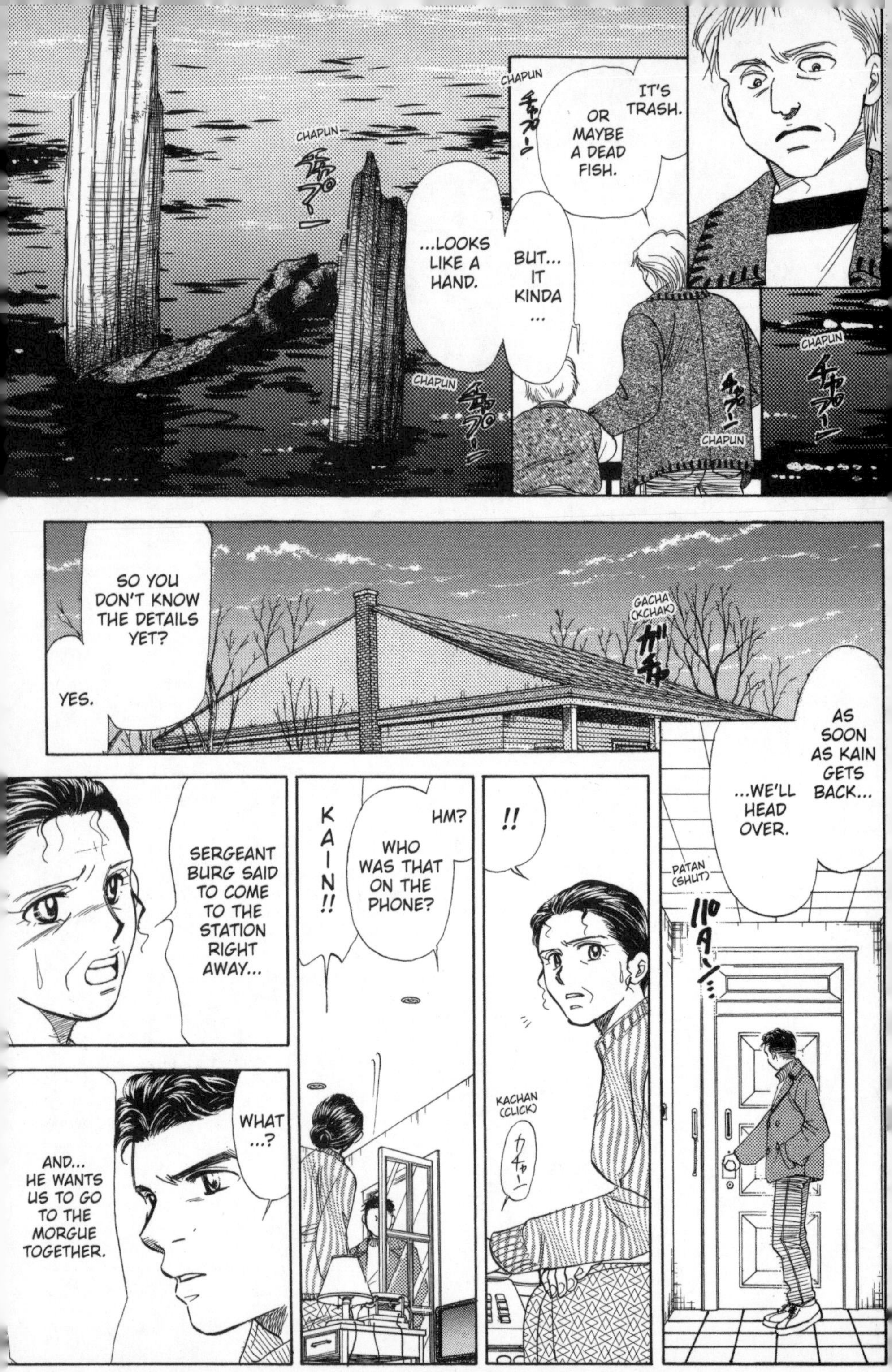
CHAPUN
CHAPUN
IT'S TRASH.
OR MAYBE A DEAD FISH.
BUT... IT KINDA ...
CHAPUN
CHAPUN
...LOOKS LIKE A HAND.
CHAPUN
GACHA (KCHAK)
SO YOU DON'T KNOW THE DETAILS YET?
YES.
AS SOON AS KAIN GETS BACK...
...WE'LL HEAD OVER.
PATAN (SHUT)
!!
KACHAN (CLICK)
HM?
WHO WAS THAT ON THE PHONE?
KAIN!!
SERGEANT BURG SAID TO COME TO THE STATION RIGHT AWAY...
WHAT ...?
AND... HE WANTS US TO GO TO THE MORGUE TOGETHER.

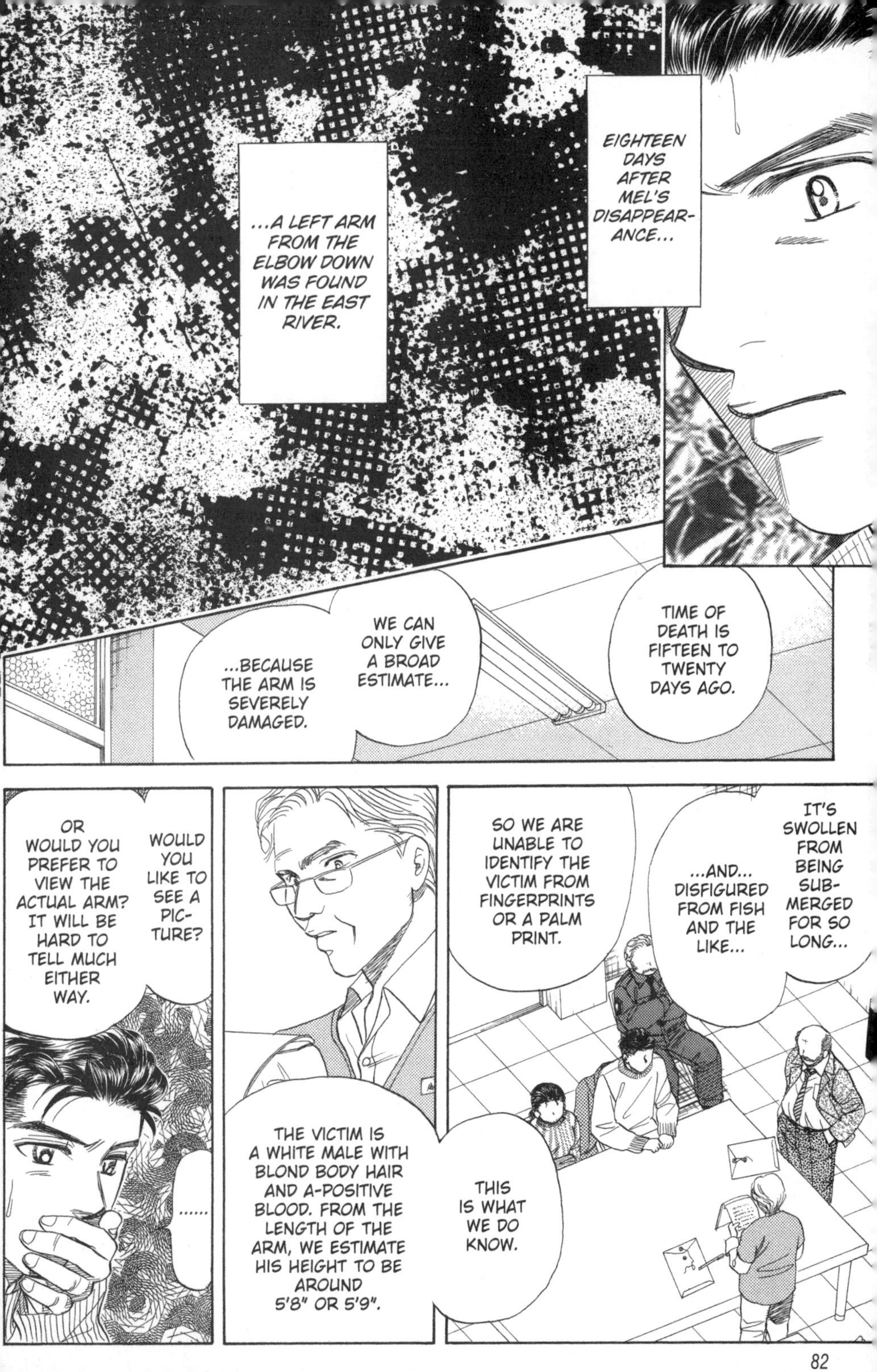
EIGHTEEN DAYS AFTER MEL'S DISAPPEAR-ANCE...
...A LEFT ARM FROM THE ELBOW DOWN WAS FOUND IN THE EAST RIVER.
TIME OF DEATH IS FIFTEEN TO TWENTY DAYS AGO.
WE CAN ONLY GIVE A BROAD ESTIMATE...
...BECAUSE THE ARM IS SEVERELY DAMAGED.
IT'S SWOLLEN FROM BEING SUB-MERGED FOR SO LONG...
...AND... DISFIGURED FROM FISH AND THE LIKE...
SO WE ARE UNABLE TO IDENTIFY THE VICTIM FROM FINGERPRINTS OR A PALM PRINT.
THIS IS WHAT WE DO KNOW.
THE VICTIM IS A WHITE MALE WITH BLOND BODY HAIR AND A-POSITIVE BLOOD. FROM THE LENGTH OF THE ARM, WE ESTIMATE HIS HEIGHT TO BE AROUND 5'8" OR 5'9".
WOULD YOU LIKE TO SEE A PIC-TURE?
OR WOULD YOU PREFER TO VIEW THE ACTUAL ARM? IT WILL BE HARD TO TELL MUCH EITHER WAY.
......

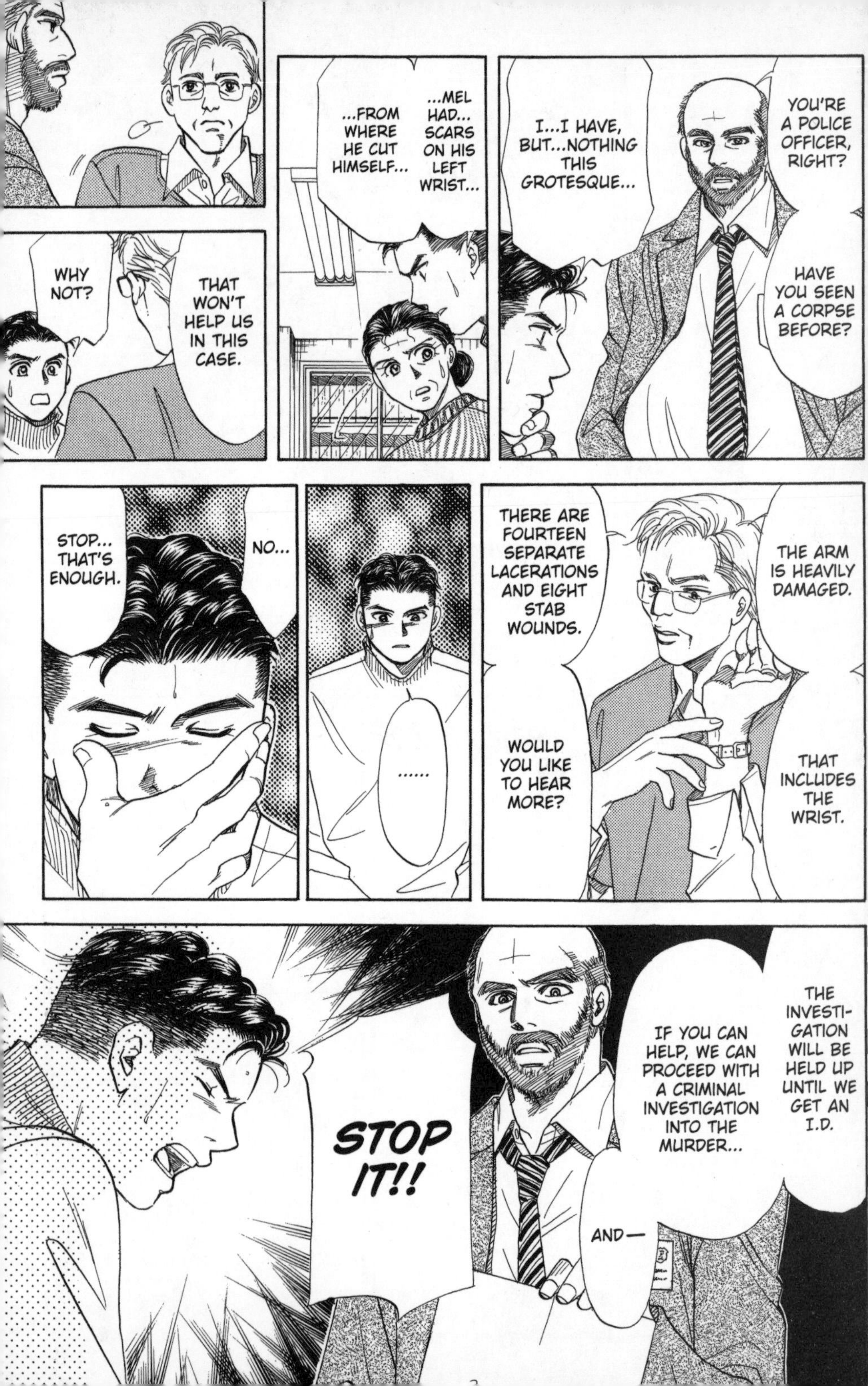
YOU'RE A POLICE OFFICER, RIGHT?
HAVE YOU SEEN A CORPSE BEFORE?
I...I HAVE, BUT...NOTHING THIS GROTESQUE...
...MEL HAD... SCARS ON HIS LEFT WRIST...
...FROM WHERE HE CUT HIMSELF...
THAT WON'T HELP US IN THIS CASE.
WHY NOT?
THE ARM IS HEAVILY DAMAGED.
THERE ARE FOURTEEN SEPARATE LACERATIONS AND EIGHT STAB WOUNDS.
THAT INCLUDES THE WRIST.
WOULD YOU LIKE TO HEAR MORE?
......
NO...
STOP... THAT'S ENOUGH.
THE INVESTI-GATION WILL BE HELD UP UNTIL WE GET AN I.D.
IF YOU CAN HELP, WE CAN PROCEED WITH A CRIMINAL INVESTIGATION INTO THE MURDER...
AND—
STOP IT!!

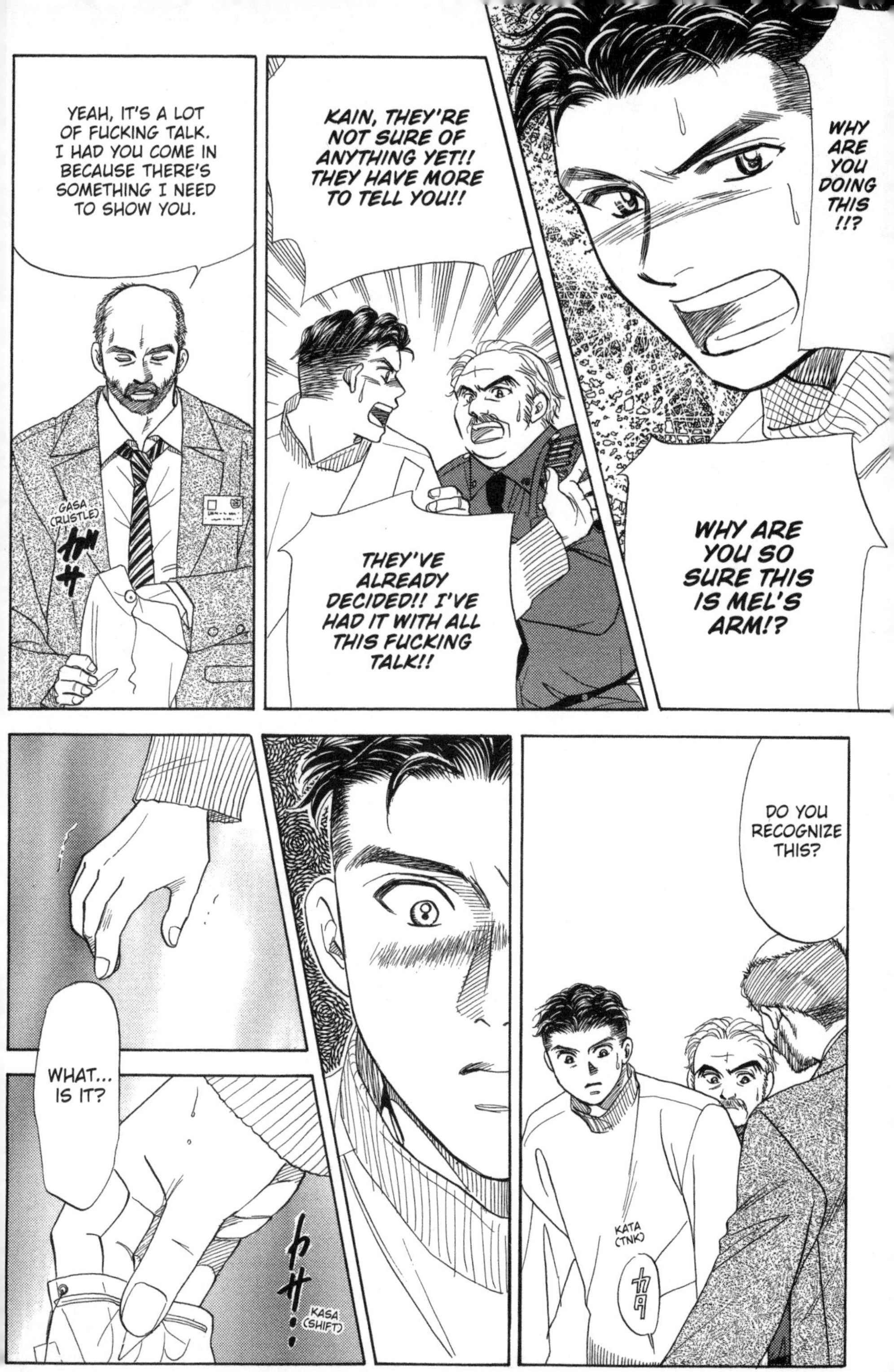
WHY ARE YOU DOING THIS !!?
WHY ARE YOU SO SURE THIS IS MEL'S ARM!?
KAIN, THEY'RE NOT SURE OF ANYTHING YET!! THEY HAVE MORE TO TELL YOU!!
THEY'VE ALREADY DECIDED!! I'VE HAD IT WITH ALL THIS FUCKING TALK!!
YEAH, IT'S A LOT OF FUCKING TALK. I HAD YOU COME IN BECAUSE THERE'S SOMETHING I NEED TO SHOW YOU.
GASA (RUSTLE)
DO YOU RECOGNIZE THIS?
KATA (TNK)
WHAT... IS IT?
KASA (SHIFT)

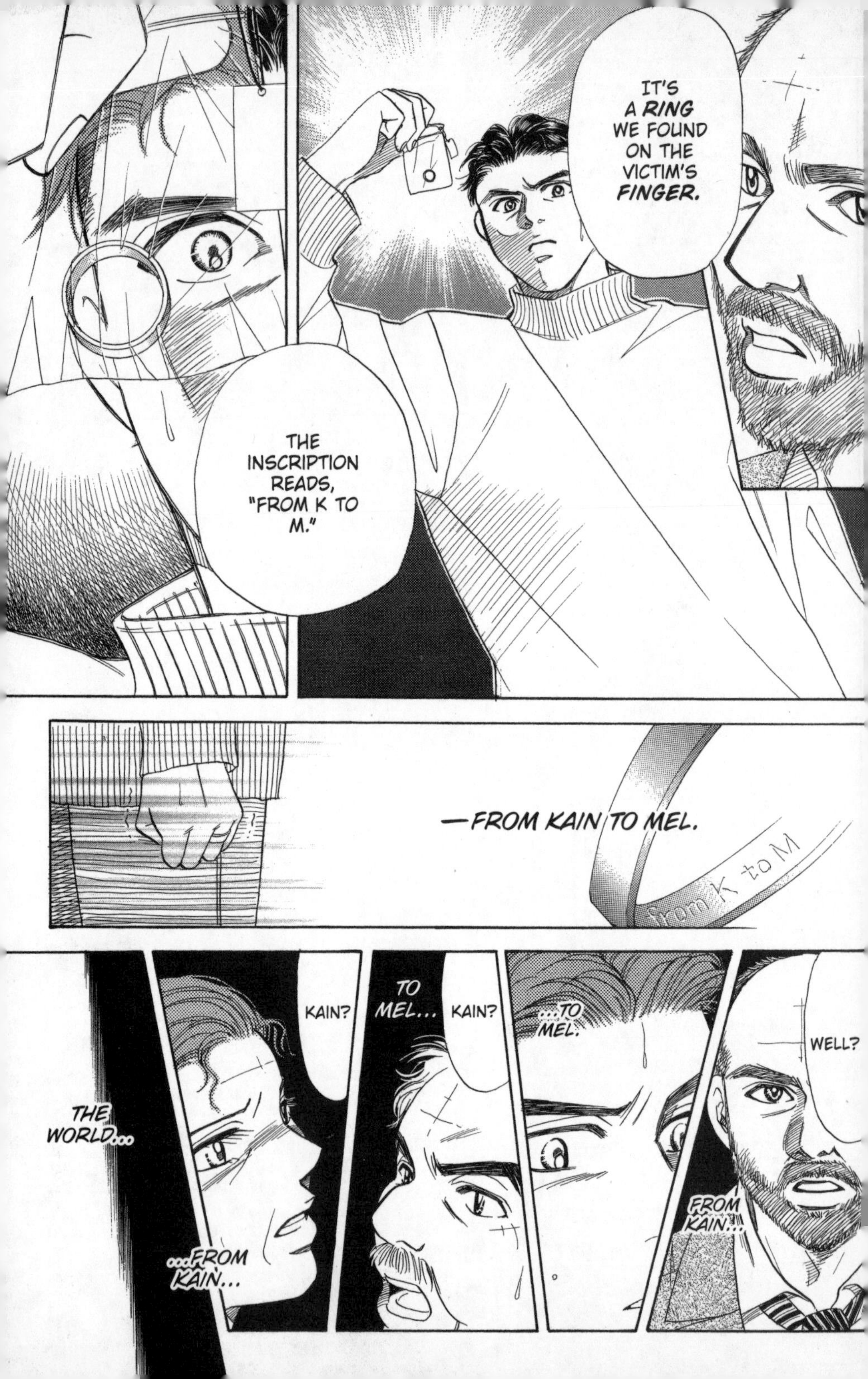
IT'S A RING WE FOUND ON THE VICTIM'S FINGER.
THE INSCRIPTION READS, "FROM K TO M."
—FROM KAIN TO MEL.
from K to M
WELL?
FROM KAIN...
...TO MEL.
KAIN?
TO MEL...
KAIN?
THE WORLD...
...FROM KAIN...

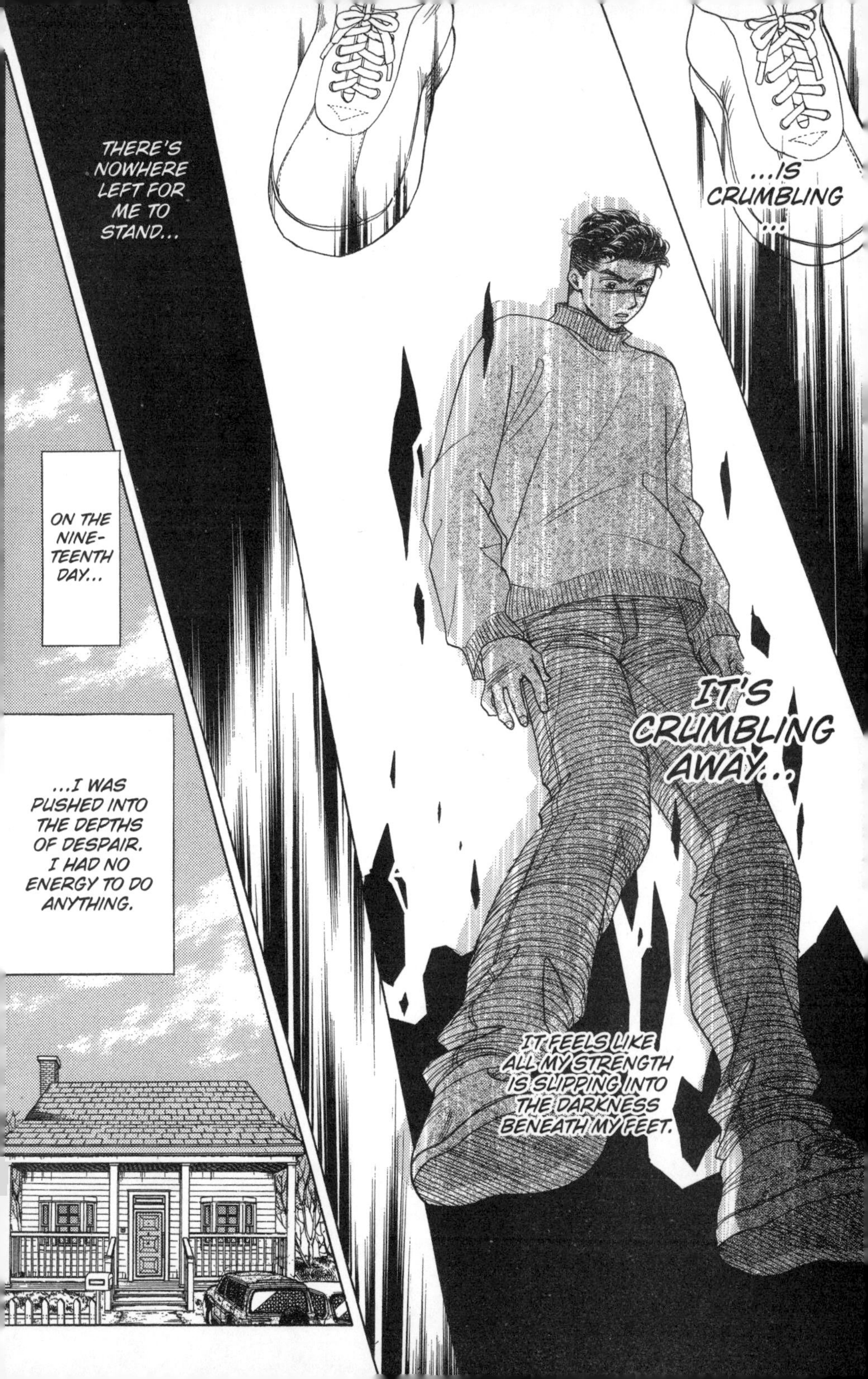
...IS CRUMBLING ...
IT'S CRUMBLING AWAY...
IT FEELS LIKE ALL MY STRENGTH IS SLIPPING INTO THE DARKNESS BENEATH MY FEET.
THERE'S NOWHERE LEFT FOR ME TO STAND...
ON THE NINE-TEENTH DAY...
...I WAS PUSHED INTO THE DEPTHS OF DESPAIR. I HAD NO ENERGY TO DO ANYTHING.

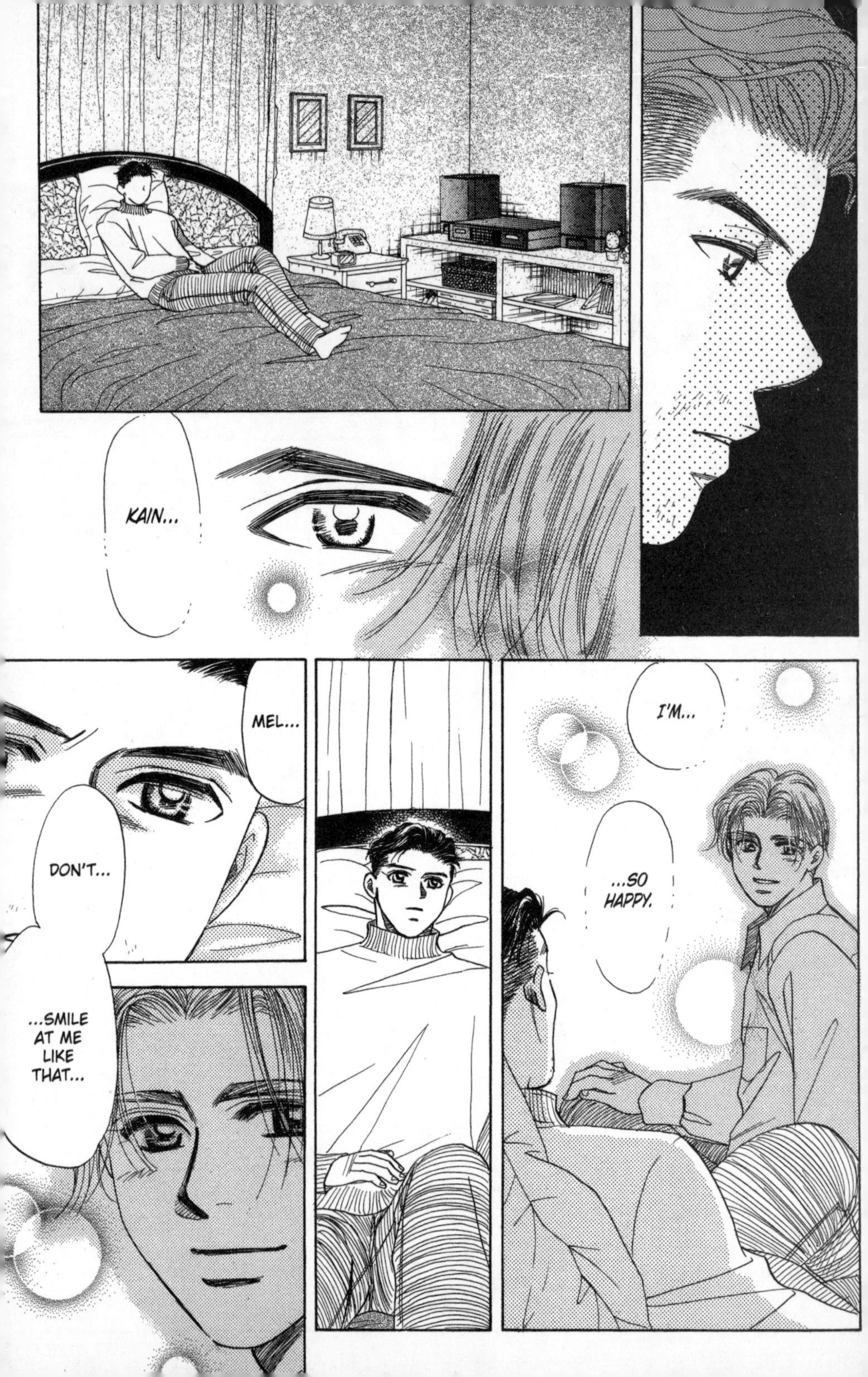
KAIN...
I'M...
...SO HAPPY.
MEL...
DON'T...
...SMILE AT ME LIKE THAT...

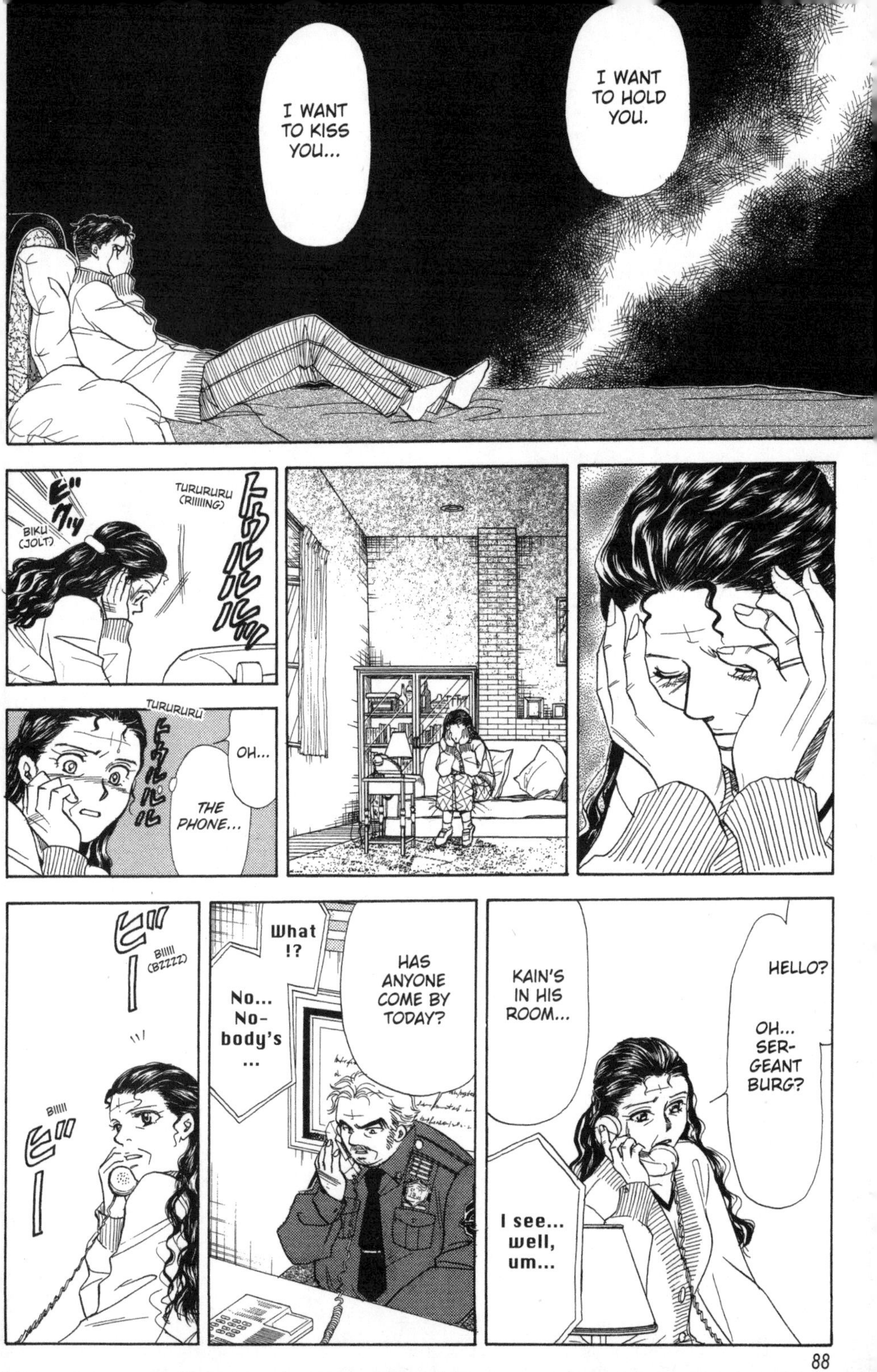
I WANT TO HOLD YOU.
I WANT TO KISS YOU...
TURURURU (RIIIIING)
BIKU (JOLT)
TURURURU
OH...
THE PHONE...
HELLO?
OH... SER-GEANT BURG?
KAIN'S IN HIS ROOM...
I see... well, um...
HAS ANYONE COME BY TODAY?
What !?
No... No-body's ...
BIIII (BZZZZ)
BIIII

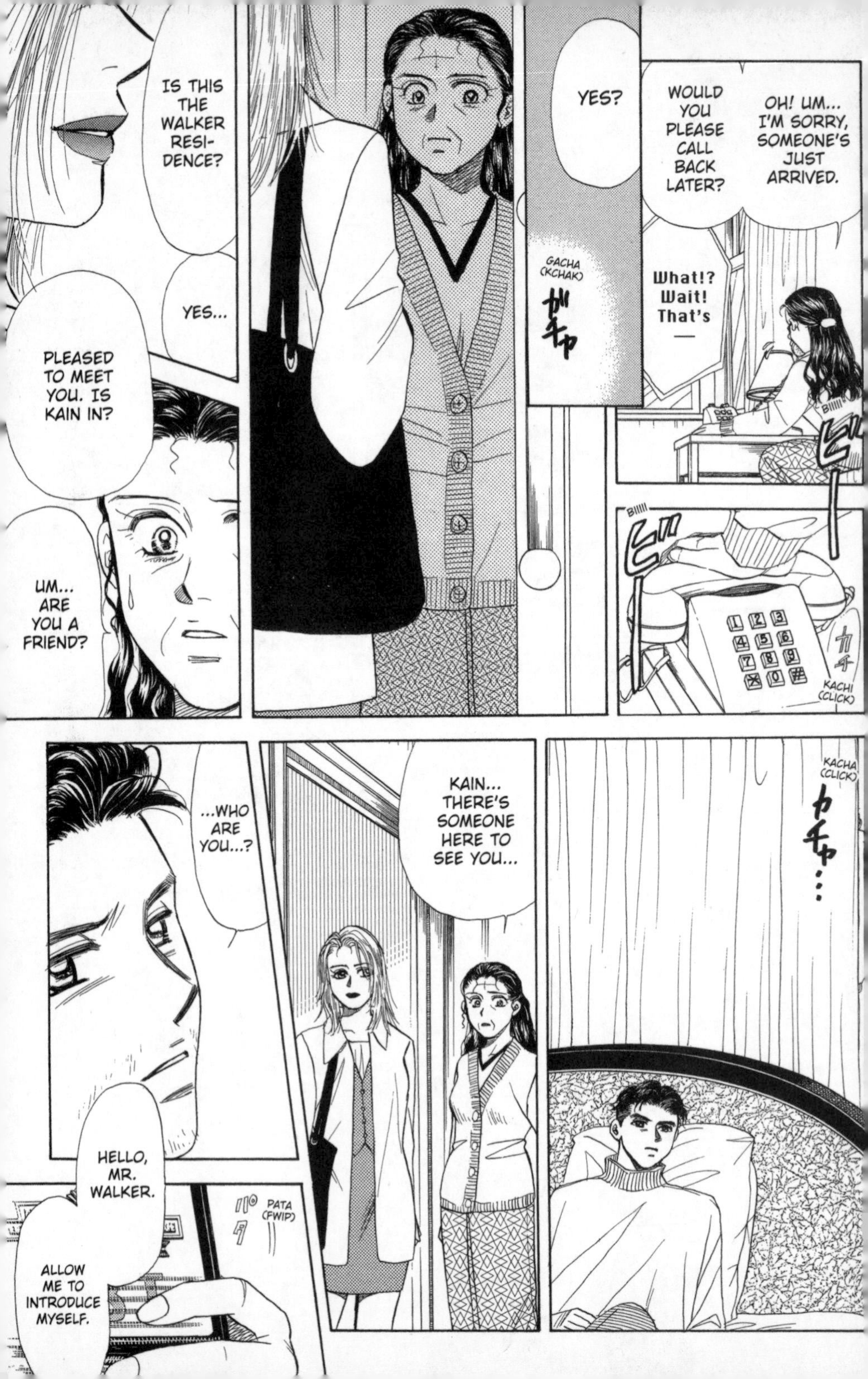
OH! UM... I'M SORRY, SOMEONE'S JUST ARRIVED.
WOULD YOU PLEASE CALL BACK LATER?
What!? Wait! That's —
BIIIII
BIIIII
KACHI (CLICK)
YES?
GACHA (KCHAK)
IS THIS THE WALKER RESIDENCE?
YES...
PLEASED TO MEET YOU. IS KAIN IN?
UM... ARE YOU A FRIEND?
KACHA (CLICK)
KAIN... THERE'S SOMEONE HERE TO SEE YOU...
...WHO ARE YOU...?
HELLO, MR. WALKER.
PATA (FWIP)
ALLOW ME TO INTRODUCE MYSELF.

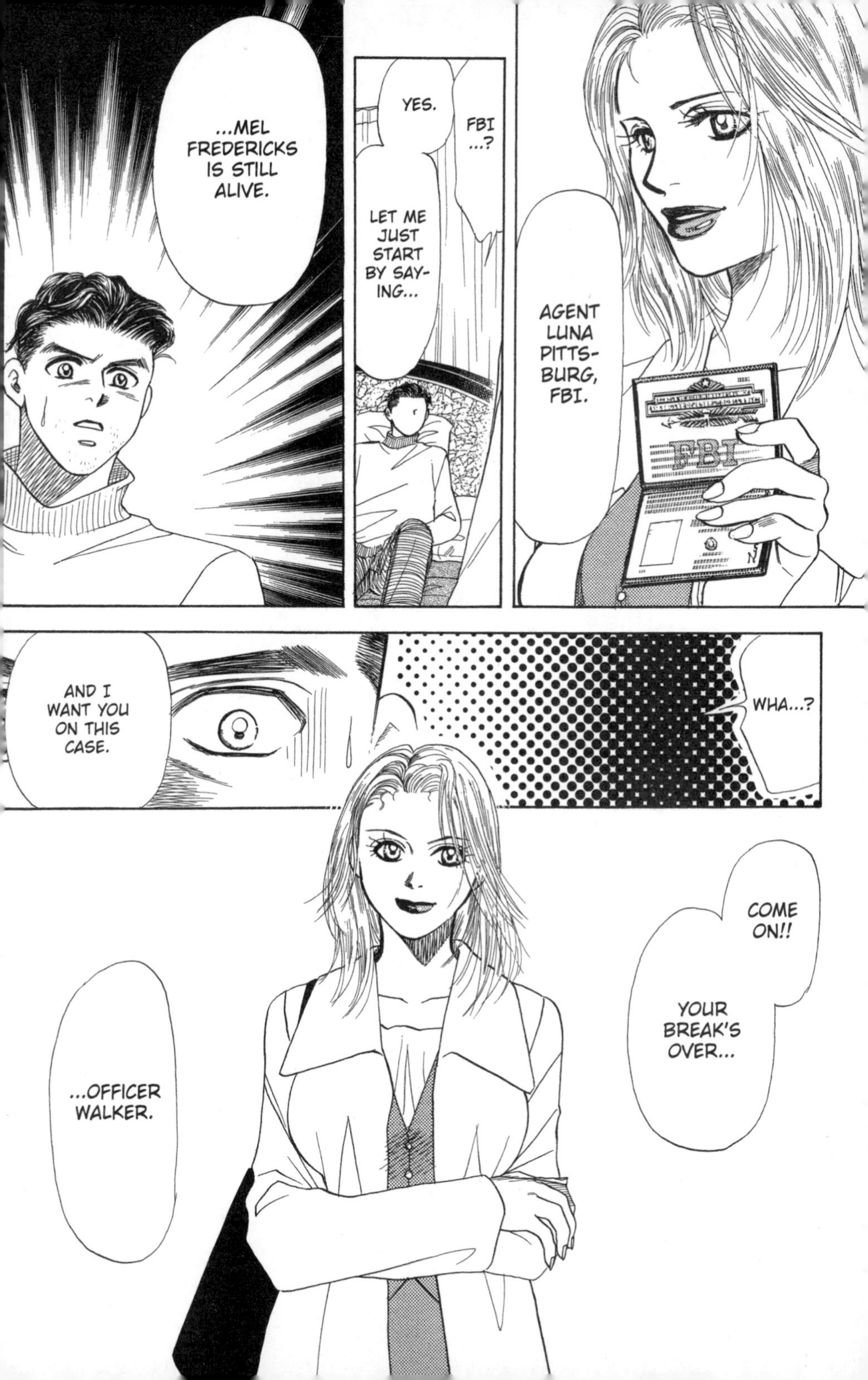

AGENT LUNA PITTS-BURG, FBI.
FBI ...?
YES.
LET ME JUST START BY SAY-ING...
...MEL FREDERICKS IS STILL ALIVE.
WHA...?
AND I WANT YOU ON THIS CASE.
COME ON!!
YOUR BREAK'S OVER...
...OFFICER WALKER.

EPISODE IV

SCENE 2

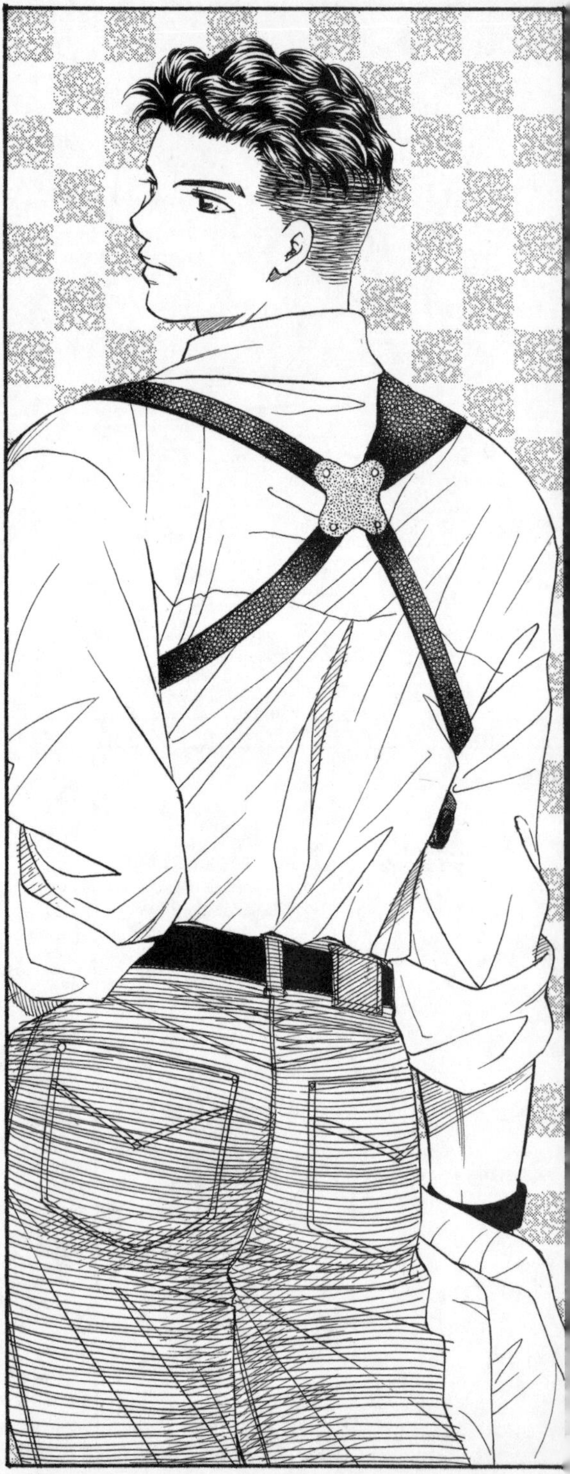

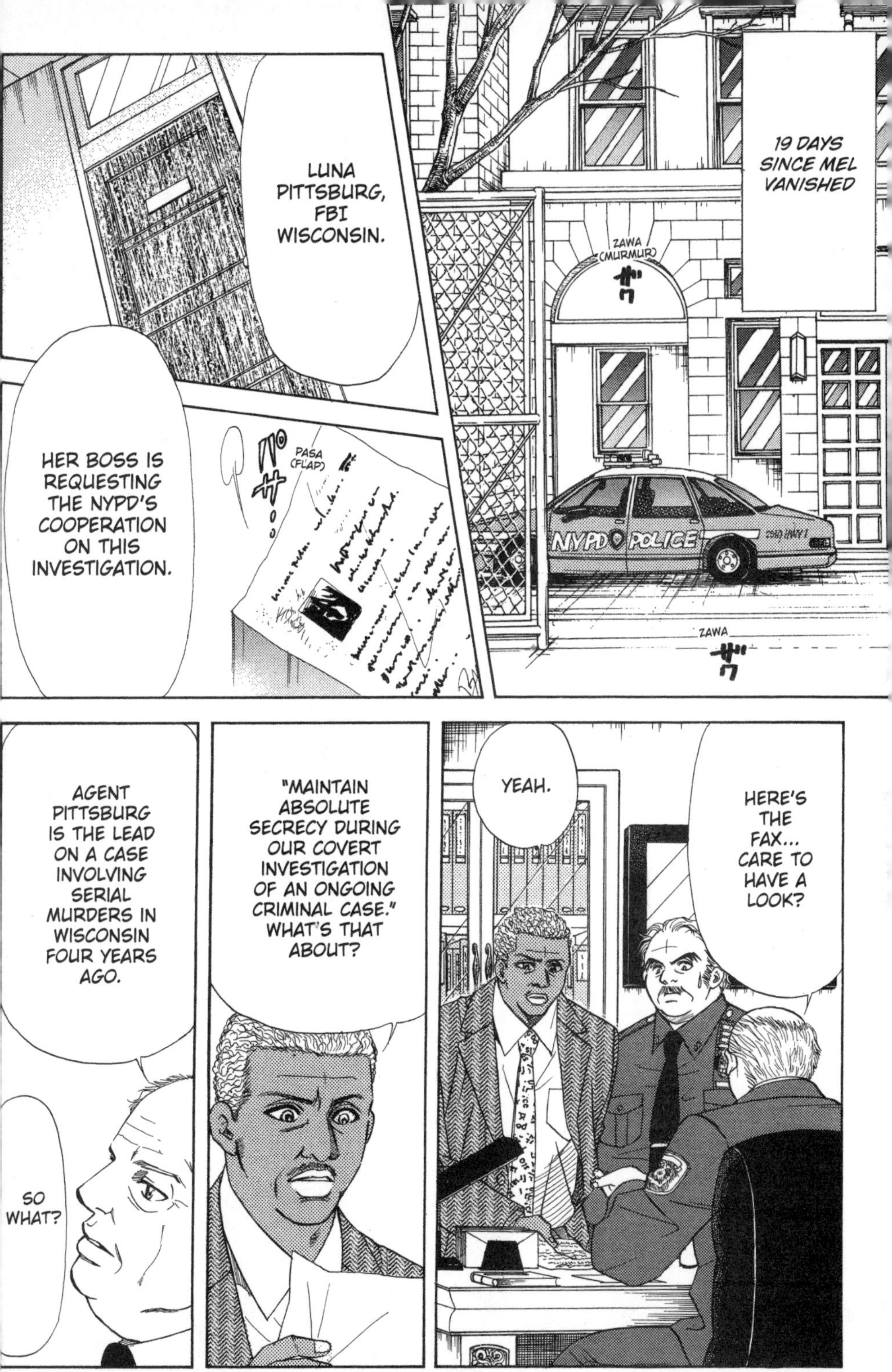
19 DAYS SINCE MEL VANISHED
ZAWA (MURMUR)
ZAWA
LUNA PITTSBURG, FBI WISCONSIN.
PASA (FLAP)
HER BOSS IS REQUESTING THE NYPD'S COOPERATION ON THIS INVESTIGATION.
HERE'S THE FAX... CARE TO HAVE A LOOK?
YEAH.
"MAINTAIN ABSOLUTE SECRECY DURING OUR COVERT INVESTIGATION OF AN ONGOING CRIMINAL CASE." WHAT'S THAT ABOUT?
AGENT PITTSBURG IS THE LEAD ON A CASE INVOLVING SERIAL MURDERS IN WISCONSIN FOUR YEARS AGO.
SO WHAT?

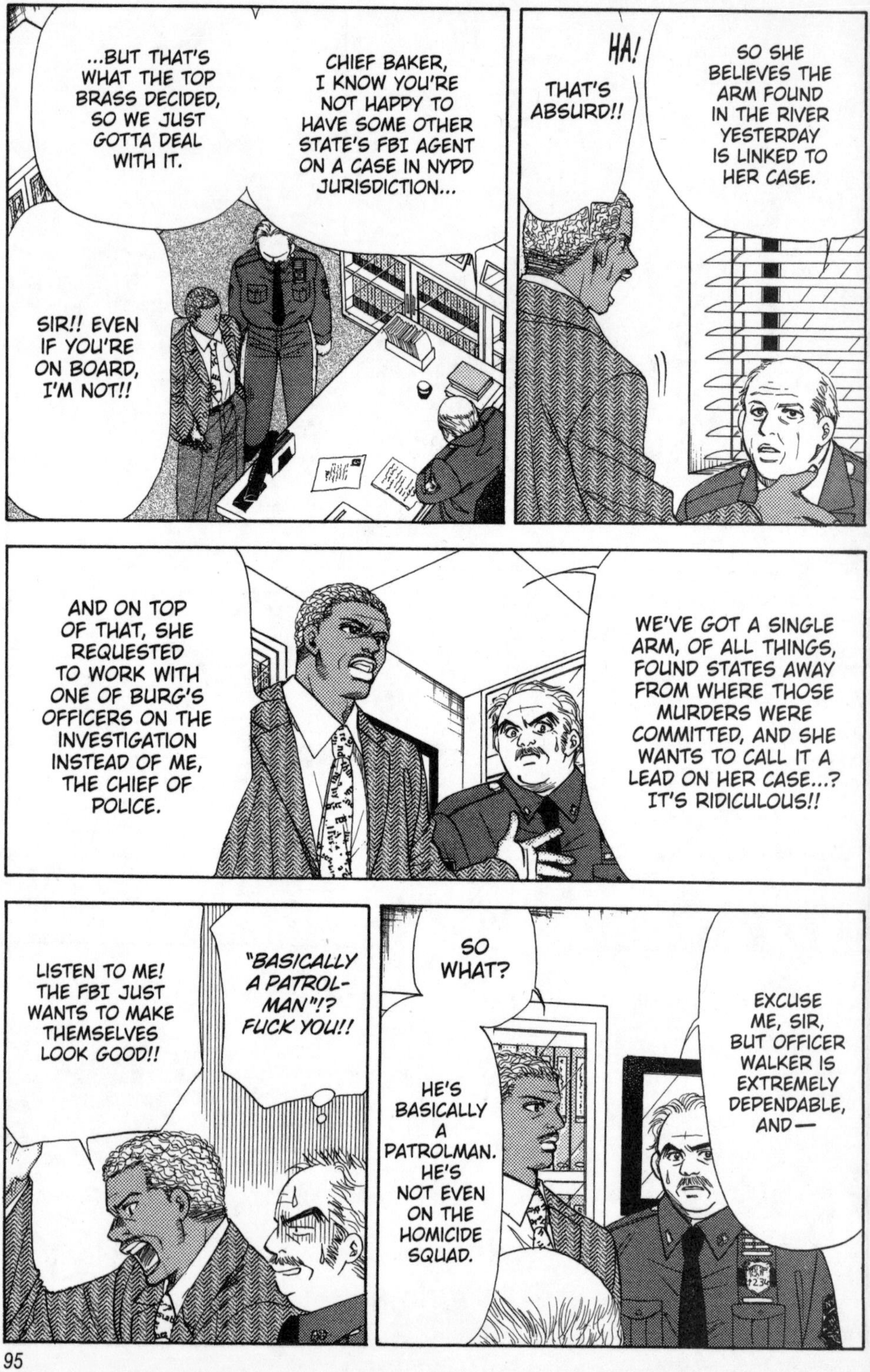
SO SHE BELIEVES THE ARM FOUND IN THE RIVER YESTERDAY IS LINKED TO HER CASE.
HA!
THAT'S ABSURD!!
CHIEF BAKER, I KNOW YOU'RE NOT HAPPY TO HAVE SOME OTHER STATE'S FBI AGENT ON A CASE IN NYPD JURISDICTION...
...BUT THAT'S WHAT THE TOP BRASS DECIDED, SO WE JUST GOTTA DEAL WITH IT.
SIR!! EVEN IF YOU'RE ON BOARD, I'M NOT!!
WE'VE GOT A SINGLE ARM, OF ALL THINGS, FOUND STATES AWAY FROM WHERE THOSE MURDERS WERE COMMITTED, AND SHE WANTS TO CALL IT A LEAD ON HER CASE...? IT'S RIDICULOUS!!
AND ON TOP OF THAT, SHE REQUESTED TO WORK WITH ONE OF BURG'S OFFICERS ON THE INVESTIGATION INSTEAD OF ME, THE CHIEF OF POLICE.
EXCUSE ME, SIR, BUT OFFICER WALKER IS EXTREMELY DEPENDABLE, AND—
SO WHAT?
HE'S BASICALLY A PATROLMAN. HE'S NOT EVEN ON THE HOMICIDE SQUAD.
"BASICALLY A PATROL-MAN"!? FUCK YOU!!
LISTEN TO ME! THE FBI JUST WANTS TO MAKE THEMSELVES LOOK GOOD!!

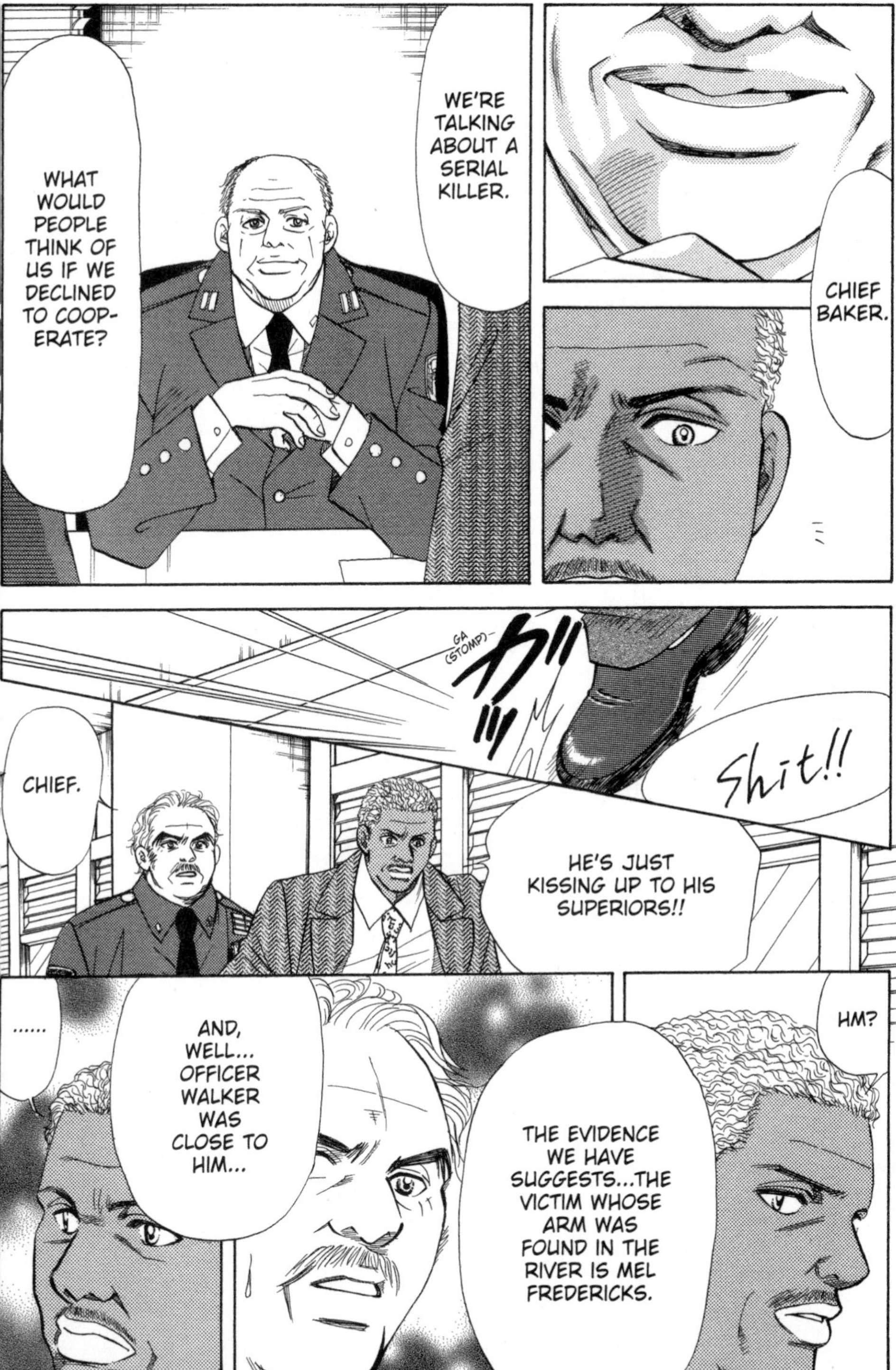
CHIEF BAKER.
WE'RE TALKING ABOUT A SERIAL KILLER.
WHAT WOULD PEOPLE THINK OF US IF WE DECLINED TO COOP-ERATE?
GA (STOMP)
Shit!!
HE'S JUST KISSING UP TO HIS SUPERIORS!!
CHIEF.
HM?
THE EVIDENCE WE HAVE SUGGESTS...THE VICTIM WHOSE ARM WAS FOUND IN THE RIVER IS MEL FREDERICKS.
AND, WELL... OFFICER WALKER WAS CLOSE TO HIM...
......

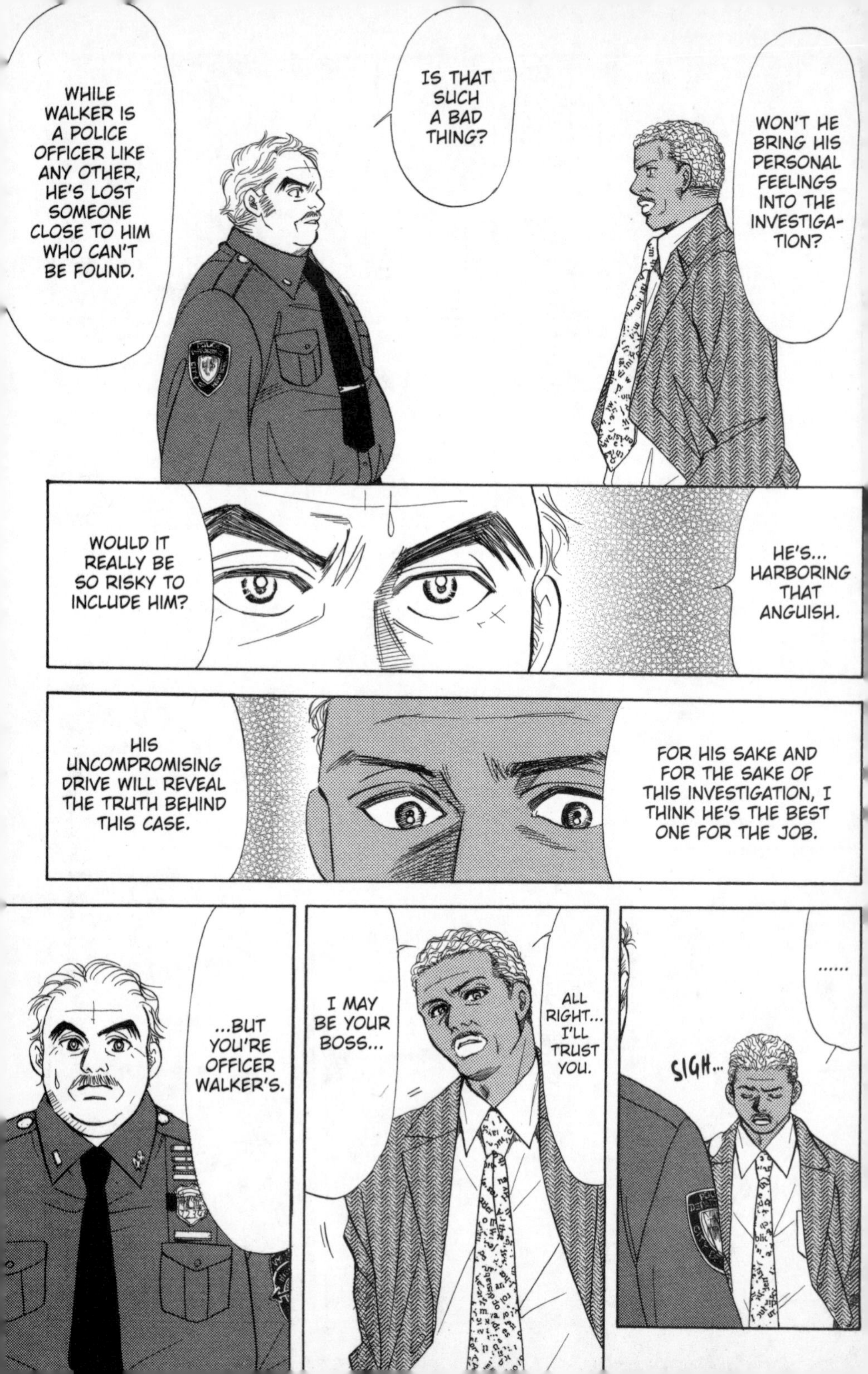
WON'T HE BRING HIS PERSONAL FEELINGS INTO THE INVESTIGA-TION?
IS THAT SUCH A BAD THING?
WHILE WALKER IS A POLICE OFFICER LIKE ANY OTHER, HE'S LOST SOMEONE CLOSE TO HIM WHO CAN'T BE FOUND.
HE'S... HARBORING THAT ANGUISH.
WOULD IT REALLY BE SO RISKY TO INCLUDE HIM?
FOR HIS SAKE AND FOR THE SAKE OF THIS INVESTIGATION, I THINK HE'S THE BEST ONE FOR THE JOB.
HIS UNCOMPROMISING DRIVE WILL REVEAL THE TRUTH BEHIND THIS CASE.
......
SIGH...
ALL RIGHT... I'LL TRUST YOU.
I MAY BE YOUR BOSS...
...BUT YOU'RE OFFICER WALKER'S.

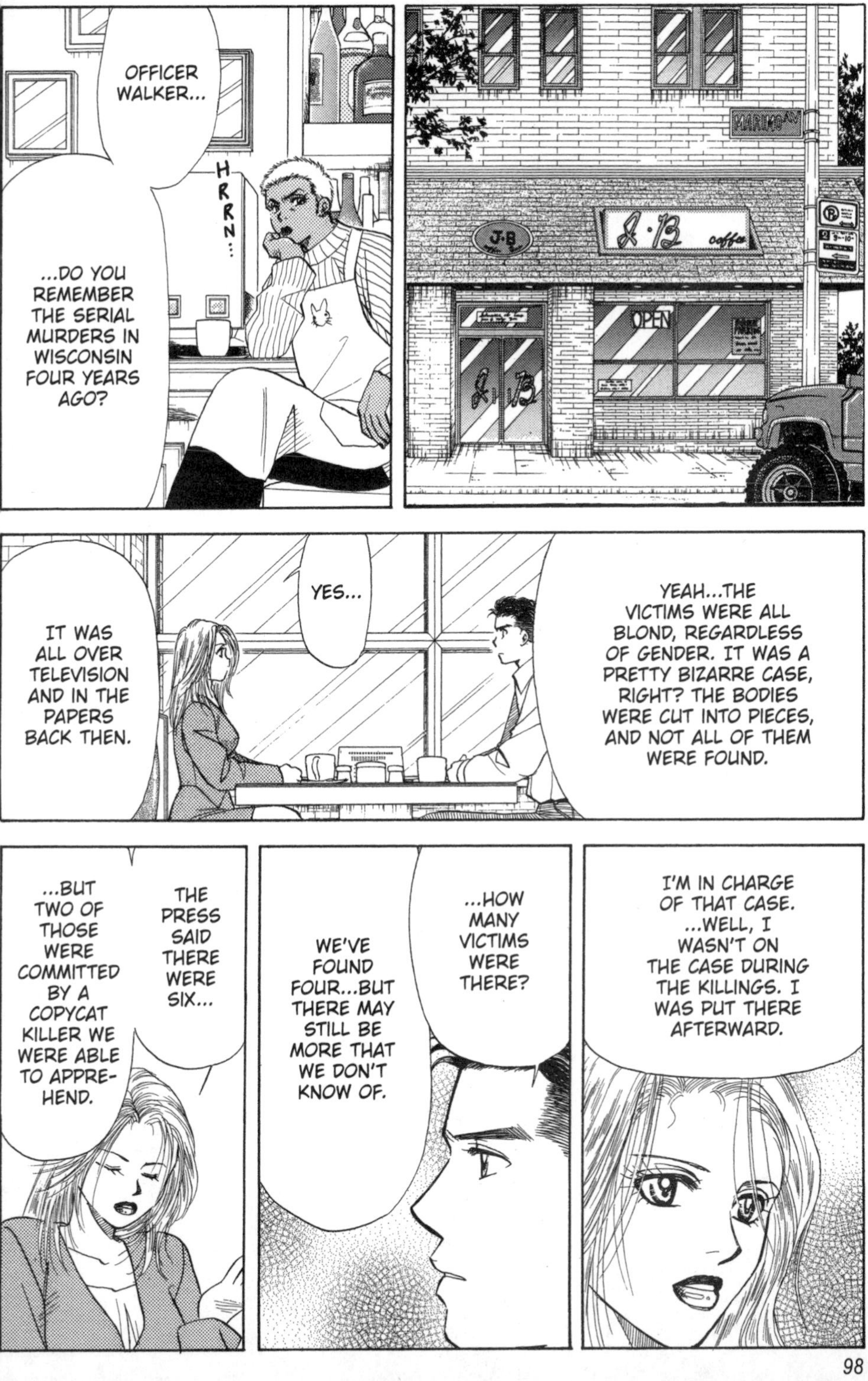
MARIMO AV
J·B
J·B coffee
OPEN
OFFICER WALKER...
HRRN...
...DO YOU REMEMBER THE SERIAL MURDERS IN WISCONSIN FOUR YEARS AGO?
YEAH...THE VICTIMS WERE ALL BLOND, REGARDLESS OF GENDER. IT WAS A PRETTY BIZARRE CASE, RIGHT? THE BODIES WERE CUT INTO PIECES, AND NOT ALL OF THEM WERE FOUND.
YES...
IT WAS ALL OVER TELEVISION AND IN THE PAPERS BACK THEN.
I'M IN CHARGE OF THAT CASE. ...WELL, I WASN'T ON THE CASE DURING THE KILLINGS. I WAS PUT THERE AFTERWARD.
...HOW MANY VICTIMS WERE THERE?
WE'VE FOUND FOUR...BUT THERE MAY STILL BE MORE THAT WE DON'T KNOW OF.
THE PRESS SAID THERE WERE SIX...
...BUT TWO OF THOSE WERE COMMITTED BY A COPYCAT KILLER WE WERE ABLE TO APPREHEND.

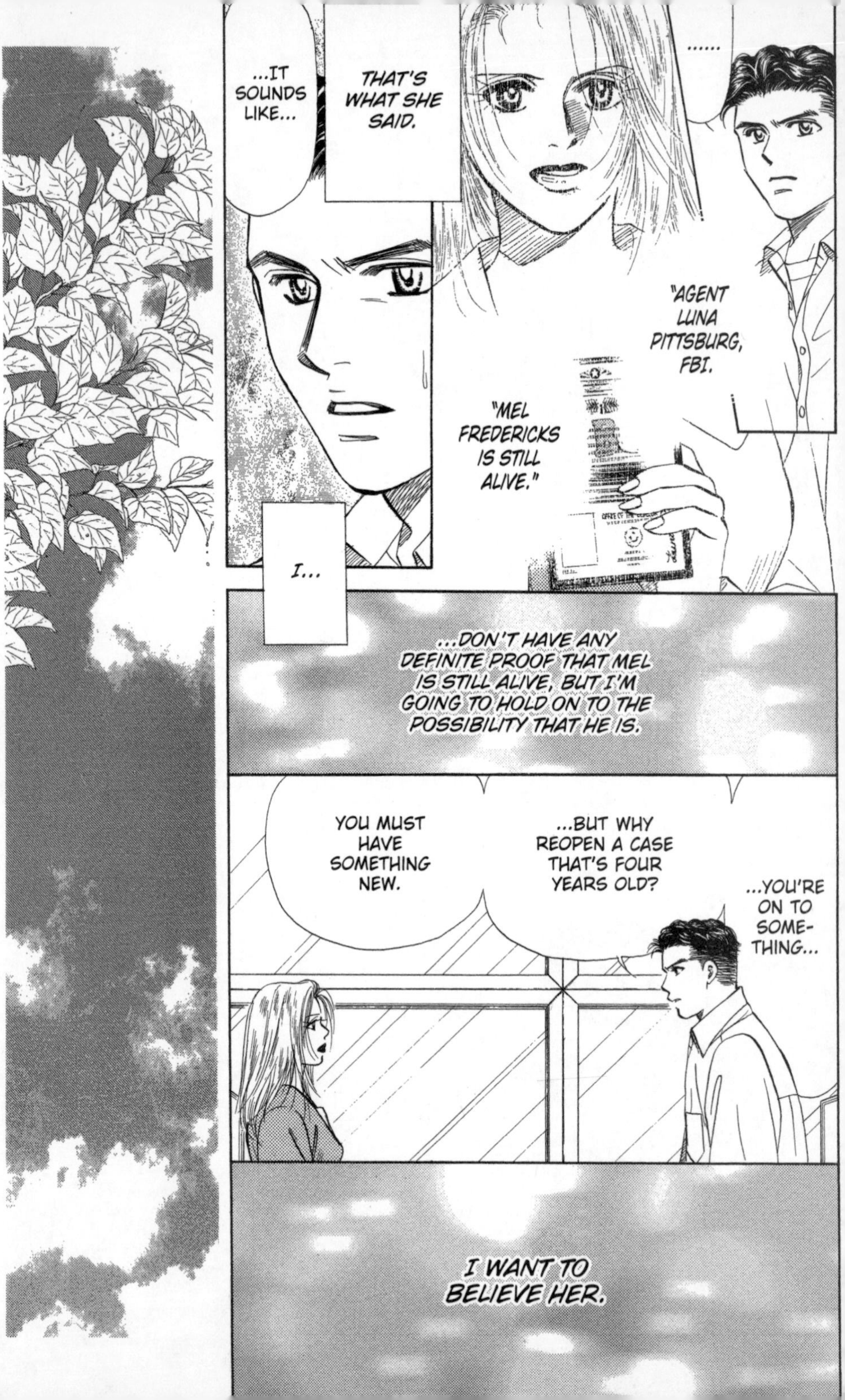
......
"AGENT LUNA PITTSBURG, FBI.
"MEL FREDERICKS IS STILL ALIVE."
THAT'S WHAT SHE SAID.
...IT SOUNDS LIKE...
I...
...DON'T HAVE ANY DEFINITE PROOF THAT MEL IS STILL ALIVE, BUT I'M GOING TO HOLD ON TO THE POSSIBILITY THAT HE IS.
...YOU'RE ON TO SOMETHING...
...BUT WHY REOPEN A CASE THAT'S FOUR YEARS OLD?
YOU MUST HAVE SOMETHING NEW.
I WANT TO BELIEVE HER.

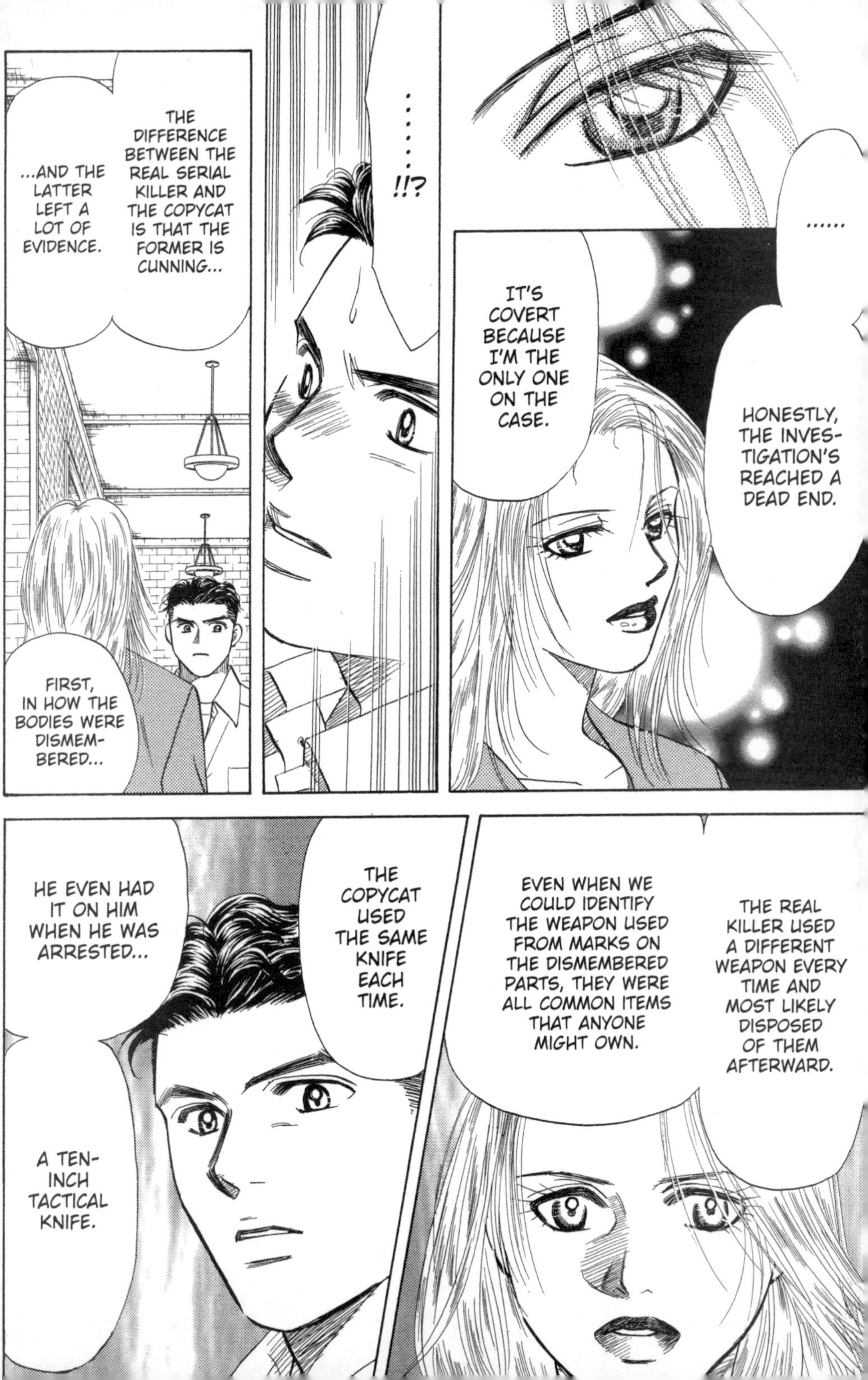
......
HONESTLY, THE INVES-TIGATION'S REACHED A DEAD END.
IT'S COVERT BECAUSE I'M THE ONLY ONE ON THE CASE.
......
!!?
THE DIFFERENCE BETWEEN THE REAL SERIAL KILLER AND THE COPYCAT IS THAT THE FORMER IS CUNNING...
...AND THE LATTER LEFT A LOT OF EVIDENCE.
FIRST, IN HOW THE BODIES WERE DISMEM-BERED...
THE REAL KILLER USED A DIFFERENT WEAPON EVERY TIME AND MOST LIKELY DISPOSED OF THEM AFTERWARD.
EVEN WHEN WE COULD IDENTIFY THE WEAPON USED FROM MARKS ON THE DISMEMBERED PARTS, THEY WERE ALL COMMON ITEMS THAT ANYONE MIGHT OWN.
THE COPYCAT USED THE SAME KNIFE EACH TIME.
HE EVEN HAD IT ON HIM WHEN HE WAS ARRESTED...
A TEN-INCH TACTICAL KNIFE.

IF YOU LOOK AT WHERE THE VICTIMS DISAPPEARED AND WHERE THEY WERE FOUND, THE COPYCAT ABDUCTED HIS VICTIMS AND DISPOSED OF THEIR REMAINS IN A SIMILAR AREA, WHEREAS THE REAL SERIAL KILLER TRANSPORTED HIS VICTIMS OVER GREAT DISTANCES, FROM ONE SIDE OF THE STATE TO THE OTHER, BEFORE DISPOSING OF THEM.
BUT THE MOST NOTABLE DIFFERENCE IS...
...MANY OF THE REAL SERIAL KILLER'S VICTIMS WERE FOUND IN BODIES OF WATER. IN PARTICULAR, THE TORSOS WERE FOUND IN WATER 100% OF THE TIME.
WE FOUND EVIDENCE OF SEXUAL ASSAULT ON ONE OF THE COPYCAT'S VICTIMS, AND WITH DNA ANALYSIS, WE SOON GOT OUR MAN.
...I SEE...
HE REALLY IS CUNNING. THE WATER GETS RID OF ALL THE EVIDENCE.
YES, THAT'S RIGHT.
IN ADDITION TO ELIMINATING SIGNS OF SEXUAL ASSAULT, THE WATER WASHES AWAY OTHER THINGS TOO.
......
... I'M ...
...AFTER THIS MAN.
SU (SSK)

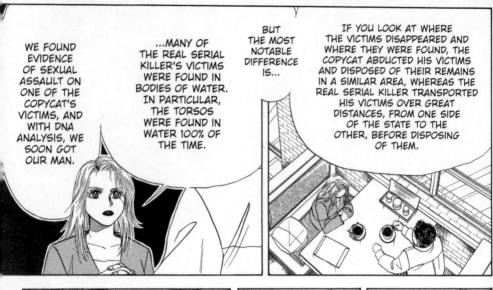

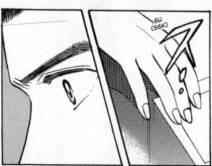

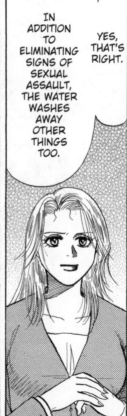

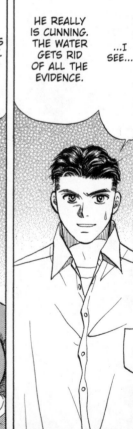

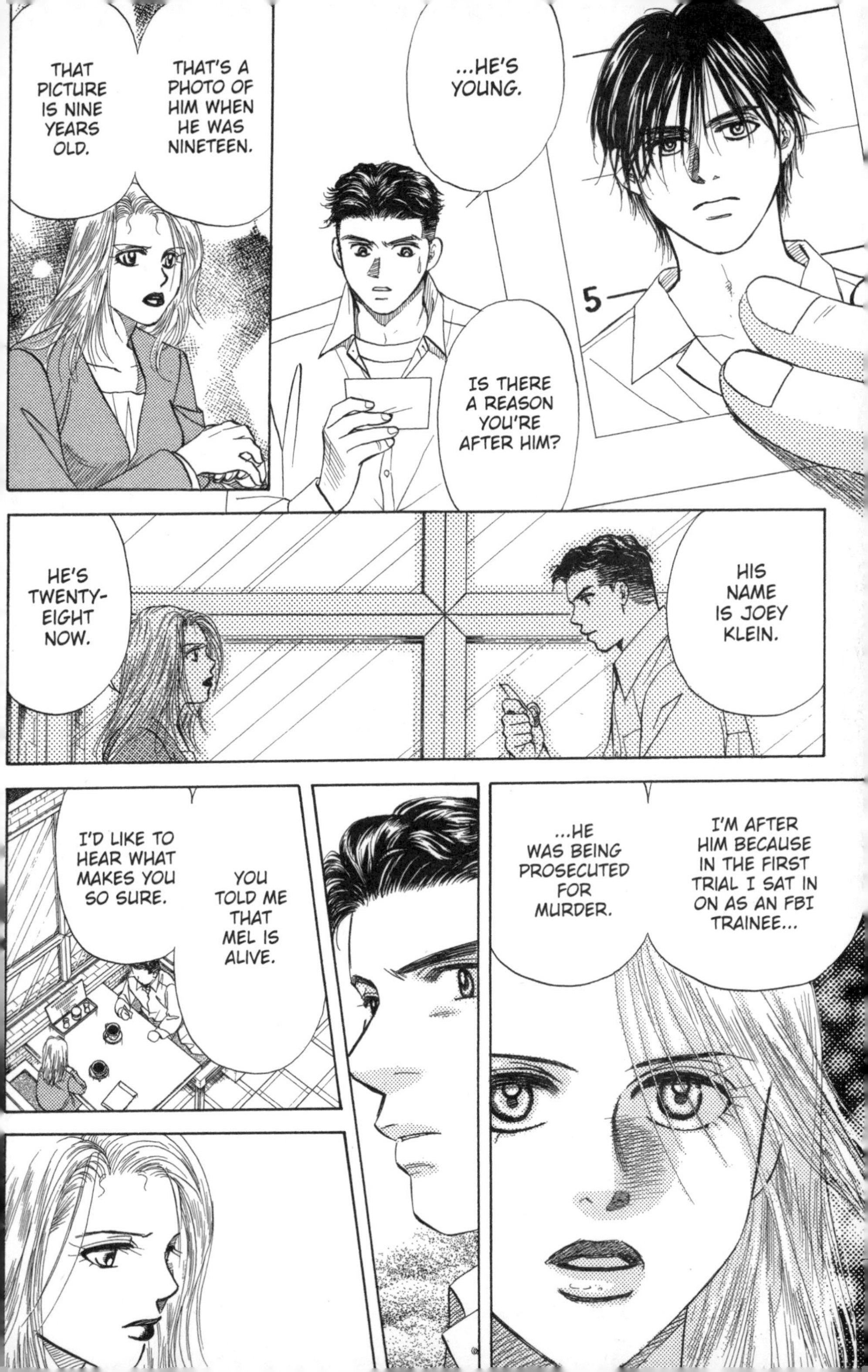
...HE'S YOUNG.
IS THERE A REASON YOU'RE AFTER HIM?
THAT'S A PHOTO OF HIM WHEN HE WAS NINETEEN.
THAT PICTURE IS NINE YEARS OLD.
5
HIS NAME IS JOEY KLEIN.
HE'S TWENTY-EIGHT NOW.
I'M AFTER HIM BECAUSE IN THE FIRST TRIAL I SAT IN ON AS AN FBI TRAINEE...
...HE WAS BEING PROSECUTED FOR MURDER.
YOU TOLD ME THAT MEL IS ALIVE.
I'D LIKE TO HEAR WHAT MAKES YOU SO SURE.

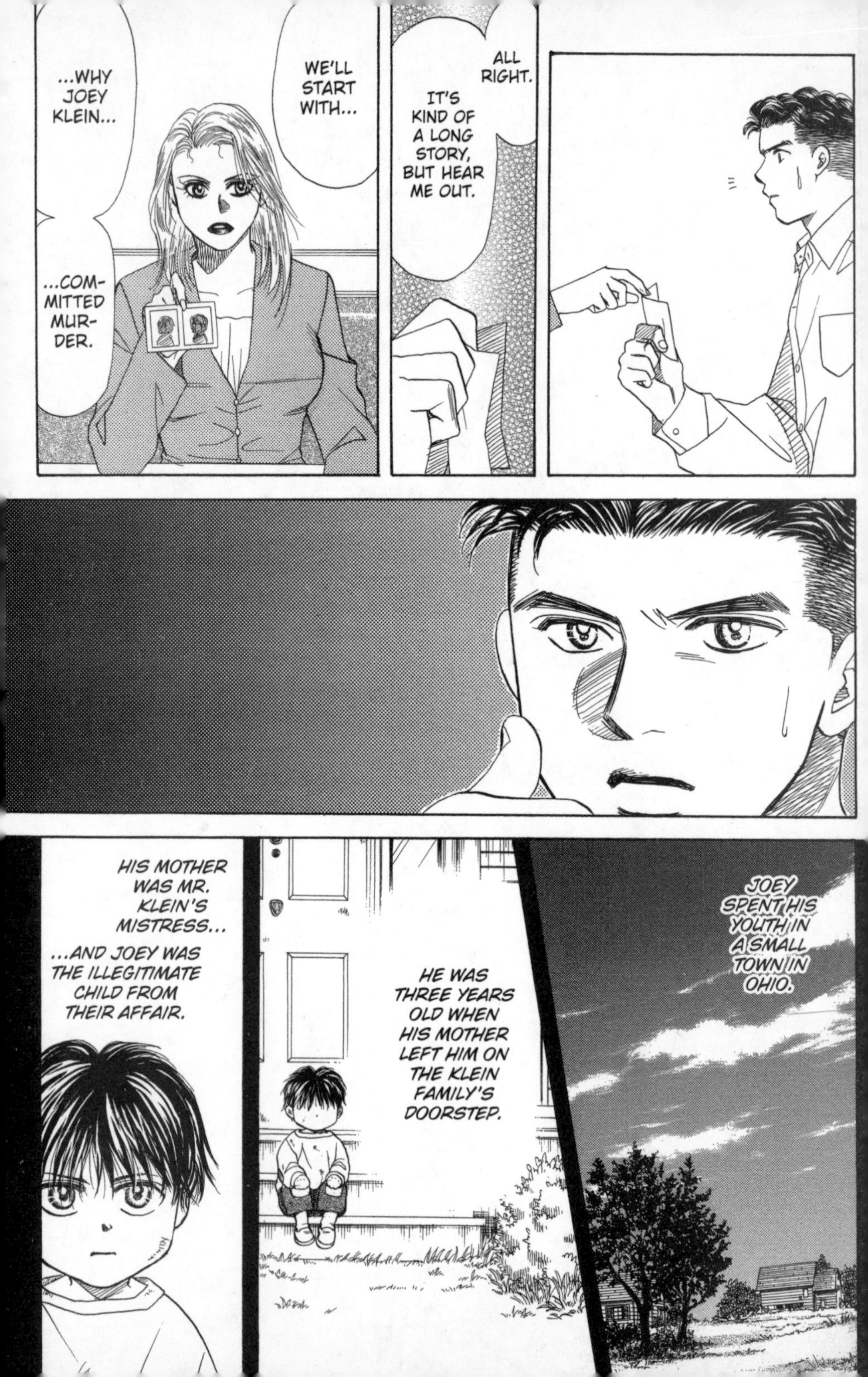
ALL RIGHT.
IT'S KIND OF A LONG STORY, BUT HEAR ME OUT.
WE'LL START WITH...
...WHY JOEY KLEIN...
...COMMITTED MURDER.
JOEY SPENT HIS YOUTH IN A SMALL TOWN IN OHIO.
HE WAS THREE YEARS OLD WHEN HIS MOTHER LEFT HIM ON THE KLEIN FAMILY'S DOORSTEP.
HIS MOTHER WAS MR. KLEIN'S MISTRESS...
...AND JOEY WAS THE ILLEGITIMATE CHILD FROM THEIR AFFAIR.

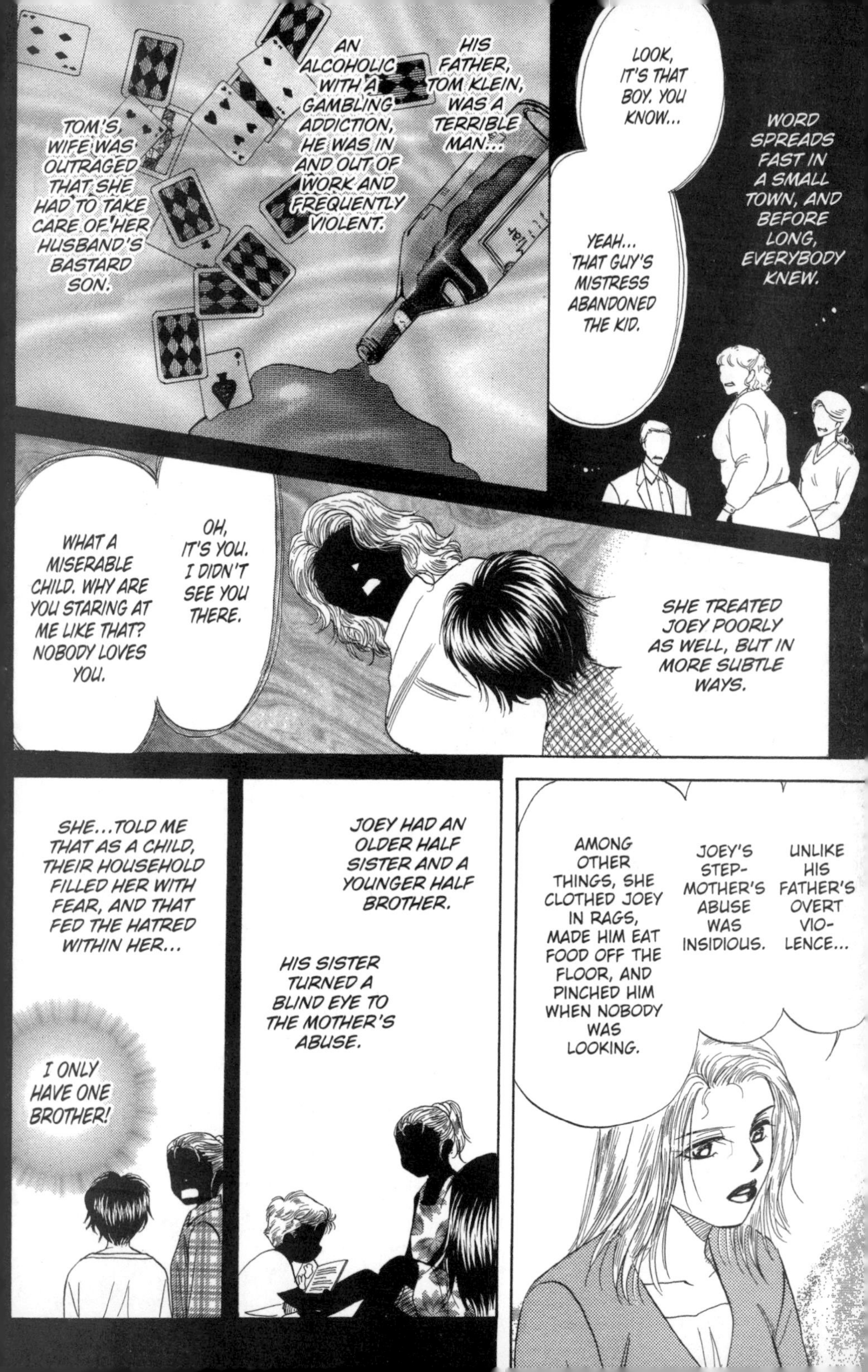
WORD SPREADS FAST IN A SMALL TOWN, AND BEFORE LONG, EVERYBODY KNEW.
LOOK, IT'S THAT BOY. YOU KNOW...
YEAH... THAT GUY'S MISTRESS ABANDONED THE KID.
HIS FATHER, TOM KLEIN, WAS A TERRIBLE MAN...
AN ALCOHOLIC WITH A GAMBLING ADDICTION, HE WAS IN AND OUT OF WORK AND FREQUENTLY VIOLENT.
TOM'S WIFE WAS OUTRAGED THAT SHE HAD TO TAKE CARE OF HER HUSBAND'S BASTARD SON.
SHE TREATED JOEY POORLY AS WELL, BUT IN MORE SUBTLE WAYS.
OH, IT'S YOU. I DIDN'T SEE YOU THERE.
WHAT A MISERABLE CHILD. WHY ARE YOU STARING AT ME LIKE THAT? NOBODY LOVES YOU.
UNLIKE HIS FATHER'S OVERT VIO-LENCE...
JOEY'S STEP-MOTHER'S ABUSE WAS INSIDIOUS.
AMONG OTHER THINGS, SHE CLOTHED JOEY IN RAGS, MADE HIM EAT FOOD OFF THE FLOOR, AND PINCHED HIM WHEN NOBODY WAS LOOKING.
JOEY HAD AN OLDER HALF SISTER AND A YOUNGER HALF BROTHER.
HIS SISTER TURNED A BLIND EYE TO THE MOTHER'S ABUSE.
SHE...TOLD ME THAT AS A CHILD, THEIR HOUSEHOLD FILLED HER WITH FEAR, AND THAT FED THE HATRED WITHIN HER...
I ONLY HAVE ONE BROTHER!

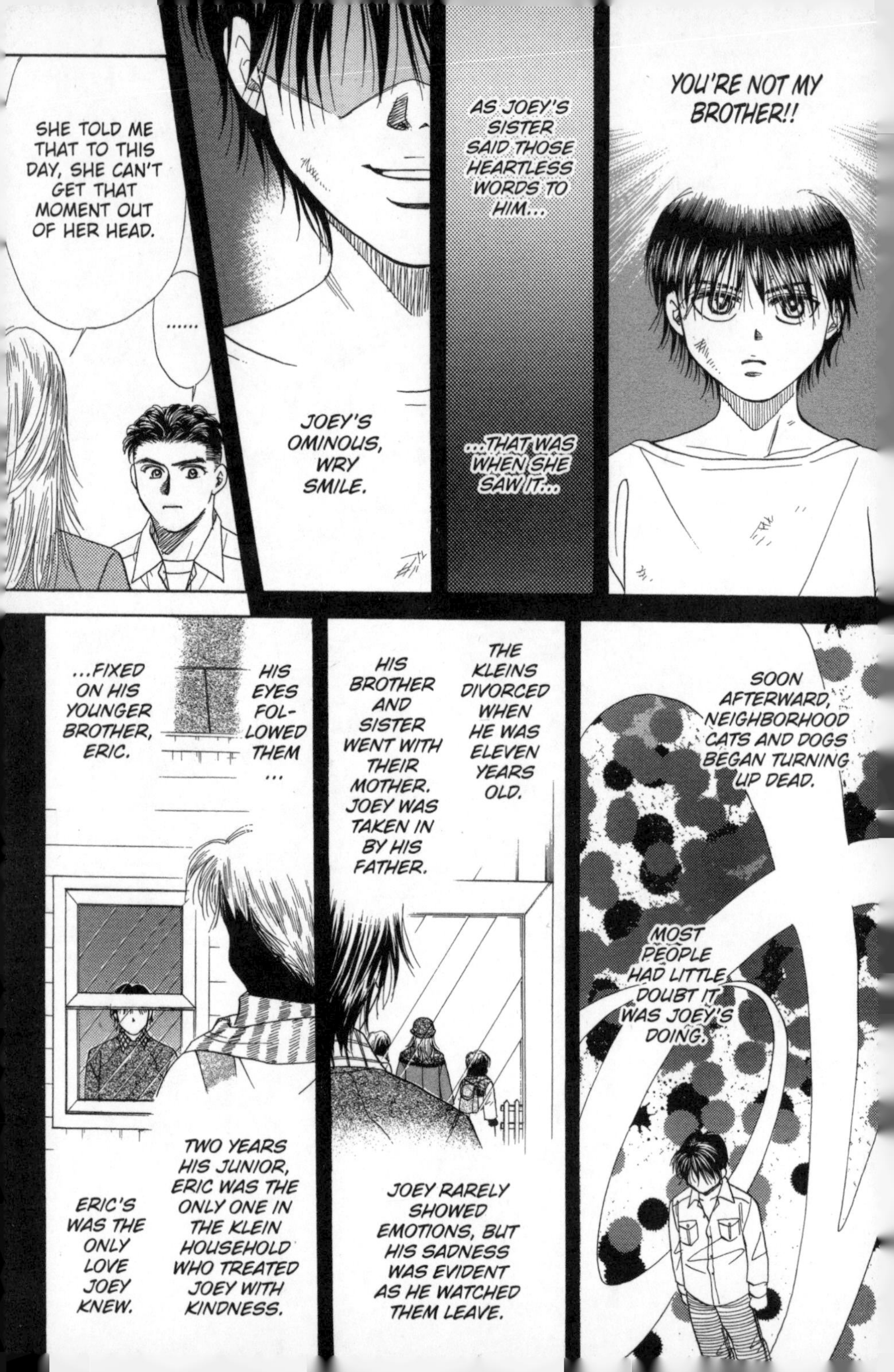
YOU'RE NOT MY BROTHER!!
AS JOEY'S SISTER SAID THOSE HEARTLESS WORDS TO HIM...
...THAT WAS WHEN SHE SAW IT...
JOEY'S OMINOUS, WRY SMILE.
SHE TOLD ME THAT TO THIS DAY, SHE CAN'T GET THAT MOMENT OUT OF HER HEAD.
......
SOON AFTERWARD, NEIGHBORHOOD CATS AND DOGS BEGAN TURNING UP DEAD.
MOST PEOPLE HAD LITTLE DOUBT IT WAS JOEY'S DOING.
THE KLEINS DIVORCED WHEN HE WAS ELEVEN YEARS OLD.
HIS BROTHER AND SISTER WENT WITH THEIR MOTHER. JOEY WAS TAKEN IN BY HIS FATHER.
JOEY RARELY SHOWED EMOTIONS, BUT HIS SADNESS WAS EVIDENT AS HE WATCHED THEM LEAVE.
HIS EYES FOL-LOWED THEM...
...FIXED ON HIS YOUNGER BROTHER, ERIC.
TWO YEARS HIS JUNIOR, ERIC WAS THE ONLY ONE IN THE KLEIN HOUSEHOLD WHO TREATED JOEY WITH KINDNESS.
ERIC'S WAS THE ONLY LOVE JOEY KNEW.

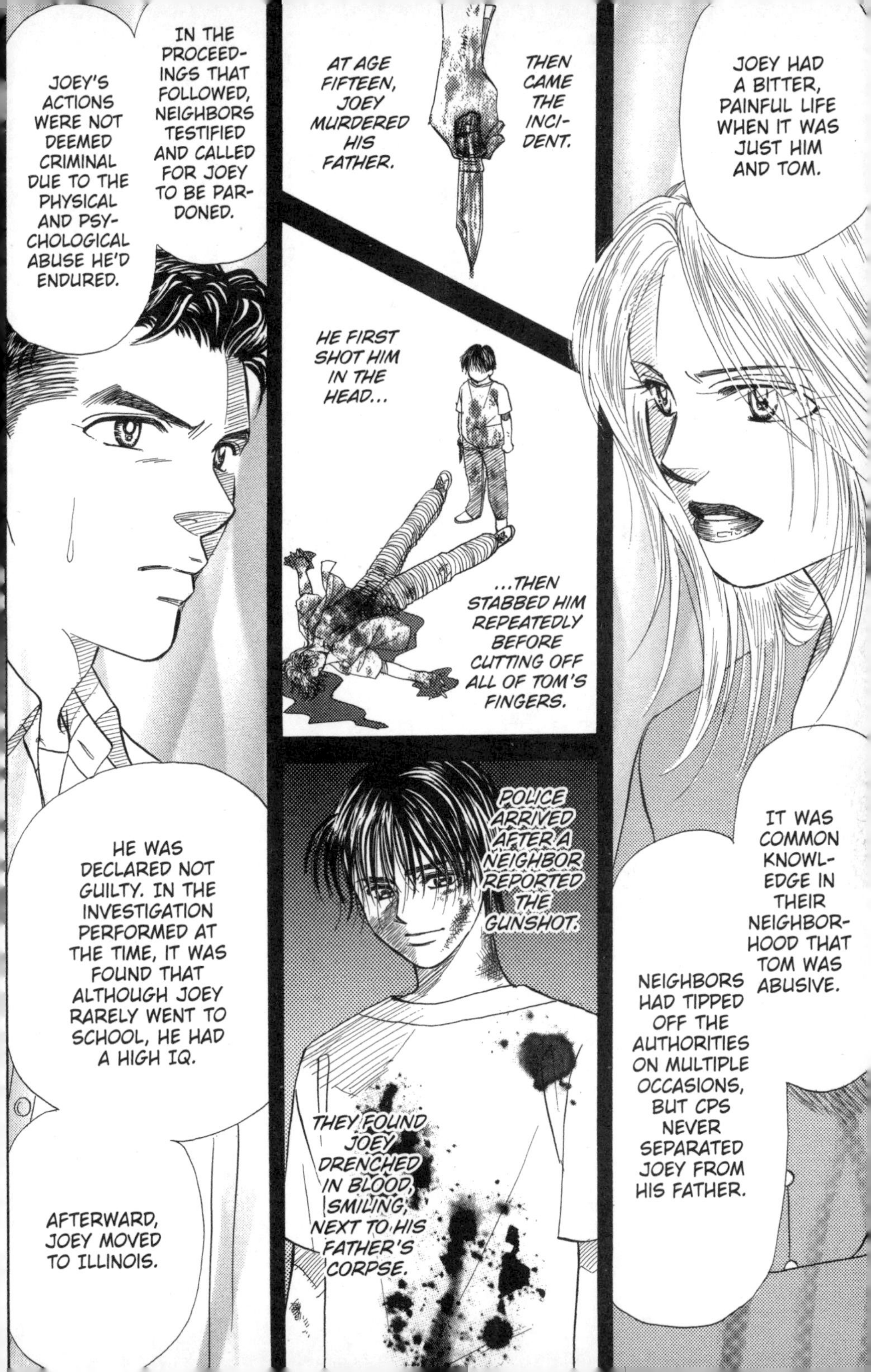
JOEY HAD A BITTER, PAINFUL LIFE WHEN IT WAS JUST HIM AND TOM.
IT WAS COMMON KNOWLEDGE IN THEIR NEIGHBORHOOD THAT TOM WAS ABUSIVE.
NEIGHBORS HAD TIPPED OFF THE AUTHORITIES ON MULTIPLE OCCASIONS, BUT CPS NEVER SEPARATED JOEY FROM HIS FATHER.
THEN CAME THE INCIDENT.
AT AGE FIFTEEN, JOEY MURDERED HIS FATHER.
HE FIRST SHOT HIM IN THE HEAD...
...THEN STABBED HIM REPEATEDLY BEFORE CUTTING OFF ALL OF TOM'S FINGERS.
POLICE ARRIVED AFTER A NEIGHBOR REPORTED THE GUNSHOT.
THEY FOUND JOEY DRENCHED IN BLOOD, SMILING, NEXT TO HIS FATHER'S CORPSE.
IN THE PROCEEDINGS THAT FOLLOWED, NEIGHBORS TESTIFIED AND CALLED FOR JOEY TO BE PARDONED.
JOEY'S ACTIONS WERE NOT DEEMED CRIMINAL DUE TO THE PHYSICAL AND PSYCHOLOGICAL ABUSE HE'D ENDURED.
HE WAS DECLARED NOT GUILTY. IN THE INVESTIGATION PERFORMED AT THE TIME, IT WAS FOUND THAT ALTHOUGH JOEY RARELY WENT TO SCHOOL, HE HAD A HIGH IQ.
AFTERWARD, JOEY MOVED TO ILLINOIS.

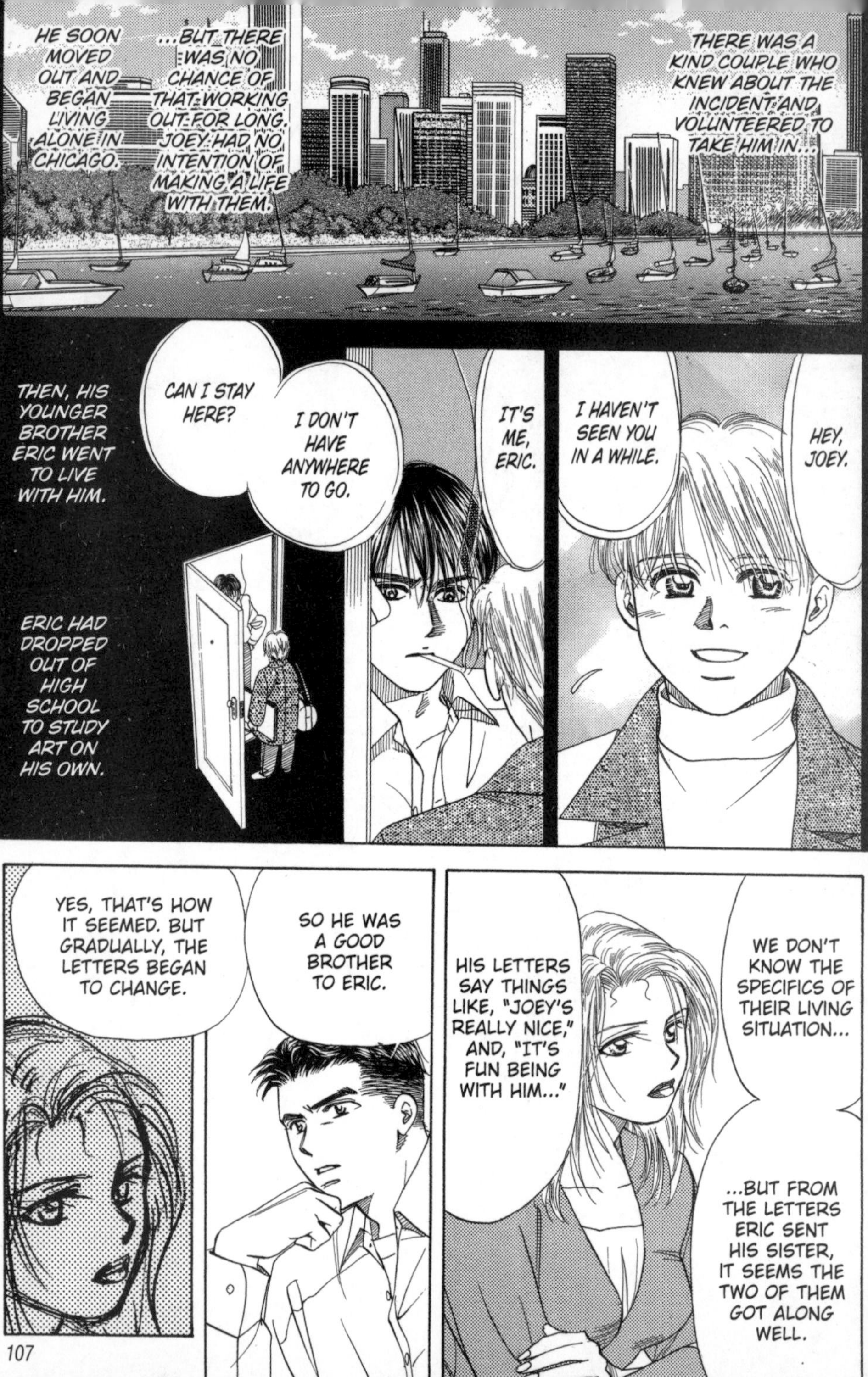
THERE WAS A KIND COUPLE WHO KNEW ABOUT THE INCIDENT AND VOLUNTEERED TO TAKE HIM IN...
...BUT THERE WAS NO CHANCE OF THAT WORKING OUT FOR LONG. JOEY HAD NO INTENTION OF MAKING A LIFE WITH THEM.
HE SOON MOVED OUT AND BEGAN LIVING ALONE IN CHICAGO.
HEY, JOEY.
I HAVEN'T SEEN YOU IN A WHILE.
IT'S ME, ERIC.
I DON'T HAVE ANYWHERE TO GO.
CAN I STAY HERE?
THEN, HIS YOUNGER BROTHER ERIC WENT TO LIVE WITH HIM.
ERIC HAD DROPPED OUT OF HIGH SCHOOL TO STUDY ART ON HIS OWN.
WE DON'T KNOW THE SPECIFICS OF THEIR LIVING SITUATION...
...BUT FROM THE LETTERS ERIC SENT HIS SISTER, IT SEEMS THE TWO OF THEM GOT ALONG WELL.
HIS LETTERS SAY THINGS LIKE, "JOEY'S REALLY NICE," AND, "IT'S FUN BEING WITH HIM..."
SO HE WAS A GOOD BROTHER TO ERIC.
YES, THAT'S HOW IT SEEMED. BUT GRADUALLY, THE LETTERS BEGAN TO CHANGE.

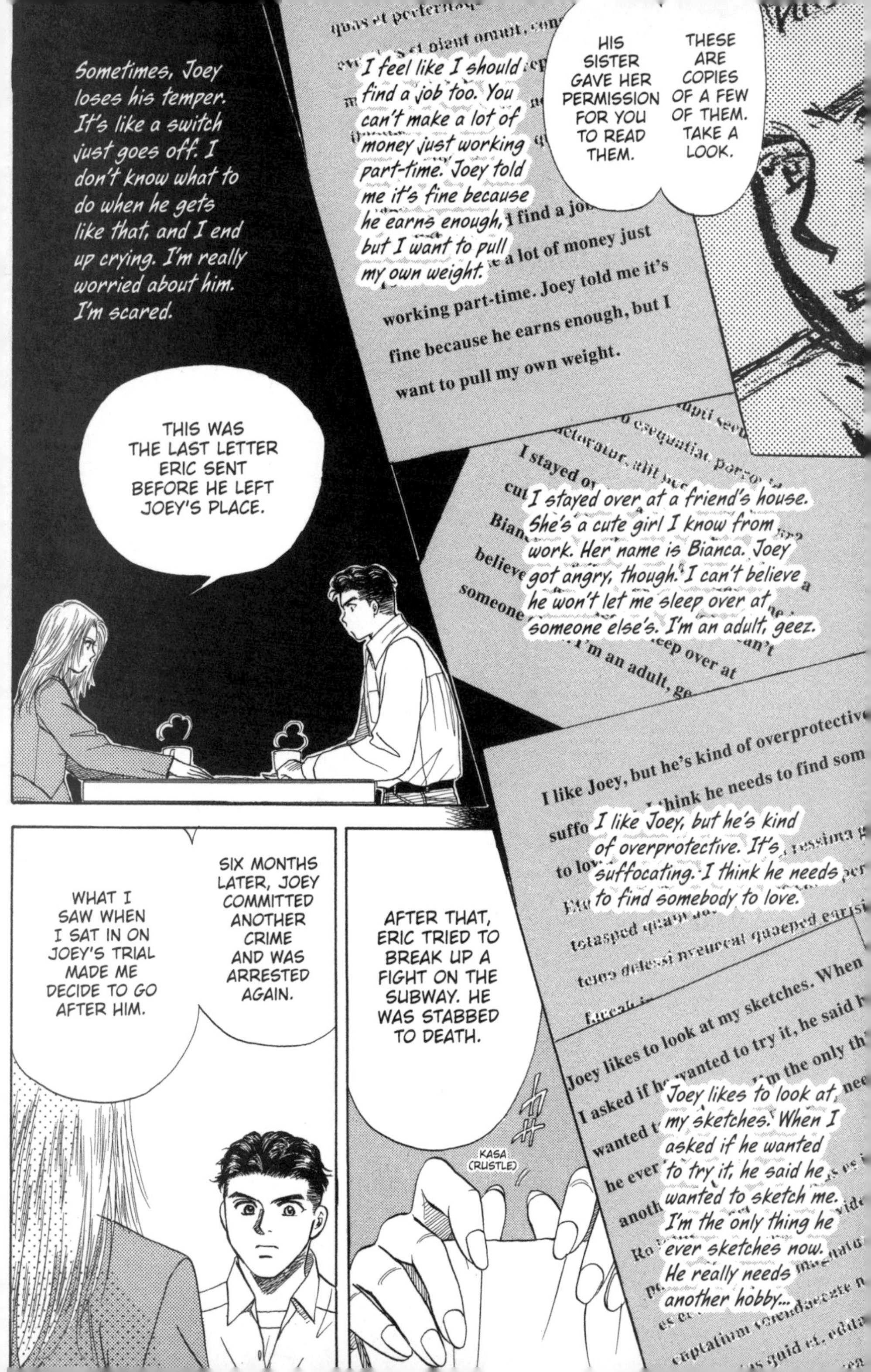
THESE ARE COPIES OF A FEW OF THEM. TAKE A LOOK.
HIS SISTER GAVE HER PERMISSION FOR YOU TO READ THEM.
I stayed over at a friend's house. She's a cute girl I know from work. Her name is Bianca. Joey got angry, though. I can't believe he won't let me sleep over at someone else's. I'm an adult, geez.
I like Joey, but he's kind of overprotective. It's suffocating. I think he needs to find somebody to love.
Joey likes to look at my sketches. When I asked if he wanted to try it, he said he wanted to sketch me. I'm the only thing he ever sketches now. He really needs another hobby...
I feel like I should find a job too. You can't make a lot of money just working part-time. Joey told me it's fine because he earns enough, but I want to pull my own weight.
Sometimes, Joey loses his temper. It's like a switch just goes off. I don't know what to do when he gets like that, and I end up crying. I'm really worried about him. I'm scared.
THIS WAS THE LAST LETTER ERIC SENT BEFORE HE LEFT JOEY'S PLACE.
AFTER THAT, ERIC TRIED TO BREAK UP A FIGHT ON THE SUBWAY. HE WAS STABBED TO DEATH.
KASA (RUSTLE)
SIX MONTHS LATER, JOEY COMMITTED ANOTHER CRIME AND WAS ARRESTED AGAIN.
WHAT I SAW WHEN I SAT IN ON JOEY'S TRIAL MADE ME DECIDE TO GO AFTER HIM.

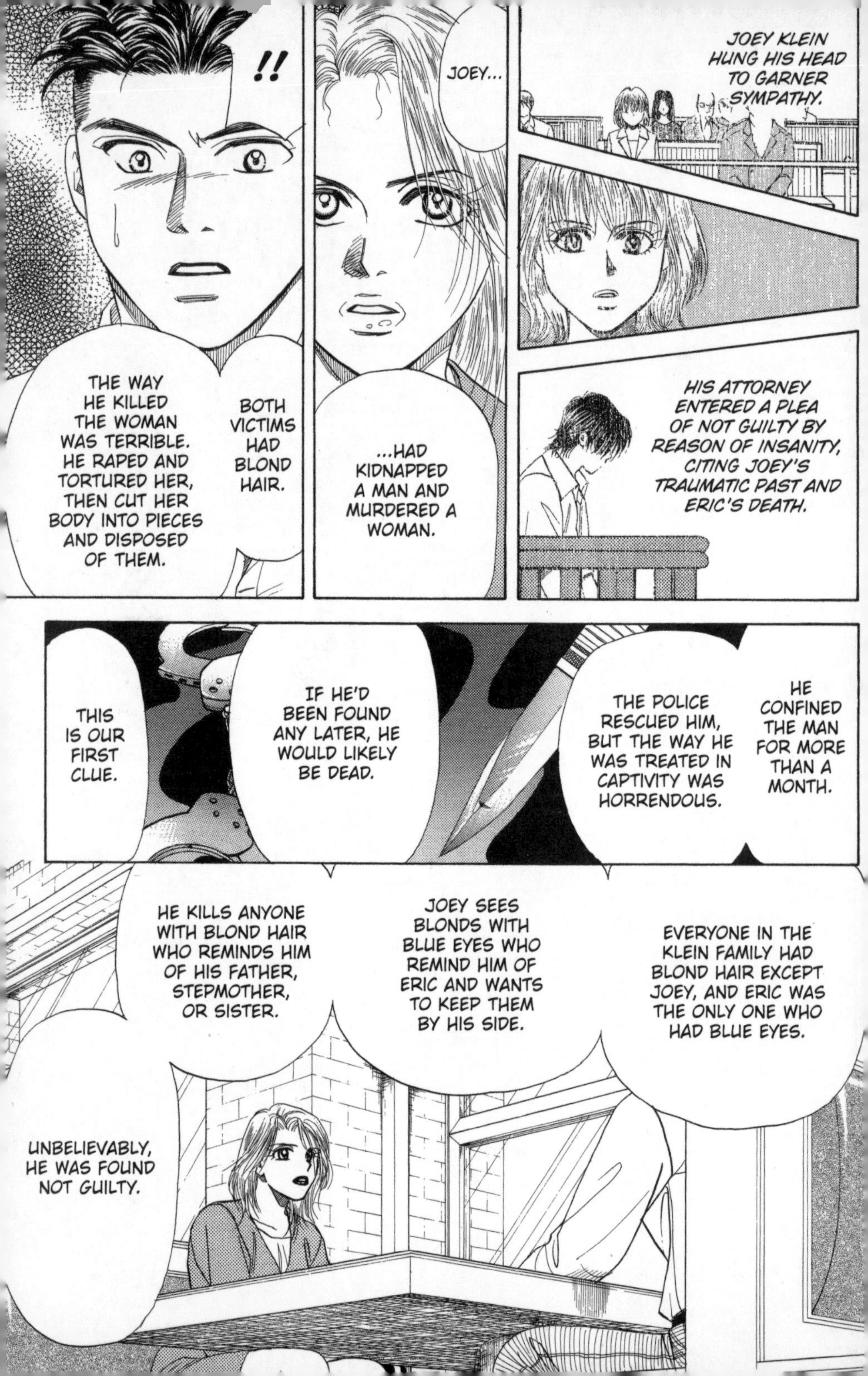
JOEY KLEIN HUNG HIS HEAD TO GARNER SYMPATHY.
HIS ATTORNEY ENTERED A PLEA OF NOT GUILTY BY REASON OF INSANITY, CITING JOEY'S TRAUMATIC PAST AND ERIC'S DEATH.
JOEY...
...HAD KIDNAPPED A MAN AND MURDERED A WOMAN.
!!
BOTH VICTIMS HAD BLOND HAIR.
THE WAY HE KILLED THE WOMAN WAS TERRIBLE. HE RAPED AND TORTURED HER, THEN CUT HER BODY INTO PIECES AND DISPOSED OF THEM.
HE CONFINED THE MAN FOR MORE THAN A MONTH.
THE POLICE RESCUED HIM, BUT THE WAY HE WAS TREATED IN CAPTIVITY WAS HORRENDOUS.
IF HE'D BEEN FOUND ANY LATER, HE WOULD LIKELY BE DEAD.
THIS IS OUR FIRST CLUE.
EVERYONE IN THE KLEIN FAMILY HAD BLOND HAIR EXCEPT JOEY, AND ERIC WAS THE ONLY ONE WHO HAD BLUE EYES.
JOEY SEES BLONDS WITH BLUE EYES WHO REMIND HIM OF ERIC AND WANTS TO KEEP THEM BY HIS SIDE.
HE KILLS ANYONE WITH BLOND HAIR WHO REMINDS HIM OF HIS FATHER, STEPMOTHER, OR SISTER.
UNBELIEVABLY, HE WAS FOUND NOT GUILTY.

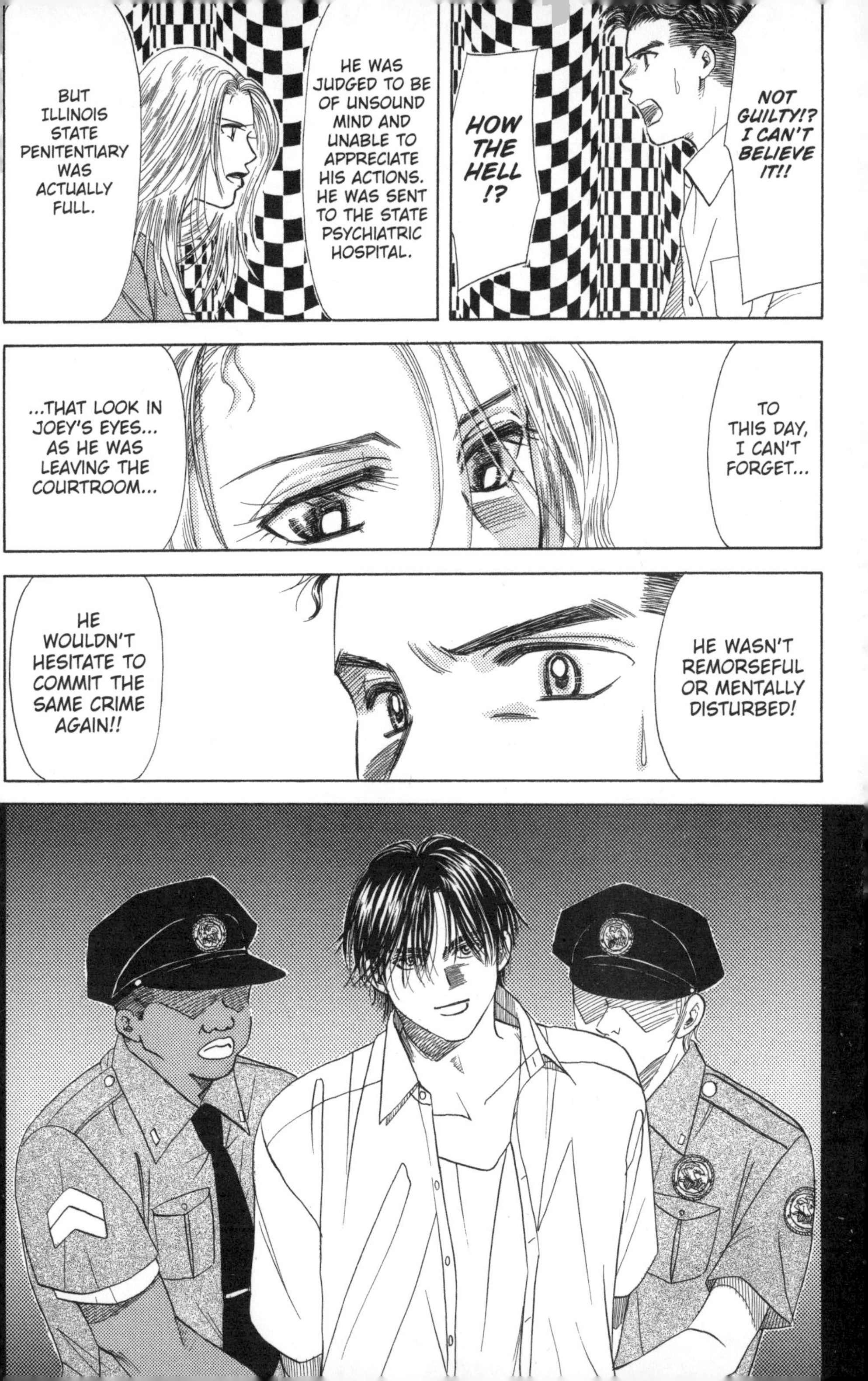
NOT GUILTY!? I CAN'T BELIEVE IT!!
HOW THE HELL!?
HE WAS JUDGED TO BE OF UNSOUND MIND AND UNABLE TO APPRECIATE HIS ACTIONS. HE WAS SENT TO THE STATE PSYCHIATRIC HOSPITAL.
BUT ILLINOIS STATE PENITENTIARY WAS ACTUALLY FULL.
TO THIS DAY, I CAN'T FORGET...
...THAT LOOK IN JOEY'S EYES... AS HE WAS LEAVING THE COURTROOM...
HE WASN'T REMORSEFUL OR MENTALLY DISTURBED!
HE WOULDN'T HESITATE TO COMMIT THE SAME CRIME AGAIN!!

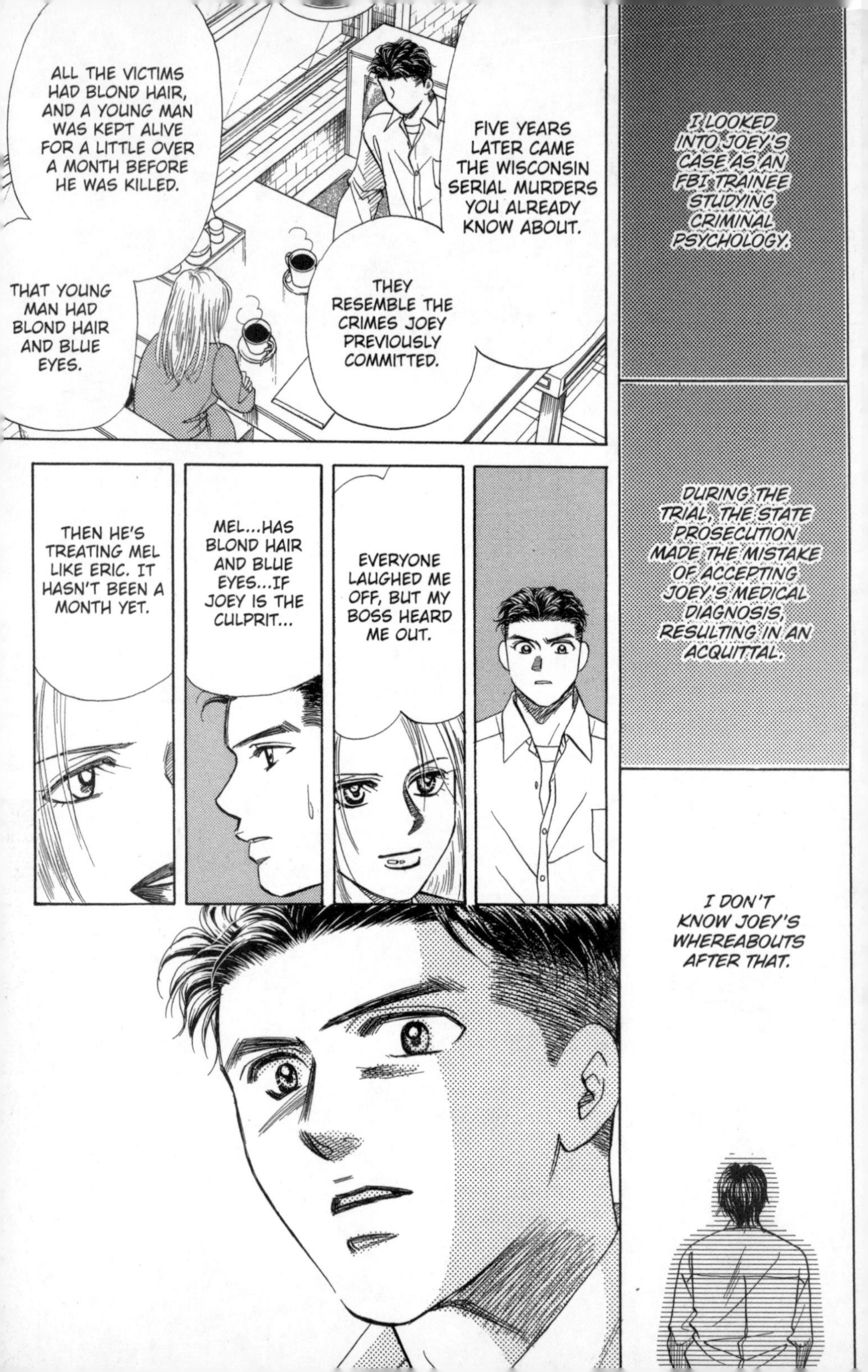
I LOOKED INTO JOEY'S CASE AS AN FBI TRAINEE STUDYING CRIMINAL PSYCHOLOGY.
DURING THE TRIAL, THE STATE PROSECUTION MADE THE MISTAKE OF ACCEPTING JOEY'S MEDICAL DIAGNOSIS, RESULTING IN AN ACQUITTAL.
I DON'T KNOW JOEY'S WHEREABOUTS AFTER THAT.
FIVE YEARS LATER CAME THE WISCONSIN SERIAL MURDERS YOU ALREADY KNOW ABOUT.
THEY RESEMBLE THE CRIMES JOEY PREVIOUSLY COMMITTED.
ALL THE VICTIMS HAD BLOND HAIR, AND A YOUNG MAN WAS KEPT ALIVE FOR A LITTLE OVER A MONTH BEFORE HE WAS KILLED.
THAT YOUNG MAN HAD BLOND HAIR AND BLUE EYES.
EVERYONE LAUGHED ME OFF, BUT MY BOSS HEARD ME OUT.
MEL...HAS BLOND HAIR AND BLUE EYES...IF JOEY IS THE CULPRIT...
THEN HE'S TREATING MEL LIKE ERIC. IT HASN'T BEEN A MONTH YET.

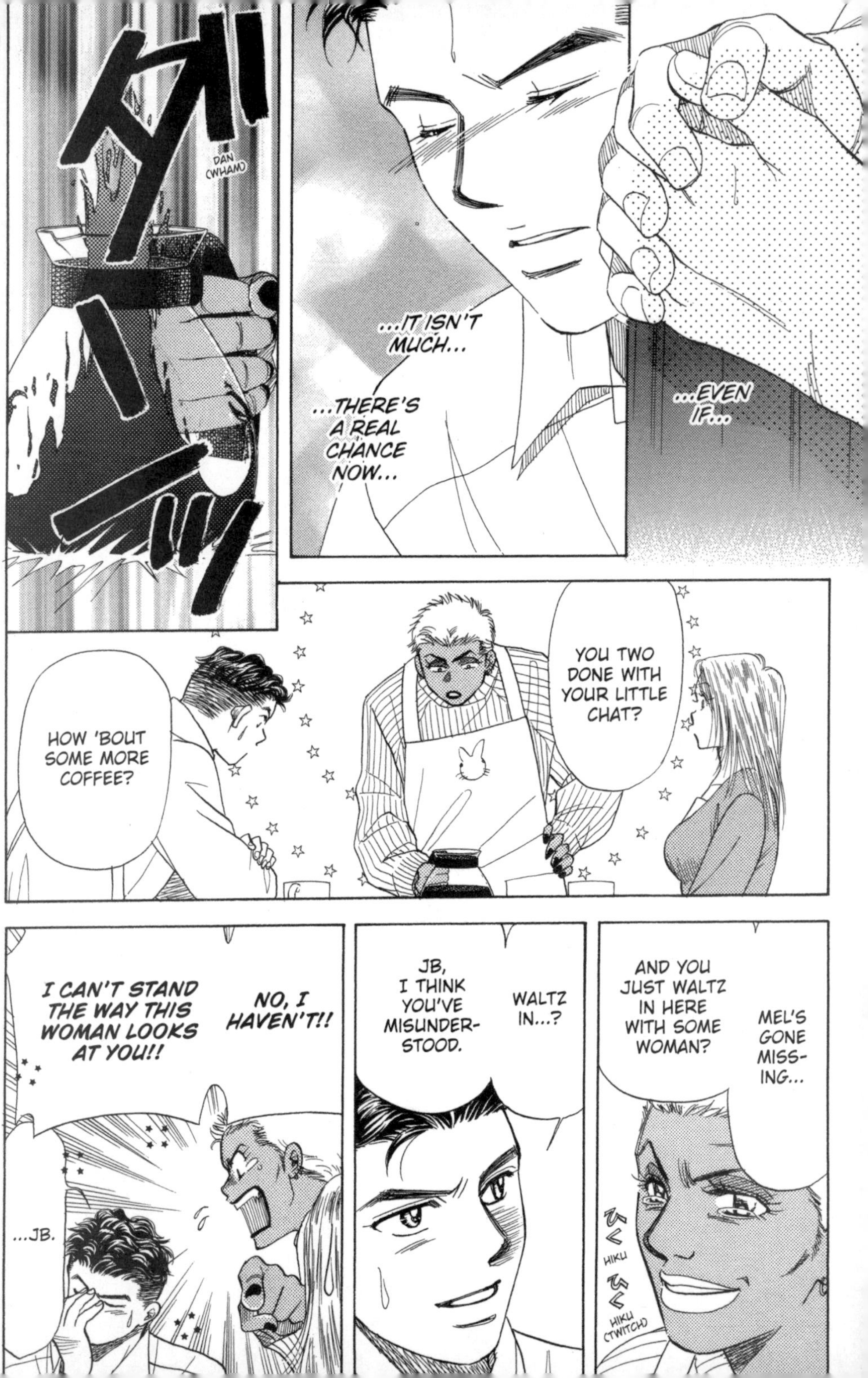
...EVEN IF...
...IT ISN'T MUCH...
...THERE'S A REAL CHANCE NOW...
DAN (WHAM)
YOU TWO DONE WITH YOUR LITTLE CHAT?
HOW 'BOUT SOME MORE COFFEE?
MEL'S GONE MISSING...
AND YOU JUST WALTZ IN HERE WITH SOME WOMAN?
HIKU
HIKU (TWITCH)
WALTZ IN...?
JB, I THINK YOU'VE MISUNDERSTOOD.
NO, I HAVEN'T!!
I CAN'T STAND THE WAY THIS WOMAN LOOKS AT YOU!!
...JB.

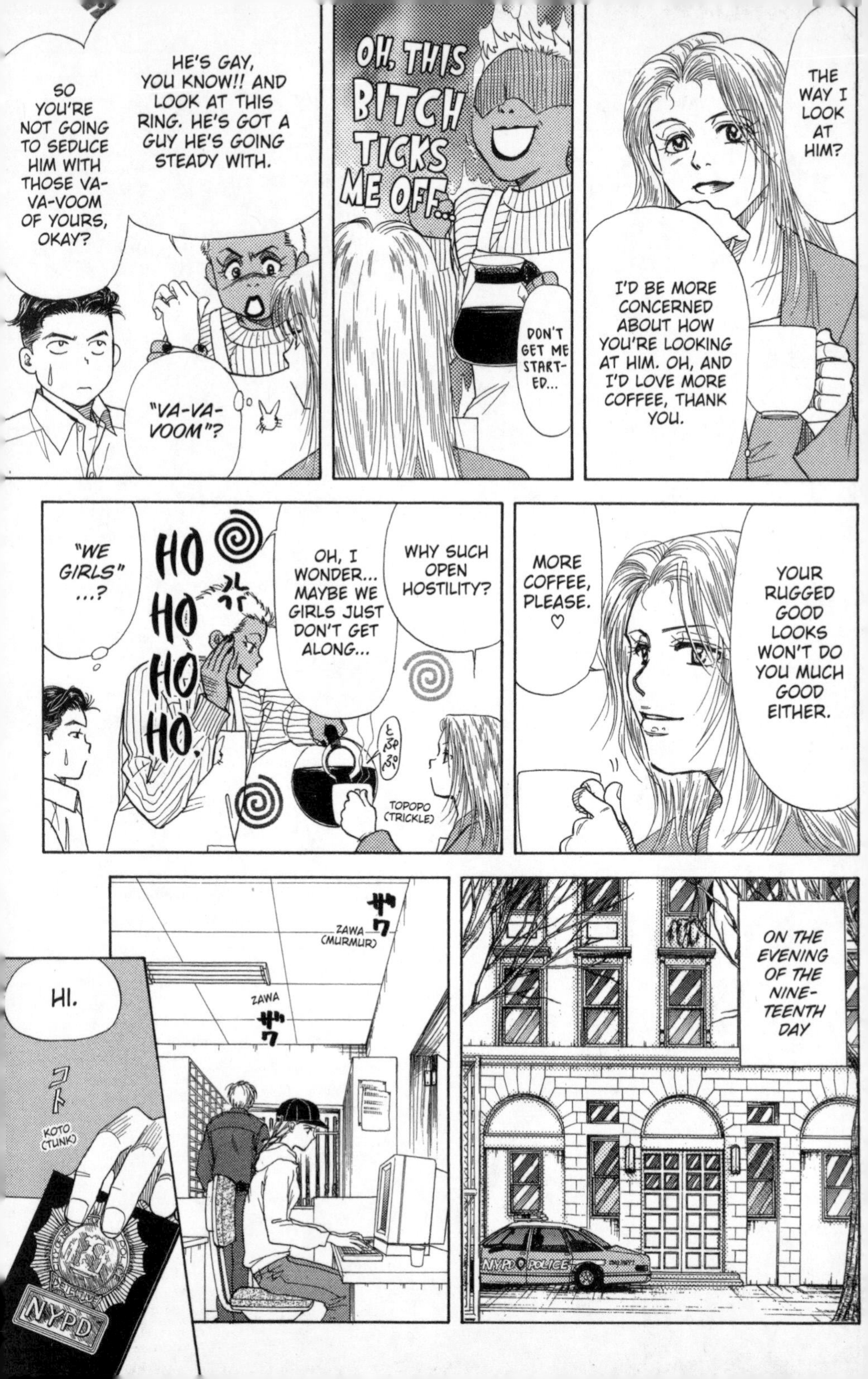
THE WAY I LOOK AT HIM?
I'D BE MORE CONCERNED ABOUT HOW YOU'RE LOOKING AT HIM. OH, AND I'D LOVE MORE COFFEE, THANK YOU.
OH, THIS BITCH TICKS ME OFF...
DON'T GET ME START-ED...
HE'S GAY, YOU KNOW!! AND LOOK AT THIS RING. HE'S GOT A GUY HE'S GOING STEADY WITH.
SO YOU'RE NOT GOING TO SEDUCE HIM WITH THOSE VA-VA-VOOM OF YOURS, OKAY?
"VA-VA-VOOM"?
YOUR RUGGED GOOD LOOKS WON'T DO YOU MUCH GOOD EITHER.
MORE COFFEE, PLEASE. ♡
WHY SUCH OPEN HOSTILITY?
OH, I WONDER... MAYBE WE GIRLS JUST DON'T GET ALONG...
HO HO HO HO.
TOPOPO (TRICKLE)
"WE GIRLS" ...?
ON THE EVENING OF THE NINE-TEENTH DAY
ZAWA (MURMUR)
ZAWA
HI.
KOTO (TUNK)
NYPD

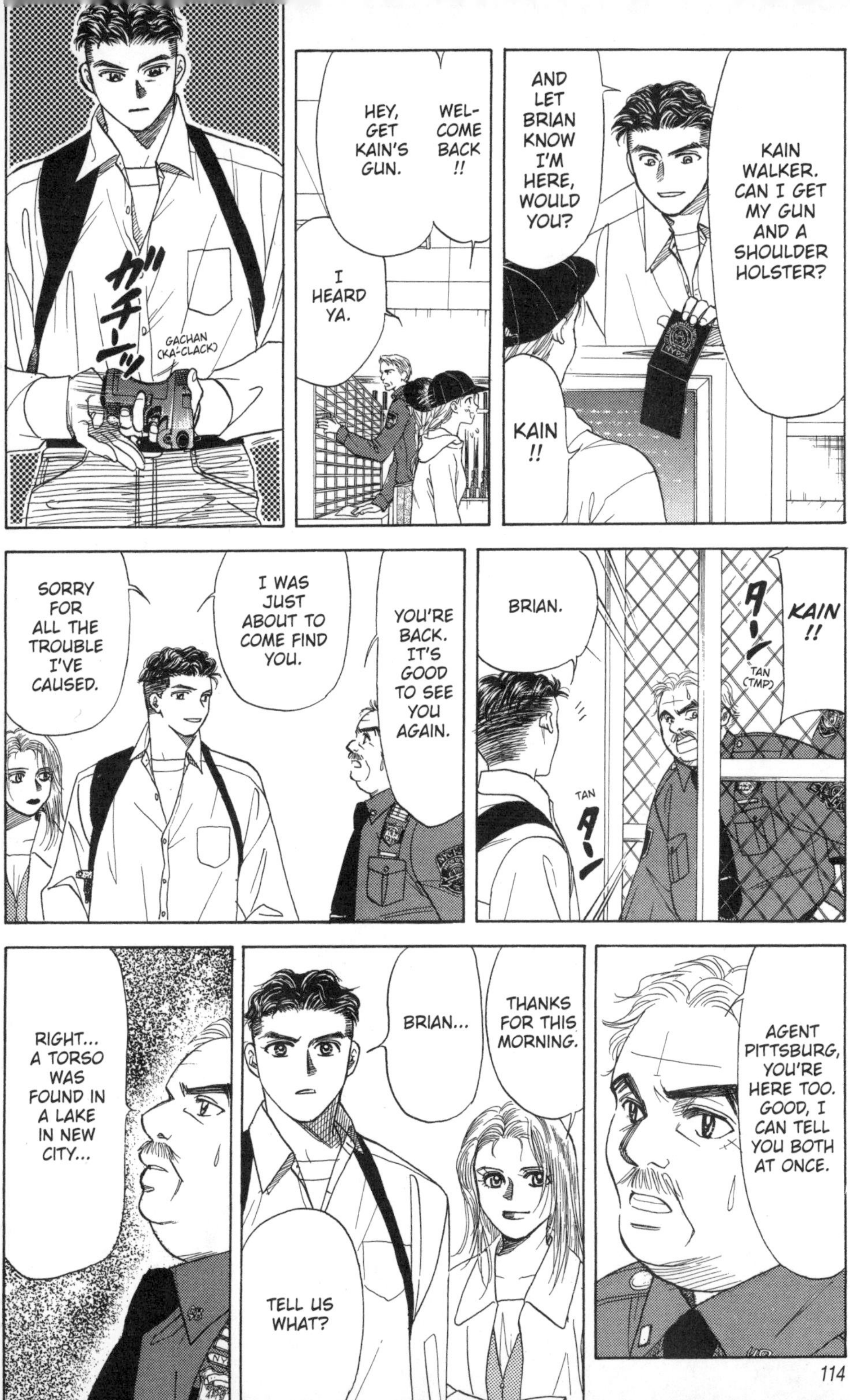
KAIN WALKER. CAN I GET MY GUN AND A SHOULDER HOLSTER?
AND LET BRIAN KNOW I'M HERE, WOULD YOU?
KAIN !!
WEL-COME BACK !!
HEY, GET KAIN'S GUN.
I HEARD YA.
ガチャーッ
GACHAN (KA-CLACK)
KAIN !!
タン
TAN (TMP)
BRIAN.
タン
TAN
YOU'RE BACK. IT'S GOOD TO SEE YOU AGAIN.
I WAS JUST ABOUT TO COME FIND YOU.
SORRY FOR ALL THE TROUBLE I'VE CAUSED.
AGENT PITTSBURG, YOU'RE HERE TOO. GOOD, I CAN TELL YOU BOTH AT ONCE.
THANKS FOR THIS MORNING.
BRIAN...
TELL US WHAT?
RIGHT... A TORSO WAS FOUND IN A LAKE IN NEW CITY...

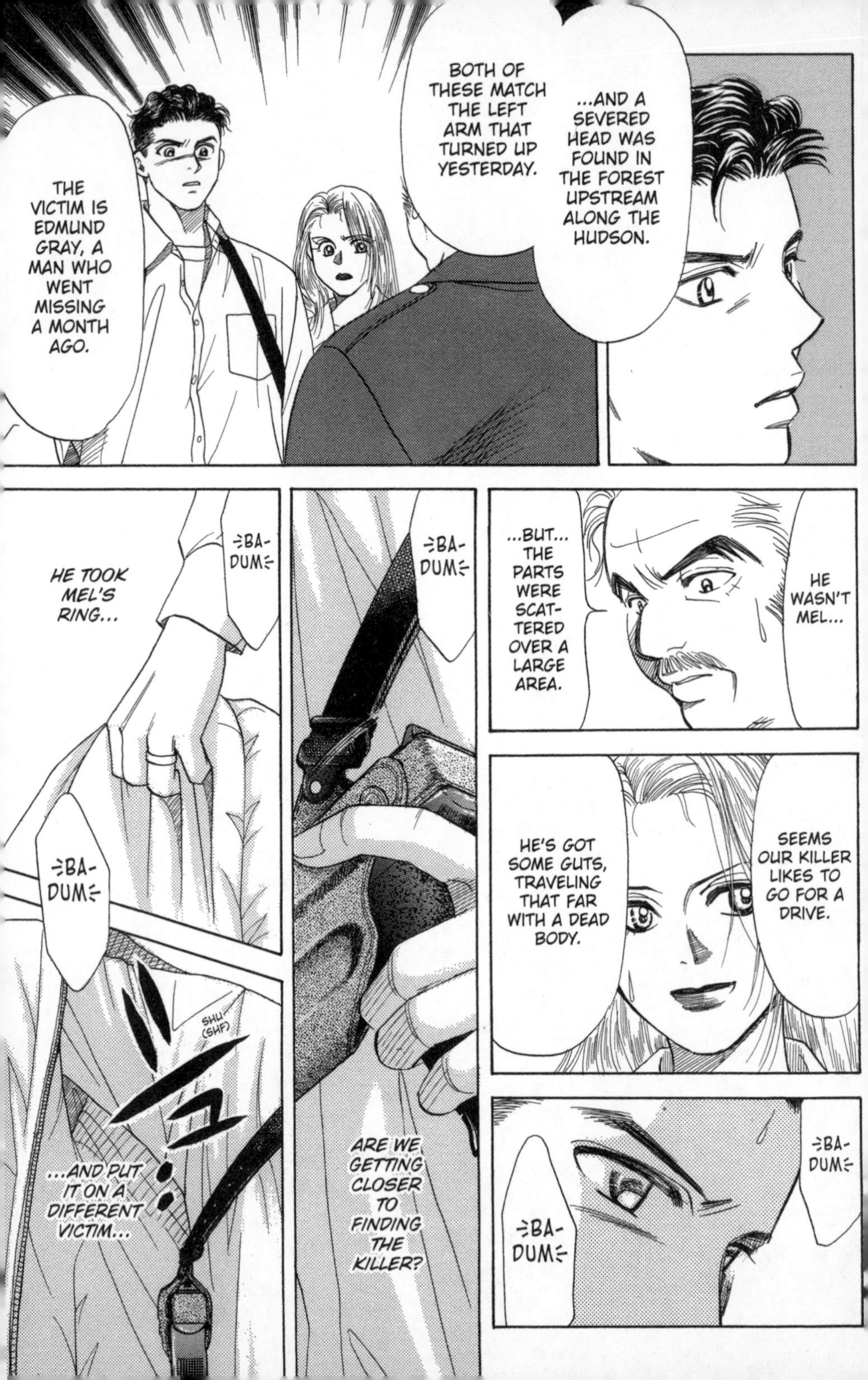
...AND A SEVERED HEAD WAS FOUND IN THE FOREST UPSTREAM ALONG THE HUDSON.
BOTH OF THESE MATCH THE LEFT ARM THAT TURNED UP YESTERDAY.
THE VICTIM IS EDMUND GRAY, A MAN WHO WENT MISSING A MONTH AGO.
HE WASN'T MEL...
...BUT... THE PARTS WERE SCATTERED OVER A LARGE AREA.
SEEMS OUR KILLER LIKES TO GO FOR A DRIVE.
HE'S GOT SOME GUTS, TRAVELING THAT FAR WITH A DEAD BODY.
BA-DUM
BA-DUM
BA-DUM
ARE WE GETTING CLOSER TO FINDING THE KILLER?
BA-DUM
HE TOOK MEL'S RING...
BA-DUM
SHU (SHF)
...AND PUT IT ON A DIFFERENT VICTIM...

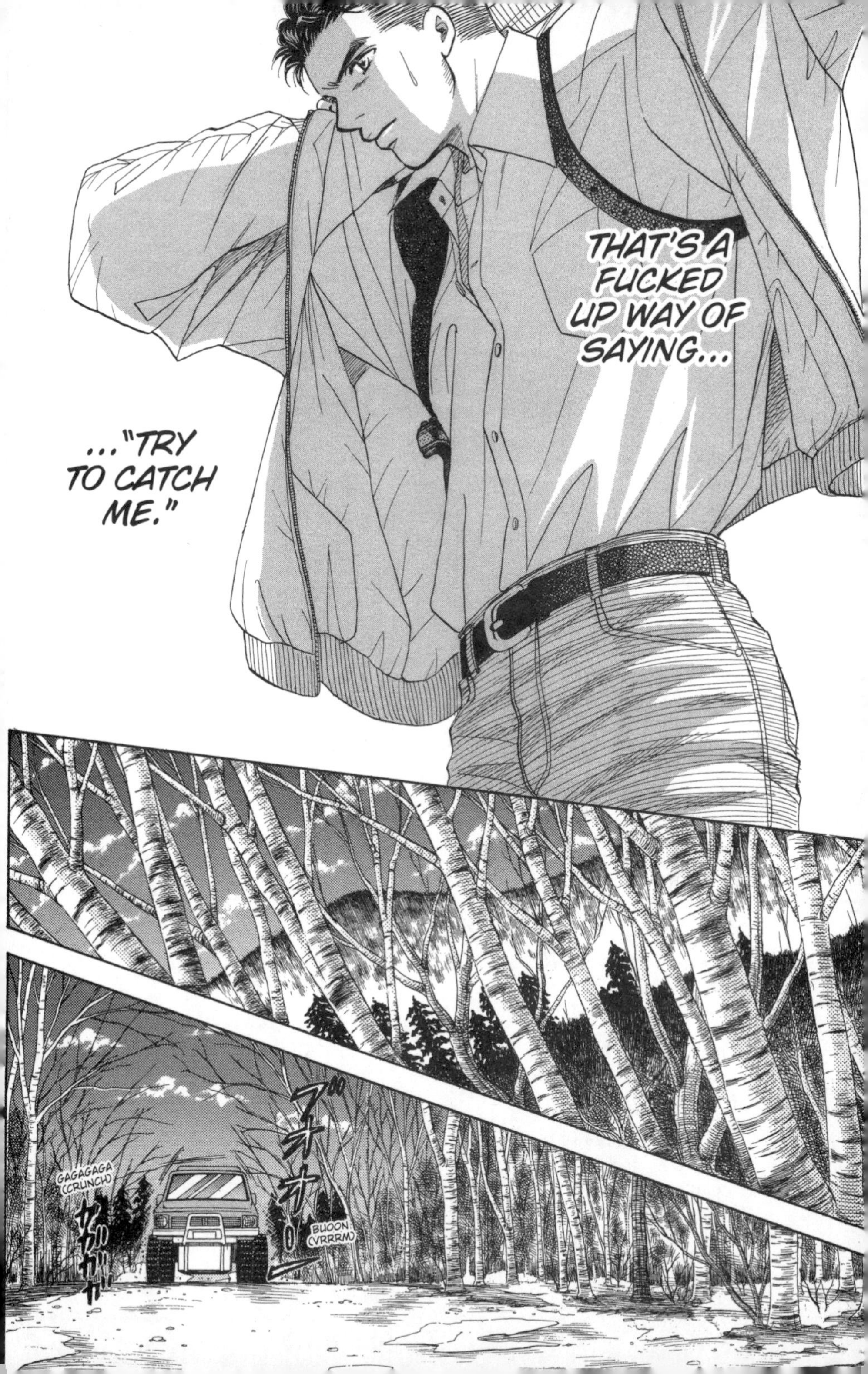
THAT'S A FUCKED UP WAY OF SAYING...
..."TRY TO CATCH ME."
BUOON (VRRRM)
GAGAGAGA (CRUNCH)

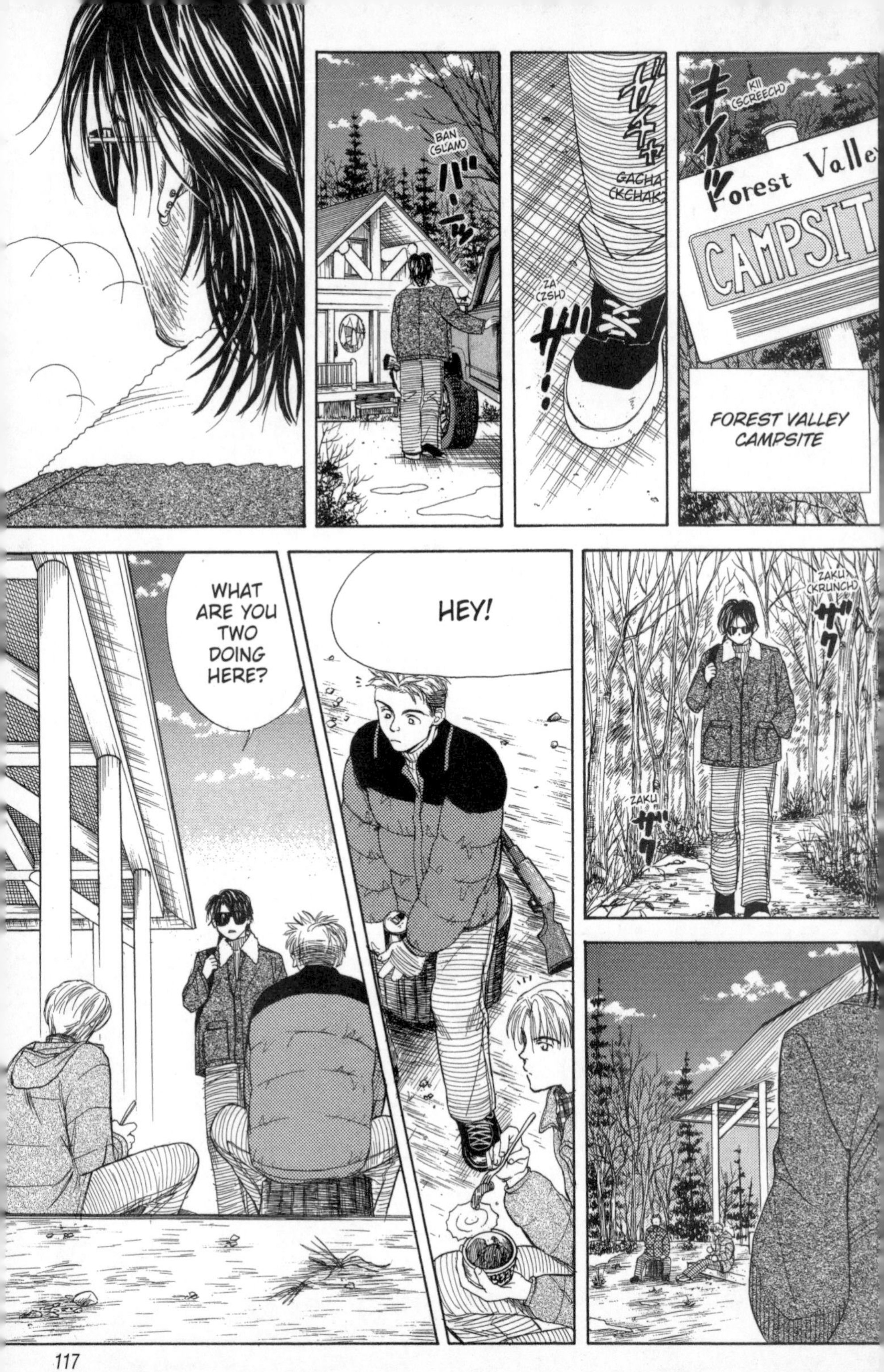
KII (SCREECH)
Forest Valle
CAMPSIT
FOREST VALLEY CAMPSITE
GACHA (KCHAK)
ZA (ZSH)
BAN (SLAM)
ZAKU (KRUNCH)
ZAKU
HEY!
WHAT ARE YOU TWO DOING HERE?

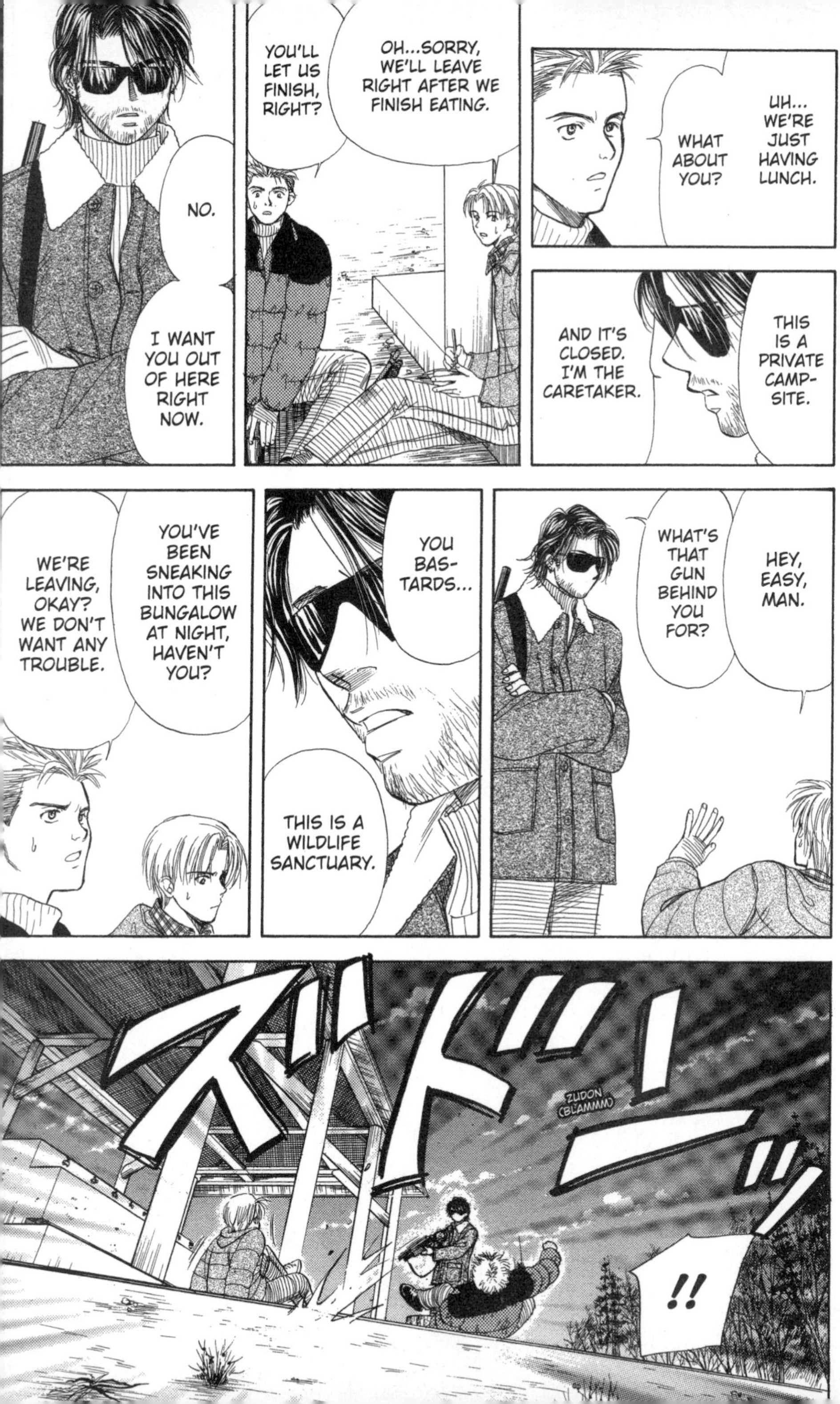
UH... WE'RE JUST HAVING LUNCH.
WHAT ABOUT YOU?
THIS IS A PRIVATE CAMP-SITE.
AND IT'S CLOSED. I'M THE CARETAKER.
OH...SORRY, WE'LL LEAVE RIGHT AFTER WE FINISH EATING.
YOU'LL LET US FINISH, RIGHT?
NO.
I WANT YOU OUT OF HERE RIGHT NOW.
HEY, EASY, MAN.
WHAT'S THAT GUN BEHIND YOU FOR?
YOU BAS-TARDS...
THIS IS A WILDLIFE SANCTUARY.
YOU'VE BEEN SNEAKING INTO THIS BUNGALOW AT NIGHT, HAVEN'T YOU?
WE'RE LEAVING, OKAY? WE DON'T WANT ANY TROUBLE.
ZUDON (BLAMMM)
!!

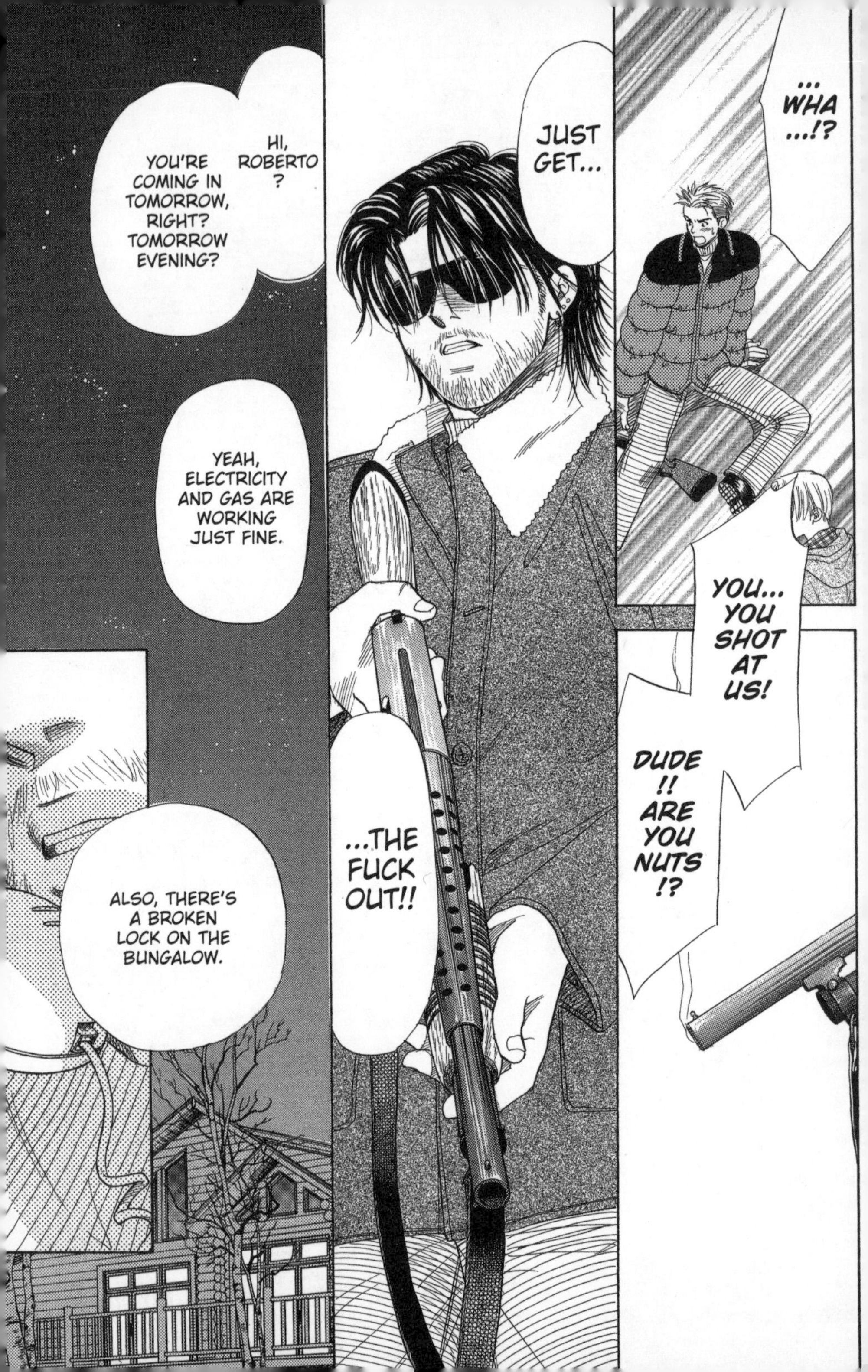
...WHA...!?
YOU... YOU SHOT AT US!
DUDE!! ARE YOU NUTS!?
JUST GET...
...THE FUCK OUT!!
HI, ROBERTO?
YOU'RE COMING IN TOMORROW, RIGHT? TOMORROW EVENING?
YEAH, ELECTRICITY AND GAS ARE WORKING JUST FINE.
ALSO, THERE'S A BROKEN LOCK ON THE BUNGALOW.

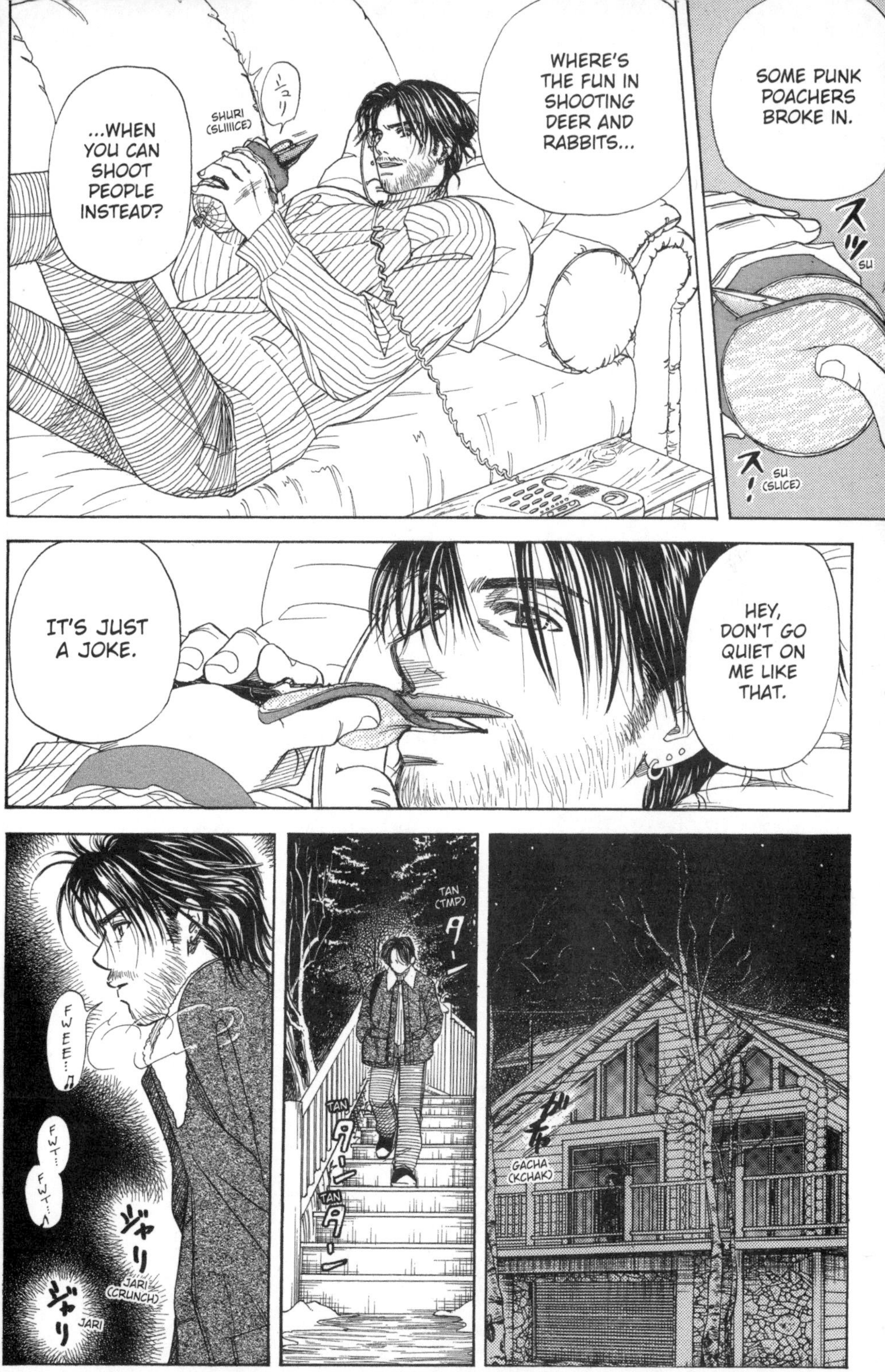
SOME PUNK POACHERS BROKE IN.
SU
SU (SLICE)
WHERE'S THE FUN IN SHOOTING DEER AND RABBITS...
SHURI (SLIIIICE)
...WHEN YOU CAN SHOOT PEOPLE INSTEAD?
HEY, DON'T GO QUIET ON ME LIKE THAT.
IT'S JUST A JOKE.
GACHA (KCHAK)
TAN (TMP)
TAN
TAN
FWEEE...♪
FWT...
FWT...♪
JARI (CRUNCH)
JARI

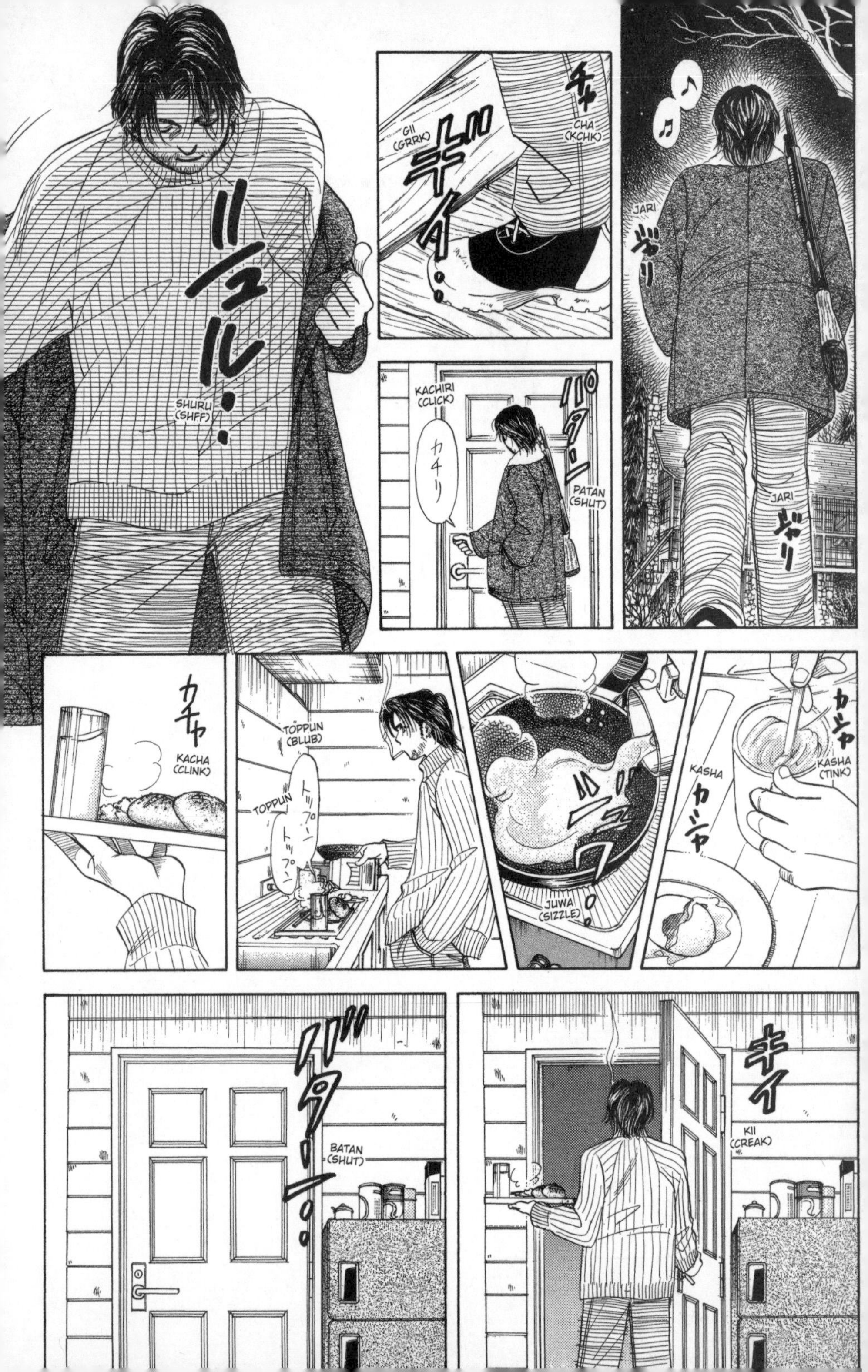
♪
♪
JARI
ジャリ
JARI
ジャリ
CHA (KCHK)
チャ
GII (GRRK)
ギイ
PATAN (SHUT)
パタン
KACHIRI (CLICK)
カチリ
SHURU (SHFF)
シュル
KASHA (TINK)
カシャ
KASHA
カシャ
JUWA (SIZZLE)
ジュワ
TOPPUN (BLUB)
トップン
TOPPUN
トップン
KACHA (CLINK)
カチャ
KII (CREAK)
キイ
BATAN (SHUT)
バタン

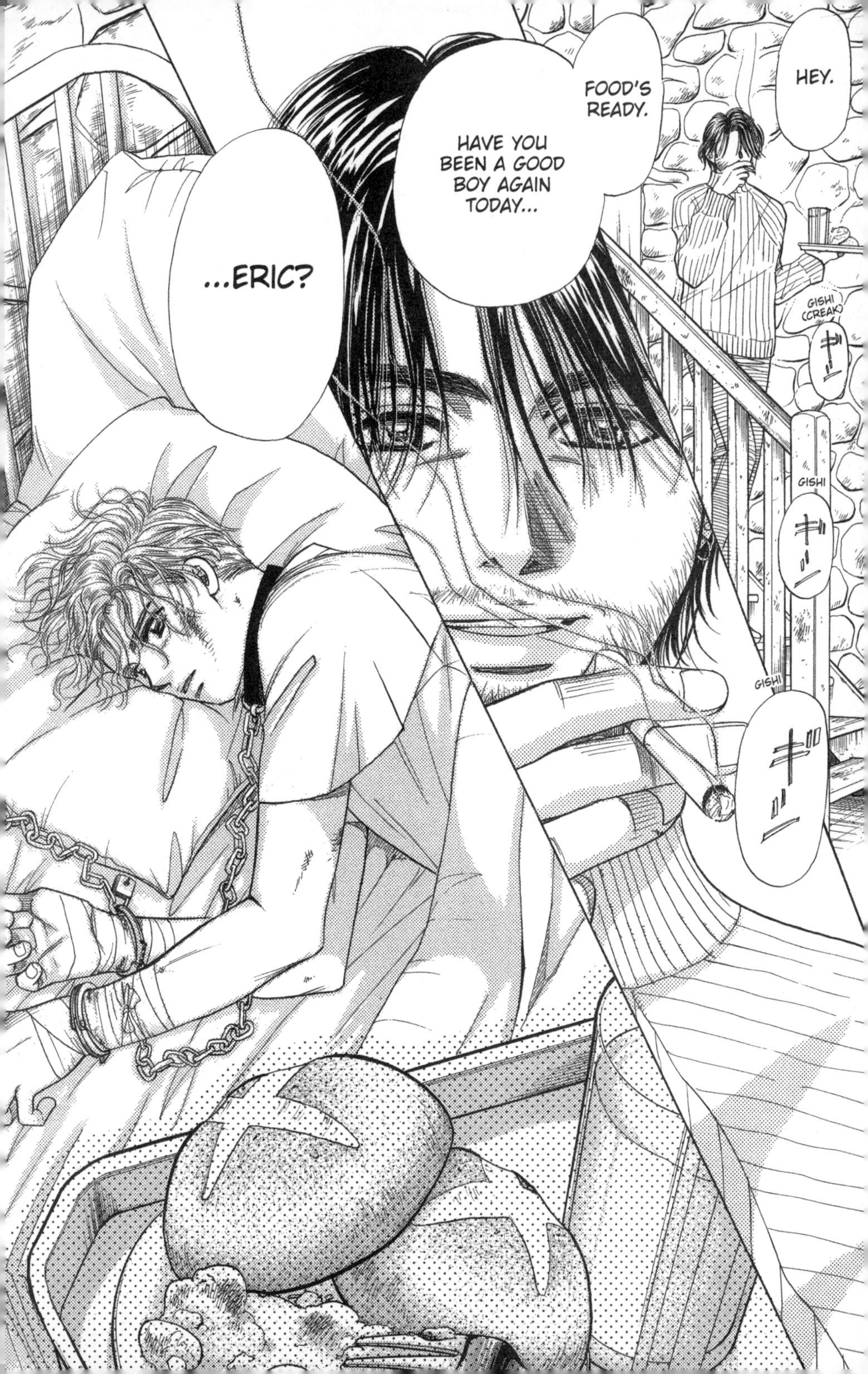
HEY.
GISHI (CREAK)
GISHI
GISHI
FOOD'S READY.
HAVE YOU BEEN A GOOD BOY AGAIN TODAY...
...ERIC?

EPISODE IV

SCENE 3

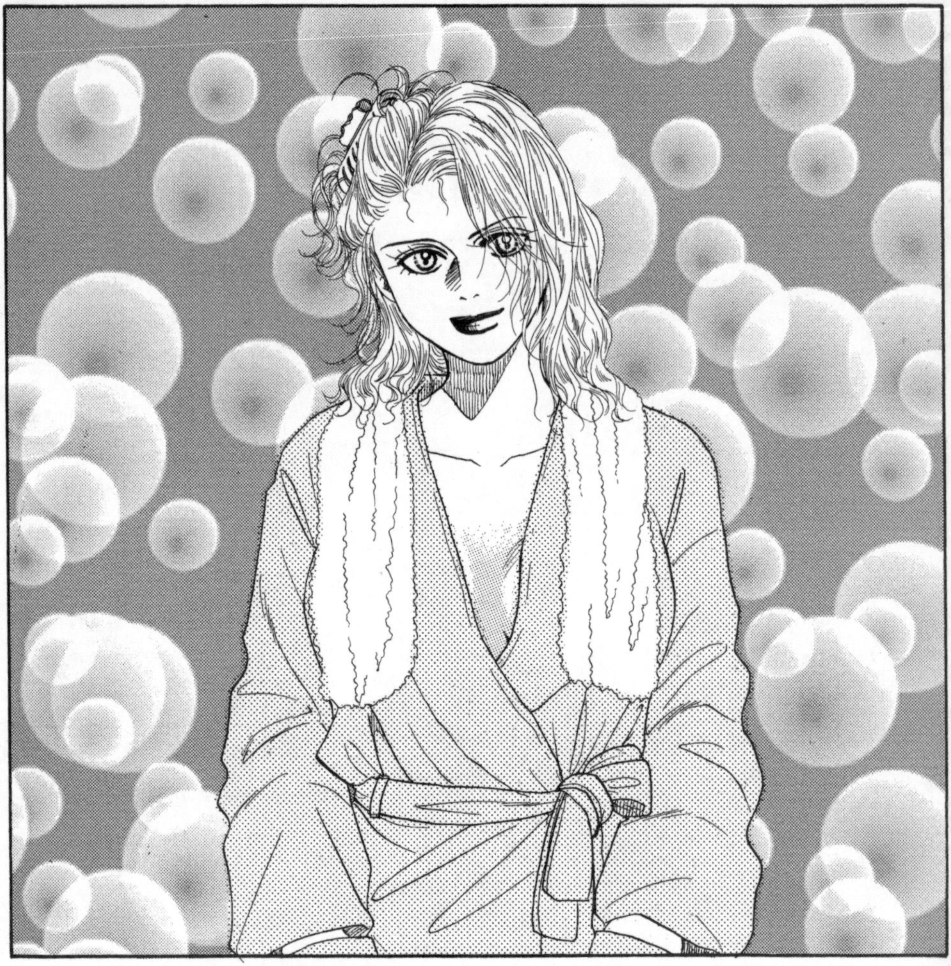

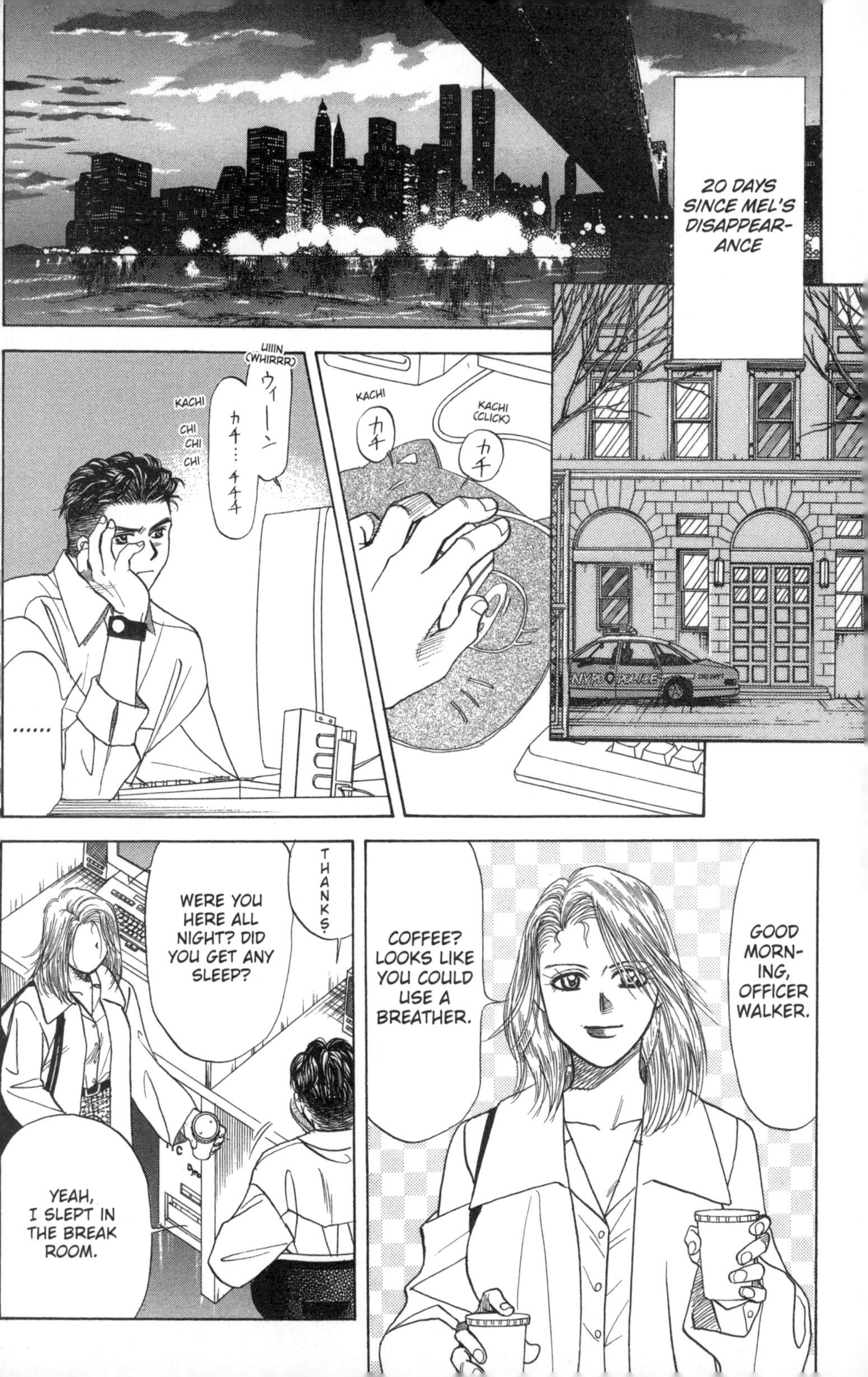
20 DAYS SINCE MEL'S DISAPPEAR-ANCE
KACHI (CLICK)
カチ
KACHI
カチ
UIIIN (WHIRRR)
ウィーン
KACHI CHI CHI CHI
カチ… チチチ
……
GOOD MORN-ING, OFFICER WALKER.
COFFEE? LOOKS LIKE YOU COULD USE A BREATHER.
THANKS.
WERE YOU HERE ALL NIGHT? DID YOU GET ANY SLEEP?
YEAH, I SLEPT IN THE BREAK ROOM.

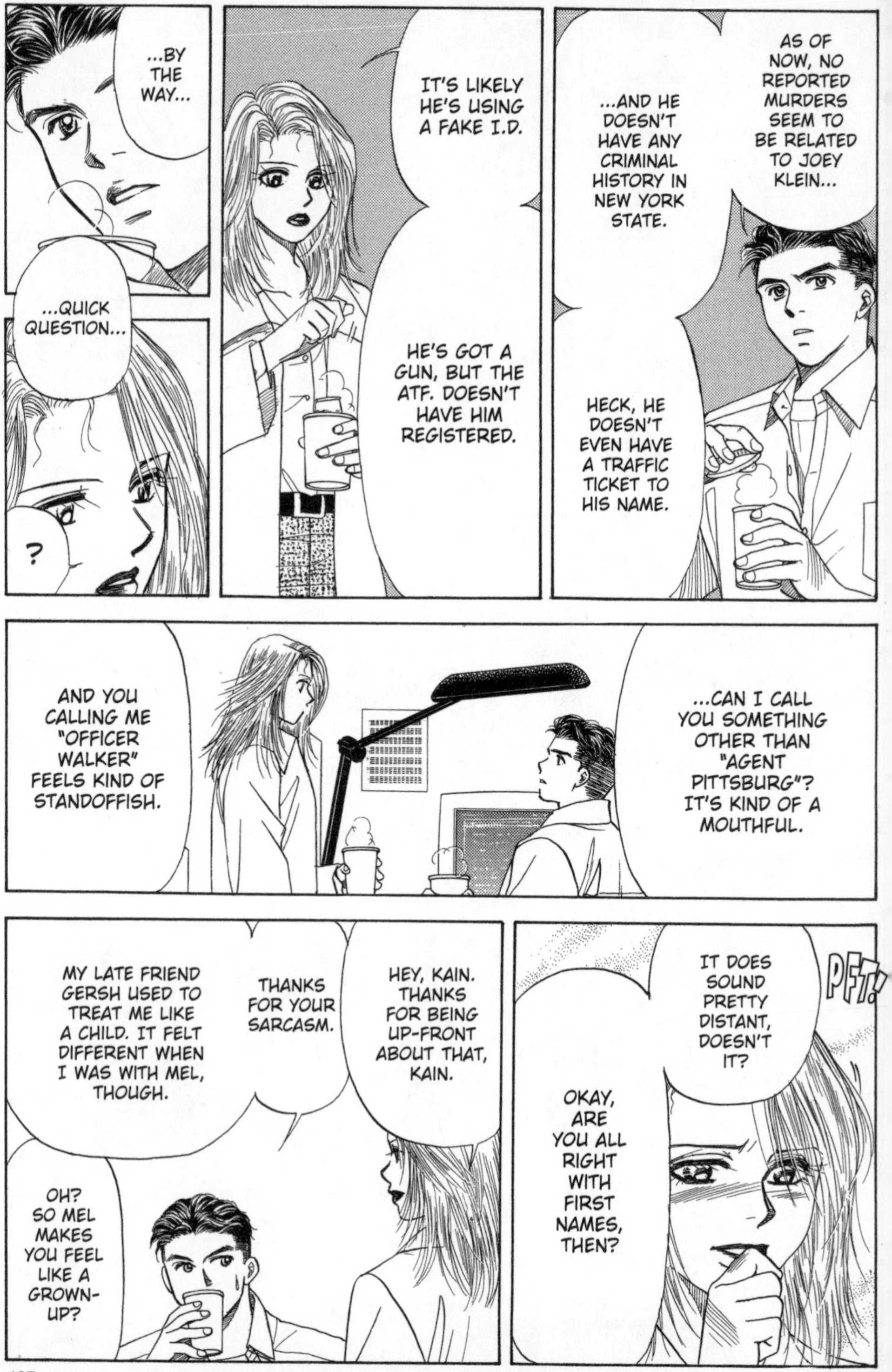
AS OF NOW, NO REPORTED MURDERS SEEM TO BE RELATED TO JOEY KLEIN...
...AND HE DOESN'T HAVE ANY CRIMINAL HISTORY IN NEW YORK STATE.
HECK, HE DOESN'T EVEN HAVE A TRAFFIC TICKET TO HIS NAME.
IT'S LIKELY HE'S USING A FAKE I.D.
HE'S GOT A GUN, BUT THE ATF. DOESN'T HAVE HIM REGISTERED.
...BY THE WAY...
...QUICK QUESTION...
?
...CAN I CALL YOU SOMETHING OTHER THAN "AGENT PITTSBURG"? IT'S KIND OF A MOUTHFUL.
AND YOU CALLING ME "OFFICER WALKER" FEELS KIND OF STANDOFFISH.
PFT!
IT DOES SOUND PRETTY DISTANT, DOESN'T IT?
OKAY, ARE YOU ALL RIGHT WITH FIRST NAMES, THEN?
HEY, KAIN. THANKS FOR BEING UP-FRONT ABOUT THAT, KAIN.
THANKS FOR YOUR SARCASM.
MY LATE FRIEND GERSH USED TO TREAT ME LIKE A CHILD. IT FELT DIFFERENT WHEN I WAS WITH MEL, THOUGH.
OH? SO MEL MAKES YOU FEEL LIKE A GROWN-UP?

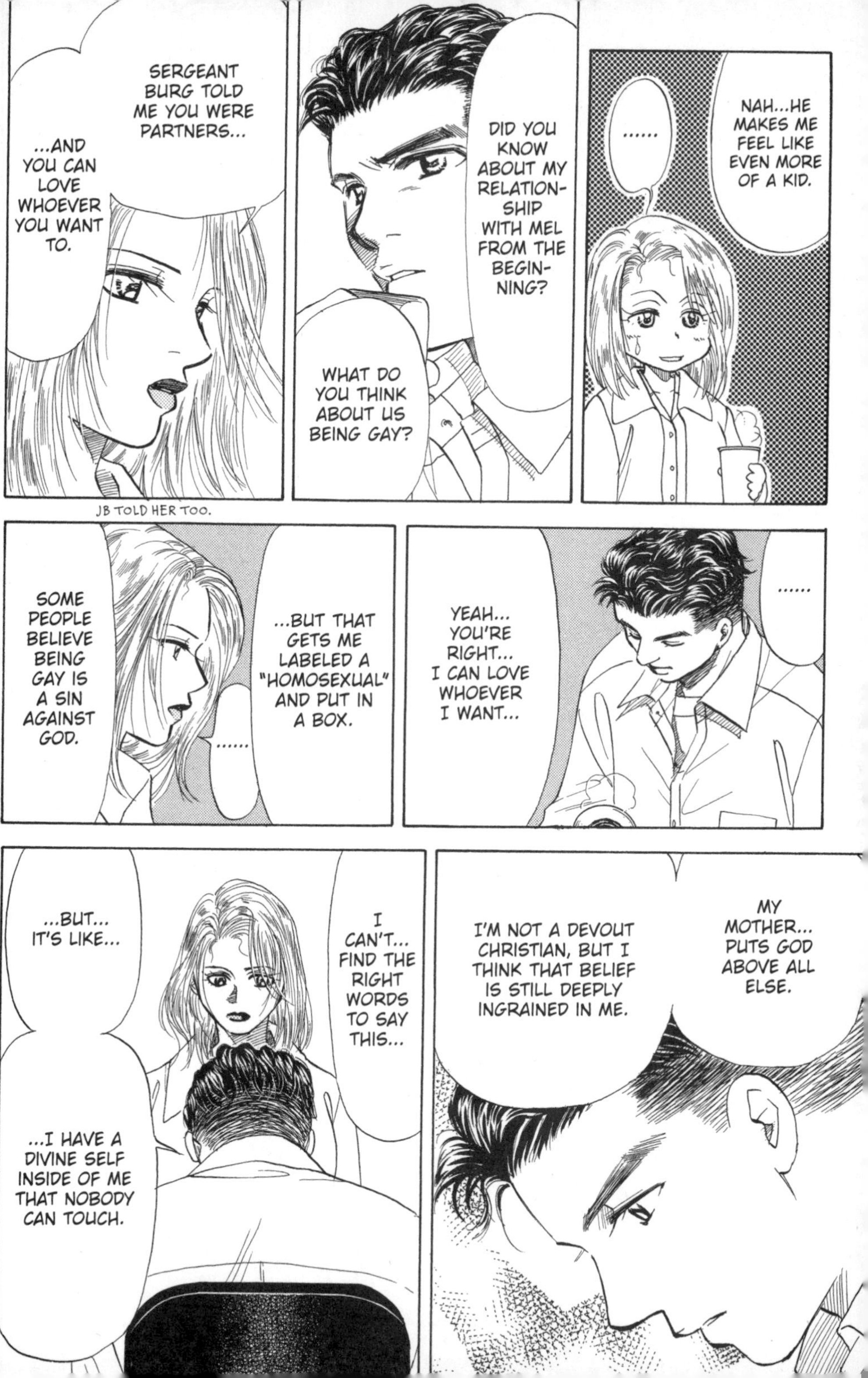
NAH...HE MAKES ME FEEL LIKE EVEN MORE OF A KID.
......
DID YOU KNOW ABOUT MY RELATIONSHIP WITH MEL FROM THE BEGINNING?
WHAT DO YOU THINK ABOUT US BEING GAY?
SERGEANT BURG TOLD ME YOU WERE PARTNERS...
...AND YOU CAN LOVE WHOEVER YOU WANT TO.
JB TOLD HER TOO.
......
YEAH... YOU'RE RIGHT... I CAN LOVE WHOEVER I WANT...
...BUT THAT GETS ME LABELED A "HOMOSEXUAL" AND PUT IN A BOX.
......
SOME PEOPLE BELIEVE BEING GAY IS A SIN AGAINST GOD.
MY MOTHER... PUTS GOD ABOVE ALL ELSE.
I'M NOT A DEVOUT CHRISTIAN, BUT I THINK THAT BELIEF IS STILL DEEPLY INGRAINED IN ME.
I CAN'T... FIND THE RIGHT WORDS TO SAY THIS...
...BUT... IT'S LIKE...
...I HAVE A DIVINE SELF INSIDE OF ME THAT NOBODY CAN TOUCH.

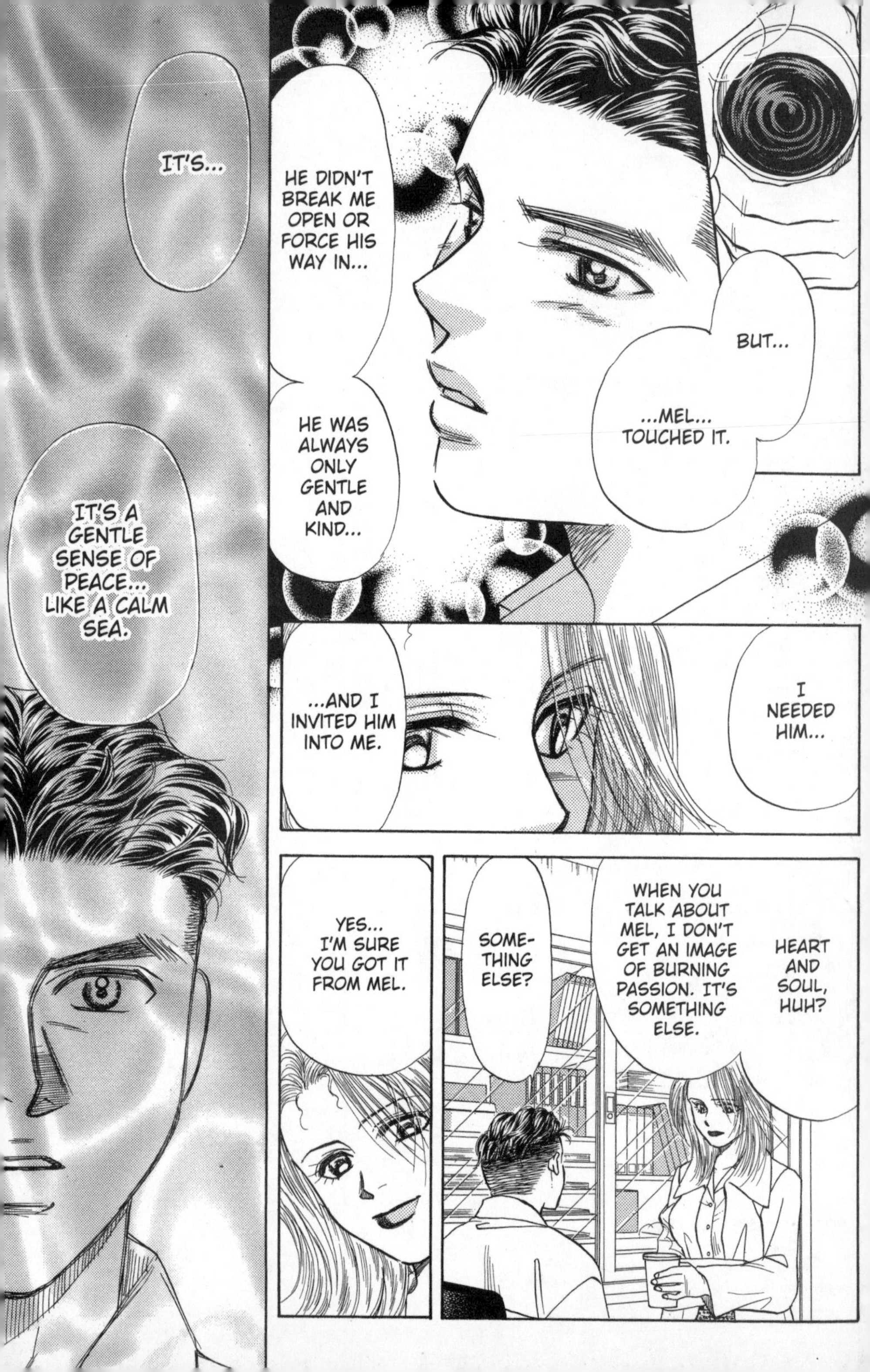
BUT...
...MEL... TOUCHED IT.
HE DIDN'T BREAK ME OPEN OR FORCE HIS WAY IN...
HE WAS ALWAYS ONLY GENTLE AND KIND...
I NEEDED HIM...
...AND I INVITED HIM INTO ME.
HEART AND SOUL, HUH?
WHEN YOU TALK ABOUT MEL, I DON'T GET AN IMAGE OF BURNING PASSION. IT'S SOMETHING ELSE.
SOME-THING ELSE?
YES... I'M SURE YOU GOT IT FROM MEL.
IT'S...
IT'S A GENTLE SENSE OF PEACE... LIKE A CALM SEA.

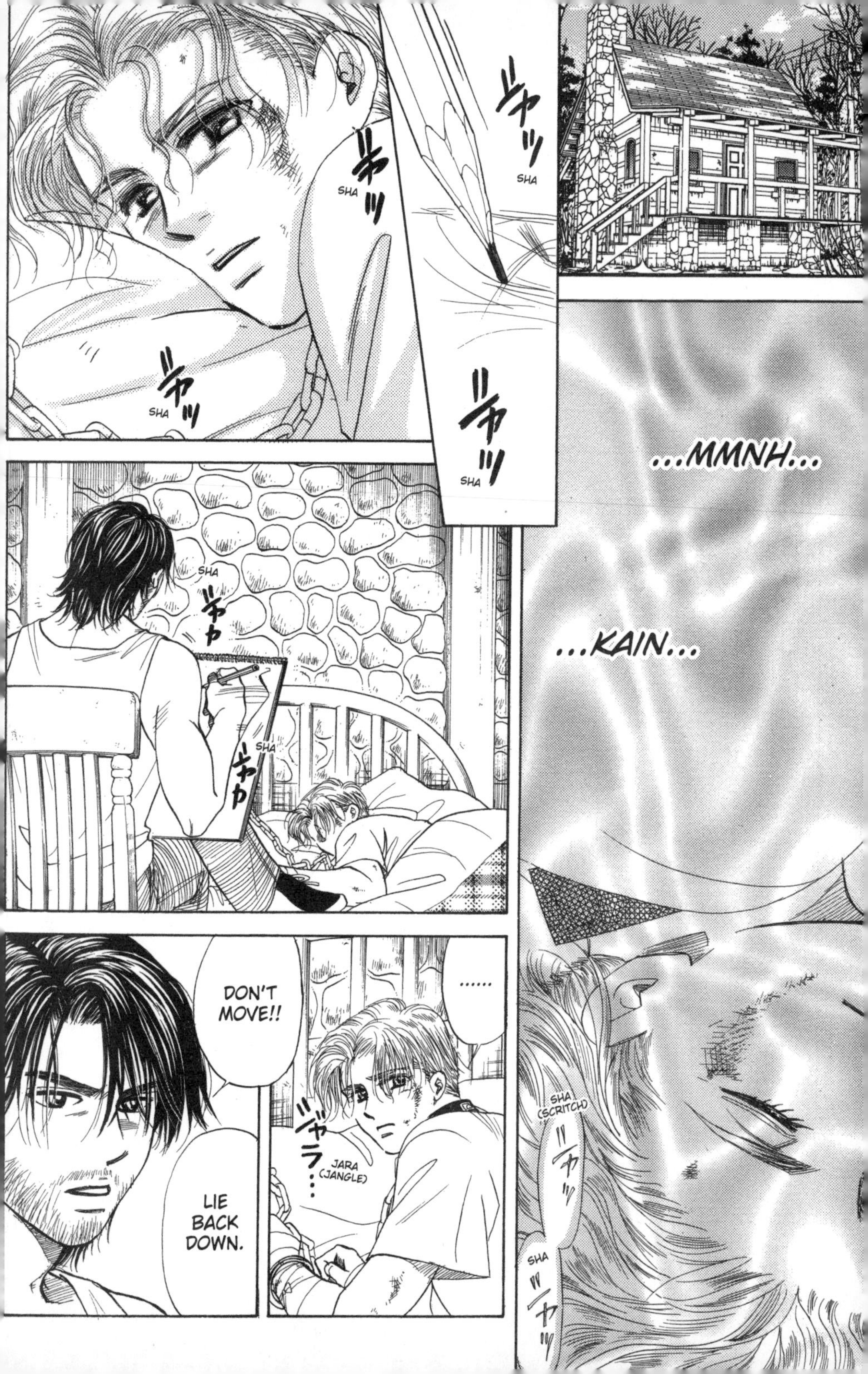

...MMNH...
...KAIN...
SHA (SCRITCH)
SHA
SHA
SHA
SHA
SHA
SHA
......
DON'T MOVE!!
LIE BACK DOWN.
JARA (JANGLE)

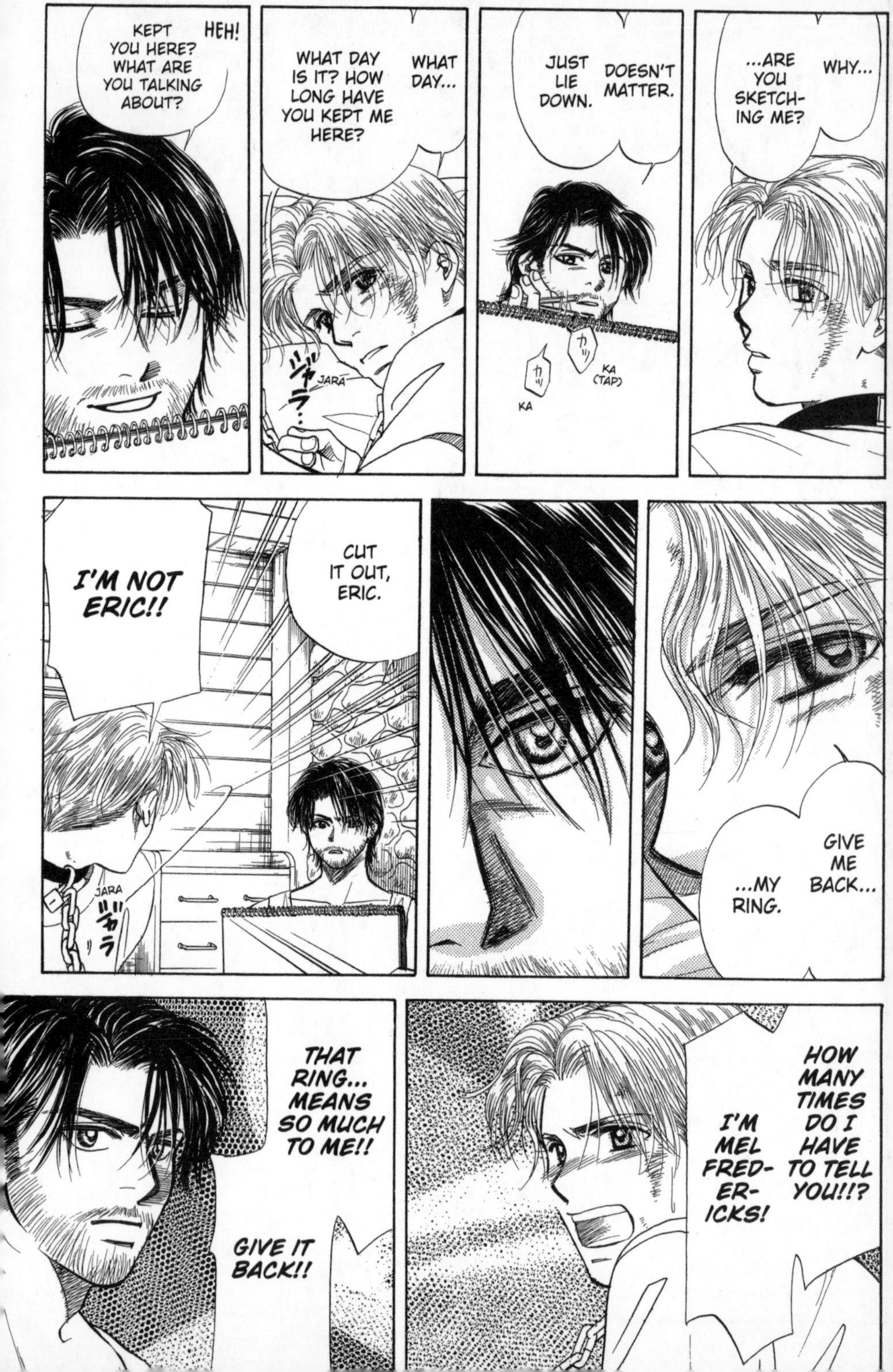
WHY...
...ARE YOU SKETCH-ING ME?
DOESN'T MATTER.
JUST LIE DOWN.
カッ
KA (TAP)
カッ
KA
WHAT DAY...
WHAT DAY IS IT? HOW LONG HAVE YOU KEPT ME HERE?
ジャラ
JARA
HEH!
KEPT YOU HERE? WHAT ARE YOU TALKING ABOUT?
GIVE ME BACK...
...MY RING.
CUT IT OUT, ERIC.
I'M NOT ERIC!!
ジャラ
JARA
HOW MANY TIMES DO I HAVE TO TELL YOU!!?
I'M MEL FRED-ER-ICKS!
THAT RING... MEANS SO MUCH TO ME!!
GIVE IT BACK!!

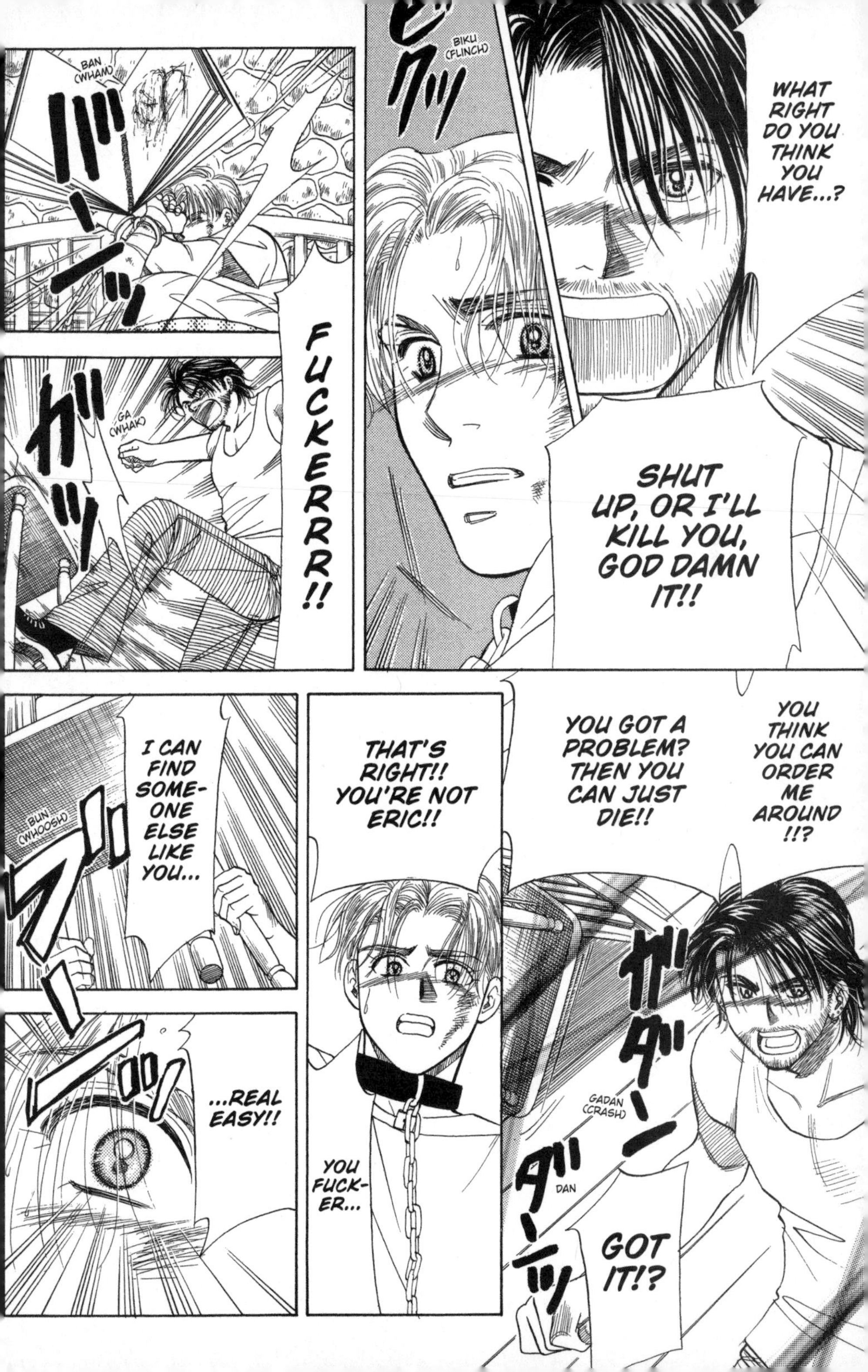
WHAT RIGHT DO YOU THINK YOU HAVE...?
BIKU (FLINCH)
SHUT UP, OR I'LL KILL YOU, GOD DAMN IT!!
BAN (WHAM)
FUCKERRRR!!
GA (WHAK)
YOU THINK YOU CAN ORDER ME AROUND!!?
YOU GOT A PROBLEM? THEN YOU CAN JUST DIE!!
GADAN (CRASH)
DAN
GOT IT!?
THAT'S RIGHT!! YOU'RE NOT ERIC!!
YOU FUCK-ER...
I CAN FIND SOME-ONE ELSE LIKE YOU...
BUN (WHOOSH)
...REAL EASY!!

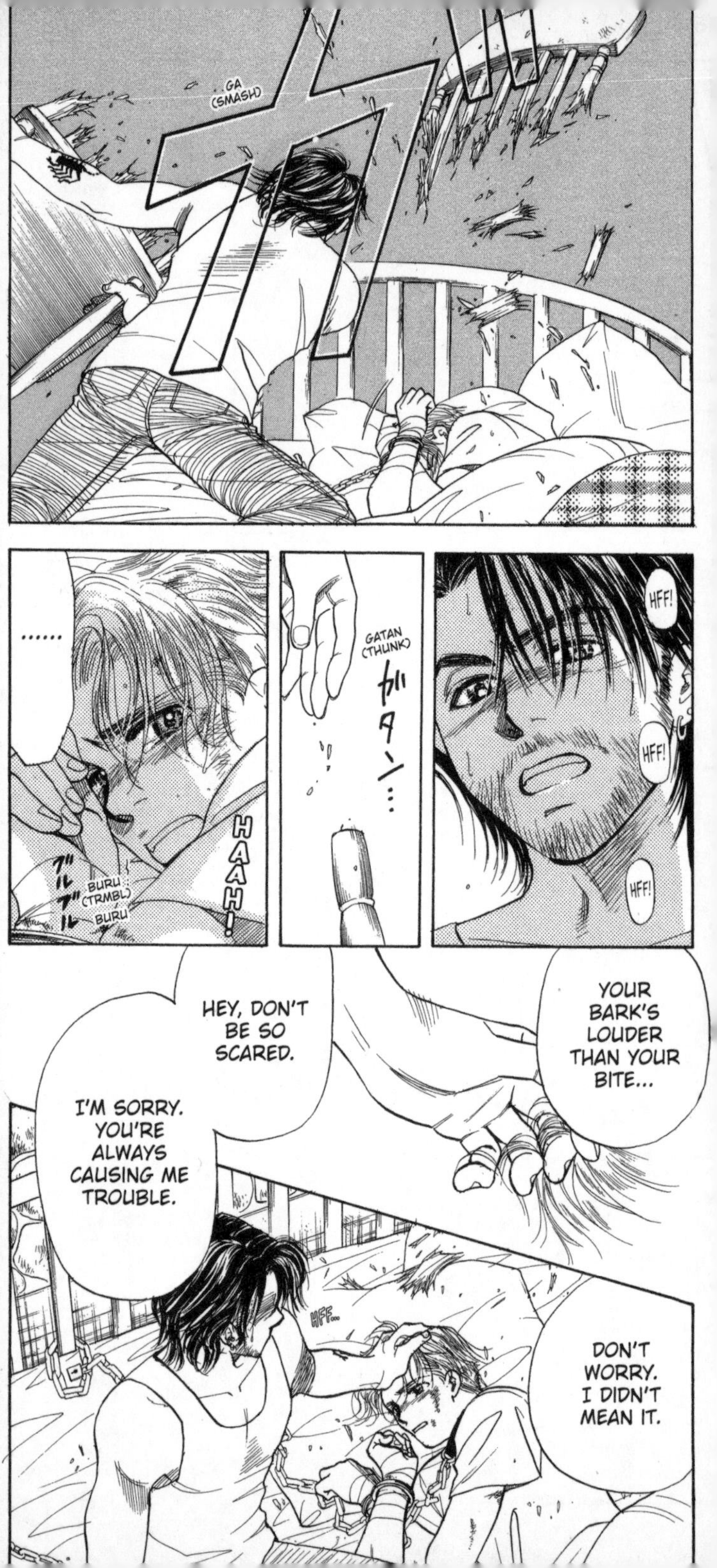
GA (SMASH)
HFF!
HFF!
HFF!
GATAN (THUNK)
......
BURU (TRMBL) BURU
HAAAH!
YOUR BARK'S LOUDER THAN YOUR BITE...
HEY, DON'T BE SO SCARED.
I'M SORRY. YOU'RE ALWAYS CAUSING ME TROUBLE.
DON'T WORRY. I DIDN'T MEAN IT.
HFF...
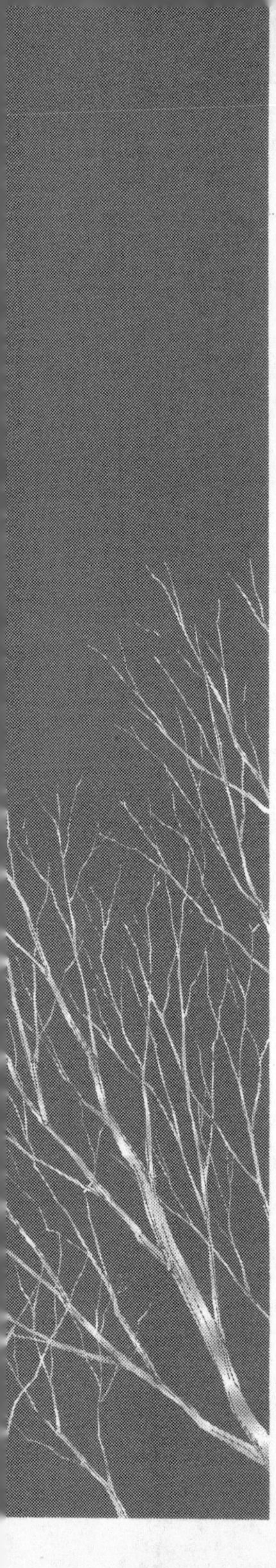

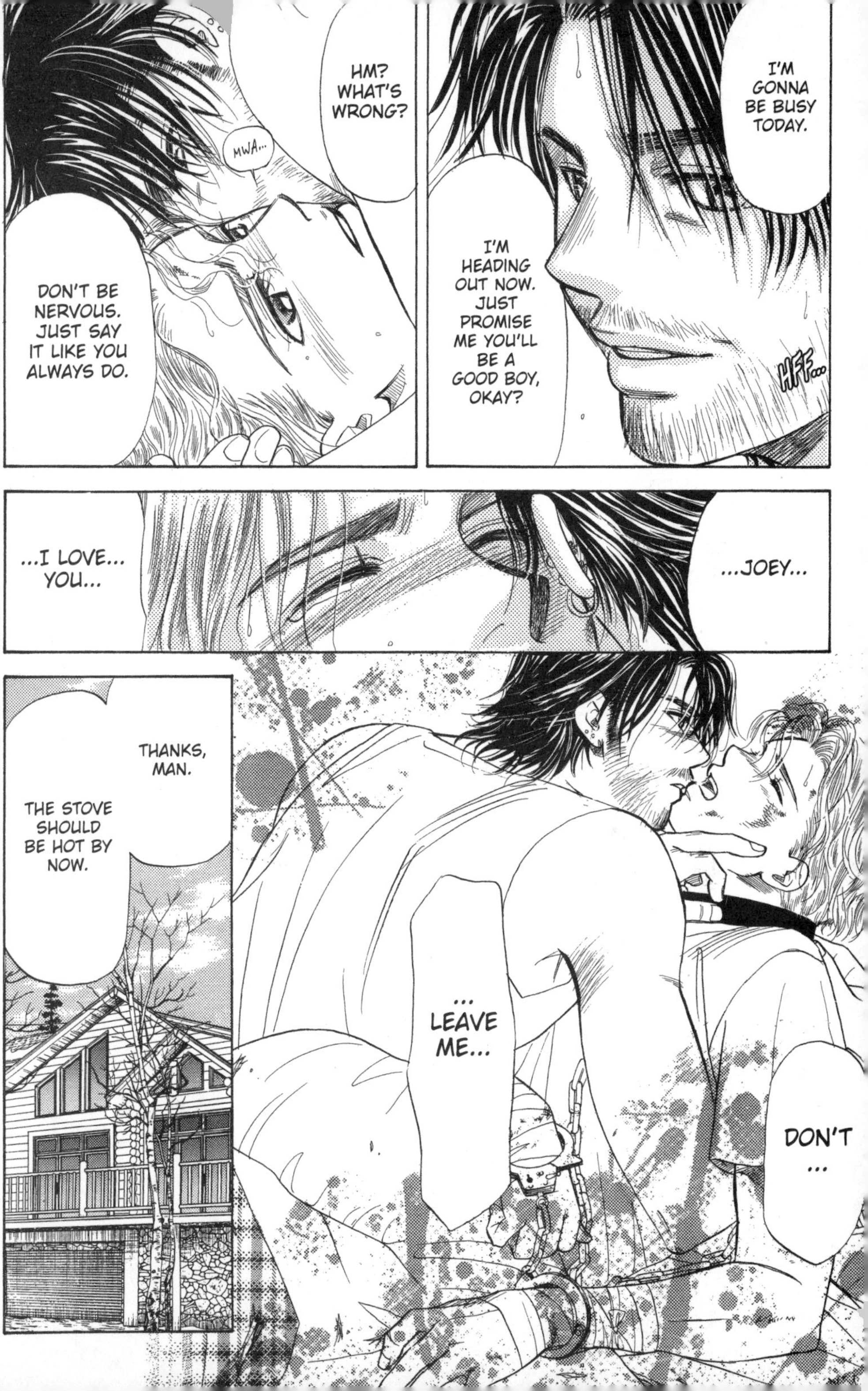
I'M GONNA BE BUSY TODAY.
HFF...
I'M HEADING OUT NOW. JUST PROMISE ME YOU'LL BE A GOOD BOY, OKAY?
HM? WHAT'S WRONG?
MWA...
DON'T BE NERVOUS. JUST SAY IT LIKE YOU ALWAYS DO.
...JOEY...
...I LOVE... YOU...
DON'T ...
... LEAVE ME...
THANKS, MAN.
THE STOVE SHOULD BE HOT BY NOW.

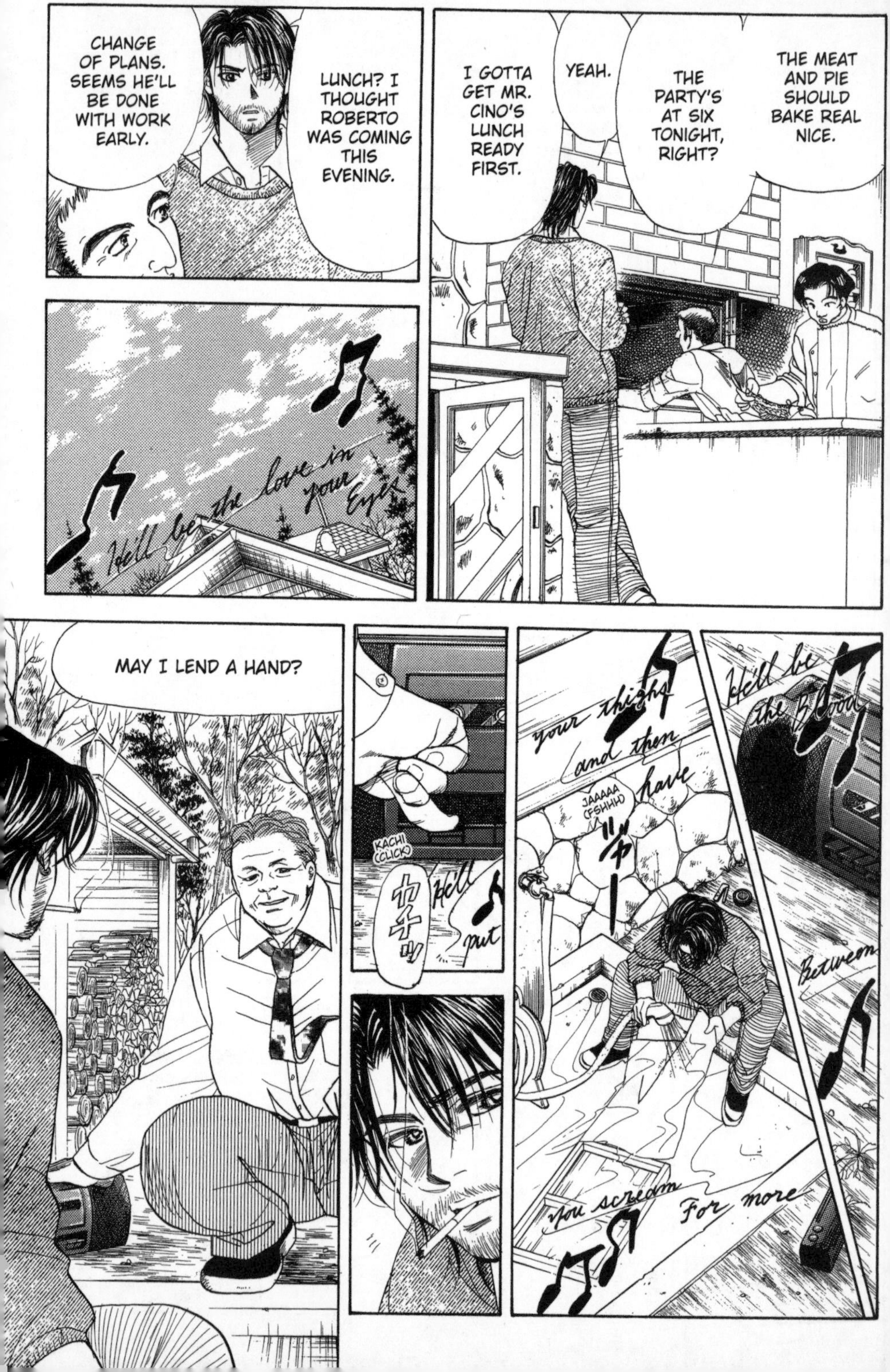

THE MEAT AND PIE SHOULD BAKE REAL NICE.
THE PARTY'S AT SIX TONIGHT, RIGHT?
YEAH.
I GOTTA GET MR. CINO'S LUNCH READY FIRST.
LUNCH? I THOUGHT ROBERTO WAS COMING THIS EVENING.
CHANGE OF PLANS. SEEMS HE'LL BE DONE WITH WORK EARLY.
He'll be the love in your Eyes
He'll be the Blood
Between
your thighs and then have
JAAAAA (FSHHH)
ジャー
you scream For more
KACHI (CLICK)
カチッ
He'll put
MAY I LEND A HAND?

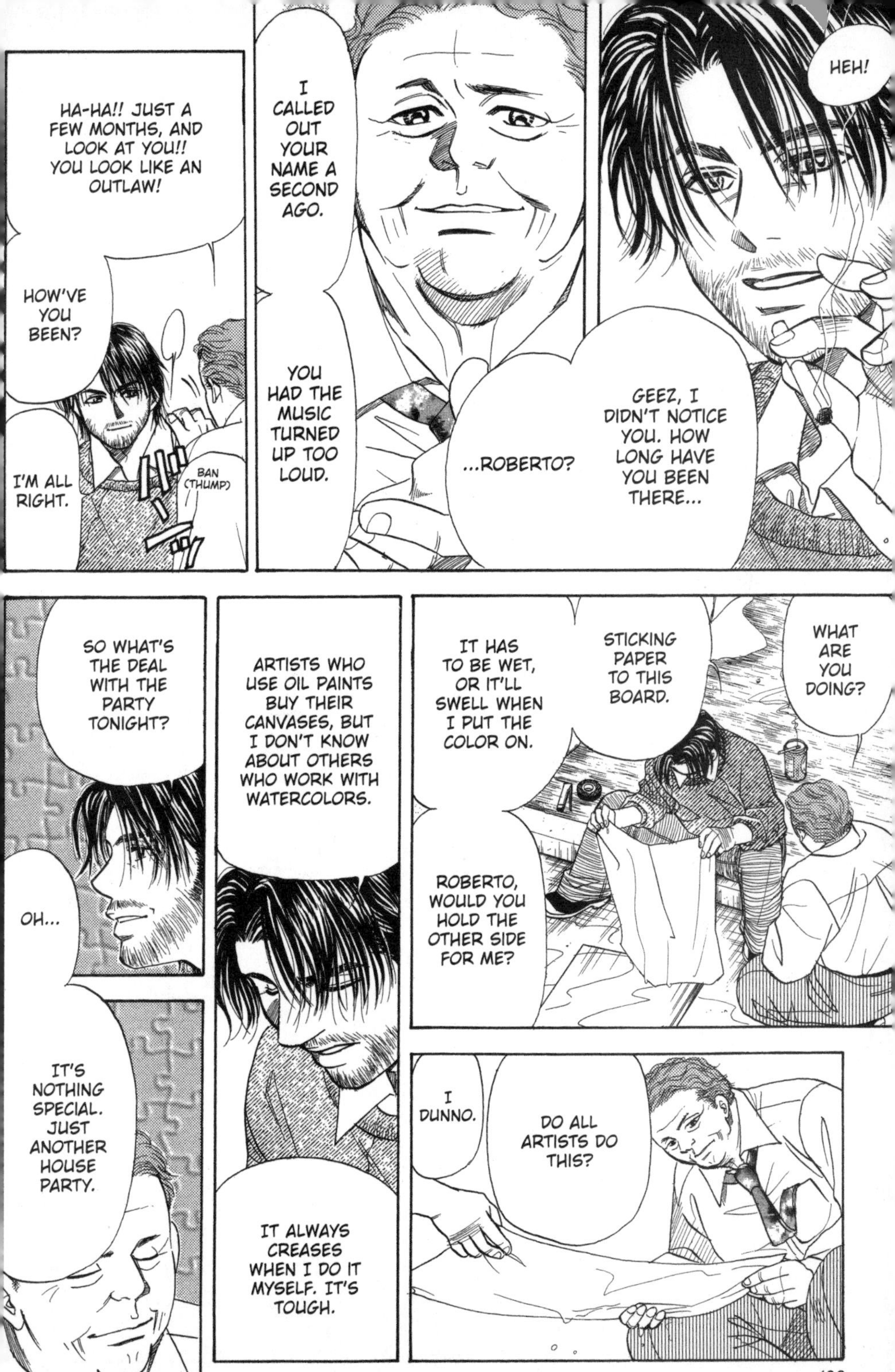
HEH!
GEEZ, I DIDN'T NOTICE YOU. HOW LONG HAVE YOU BEEN THERE...
...ROBERTO?
I CALLED OUT YOUR NAME A SECOND AGO.
YOU HAD THE MUSIC TURNED UP TOO LOUD.
HA-HA!! JUST A FEW MONTHS, AND LOOK AT YOU!! YOU LOOK LIKE AN OUTLAW!
HOW'VE YOU BEEN?
I'M ALL RIGHT.
BAN (THUMP)
WHAT ARE YOU DOING?
STICKING PAPER TO THIS BOARD.
IT HAS TO BE WET, OR IT'LL SWELL WHEN I PUT THE COLOR ON.
ROBERTO, WOULD YOU HOLD THE OTHER SIDE FOR ME?
DO ALL ARTISTS DO THIS?
I DUNNO.
ARTISTS WHO USE OIL PAINTS BUY THEIR CANVASES, BUT I DON'T KNOW ABOUT OTHERS WHO WORK WITH WATERCOLORS.
IT ALWAYS CREASES WHEN I DO IT MYSELF. IT'S TOUGH.
SO WHAT'S THE DEAL WITH THE PARTY TONIGHT?
OH...
IT'S NOTHING SPECIAL. JUST ANOTHER HOUSE PARTY.

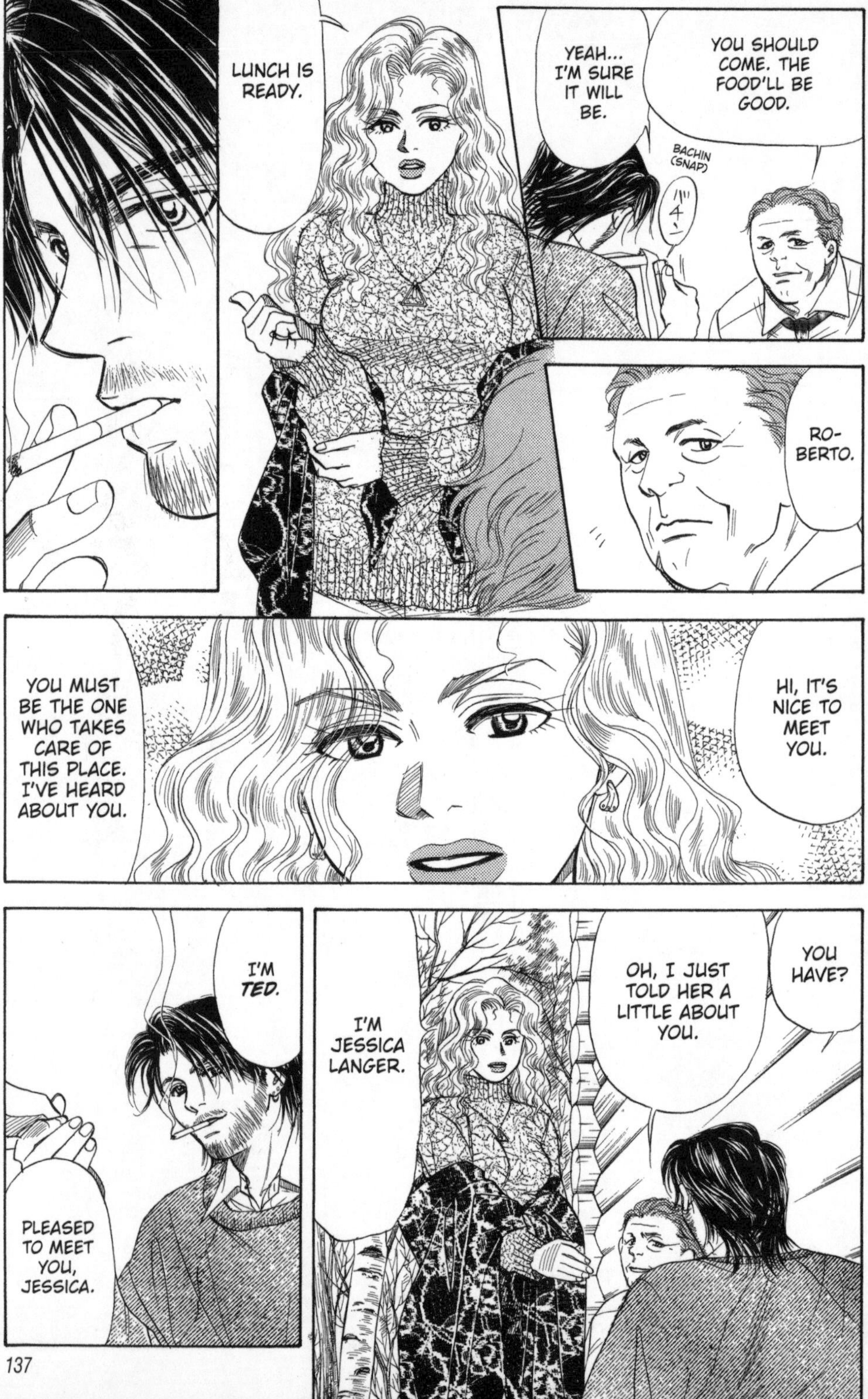
YOU SHOULD COME. THE FOOD'LL BE GOOD.
YEAH... I'M SURE IT WILL BE.
BACHIN (SNAP)
RO-BERTO.
LUNCH IS READY.
HI, IT'S NICE TO MEET YOU.
YOU MUST BE THE ONE WHO TAKES CARE OF THIS PLACE. I'VE HEARD ABOUT YOU.
YOU HAVE?
OH, I JUST TOLD HER A LITTLE ABOUT YOU.
I'M JESSICA LANGER.
I'M *TED*.
PLEASED TO MEET YOU, JESSICA.

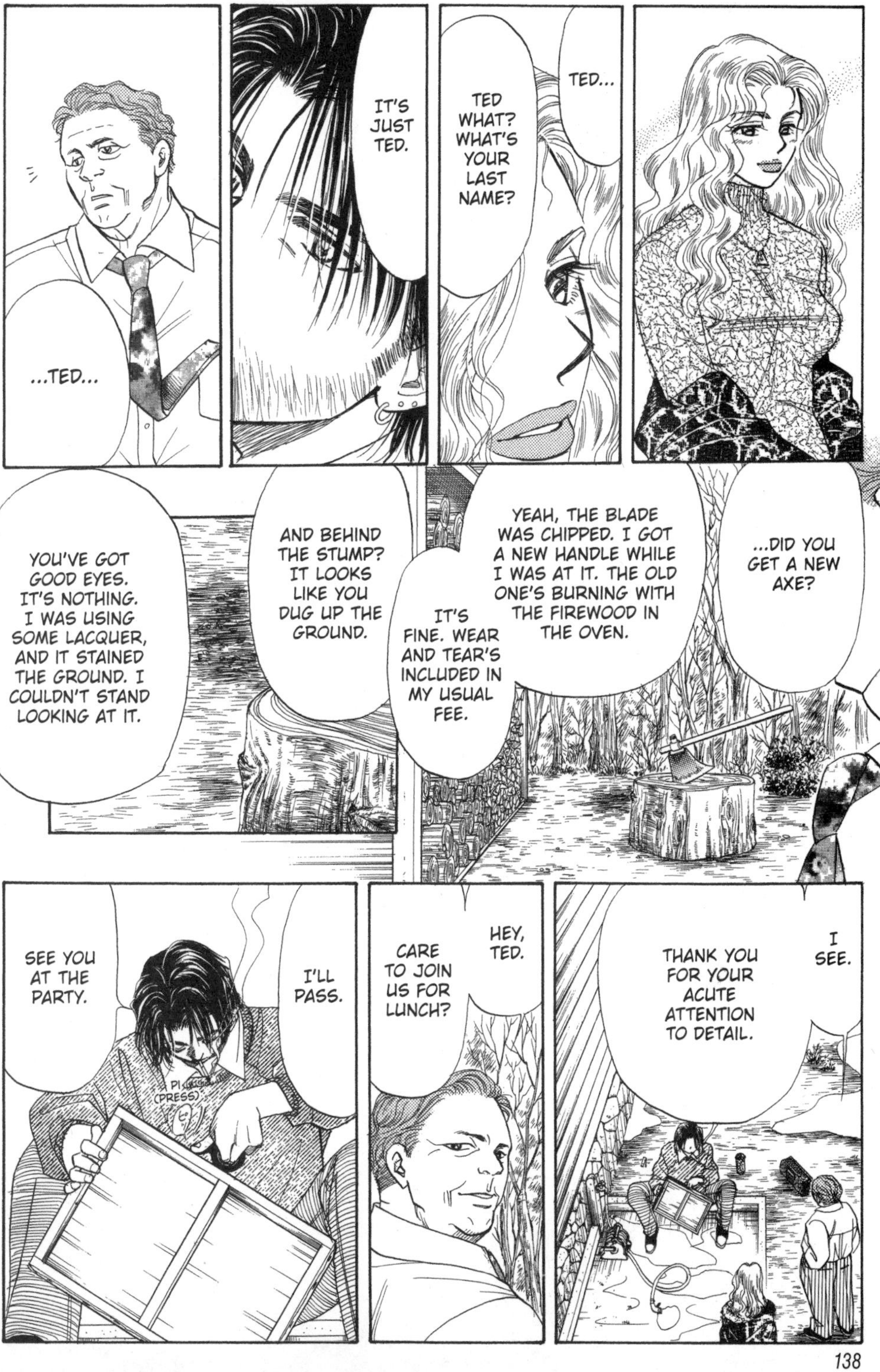
TED...
TED WHAT? WHAT'S YOUR LAST NAME?
IT'S JUST TED.
...TED...
...DID YOU GET A NEW AXE?
YEAH, THE BLADE WAS CHIPPED. I GOT A NEW HANDLE WHILE I WAS AT IT. THE OLD ONE'S BURNING WITH THE FIREWOOD IN THE OVEN.
IT'S FINE. WEAR AND TEAR'S INCLUDED IN MY USUAL FEE.
AND BEHIND THE STUMP? IT LOOKS LIKE YOU DUG UP THE GROUND.
YOU'VE GOT GOOD EYES. IT'S NOTHING. I WAS USING SOME LACQUER, AND IT STAINED THE GROUND. I COULDN'T STAND LOOKING AT IT.
I SEE.
THANK YOU FOR YOUR ACUTE ATTENTION TO DETAIL.
HEY, TED.
CARE TO JOIN US FOR LUNCH?
I'LL PASS.
PI (PRESS)
SEE YOU AT THE PARTY.

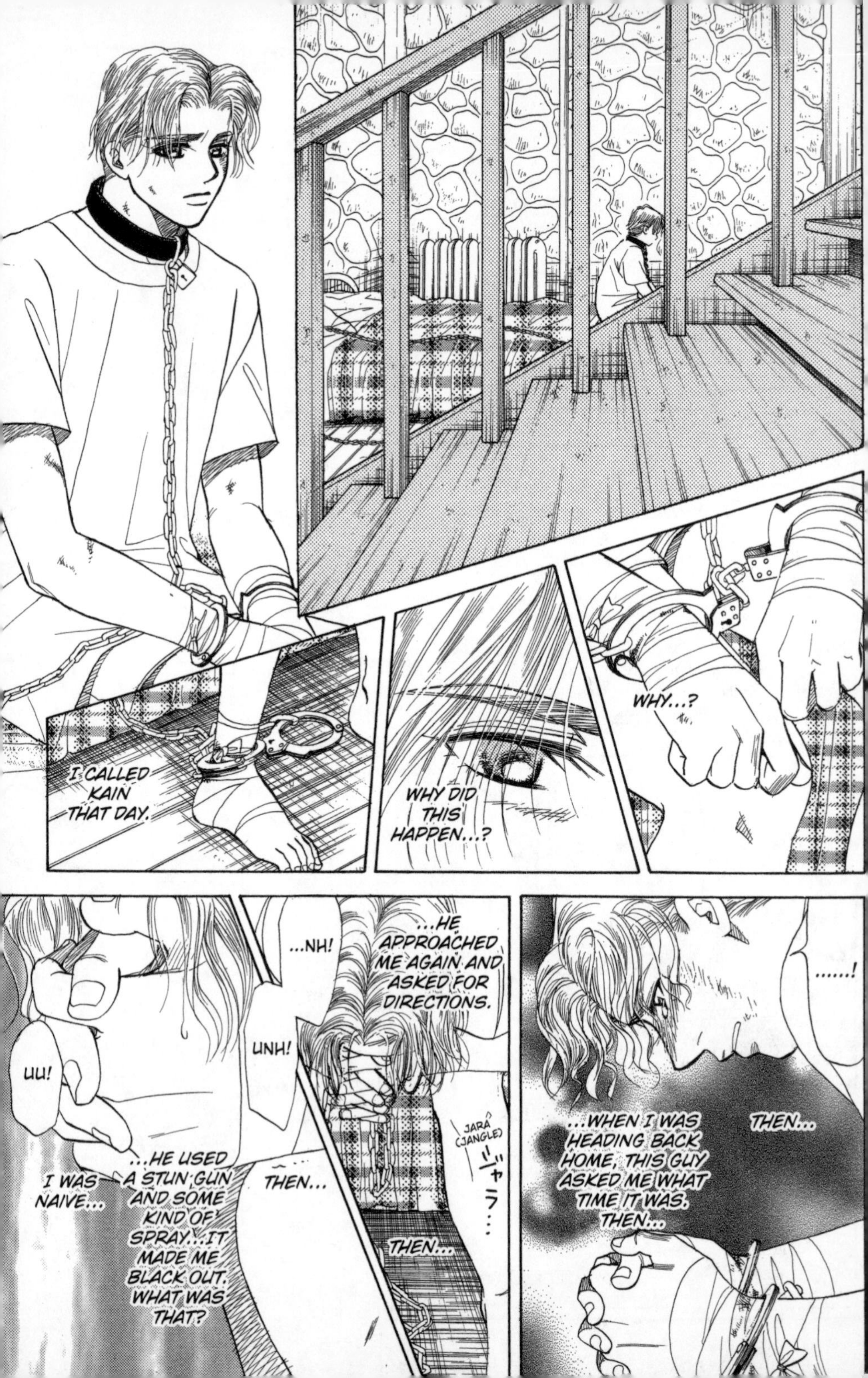
WHY...?
WHY DID THIS HAPPEN...?
I CALLED KAIN THAT DAY.
......!
THEN...
...WHEN I WAS HEADING BACK HOME, THIS GUY ASKED ME WHAT TIME IT WAS. THEN...
...HE APPROACHED ME AGAIN AND ASKED FOR DIRECTIONS.
...NH!
UNH!
JARA (JANGLE)
ジャラ...
THEN...
THEN...
UU!
...HE USED A STUN GUN AND SOME KIND OF SPRAY...IT MADE ME BLACK OUT. WHAT WAS THAT?
I WAS NAIVE...

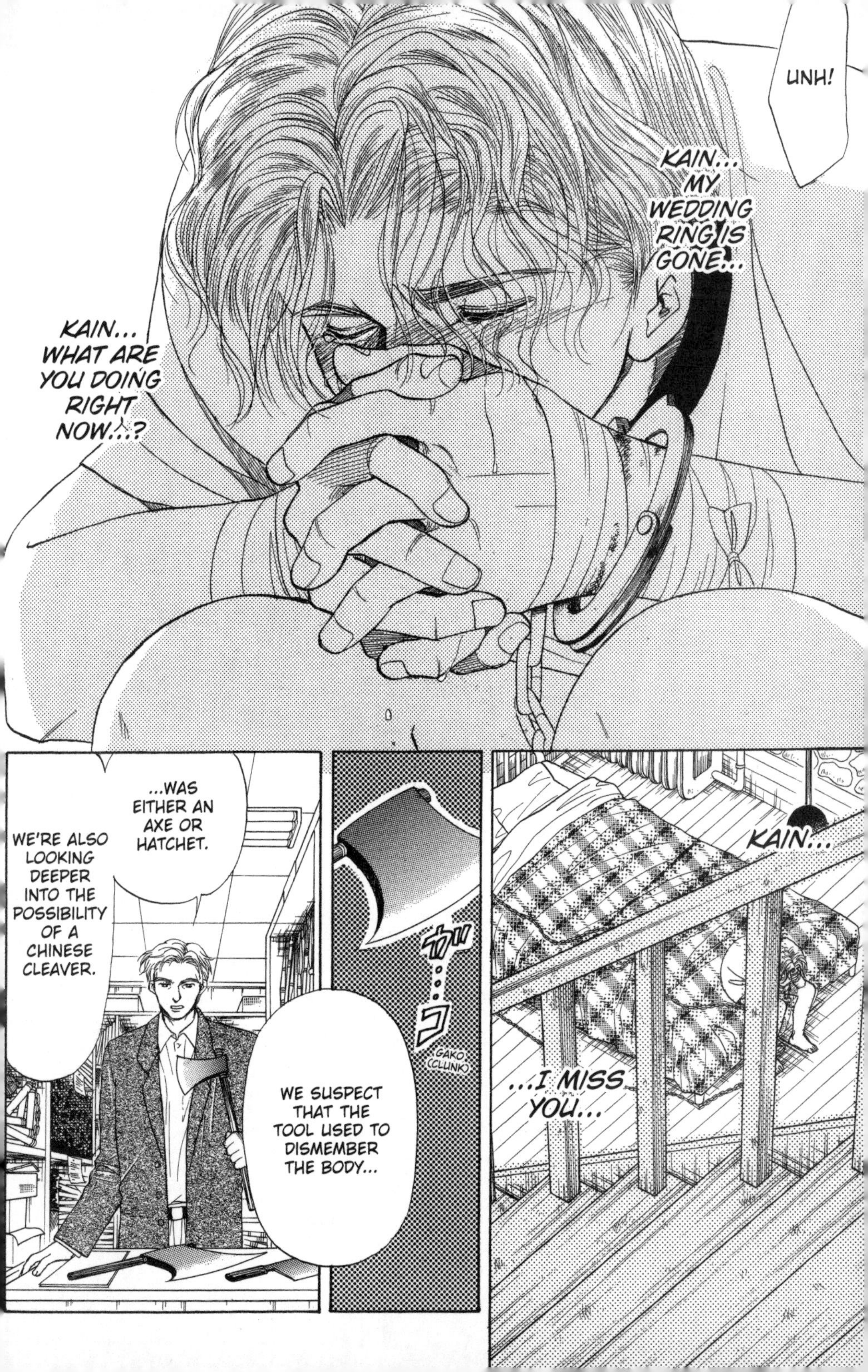
UNH!
KAIN... MY WEDDING RING IS GONE...
KAIN... WHAT ARE YOU DOING RIGHT NOW...?
KAIN...
...I MISS YOU...
GAKO (CLUNK)
WE SUSPECT THAT THE TOOL USED TO DISMEMBER THE BODY...
...WAS EITHER AN AXE OR HATCHET.
WE'RE ALSO LOOKING DEEPER INTO THE POSSIBILITY OF A CHINESE CLEAVER.

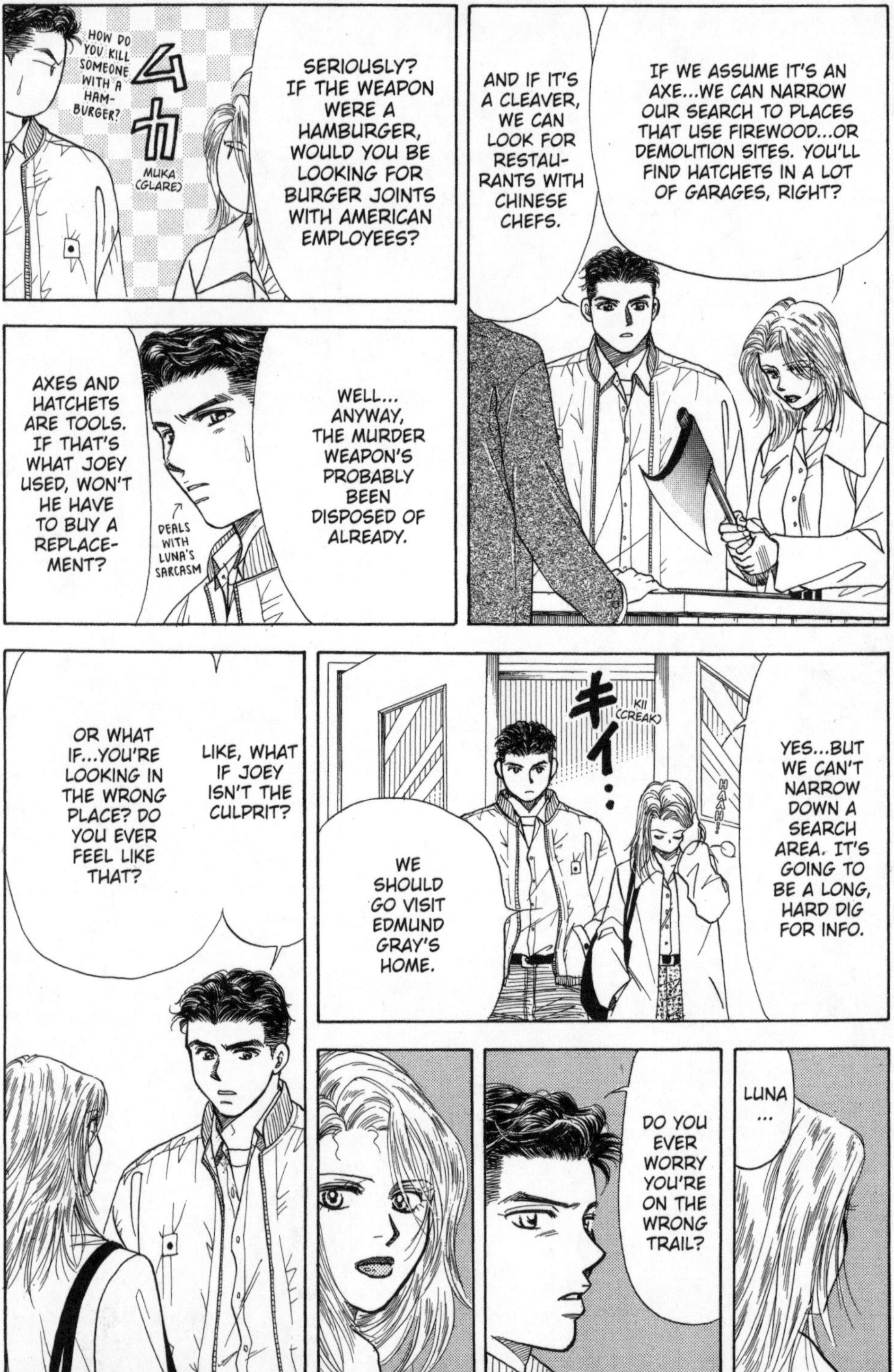

IF WE ASSUME IT'S AN AXE...WE CAN NARROW OUR SEARCH TO PLACES THAT USE FIREWOOD...OR DEMOLITION SITES. YOU'LL FIND HATCHETS IN A LOT OF GARAGES, RIGHT?
AND IF IT'S A CLEAVER, WE CAN LOOK FOR RESTAU-RANTS WITH CHINESE CHEFS.
SERIOUSLY? IF THE WEAPON WERE A HAMBURGER, WOULD YOU BE LOOKING FOR BURGER JOINTS WITH AMERICAN EMPLOYEES?
ムカ
MUKA (GLARE)
HOW DO YOU KILL SOMEONE WITH A HAM-BURGER?
WELL... ANYWAY, THE MURDER WEAPON'S PROBABLY BEEN DISPOSED OF ALREADY.
DEALS WITH LUNA'S SARCASM
AXES AND HATCHETS ARE TOOLS. IF THAT'S WHAT JOEY USED, WON'T HE HAVE TO BUY A REPLACE-MENT?
YES...BUT WE CAN'T NARROW DOWN A SEARCH AREA. IT'S GOING TO BE A LONG, HARD DIG FOR INFO.
HAAH...
キイ
KII (CREAK)
WE SHOULD GO VISIT EDMUND GRAY'S HOME.
LUNA ...
DO YOU EVER WORRY YOU'RE ON THE WRONG TRAIL?
LIKE, WHAT IF JOEY ISN'T THE CULPRIT?
OR WHAT IF...YOU'RE LOOKING IN THE WRONG PLACE? DO YOU EVER FEEL LIKE THAT?

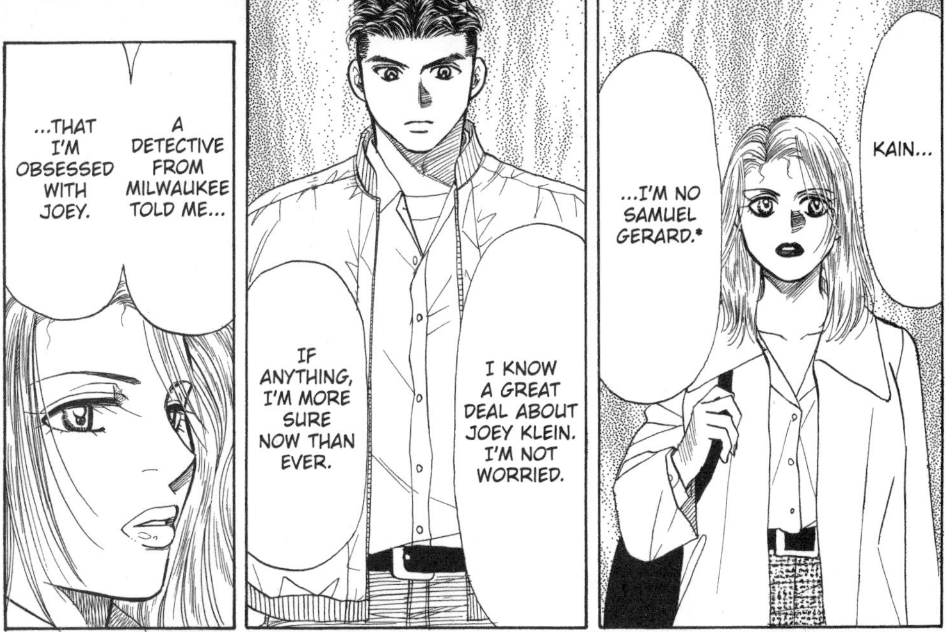
KAIN...
...I'M NO SAMUEL GERARD.*
I KNOW A GREAT DEAL ABOUT JOEY KLEIN. I'M NOT WORRIED.
IF ANYTHING, I'M MORE SURE NOW THAN EVER.
A DETECTIVE FROM MILWAUKEE TOLD ME...
...THAT I'M OBSESSED WITH JOEY.

*IN THE FILM THE FUGITIVE, DEPUTY U.S. MARSHAL SAMUEL GERARD MISTAKENLY PURSUES THE INNOCENT DR. RICHARD KIMBLE.

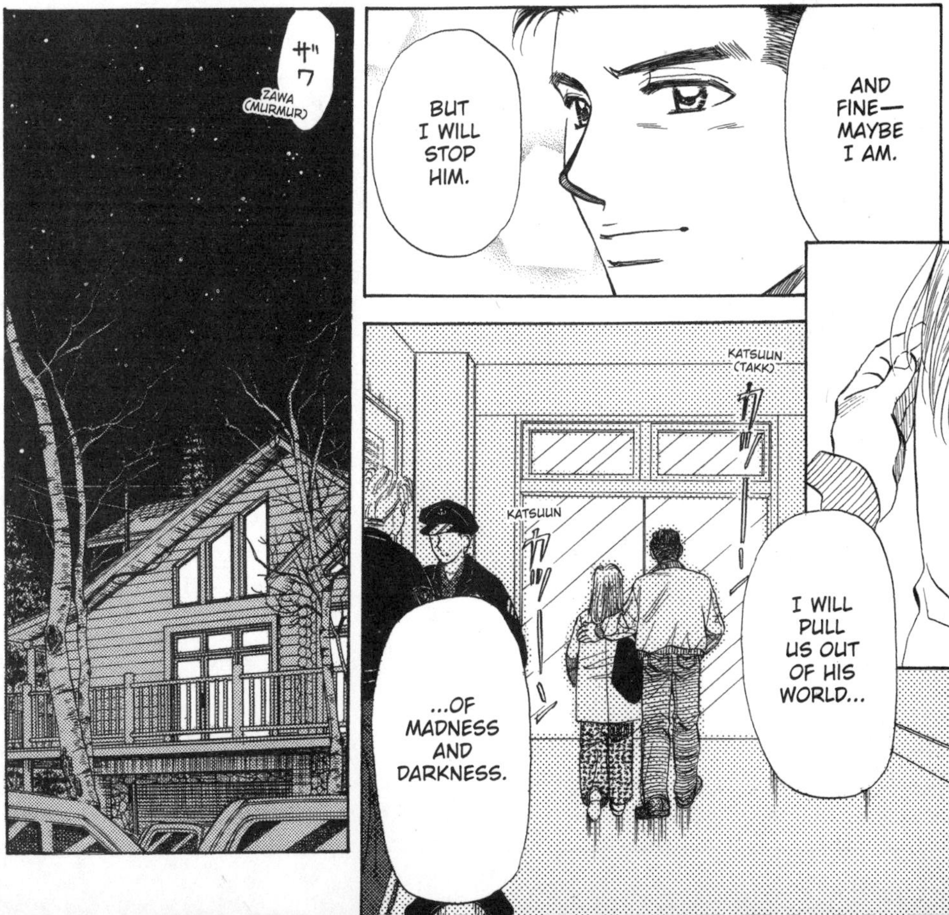
AND FINE—MAYBE I AM.
BUT I WILL STOP HIM.
I WILL PULL US OUT OF HIS WORLD...
カッ
KATSUUN (TAKK)
カッ
KATSUUN
...OF MADNESS AND DARKNESS.
ザワ
ZAWA (MURMUR)

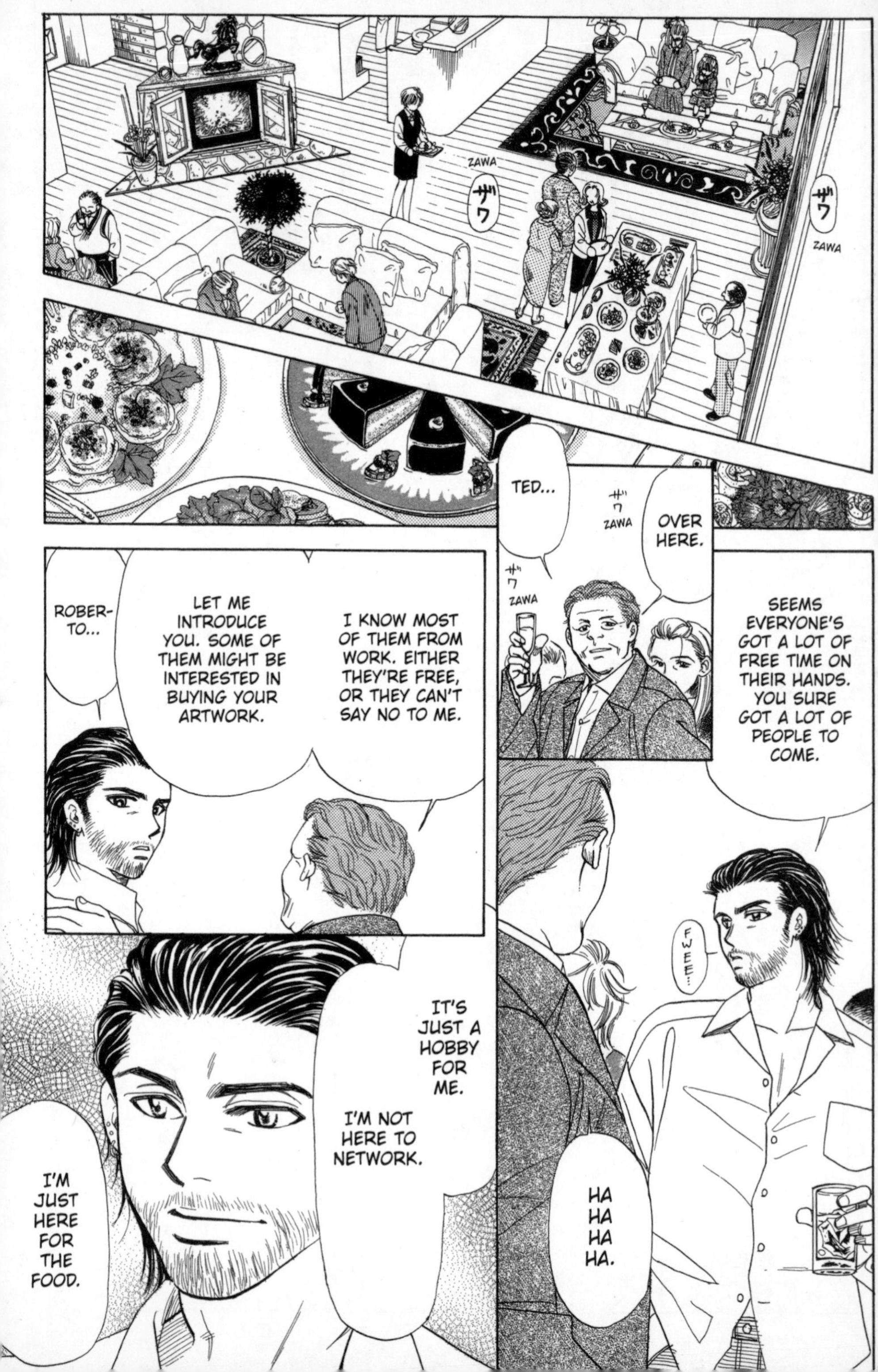

ザワ ZAWA
ザワ ZAWA
OVER HERE.
TED...
ザワ ZAWA
ザワ ZAWA
SEEMS EVERYONE'S GOT A LOT OF FREE TIME ON THEIR HANDS. YOU SURE GOT A LOT OF PEOPLE TO COME.
FWEE...
HA HA HA HA.
I KNOW MOST OF THEM FROM WORK. EITHER THEY'RE FREE, OR THEY CAN'T SAY NO TO ME.
ROBERTO...
LET ME INTRODUCE YOU. SOME OF THEM MIGHT BE INTERESTED IN BUYING YOUR ARTWORK.
IT'S JUST A HOBBY FOR ME.
I'M NOT HERE TO NETWORK.
I'M JUST HERE FOR THE FOOD.

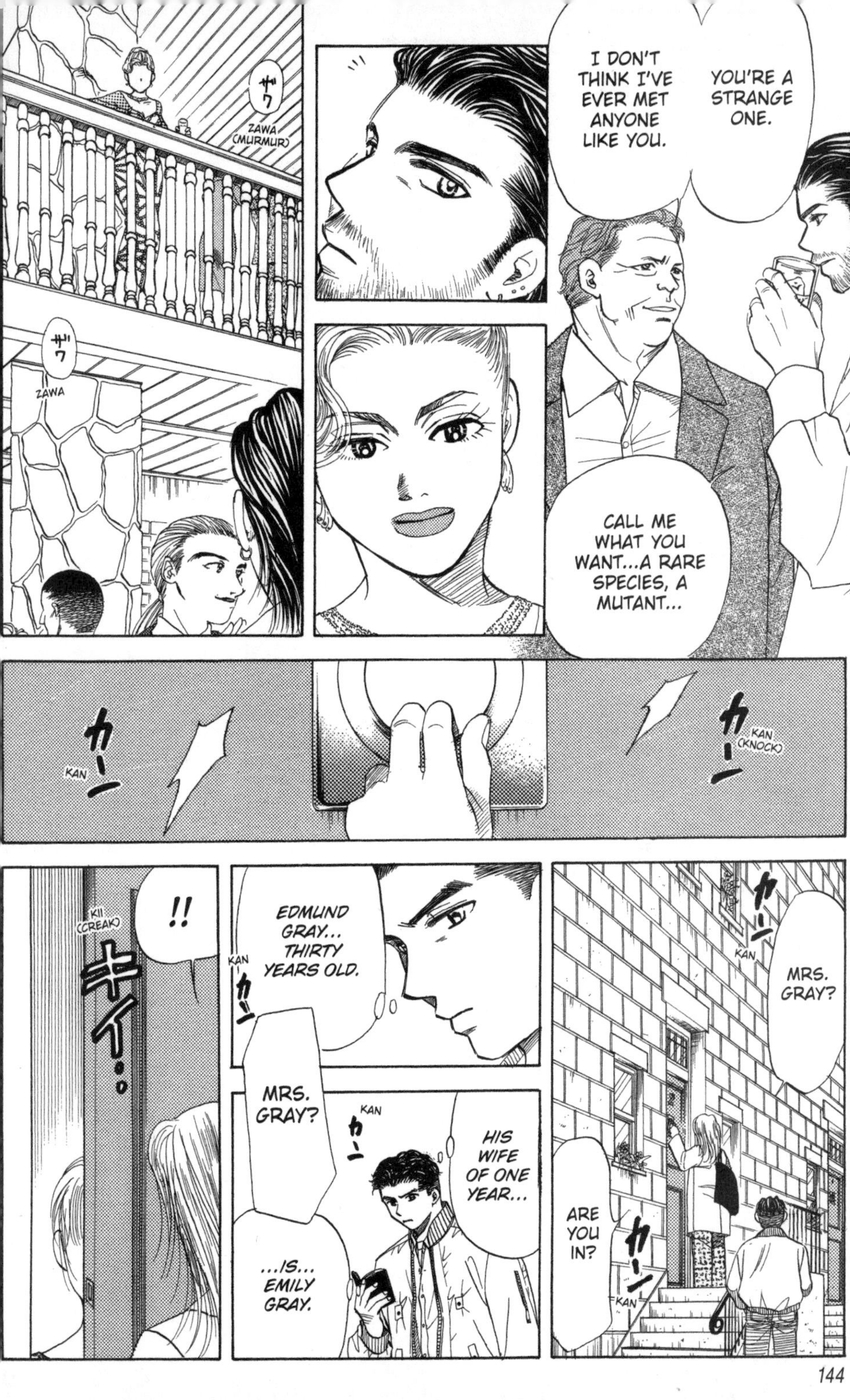
YOU'RE A STRANGE ONE.
I DON'T THINK I'VE EVER MET ANYONE LIKE YOU.
CALL ME WHAT YOU WANT...A RARE SPECIES, A MUTANT...
ザワ
ZAWA (MURMUR)
ザワ
ZAWA
カーン
KAN (KNOCK)
カーン
KAN
カーン
KAN
MRS. GRAY?
ARE YOU IN?
カーン
KAN
EDMUND GRAY... THIRTY YEARS OLD.
カン
KAN
HIS WIFE OF ONE YEAR...
カー
KAN
MRS. GRAY?
...IS... EMILY GRAY.
!!
キイ
KII (CREAK)

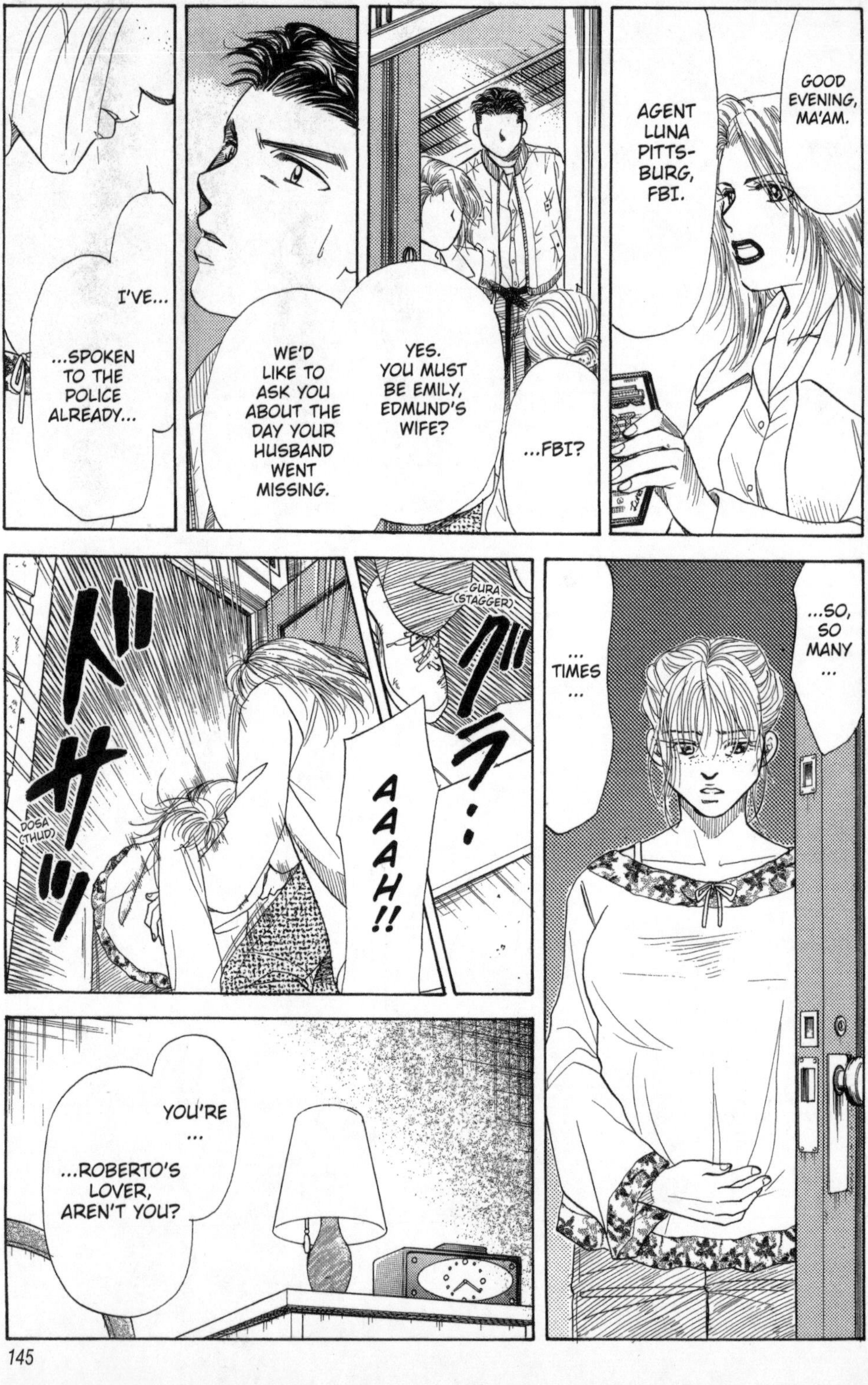
GOOD EVENING, MA'AM.
AGENT LUNA PITTSBURG, FBI.
...FBI?
YES. YOU MUST BE EMILY, EDMUND'S WIFE?
WE'D LIKE TO ASK YOU ABOUT THE DAY YOUR HUSBAND WENT MISSING.
I'VE...
...SPOKEN TO THE POLICE ALREADY...
...SO, SO MANY ...
... TIMES ...
グラ…
GURA (STAGGER)
AAAAH!!
ドサッ
DOSA (THUD)
YOU'RE ...
...ROBERTO'S LOVER, AREN'T YOU?

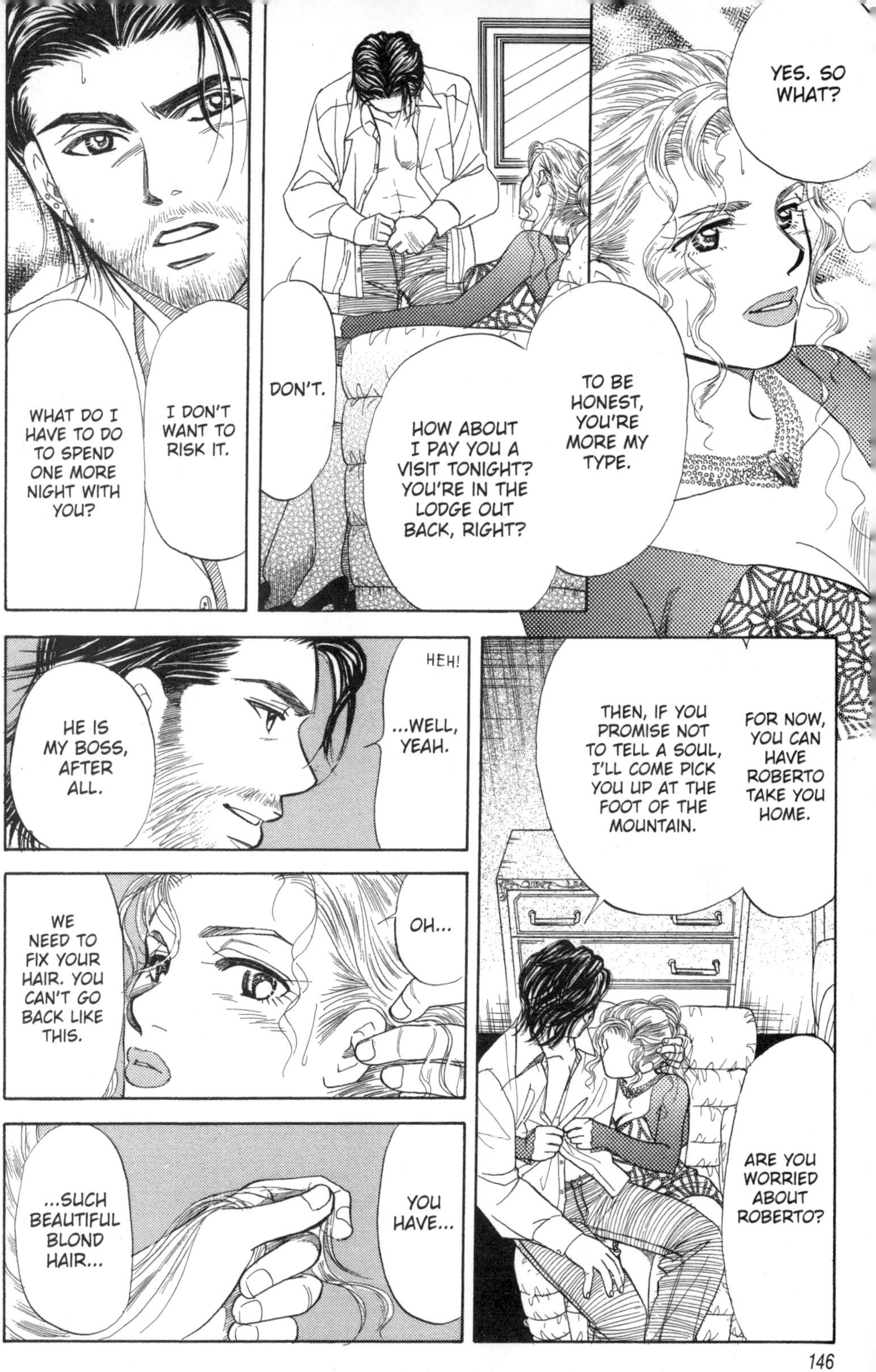
YES. SO WHAT?
TO BE HONEST, YOU'RE MORE MY TYPE.
HOW ABOUT I PAY YOU A VISIT TONIGHT? YOU'RE IN THE LODGE OUT BACK, RIGHT?
DON'T.
I DON'T WANT TO RISK IT.
WHAT DO I HAVE TO DO TO SPEND ONE MORE NIGHT WITH YOU?
FOR NOW, YOU CAN HAVE ROBERTO TAKE YOU HOME.
THEN, IF YOU PROMISE NOT TO TELL A SOUL, I'LL COME PICK YOU UP AT THE FOOT OF THE MOUNTAIN.
ARE YOU WORRIED ABOUT ROBERTO?
HEH!
...WELL, YEAH.
HE IS MY BOSS, AFTER ALL.
OH...
WE NEED TO FIX YOUR HAIR. YOU CAN'T GO BACK LIKE THIS.
YOU HAVE...
...SUCH BEAUTIFUL BLOND HAIR...

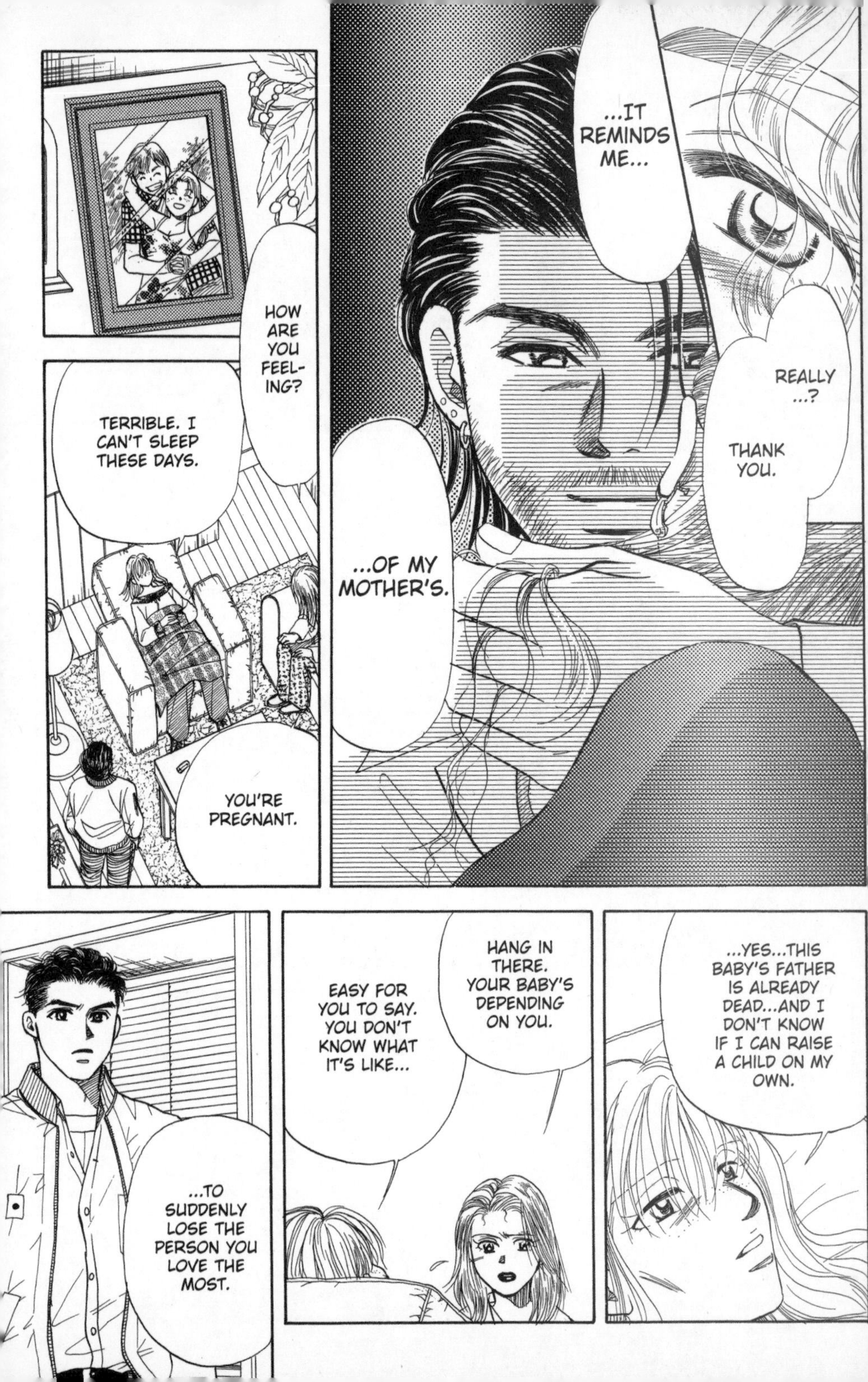
...IT REMINDS ME...
...OF MY MOTHER'S.
REALLY ...? THANK YOU.
HOW ARE YOU FEEL-ING?
TERRIBLE. I CAN'T SLEEP THESE DAYS.
YOU'RE PREGNANT.
...YES...THIS BABY'S FATHER IS ALREADY DEAD...AND I DON'T KNOW IF I CAN RAISE A CHILD ON MY OWN.
HANG IN THERE. YOUR BABY'S DEPENDING ON YOU.
EASY FOR YOU TO SAY. YOU DON'T KNOW WHAT IT'S LIKE...
...TO SUDDENLY LOSE THE PERSON YOU LOVE THE MOST.

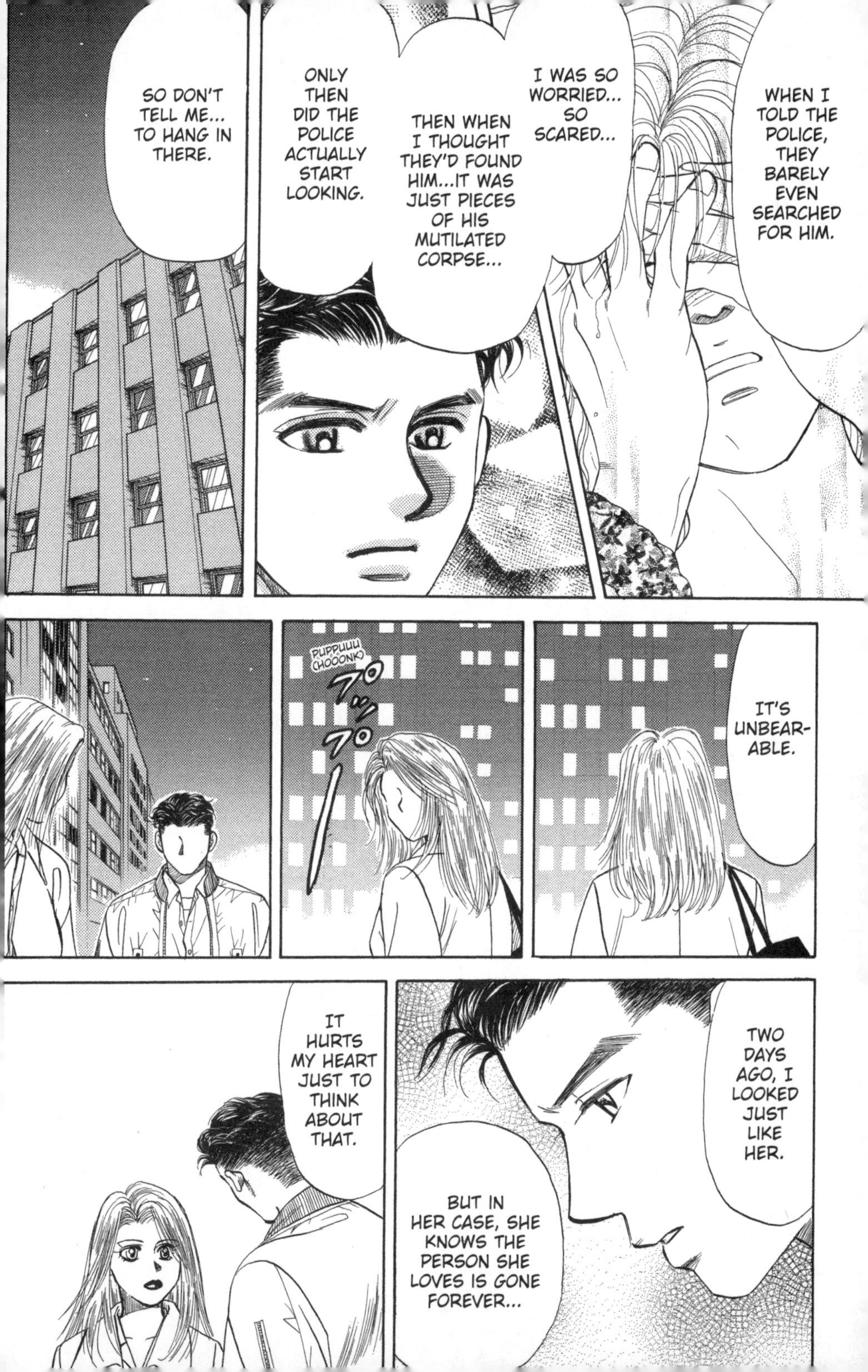
WHEN I TOLD THE POLICE, THEY BARELY EVEN SEARCHED FOR HIM.
I WAS SO WORRIED... SO SCARED...
THEN WHEN I THOUGHT THEY'D FOUND HIM...IT WAS JUST PIECES OF HIS MUTILATED CORPSE...
ONLY THEN DID THE POLICE ACTUALLY START LOOKING.
SO DON'T TELL ME... TO HANG IN THERE.
IT'S UNBEAR-ABLE.
PUPPUUU (HOOONK)
TWO DAYS AGO, I LOOKED JUST LIKE HER.
BUT IN HER CASE, SHE KNOWS THE PERSON SHE LOVES IS GONE FOREVER...
IT HURTS MY HEART JUST TO THINK ABOUT THAT.

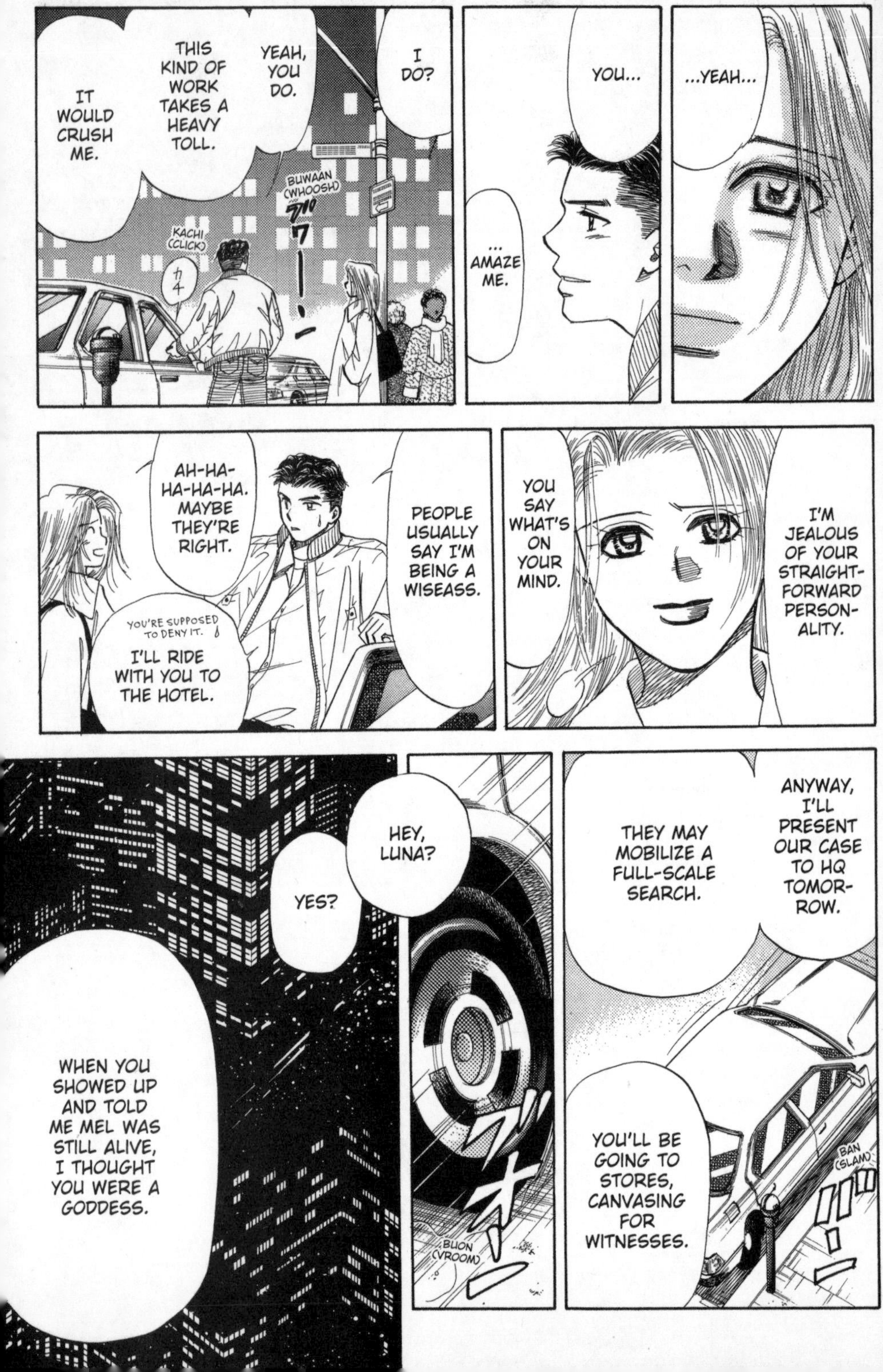
...YEAH...
YOU...
...AMAZE ME.
I DO?
YEAH, YOU DO.
THIS KIND OF WORK TAKES A HEAVY TOLL.
IT WOULD CRUSH ME.
BUWAAN (WHOOSH)
KACHI (CLICK)
I'M JEALOUS OF YOUR STRAIGHT-FORWARD PERSON-ALITY.
YOU SAY WHAT'S ON YOUR MIND.
PEOPLE USUALLY SAY I'M BEING A WISEASS.
AH-HA-HA-HA-HA. MAYBE THEY'RE RIGHT.
YOU'RE SUPPOSED TO DENY IT.
I'LL RIDE WITH YOU TO THE HOTEL.
ANYWAY, I'LL PRESENT OUR CASE TO HQ TOMOR-ROW.
THEY MAY MOBILIZE A FULL-SCALE SEARCH.
YOU'LL BE GOING TO STORES, CANVASING FOR WITNESSES.
BAN (SLAM)
BUON (VROOM)
HEY, LUNA?
YES?
WHEN YOU SHOWED UP AND TOLD ME MEL WAS STILL ALIVE, I THOUGHT YOU WERE A GODDESS.

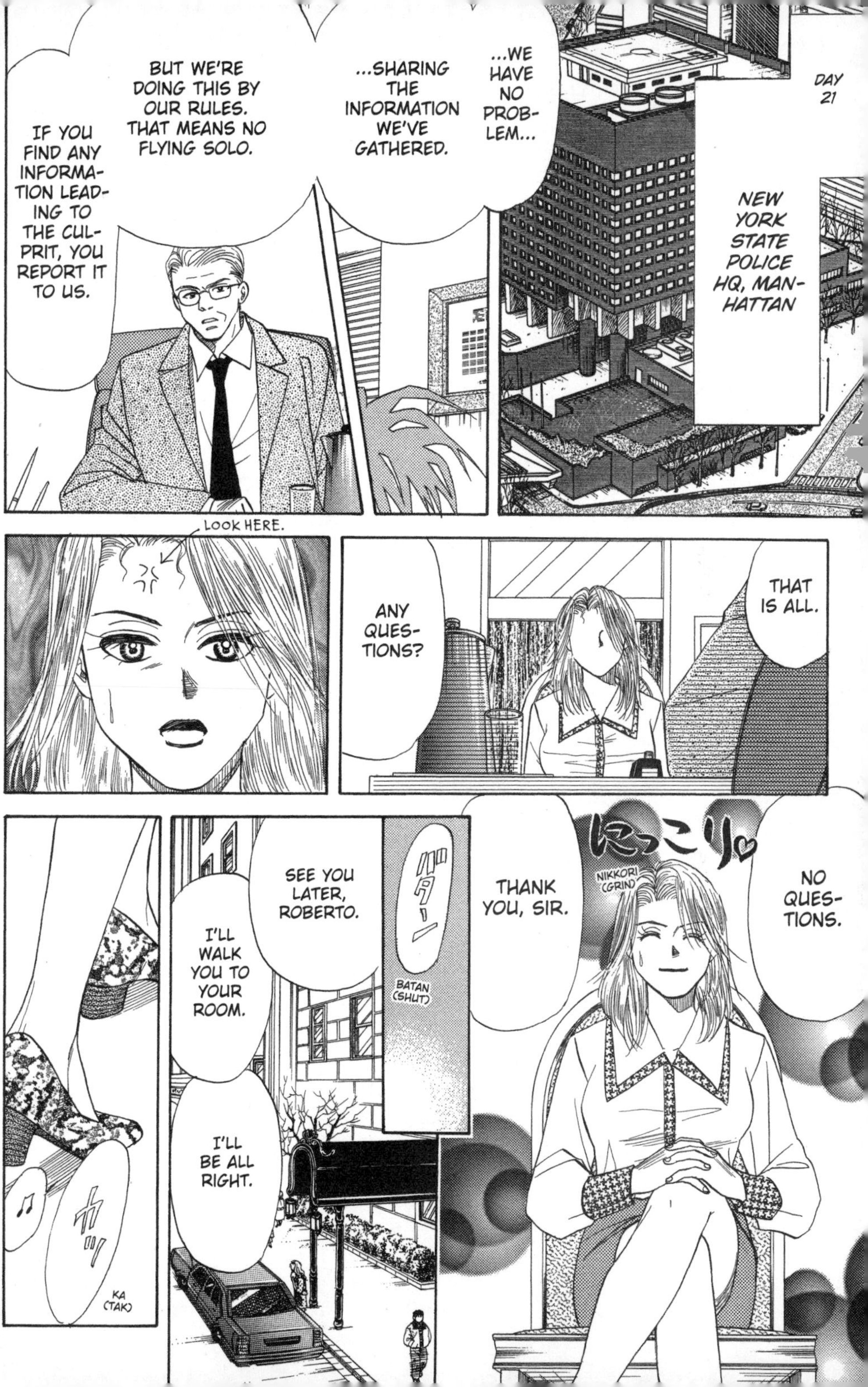
DAY 21
NEW YORK STATE POLICE HQ, MANHATTAN
...WE HAVE NO PROBLEM...
...SHARING THE INFORMATION WE'VE GATHERED.
BUT WE'RE DOING THIS BY OUR RULES. THAT MEANS NO FLYING SOLO.
IF YOU FIND ANY INFORMATION LEADING TO THE CULPRIT, YOU REPORT IT TO US.
THAT IS ALL.
ANY QUESTIONS?
LOOK HERE.
NO QUESTIONS.
にっこり
NIKKORI (GRIN)
THANK YOU, SIR.
バタン
BATAN (SHUT)
SEE YOU LATER, ROBERTO.
I'LL WALK YOU TO YOUR ROOM.
I'LL BE ALL RIGHT.
♪
カツ
KA (TAK)

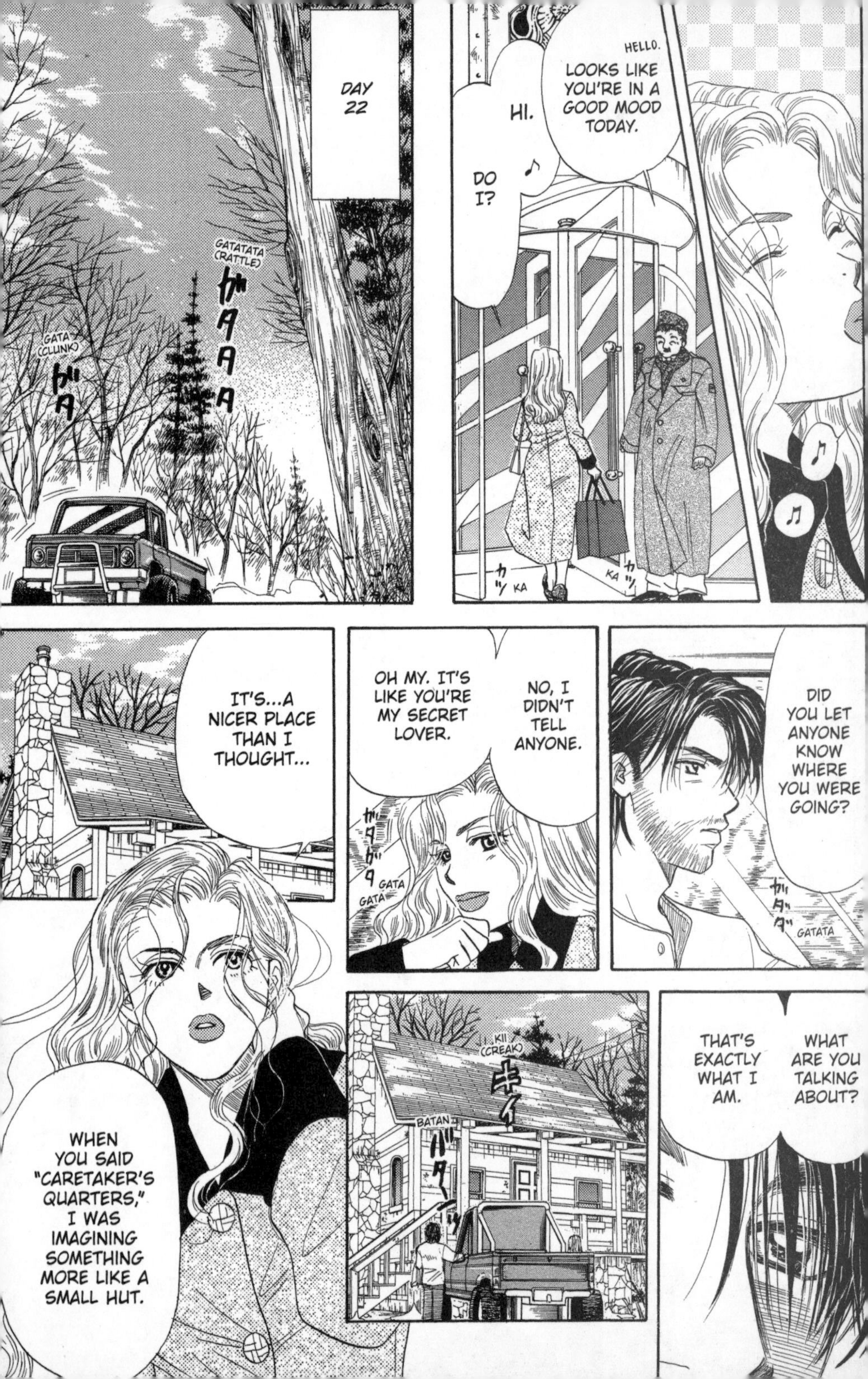
HELLO.
LOOKS LIKE YOU'RE IN A GOOD MOOD TODAY.
HI.
DO I?
KA
KA
DAY 22
GATATATA (RATTLE)
GATA (CLUNK)
DID YOU LET ANYONE KNOW WHERE YOU WERE GOING?
GATATA
NO, I DIDN'T TELL ANYONE.
OH MY. IT'S LIKE YOU'RE MY SECRET LOVER.
GATA GATA
WHAT ARE YOU TALKING ABOUT?
THAT'S EXACTLY WHAT I AM.
KII (CREAK)
BATAN
IT'S...A NICER PLACE THAN I THOUGHT...
WHEN YOU SAID "CARETAKER'S QUARTERS," I WAS IMAGINING SOMETHING MORE LIKE A SMALL HUT.

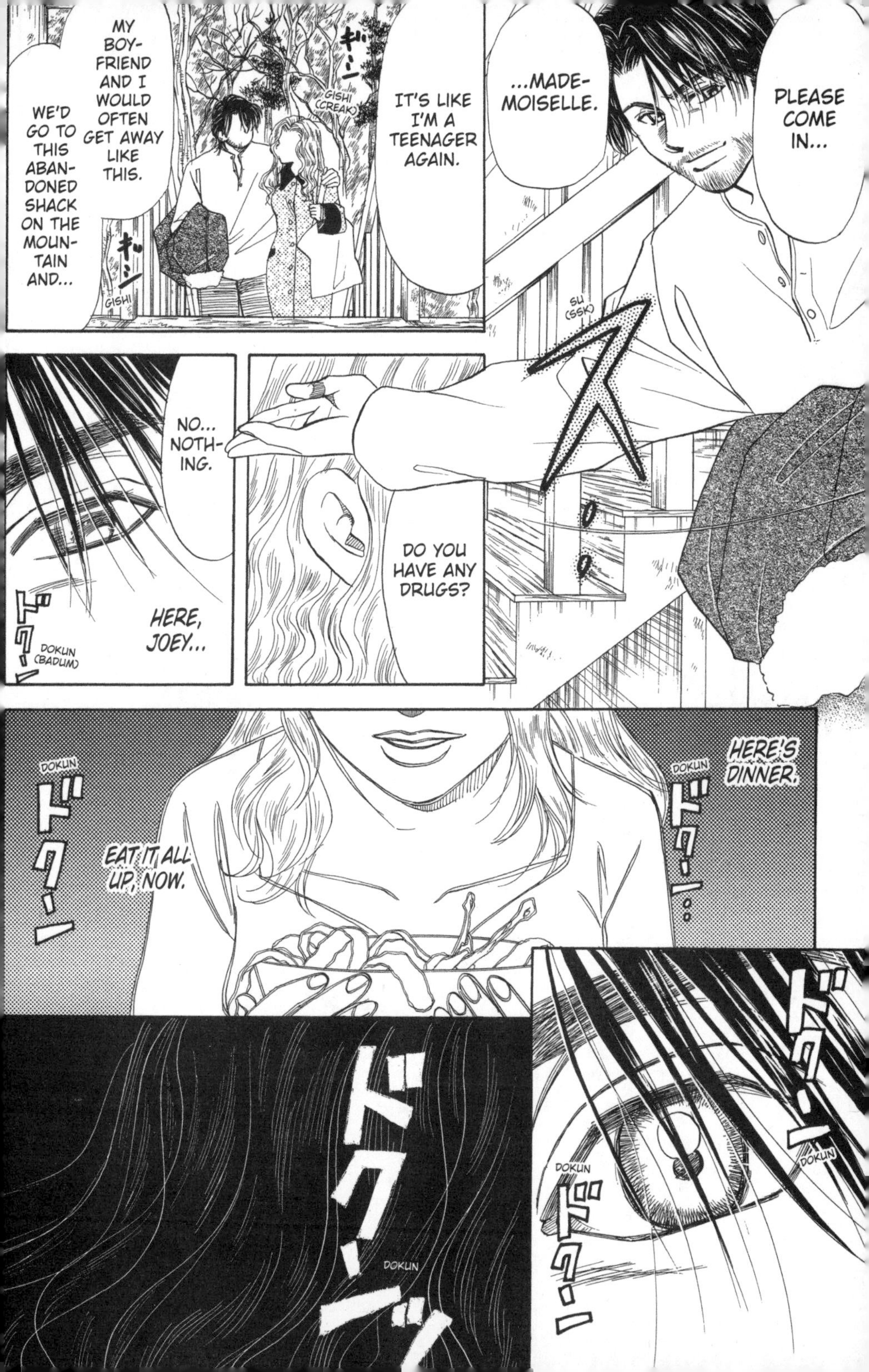
PLEASE COME IN...
...MADEMOISELLE.
SU (SSK)
IT'S LIKE I'M A TEENAGER AGAIN.
GISHI (CREAK)
MY BOYFRIEND AND I WOULD OFTEN GET AWAY LIKE THIS.
WE'D GO TO THIS ABANDONED SHACK ON THE MOUNTAIN AND...
GISHI
DO YOU HAVE ANY DRUGS?
NO... NOTHING.
HERE, JOEY...
DOKUN (BADUM)
HERE'S DINNER.
DOKUN
EAT IT ALL UP, NOW.
DOKUN
DOKUN
DOKUN
DOKUN

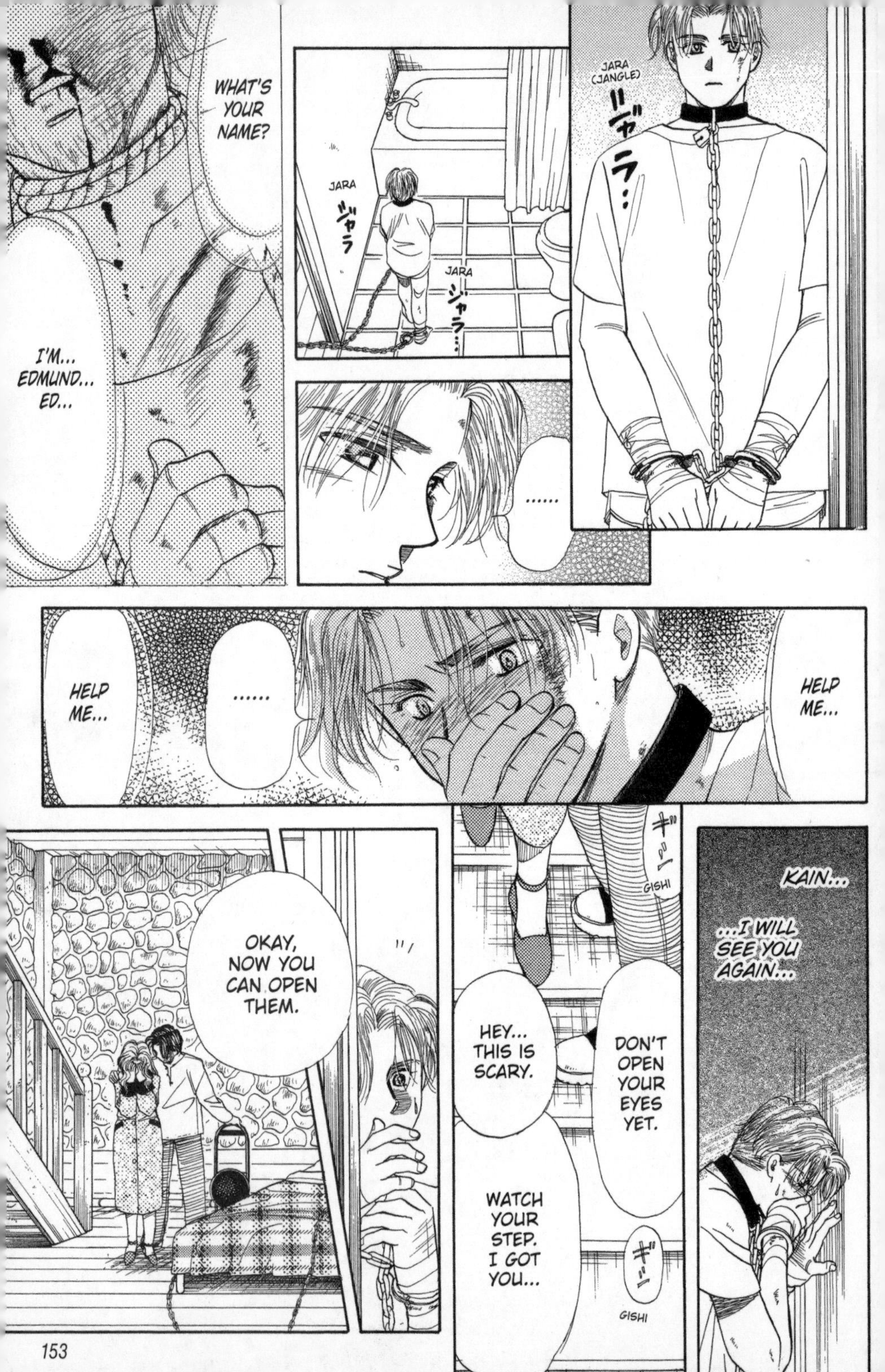
JARA (JANGLE)
ジャラ…
JARA
ジャラ
JARA
ジャラ…
……
WHAT'S YOUR NAME?
I'M... EDMUND... ED...
HELP ME...
……
HELP ME...
KAIN...
...I WILL SEE YOU AGAIN...
ギシ
GISHI
DON'T OPEN YOUR EYES YET.
HEY... THIS IS SCARY.
WATCH YOUR STEP. I GOT YOU...
ギシ
GISHI
OKAY, NOW YOU CAN OPEN THEM.

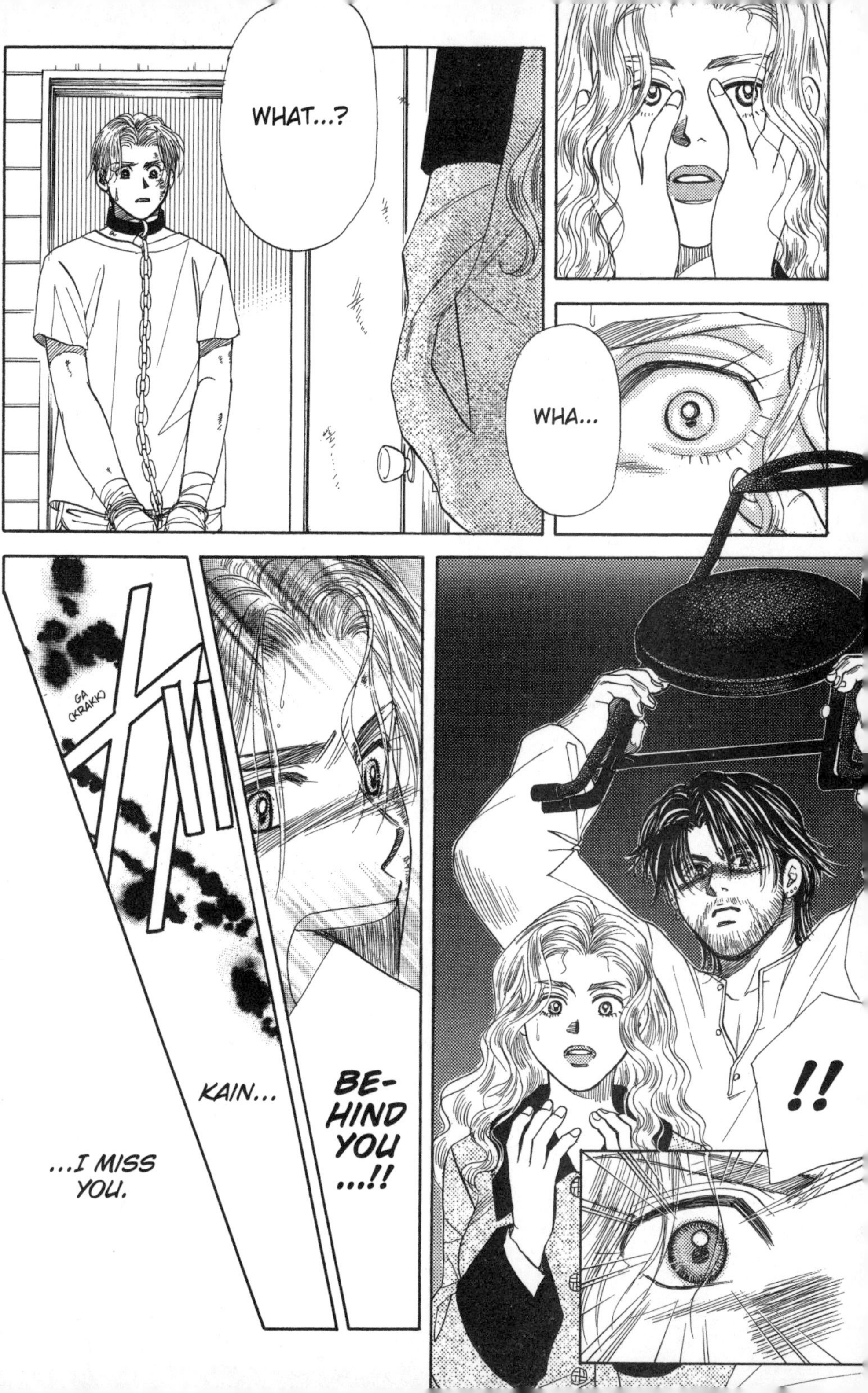
WHA...
WHAT...?
!!
BE-HIND YOU...!!
GA (KRAKK)
KAIN...
...I MISS YOU.

EPISODE IV

SCENE 4

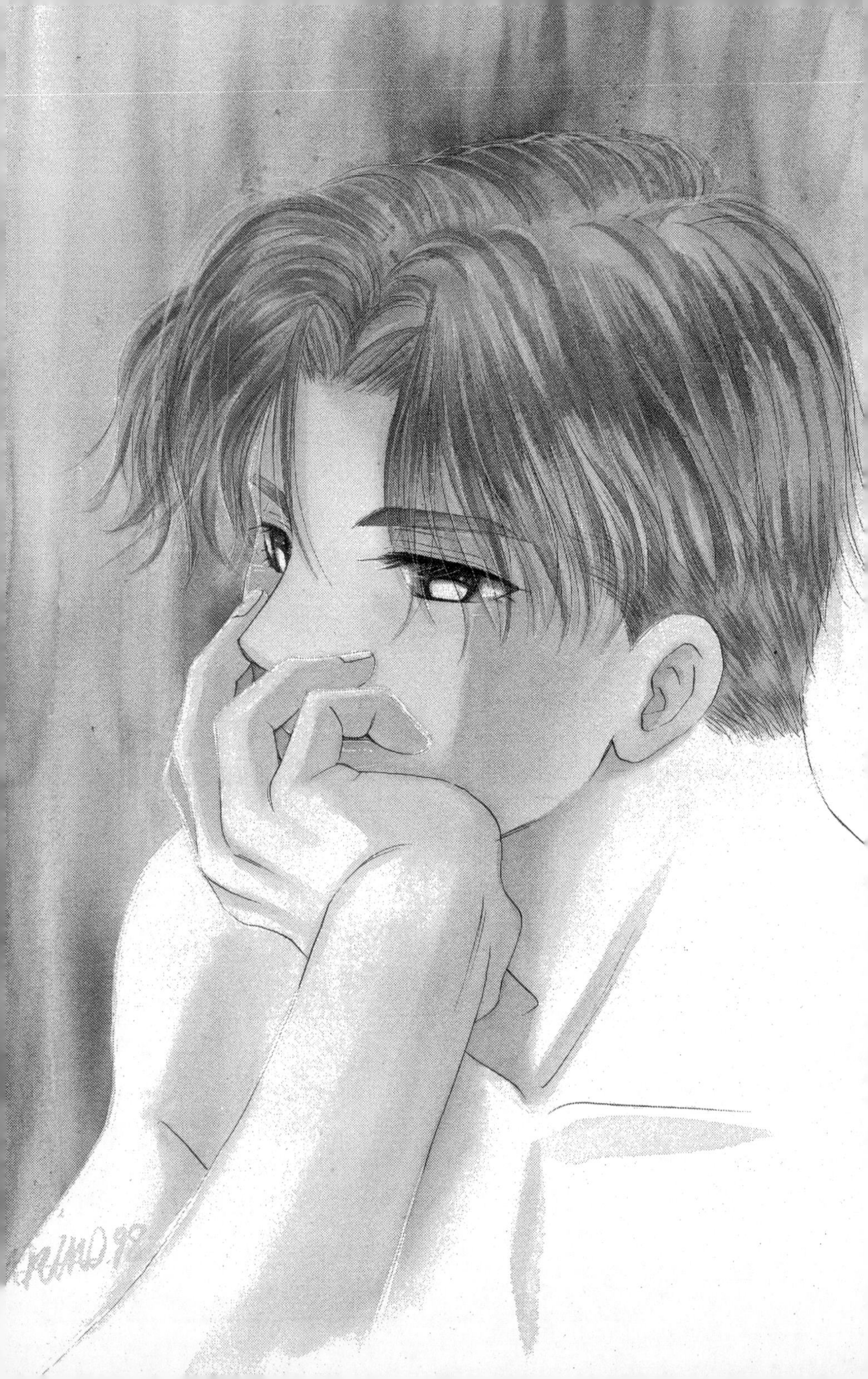

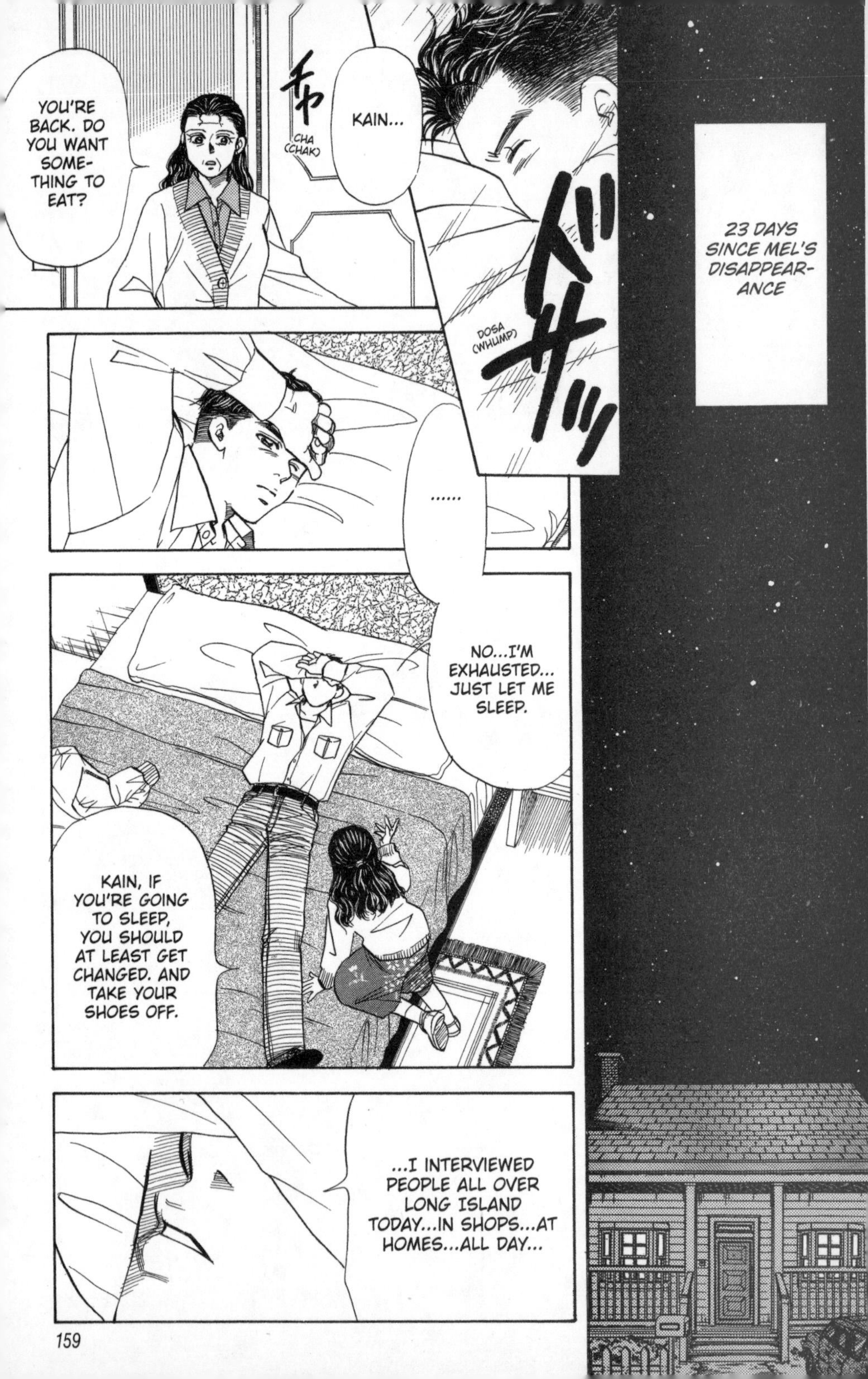
23 DAYS SINCE MEL'S DISAPPEARANCE
DOSA (WHUMP)
KAIN...
CHA (CHAK)
YOU'RE BACK. DO YOU WANT SOMETHING TO EAT?
......
NO...I'M EXHAUSTED... JUST LET ME SLEEP.
KAIN, IF YOU'RE GOING TO SLEEP, YOU SHOULD AT LEAST GET CHANGED. AND TAKE YOUR SHOES OFF.
...I INTERVIEWED PEOPLE ALL OVER LONG ISLAND TODAY...IN SHOPS...AT HOMES...ALL DAY...

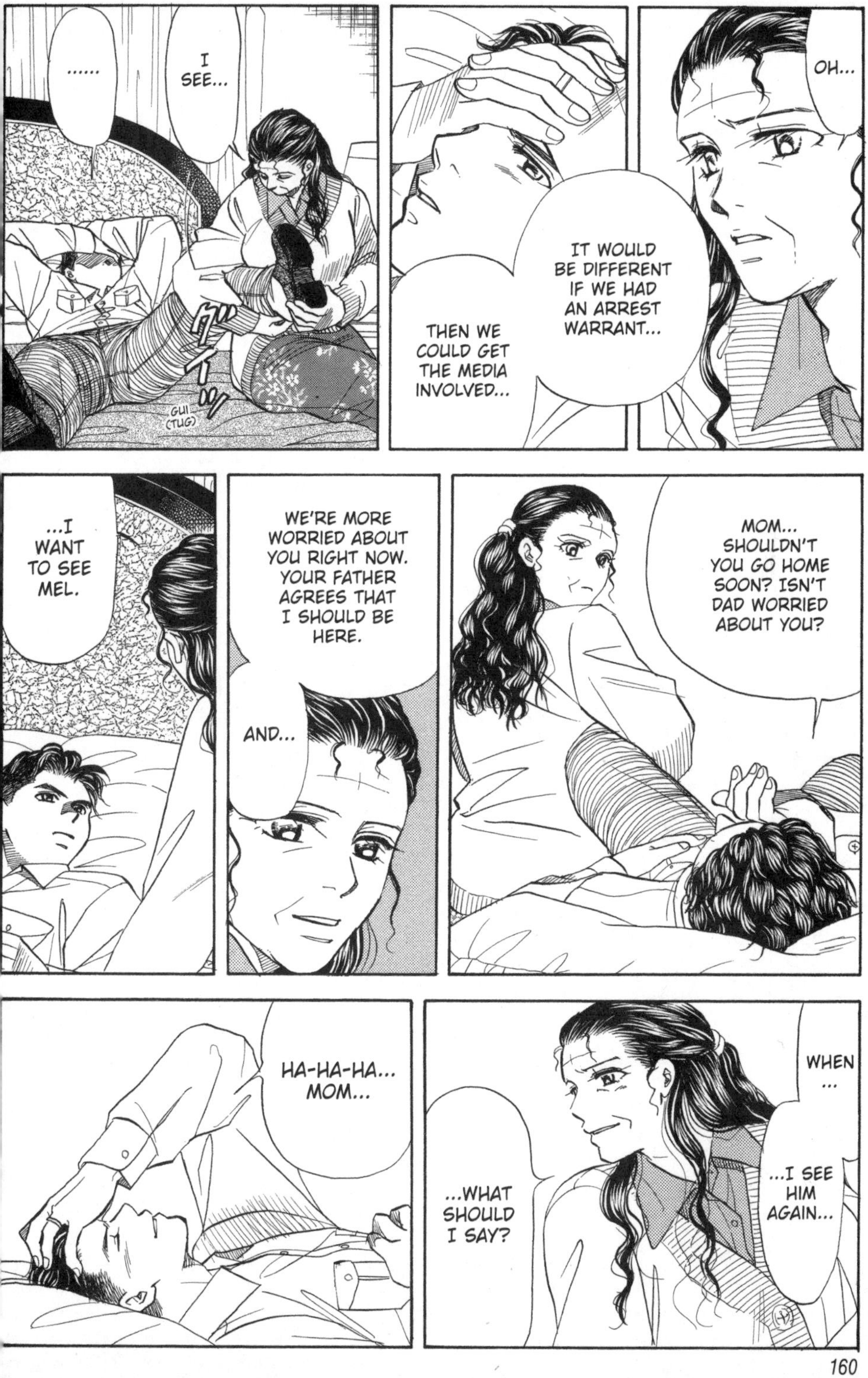
OH...
IT WOULD BE DIFFERENT IF WE HAD AN ARREST WARRANT...
THEN WE COULD GET THE MEDIA INVOLVED...
I SEE...
......
GUI (TUG)
MOM... SHOULDN'T YOU GO HOME SOON? ISN'T DAD WORRIED ABOUT YOU?
WE'RE MORE WORRIED ABOUT YOU RIGHT NOW. YOUR FATHER AGREES THAT I SHOULD BE HERE.
AND...
...I WANT TO SEE MEL.
WHEN...
...I SEE HIM AGAIN...
...WHAT SHOULD I SAY?
HA-HA-HA... MOM...

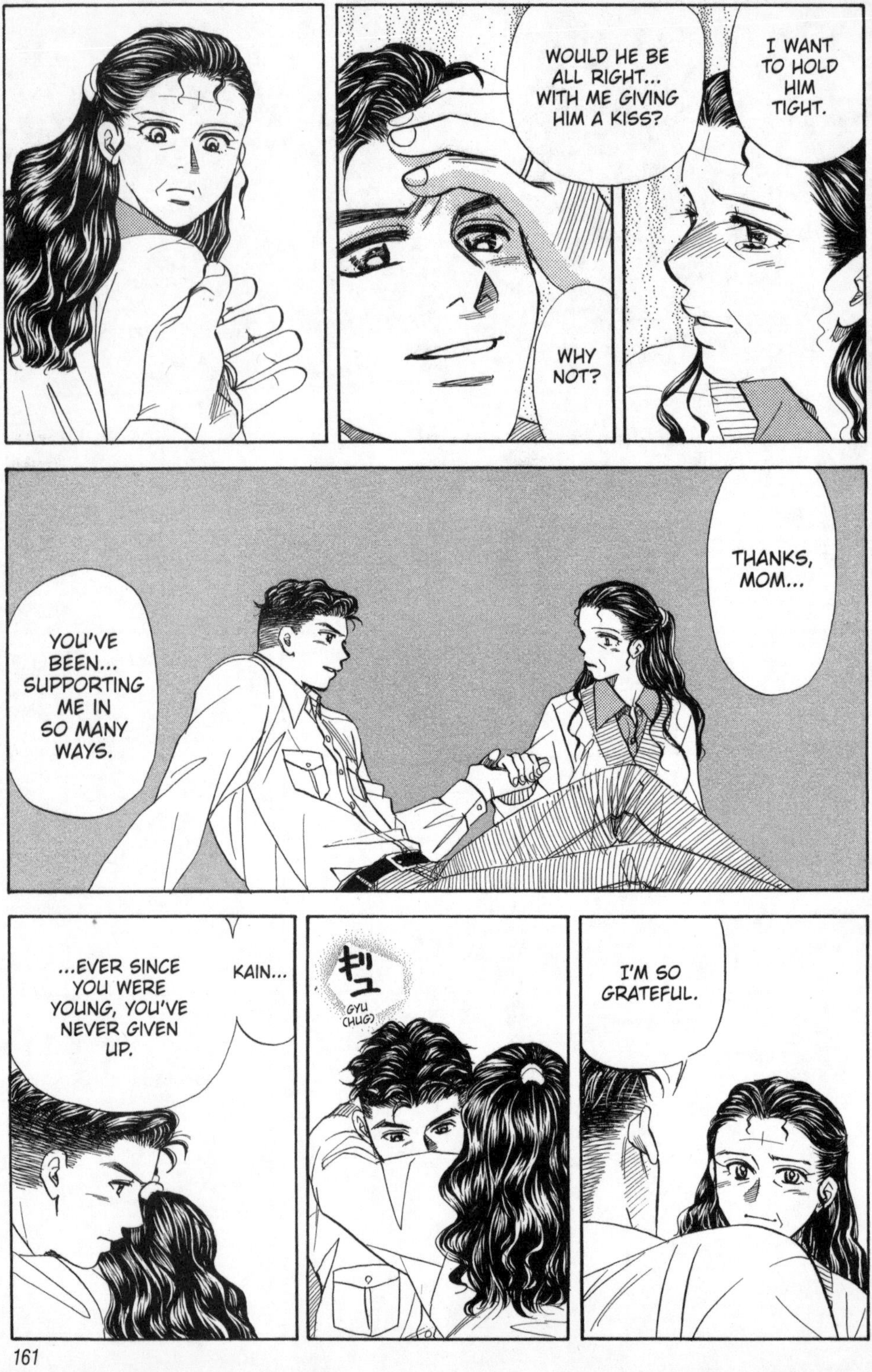
I WANT TO HOLD HIM TIGHT.
WOULD HE BE ALL RIGHT... WITH ME GIVING HIM A KISS?
WHY NOT?
THANKS, MOM...
YOU'VE BEEN... SUPPORTING ME IN SO MANY WAYS.
I'M SO GRATEFUL.
ギュ
GYU (HUG)
KAIN...
...EVER SINCE YOU WERE YOUNG, YOU'VE NEVER GIVEN UP.

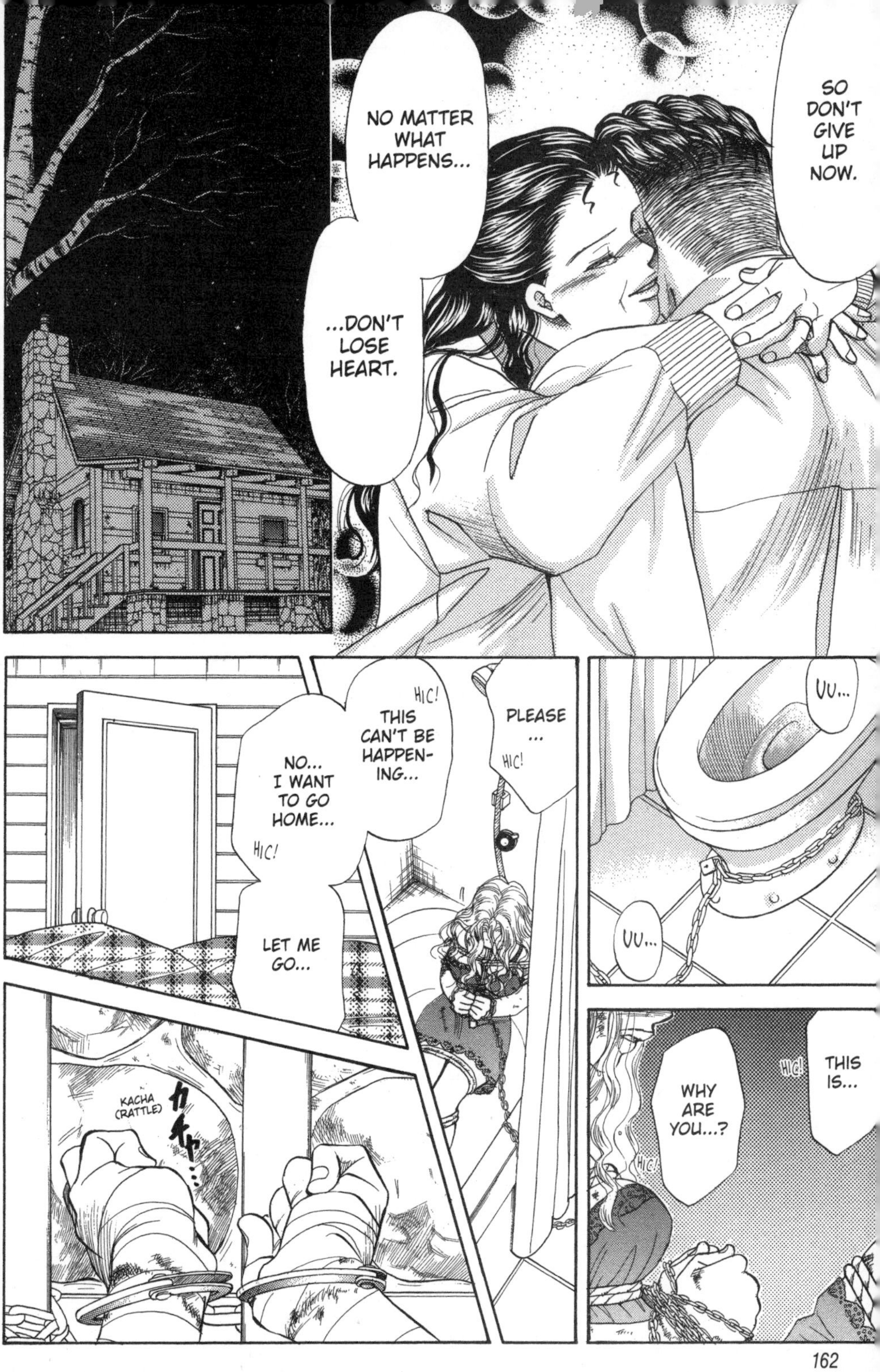
SO DON'T GIVE UP NOW.
NO MATTER WHAT HAPPENS...
...DON'T LOSE HEART.
UU...
UU...
THIS IS...
HIC!
WHY ARE YOU...?
HIC!
PLEASE ...
HIC!
HIC!
THIS CAN'T BE HAPPEN-ING...
NO... I WANT TO GO HOME...
HIC!
LET ME GO...
KACHA (RATTLE)
カチャ...

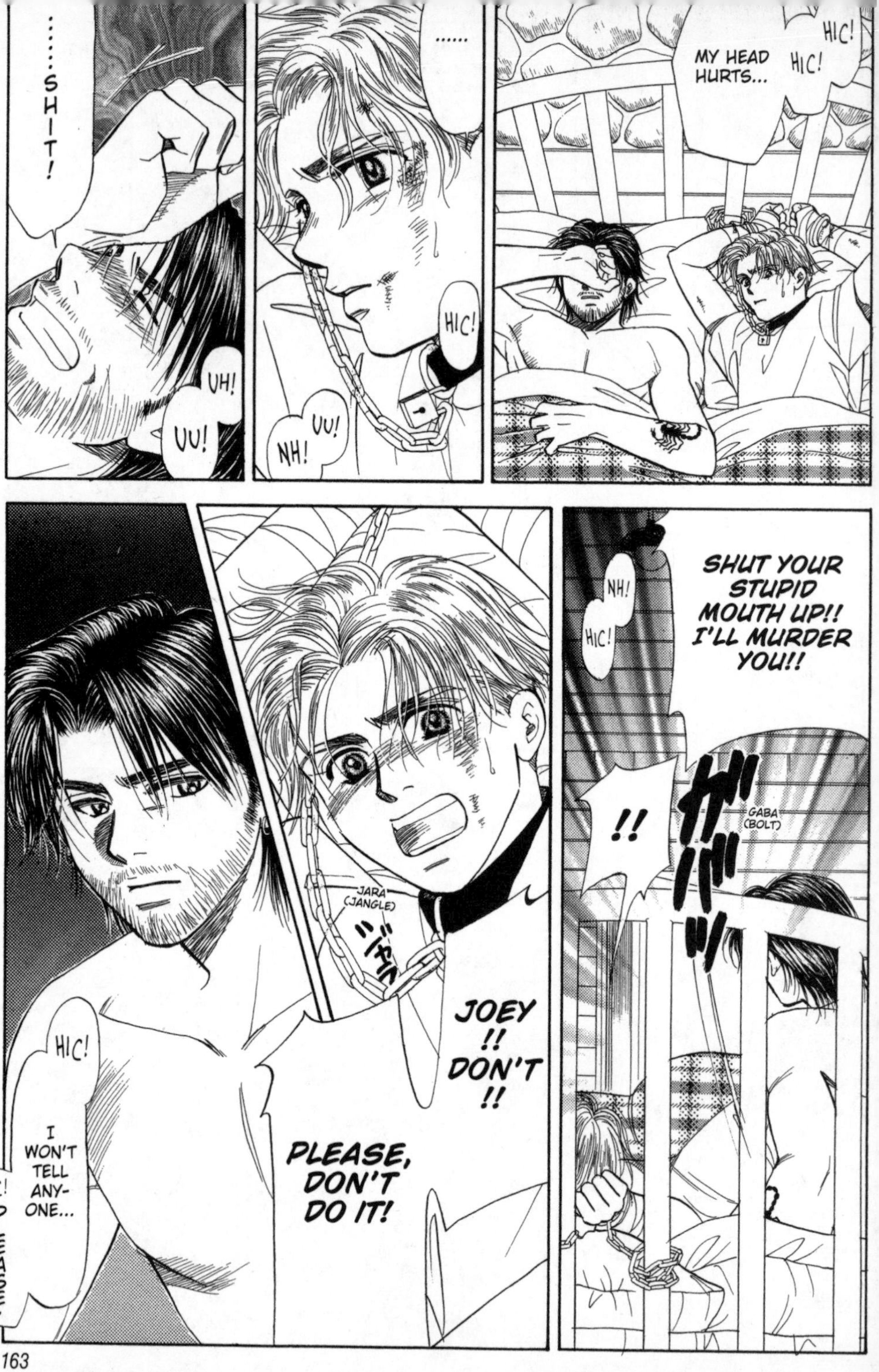
HIC!
HIC!
MY HEAD HURTS...
......
HIC!
UU!
NH!
......SHIT!
UH!
UU!
SHUT YOUR STUPID MOUTH UP!! I'LL MURDER YOU!!
NH!
HIC!
GABA (BOLT)
!!
JOEY!! DON'T!!
JARA (JANGLE)
PLEASE, DON'T DO IT!
HIC!
I WON'T TELL ANY-ONE...
HIC! PLEASE.

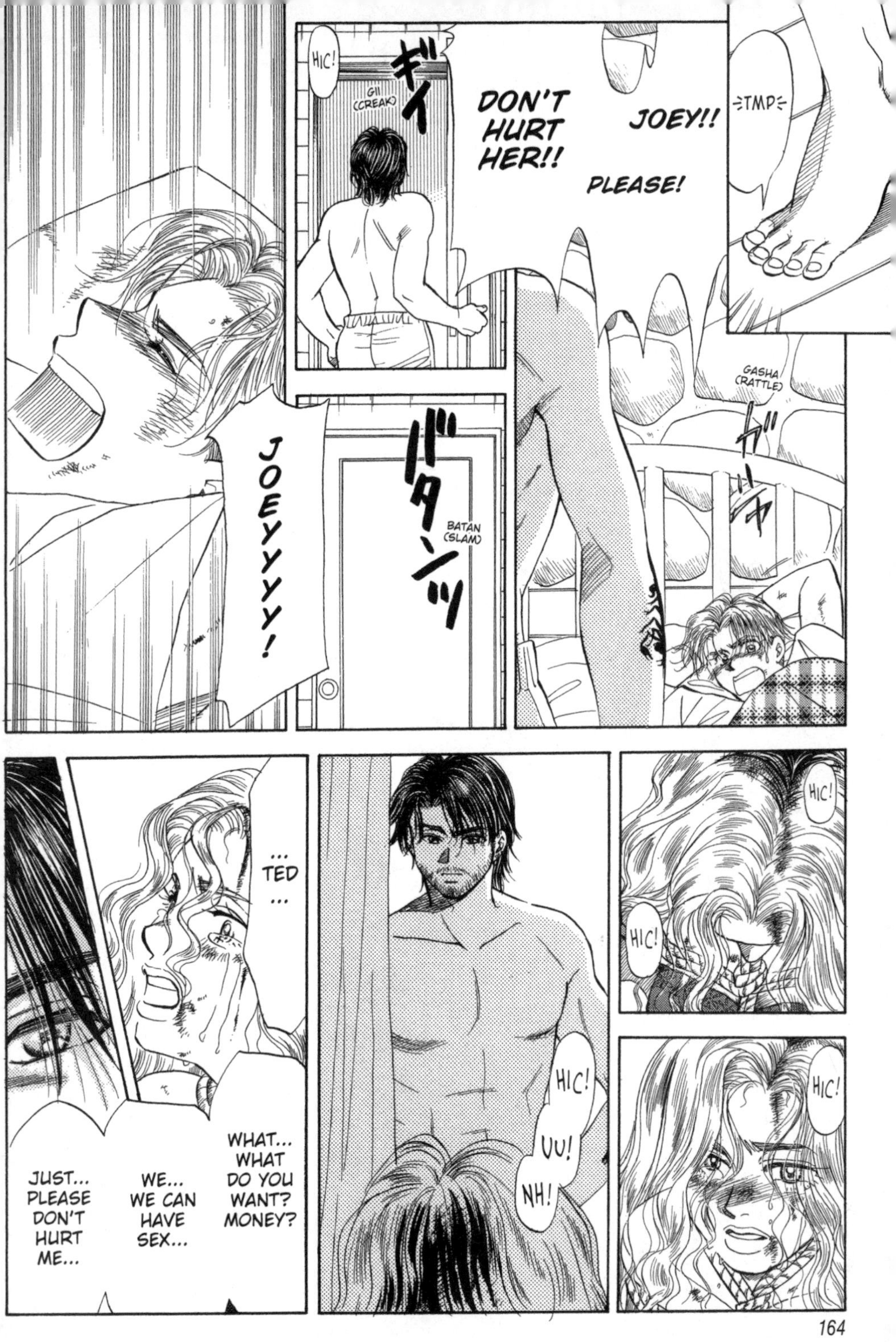
TMP
DON'T HURT HER!!
JOEY!!
PLEASE!
ガシャ
GASHA (RATTLE)
HIC!
ギイ
GII (CREAK)
バタンッ
BATAN (SLAM)
JOEYYYYY!
HIC!
HIC!
HIC!
HIC!
UU!
NH!
... TED ...
WHAT... WHAT DO YOU WANT? MONEY?
WE... WE CAN HAVE SEX...
JUST... PLEASE DON'T HURT ME...

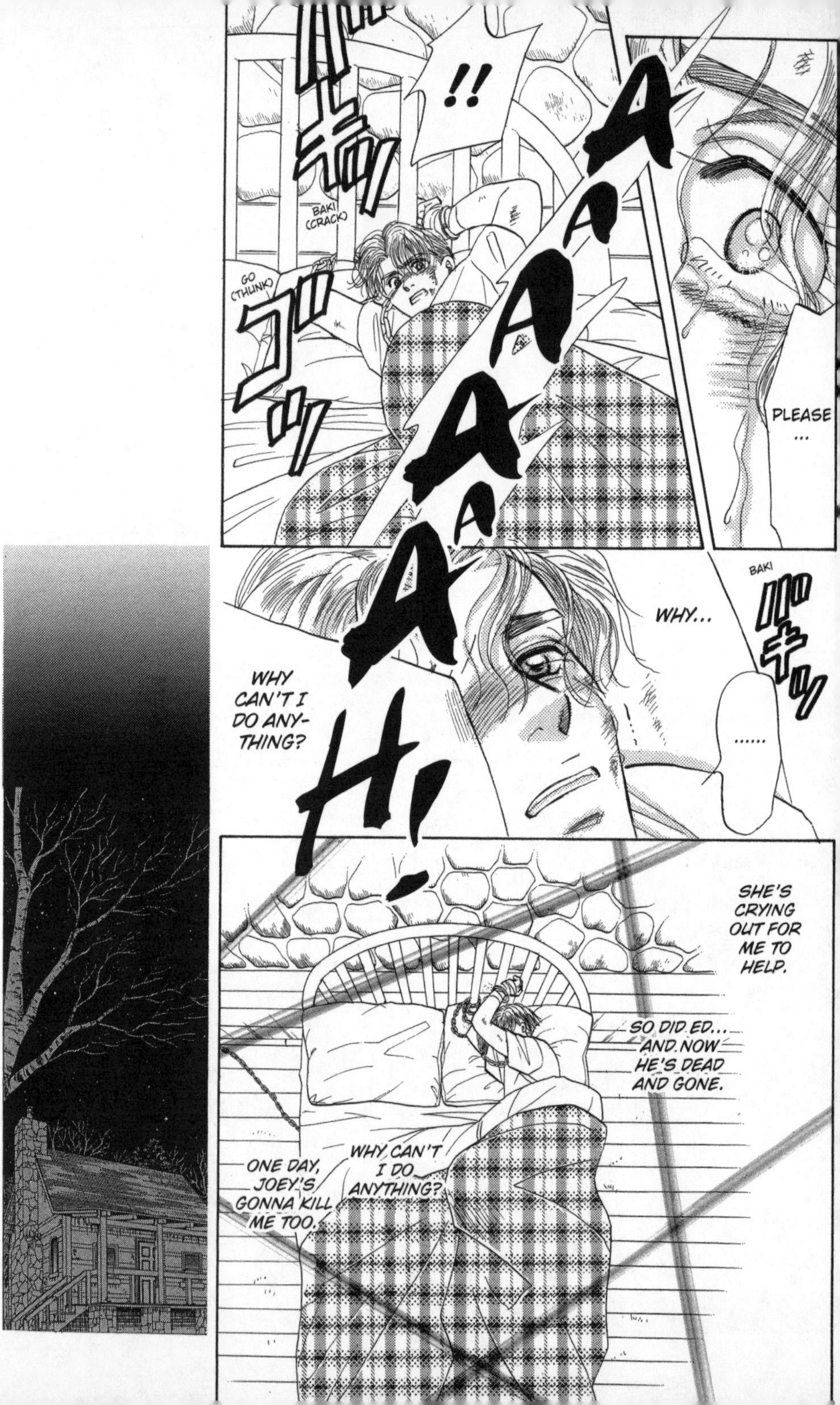
PLEASE...
!!
BAKI (CRACK)
GO (THUNK)
AAAAAAAH!
BAKI
......
WHY...
WHY CAN'T I DO ANYTHING?
SHE'S CRYING OUT FOR ME TO HELP.
SO DID ED... AND NOW HE'S DEAD AND GONE.
WHY CAN'T I DO ANYTHING?
ONE DAY, JOEY'S GONNA KILL ME TOO.

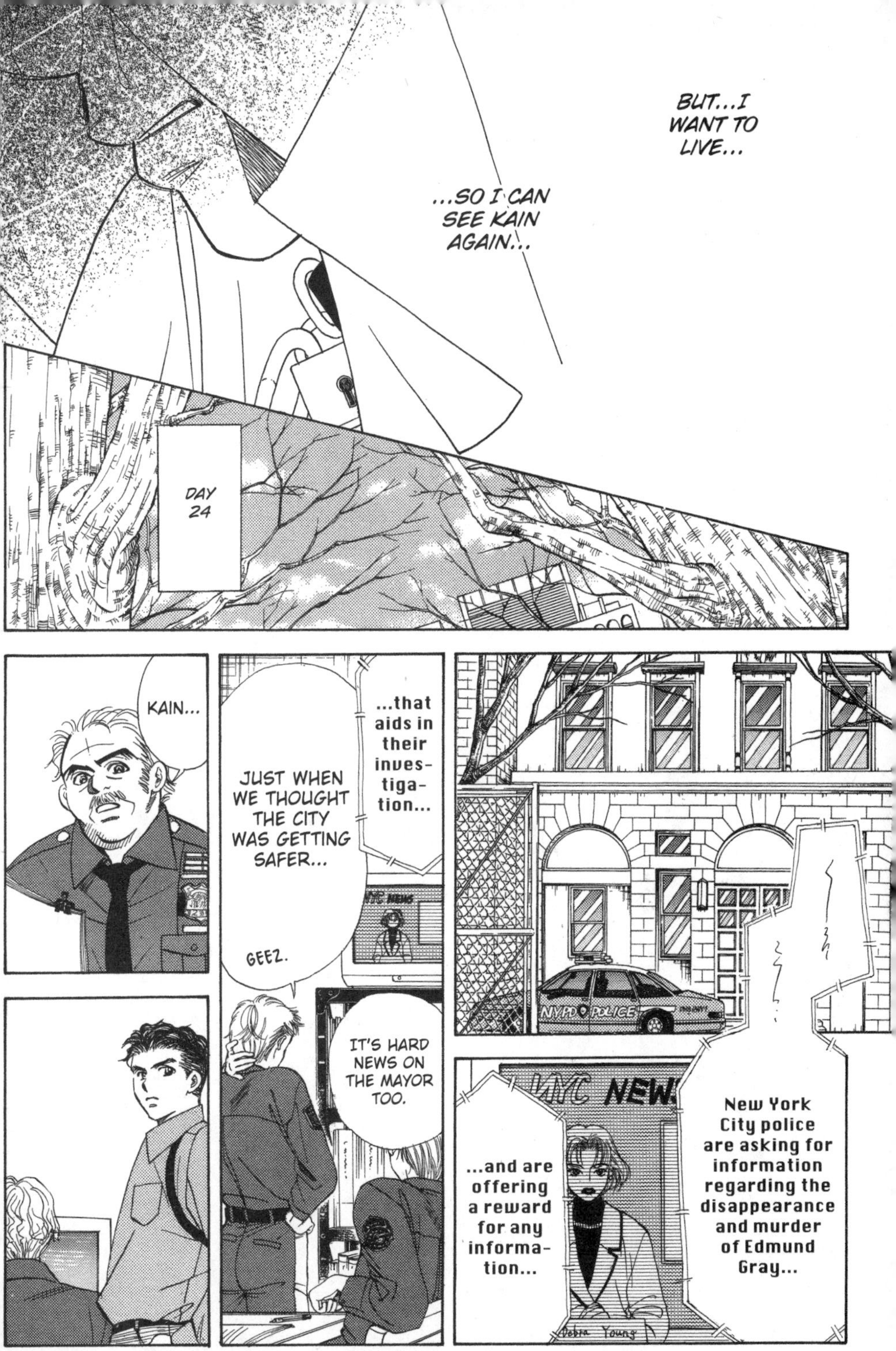
BUT...I WANT TO LIVE...
...SO I CAN SEE KAIN AGAIN...
DAY 24
NYPD POLICE
New York City police are asking for information regarding the disappearance and murder of Edmund Gray...
...and are offering a reward for any information...
Debra Young
...that aids in their investigation...
JUST WHEN WE THOUGHT THE CITY WAS GETTING SAFER...
GEEZ.
IT'S HARD NEWS ON THE MAYOR TOO.
KAIN...

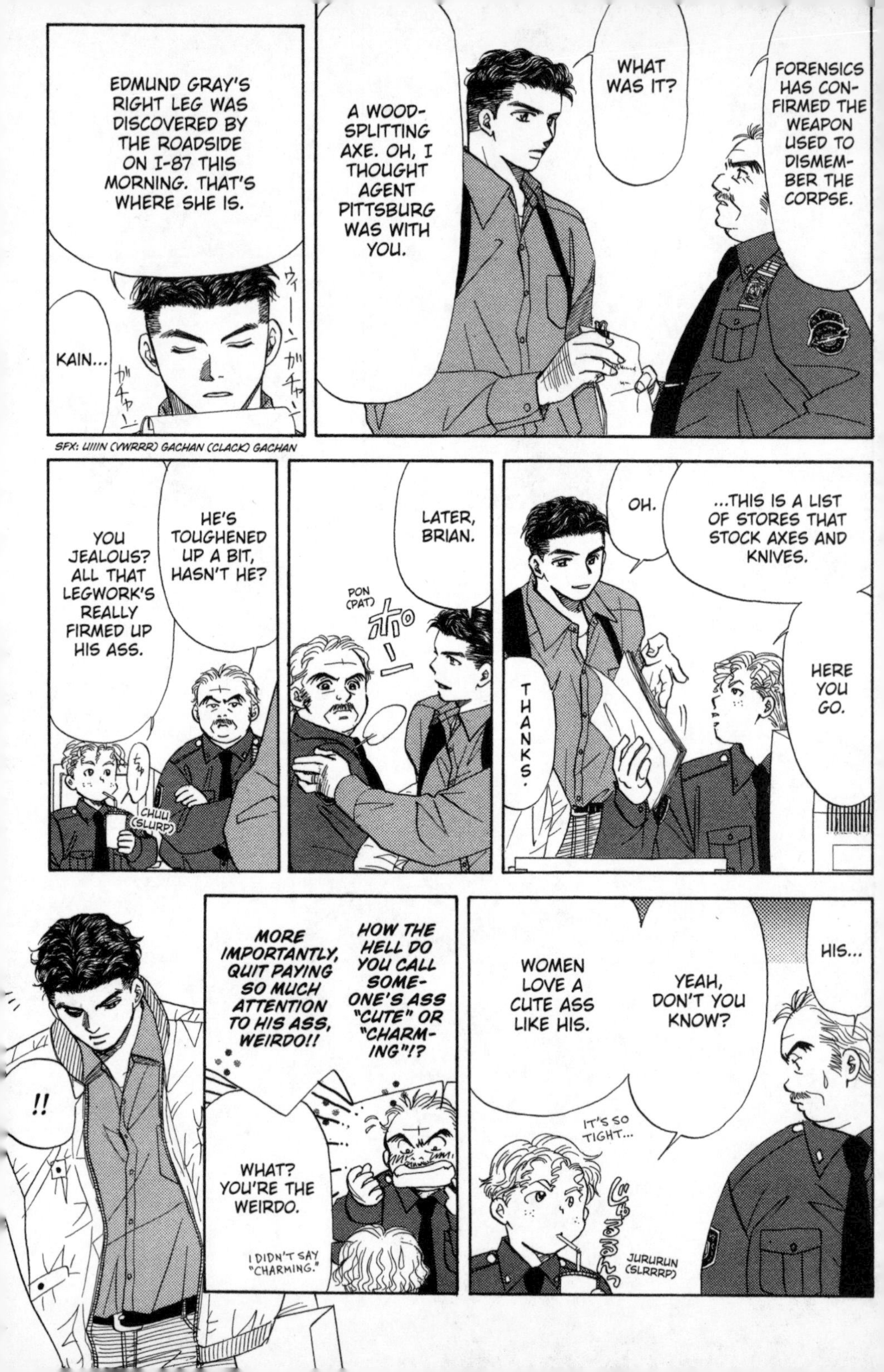

FORENSICS HAS CONFIRMED THE WEAPON USED TO DISMEMBER THE CORPSE.
WHAT WAS IT?
A WOOD-SPLITTING AXE. OH, I THOUGHT AGENT PITTSBURG WAS WITH YOU.
EDMUND GRAY'S RIGHT LEG WAS DISCOVERED BY THE ROADSIDE ON I-87 THIS MORNING. THAT'S WHERE SHE IS.
KAIN...
SFX: UIIIN (VWRRR) GACHAN (CLACK) GACHAN
...THIS IS A LIST OF STORES THAT STOCK AXES AND KNIVES.
OH.
HERE YOU GO.
THANKS.
LATER, BRIAN.
PON (PAT)
HE'S TOUGHENED UP A BIT, HASN'T HE?
YOU JEALOUS? ALL THAT LEGWORK'S REALLY FIRMED UP HIS ASS.
CHUU (SLURP)
HIS...
YEAH, DON'T YOU KNOW?
WOMEN LOVE A CUTE ASS LIKE HIS.
IT'S SO TIGHT...
JURURUN (SLRRRP)
HOW THE HELL DO YOU CALL SOMEONE'S ASS "CUTE" OR "CHARMING"!?
MORE IMPORTANTLY, QUIT PAYING SO MUCH ATTENTION TO HIS ASS, WEIRDO!!
WHAT? YOU'RE THE WEIRDO.
I DIDN'T SAY "CHARMING."
!!

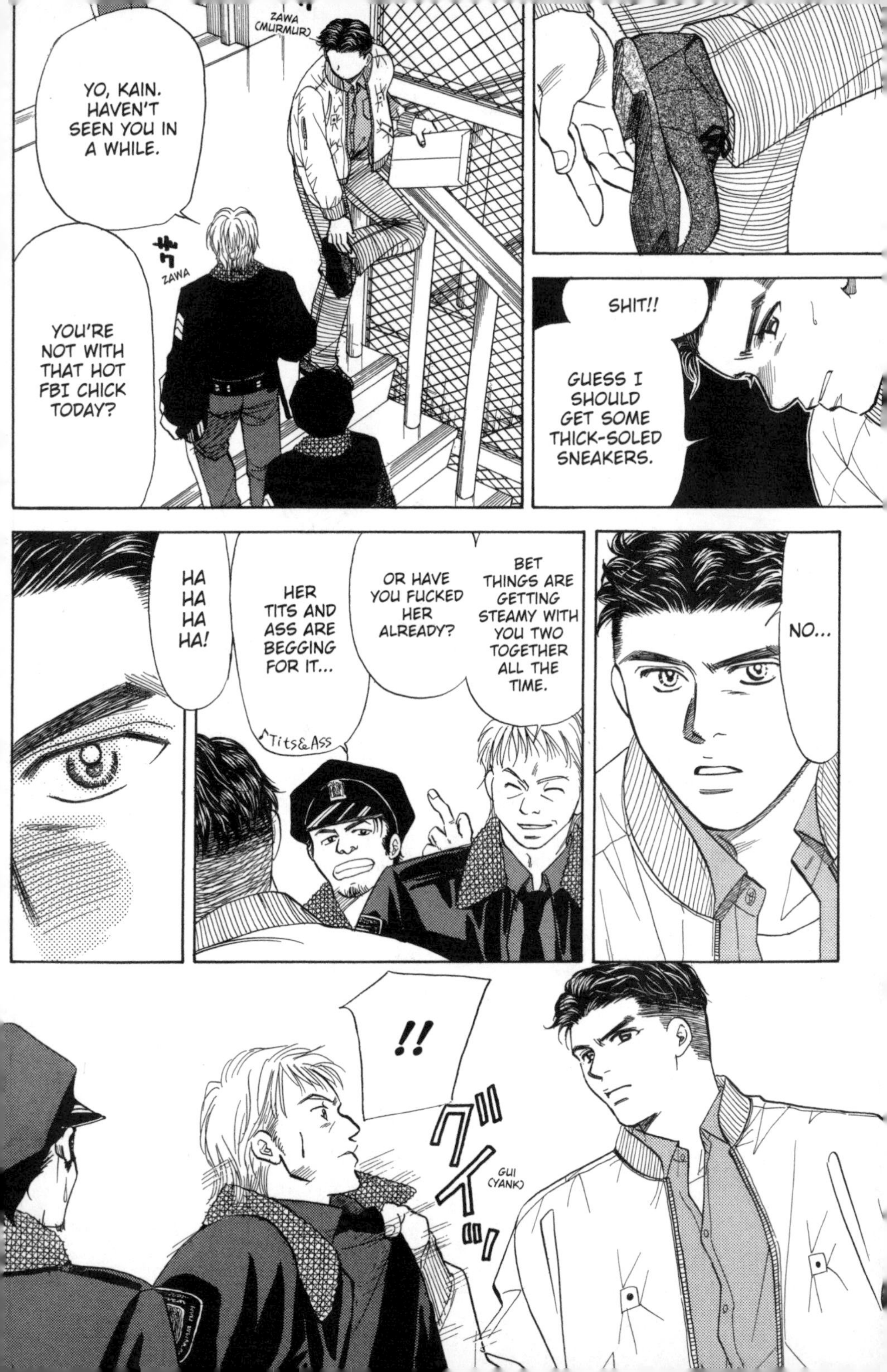
SHIT!!
GUESS I SHOULD GET SOME THICK-SOLED SNEAKERS.
ZAWA (MURMUR)
YO, KAIN. HAVEN'T SEEN YOU IN A WHILE.
ZAWA
YOU'RE NOT WITH THAT HOT FBI CHICK TODAY?
NO...
BET THINGS ARE GETTING STEAMY WITH YOU TWO TOGETHER ALL THE TIME.
OR HAVE YOU FUCKED HER ALREADY?
HER TITS AND ASS ARE BEGGING FOR IT...
♪Tits&Ass
HA HA HA HA!
!!
GUI (YANK)

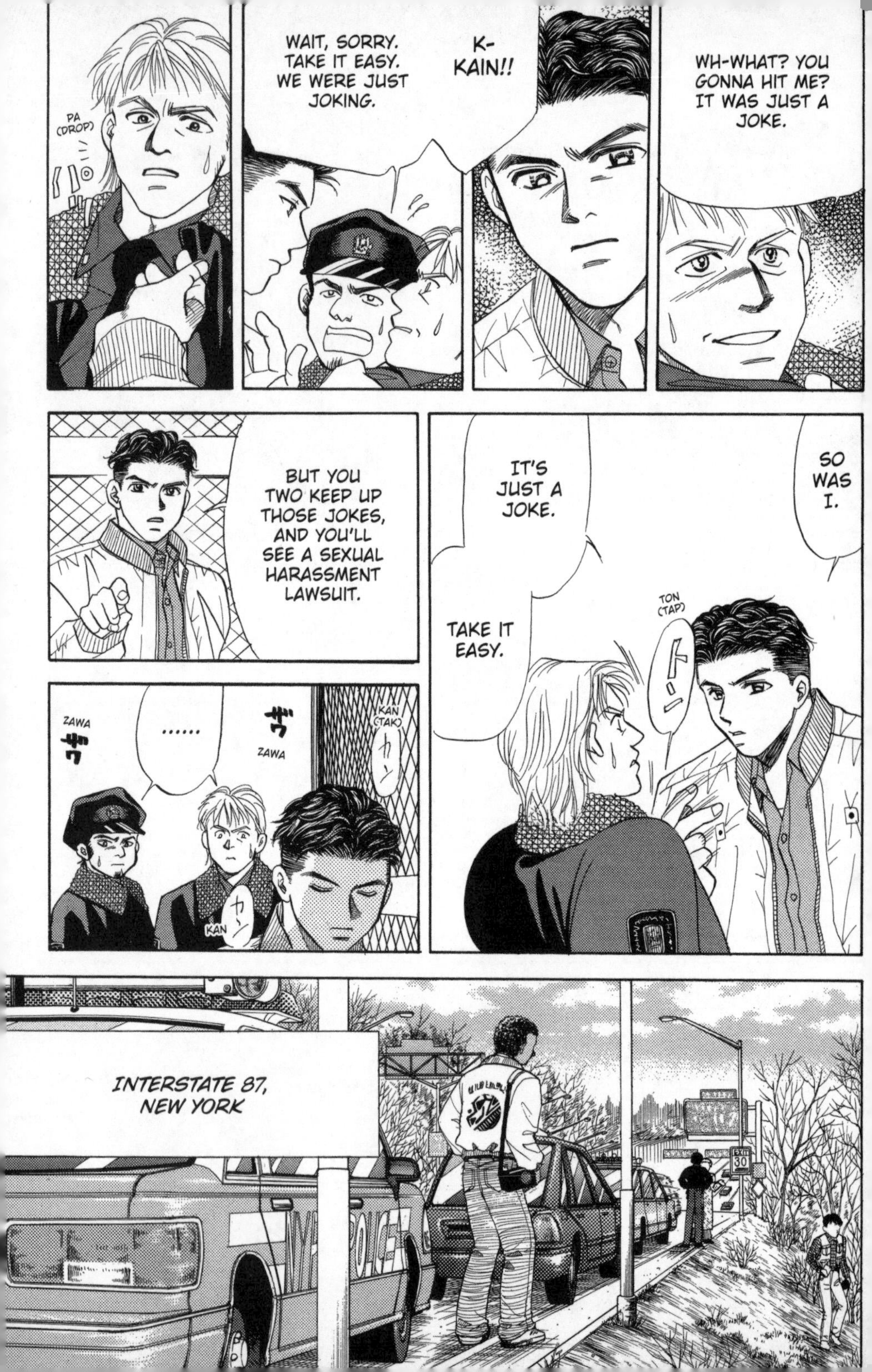
WH-WHAT? YOU GONNA HIT ME? IT WAS JUST A JOKE.
K-KAIN!!
WAIT, SORRY. TAKE IT EASY. WE WERE JUST JOKING.
PA (DROP)
SO WAS I.
IT'S JUST A JOKE.
TAKE IT EASY.
TON (TAP)
BUT YOU TWO KEEP UP THOSE JOKES, AND YOU'LL SEE A SEXUAL HARASSMENT LAWSUIT.
KAN (TAK)
ZAWA
......
ZAWA
KAN
INTERSTATE 87, NEW YORK

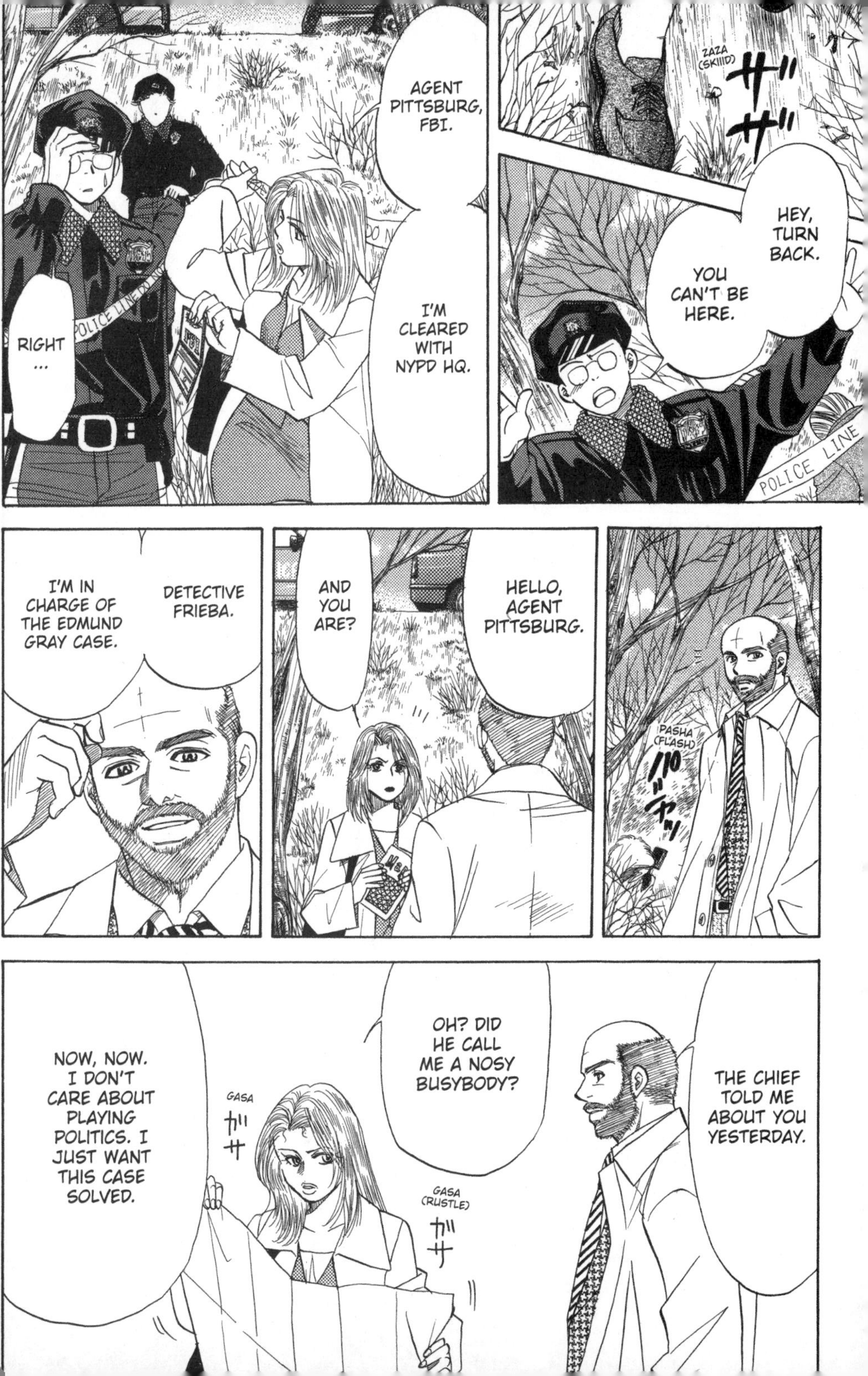
ZAZA (SKIIID)
HEY, TURN BACK.
YOU CAN'T BE HERE.
AGENT PITTSBURG, FBI.
I'M CLEARED WITH NYPD HQ.
RIGHT ...
PASHA (FLASH)
HELLO, AGENT PITTSBURG.
AND YOU ARE?
DETECTIVE FRIEBA.
I'M IN CHARGE OF THE EDMUND GRAY CASE.
THE CHIEF TOLD ME ABOUT YOU YESTERDAY.
OH? DID HE CALL ME A NOSY BUSYBODY?
GASA (RUSTLE)
GASA
NOW, NOW. I DON'T CARE ABOUT PLAYING POLITICS. I JUST WANT THIS CASE SOLVED.

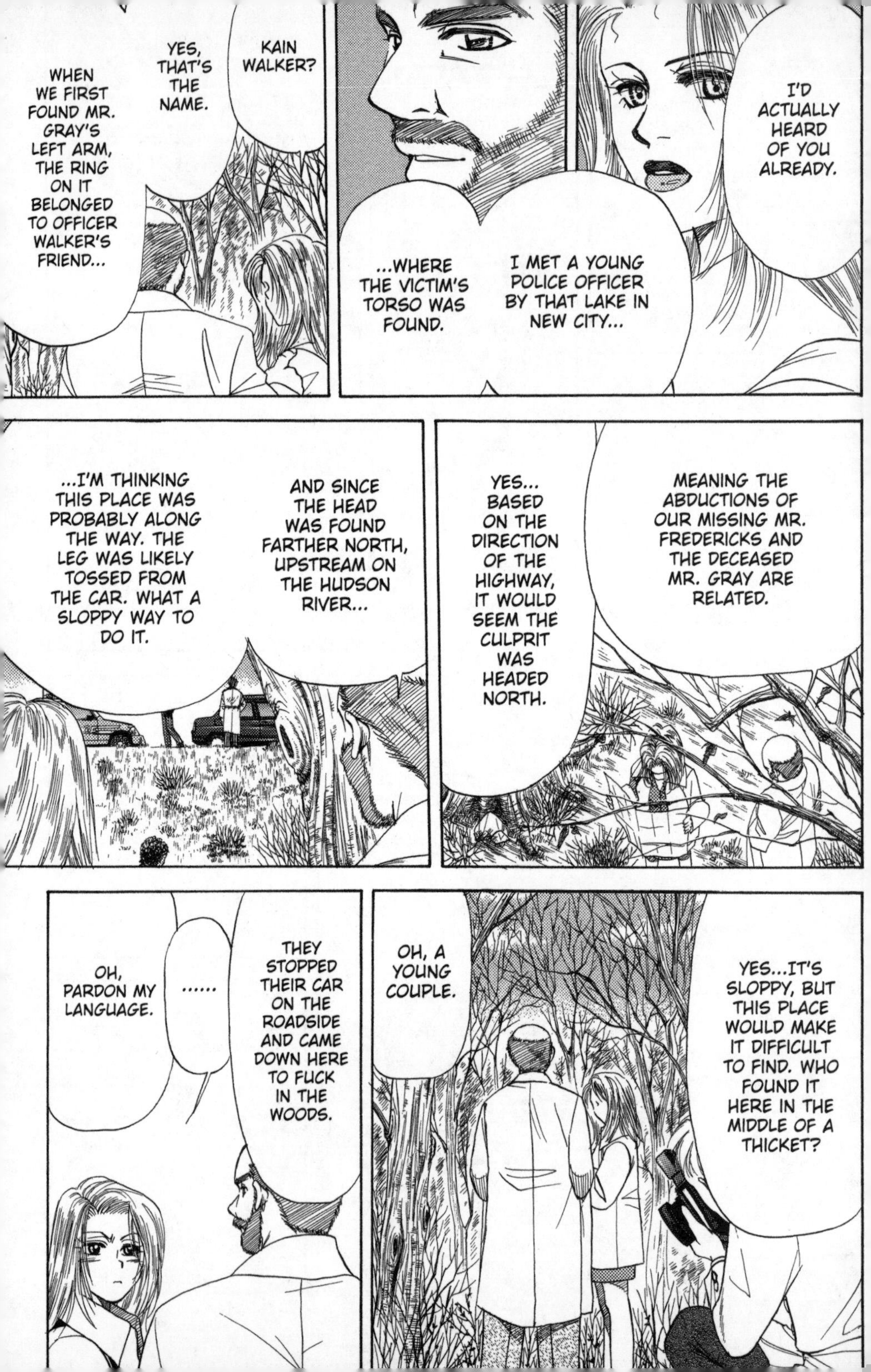
I'D ACTUALLY HEARD OF YOU ALREADY.
I MET A YOUNG POLICE OFFICER BY THAT LAKE IN NEW CITY...
...WHERE THE VICTIM'S TORSO WAS FOUND.
KAIN WALKER?
YES, THAT'S THE NAME.
WHEN WE FIRST FOUND MR. GRAY'S LEFT ARM, THE RING ON IT BELONGED TO OFFICER WALKER'S FRIEND...
MEANING THE ABDUCTIONS OF OUR MISSING MR. FREDERICKS AND THE DECEASED MR. GRAY ARE RELATED.
YES... BASED ON THE DIRECTION OF THE HIGHWAY, IT WOULD SEEM THE CULPRIT WAS HEADED NORTH.
AND SINCE THE HEAD WAS FOUND FARTHER NORTH, UPSTREAM ON THE HUDSON RIVER...
...I'M THINKING THIS PLACE WAS PROBABLY ALONG THE WAY. THE LEG WAS LIKELY TOSSED FROM THE CAR. WHAT A SLOPPY WAY TO DO IT.
YES...IT'S SLOPPY, BUT THIS PLACE WOULD MAKE IT DIFFICULT TO FIND. WHO FOUND IT HERE IN THE MIDDLE OF A THICKET?
OH, A YOUNG COUPLE.
THEY STOPPED THEIR CAR ON THE ROADSIDE AND CAME DOWN HERE TO FUCK IN THE WOODS.
......
OH, PARDON MY LANGUAGE.

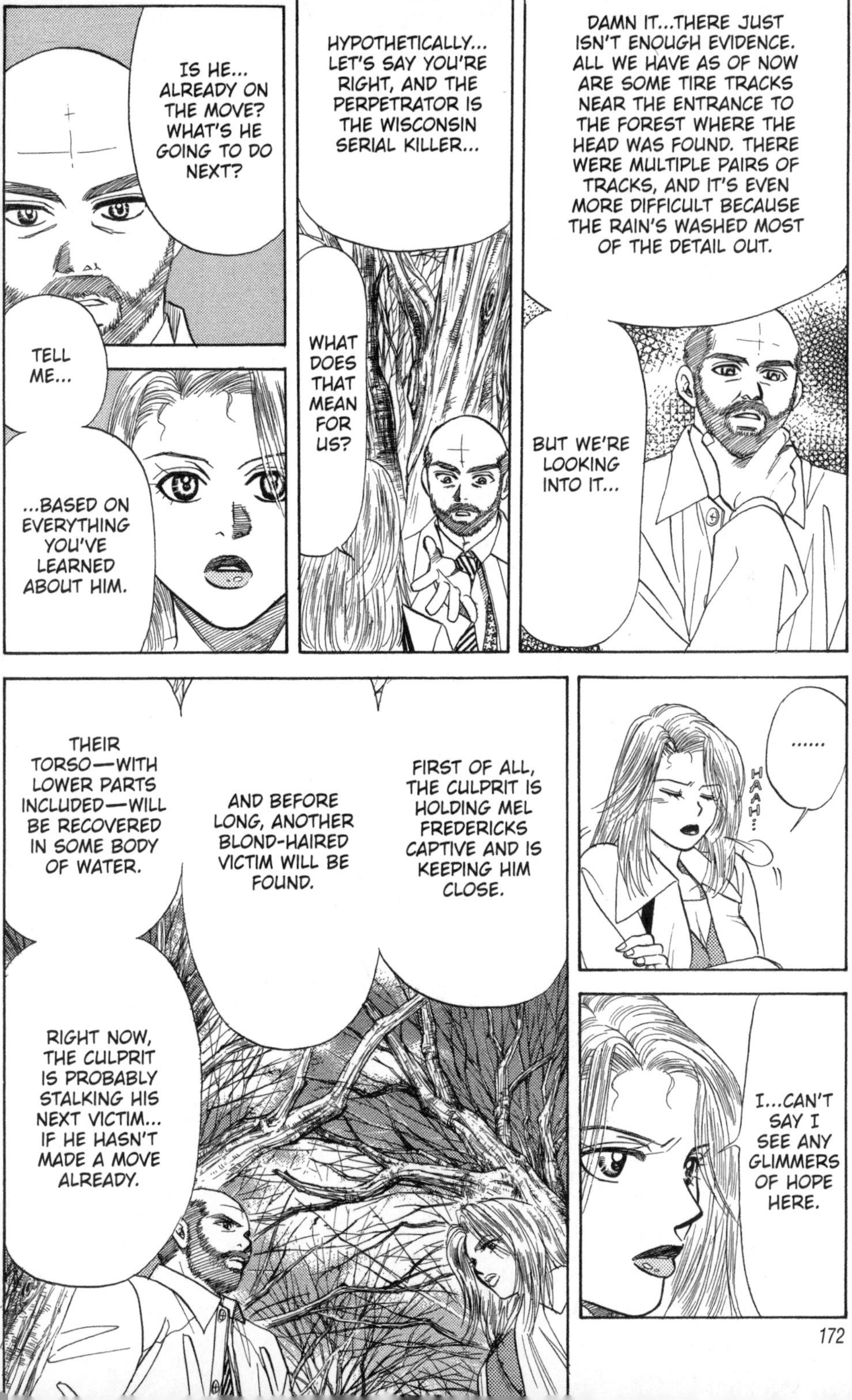
DAMN IT...THERE JUST ISN'T ENOUGH EVIDENCE. ALL WE HAVE AS OF NOW ARE SOME TIRE TRACKS NEAR THE ENTRANCE TO THE FOREST WHERE THE HEAD WAS FOUND. THERE WERE MULTIPLE PAIRS OF TRACKS, AND IT'S EVEN MORE DIFFICULT BECAUSE THE RAIN'S WASHED MOST OF THE DETAIL OUT.
BUT WE'RE LOOKING INTO IT...
HYPOTHETICALLY... LET'S SAY YOU'RE RIGHT, AND THE PERPETRATOR IS THE WISCONSIN SERIAL KILLER...
WHAT DOES THAT MEAN FOR US?
IS HE... ALREADY ON THE MOVE? WHAT'S HE GOING TO DO NEXT?
TELL ME...
...BASED ON EVERYTHING YOU'VE LEARNED ABOUT HIM.
......
HAAH...
I...CAN'T SAY I SEE ANY GLIMMERS OF HOPE HERE.
FIRST OF ALL, THE CULPRIT IS HOLDING MEL FREDERICKS CAPTIVE AND IS KEEPING HIM CLOSE.
AND BEFORE LONG, ANOTHER BLOND-HAIRED VICTIM WILL BE FOUND.
THEIR TORSO—WITH LOWER PARTS INCLUDED—WILL BE RECOVERED IN SOME BODY OF WATER.
RIGHT NOW, THE CULPRIT IS PROBABLY STALKING HIS NEXT VICTIM... IF HE HASN'T MADE A MOVE ALREADY.

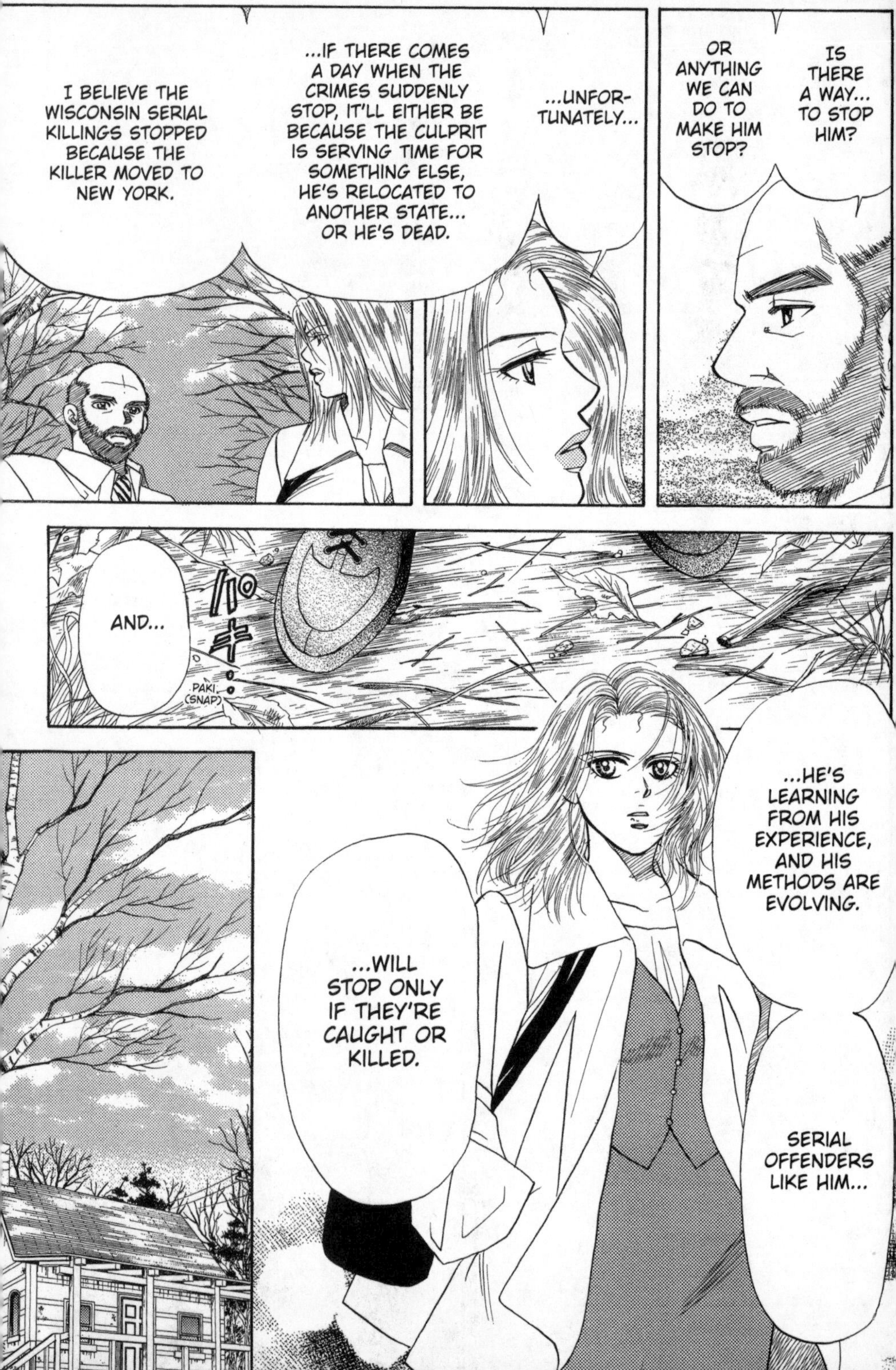
IS THERE A WAY... TO STOP HIM?
OR ANYTHING WE CAN DO TO MAKE HIM STOP?
...UNFOR-TUNATELY...
...IF THERE COMES A DAY WHEN THE CRIMES SUDDENLY STOP, IT'LL EITHER BE BECAUSE THE CULPRIT IS SERVING TIME FOR SOMETHING ELSE, HE'S RELOCATED TO ANOTHER STATE... OR HE'S DEAD.
I BELIEVE THE WISCONSIN SERIAL KILLINGS STOPPED BECAUSE THE KILLER MOVED TO NEW YORK.
パキ
PAKI (SNAP)
AND...
...HE'S LEARNING FROM HIS EXPERIENCE, AND HIS METHODS ARE EVOLVING.
SERIAL OFFENDERS LIKE HIM...
...WILL STOP ONLY IF THEY'RE CAUGHT OR KILLED.

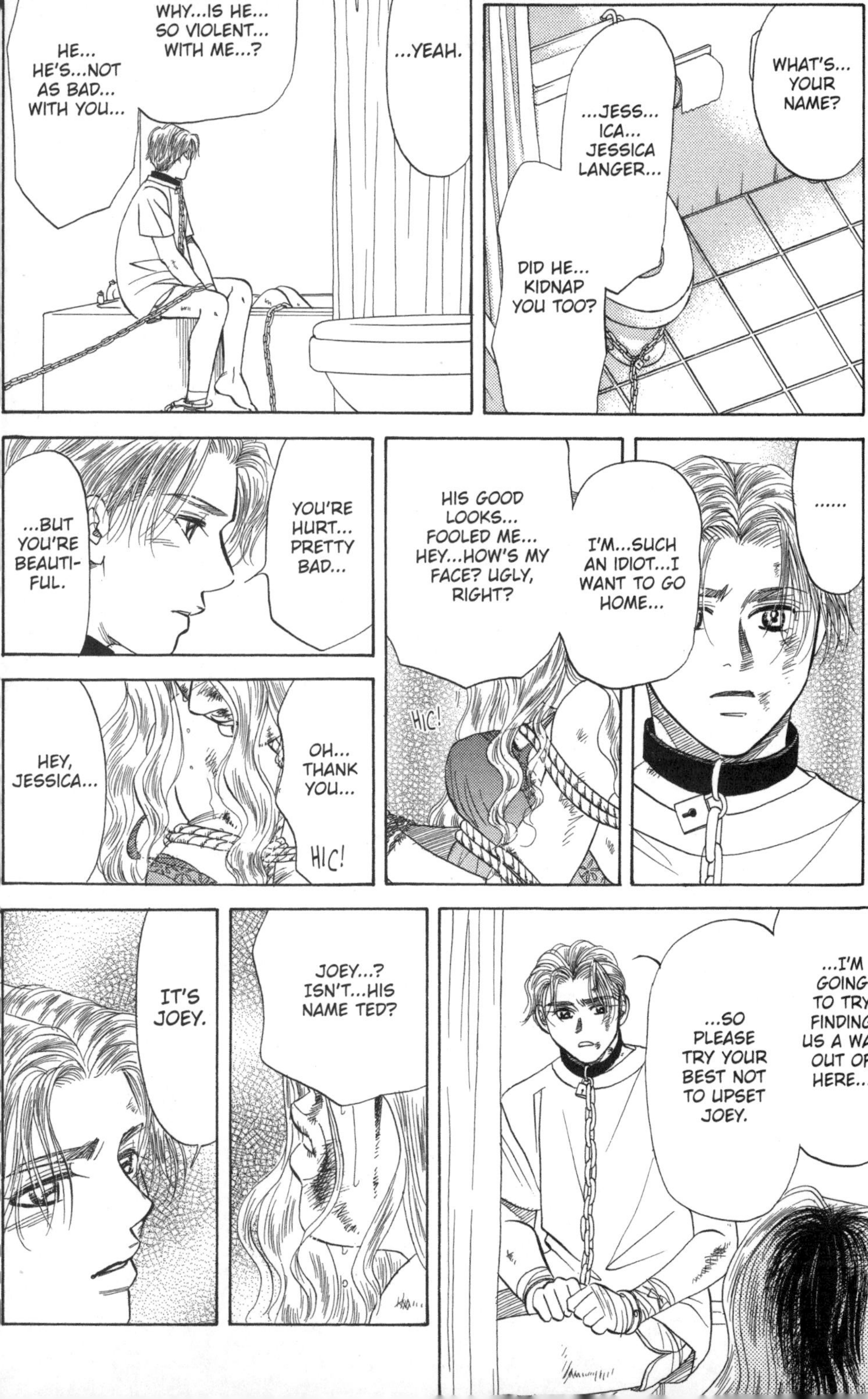
WHAT'S... YOUR NAME?
...JESS... ICA... JESSICA LANGER...
DID HE... KIDNAP YOU TOO?
...YEAH.
WHY...IS HE... SO VIOLENT... WITH ME...?
HE... HE'S...NOT AS BAD... WITH YOU...
......
I'M...SUCH AN IDIOT...I WANT TO GO HOME...
HIS GOOD LOOKS... FOOLED ME... HEY...HOW'S MY FACE? UGLY, RIGHT?
HIC!
YOU'RE HURT... PRETTY BAD...
...BUT YOU'RE BEAUTI-FUL.
OH... THANK YOU...
HIC!
HEY, JESSICA...
...I'M GOING TO TRY FINDING US A WAY OUT OF HERE...
...SO PLEASE TRY YOUR BEST NOT TO UPSET JOEY.
JOEY...? ISN'T...HIS NAME TED?
IT'S JOEY.

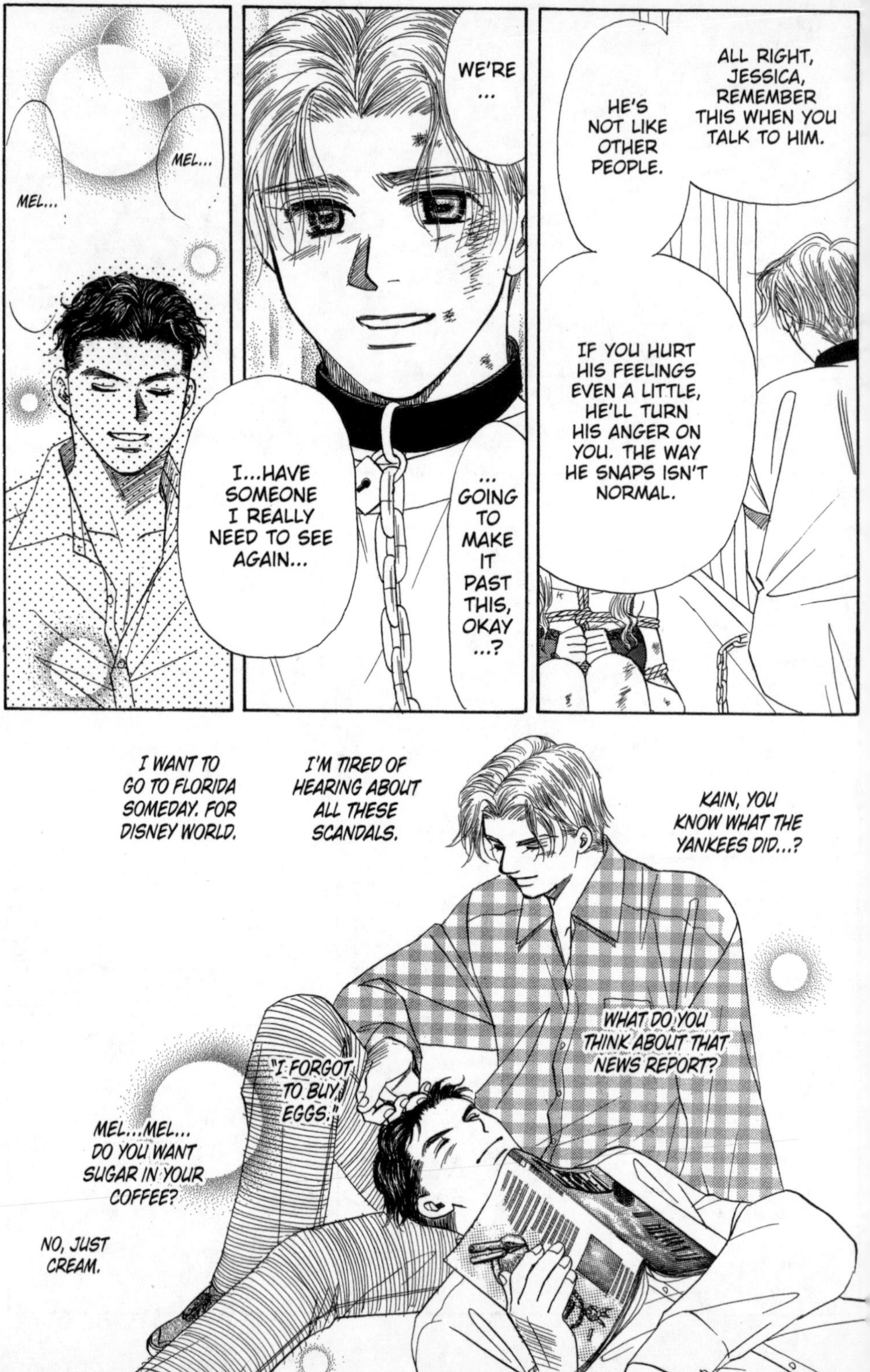
ALL RIGHT, JESSICA, REMEMBER THIS WHEN YOU TALK TO HIM.
HE'S NOT LIKE OTHER PEOPLE.
IF YOU HURT HIS FEELINGS EVEN A LITTLE, HE'LL TURN HIS ANGER ON YOU. THE WAY HE SNAPS ISN'T NORMAL.
WE'RE ...
... GOING TO MAKE IT PAST THIS, OKAY ...?
I...HAVE SOMEONE I REALLY NEED TO SEE AGAIN...
MEL...
MEL...
KAIN, YOU KNOW WHAT THE YANKEES DID...?
I'M TIRED OF HEARING ABOUT ALL THESE SCANDALS.
I WANT TO GO TO FLORIDA SOMEDAY. FOR DISNEY WORLD.
WHAT DO YOU THINK ABOUT THAT NEWS REPORT?
"I FORGOT TO BUY EGGS."
MEL...MEL... DO YOU WANT SUGAR IN YOUR COFFEE?
NO, JUST CREAM.

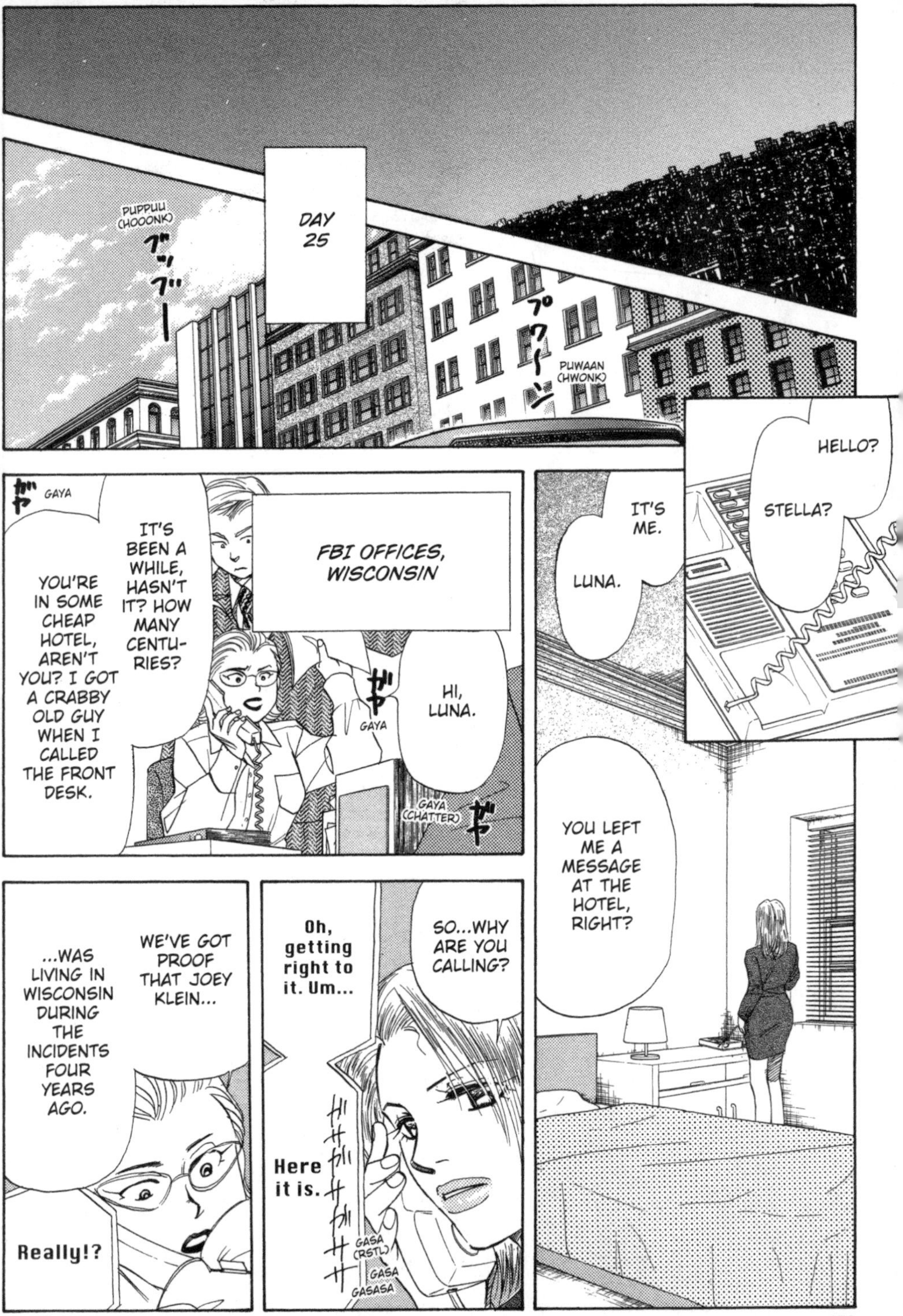
DAY 25
PUWAAN (HWONK)
プワーン
PUPPUU (HOOONK)
ブッブー
HELLO?
STELLA?
IT'S ME.
LUNA.
YOU LEFT ME A MESSAGE AT THE HOTEL, RIGHT?
FBI OFFICES, WISCONSIN
HI, LUNA.
ガヤ
GAYA
IT'S BEEN A WHILE, HASN'T IT? HOW MANY CENTURIES?
ガヤ
GAYA
YOU'RE IN SOME CHEAP HOTEL, AREN'T YOU? I GOT A CRABBY OLD GUY WHEN I CALLED THE FRONT DESK.
ガヤ
GAYA (CHATTER)
SO...WHY ARE YOU CALLING?
Oh, getting right to it. Um...
Here it is.
GASA (RSTL) GASA GASASA
WE'VE GOT PROOF THAT JOEY KLEIN...
...WAS LIVING IN WISCONSIN DURING THE INCIDENTS FOUR YEARS AGO.
Really!?

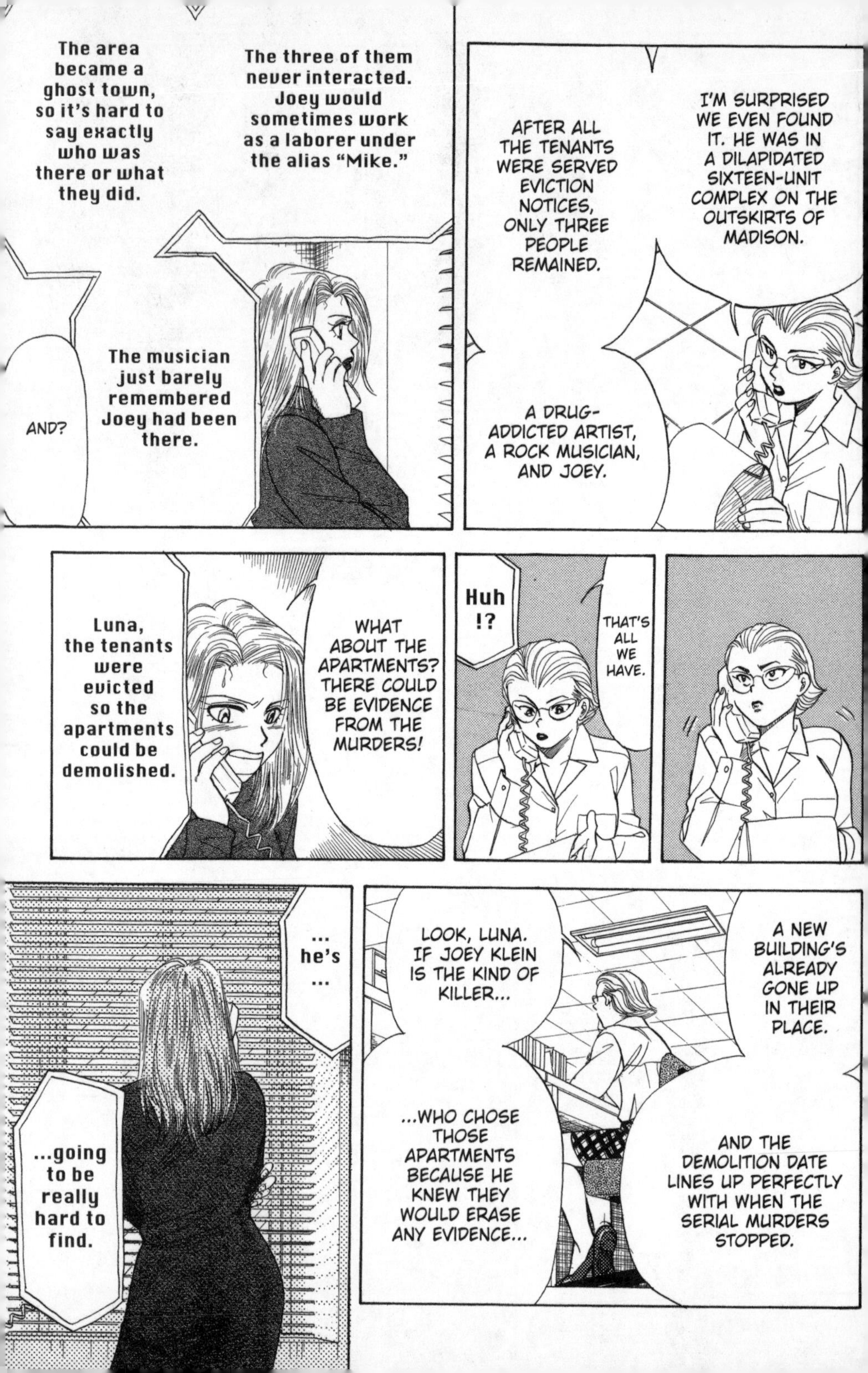
I'M SURPRISED WE EVEN FOUND IT. HE WAS IN A DILAPIDATED SIXTEEN-UNIT COMPLEX ON THE OUTSKIRTS OF MADISON.
AFTER ALL THE TENANTS WERE SERVED EVICTION NOTICES, ONLY THREE PEOPLE REMAINED.
A DRUG-ADDICTED ARTIST, A ROCK MUSICIAN, AND JOEY.
The three of them never interacted. Joey would sometimes work as a laborer under the alias "Mike."
The area became a ghost town, so it's hard to say exactly who was there or what they did.
The musician just barely remembered Joey had been there.
AND?
THAT'S ALL WE HAVE.
Huh !?
WHAT ABOUT THE APARTMENTS? THERE COULD BE EVIDENCE FROM THE MURDERS!
Luna, the tenants were evicted so the apartments could be demolished.
A NEW BUILDING'S ALREADY GONE UP IN THEIR PLACE.
LOOK, LUNA. IF JOEY KLEIN IS THE KIND OF KILLER...
AND THE DEMOLITION DATE LINES UP PERFECTLY WITH WHEN THE SERIAL MURDERS STOPPED.
...WHO CHOSE THOSE APARTMENTS BECAUSE HE KNEW THEY WOULD ERASE ANY EVIDENCE...
... he's ...
...going to be really hard to find.

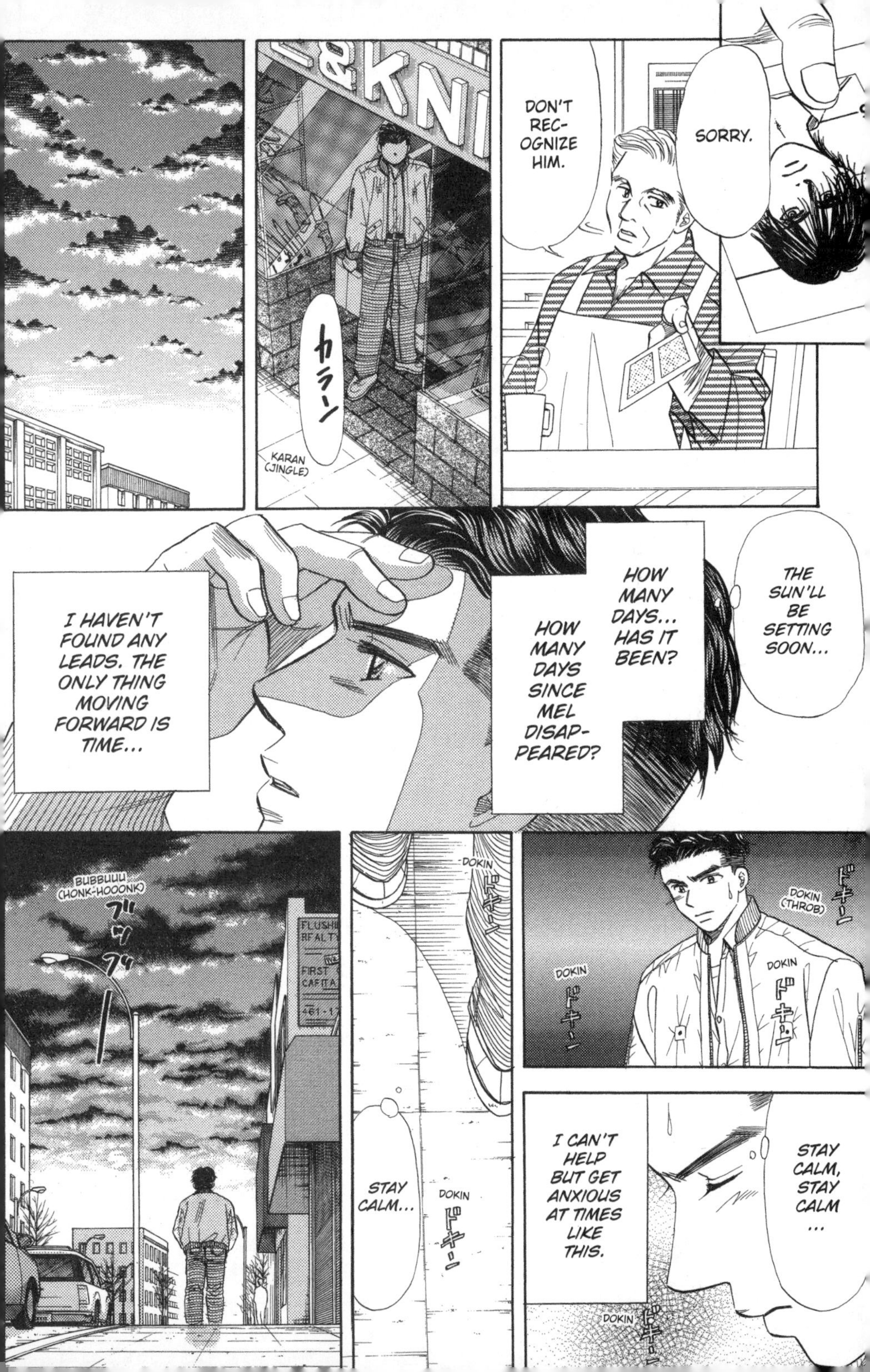
SORRY.
DON'T RECOGNIZE HIM.
カラーン
KARAN (JINGLE)
THE SUN'LL BE SETTING SOON...
HOW MANY DAYS... HAS IT BEEN?
HOW MANY DAYS SINCE MEL DISAPPEARED?
I HAVEN'T FOUND ANY LEADS. THE ONLY THING MOVING FORWARD IS TIME...
ドキー
DOKIN (THROB)
DOKIN
ドキー
DOKIN
ドキー
STAY CALM, STAY CALM...
I CAN'T HELP BUT GET ANXIOUS AT TIMES LIKE THIS.
DOKIN
ドキー
DOKIN
ドキー
STAY CALM...
DOKIN
ドキー
BUBBUUU (HONK-HOOONK)
ブッブー

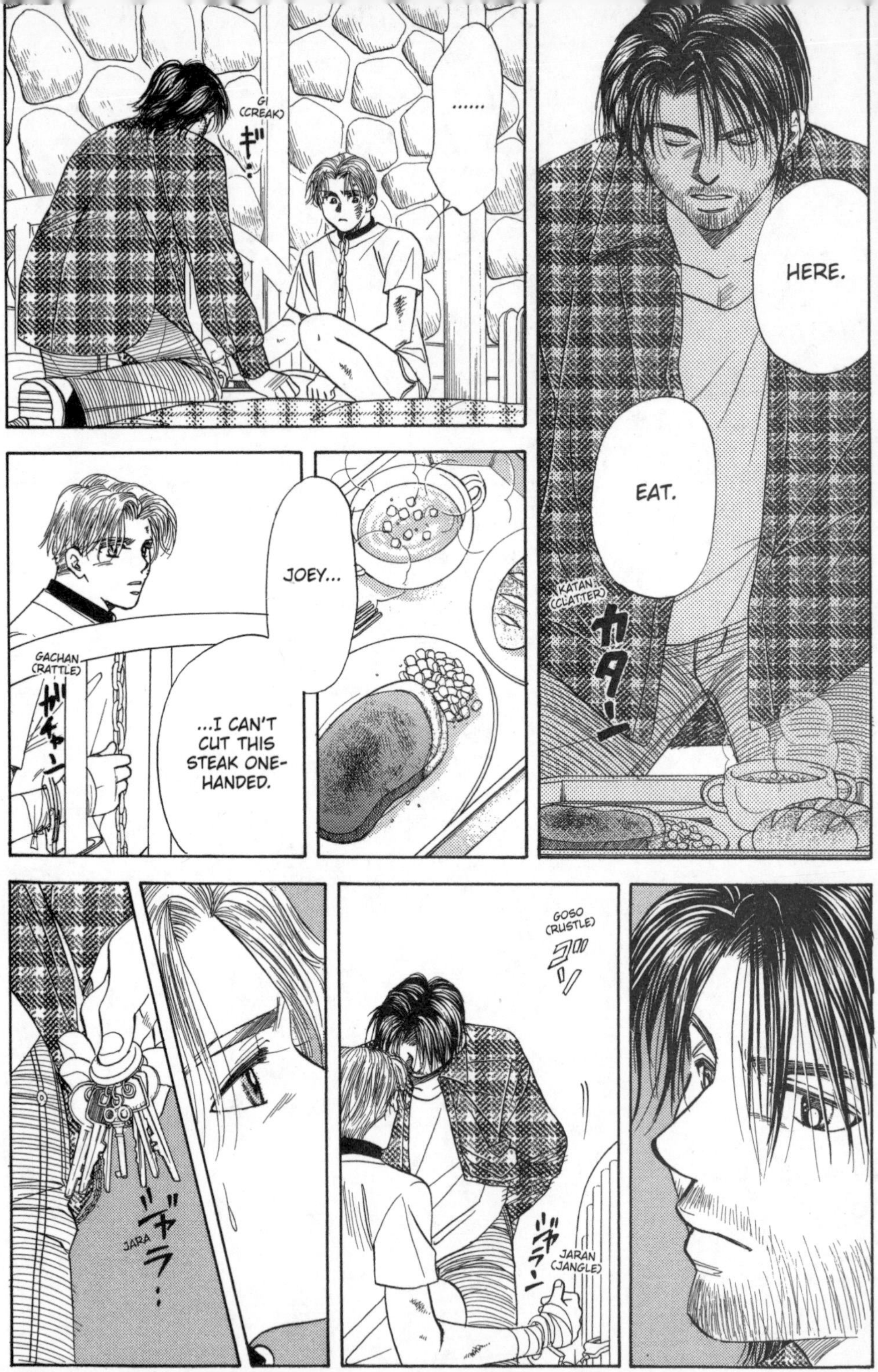

HERE.
EAT.
KATAN (CLATTER)
カターン
......
GI (CREAK)
ギ
JOEY...
...I CAN'T CUT THIS STEAK ONE-HANDED.
GACHAN (RATTLE)
ガチャン
GOSO (RUSTLE)
ゴソ
JARAN (JANGLE)
ジャラーン
JARA
ジャラ

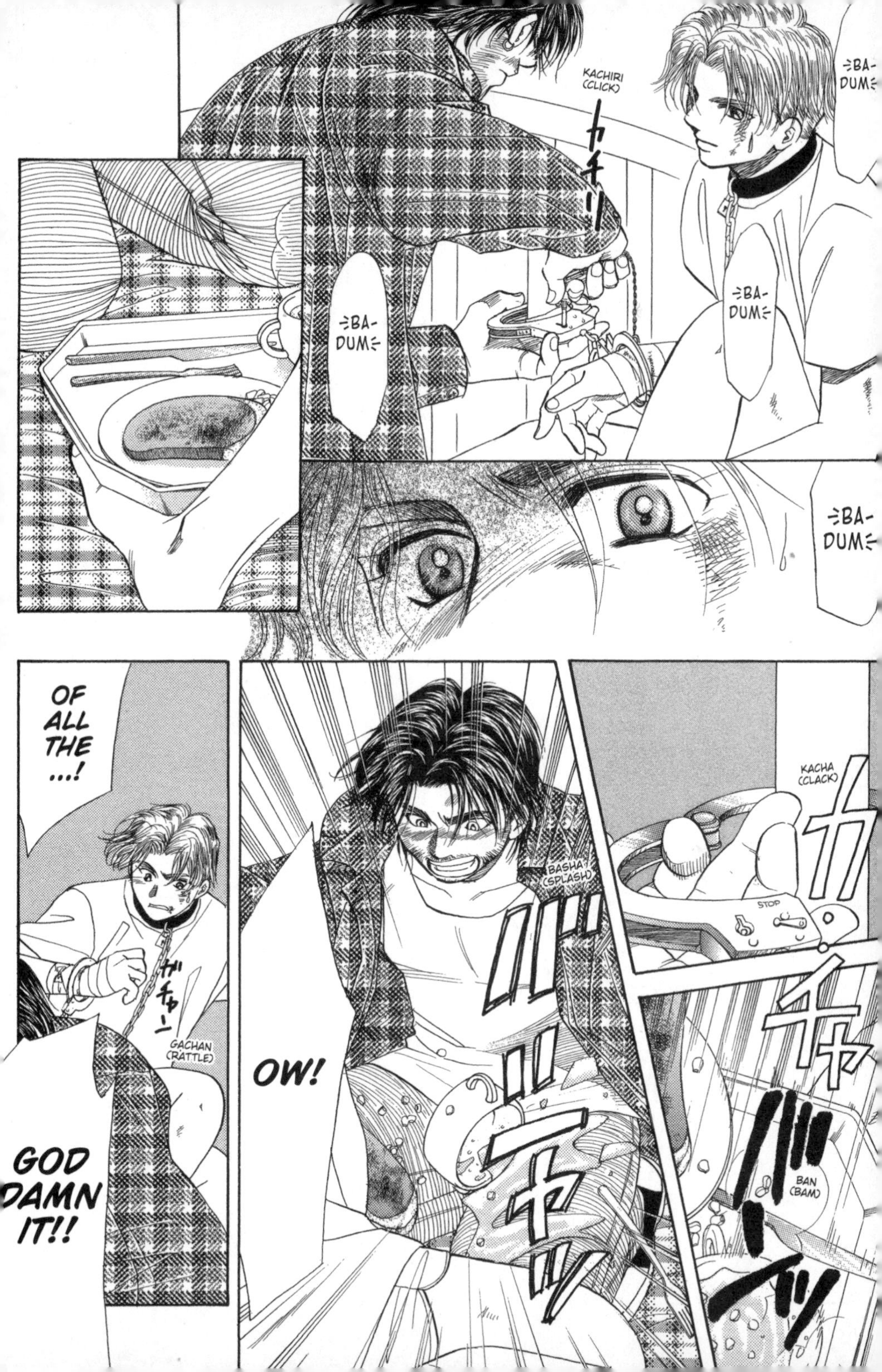
=BA-DUM=
KACHIRI (CLICK)
カチー
=BA-DUM=
=BA-DUM=
=BA-DUM=
KACHA (CLICK)
カチャ
STOP
BAN (BAM)
BASHA (SPLASH)
OW!
OF ALL THE ...!
ガチャン
GACHAN (RATTLE)
GOD DAMN IT!!

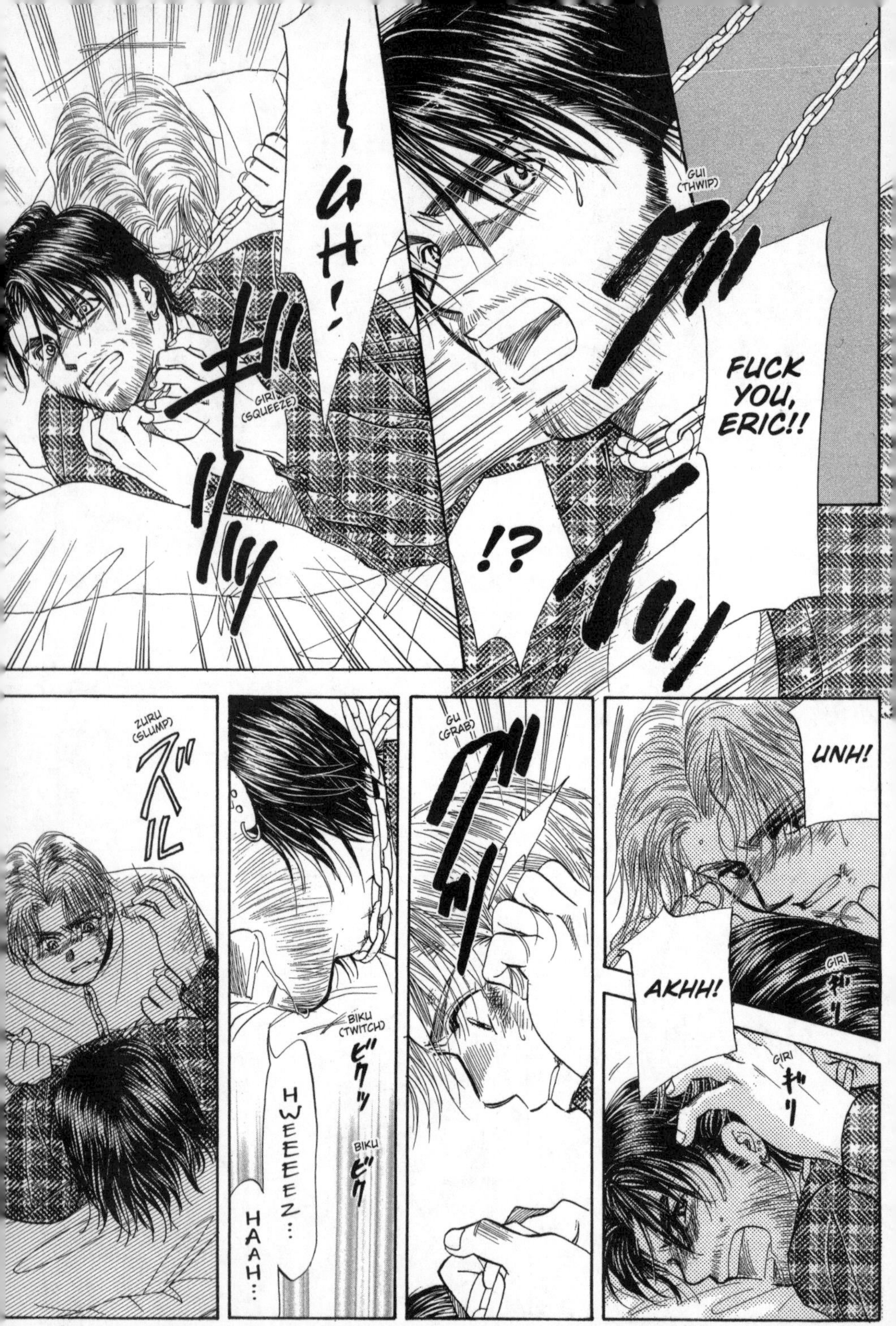
GUI (THWIP)
グイッ
FUCK YOU, ERIC!!
!?
...UGH!!
GIRI (SQUEEZE)
ギリッ
UNH!
GIRI
ギリ
AKHH!
GIRI
ギリ
GU (GRAB)
グッ
BIKU (TWITCH)
ビクッ
BIKU
ビク
HWEEEEZ...
HAAAH...
ZURU (SLUMP)
ズル

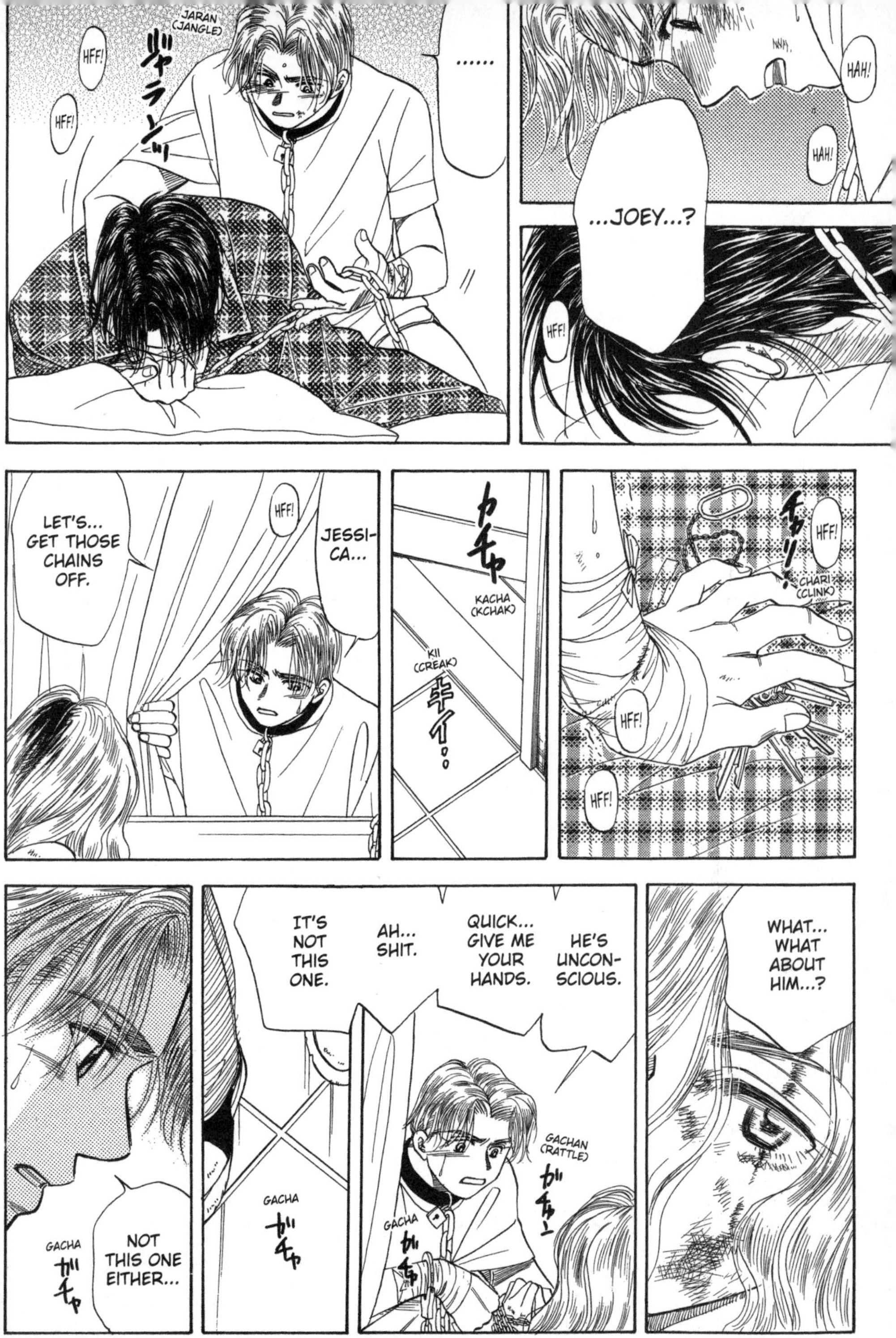
HAH!
HAH!
...JOEY...?
HFF!
......
JARAN (JANGLE)
HFF!
HFF!
CHARI (CLINK)
HFF!
HFF!
HFF!
KACHA (KCHAK)
KII (CREAK)
JESSI-CA...
HFF!
LET'S... GET THOSE CHAINS OFF.
WHAT... WHAT ABOUT HIM...?
HE'S UNCON-SCIOUS.
QUICK... GIVE ME YOUR HANDS.
AH... SHIT.
IT'S NOT THIS ONE.
GACHAN (RATTLE)
GACHA
GACHA
NOT THIS ONE EITHER...
GACHA

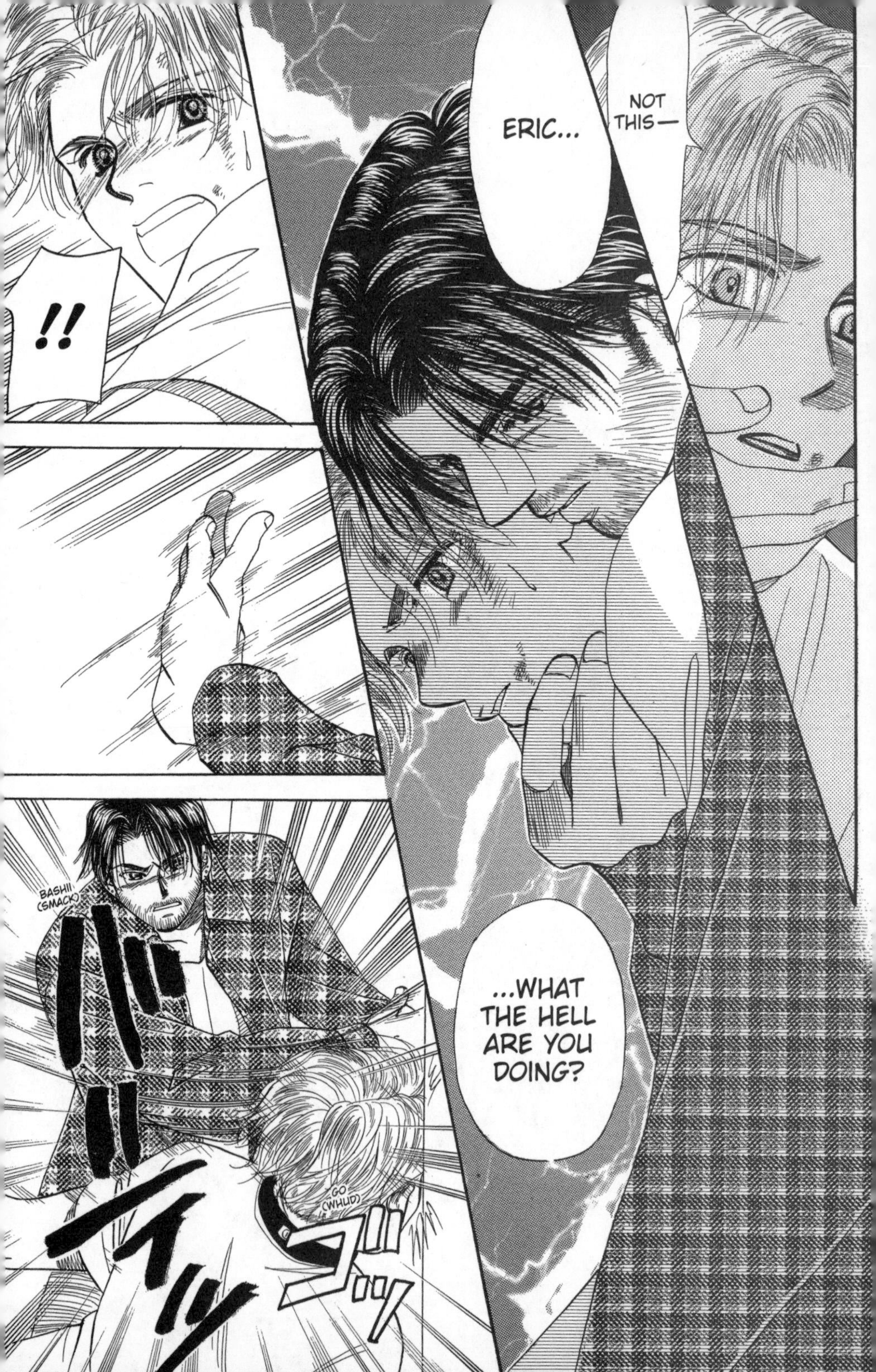
ERIC...
NOT THIS—
...WHAT THE HELL ARE YOU DOING?
!!
BASHI (SMACK)
GO (WHUD)

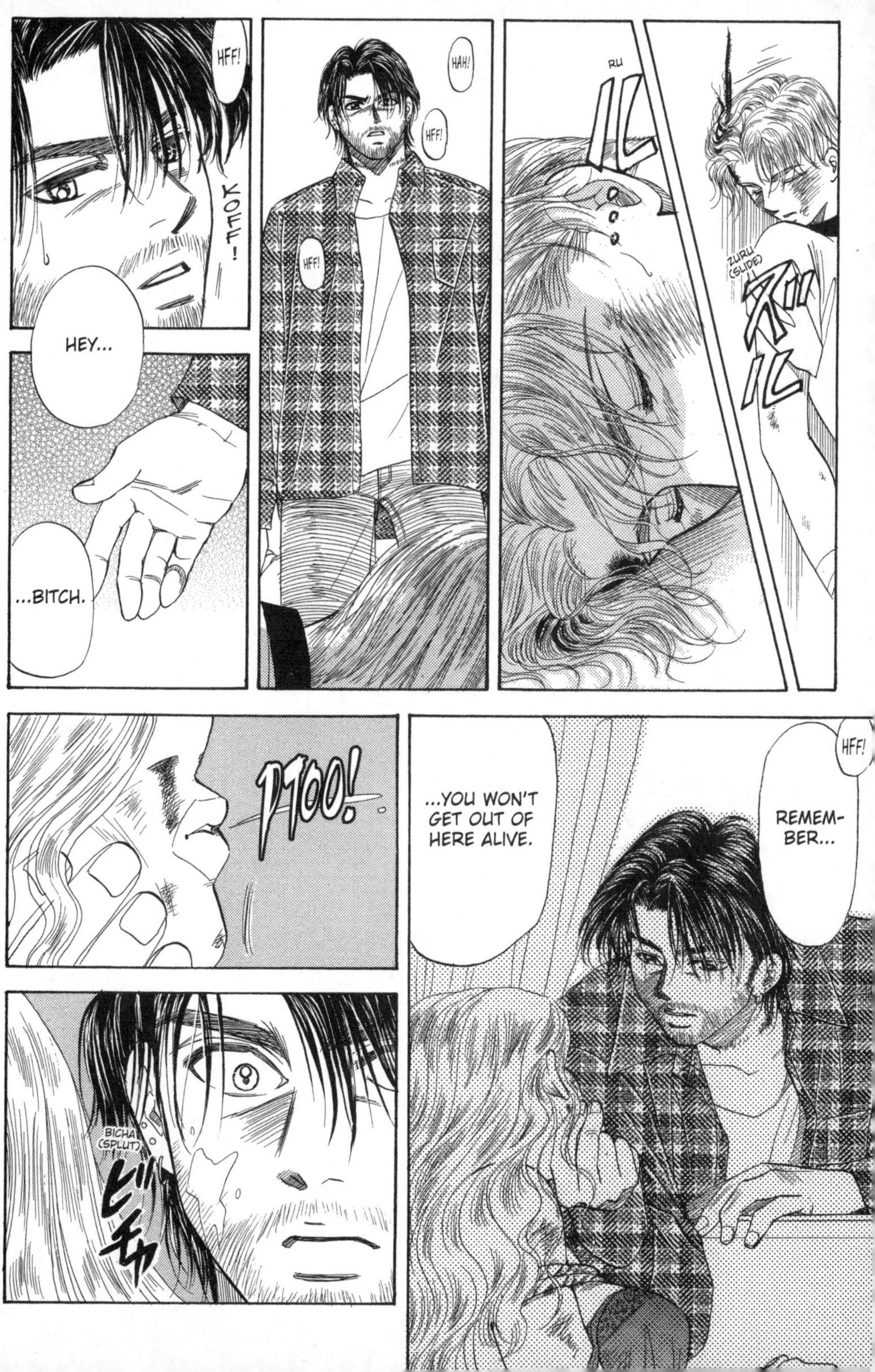
ZURU (SLIDE)
RU
HAH!
HFF!
HFF!
HFF!
KOFF!
HEY...
...BITCH.
HFF!
REMEM-BER...
...YOU WON'T GET OUT OF HERE ALIVE.
PTOO!
BICHA (SPLUT)

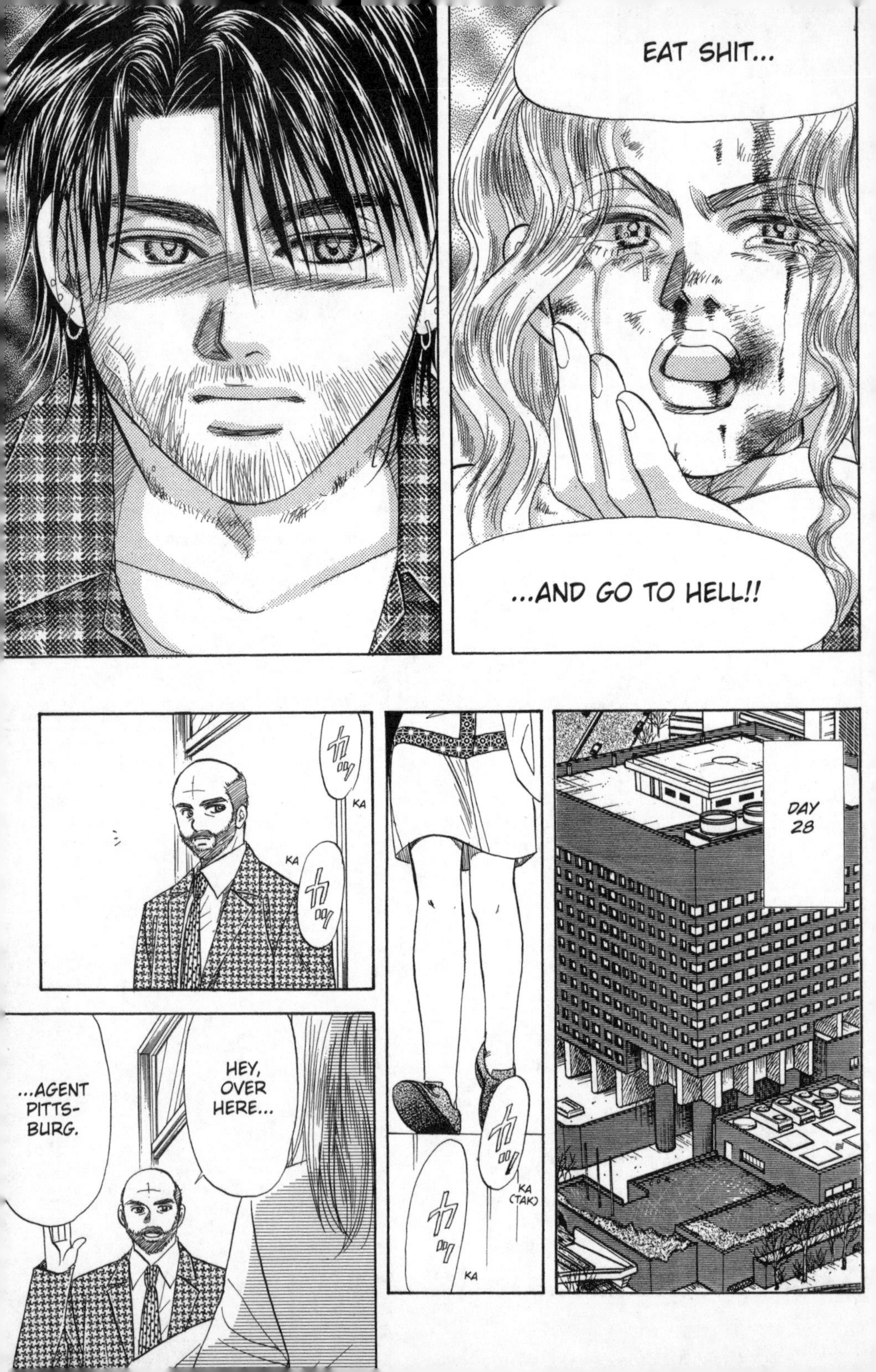
EAT SHIT...
...AND GO TO HELL!!
DAY 28
カッ
KA (TAK)
カッ
KA
カッ
KA
カッ
KA
HEY, OVER HERE...
...AGENT PITTS-BURG.

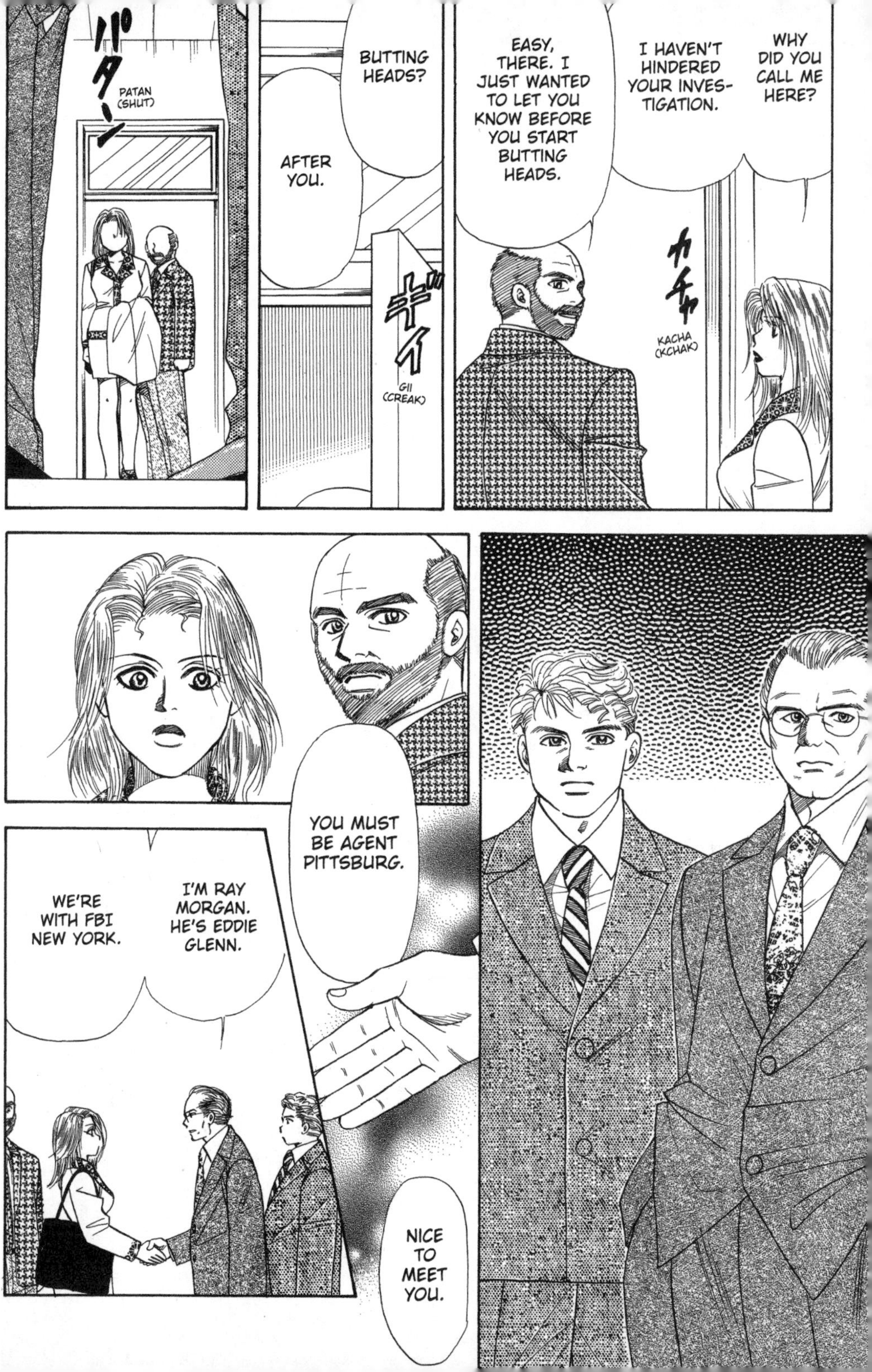
WHY DID YOU CALL ME HERE?
I HAVEN'T HINDERED YOUR INVES-TIGATION.
EASY, THERE. I JUST WANTED TO LET YOU KNOW BEFORE YOU START BUTTING HEADS.
カチャ
KACHA (KCHAK)
BUTTING HEADS?
AFTER YOU.
ギィ
GII (CREAK)
パタン
PATAN (SHUT)
YOU MUST BE AGENT PITTSBURG.
I'M RAY MORGAN. HE'S EDDIE GLENN.
WE'RE WITH FBI NEW YORK.
NICE TO MEET YOU.

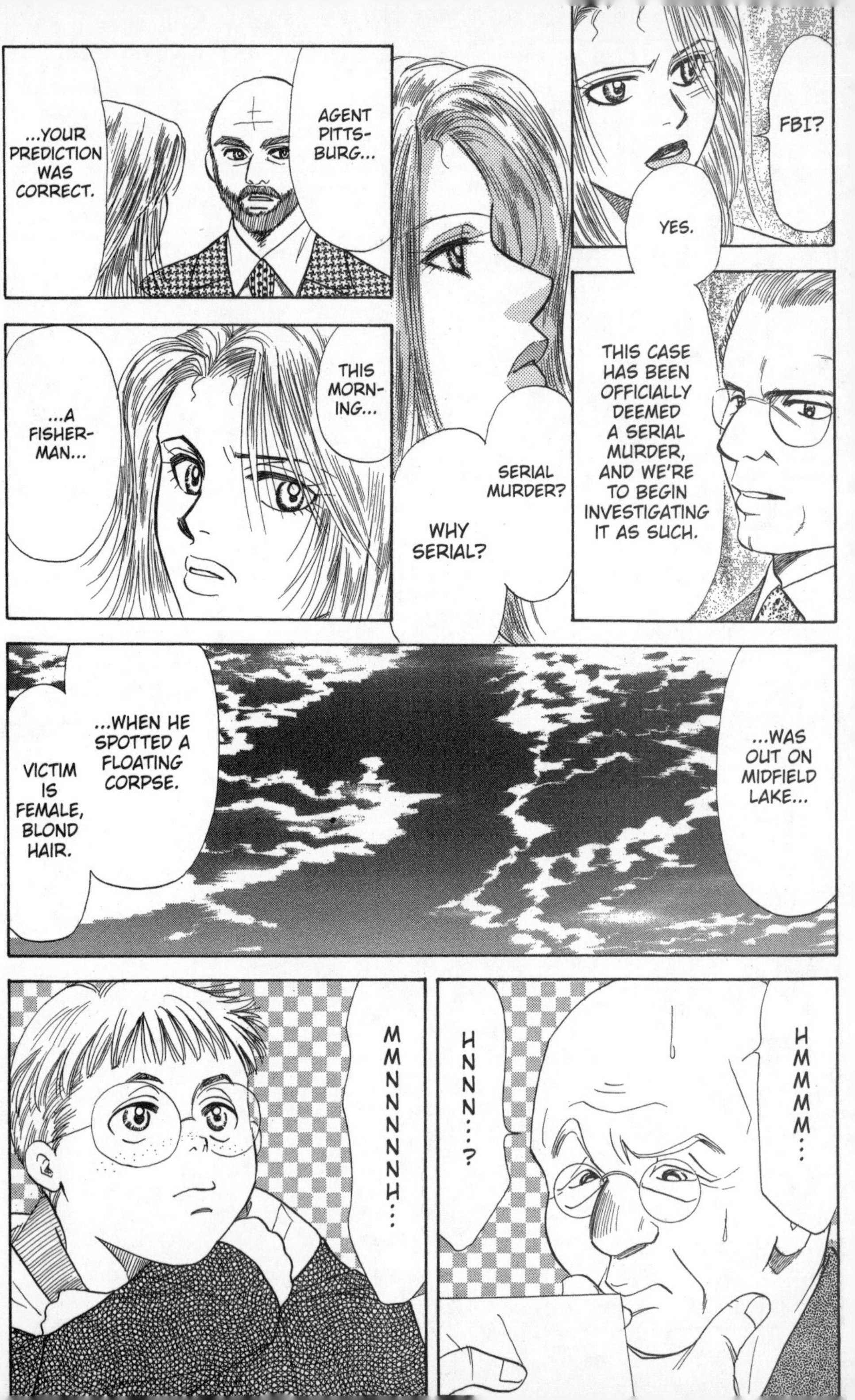
FBI?
YES.
THIS CASE HAS BEEN OFFICIALLY DEEMED A SERIAL MURDER, AND WE'RE TO BEGIN INVESTIGATING IT AS SUCH.
SERIAL MURDER?
WHY SERIAL?
AGENT PITTS-BURG...
...YOUR PREDICTION WAS CORRECT.
THIS MORN-ING...
...A FISHER-MAN...
...WAS OUT ON MIDFIELD LAKE...
...WHEN HE SPOTTED A FLOATING CORPSE.
VICTIM IS FEMALE, BLOND HAIR.
HMMMM...
HNNN...?
MNNNNNNH...

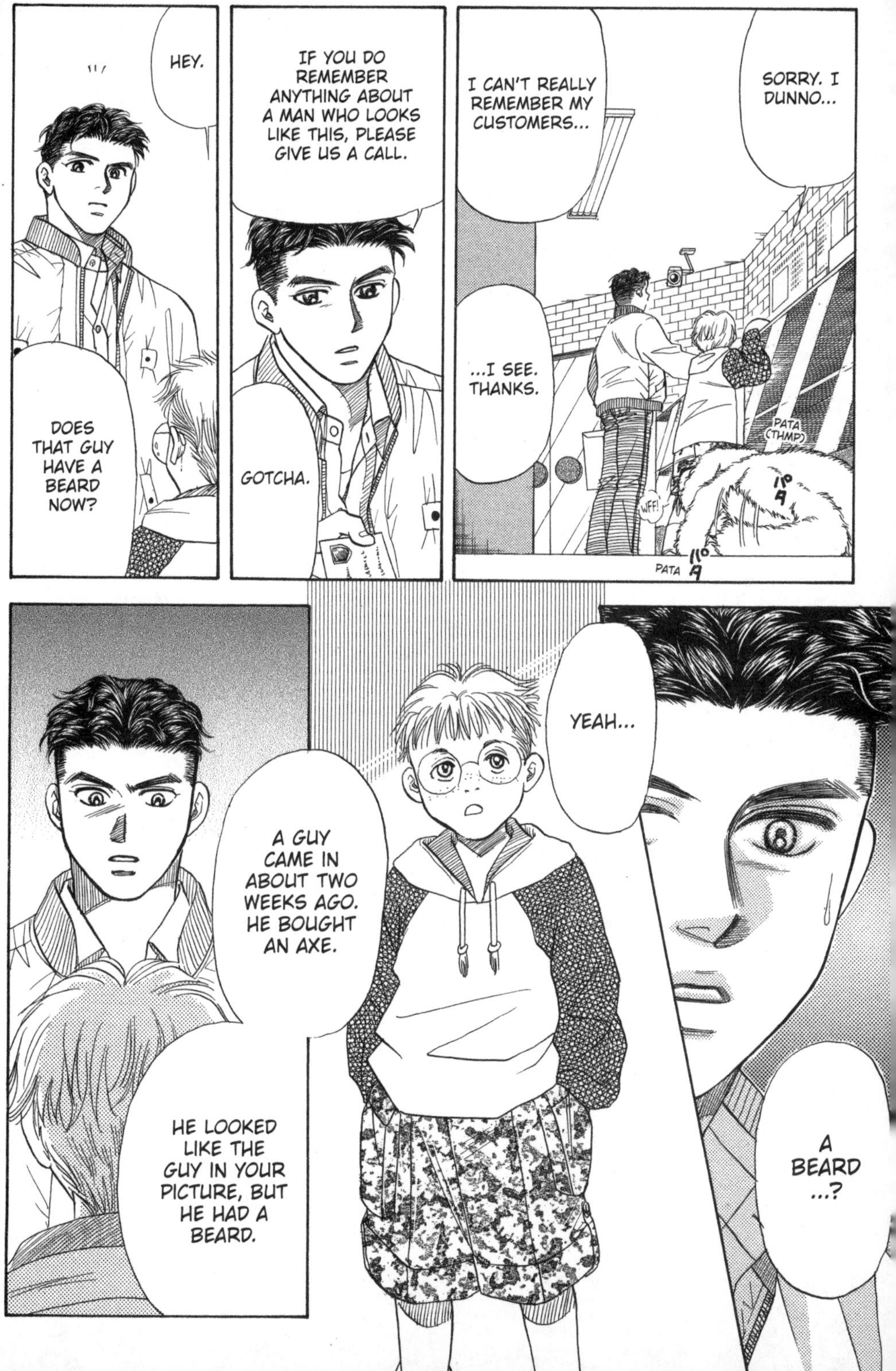
SORRY. I DUNNO...
I CAN'T REALLY REMEMBER MY CUSTOMERS...
...I SEE. THANKS.
PATA (THMP)
WFF!
PATA
IF YOU DO REMEMBER ANYTHING ABOUT A MAN WHO LOOKS LIKE THIS, PLEASE GIVE US A CALL.
GOTCHA.
HEY.
DOES THAT GUY HAVE A BEARD NOW?
YEAH...
A BEARD ...?
A GUY CAME IN ABOUT TWO WEEKS AGO. HE BOUGHT AN AXE.
HE LOOKED LIKE THE GUY IN YOUR PICTURE, BUT HE HAD A BEARD.

EPISODE IV

SCENE 5

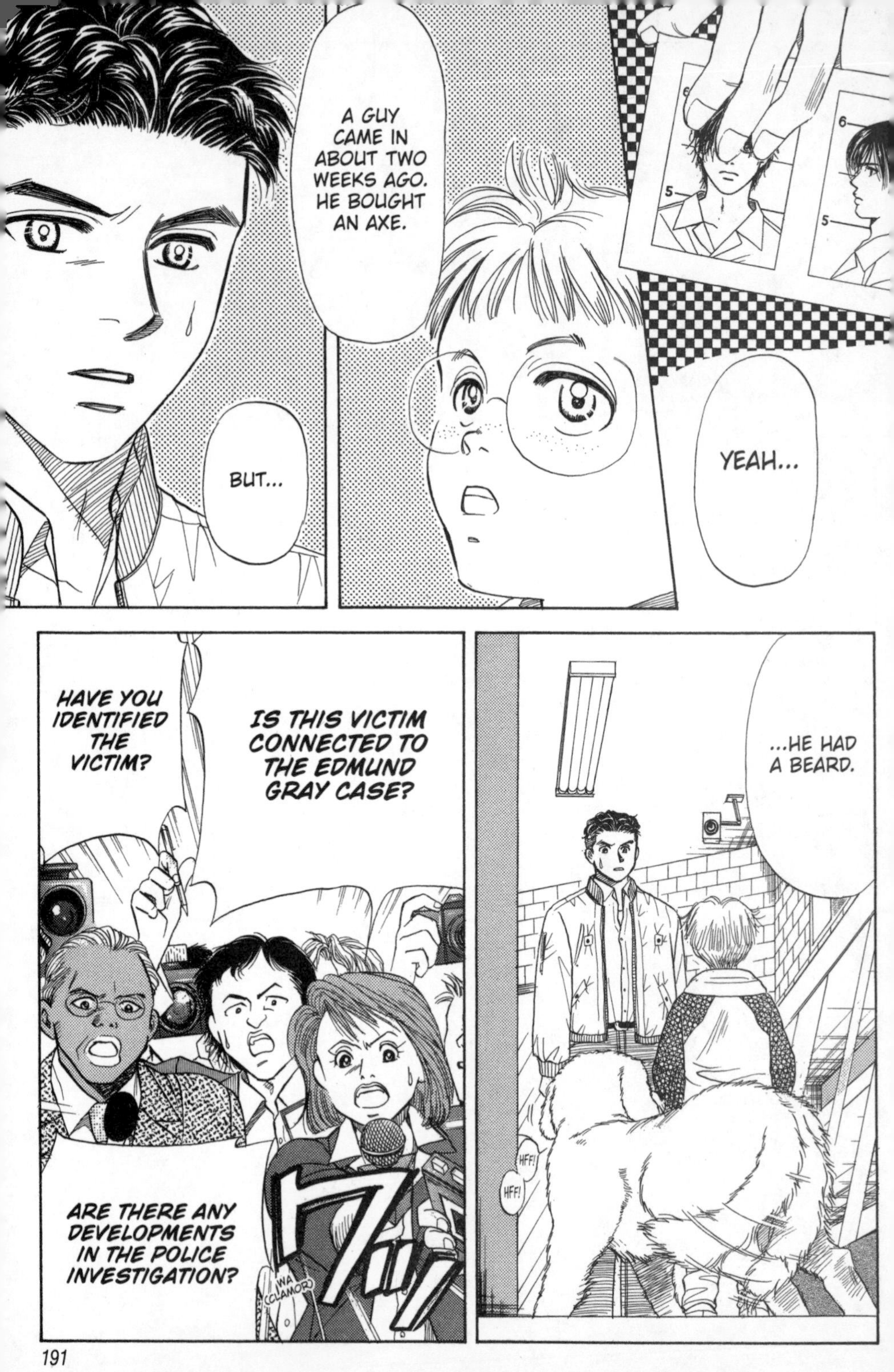
YEAH...
A GUY CAME IN ABOUT TWO WEEKS AGO. HE BOUGHT AN AXE.
BUT...
...HE HAD A BEARD.
HFF!
HFF!
IS THIS VICTIM CONNECTED TO THE EDMUND GRAY CASE?
HAVE YOU IDENTIFIED THE VICTIM?
ARE THERE ANY DEVELOPMENTS IN THE POLICE INVESTIGATION?
WA (CLAMOR)

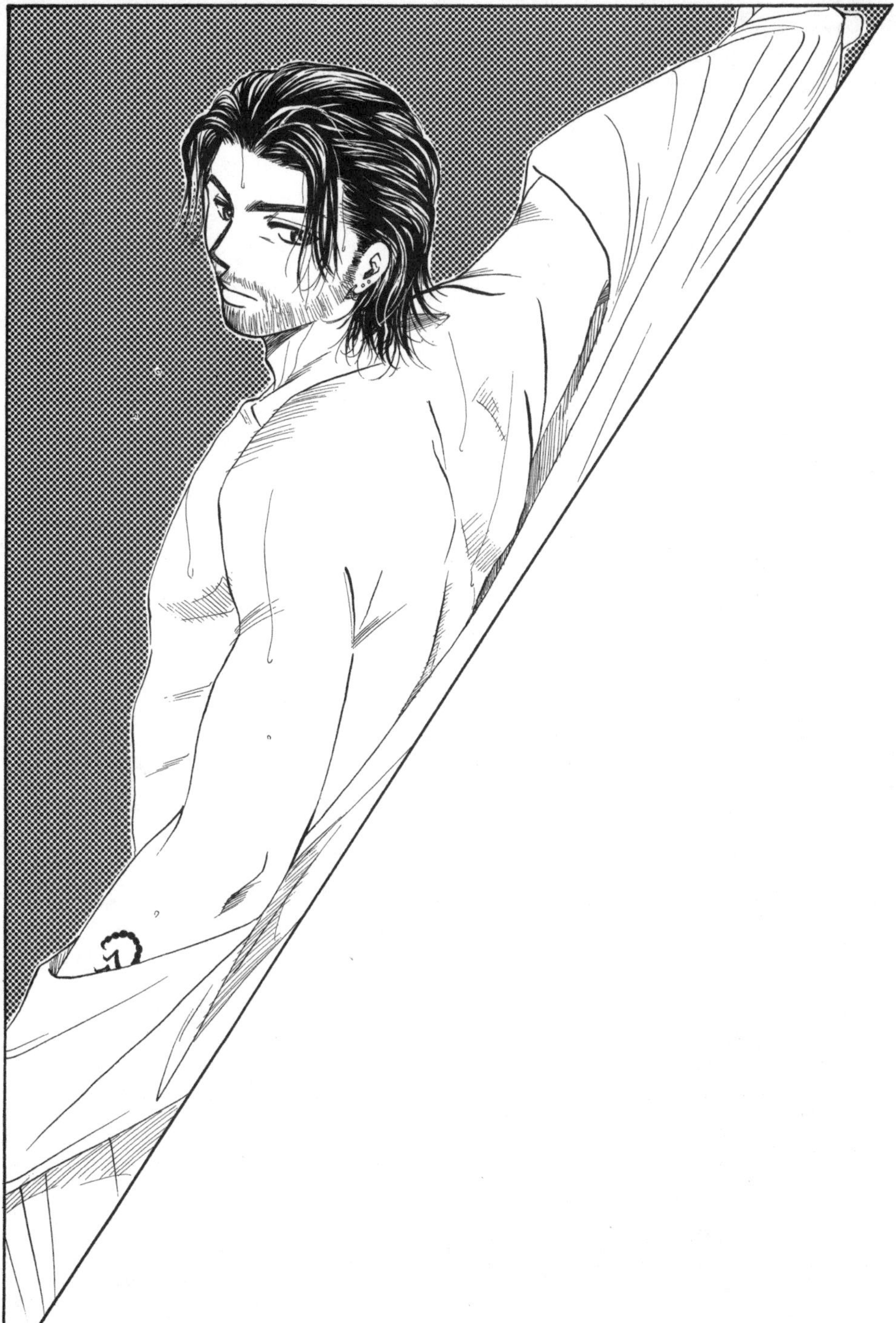

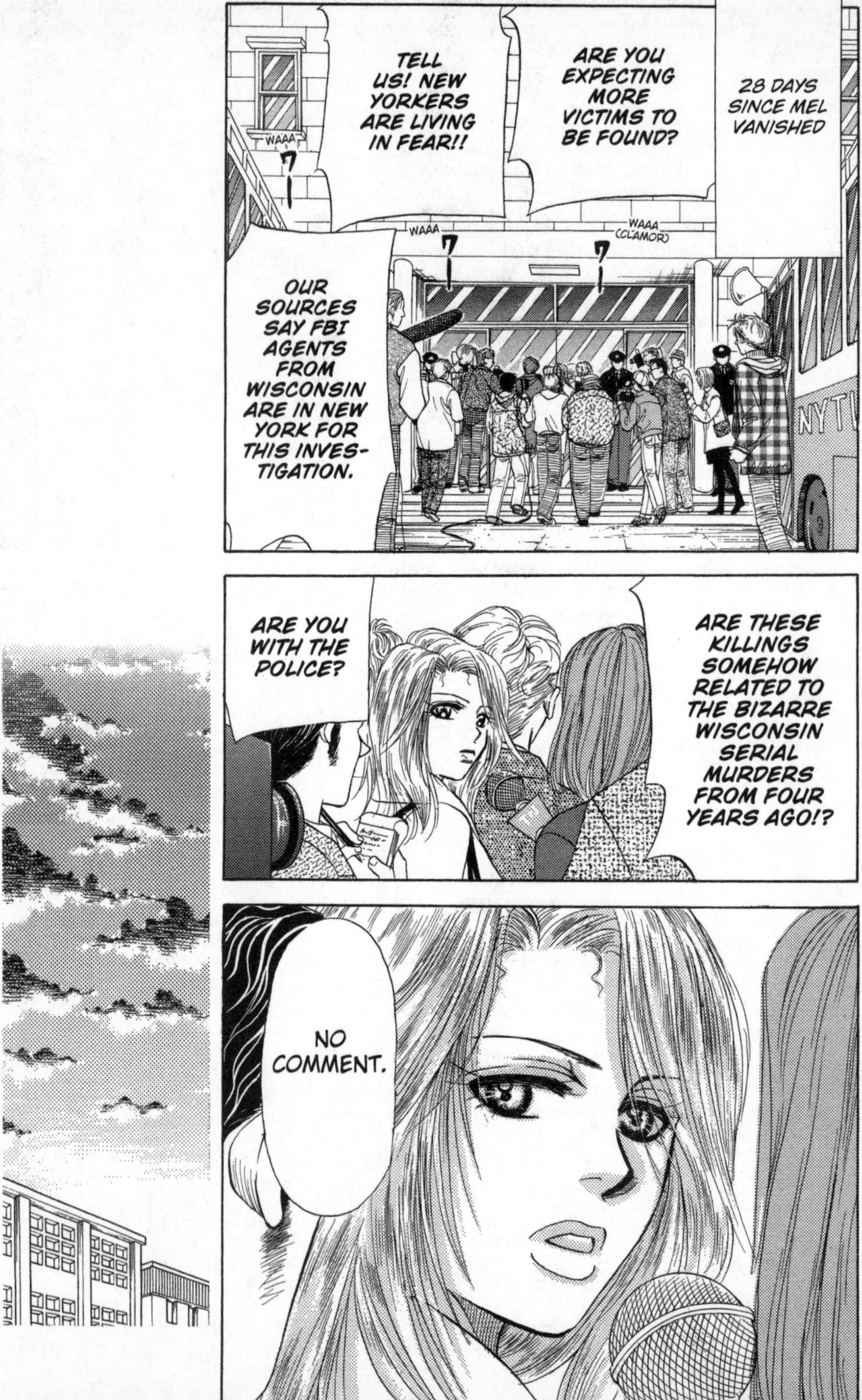
28 DAYS SINCE MEL VANISHED
ARE YOU EXPECTING MORE VICTIMS TO BE FOUND?
TELL US! NEW YORKERS ARE LIVING IN FEAR!!
WAAA
WAAA (CLAMOR)
WAAA
OUR SOURCES SAY FBI AGENTS FROM WISCONSIN ARE IN NEW YORK FOR THIS INVES-TIGATION.
ARE THESE KILLINGS SOMEHOW RELATED TO THE BIZARRE WISCONSIN SERIAL MURDERS FROM FOUR YEARS AGO!?
ARE YOU WITH THE POLICE?
NO COMMENT.

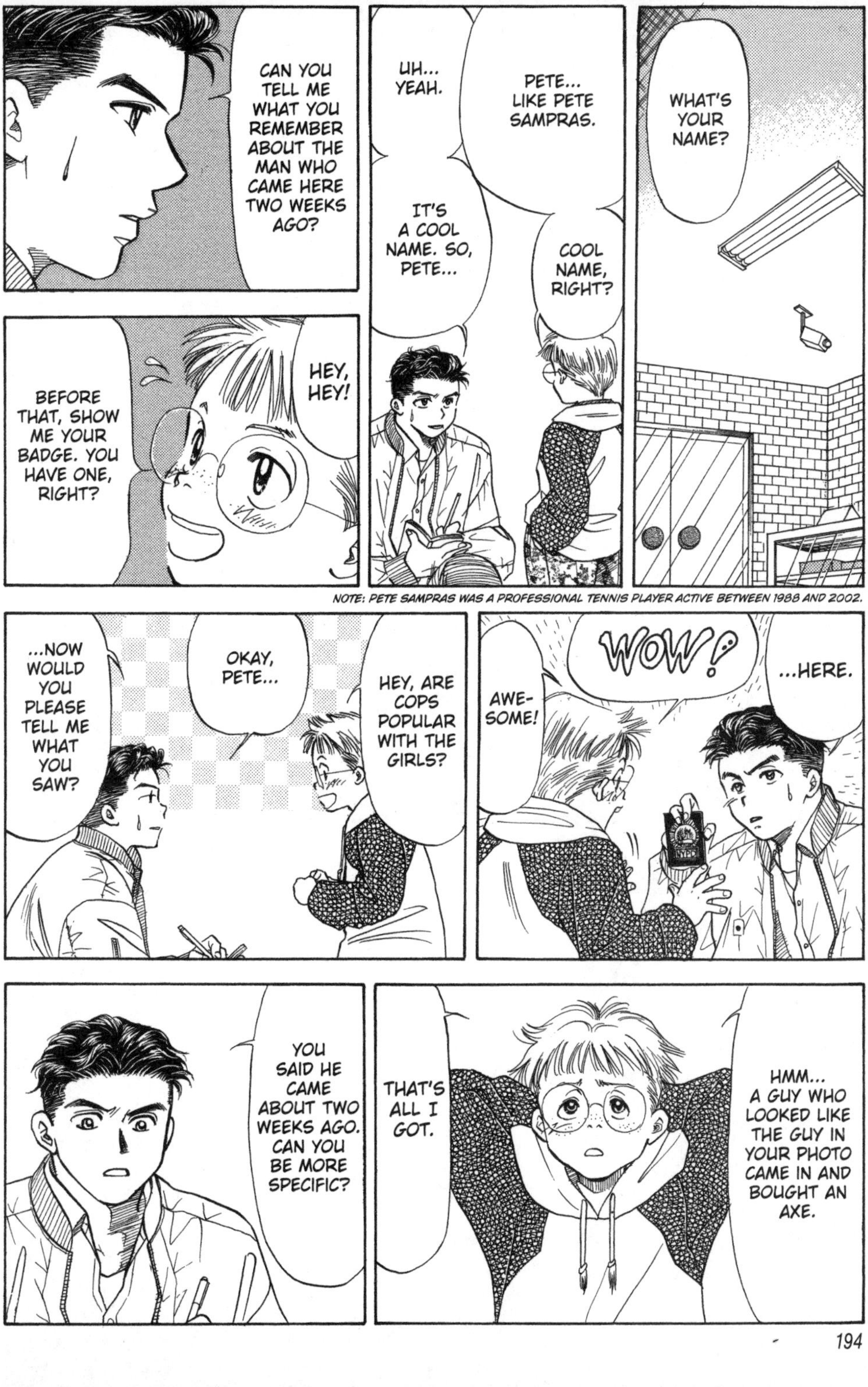
WHAT'S YOUR NAME?
PETE... LIKE PETE SAMPRAS.
COOL NAME, RIGHT?
UH... YEAH.
IT'S A COOL NAME. SO, PETE...
CAN YOU TELL ME WHAT YOU REMEMBER ABOUT THE MAN WHO CAME HERE TWO WEEKS AGO?
HEY, HEY!
BEFORE THAT, SHOW ME YOUR BADGE. YOU HAVE ONE, RIGHT?
NOTE: PETE SAMPRAS WAS A PROFESSIONAL TENNIS PLAYER ACTIVE BETWEEN 1988 AND 2002.
...HERE.
WOW!
AWE-SOME!
HEY, ARE COPS POPULAR WITH THE GIRLS?
OKAY, PETE...
...NOW WOULD YOU PLEASE TELL ME WHAT YOU SAW?
HMM... A GUY WHO LOOKED LIKE THE GUY IN YOUR PHOTO CAME IN AND BOUGHT AN AXE.
THAT'S ALL I GOT.
YOU SAID HE CAME ABOUT TWO WEEKS AGO. CAN YOU BE MORE SPECIFIC?

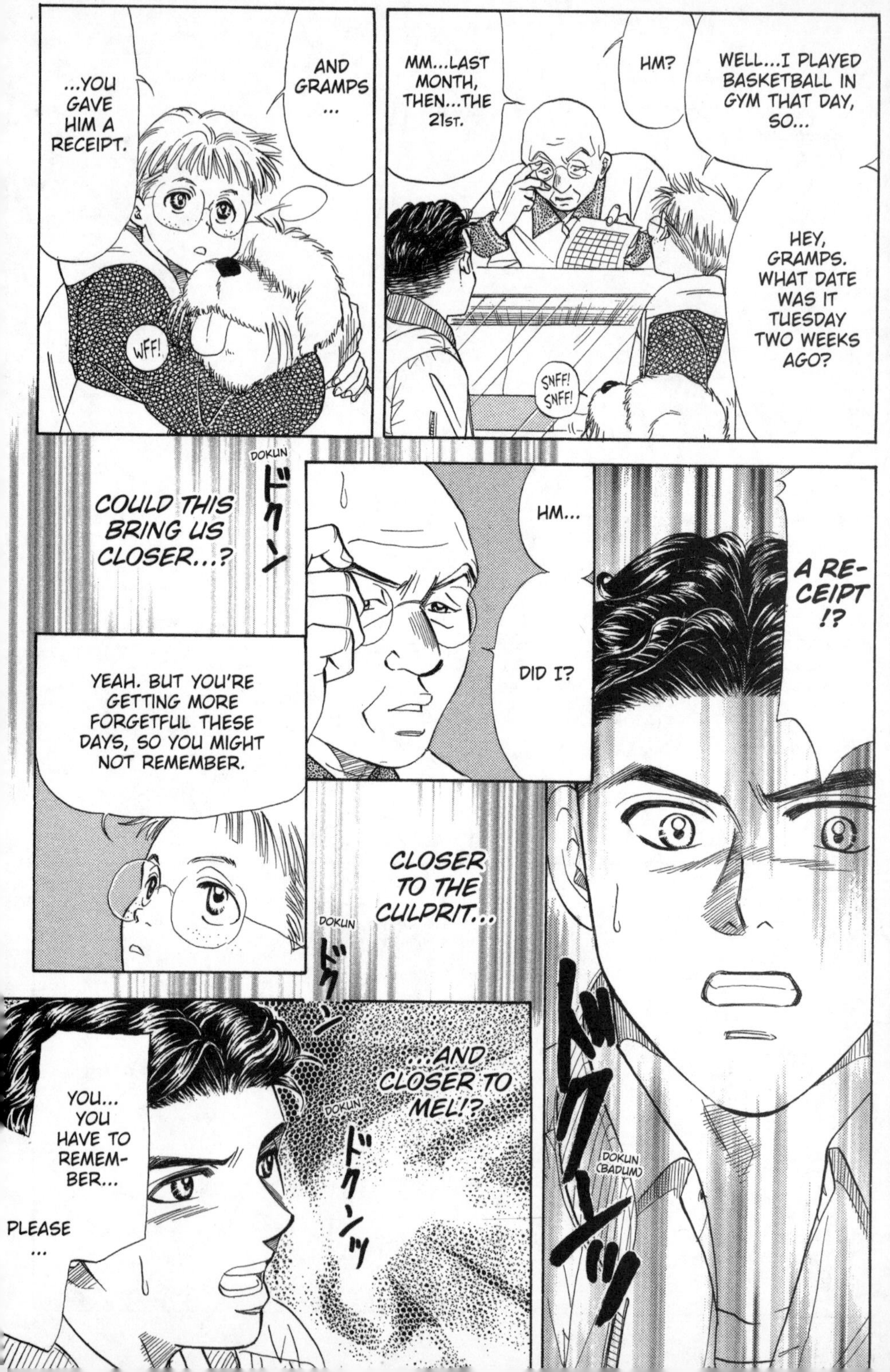
WELL...I PLAYED BASKETBALL IN GYM THAT DAY, SO...
HEY, GRAMPS. WHAT DATE WAS IT TUESDAY TWO WEEKS AGO?
HM?
MM...LAST MONTH, THEN...THE 21ST.
SNFF! SNFF!
AND GRAMPS...
...YOU GAVE HIM A RECEIPT.
WFF!
A RE-CEIPT!?
DOKUN (BADUM)
HM...
DID I?
DOKUN
COULD THIS BRING US CLOSER...?
YEAH. BUT YOU'RE GETTING MORE FORGETFUL THESE DAYS, SO YOU MIGHT NOT REMEMBER.
CLOSER TO THE CULPRIT...
DOKUN
...AND CLOSER TO MEL!?
DOKUN
YOU... YOU HAVE TO REMEMBER...
PLEASE...

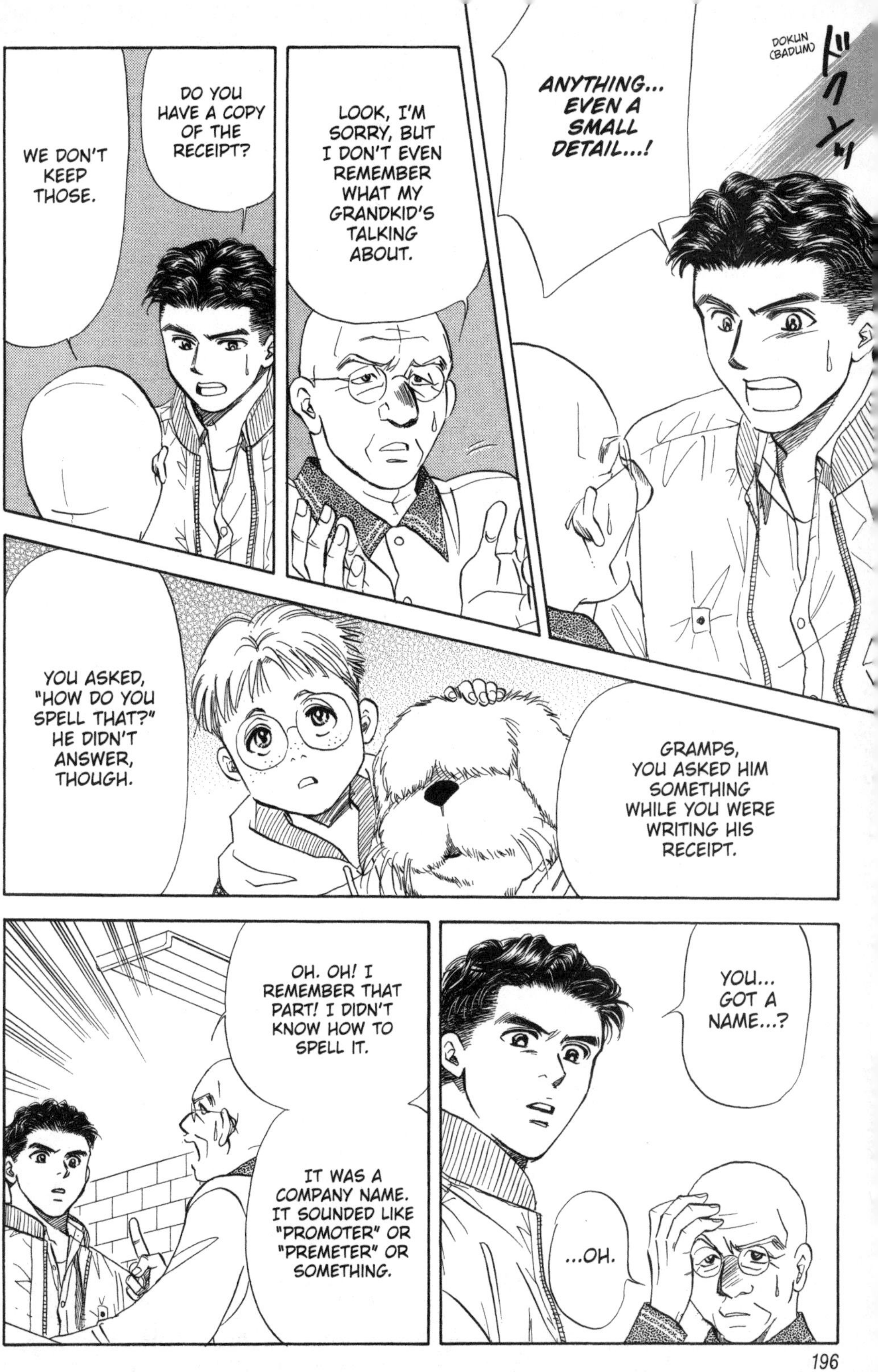
DOKUN (BADUM)
ドクン
ANYTHING... EVEN A SMALL DETAIL...!
LOOK, I'M SORRY, BUT I DON'T EVEN REMEMBER WHAT MY GRANDKID'S TALKING ABOUT.
DO YOU HAVE A COPY OF THE RECEIPT?
WE DON'T KEEP THOSE.
GRAMPS, YOU ASKED HIM SOMETHING WHILE YOU WERE WRITING HIS RECEIPT.
YOU ASKED, "HOW DO YOU SPELL THAT?" HE DIDN'T ANSWER, THOUGH.
YOU... GOT A NAME...?
...OH.
OH. OH! I REMEMBER THAT PART! I DIDN'T KNOW HOW TO SPELL IT.
IT WAS A COMPANY NAME. IT SOUNDED LIKE "PROMOTER" OR "PREMETER" OR SOMETHING.

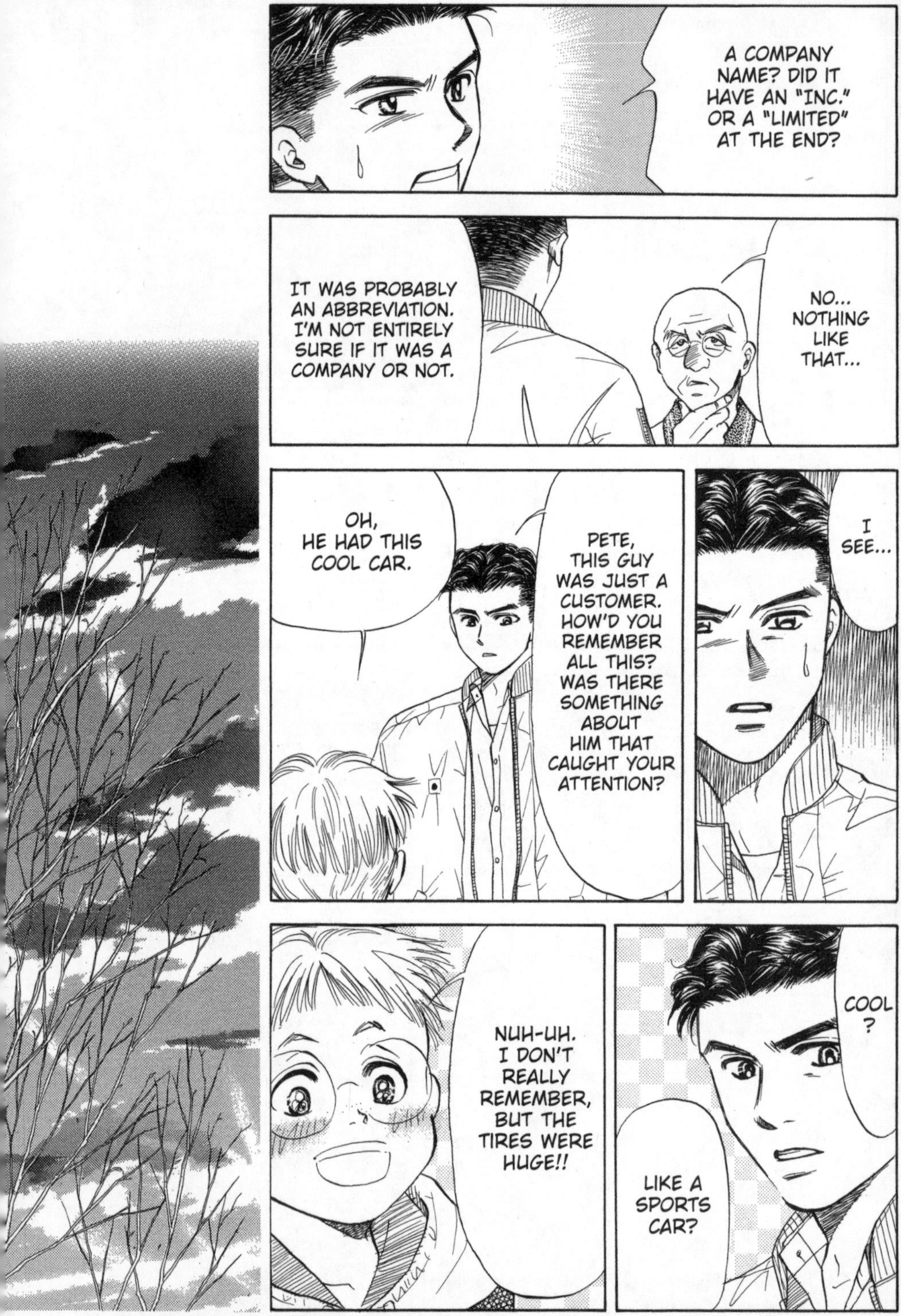
A COMPANY NAME? DID IT HAVE AN "INC." OR A "LIMITED" AT THE END?
NO... NOTHING LIKE THAT...
IT WAS PROBABLY AN ABBREVIATION. I'M NOT ENTIRELY SURE IF IT WAS A COMPANY OR NOT.
I SEE...
PETE, THIS GUY WAS JUST A CUSTOMER. HOW'D YOU REMEMBER ALL THIS? WAS THERE SOMETHING ABOUT HIM THAT CAUGHT YOUR ATTENTION?
OH, HE HAD THIS COOL CAR.
COOL?
LIKE A SPORTS CAR?
NUH-UH. I DON'T REALLY REMEMBER, BUT THE TIRES WERE HUGE!!

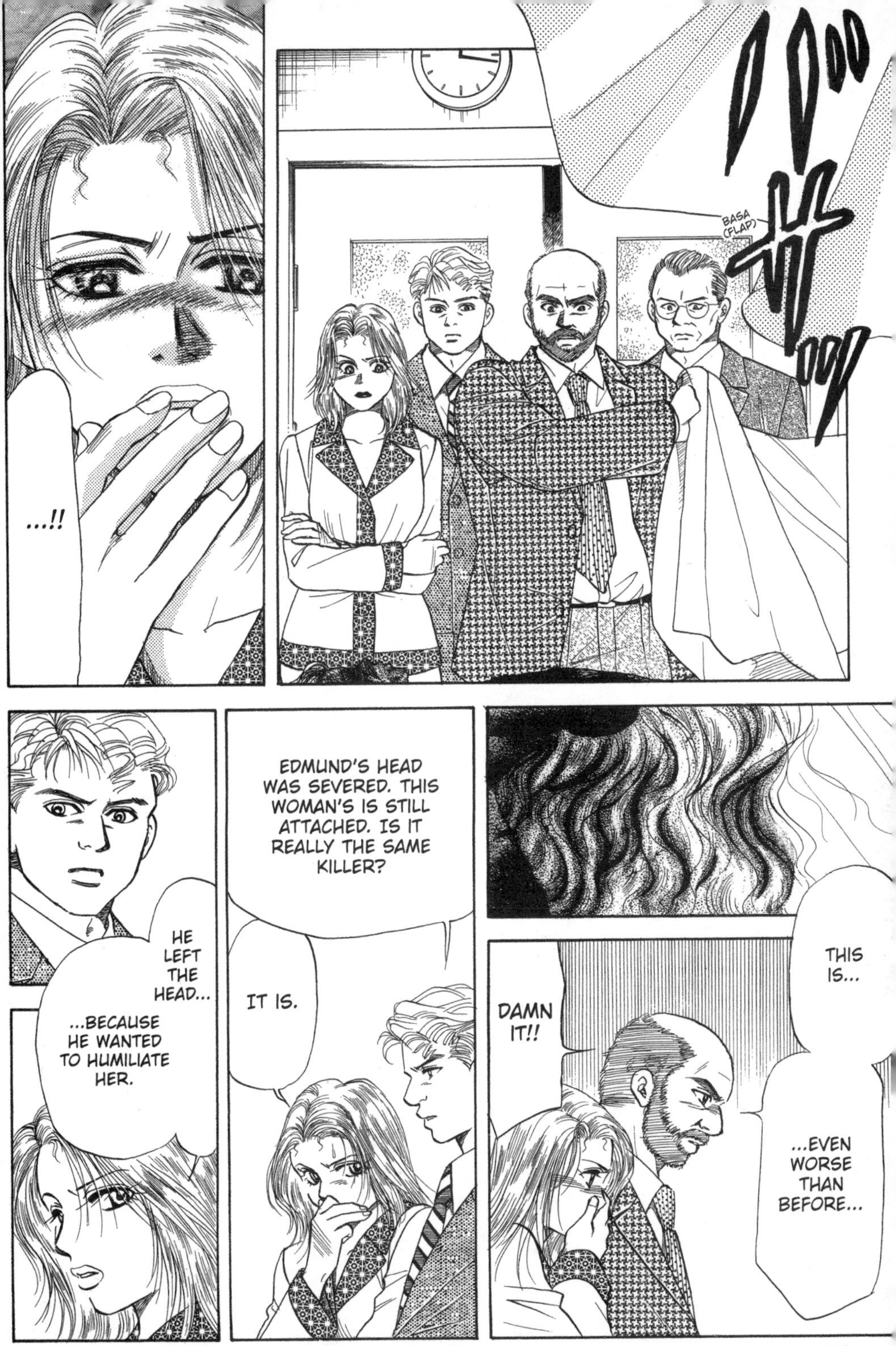
BASA (FLAP)
...!!
THIS IS...
...EVEN WORSE THAN BEFORE...
DAMN IT!!
EDMUND'S HEAD WAS SEVERED. THIS WOMAN'S IS STILL ATTACHED. IS IT REALLY THE SAME KILLER?
IT IS.
HE LEFT THE HEAD...
...BECAUSE HE WANTED TO HUMILIATE HER.

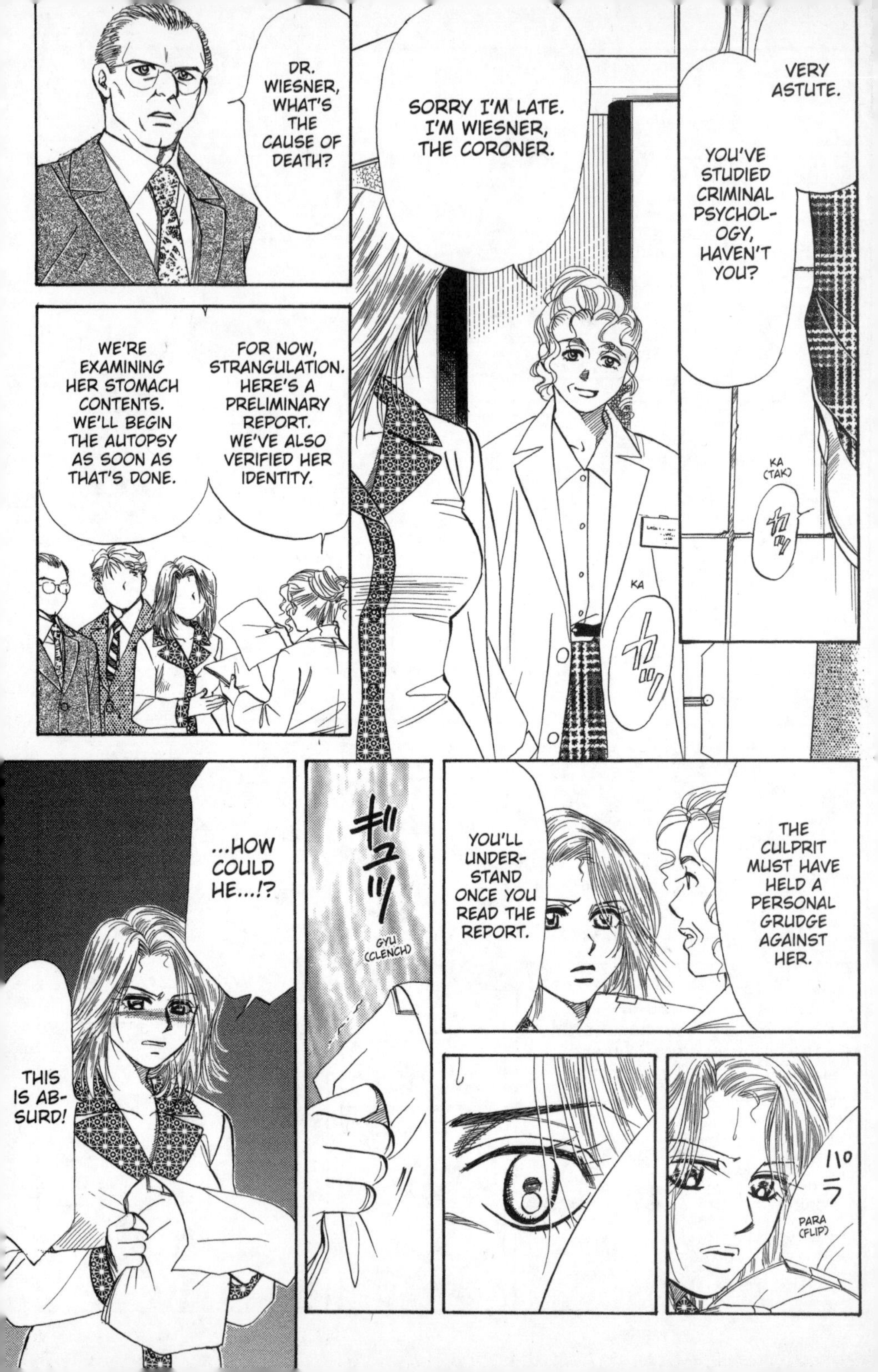
VERY ASTUTE.
YOU'VE STUDIED CRIMINAL PSYCHOLOGY, HAVEN'T YOU?
KA (TAK)
SORRY I'M LATE. I'M WIESNER, THE CORONER.
KA
DR. WIESNER, WHAT'S THE CAUSE OF DEATH?
FOR NOW, STRANGULATION. HERE'S A PRELIMINARY REPORT. WE'VE ALSO VERIFIED HER IDENTITY.
WE'RE EXAMINING HER STOMACH CONTENTS. WE'LL BEGIN THE AUTOPSY AS SOON AS THAT'S DONE.
THE CULPRIT MUST HAVE HELD A PERSONAL GRUDGE AGAINST HER.
YOU'LL UNDERSTAND ONCE YOU READ THE REPORT.
PARA (FLIP)
GYU (CLENCH)
...HOW COULD HE...!?
THIS IS ABSURD!

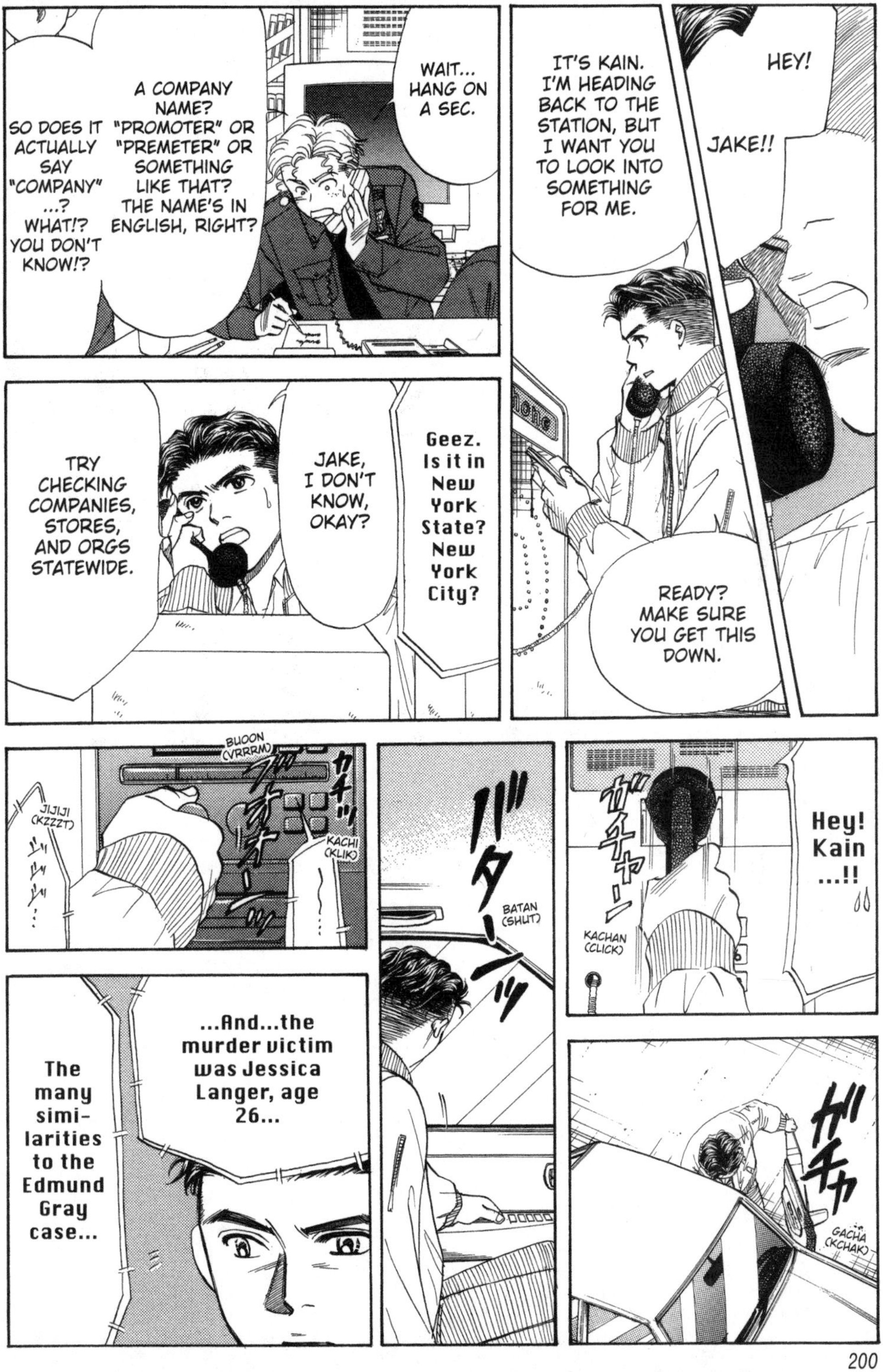
HEY!
JAKE!!
IT'S KAIN. I'M HEADING BACK TO THE STATION, BUT I WANT YOU TO LOOK INTO SOMETHING FOR ME.
READY? MAKE SURE YOU GET THIS DOWN.
WAIT... HANG ON A SEC.
A COMPANY NAME? "PROMOTER" OR "PREMETER" OR SOMETHING LIKE THAT? THE NAME'S IN ENGLISH, RIGHT?
SO DOES IT ACTUALLY SAY "COMPANY" ...? WHAT!? YOU DON'T KNOW!?
Geez. Is it in New York State? New York City?
JAKE, I DON'T KNOW, OKAY?
TRY CHECKING COMPANIES, STORES, AND ORGS STATEWIDE.
Hey! Kain ...!!
ガチャン
KACHAN (CLICK)
ガチャ
GACHA (KCHAK)
バターンッ
BATAN (SHUT)
BUOON (VRRRM)
カチッ
KACHI (KLIK)
JIJIJI (KZZZT)
...And...the murder victim was Jessica Langer, age 26...
The many simi-larities to the Edmund Gray case...

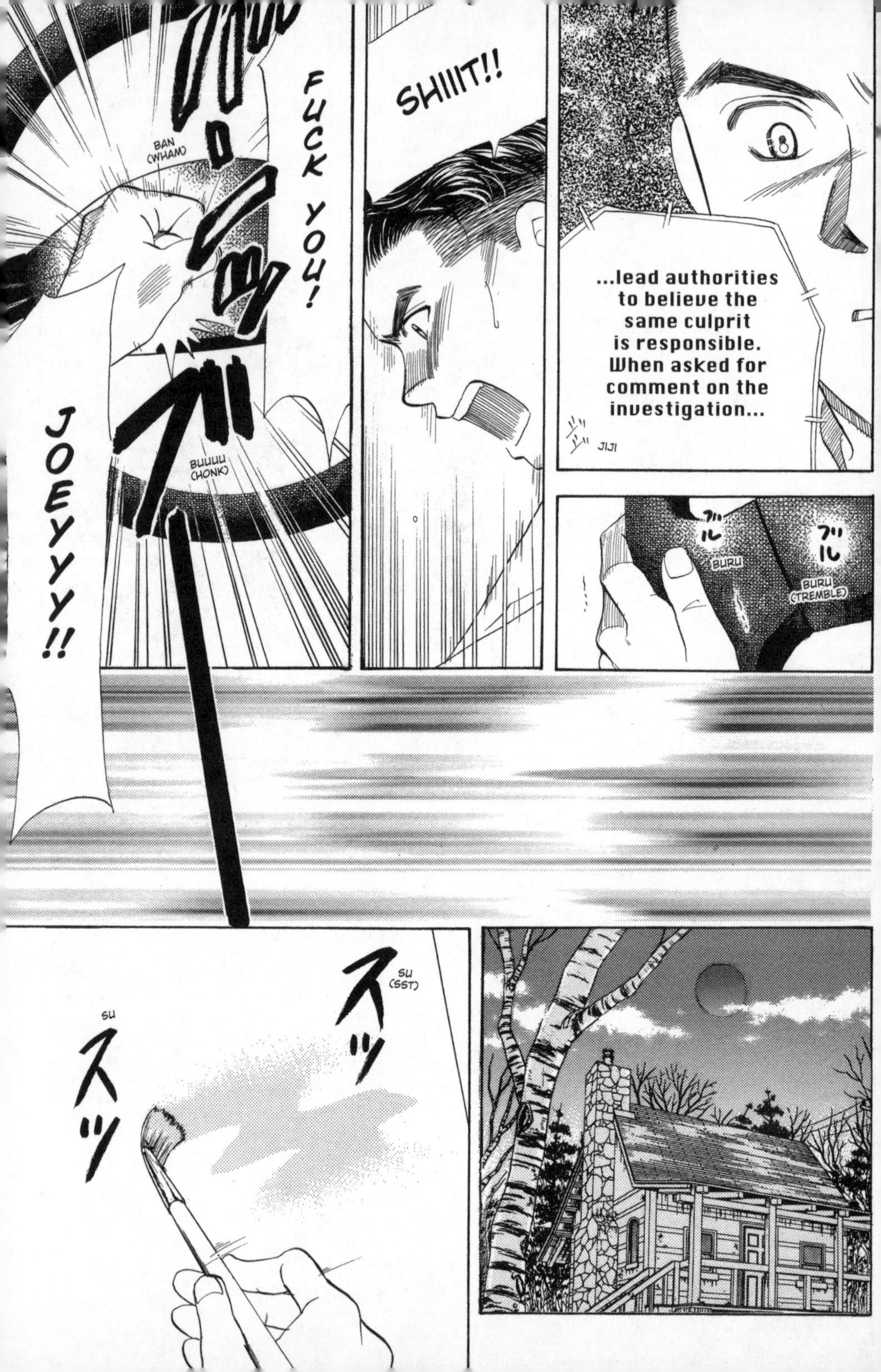
...lead authorities to believe the same culprit is responsible. When asked for comment on the investigation...
JIJI
ブル
BURU
ブル
BURU (TREMBLE)
SHIIIT!!
FUCK YOU!
BAN (WHAM)
BUUUU (HONK)
JOEYYY!!
スッ
SU (SST)
スッ
SU

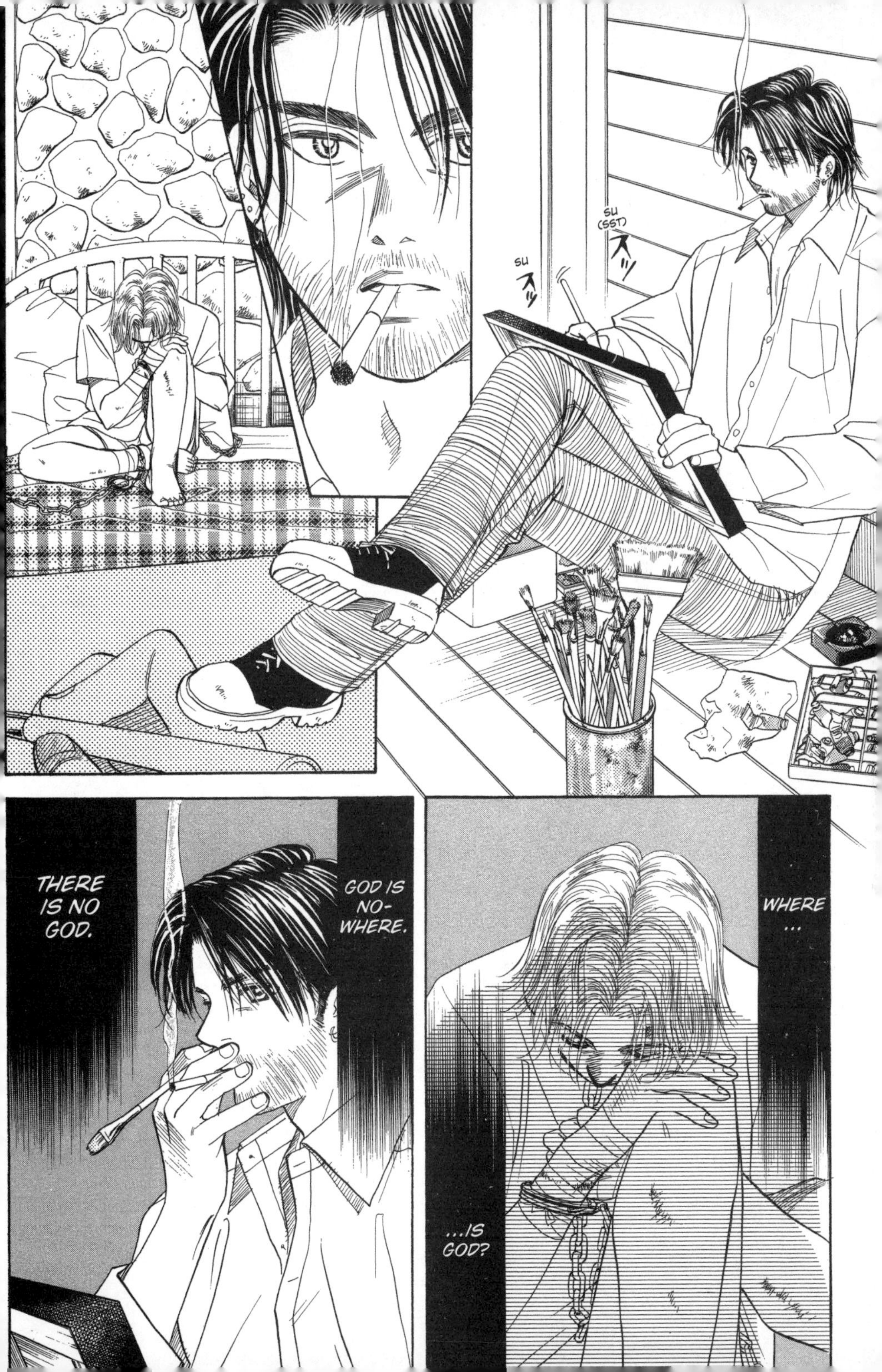

スッ
SU (SST)
スッ
SU
WHERE ...
...IS GOD?
GOD IS NO-WHERE.
THERE IS NO GOD.

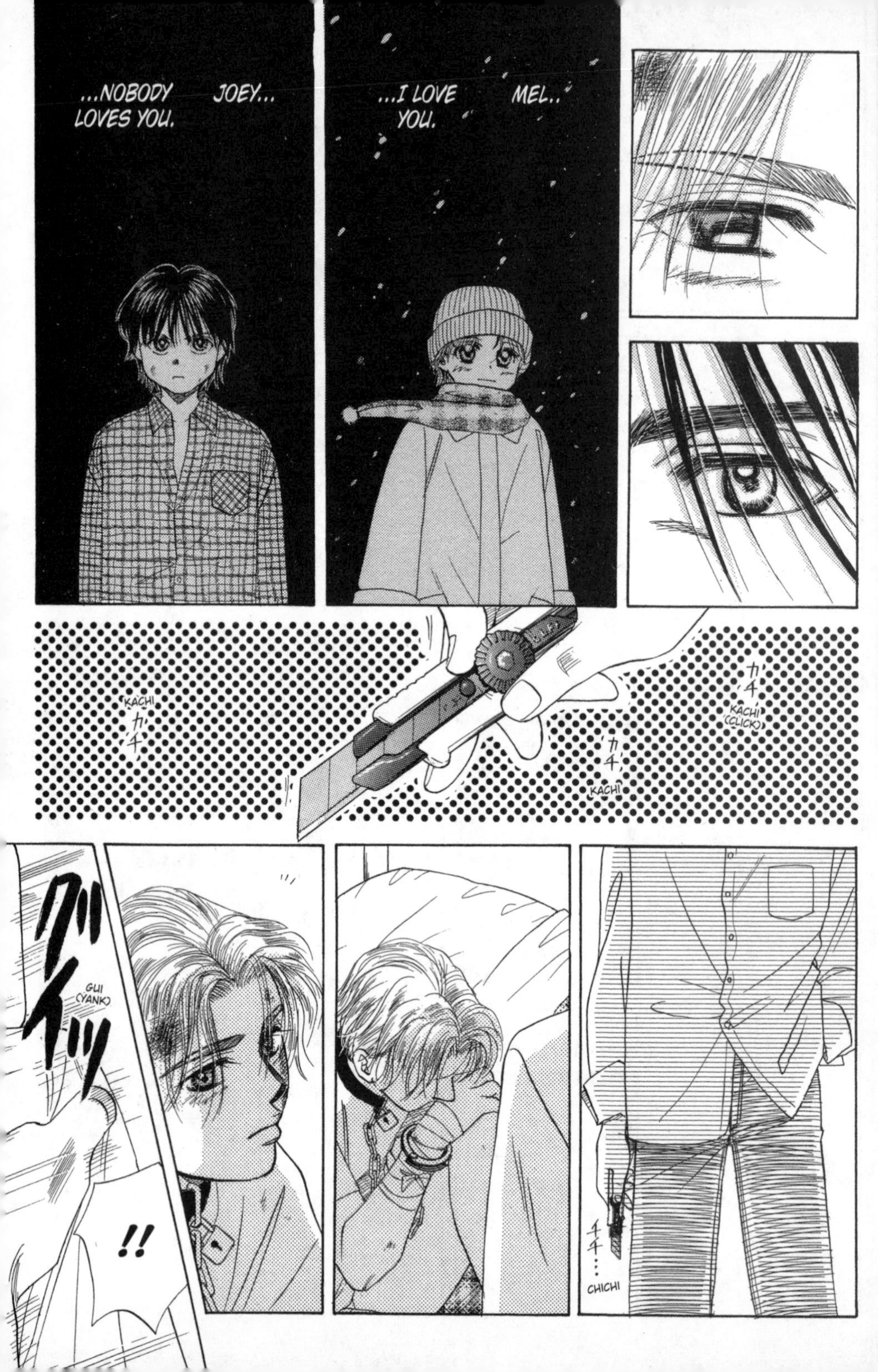
MEL..
...I LOVE YOU.
JOEY...
...NOBODY LOVES YOU.
カチ
KACHI (CLICK)
カチ
KACHI
KACHI
カチ
チチ…
CHICHI
グイッ
GUI (YANK)
!!

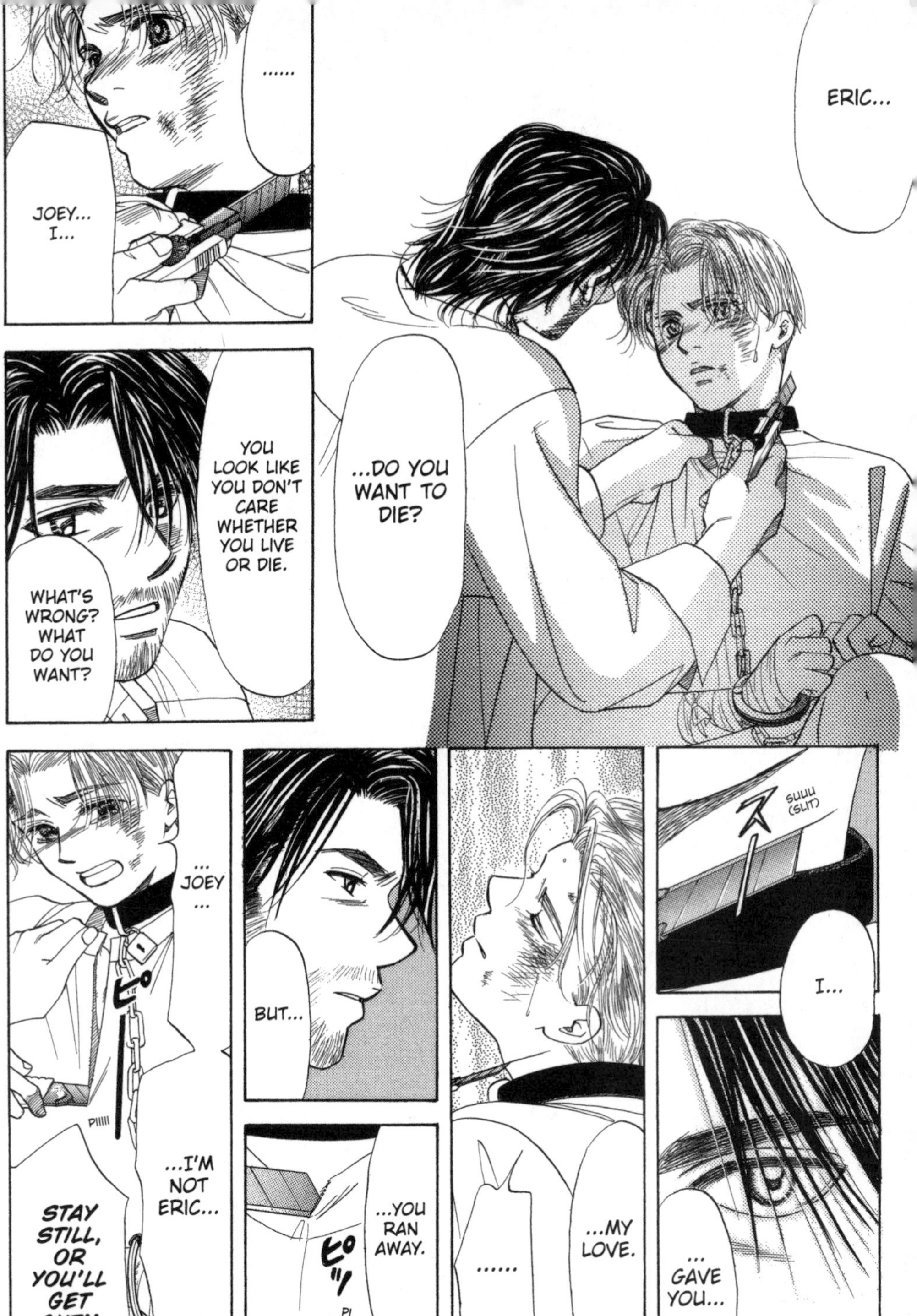

ERIC...
...DO YOU WANT TO DIE?
......
JOEY... I...
YOU LOOK LIKE YOU DON'T CARE WHETHER YOU LIVE OR DIE.
WHAT'S WRONG? WHAT DO YOU WANT?
ス
SUUU (SLIT)
I...
... GAVE YOU...
...MY LOVE.
......
BUT...
...YOU RAN AWAY.
ピッ
PI (RIP)
... JOEY ...
ピー
PIIIII
...I'M NOT ERIC...
STAY STILL, OR YOU'LL GET CUT!!

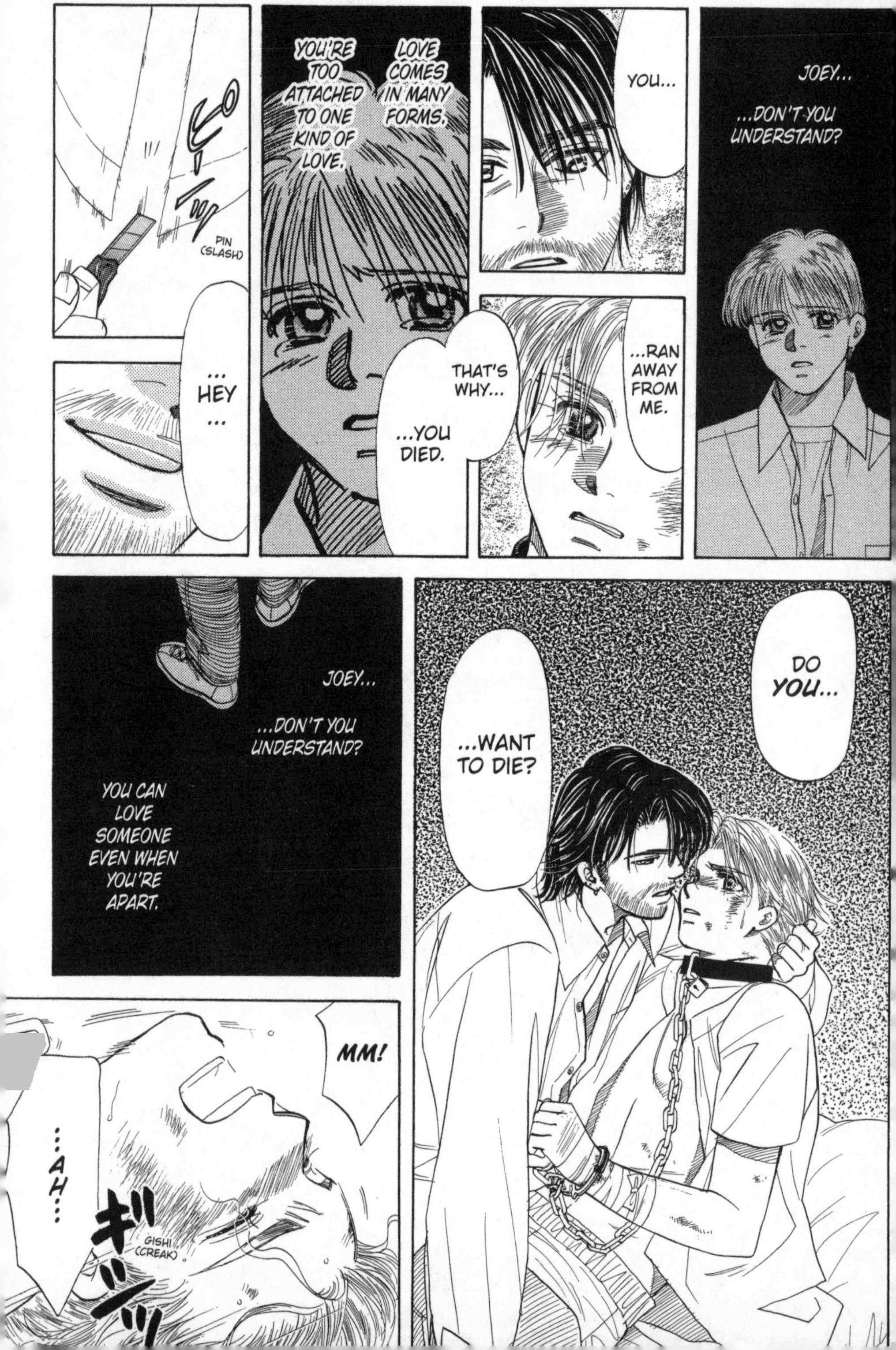
JOEY...
...DON'T YOU UNDERSTAND?
YOU...
...RAN AWAY FROM ME.
THAT'S WHY...
...YOU DIED.
LOVE COMES IN MANY FORMS.
YOU'RE TOO ATTACHED TO ONE KIND OF LOVE.
PIN (SLASH)
...HEY...
DO YOU...
...WANT TO DIE?
JOEY...
...DON'T YOU UNDERSTAND?
YOU CAN LOVE SOMEONE EVEN WHEN YOU'RE APART.
MM!
...AH...
GISHI (CREAK)

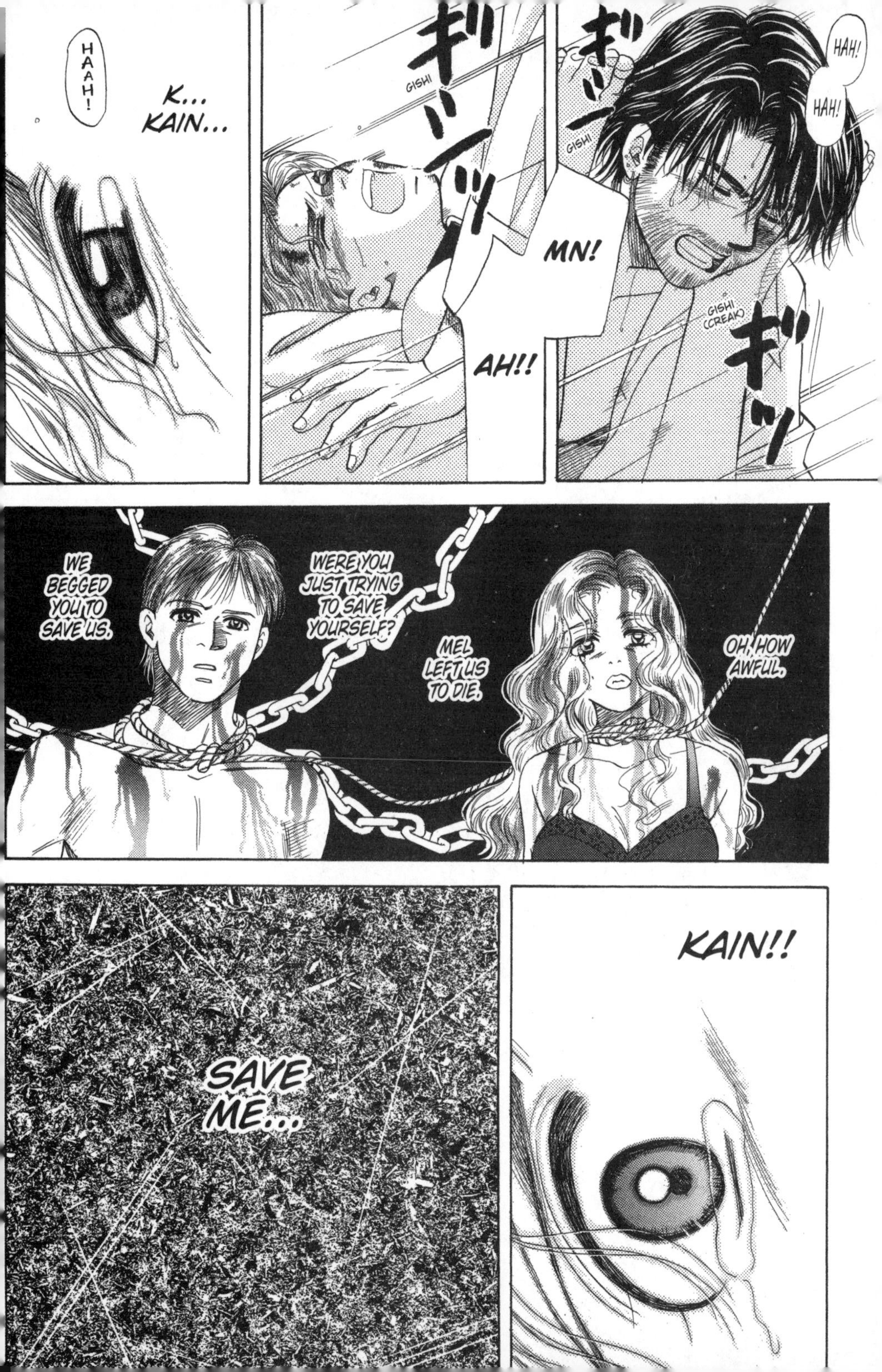
HAH!
HAH!
GISHI
GISHI (CREAK)
MN!
GISHI
AH!!
HAAAH!
K... KAIN...
OH, HOW AWFUL.
MEL LEFT US TO DIE.
WERE YOU JUST TRYING TO SAVE YOURSELF?
WE BEGGED YOU TO SAVE US.
KAIN!!
SAVE ME...

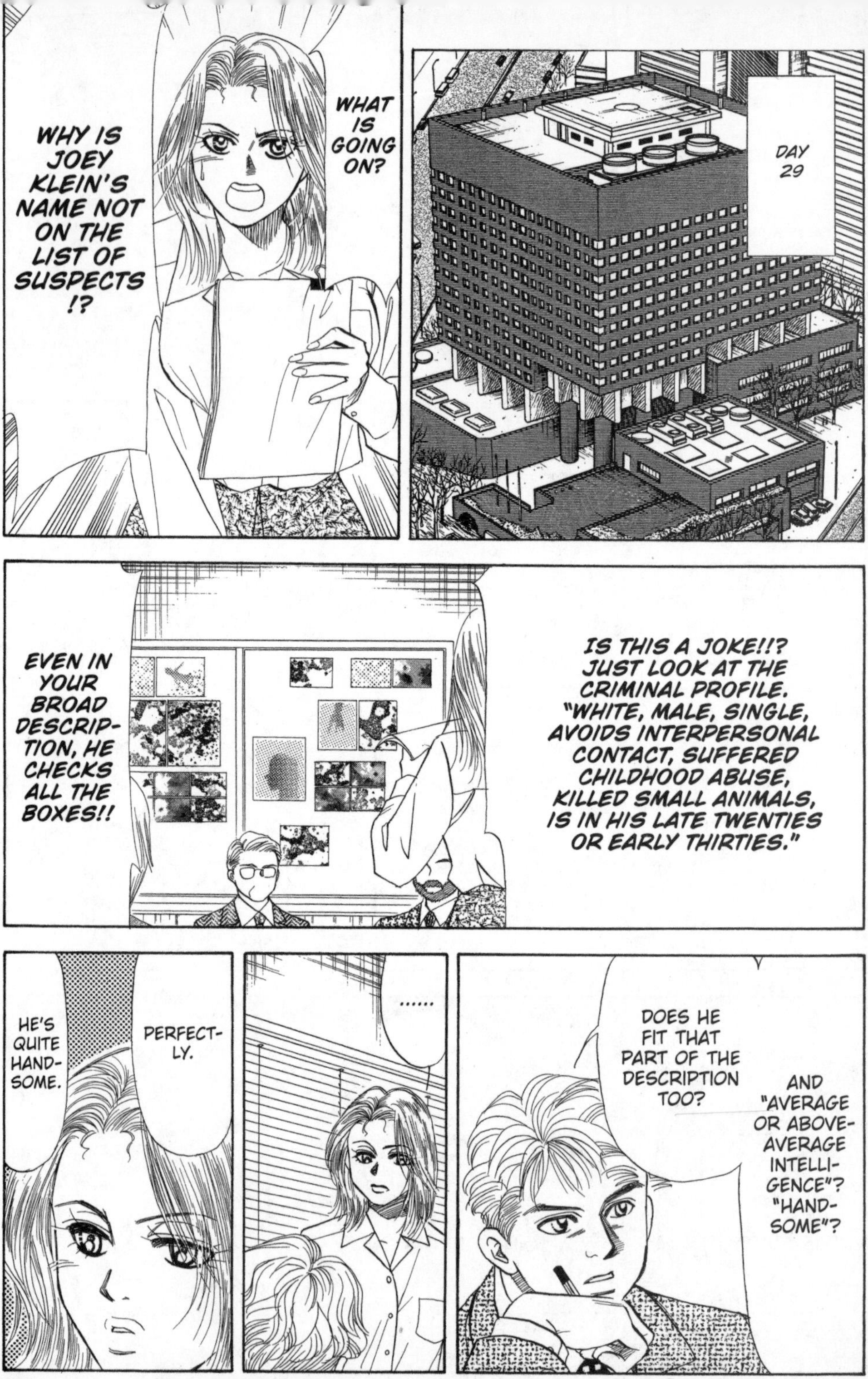
DAY 29
WHAT IS GOING ON?
WHY IS JOEY KLEIN'S NAME NOT ON THE LIST OF SUSPECTS!?
IS THIS A JOKE!!? JUST LOOK AT THE CRIMINAL PROFILE. "WHITE, MALE, SINGLE, AVOIDS INTERPERSONAL CONTACT, SUFFERED CHILDHOOD ABUSE, KILLED SMALL ANIMALS, IS IN HIS LATE TWENTIES OR EARLY THIRTIES."
EVEN IN YOUR BROAD DESCRIPTION, HE CHECKS ALL THE BOXES!!
AND "AVERAGE OR ABOVE-AVERAGE INTELLIGENCE"? "HANDSOME"?
DOES HE FIT THAT PART OF THE DESCRIPTION TOO?
......
PERFECTLY.
HE'S QUITE HANDSOME.

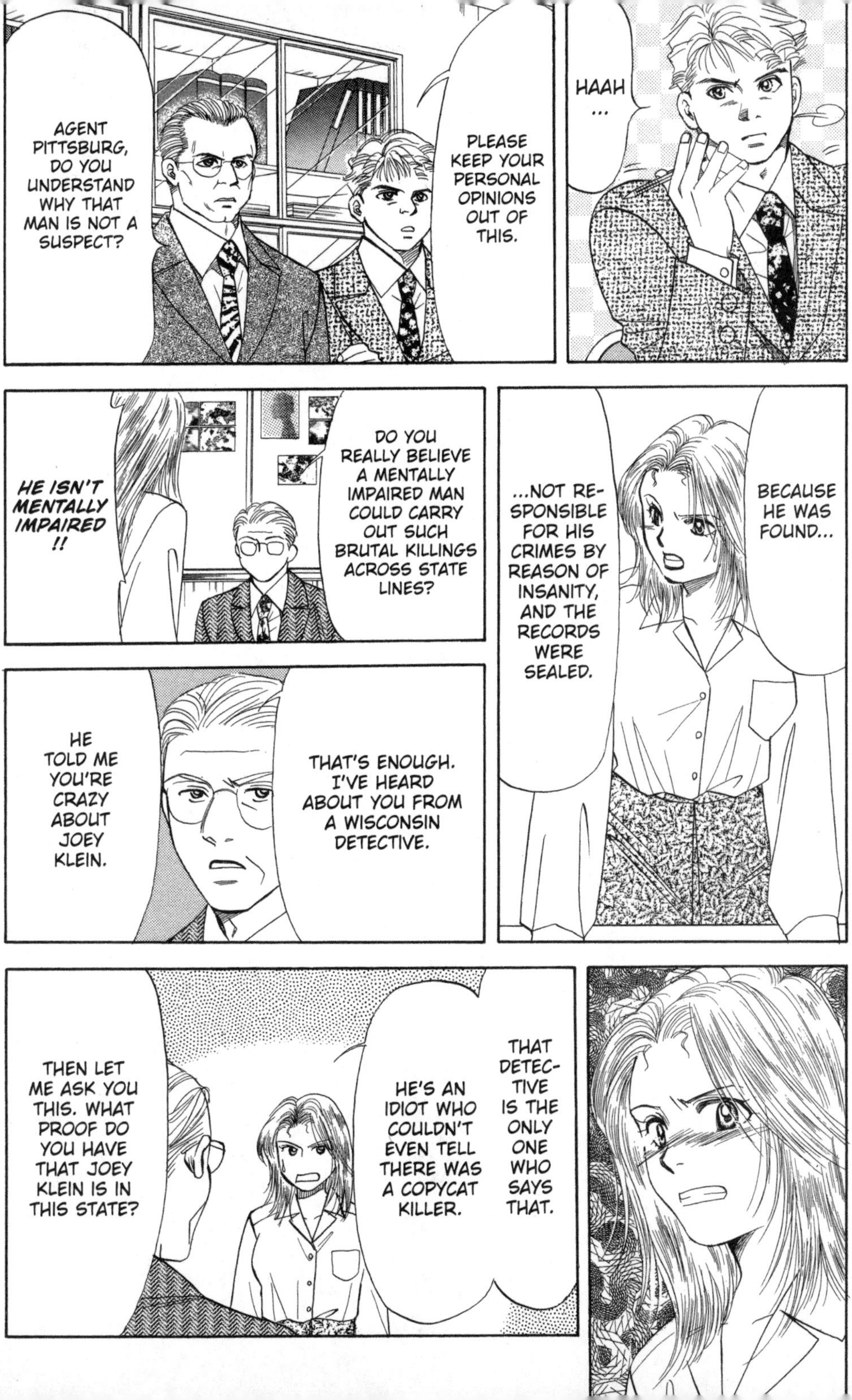
HAAH ...
PLEASE KEEP YOUR PERSONAL OPINIONS OUT OF THIS.
AGENT PITTSBURG, DO YOU UNDERSTAND WHY THAT MAN IS NOT A SUSPECT?
BECAUSE HE WAS FOUND...
...NOT RE-SPONSIBLE FOR HIS CRIMES BY REASON OF INSANITY, AND THE RECORDS WERE SEALED.
DO YOU REALLY BELIEVE A MENTALLY IMPAIRED MAN COULD CARRY OUT SUCH BRUTAL KILLINGS ACROSS STATE LINES?
HE ISN'T MENTALLY IMPAIRED!!
THAT'S ENOUGH. I'VE HEARD ABOUT YOU FROM A WISCONSIN DETECTIVE.
HE TOLD ME YOU'RE CRAZY ABOUT JOEY KLEIN.
THAT DETEC-TIVE IS THE ONLY ONE WHO SAYS THAT.
HE'S AN IDIOT WHO COULDN'T EVEN TELL THERE WAS A COPYCAT KILLER.
THEN LET ME ASK YOU THIS. WHAT PROOF DO YOU HAVE THAT JOEY KLEIN IS IN THIS STATE?

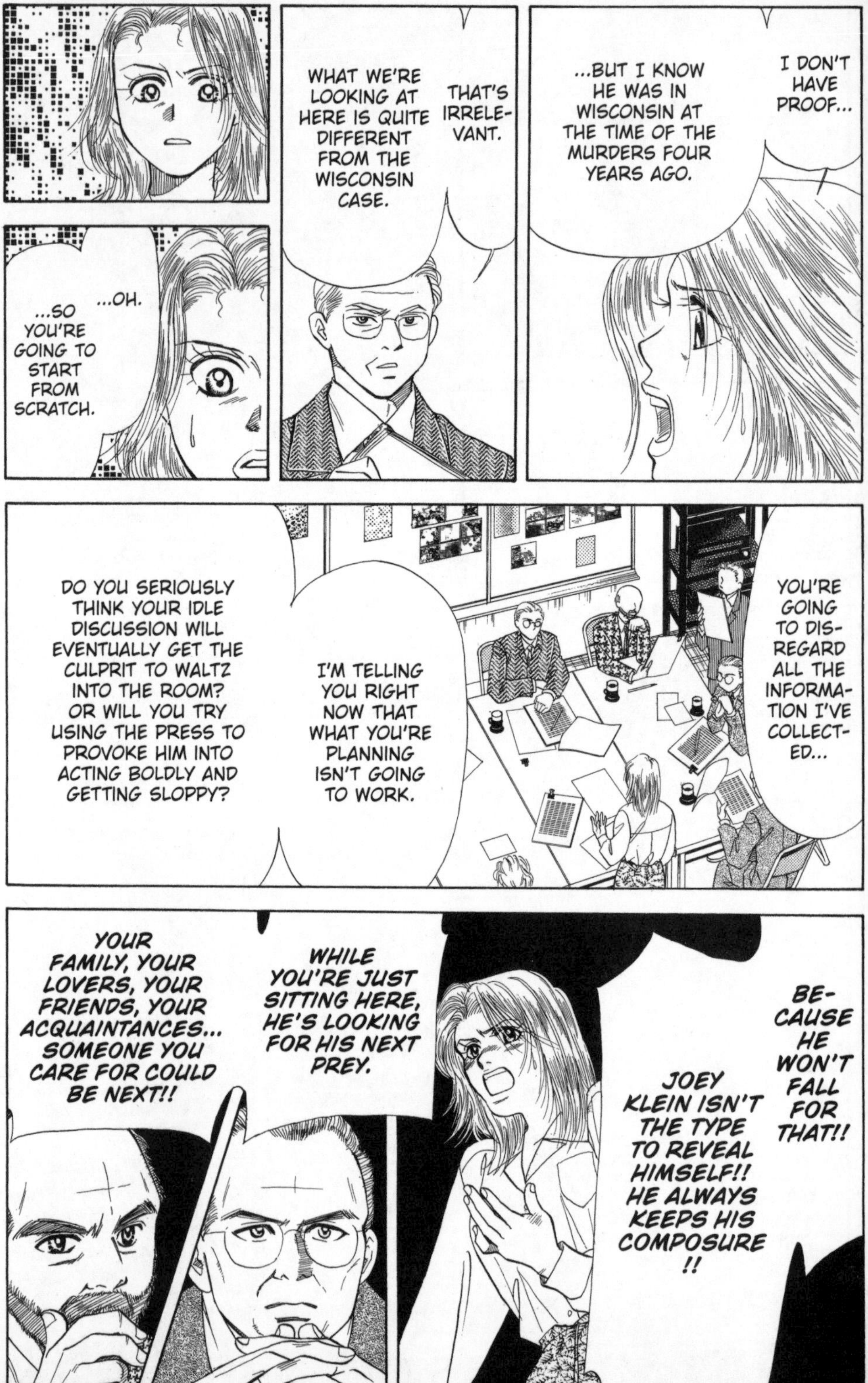
I DON'T HAVE PROOF...
...BUT I KNOW HE WAS IN WISCONSIN AT THE TIME OF THE MURDERS FOUR YEARS AGO.
THAT'S IRRELEVANT.
WHAT WE'RE LOOKING AT HERE IS QUITE DIFFERENT FROM THE WISCONSIN CASE.
...OH.
...SO YOU'RE GOING TO START FROM SCRATCH.
YOU'RE GOING TO DISREGARD ALL THE INFORMATION I'VE COLLECTED...
I'M TELLING YOU RIGHT NOW THAT WHAT YOU'RE PLANNING ISN'T GOING TO WORK.
DO YOU SERIOUSLY THINK YOUR IDLE DISCUSSION WILL EVENTUALLY GET THE CULPRIT TO WALTZ INTO THE ROOM? OR WILL YOU TRY USING THE PRESS TO PROVOKE HIM INTO ACTING BOLDLY AND GETTING SLOPPY?
BECAUSE HE WON'T FALL FOR THAT!!
JOEY KLEIN ISN'T THE TYPE TO REVEAL HIMSELF!! HE ALWAYS KEEPS HIS COMPOSURE!!
WHILE YOU'RE JUST SITTING HERE, HE'S LOOKING FOR HIS NEXT PREY.
YOUR FAMILY, YOUR LOVERS, YOUR FRIENDS, YOUR ACQUAINTANCES... SOMEONE YOU CARE FOR COULD BE NEXT!!

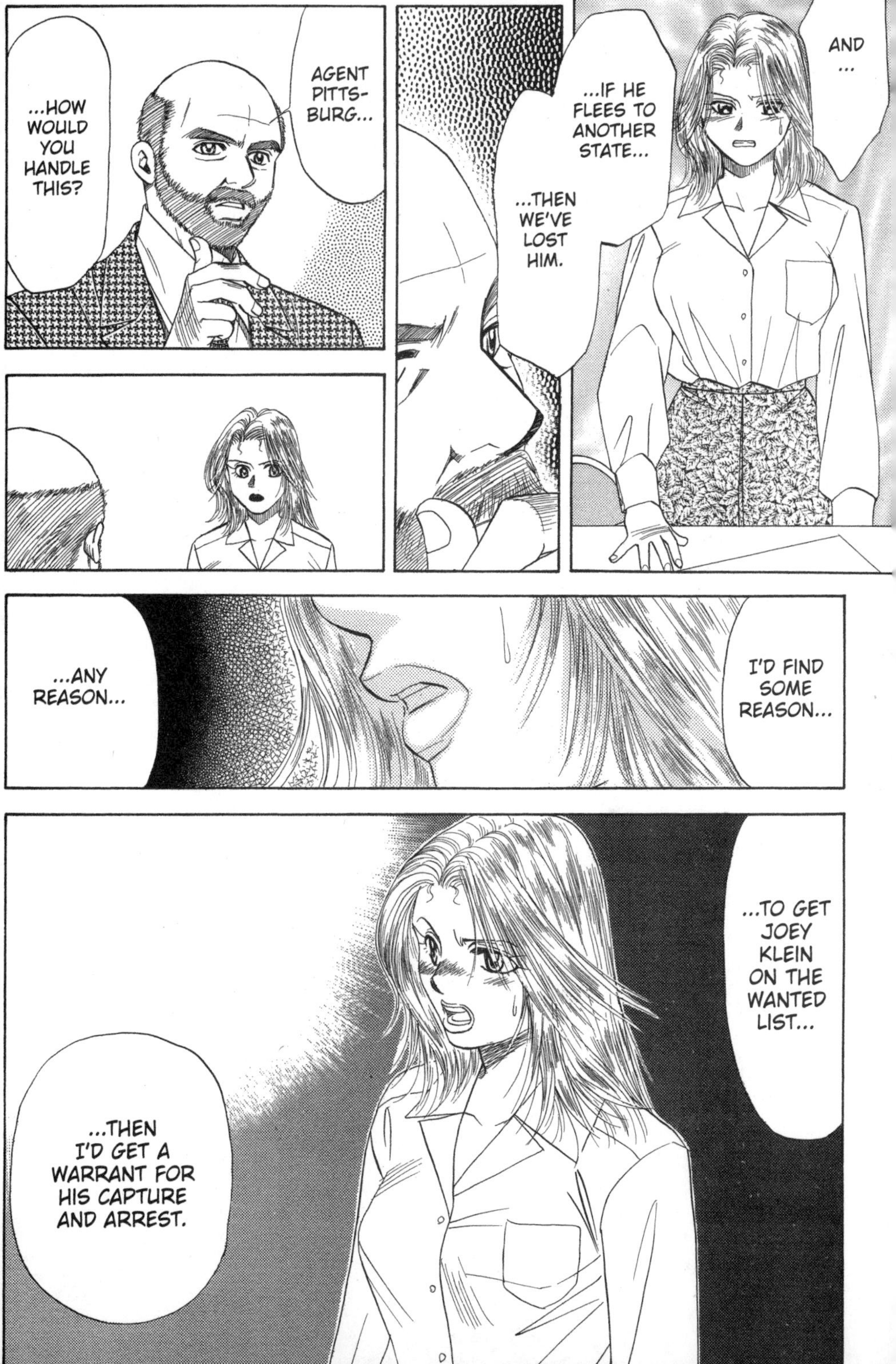
AND ...
...IF HE FLEES TO ANOTHER STATE...
...THEN WE'VE LOST HIM.
AGENT PITTSBURG...
...HOW WOULD YOU HANDLE THIS?
I'D FIND SOME REASON...
...ANY REASON...
...TO GET JOEY KLEIN ON THE WANTED LIST...
...THEN I'D GET A WARRANT FOR HIS CAPTURE AND ARREST.

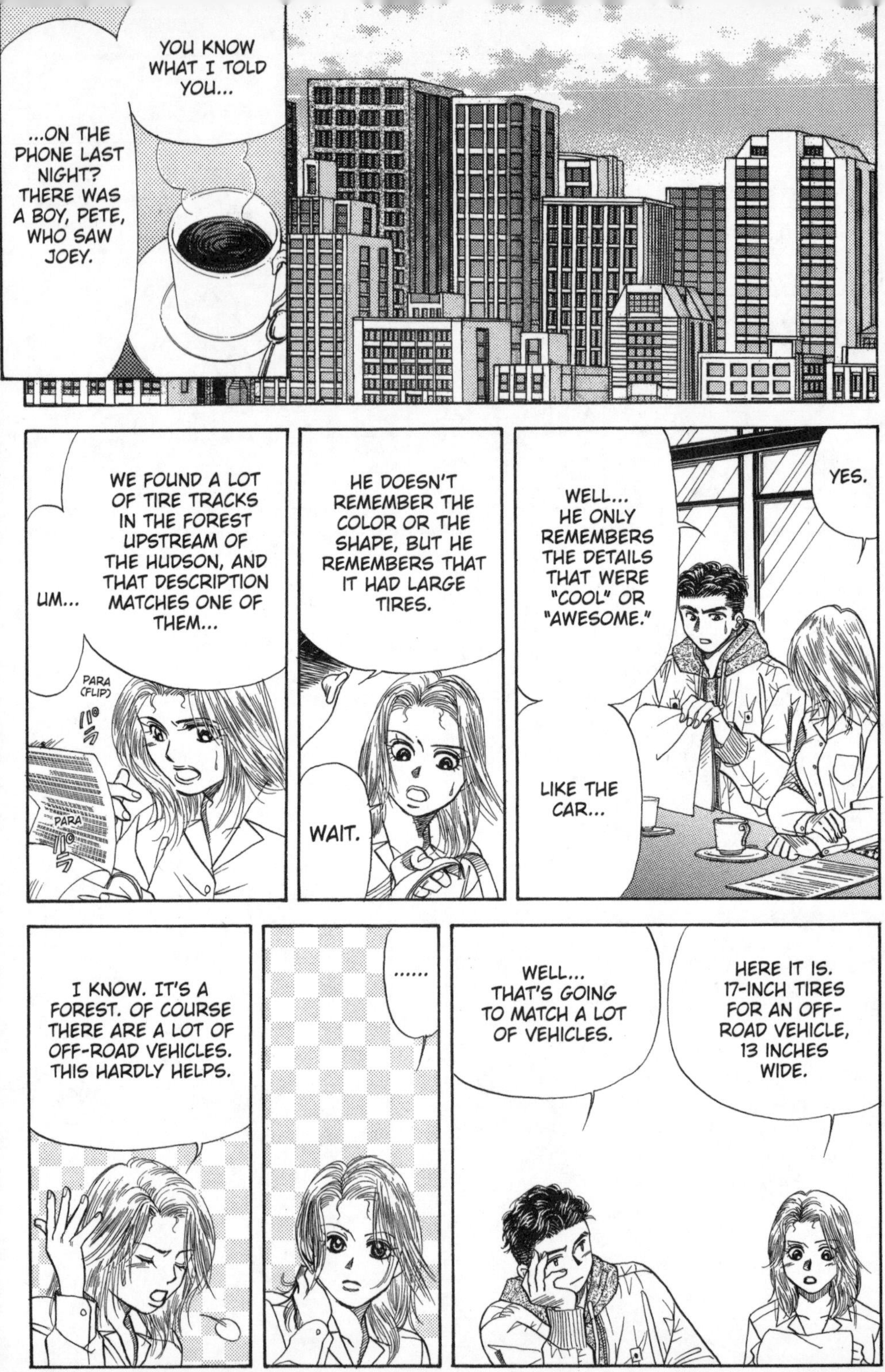
YOU KNOW WHAT I TOLD YOU...
...ON THE PHONE LAST NIGHT? THERE WAS A BOY, PETE, WHO SAW JOEY.
YES.
WELL... HE ONLY REMEMBERS THE DETAILS THAT WERE "COOL" OR "AWESOME."
LIKE THE CAR...
HE DOESN'T REMEMBER THE COLOR OR THE SHAPE, BUT HE REMEMBERS THAT IT HAD LARGE TIRES.
WAIT.
WE FOUND A LOT OF TIRE TRACKS IN THE FOREST UPSTREAM OF THE HUDSON, AND THAT DESCRIPTION MATCHES ONE OF THEM...
UM...
PARA (FLIP)
PARA
HERE IT IS. 17-INCH TIRES FOR AN OFF-ROAD VEHICLE, 13 INCHES WIDE.
WELL... THAT'S GOING TO MATCH A LOT OF VEHICLES.
......
I KNOW. IT'S A FOREST. OF COURSE THERE ARE A LOT OF OFF-ROAD VEHICLES. THIS HARDLY HELPS.

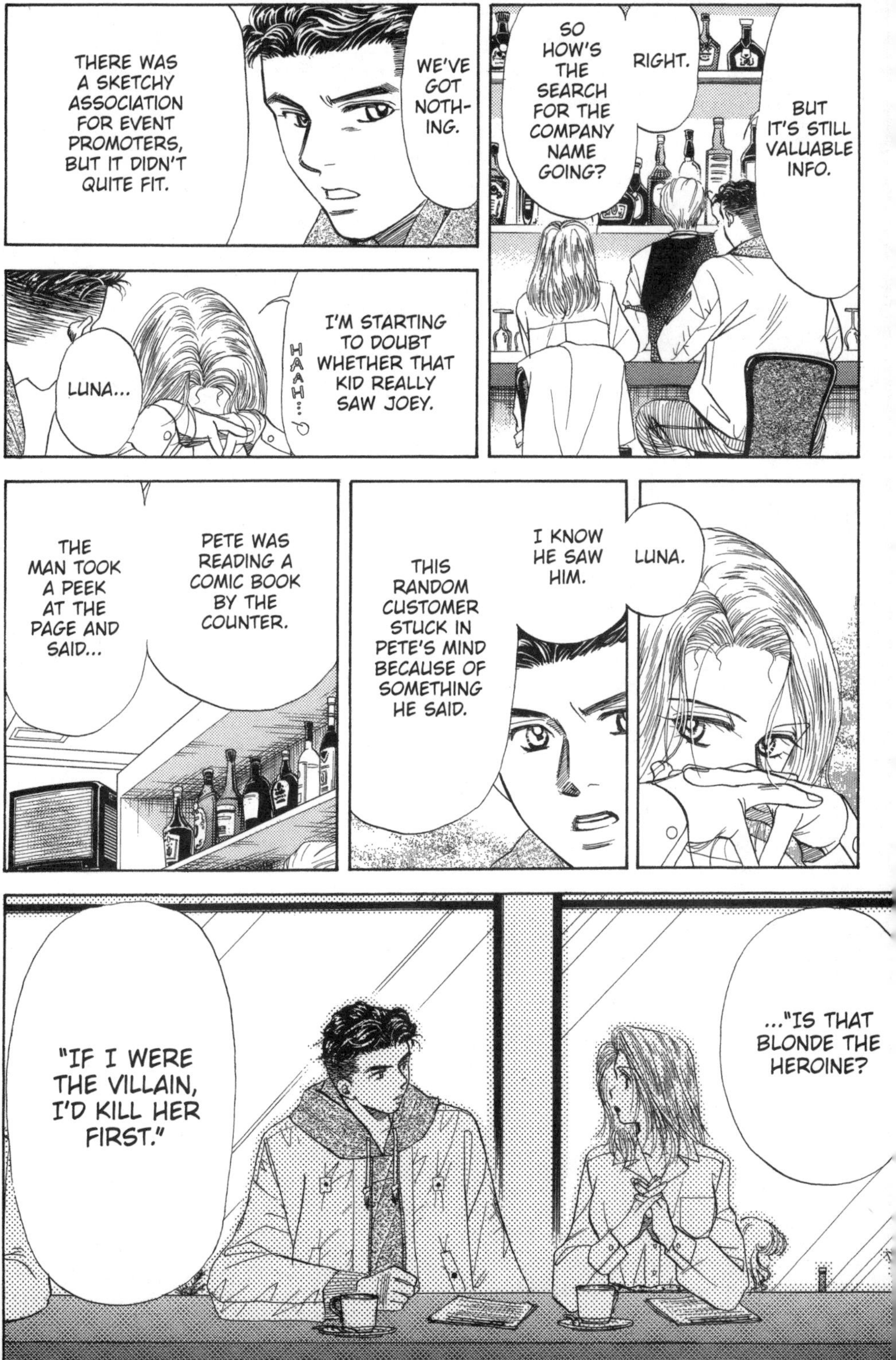
SO HOW'S THE SEARCH FOR THE COMPANY NAME GOING?
RIGHT.
BUT IT'S STILL VALUABLE INFO.
WE'VE GOT NOTH-ING.
THERE WAS A SKETCHY ASSOCIATION FOR EVENT PROMOTERS, BUT IT DIDN'T QUITE FIT.
I'M STARTING TO DOUBT WHETHER THAT KID REALLY SAW JOEY.
HAAAH...
LUNA...
LUNA.
I KNOW HE SAW HIM.
THIS RANDOM CUSTOMER STUCK IN PETE'S MIND BECAUSE OF SOMETHING HE SAID.
PETE WAS READING A COMIC BOOK BY THE COUNTER.
THE MAN TOOK A PEEK AT THE PAGE AND SAID...
..."IS THAT BLONDE THE HEROINE?
"IF I WERE THE VILLAIN, I'D KILL HER FIRST."

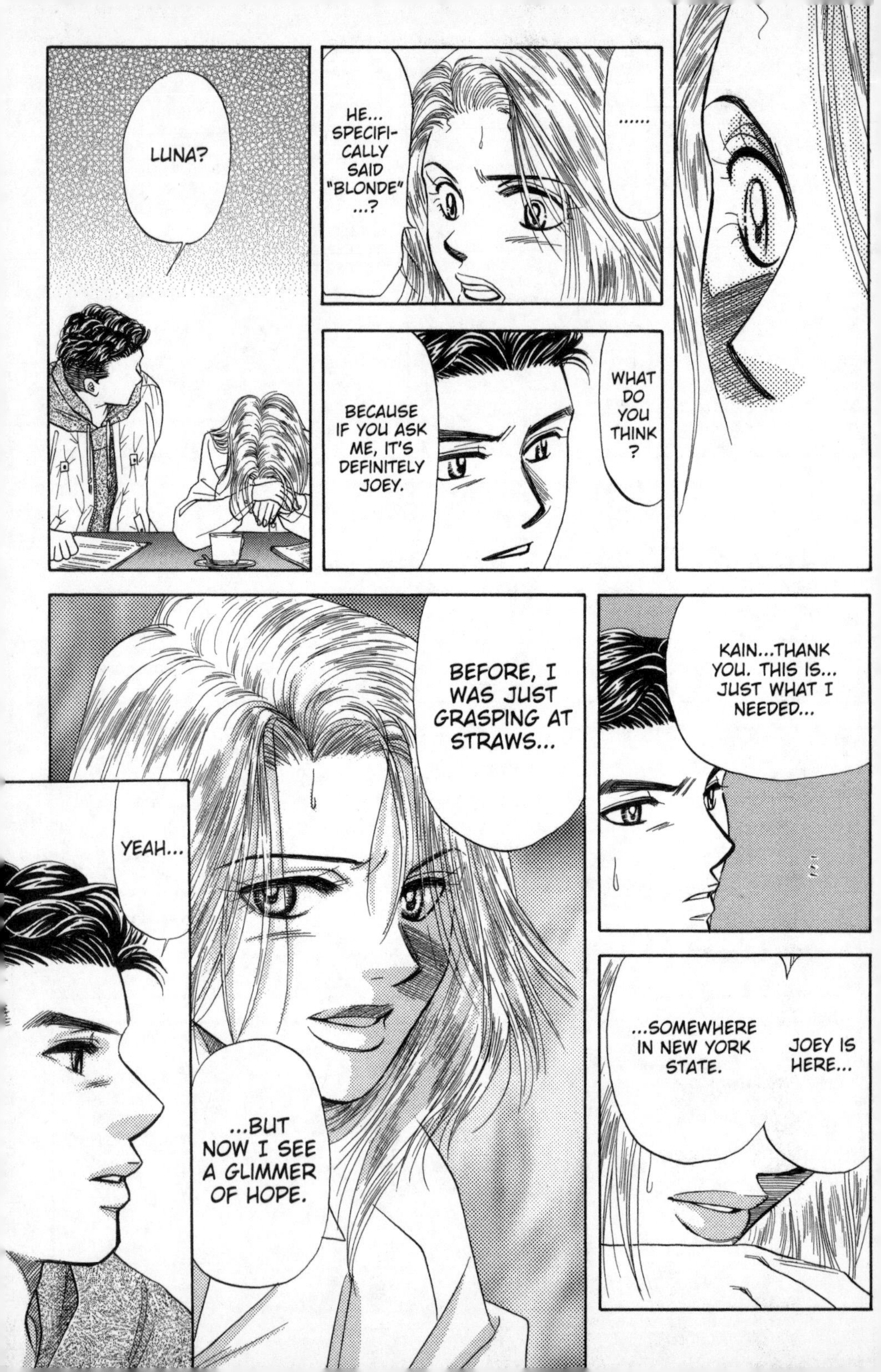
......
HE... SPECIFI-CALLY SAID "BLONDE" ...?
WHAT DO YOU THINK?
BECAUSE IF YOU ASK ME, IT'S DEFINITELY JOEY.
LUNA?
KAIN...THANK YOU. THIS IS... JUST WHAT I NEEDED...
JOEY IS HERE...
...SOMEWHERE IN NEW YORK STATE.
BEFORE, I WAS JUST GRASPING AT STRAWS...
...BUT NOW I SEE A GLIMMER OF HOPE.
YEAH...

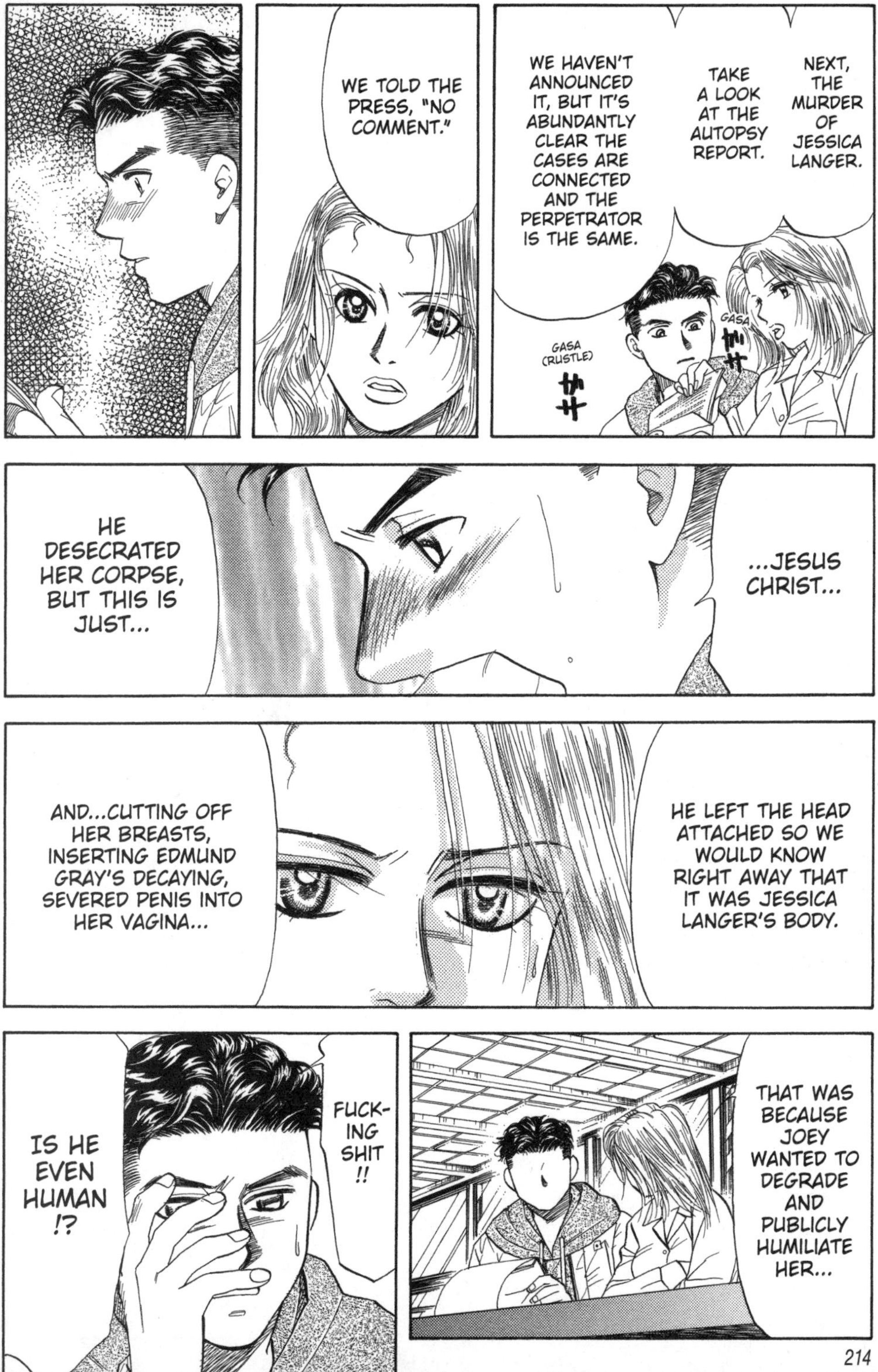
NEXT, THE MURDER OF JESSICA LANGER.
TAKE A LOOK AT THE AUTOPSY REPORT.
WE HAVEN'T ANNOUNCED IT, BUT IT'S ABUNDANTLY CLEAR THE CASES ARE CONNECTED AND THE PERPETRATOR IS THE SAME.
GASA ガサ
GASA (RUSTLE) ガサ
WE TOLD THE PRESS, "NO COMMENT."
...JESUS CHRIST...
HE DESECRATED HER CORPSE, BUT THIS IS JUST...
HE LEFT THE HEAD ATTACHED SO WE WOULD KNOW RIGHT AWAY THAT IT WAS JESSICA LANGER'S BODY.
AND...CUTTING OFF HER BREASTS, INSERTING EDMUND GRAY'S DECAYING, SEVERED PENIS INTO HER VAGINA...
THAT WAS BECAUSE JOEY WANTED TO DEGRADE AND PUBLICLY HUMILIATE HER...
FUCK-ING SHIT !!
IS HE EVEN HUMAN !?

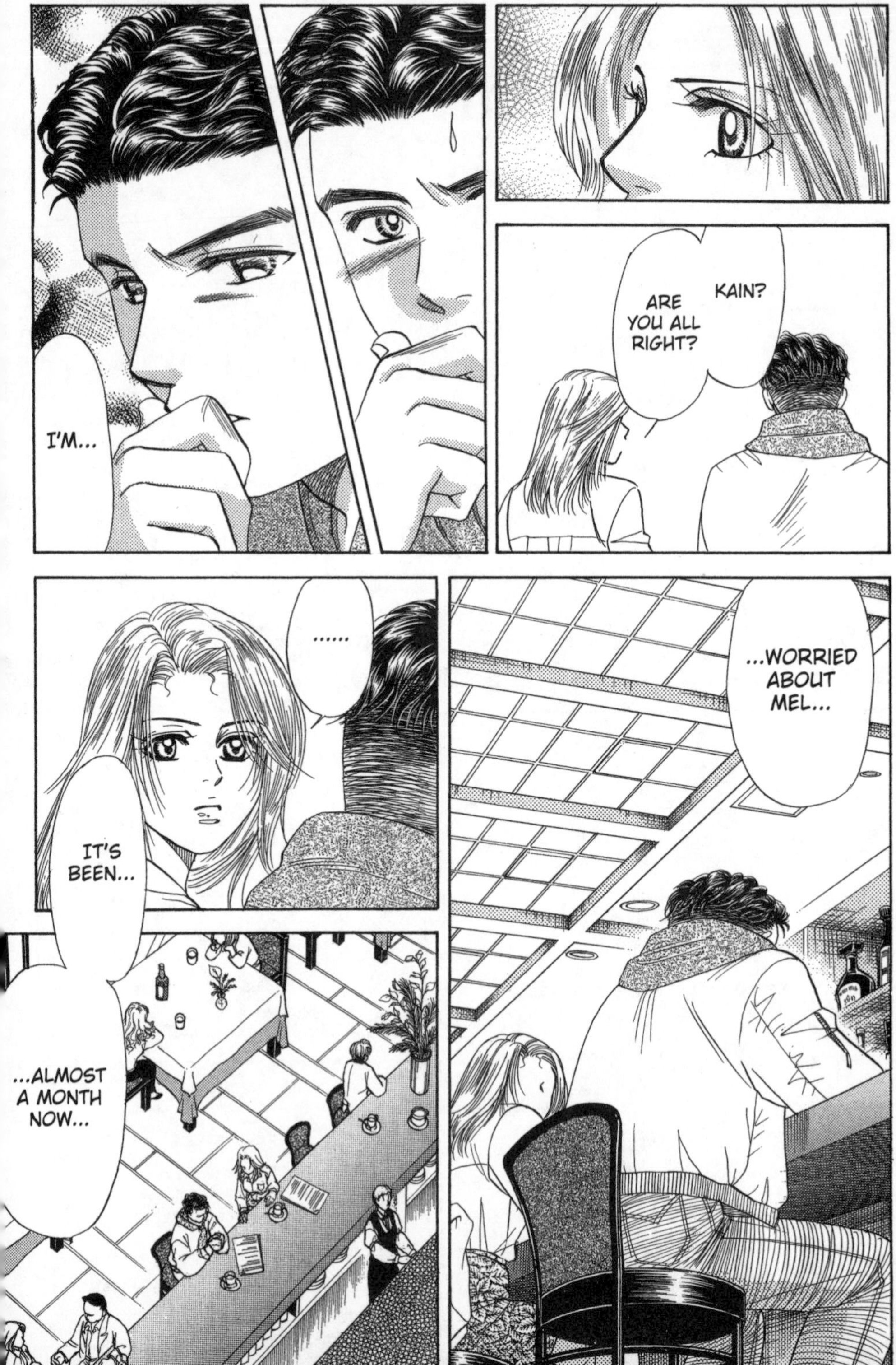
KAIN?
ARE YOU ALL RIGHT?
I'M...
...WORRIED ABOUT MEL...
......
IT'S BEEN...
...ALMOST A MONTH NOW...

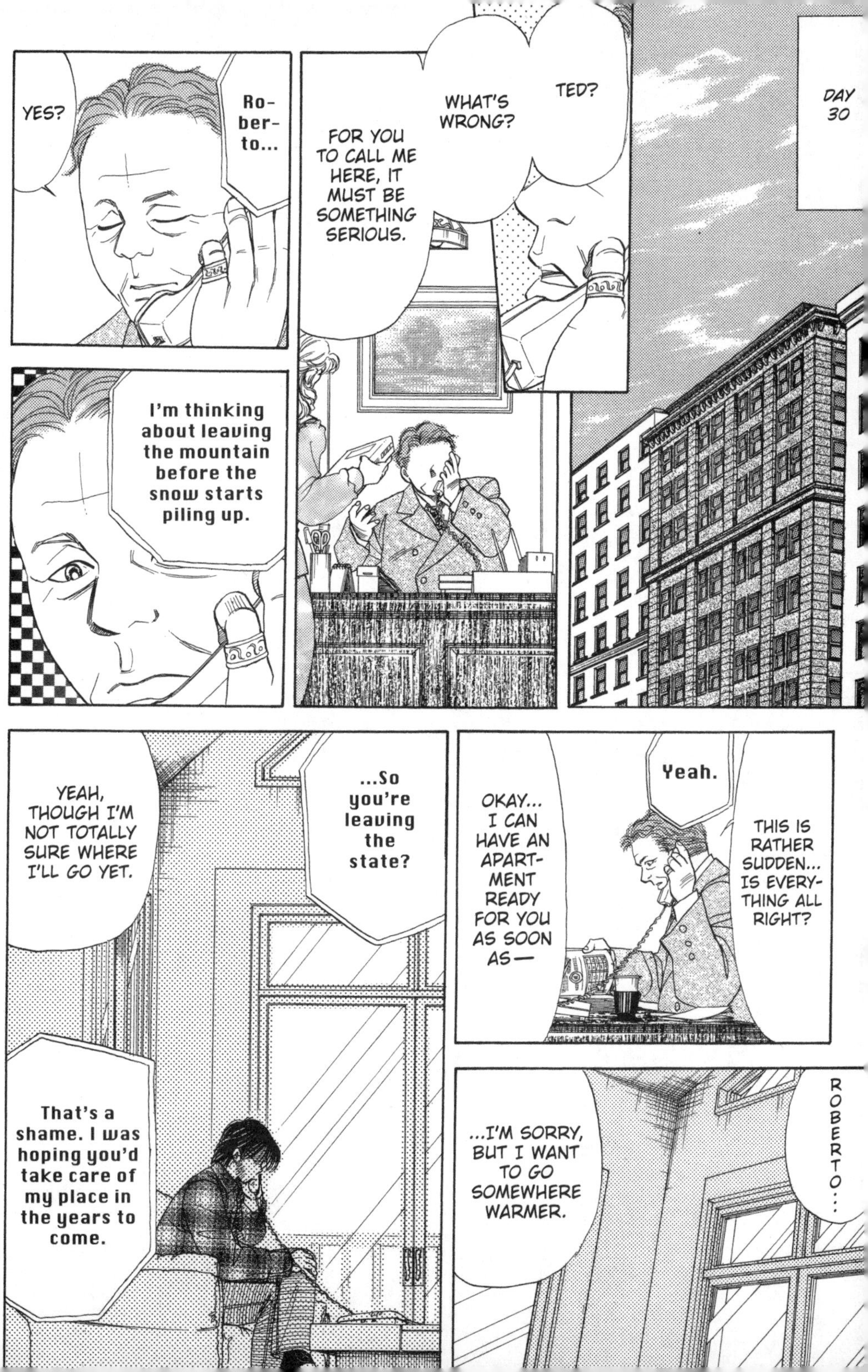
DAY 30
TED?
WHAT'S WRONG?
FOR YOU TO CALL ME HERE, IT MUST BE SOMETHING SERIOUS.
Ro-ber-to...
YES?
I'm thinking about leaving the mountain before the snow starts piling up.
THIS IS RATHER SUDDEN... IS EVERYTHING ALL RIGHT?
Yeah.
OKAY... I CAN HAVE AN APART-MENT READY FOR YOU AS SOON AS—
...I'M SORRY, BUT I WANT TO GO SOMEWHERE WARMER.
ROBERTO...
...So you're leaving the state?
YEAH, THOUGH I'M NOT TOTALLY SURE WHERE I'LL GO YET.
That's a shame. I was hoping you'd take care of my place in the years to come.

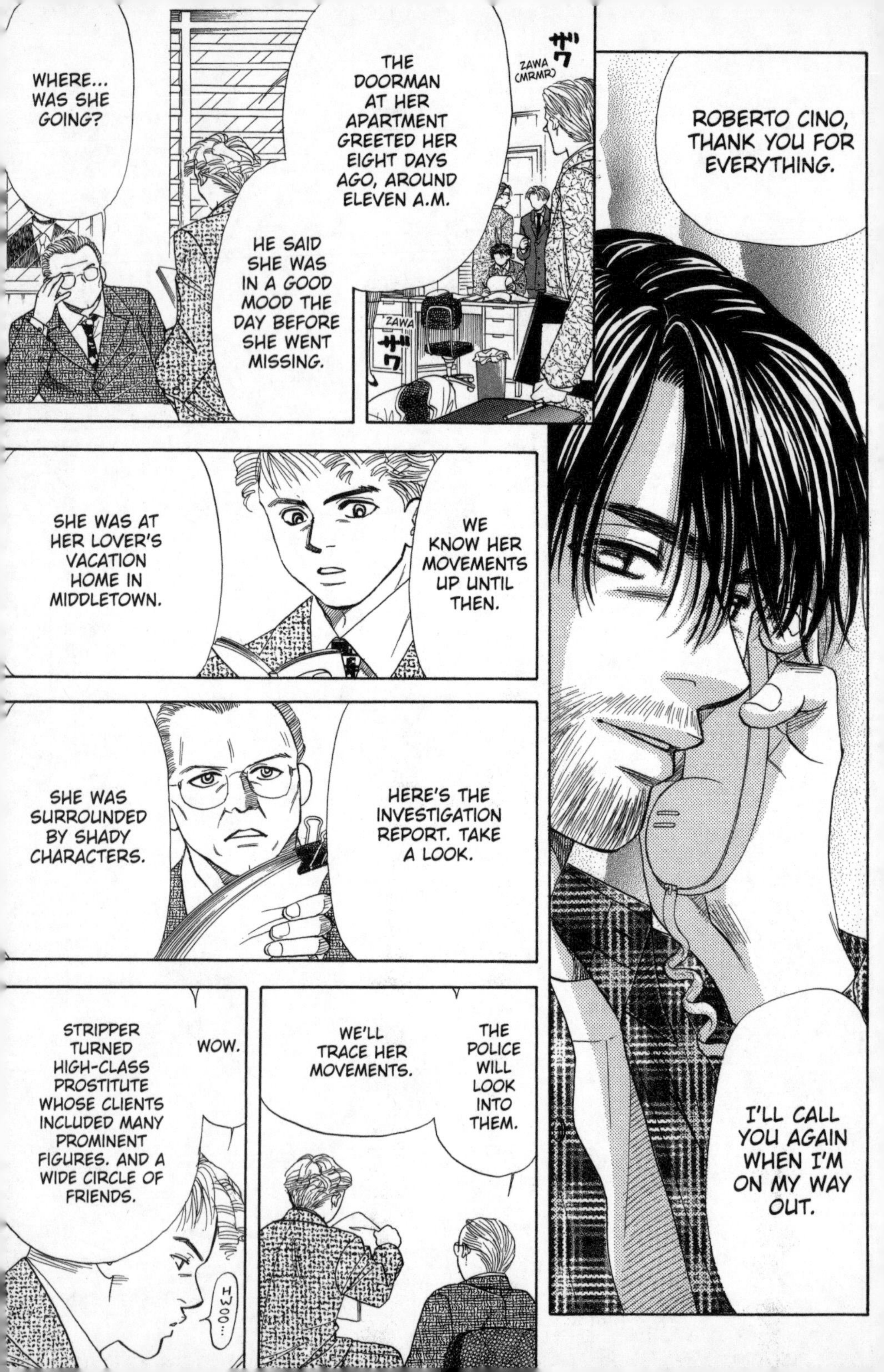
ROBERTO CINO, THANK YOU FOR EVERYTHING.
I'LL CALL YOU AGAIN WHEN I'M ON MY WAY OUT.
ザワ
ZAWA (MRMR)
ZAWA
ザワ
THE DOORMAN AT HER APARTMENT GREETED HER EIGHT DAYS AGO, AROUND ELEVEN A.M.
HE SAID SHE WAS IN A GOOD MOOD THE DAY BEFORE SHE WENT MISSING.
WHERE... WAS SHE GOING?
WE KNOW HER MOVEMENTS UP UNTIL THEN.
SHE WAS AT HER LOVER'S VACATION HOME IN MIDDLETOWN.
HERE'S THE INVESTIGATION REPORT. TAKE A LOOK.
SHE WAS SURROUNDED BY SHADY CHARACTERS.
THE POLICE WILL LOOK INTO THEM.
WE'LL TRACE HER MOVEMENTS.
WOW.
STRIPPER TURNED HIGH-CLASS PROSTITUTE WHOSE CLIENTS INCLUDED MANY PROMINENT FIGURES. AND A WIDE CIRCLE OF FRIENDS.
HWOO...

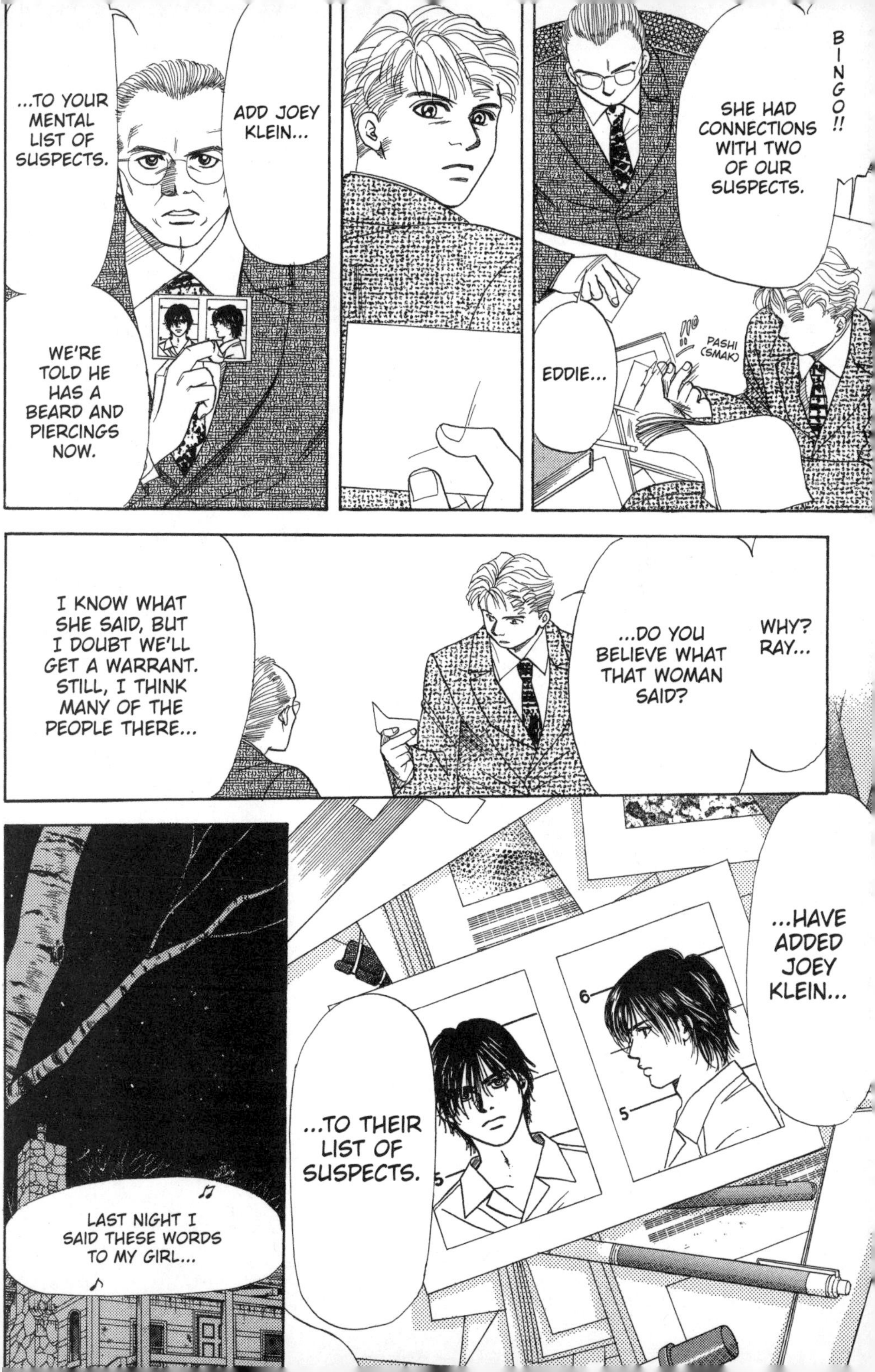
BINGO!!
SHE HAD CONNECTIONS WITH TWO OF OUR SUSPECTS.
PASHI (SMAK)
EDDIE...
ADD JOEY KLEIN...
...TO YOUR MENTAL LIST OF SUSPECTS.
WE'RE TOLD HE HAS A BEARD AND PIERCINGS NOW.
WHY? RAY...
...DO YOU BELIEVE WHAT THAT WOMAN SAID?
I KNOW WHAT SHE SAID, BUT I DOUBT WE'LL GET A WARRANT. STILL, I THINK MANY OF THE PEOPLE THERE...
...HAVE ADDED JOEY KLEIN...
...TO THEIR LIST OF SUSPECTS.
LAST NIGHT I SAID THESE WORDS TO MY GIRL...

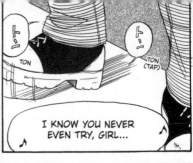

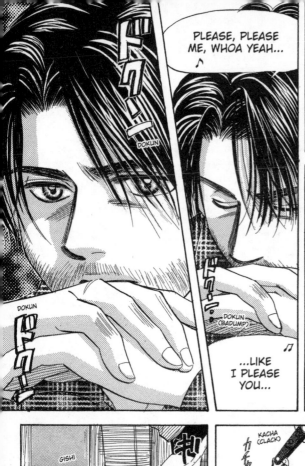

トン
TON
トン
TON (TAP)
I KNOW YOU NEVER EVEN TRY, GIRL...
COME ON.
トン
TON
COME ON.
トン
TON
COME ON.
COME ON.
PLEASE, PLEASE ME, WHOA YEAH...
ドクーン
DOKUN (BADUMP)
...LIKE I PLEASE YOU...
ドクーン
DOKUN
DOKUN
ドクーン
DOKUN
ドクーッ
DOKUN
ドクーッ
KACHA (CLACK)
カチャ...
ドクーッ
DOKUN
ギッ
GI (CREAK)
GISHI
ギシ
GISHI
ギシ
DOKUN
ドクーーッ
ギシーー
GISHI

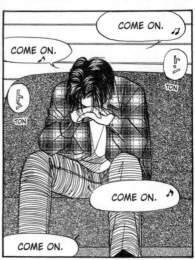

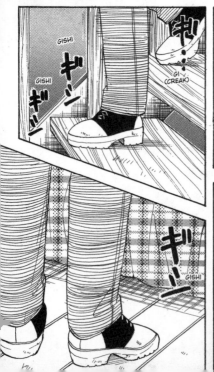

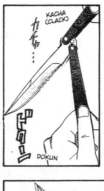

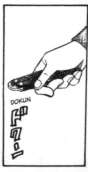

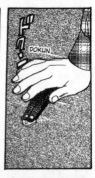

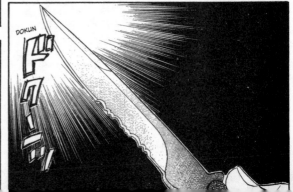

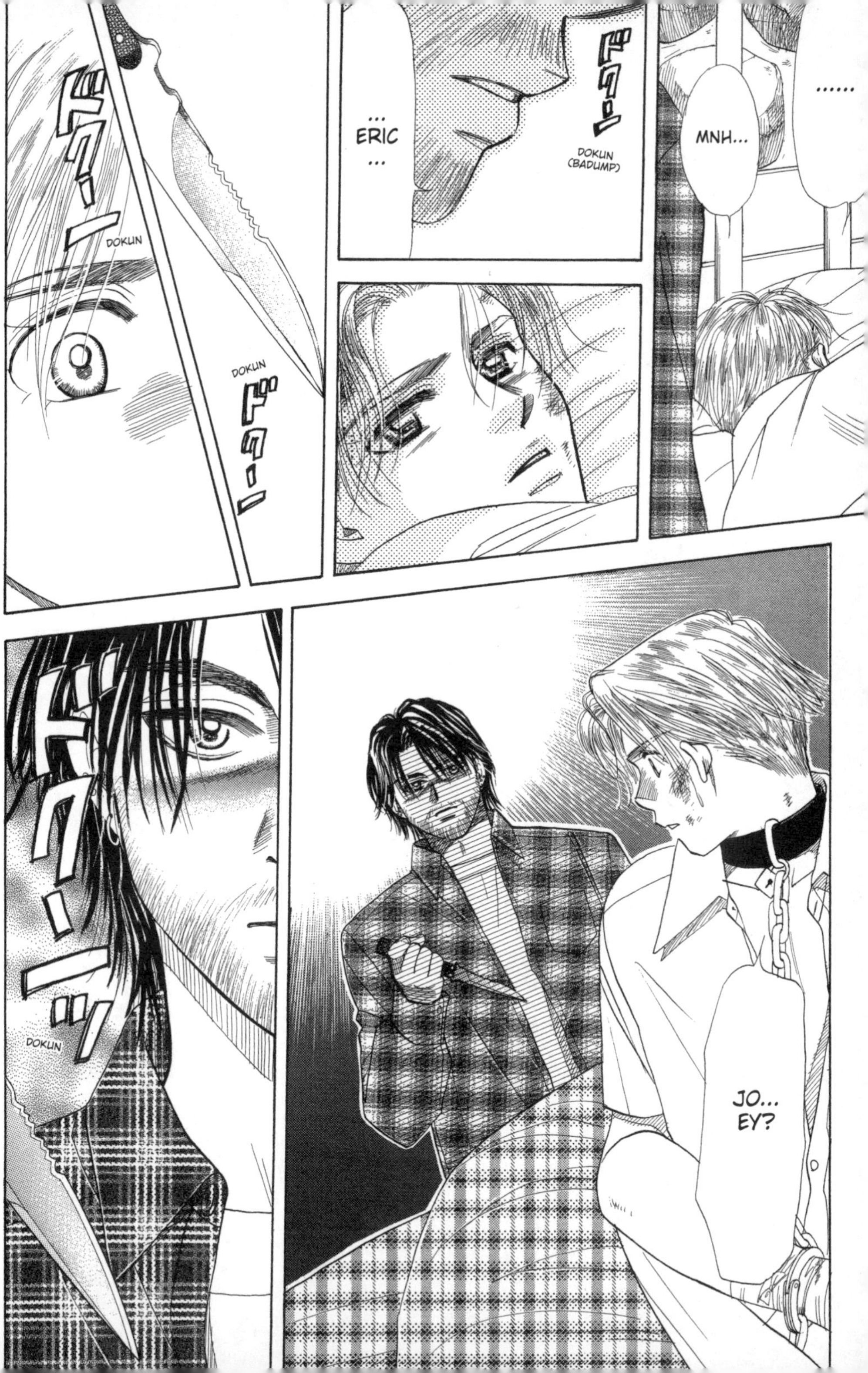
......
MNH...
DOKUN (BADUMP)
... ERIC ...
DOKUN
DOKUN
JO... EY?
DOKUN

EPISODE IV

SCENE 6

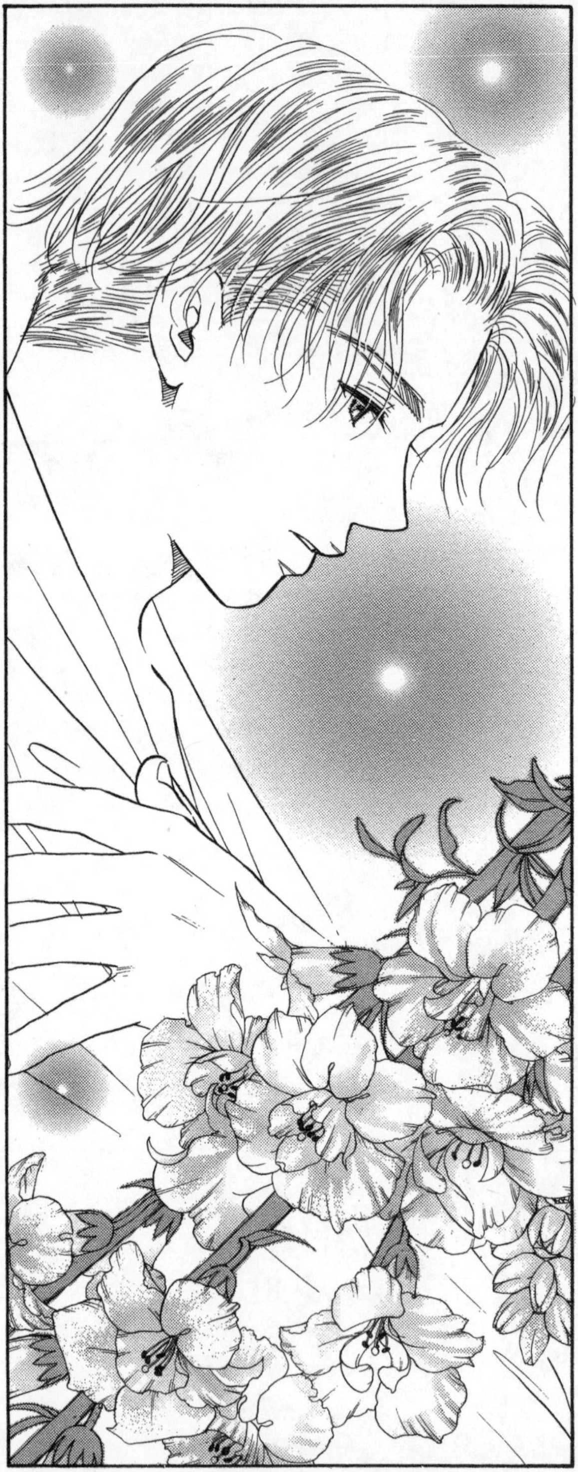

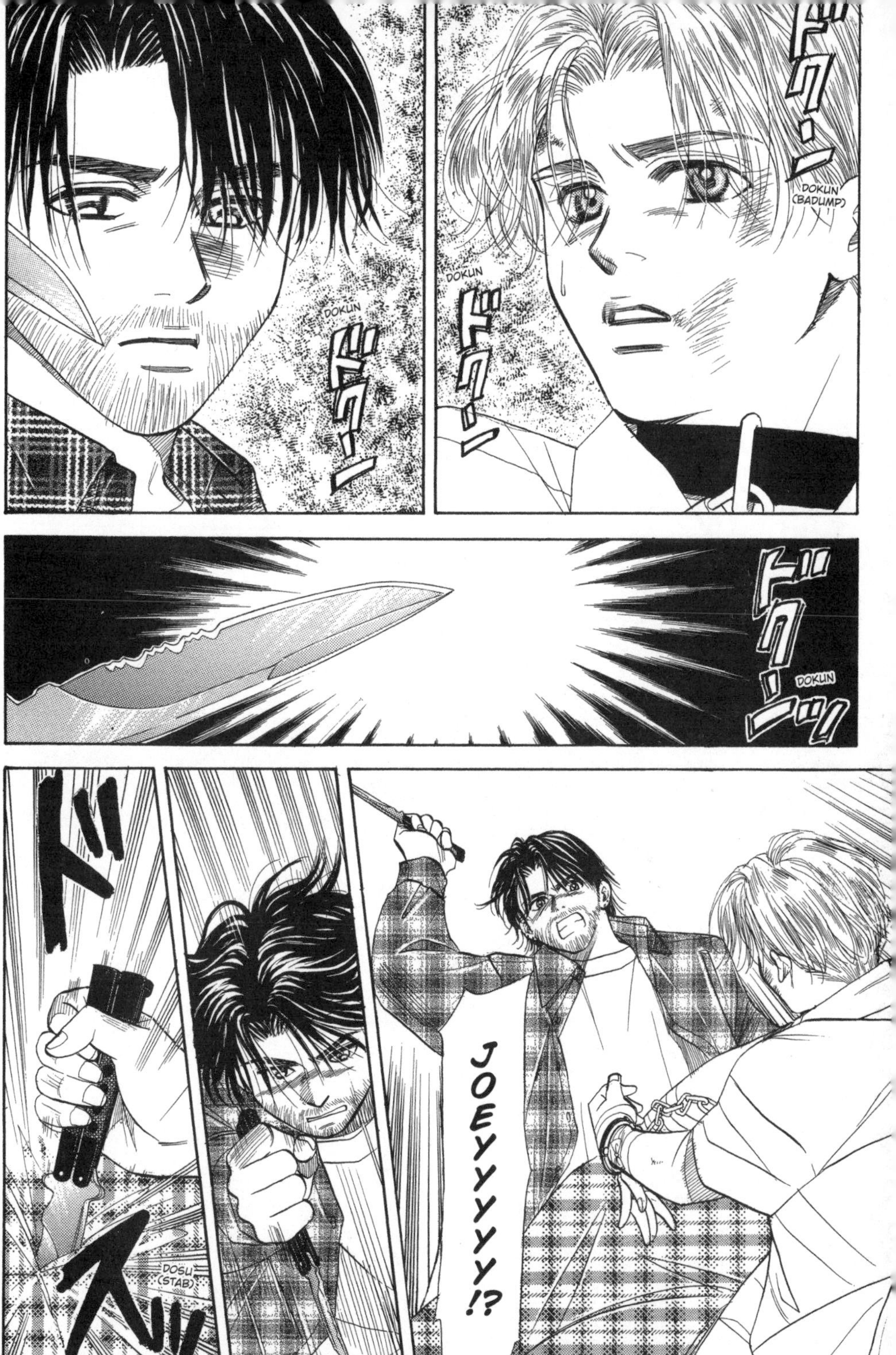
DOKUN (BADUMP)
DOKUN
DOKUN
DOKUN
JOEYYYYYY!?
DOSU (STAB)

ZURU (SLIP)
DOSA (FWUMP)
DO (THUD)
HAH!
HAH!
HAH!
HAH!

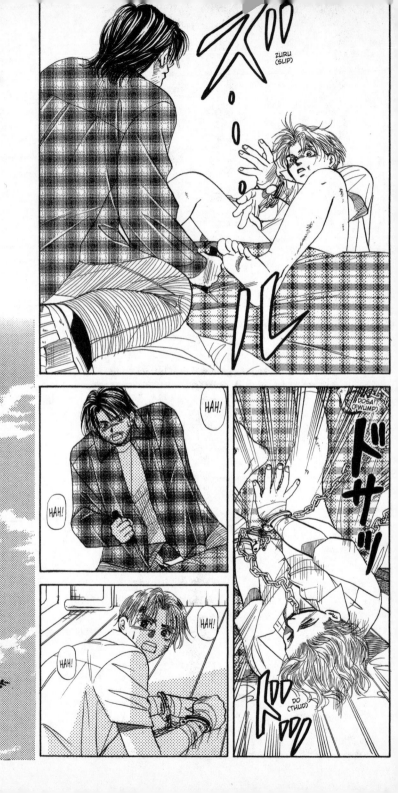

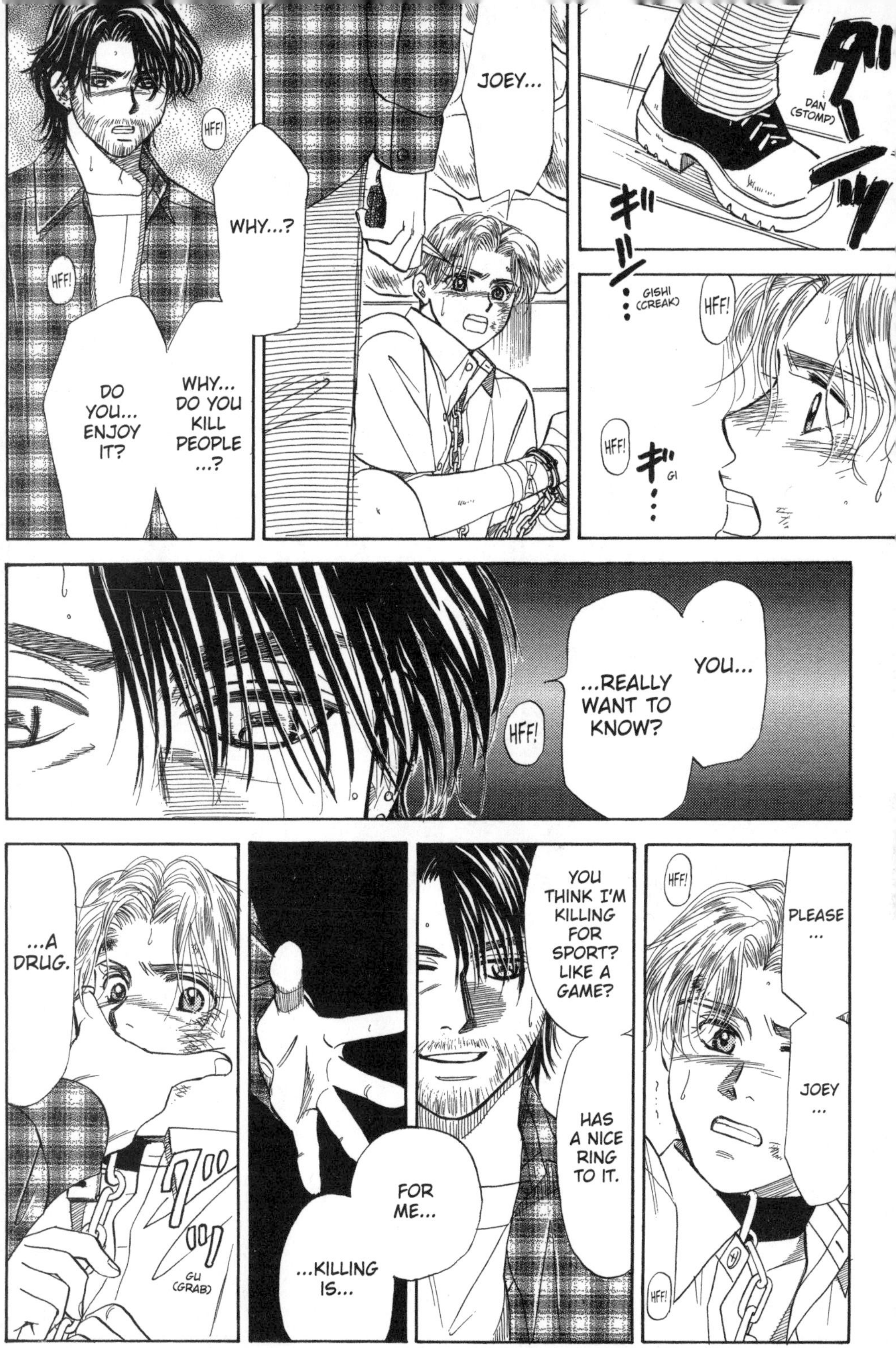
DAN (STOMP)
GISHI (CREAK)
HFF!
HFF!
GI
JOEY...
HFF!
WHY...?
HFF!
WHY... DO YOU KILL PEOPLE ...?
DO YOU... ENJOY IT?
YOU...
...REALLY WANT TO KNOW?
HFF!
HFF!
PLEASE ...
JOEY ...
HFF!
YOU THINK I'M KILLING FOR SPORT? LIKE A GAME?
HAS A NICE RING TO IT.
FOR ME...
...KILLING IS...
...A DRUG.
GU (GRAB)

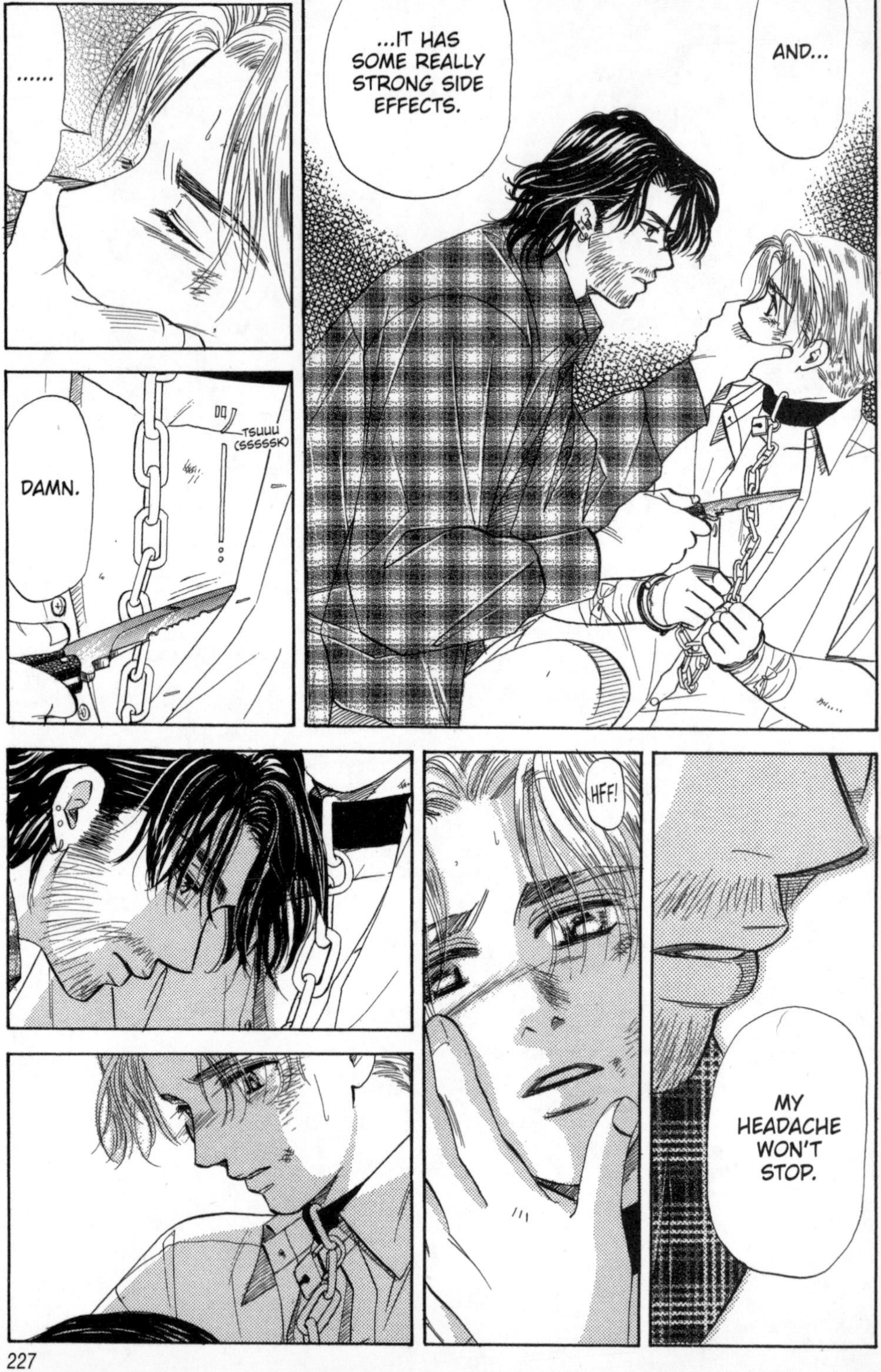
...IT HAS SOME REALLY STRONG SIDE EFFECTS.
AND...
......
TSUUU (SSSSSK)
DAMN.
MY HEADACHE WON'T STOP.
HFF!

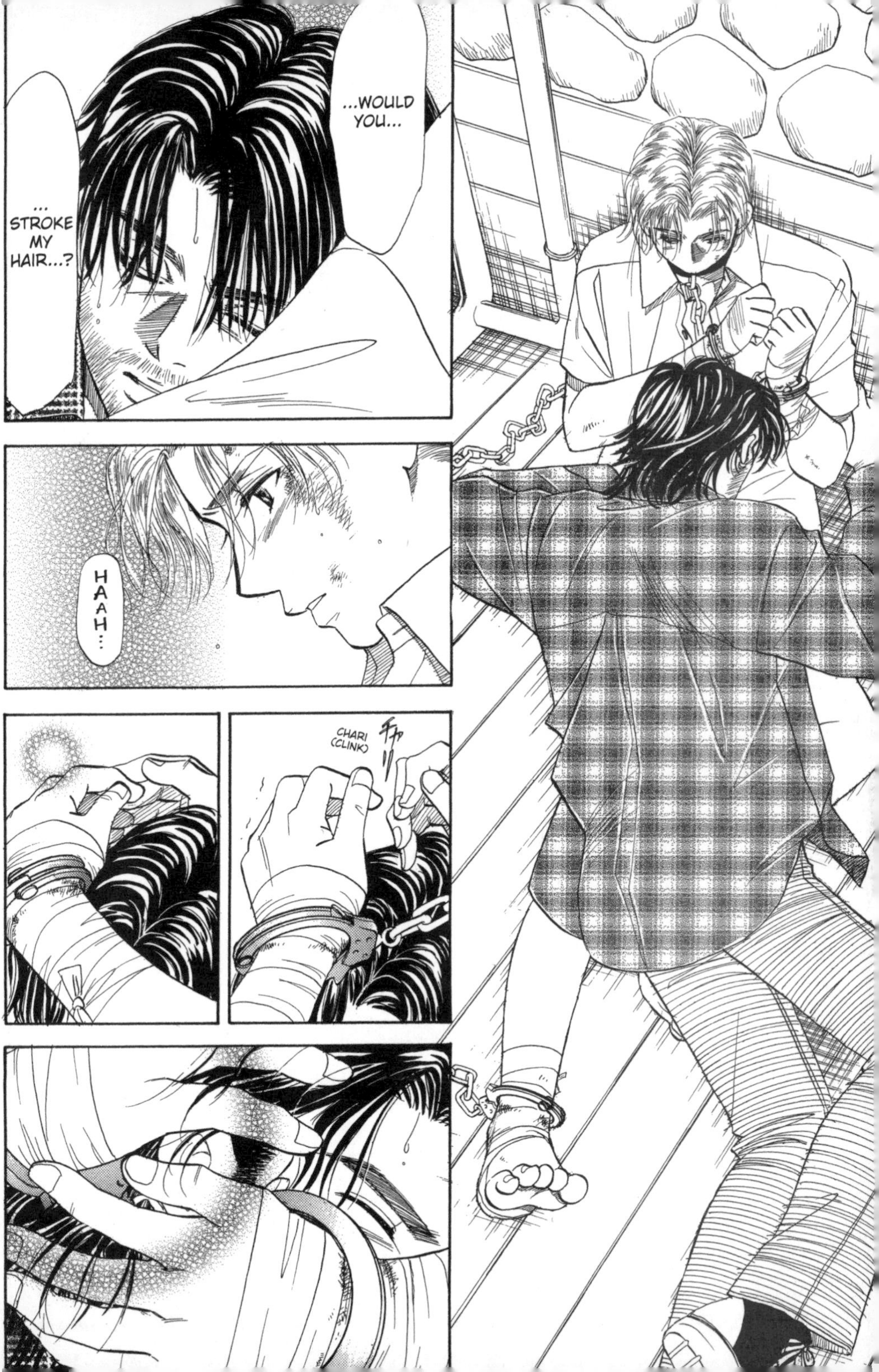
...WOULD YOU...
...STROKE MY HAIR...?
HAAH...
CHARI (CLINK)

......

HAH...

TP!!
CHARI

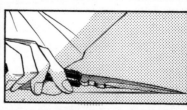

SHIT!!

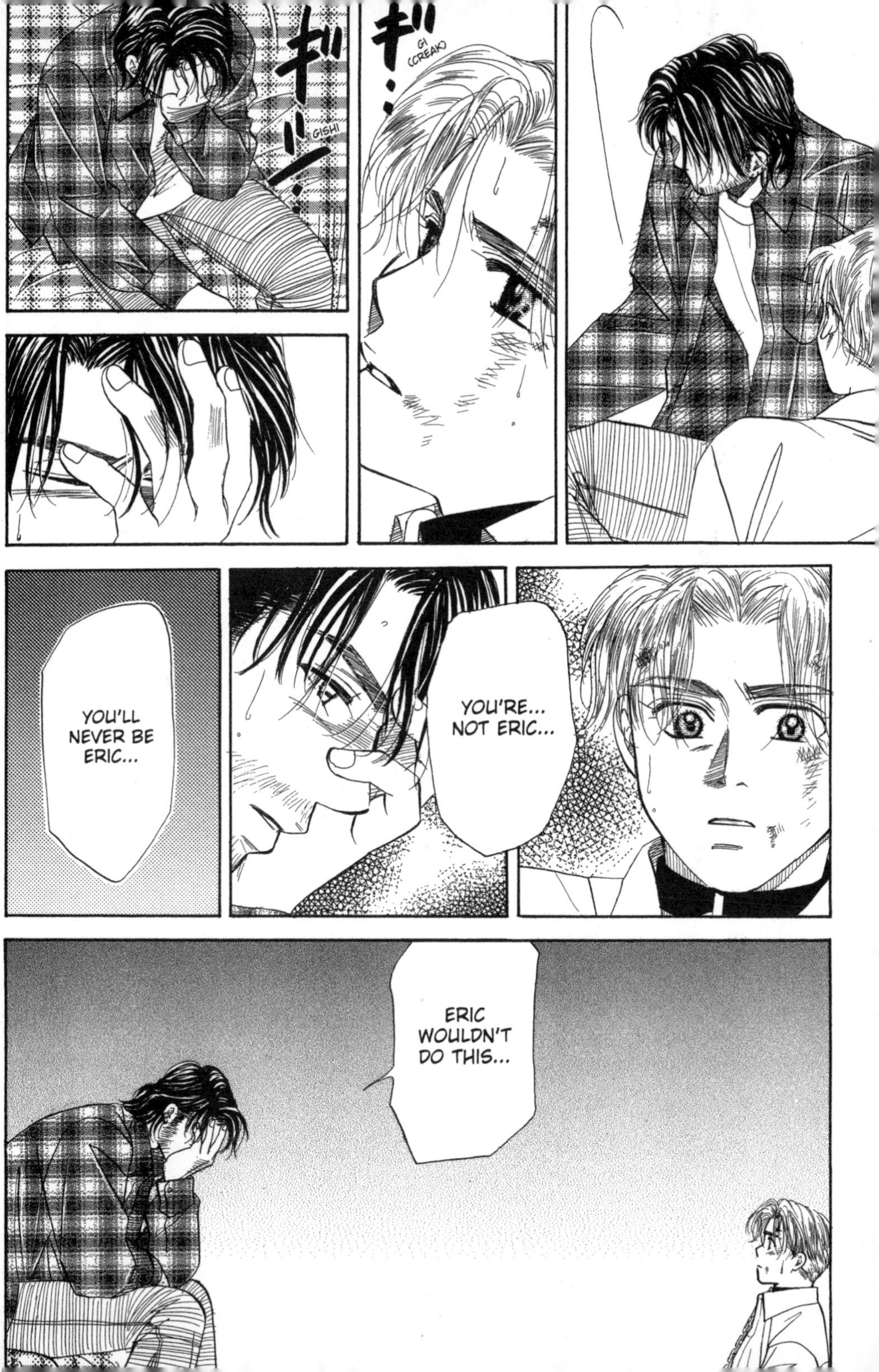
GI (CREAK)
GISHI
YOU'RE... NOT ERIC...
YOU'LL NEVER BE ERIC...
ERIC WOULDN'T DO THIS...

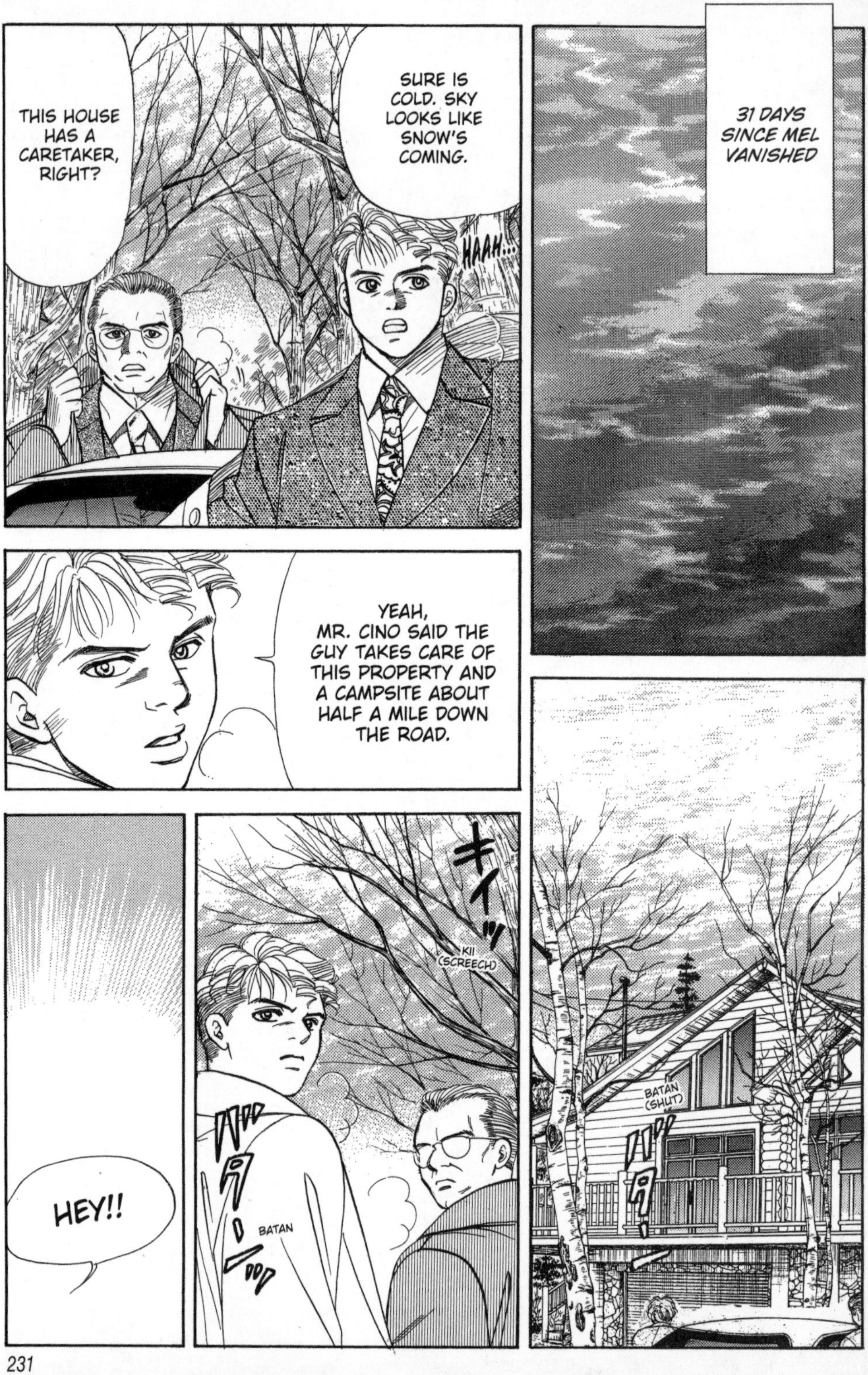
31 DAYS SINCE MEL VANISHED
SURE IS COLD. SKY LOOKS LIKE SNOW'S COMING.
THIS HOUSE HAS A CARETAKER, RIGHT?
HAAH...
YEAH, MR. CINO SAID THE GUY TAKES CARE OF THIS PROPERTY AND A CAMPSITE ABOUT HALF A MILE DOWN THE ROAD.
BATAN (SHUT)
キイッ
KII (SCREECH)
バタン
BATAN
HEY!!

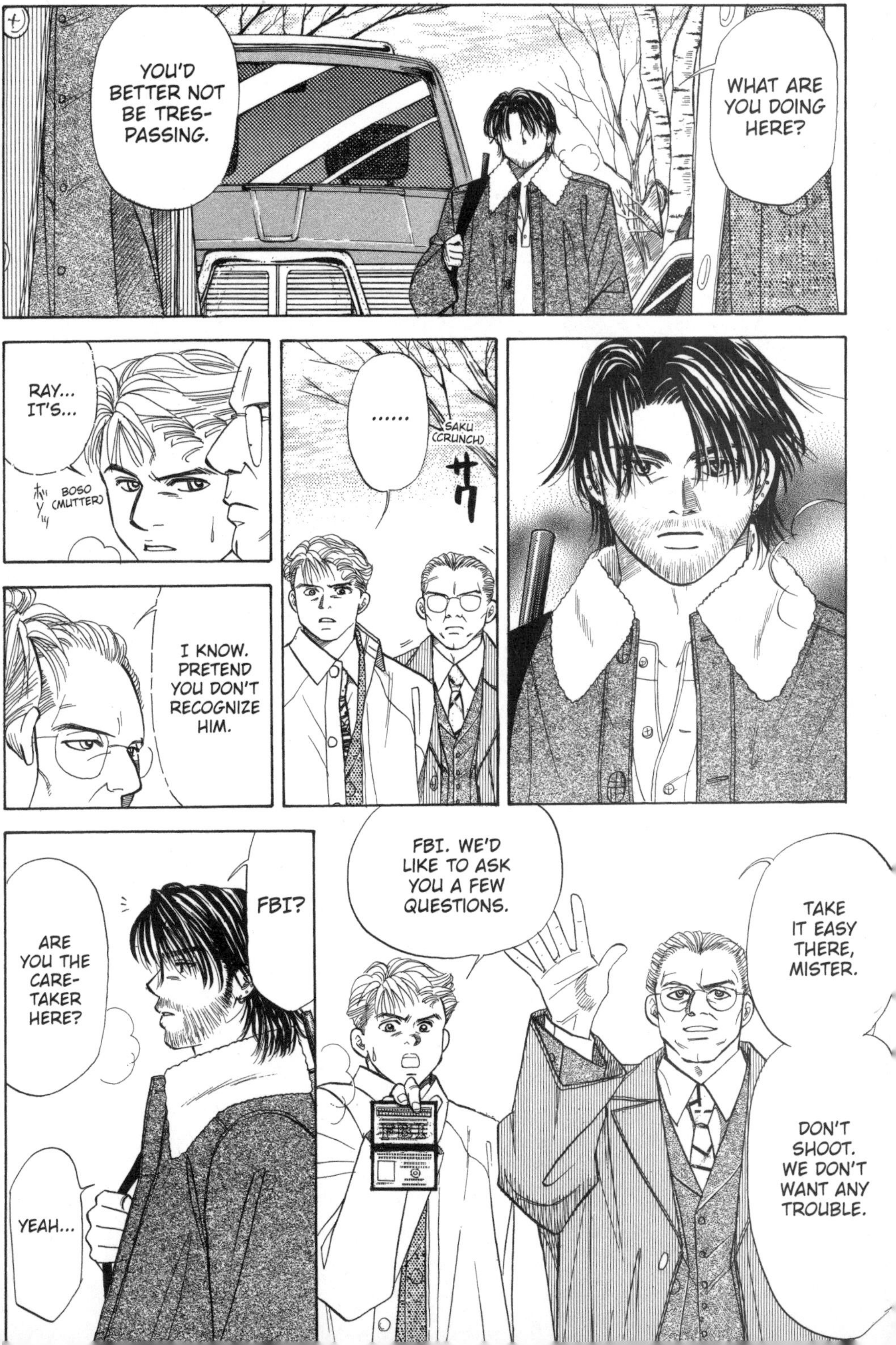
WHAT ARE YOU DOING HERE?
YOU'D BETTER NOT BE TRES-PASSING.
......
サク
SAKU (CRUNCH)
RAY... IT'S...
BOSO (MUTTER)
I KNOW. PRETEND YOU DON'T RECOGNIZE HIM.
TAKE IT EASY THERE, MISTER.
DON'T SHOOT. WE DON'T WANT ANY TROUBLE.
FBI. WE'D LIKE TO ASK YOU A FEW QUESTIONS.
FBI?
ARE YOU THE CARE-TAKER HERE?
YEAH...

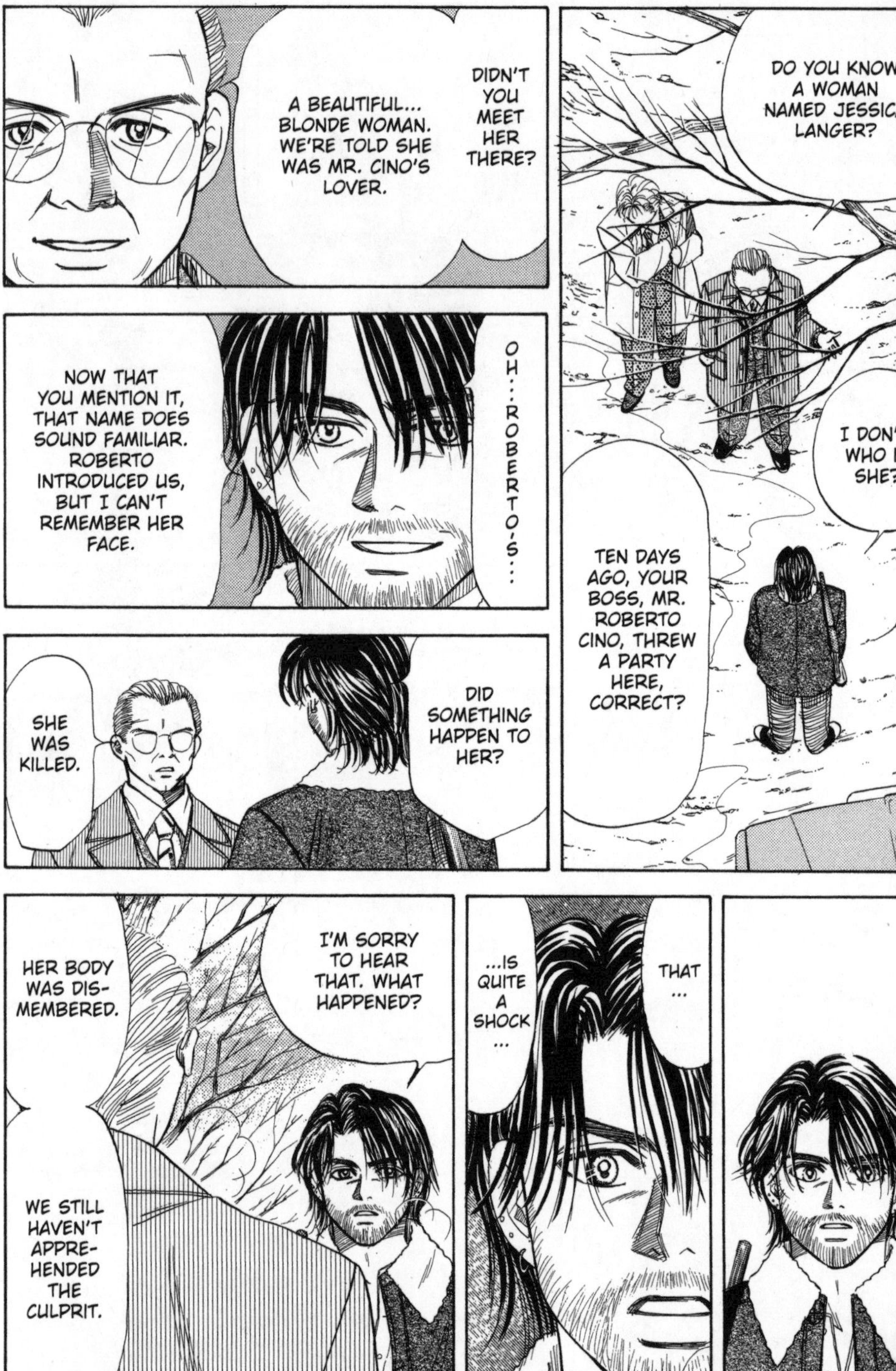
DO YOU KNOW A WOMAN NAMED JESSICA LANGER?
I DON'T. WHO IS SHE?
TEN DAYS AGO, YOUR BOSS, MR. ROBERTO CINO, THREW A PARTY HERE, CORRECT?
DIDN'T YOU MEET HER THERE?
A BEAUTIFUL... BLONDE WOMAN. WE'RE TOLD SHE WAS MR. CINO'S LOVER.
OH...ROBERTO'S...
NOW THAT YOU MENTION IT, THAT NAME DOES SOUND FAMILIAR. ROBERTO INTRODUCED US, BUT I CAN'T REMEMBER HER FACE.
DID SOMETHING HAPPEN TO HER?
SHE WAS KILLED.
THAT ...
...IS QUITE A SHOCK ...
I'M SORRY TO HEAR THAT. WHAT HAPPENED?
HER BODY WAS DIS-MEMBERED.
WE STILL HAVEN'T APPRE-HENDED THE CULPRIT.

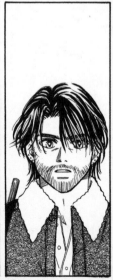

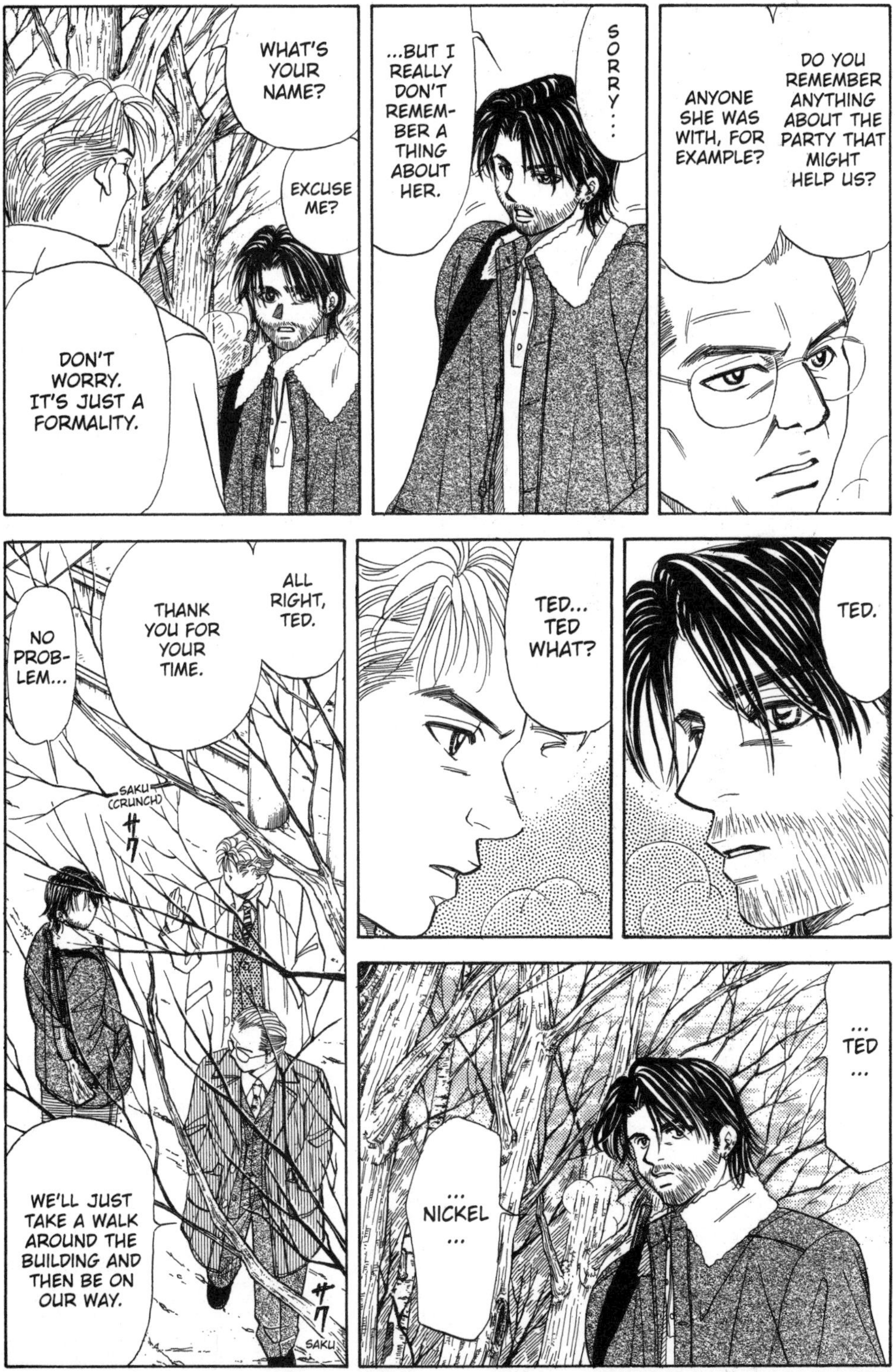
DO YOU REMEMBER ANYTHING ABOUT THE PARTY THAT MIGHT HELP US?
ANYONE SHE WAS WITH, FOR EXAMPLE?
SORRY...
...BUT I REALLY DON'T REMEMBER A THING ABOUT HER.
WHAT'S YOUR NAME?
EXCUSE ME?
DON'T WORRY. IT'S JUST A FORMALITY.
TED.
TED... TED WHAT?
...TED...
...NICKEL...
ALL RIGHT, TED.
THANK YOU FOR YOUR TIME.
NO PROBLEM...
SAKU (CRUNCH)
WE'LL JUST TAKE A WALK AROUND THE BUILDING AND THEN BE ON OUR WAY.
SAKU

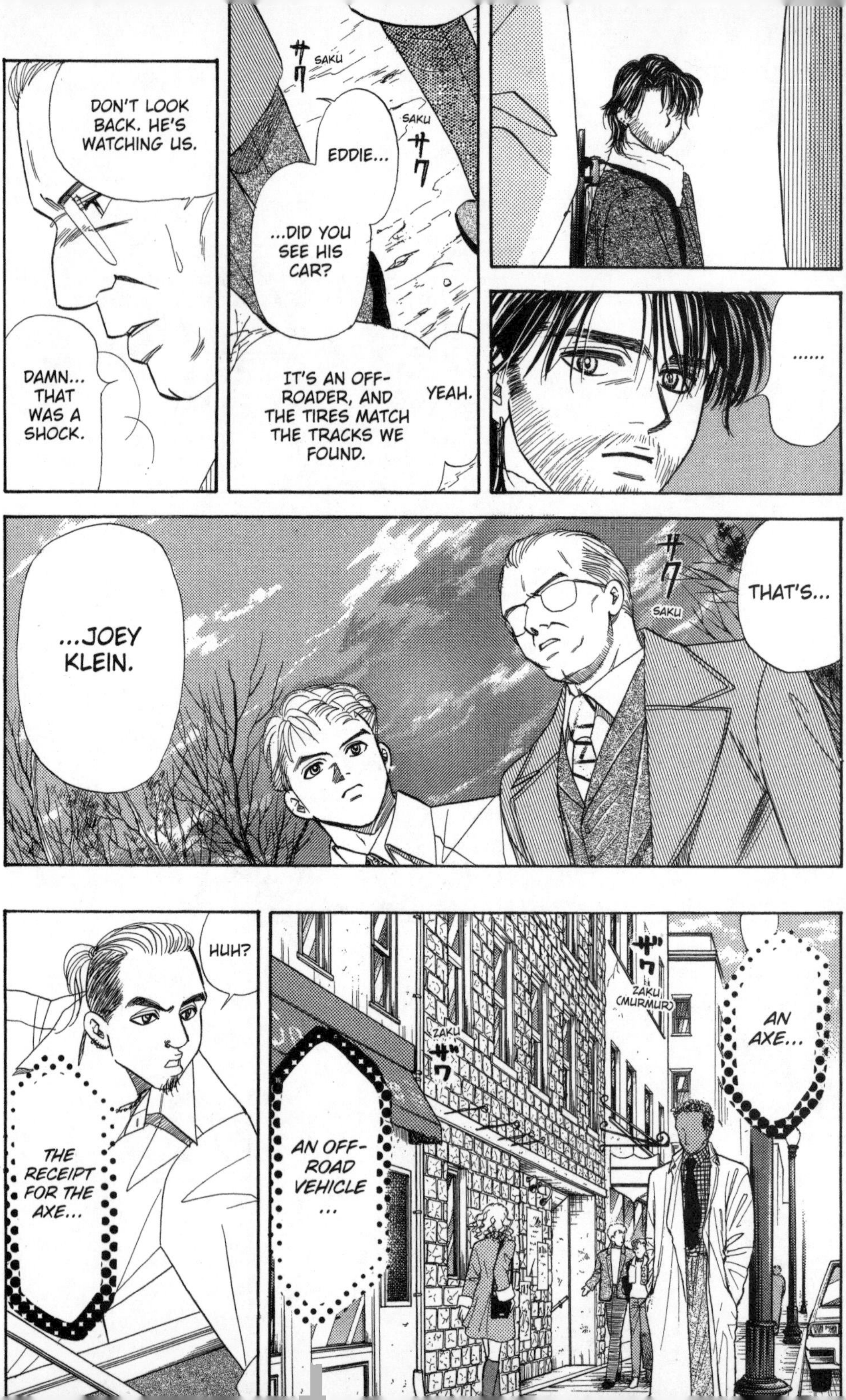

......
サク
SAKU
EDDIE...
...DID YOU SEE HIS CAR?
サク
SAKU
YEAH.
IT'S AN OFF-ROADER, AND THE TIRES MATCH THE TRACKS WE FOUND.
DON'T LOOK BACK. HE'S WATCHING US.
DAMN... THAT WAS A SHOCK.
THAT'S...
サク
SAKU
...JOEY KLEIN.
AN AXE...
ザワ
ZAKU (MURMUR)
ザワ
ZAKU
AN OFF-ROAD VEHICLE ...
HUH?
THE RECEIPT FOR THE AXE...

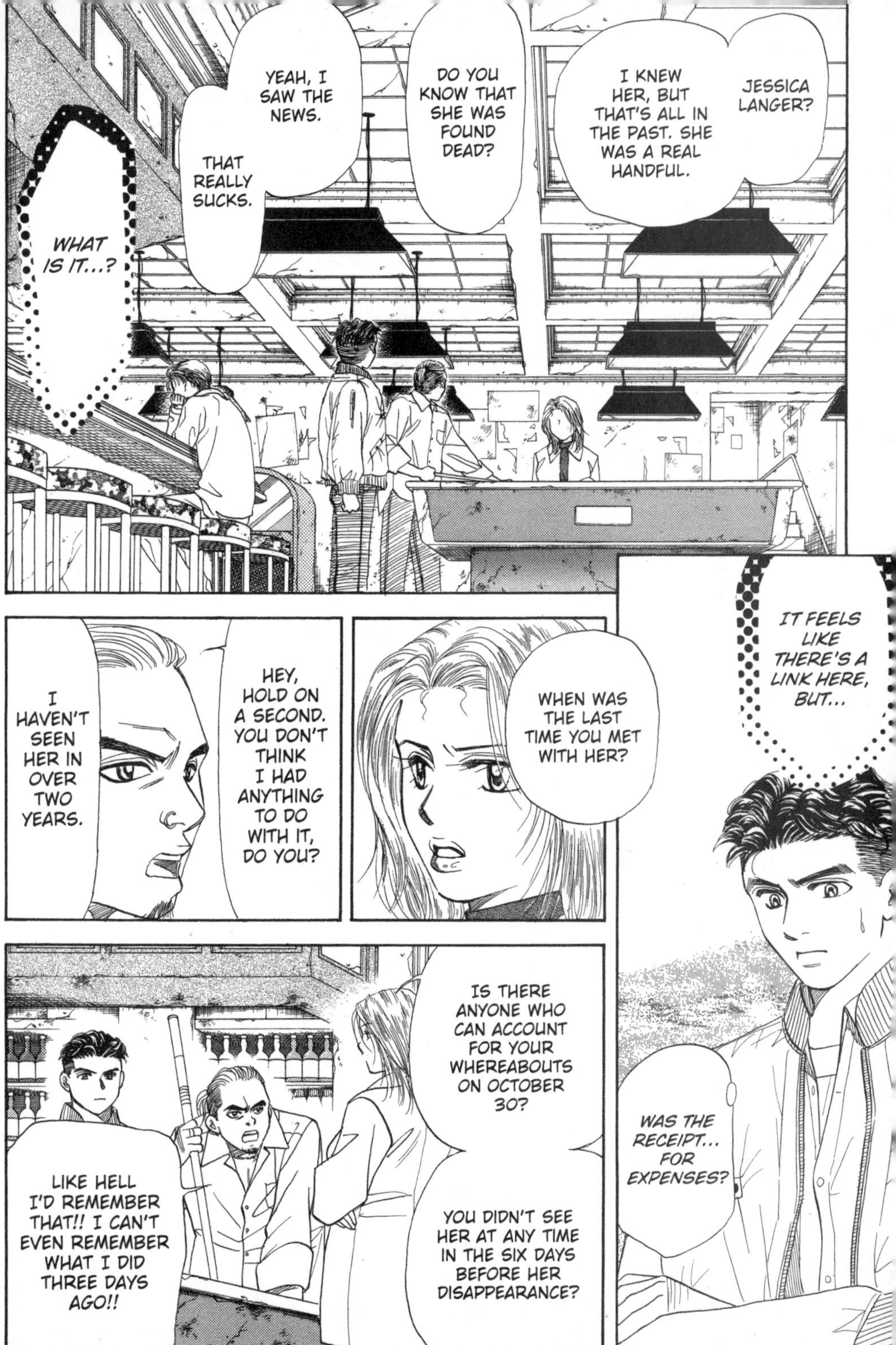
JESSICA LANGER?
I KNEW HER, BUT THAT'S ALL IN THE PAST. SHE WAS A REAL HANDFUL.
DO YOU KNOW THAT SHE WAS FOUND DEAD?
YEAH, I SAW THE NEWS.
THAT REALLY SUCKS.
WHAT IS IT...?
IT FEELS LIKE THERE'S A LINK HERE, BUT...
WAS THE RECEIPT... FOR EXPENSES?
WHEN WAS THE LAST TIME YOU MET WITH HER?
HEY, HOLD ON A SECOND. YOU DON'T THINK I HAD ANYTHING TO DO WITH IT, DO YOU?
I HAVEN'T SEEN HER IN OVER TWO YEARS.
IS THERE ANYONE WHO CAN ACCOUNT FOR YOUR WHEREABOUTS ON OCTOBER 30?
YOU DIDN'T SEE HER AT ANY TIME IN THE SIX DAYS BEFORE HER DISAPPEARANCE?
LIKE HELL I'D REMEMBER THAT!! I CAN'T EVEN REMEMBER WHAT I DID THREE DAYS AGO!!

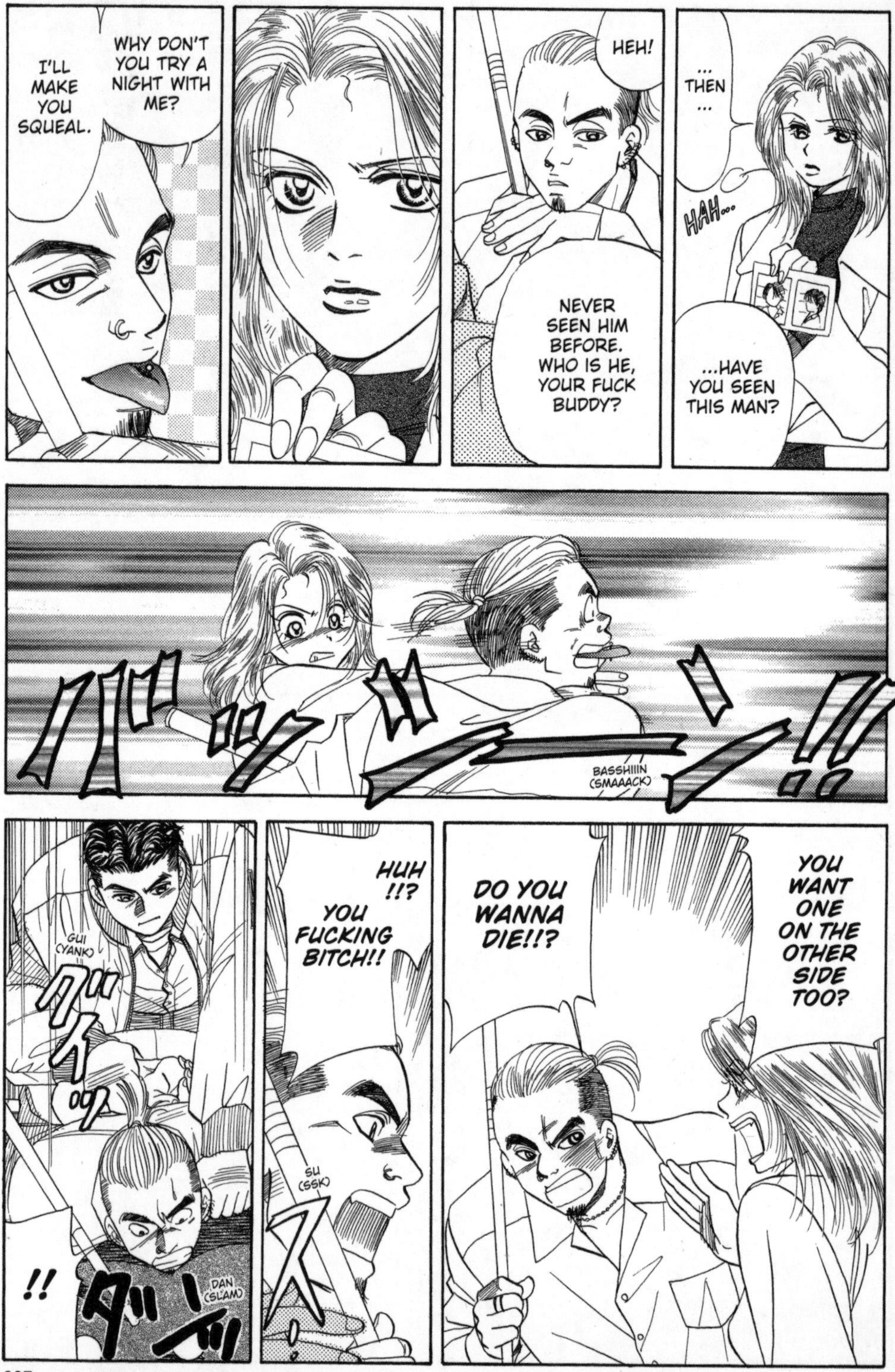
...THEN ...
HAH...
...HAVE YOU SEEN THIS MAN?
HEH!
NEVER SEEN HIM BEFORE. WHO IS HE, YOUR FUCK BUDDY?
WHY DON'T YOU TRY A NIGHT WITH ME?
I'LL MAKE YOU SQUEAL.
BASSHIIIN (SMAAACK)
YOU WANT ONE ON THE OTHER SIDE TOO?
DO YOU WANNA DIE!!?
HUH!!? YOU FUCKING BITCH!!
SU (SSK)
GUI (YANK)
!!
DAN (SLAM)

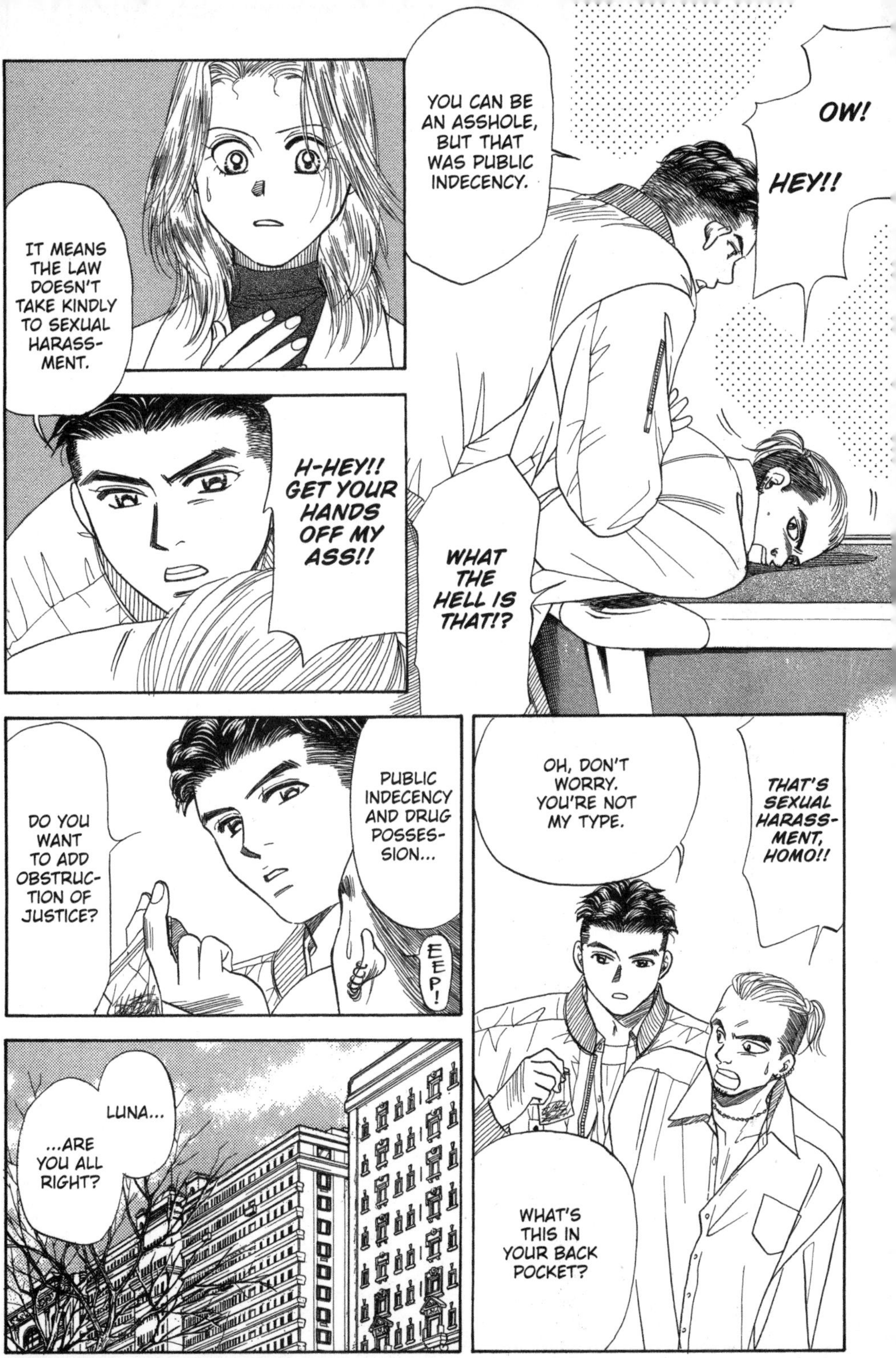
OW!
HEY!!
YOU CAN BE AN ASSHOLE, BUT THAT WAS PUBLIC INDECENCY.
WHAT THE HELL IS THAT!?
IT MEANS THE LAW DOESN'T TAKE KINDLY TO SEXUAL HARASS-MENT.
H-HEY!! GET YOUR HANDS OFF MY ASS!!
THAT'S SEXUAL HARASS-MENT, HOMO!!
OH, DON'T WORRY. YOU'RE NOT MY TYPE.
WHAT'S THIS IN YOUR BACK POCKET?
PUBLIC INDECENCY AND DRUG POSSES-SION...
DO YOU WANT TO ADD OBSTRUC-TION OF JUSTICE?
EEP!
LUNA...
...ARE YOU ALL RIGHT?

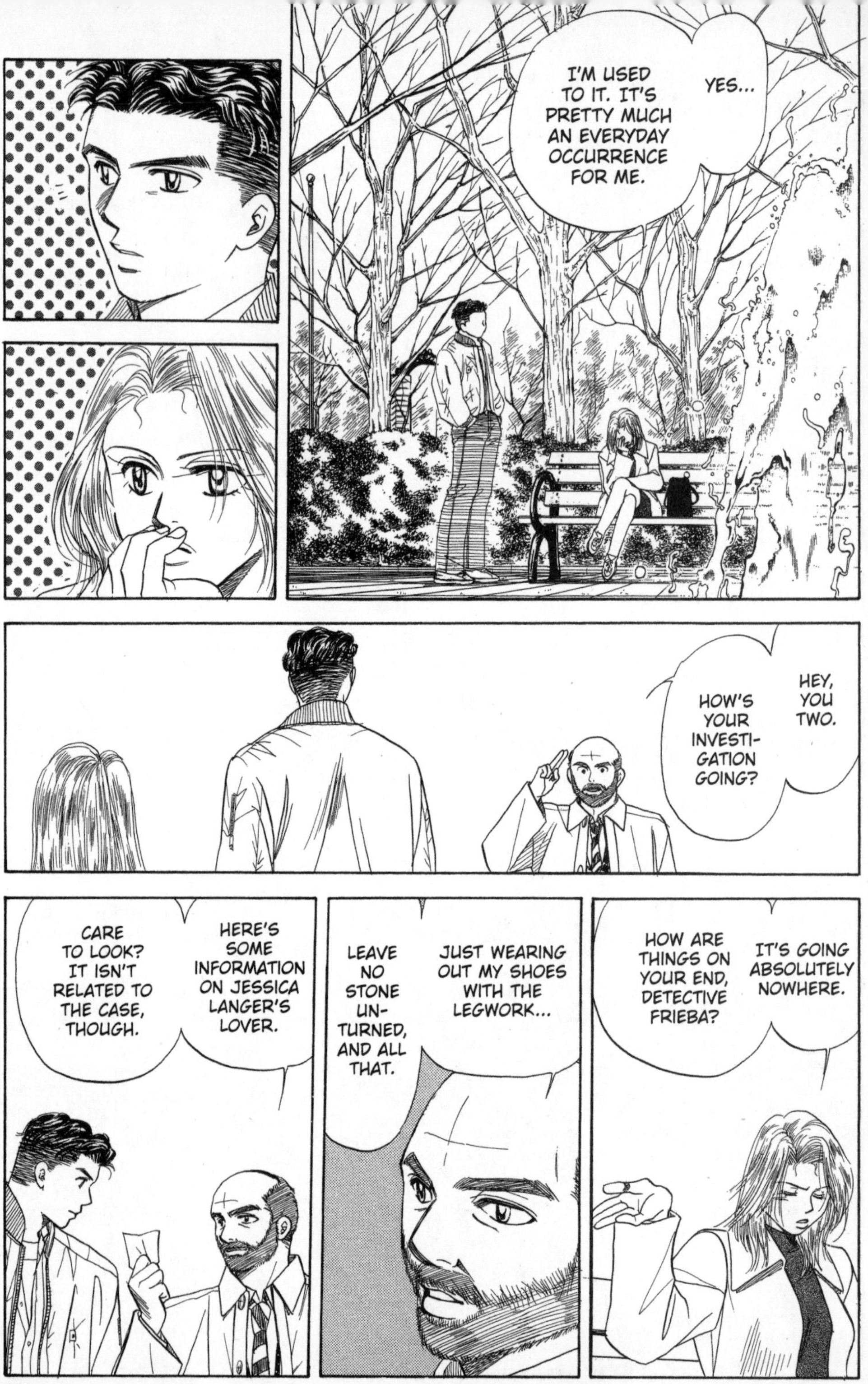
YES...
I'M USED TO IT. IT'S PRETTY MUCH AN EVERYDAY OCCURRENCE FOR ME.
HEY, YOU TWO.
HOW'S YOUR INVESTIGATION GOING?
IT'S GOING ABSOLUTELY NOWHERE.
HOW ARE THINGS ON YOUR END, DETECTIVE FRIEBA?
JUST WEARING OUT MY SHOES WITH THE LEGWORK...
LEAVE NO STONE UNTURNED, AND ALL THAT.
HERE'S SOME INFORMATION ON JESSICA LANGER'S LOVER.
CARE TO LOOK? IT ISN'T RELATED TO THE CASE, THOUGH.

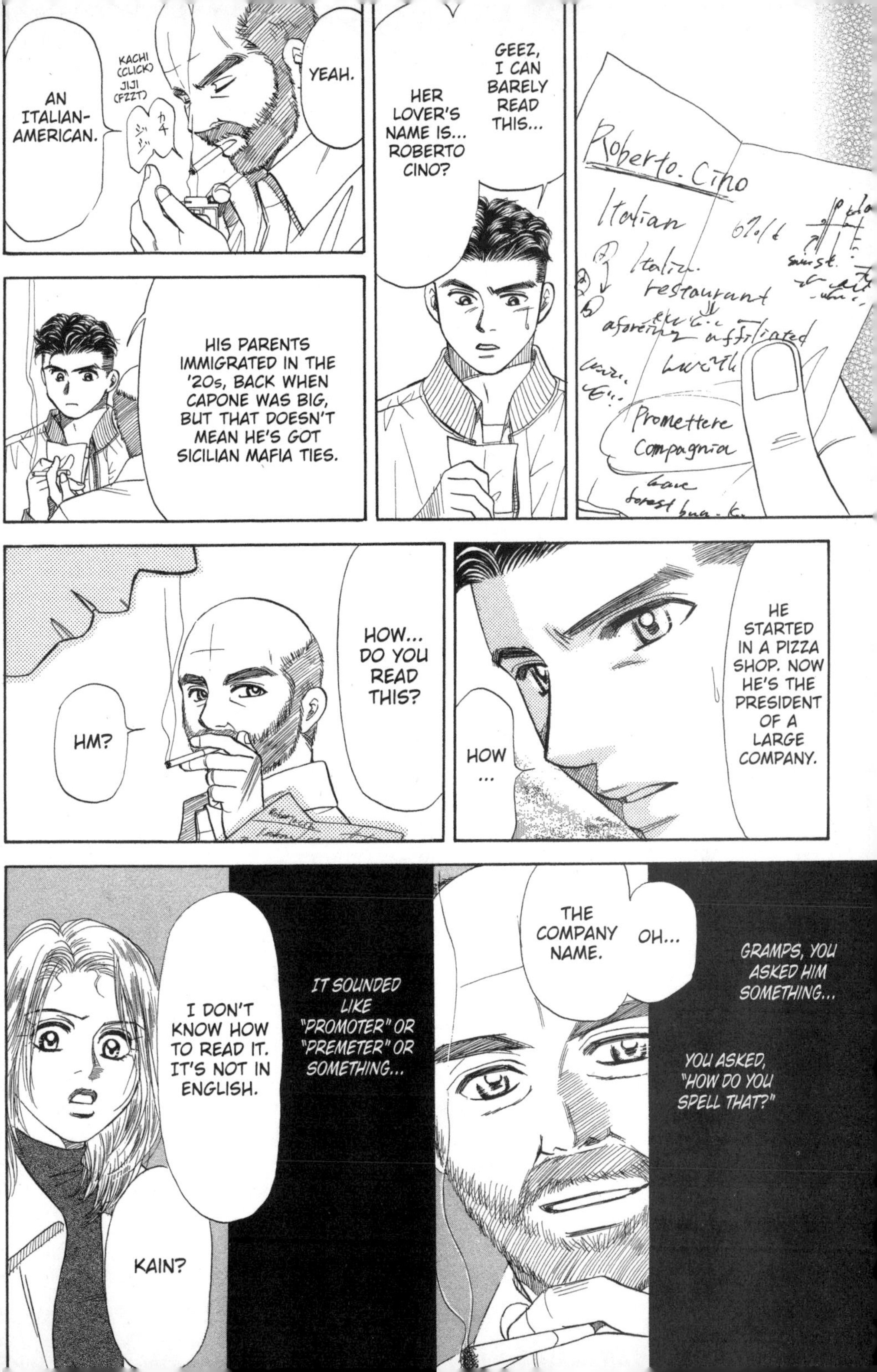
Roberto. Cino
Italian
restaurant
affiliated
Promettere Compagnia
GEEZ, I CAN BARELY READ THIS...
HER LOVER'S NAME IS... ROBERTO CINO?
YEAH.
KACHI (CLICK) JIJI (FZZT)
カチ ジジ
AN ITALIAN-AMERICAN.
HIS PARENTS IMMIGRATED IN THE '20s, BACK WHEN CAPONE WAS BIG, BUT THAT DOESN'T MEAN HE'S GOT SICILIAN MAFIA TIES.
HE STARTED IN A PIZZA SHOP. NOW HE'S THE PRESIDENT OF A LARGE COMPANY.
HOW ...
HOW... DO YOU READ THIS?
HM?
GRAMPS, YOU ASKED HIM SOMETHING...
YOU ASKED, "HOW DO YOU SPELL THAT?"
OH...
THE COMPANY NAME.
IT SOUNDED LIKE "PROMOTER" OR "PREMETER" OR SOMETHING...
I DON'T KNOW HOW TO READ IT. IT'S NOT IN ENGLISH.
KAIN?

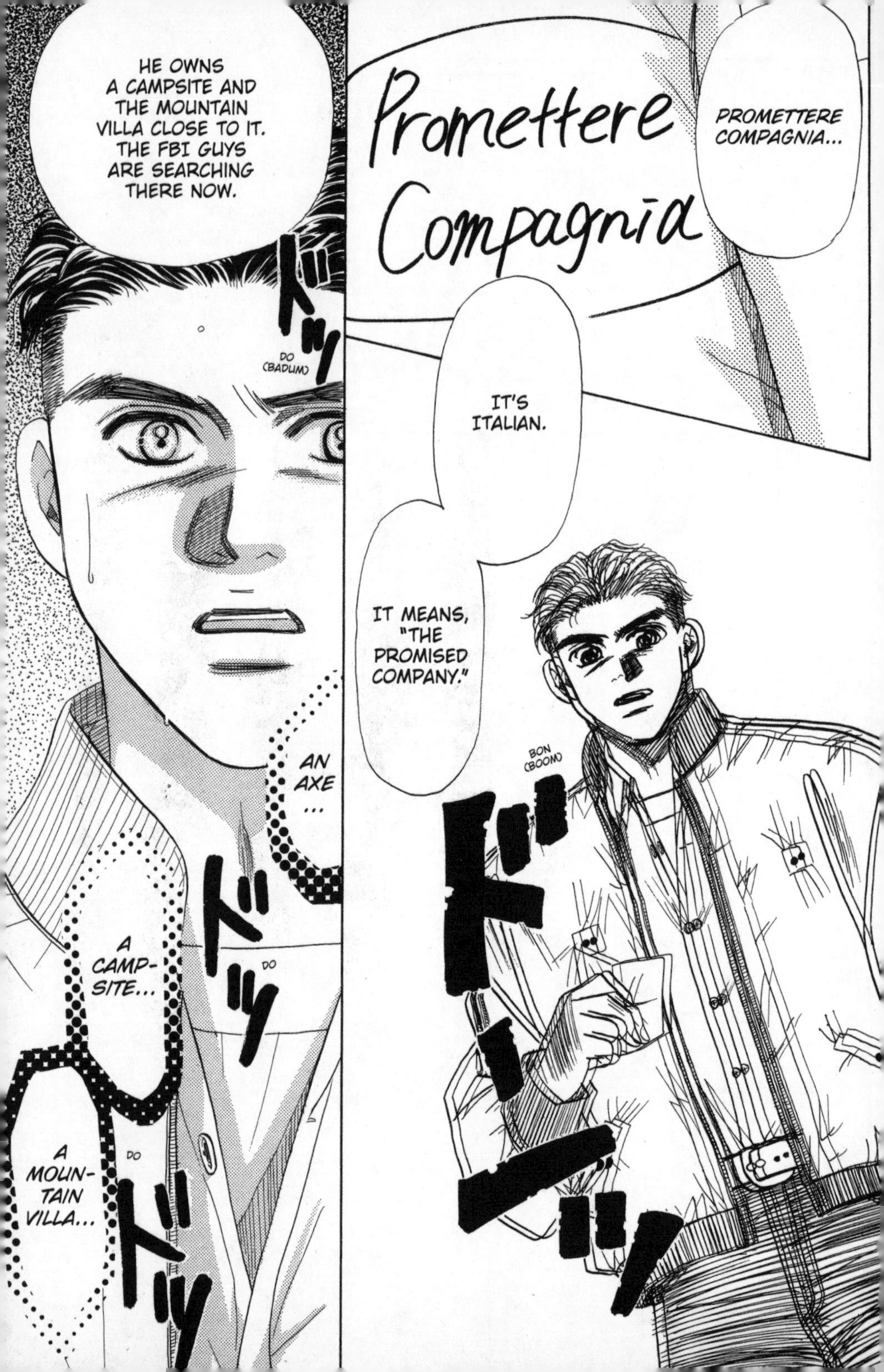

Promettere Compagnia
PROMETTERE COMPAGNIA...
IT'S ITALIAN.
IT MEANS, "THE PROMISED COMPANY."
BON (BOOM)
HE OWNS A CAMPSITE AND THE MOUNTAIN VILLA CLOSE TO IT. THE FBI GUYS ARE SEARCHING THERE NOW.
DO (BADUM)
AN AXE ...
DO
A CAMP-SITE...
DO
A MOUN-TAIN VILLA...

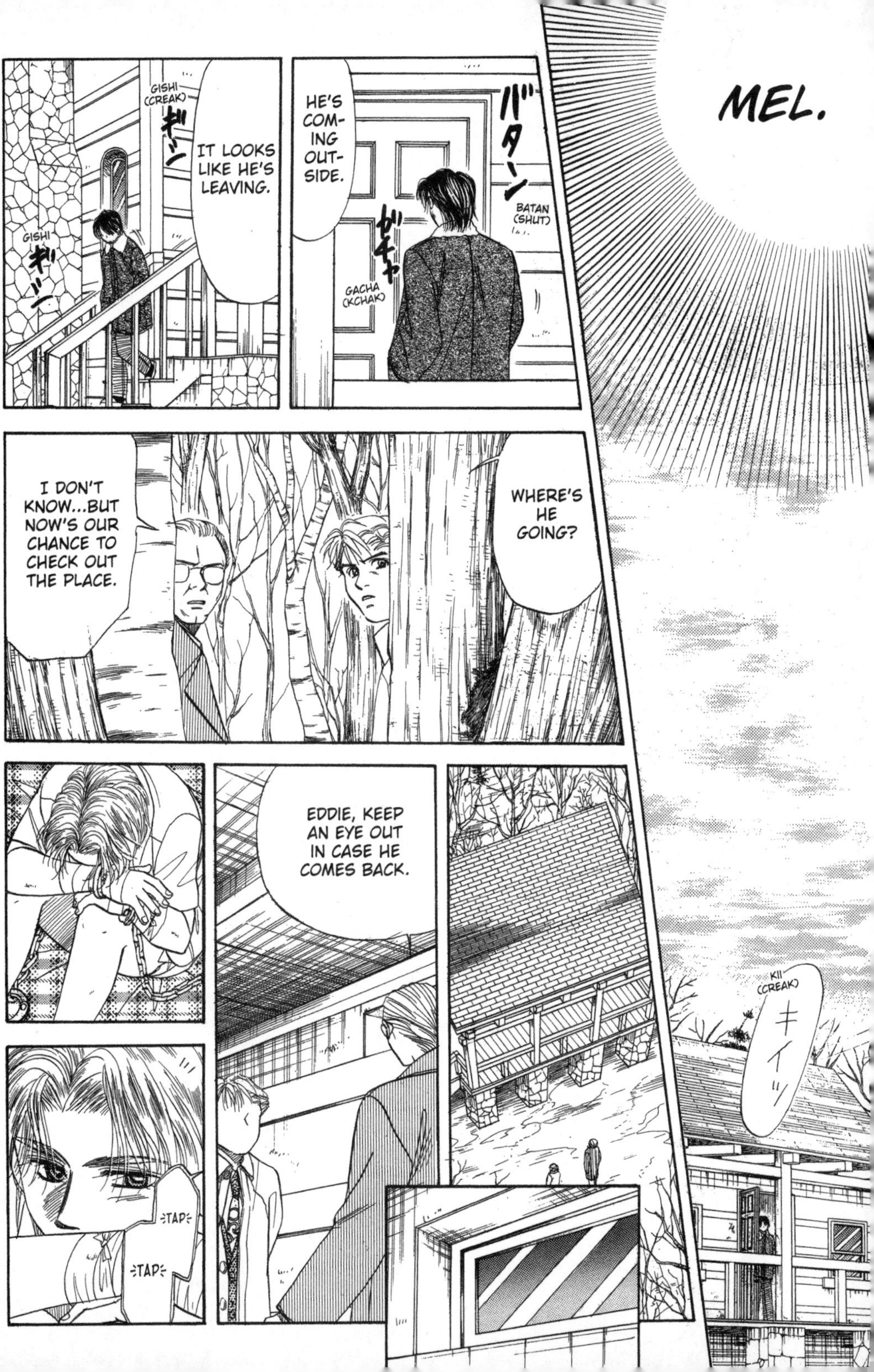
MEL.
KII (CREAK)
キイッ
HE'S COMING OUTSIDE.
バタン
BATAN (SHUT)
ガチャ
GACHA (KCHAK)
GISHI (CREAK)
IT LOOKS LIKE HE'S LEAVING.
GISHI
WHERE'S HE GOING?
I DON'T KNOW...BUT NOW'S OUR CHANCE TO CHECK OUT THE PLACE.
EDDIE, KEEP AN EYE OUT IN CASE HE COMES BACK.
TAP
TAP

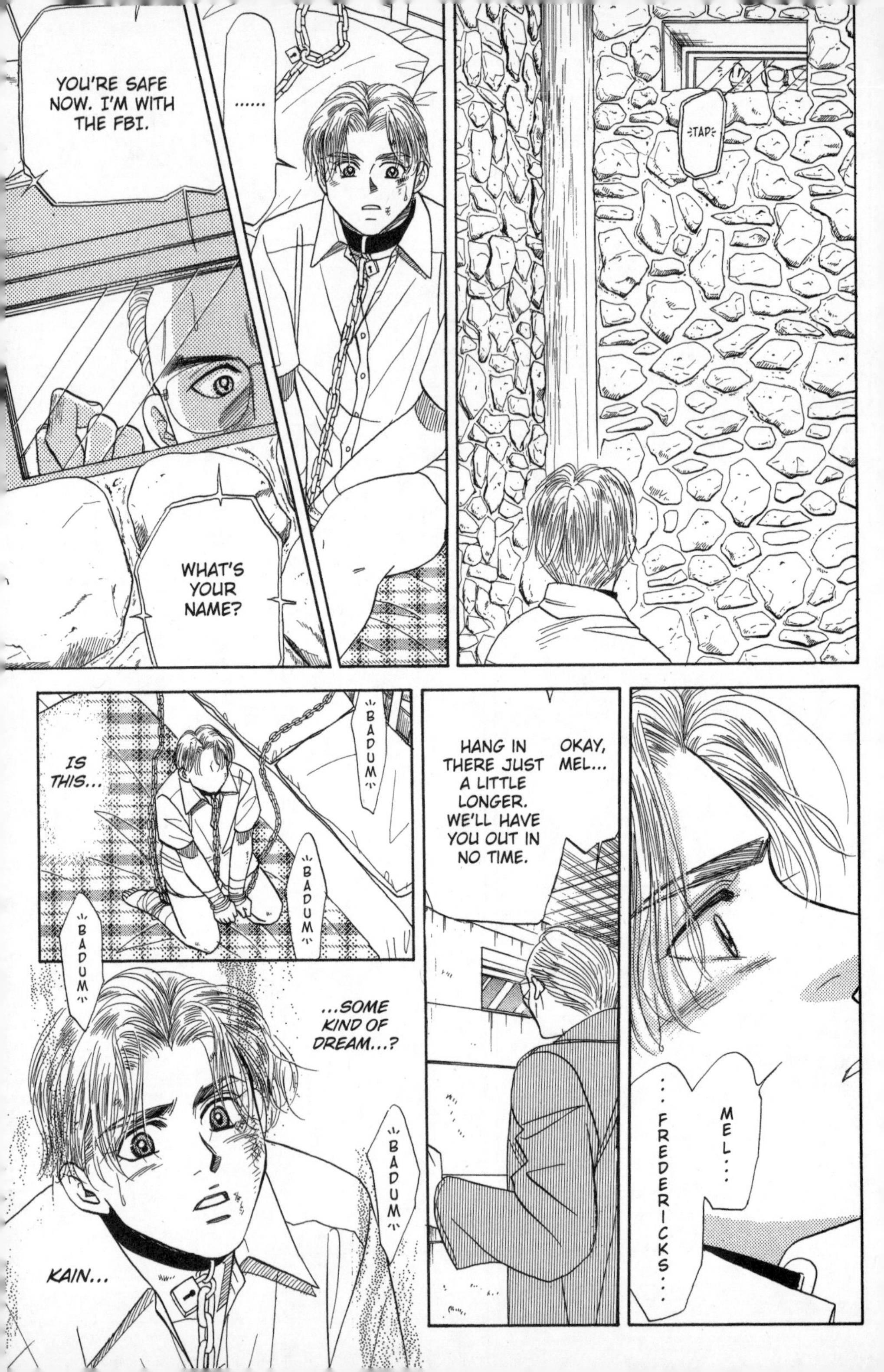
TAP
......
YOU'RE SAFE NOW. I'M WITH THE FBI.
WHAT'S YOUR NAME?
MEL...
...FREDERICKS...
OKAY, MEL...
HANG IN THERE JUST A LITTLE LONGER. WE'LL HAVE YOU OUT IN NO TIME.
BADUM
IS THIS...
BADUM
BADUM
...SOME KIND OF DREAM...?
BADUM
KAIN...

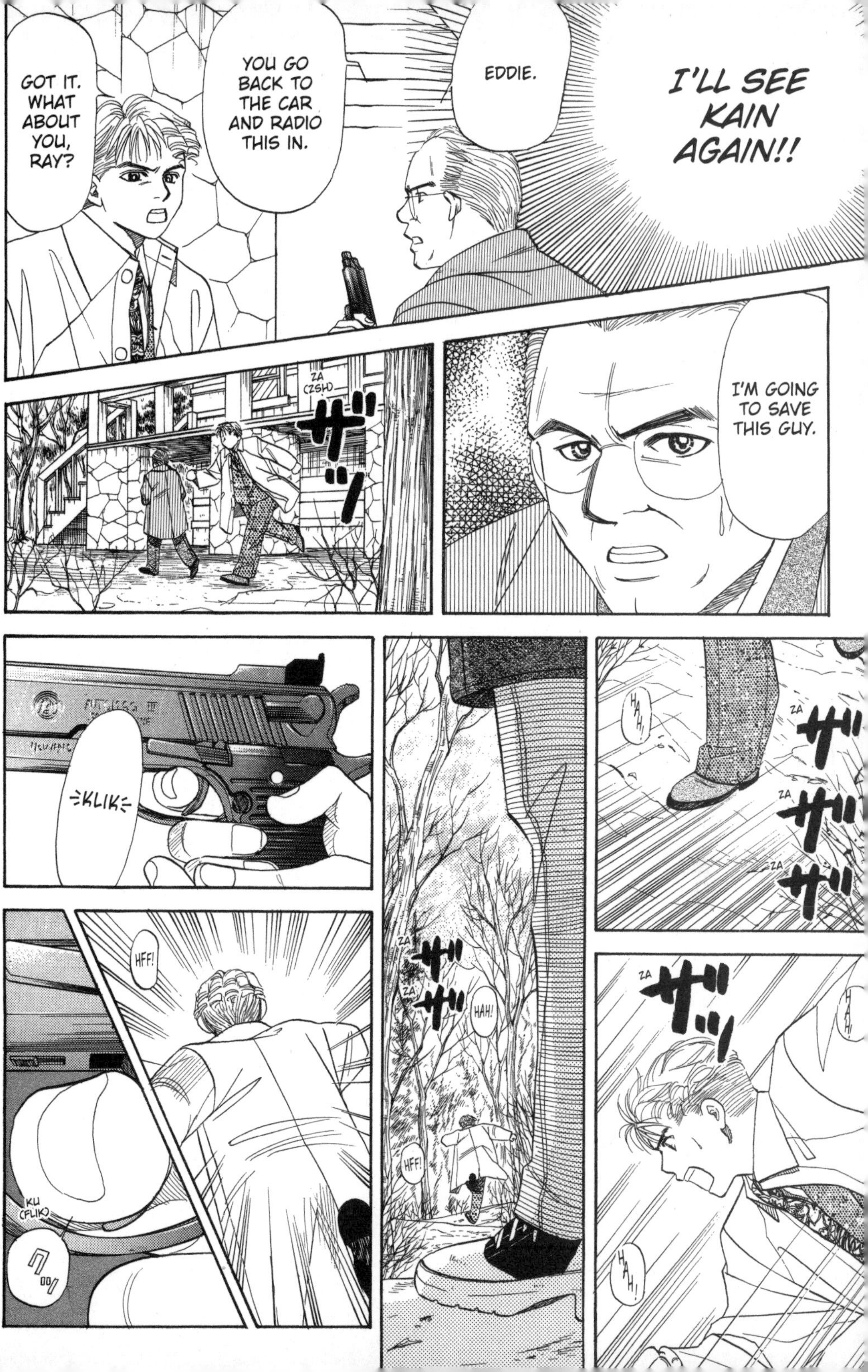
I'LL SEE KAIN AGAIN!!
EDDIE.
YOU GO BACK TO THE CAR AND RADIO THIS IN.
GOT IT. WHAT ABOUT YOU, RAY?
I'M GOING TO SAVE THIS GUY.
ZA (ZSH)
ザッ
HAH!
ZA
ザ
ZA
ザ
ZA
ザ
ZA
ザッ
HAH!
HAH!
ZA
ザ
ZA
ザ
HAH!
HFF!
KLIK
HFF!
KU (FLIK)

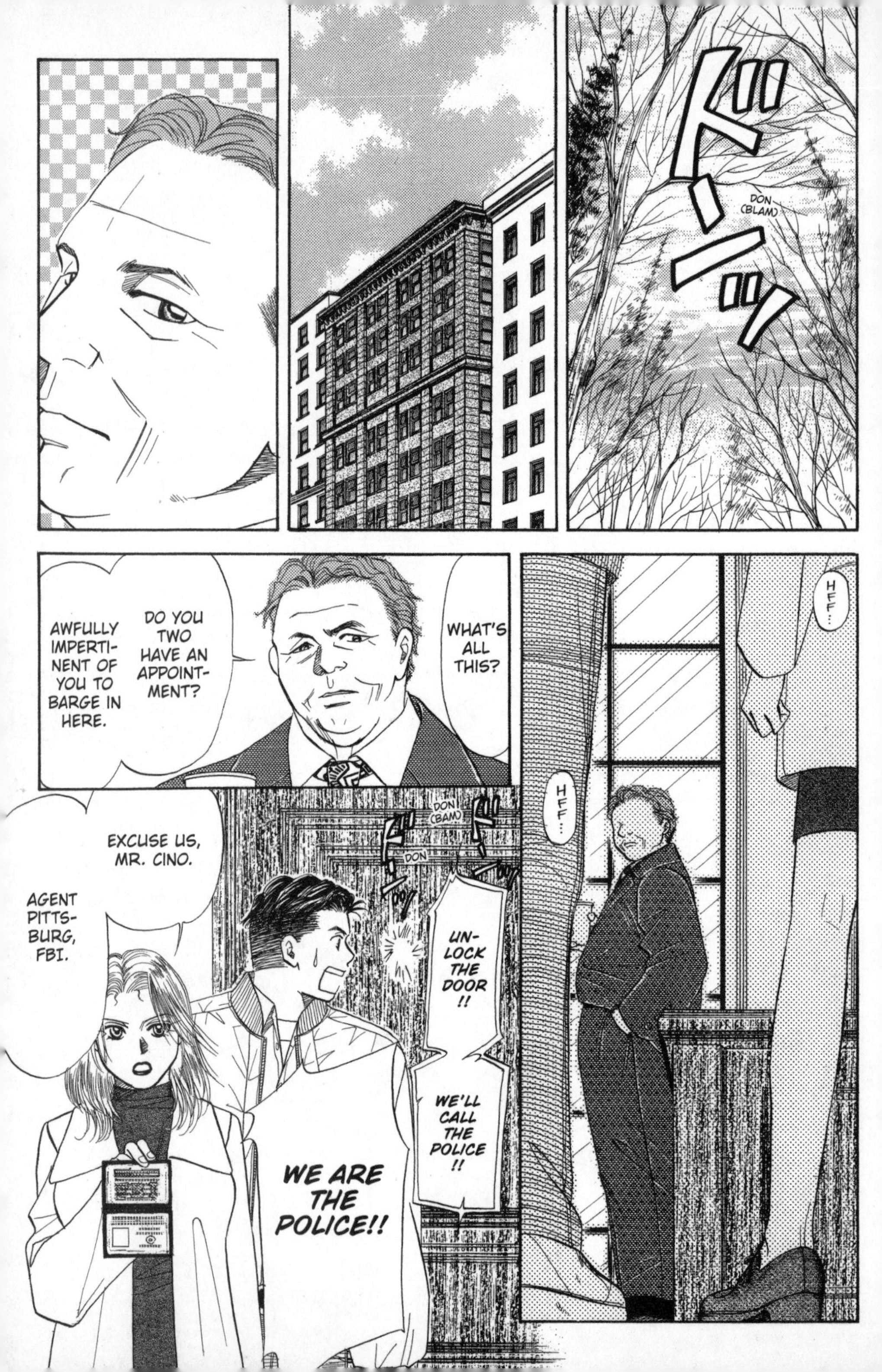
DON (BLAM)
HFF...
HFF...
WHAT'S ALL THIS?
DO YOU TWO HAVE AN APPOINTMENT?
AWFULLY IMPERTINENT OF YOU TO BARGE IN HERE.
DON (BAM)
DON
UNLOCK THE DOOR!!
WE'LL CALL THE POLICE!!
WE ARE THE POLICE!!
EXCUSE US, MR. CINO.
AGENT PITTSBURG, FBI.

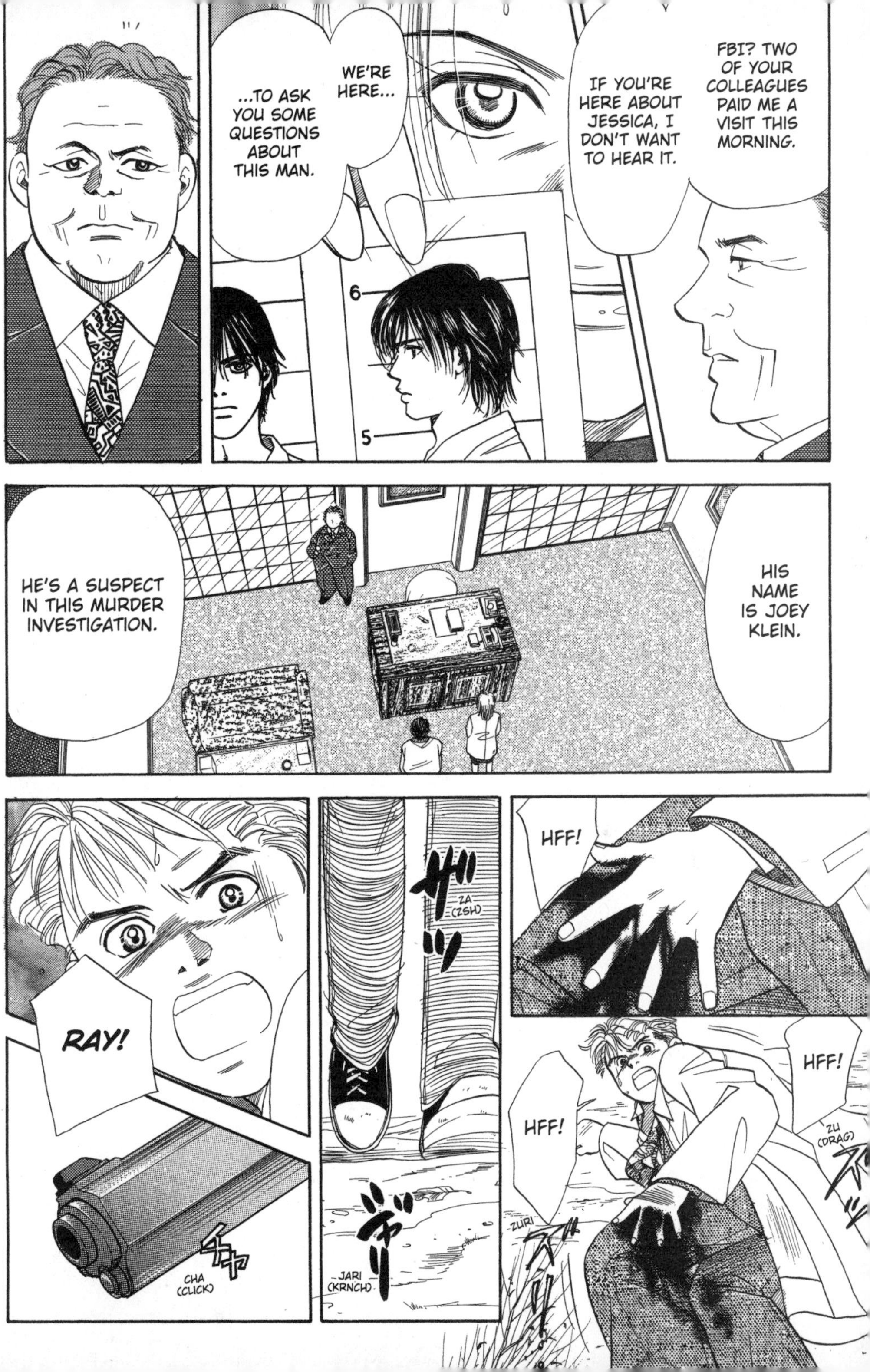
FBI? TWO OF YOUR COLLEAGUES PAID ME A VISIT THIS MORNING.
IF YOU'RE HERE ABOUT JESSICA, I DON'T WANT TO HEAR IT.
WE'RE HERE...
...TO ASK YOU SOME QUESTIONS ABOUT THIS MAN.
6
5
HIS NAME IS JOEY KLEIN.
HE'S A SUSPECT IN THIS MURDER INVESTIGATION.
HFF!
HFF!
ZU (DRAG)
HFF!
ZURI
ZA (ZSH)
JARI (KRNCH)
RAY!
CHA (CLICK)

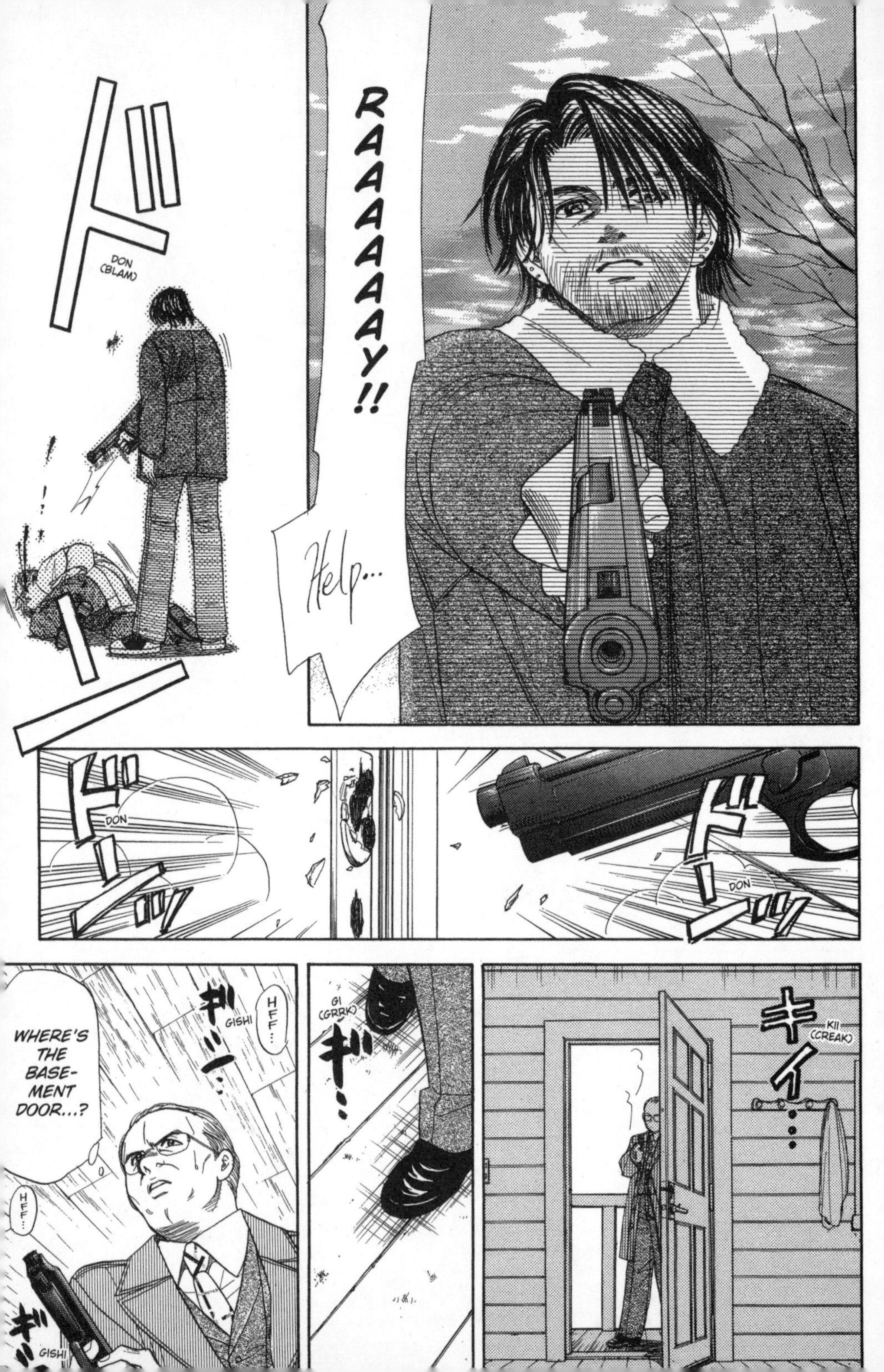
RAAAAAAAAY!!
Help...
ド
DON (BLAM)
ドン
DON
ドン
DON
キイ…
KII (CREAK)
ギ
GI (GRRK)
ギッ
GISHI
HFF...
WHERE'S THE BASEMENT DOOR...?
HFF...
ギッ
GISHI

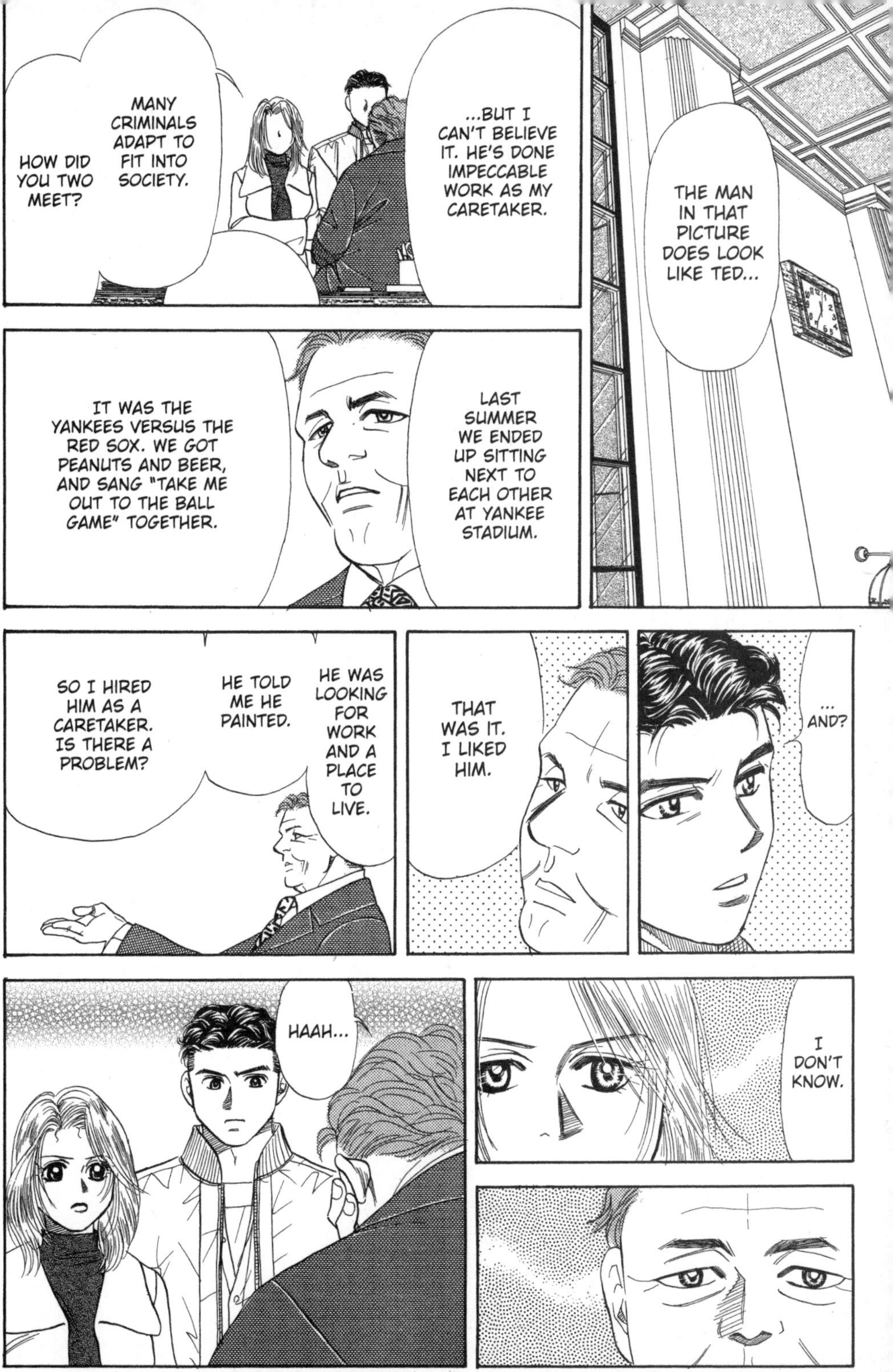
THE MAN IN THAT PICTURE DOES LOOK LIKE TED...
...BUT I CAN'T BELIEVE IT. HE'S DONE IMPECCABLE WORK AS MY CARETAKER.
MANY CRIMINALS ADAPT TO FIT INTO SOCIETY.
HOW DID YOU TWO MEET?
LAST SUMMER WE ENDED UP SITTING NEXT TO EACH OTHER AT YANKEE STADIUM.
IT WAS THE YANKEES VERSUS THE RED SOX. WE GOT PEANUTS AND BEER, AND SANG "TAKE ME OUT TO THE BALL GAME" TOGETHER.
...AND?
THAT WAS IT. I LIKED HIM.
HE WAS LOOKING FOR WORK AND A PLACE TO LIVE.
HE TOLD ME HE PAINTED.
SO I HIRED HIM AS A CARETAKER. IS THERE A PROBLEM?
I DON'T KNOW.
HAAH...

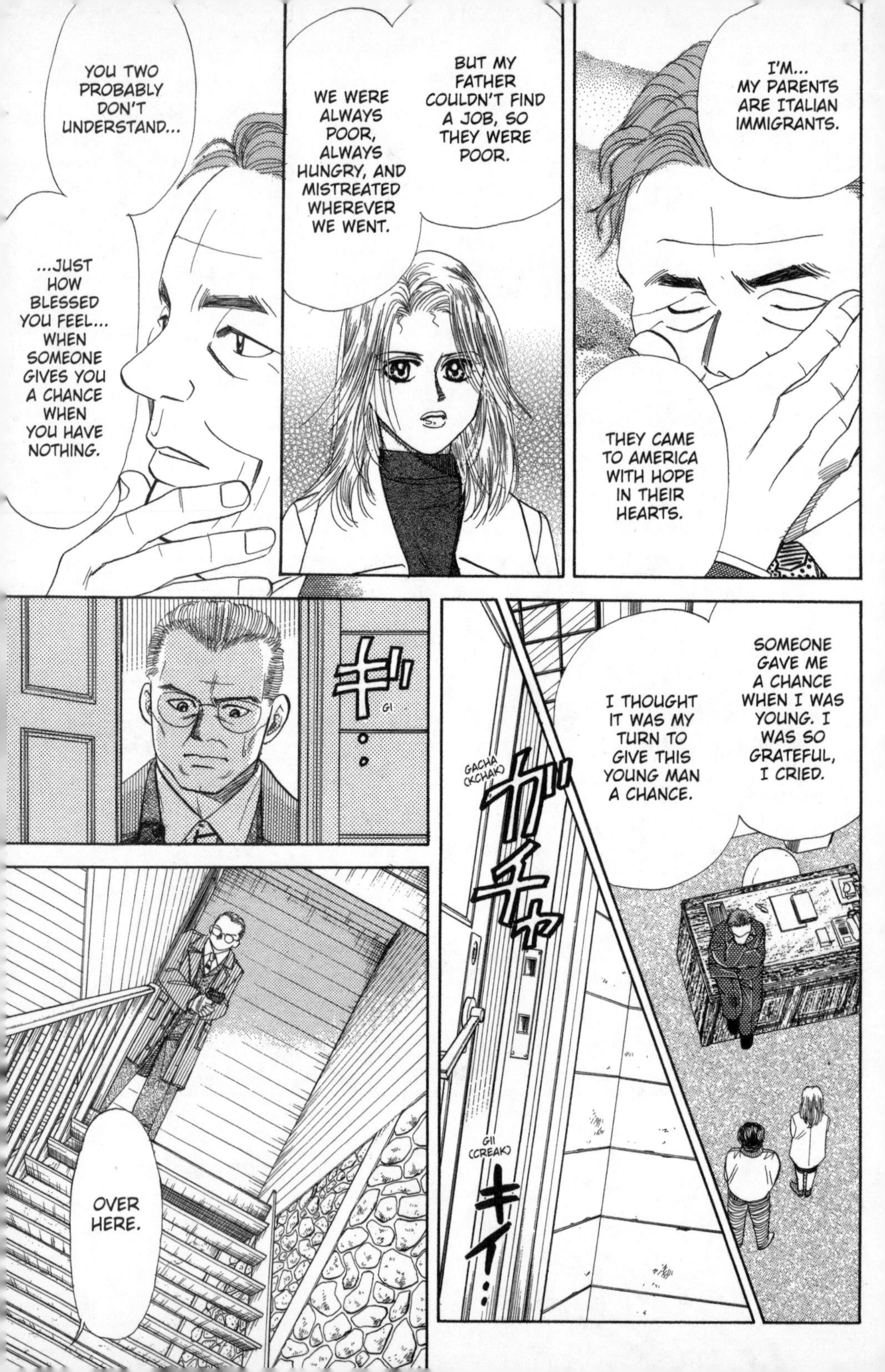
I'M... MY PARENTS ARE ITALIAN IMMIGRANTS.
THEY CAME TO AMERICA WITH HOPE IN THEIR HEARTS.
BUT MY FATHER COULDN'T FIND A JOB, SO THEY WERE POOR.
WE WERE ALWAYS POOR, ALWAYS HUNGRY, AND MISTREATED WHEREVER WE WENT.
YOU TWO PROBABLY DON'T UNDERSTAND...
...JUST HOW BLESSED YOU FEEL... WHEN SOMEONE GIVES YOU A CHANCE WHEN YOU HAVE NOTHING.
SOMEONE GAVE ME A CHANCE WHEN I WAS YOUNG. I WAS SO GRATEFUL, I CRIED.
I THOUGHT IT WAS MY TURN TO GIVE THIS YOUNG MAN A CHANCE.
GACHA (KCHAK)
GII (CREAK)
GI
OVER HERE.

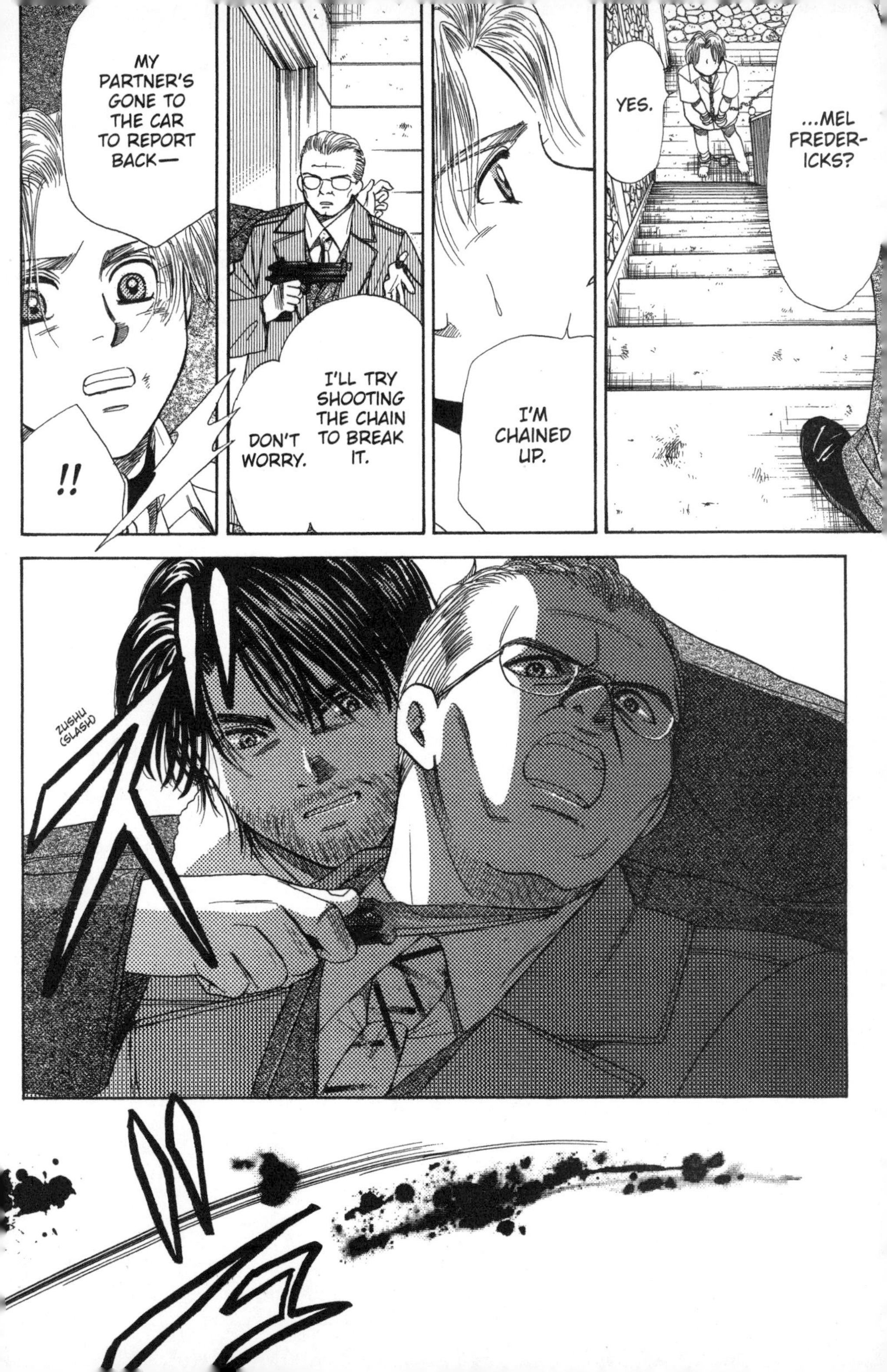
...MEL FREDER-ICKS?
YES.
I'M CHAINED UP.
I'LL TRY SHOOTING THE CHAIN TO BREAK IT.
DON'T WORRY.
MY PARTNER'S GONE TO THE CAR TO REPORT BACK—
!!
ZUSHU (SLASH)

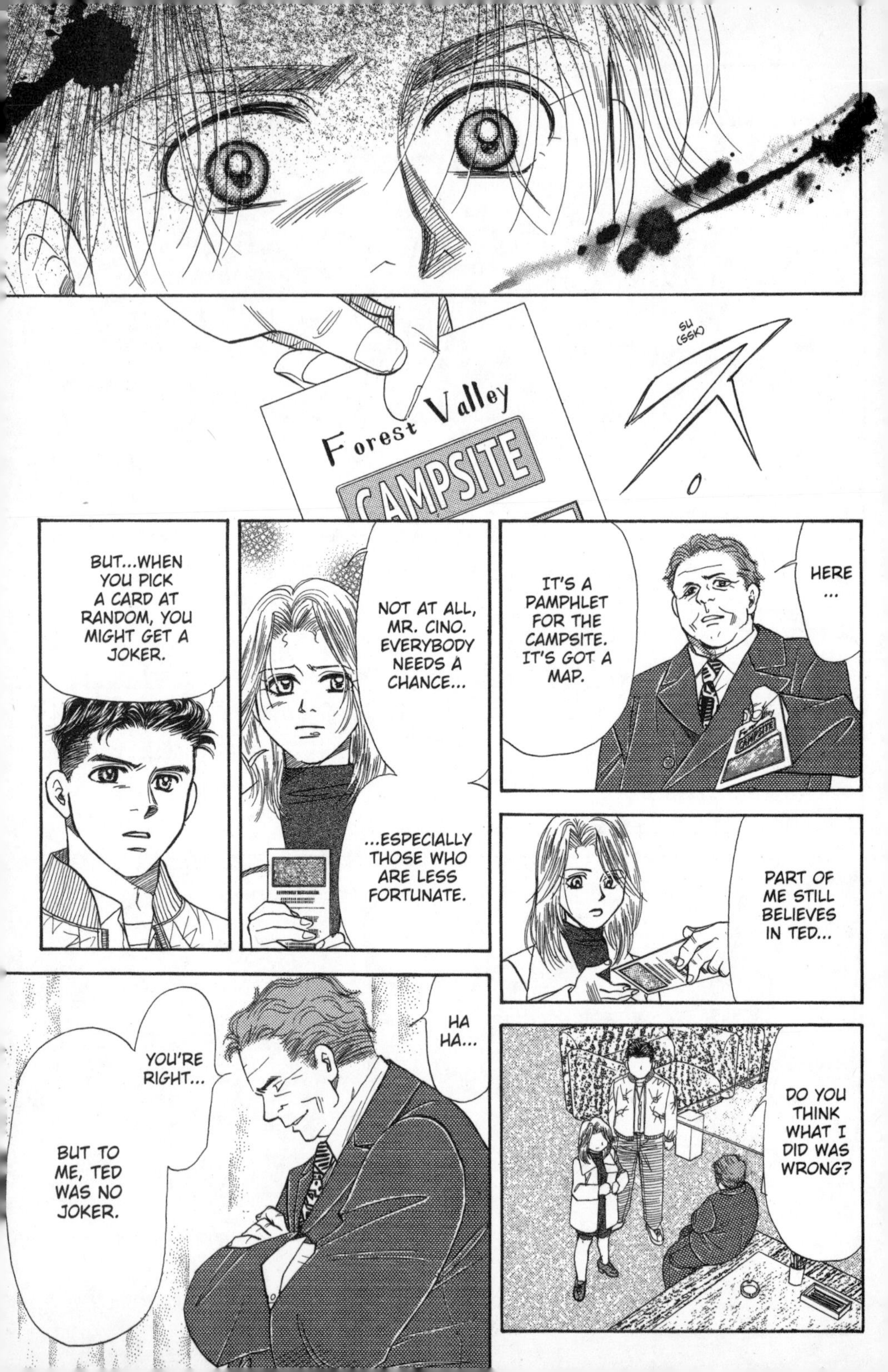
SU (SSK)
Forest Valley
CAMPSITE
HERE...
IT'S A PAMPHLET FOR THE CAMPSITE. IT'S GOT A MAP.
PART OF ME STILL BELIEVES IN TED...
NOT AT ALL, MR. CINO. EVERYBODY NEEDS A CHANCE...
...ESPECIALLY THOSE WHO ARE LESS FORTUNATE.
BUT...WHEN YOU PICK A CARD AT RANDOM, YOU MIGHT GET A JOKER.
DO YOU THINK WHAT I DID WAS WRONG?
HA HA...
YOU'RE RIGHT...
BUT TO ME, TED WAS NO JOKER.

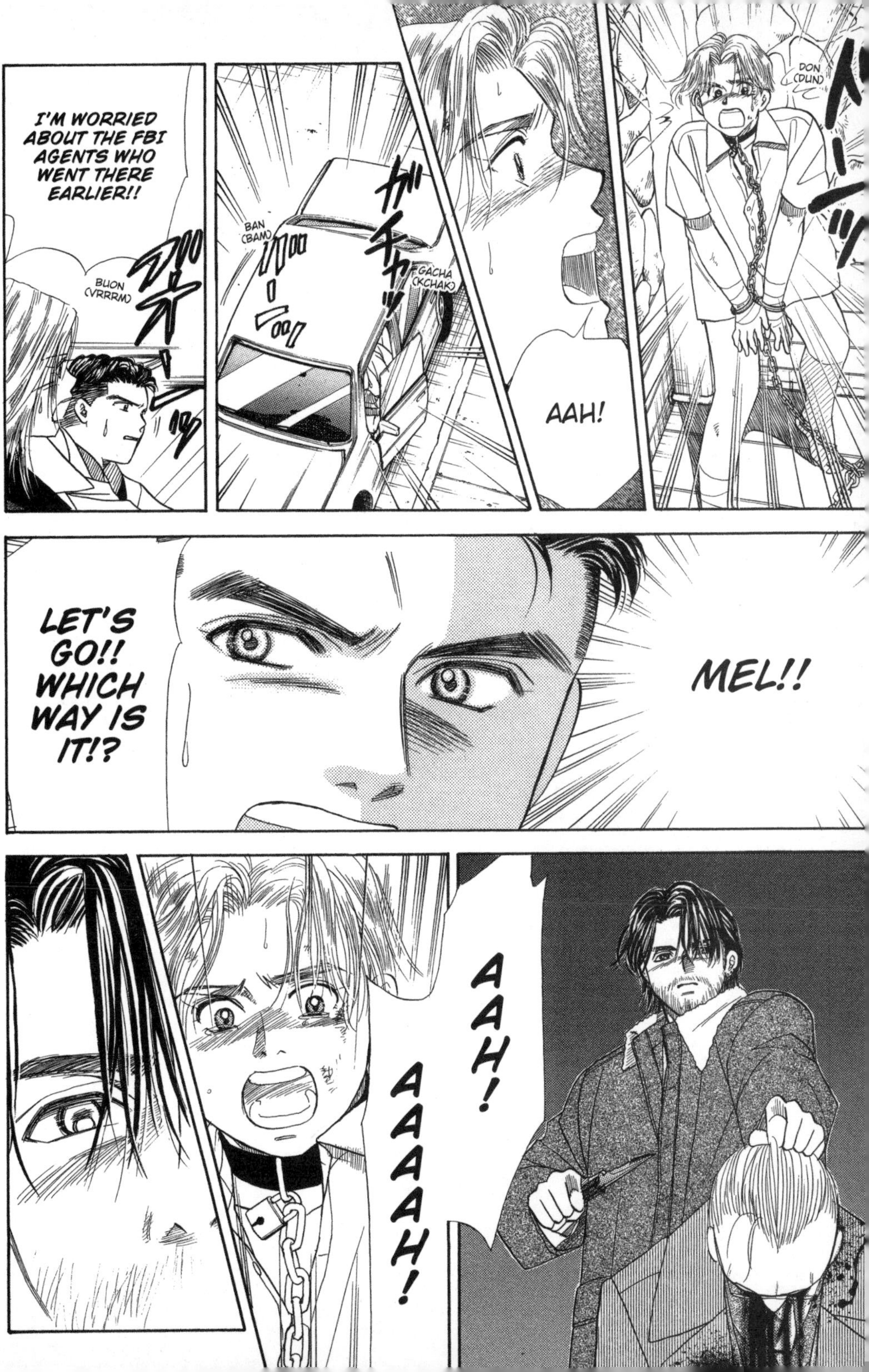
DON (DUN)
AAH!
BAN (BAM)
GACHA (KCHAK)
I'M WORRIED ABOUT THE FBI AGENTS WHO WENT THERE EARLIER!!
BUON (VRRRM)
MEL!!
LET'S GO!! WHICH WAY IS IT!?
AAH! AAAAAH!

EPISODE IV

SCENE 7

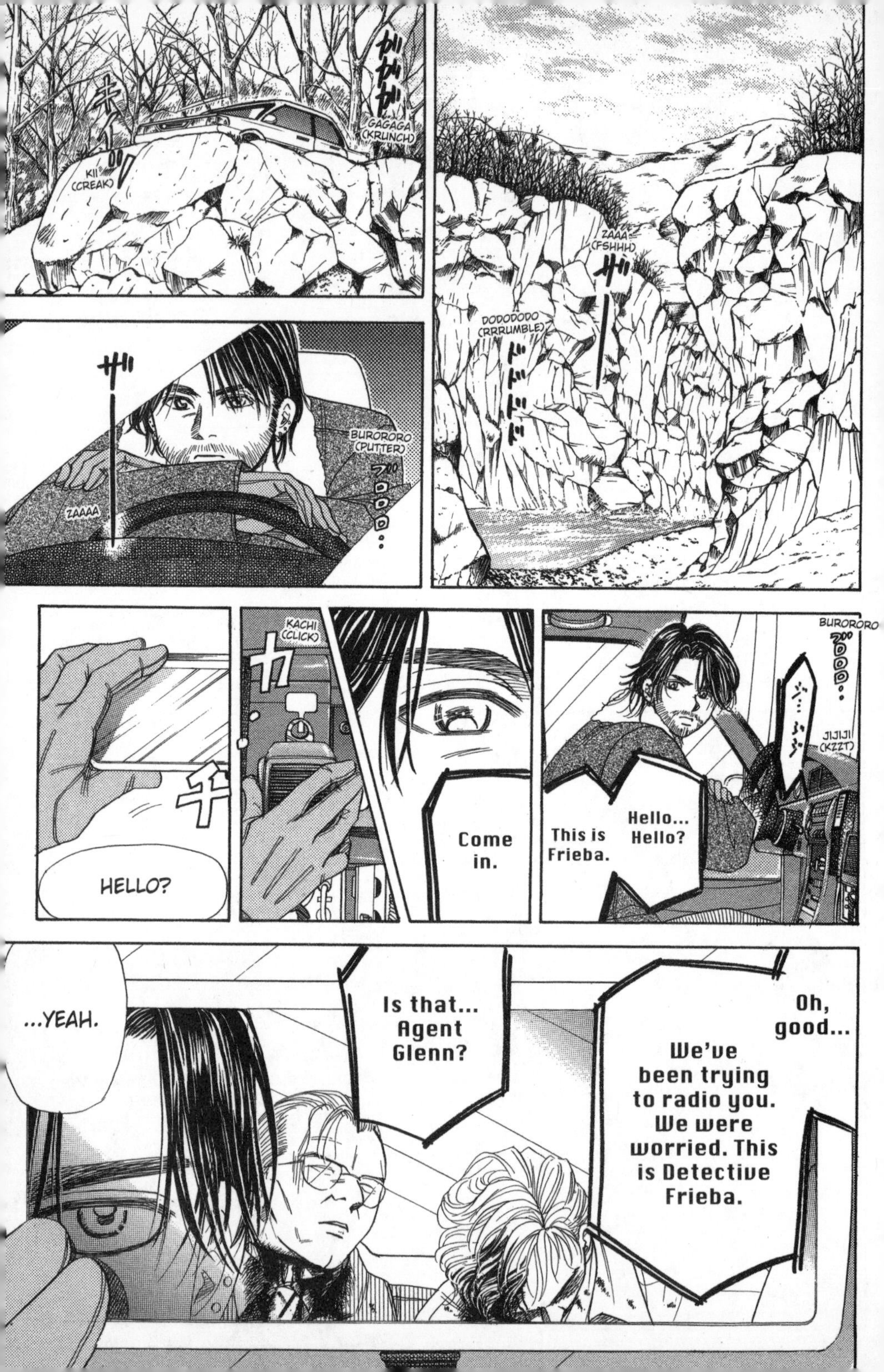
ZAAA (FSHHH)
DODODODO (RRRUMBLE)
GAGAGA (KRUNCH)
KII (CREAK)
BURORORO (PUTTER)
ZAAAA
BURORORO
JIJIJI (KZZT)
Hello... Hello?
This is Frieba.
Come in.
KACHI (CLICK)
HELLO?
Oh, good...
We've been trying to radio you. We were worried. This is Detective Frieba.
Is that... Agent Glenn?
...YEAH.

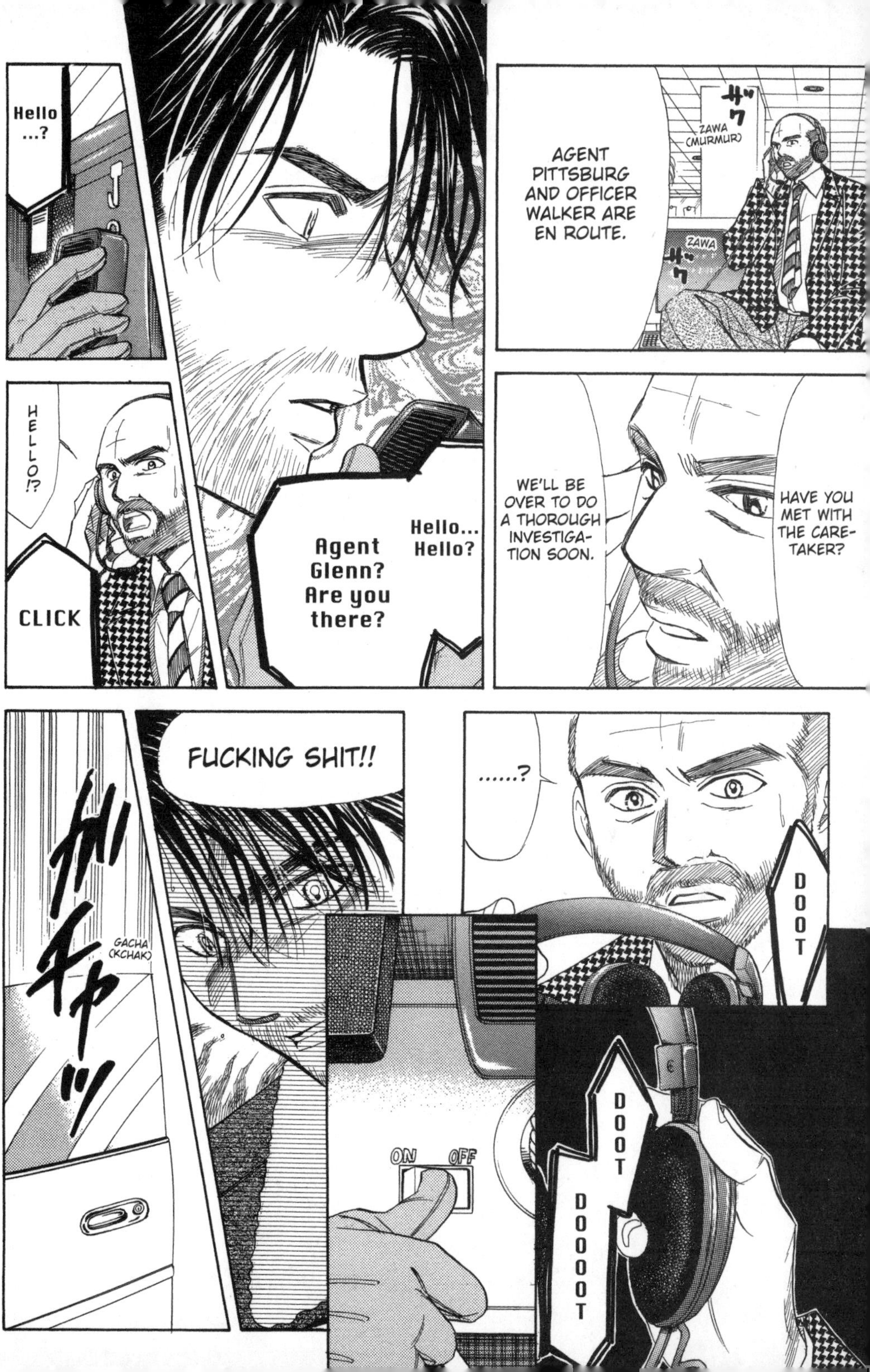
ZAWA (MURMUR)
AGENT PITTSBURG AND OFFICER WALKER ARE EN ROUTE.
ZAWA
HAVE YOU MET WITH THE CARE-TAKER?
WE'LL BE OVER TO DO A THOROUGH INVESTIGATION SOON.
Hello... Hello?
Agent Glenn? Are you there?
Hello ...?
HELLO!?
CLICK
......?
DOOT
DOOT
DOOOOOOT
FUCKING SHIT!!
GACHA (KCHAK)

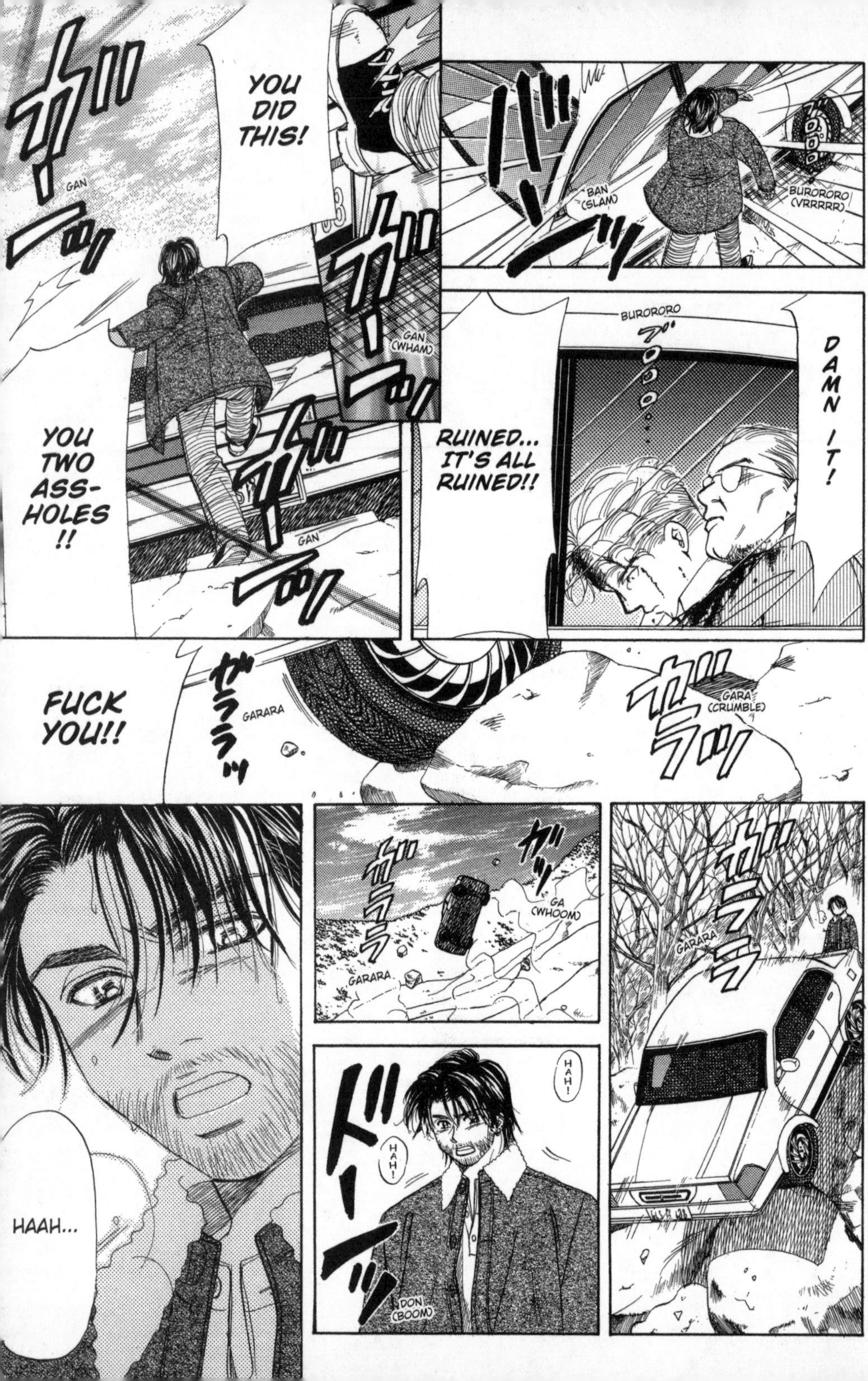
BURORORO (VRRRRR)
BAN (SLAM)
DAMN IT!
BURORORO
RUINED... IT'S ALL RUINED!!
YOU DID THIS!
GAN (WHAM)
GAN
YOU TWO ASSHOLES!!
GAN
GARA (CRUMBLE)
GARARA
FUCK YOU!!
GARARA
GA (WHOOM)
GARARA
HAH!
HAH!
DON (BOOM)
HAAH...

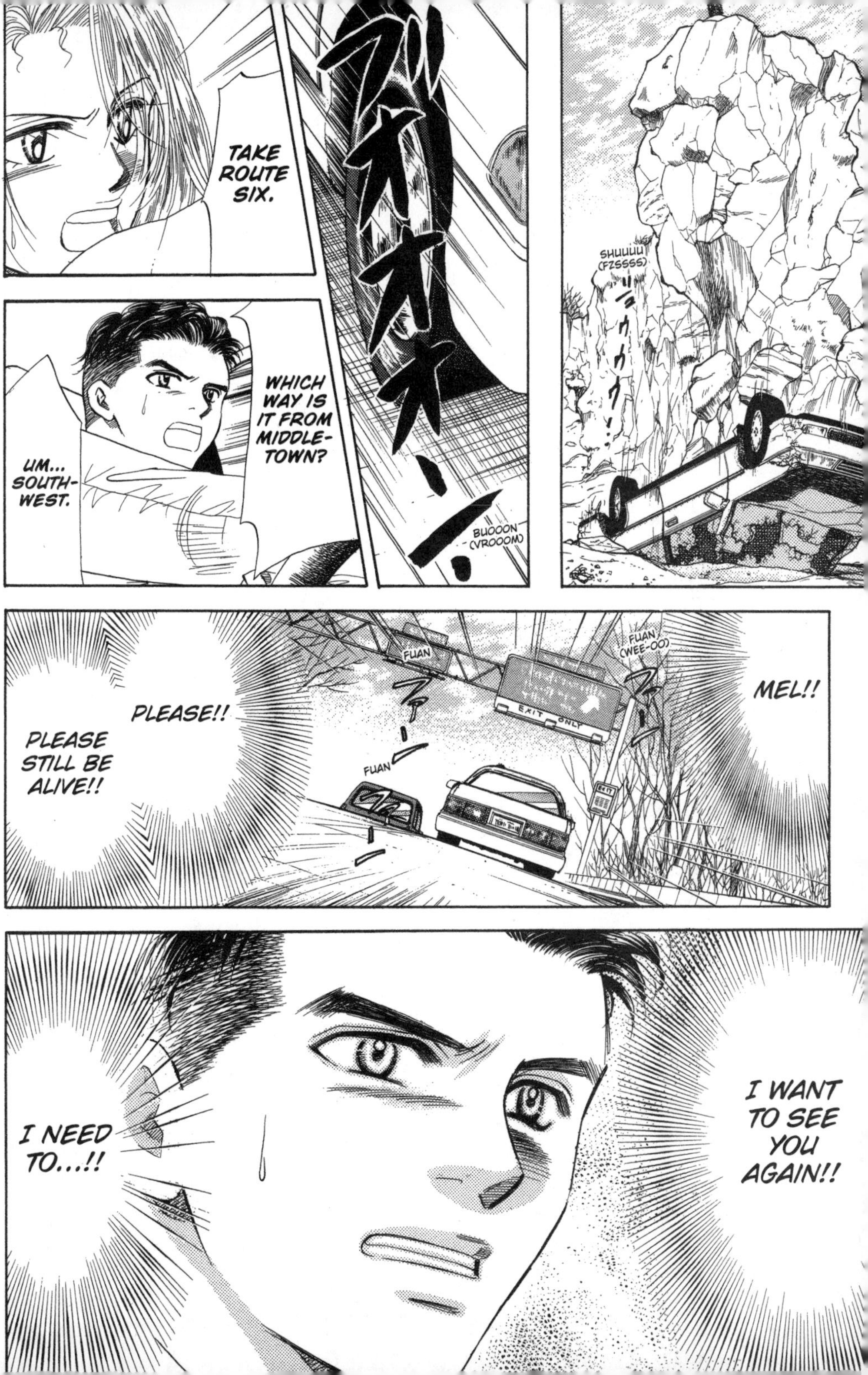
SHUUUU (FZSSSS)
BUOOON (VROOOM)
TAKE ROUTE SIX.
WHICH WAY IS IT FROM MIDDLE-TOWN?
UM... SOUTH-WEST.
MEL!!
FUAN (WEE-OO)
FUAN
FUAN
EXIT ONLY
PLEASE!!
PLEASE STILL BE ALIVE!!
I WANT TO SEE YOU AGAIN!!
I NEED TO...!!

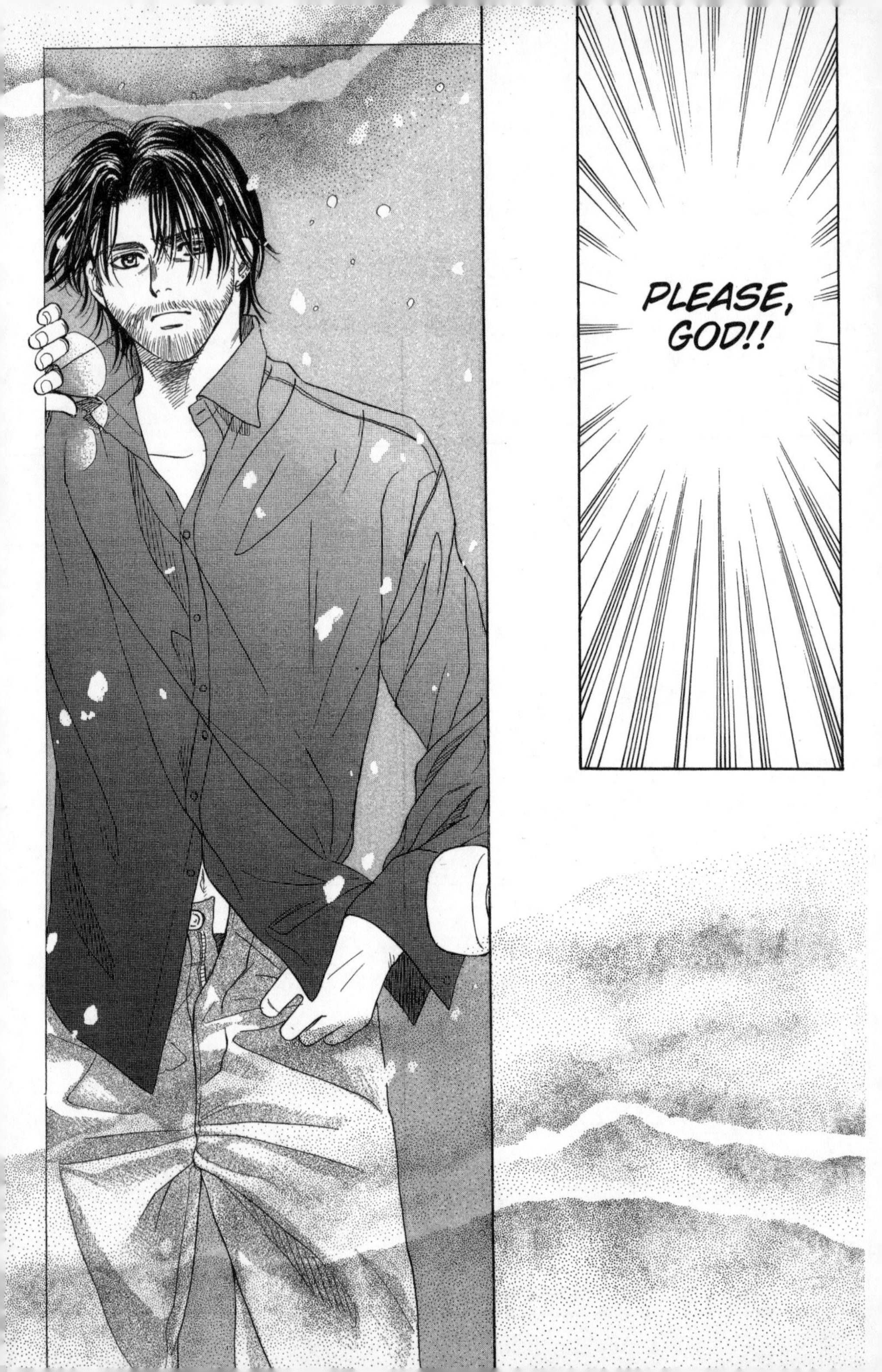
PLEASE, GOD!!

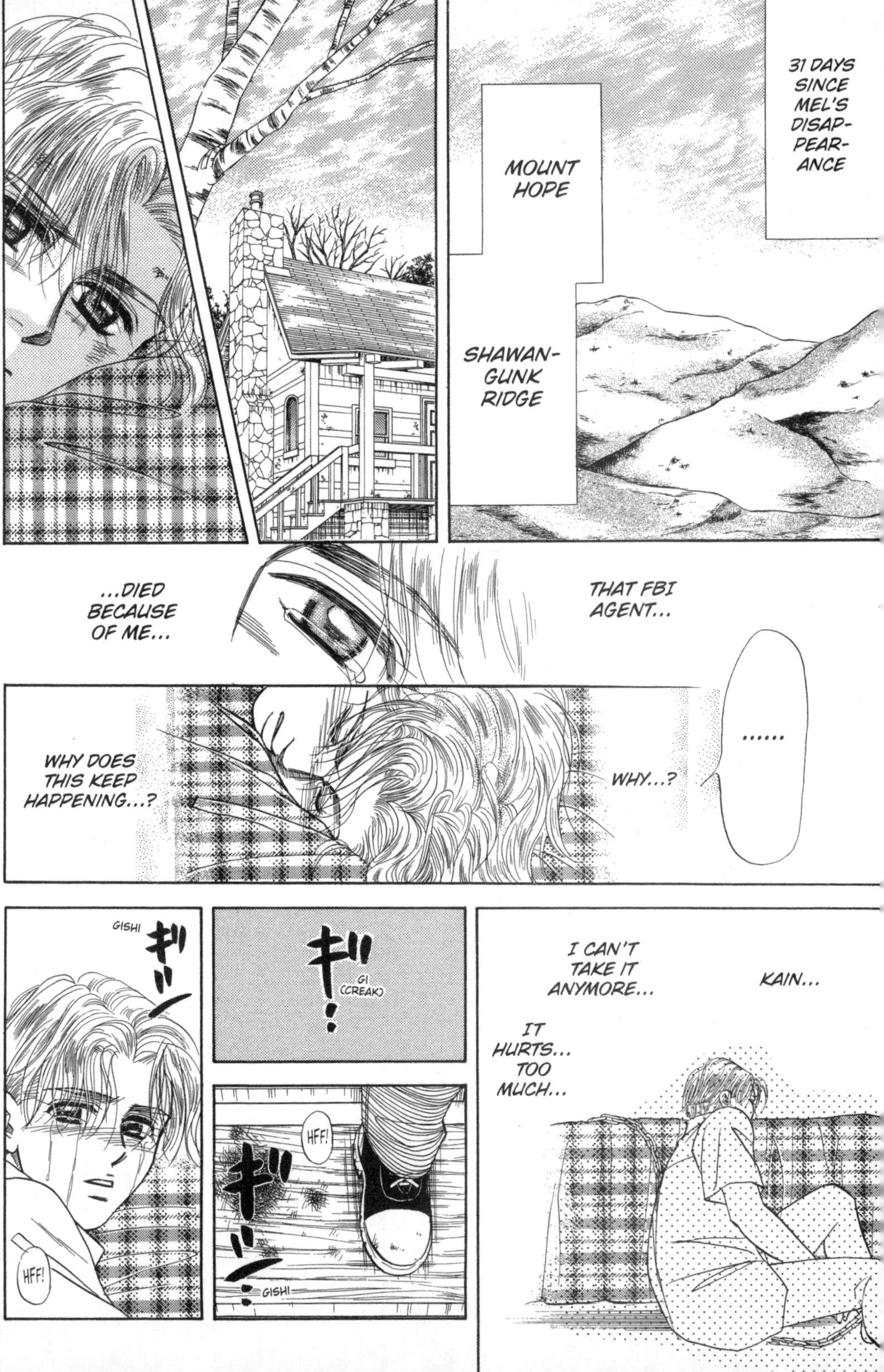

31 DAYS SINCE MEL'S DISAP-PEAR-ANCE
MOUNT HOPE
SHAWAN-GUNK RIDGE
THAT FBI AGENT...
...DIED BECAUSE OF ME...
......
WHY...?
WHY DOES THIS KEEP HAPPENING...?
KAIN...
I CAN'T TAKE IT ANYMORE...
IT HURTS... TOO MUCH...
GI (CREAK)
HFF!
GISHI
GISHI
HFF!

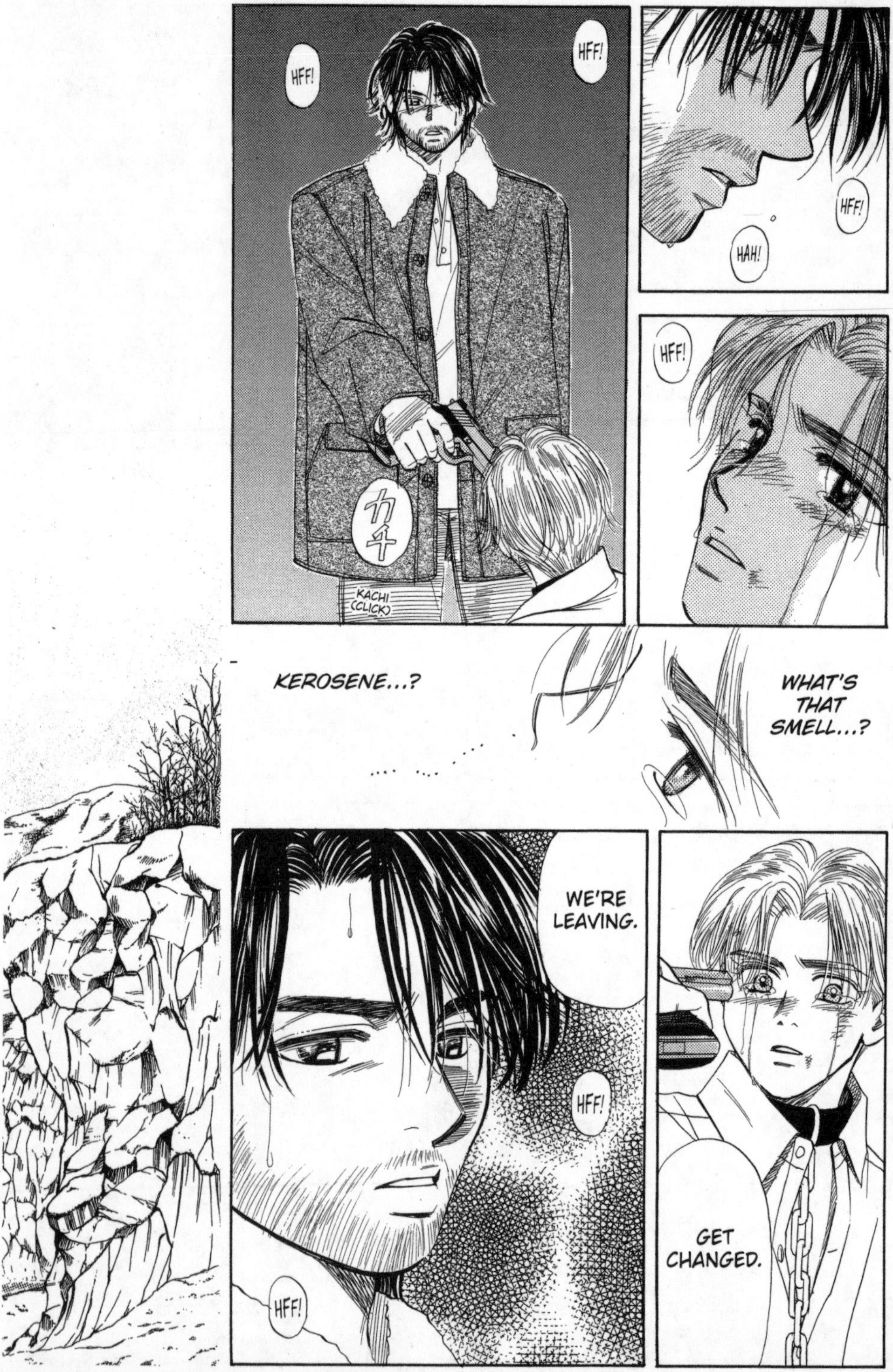
HFF!
HAH!
HFF!
HFF!
HFF!
カチ
KACHI (CLICK)
WHAT'S THAT SMELL...?
KEROSENE...?
GET CHANGED.
WE'RE LEAVING.
HFF!
HFF!

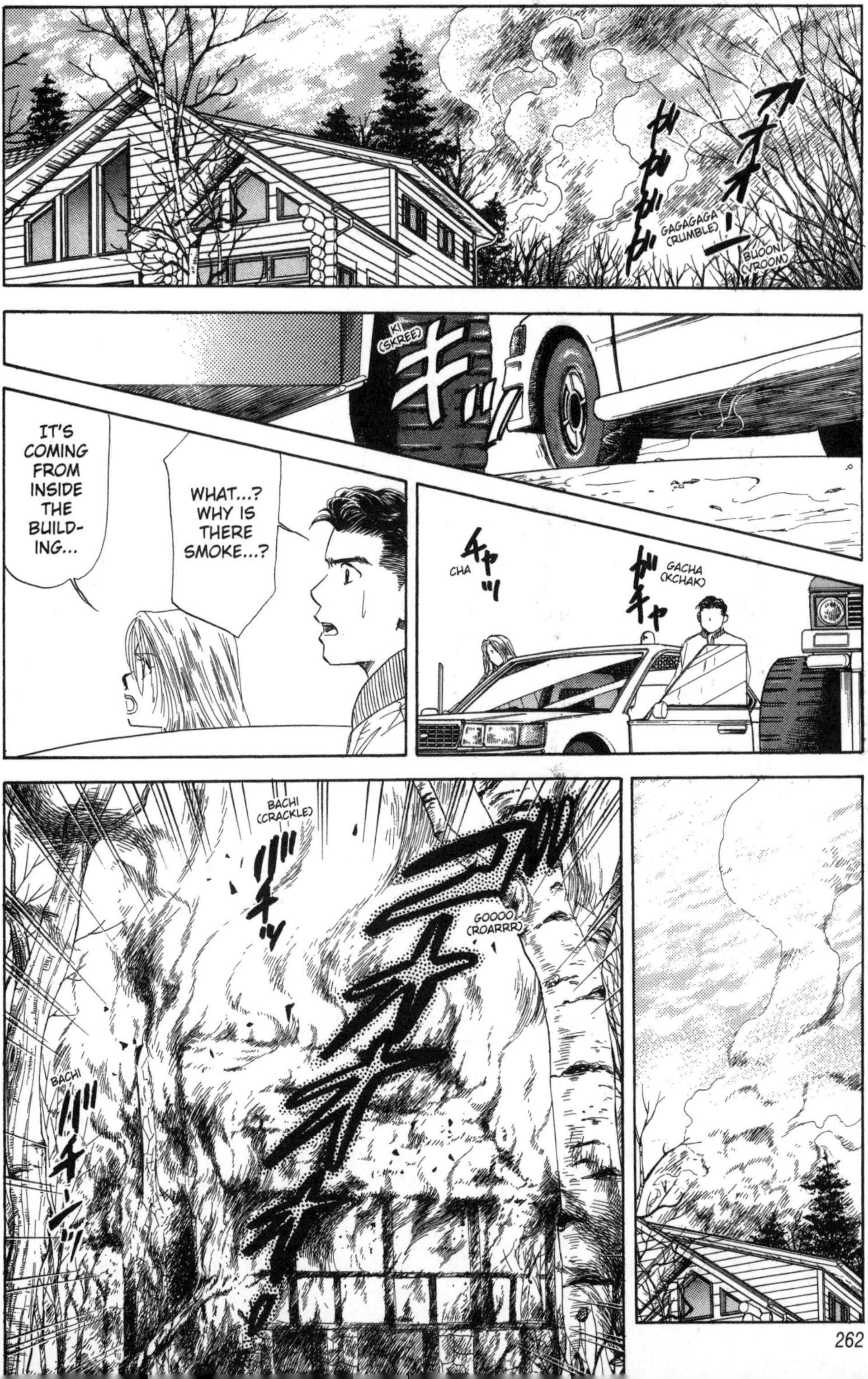
BUOON (VROOM)
GAGAGAGA (RUMBLE)
KI (SKREE)
GACHA (KCHAK)
CHA
WHAT...? WHY IS THERE SMOKE...?
IT'S COMING FROM INSIDE THE BUILD-ING...
GOOOO (ROARRR)
BACHI (CRACKLE)
BACHI

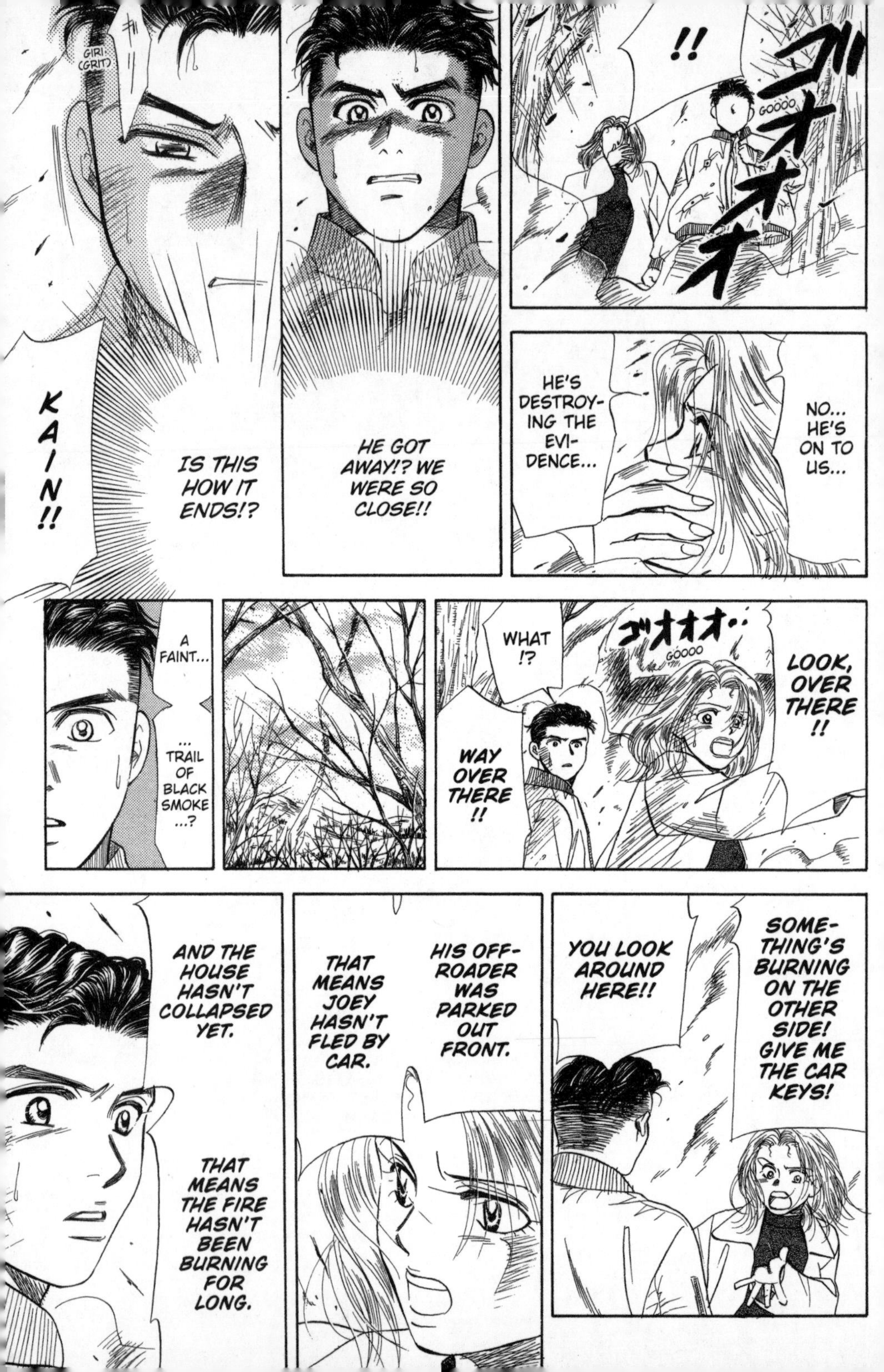
!!
ゴオオオ
GOOOO
NO... HE'S ON TO US...
HE'S DESTROYING THE EVIDENCE...
HE GOT AWAY!? WE WERE SO CLOSE!!
GIRI (GRIT)
IS THIS HOW IT ENDS!?
KAIN!!
LOOK, OVER THERE!!
ゴオオオ
GOOOO
WHAT!?
WAY OVER THERE!!
A FAINT...
...TRAIL OF BLACK SMOKE...?
SOMETHING'S BURNING ON THE OTHER SIDE! GIVE ME THE CAR KEYS!
YOU LOOK AROUND HERE!!
HIS OFF-ROADER WAS PARKED OUT FRONT.
THAT MEANS JOEY HASN'T FLED BY CAR.
AND THE HOUSE HASN'T COLLAPSED YET.
THAT MEANS THE FIRE HASN'T BEEN BURNING FOR LONG.

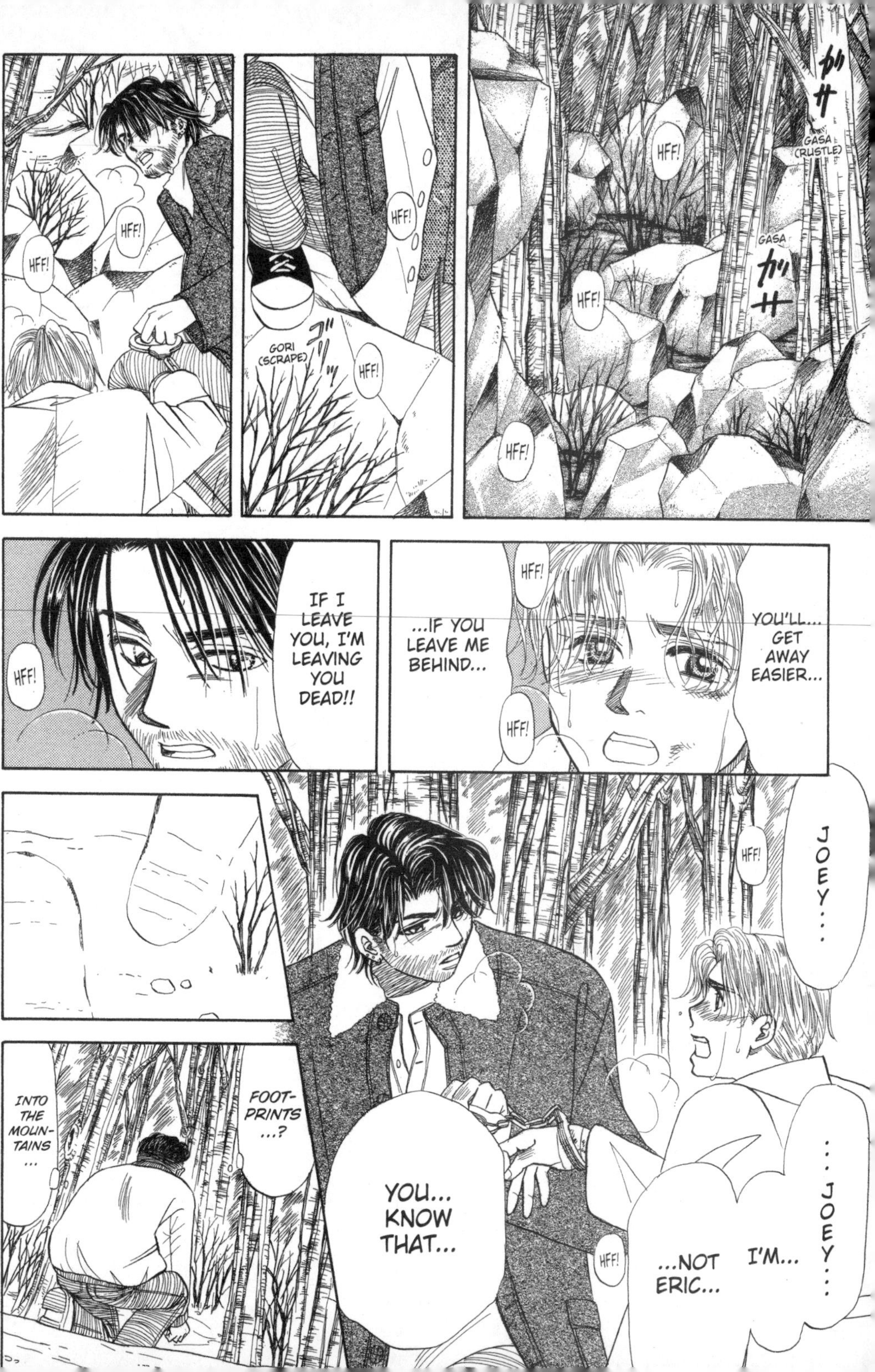

HFF!
GASA (RUSTLE)
GASA
HFF!
HFF!
HFF!
GORI (SCRAPE)
HFF!
HFF!
HFF!
YOU'LL... GET AWAY EASIER...
HFF!
...IF YOU LEAVE ME BEHIND...
HFF!
IF I LEAVE YOU, I'M LEAVING YOU DEAD!!
HFF!
JOEY...
HFF!
...JOEY...
I'M...
...NOT ERIC...
HFF!
YOU... KNOW THAT...
FOOT-PRINTS...?
INTO THE MOUN-TAINS...

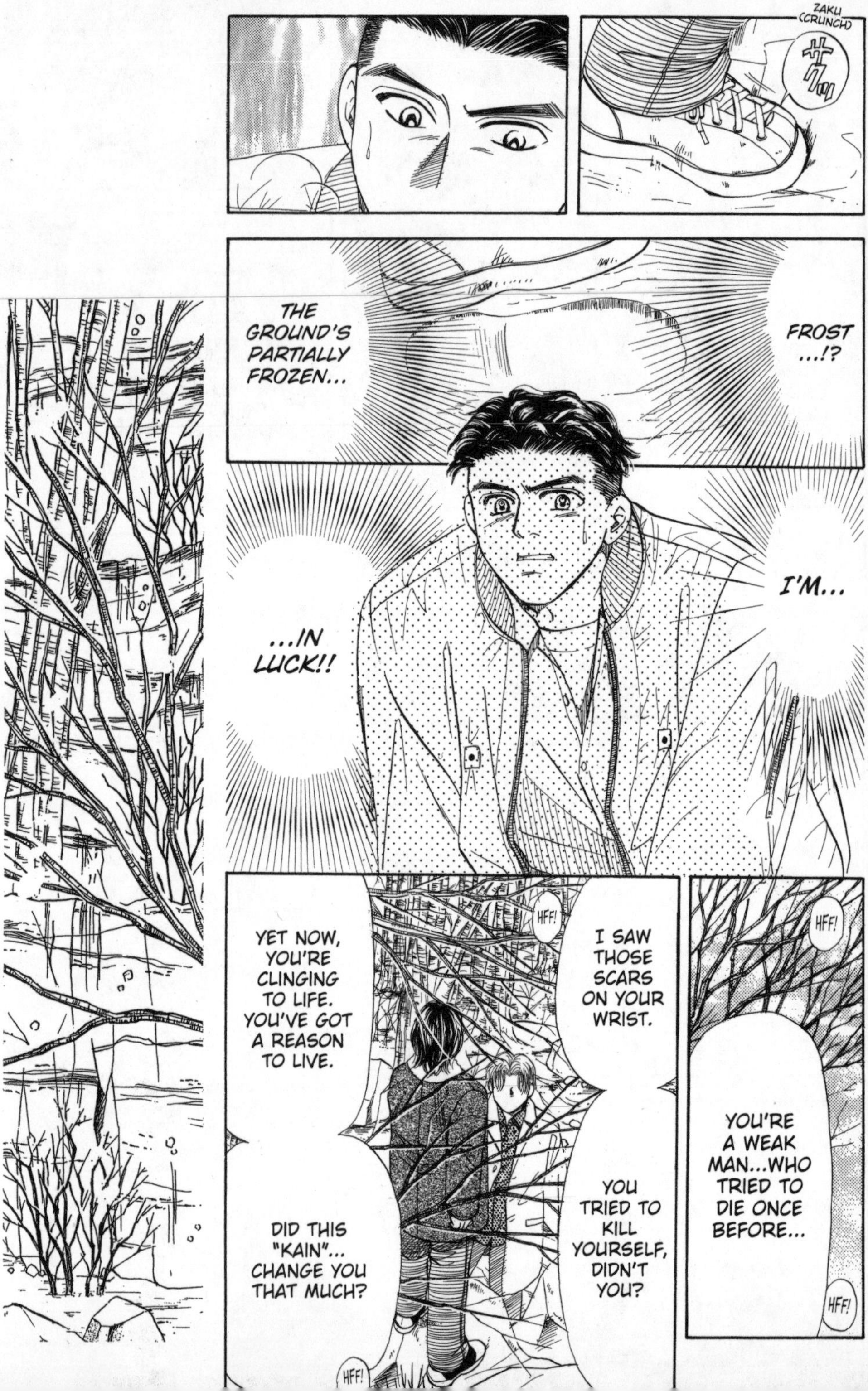
ZAKU (CRUNCH)
サクッ
FROST ...!?
THE GROUND'S PARTIALLY FROZEN...
I'M...
...IN LUCK!!
HFF!
YOU'RE A WEAK MAN...WHO TRIED TO DIE ONCE BEFORE...
HFF!
HFF!
I SAW THOSE SCARS ON YOUR WRIST.
YOU TRIED TO KILL YOURSELF, DIDN'T YOU?
YET NOW, YOU'RE CLINGING TO LIFE. YOU'VE GOT A REASON TO LIVE.
DID THIS "KAIN"... CHANGE YOU THAT MUCH?
HFF!

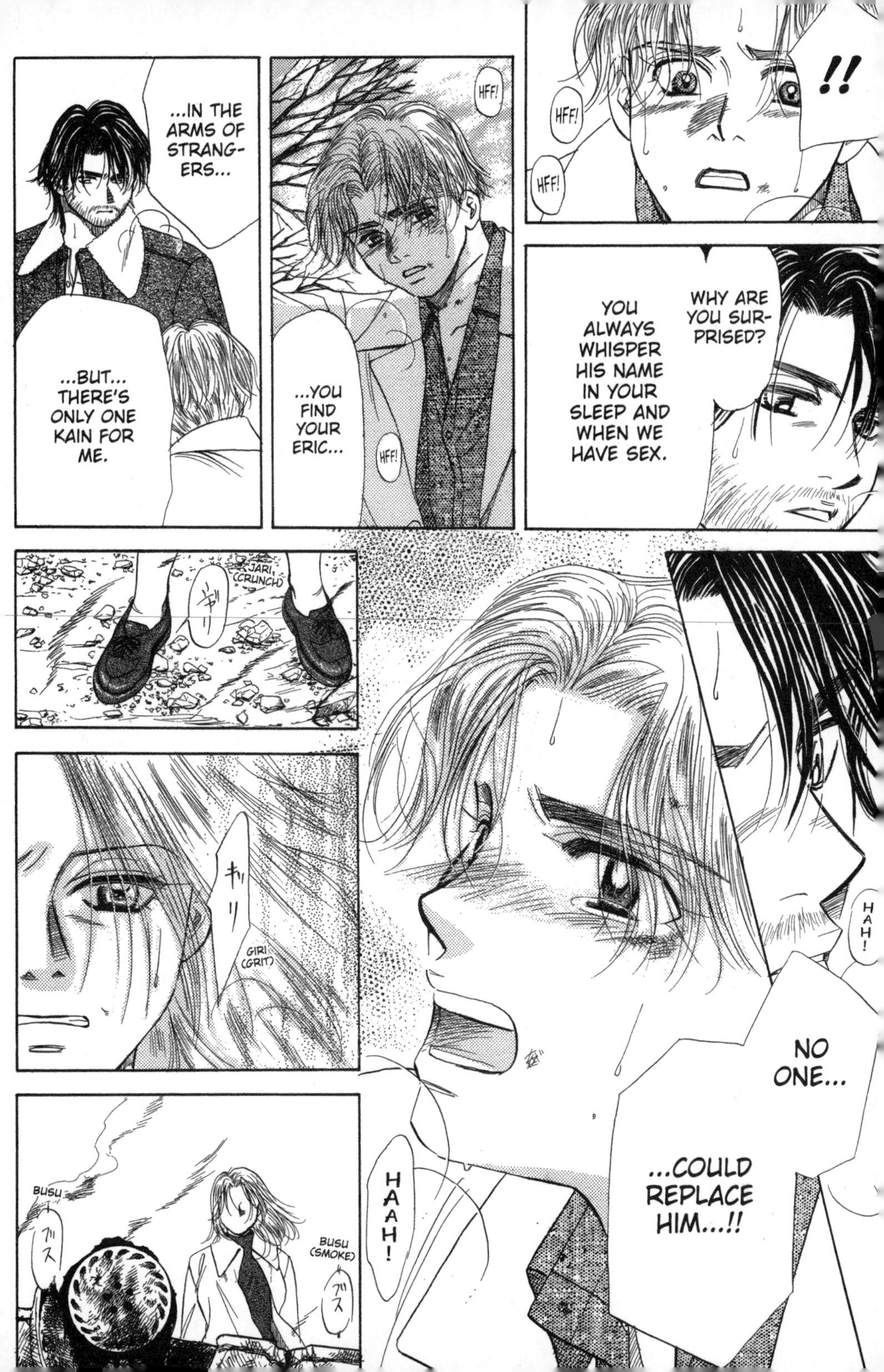
HFF!
HFF!
!!
WHY ARE YOU SURPRISED?
YOU ALWAYS WHISPER HIS NAME IN YOUR SLEEP AND WHEN WE HAVE SEX.
HFF!
...YOU FIND YOUR ERIC...
HFF!
...IN THE ARMS OF STRANGERS...
...BUT... THERE'S ONLY ONE KAIN FOR ME.
HAH!
NO ONE...
...COULD REPLACE HIM...!!
HAAAH!
JARI (CRUNCH)
ジャリ
ギリ
GIRI (GRIT)
BUSU
ブス
BUSU (SMOKE)
ブス

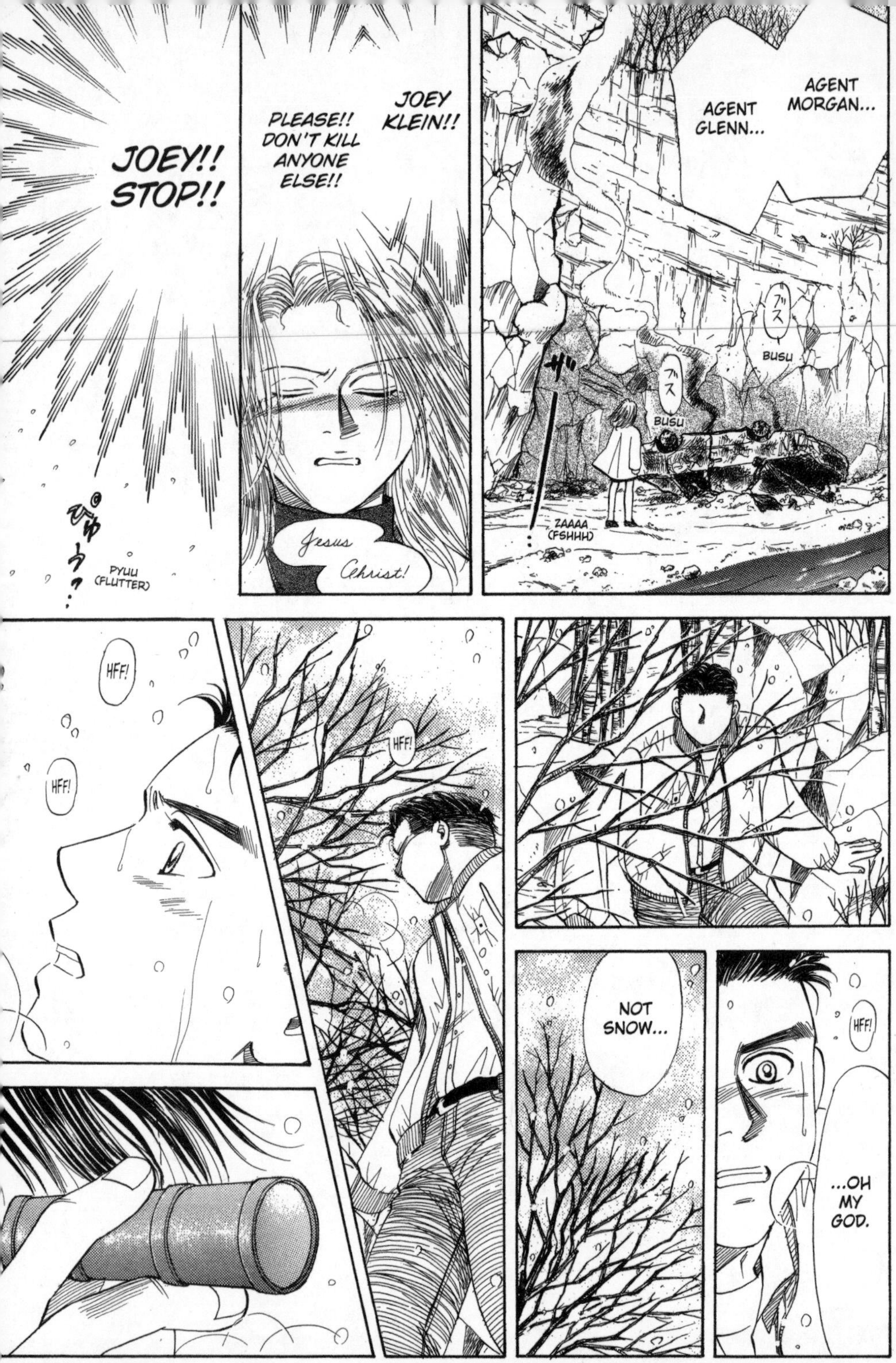
AGENT MORGAN...
AGENT GLENN...
ブス
BUSU
ブス
BUSU
ZAAAA (FSHHH)
JOEY KLEIN!!
PLEASE!! DON'T KILL ANYONE ELSE!!
Jesus Christ!
JOEY!! STOP!!
PYUU (FLUTTER)
HFF!
...OH MY GOD.
NOT SNOW...
HFF!
HFF!
HFF!

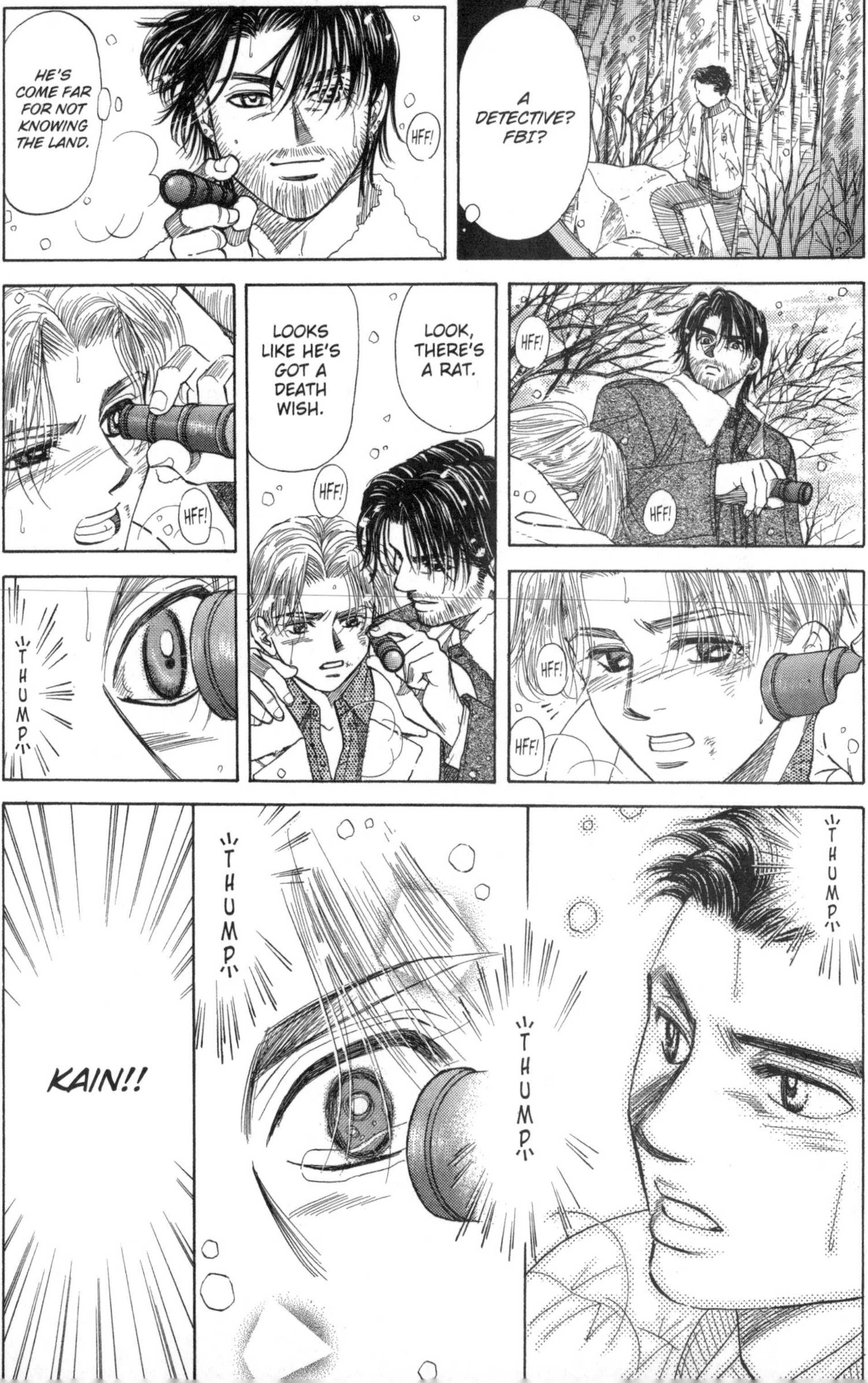
A DETECTIVE? FBI?
HE'S COME FAR FOR NOT KNOWING THE LAND.
HFF!
HFF!
HFF!
HFF!
HFF!
LOOK, THERE'S A RAT.
LOOKS LIKE HE'S GOT A DEATH WISH.
HFF!
HFF!
HFF!
THUMP
THUMP
THUMP
THUMP
KAIN!!

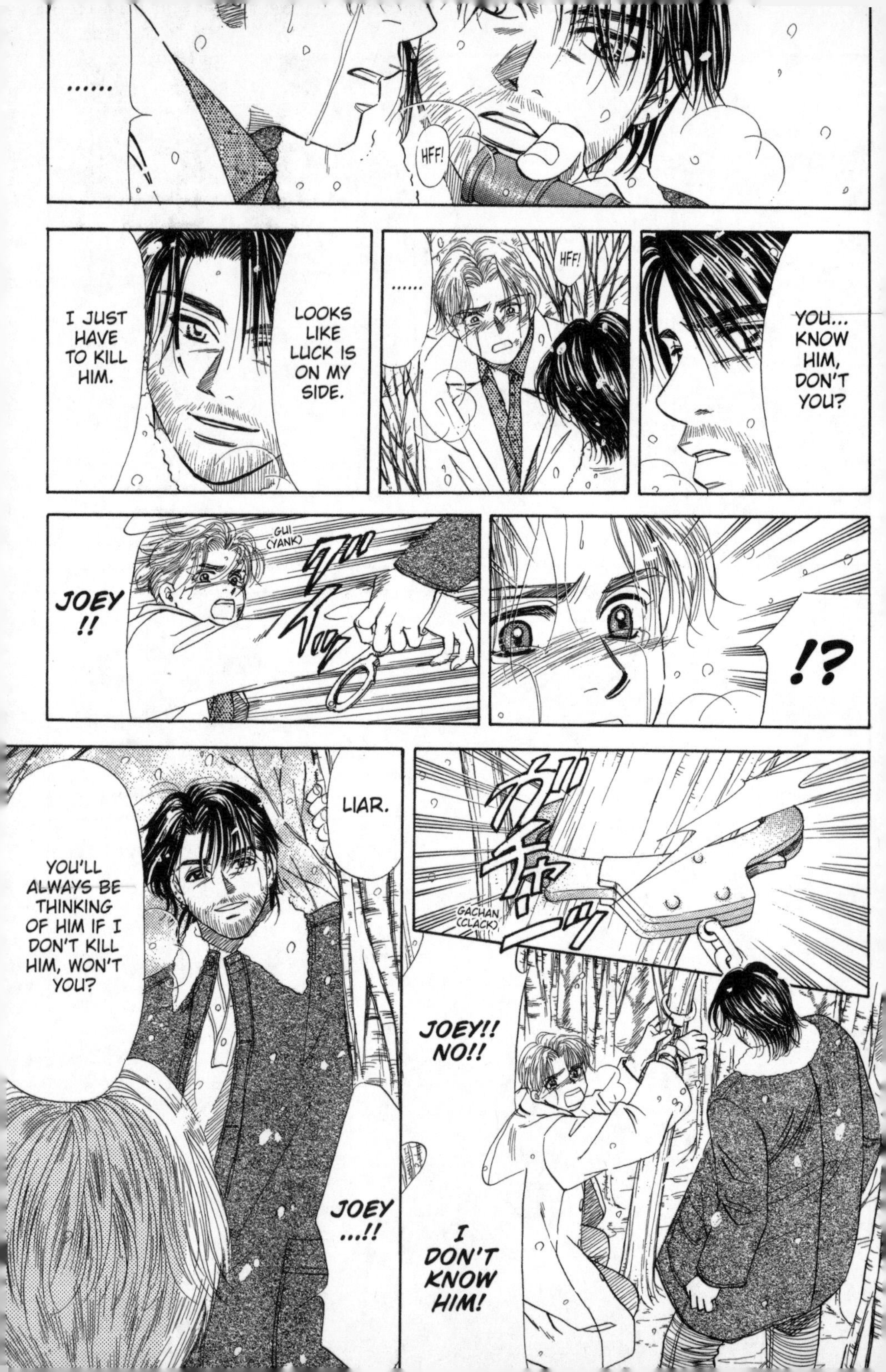
HFF!
......
YOU... KNOW HIM, DON'T YOU?
HFF!
......
LOOKS LIKE LUCK IS ON MY SIDE.
I JUST HAVE TO KILL HIM.
!?
GUI (YANK)
JOEY !!
GACHAN (CLACK)
JOEY!! NO!!
I DON'T KNOW HIM!
LIAR.
YOU'LL ALWAYS BE THINKING OF HIM IF I DON'T KILL HIM, WON'T YOU?
JOEY ...!!

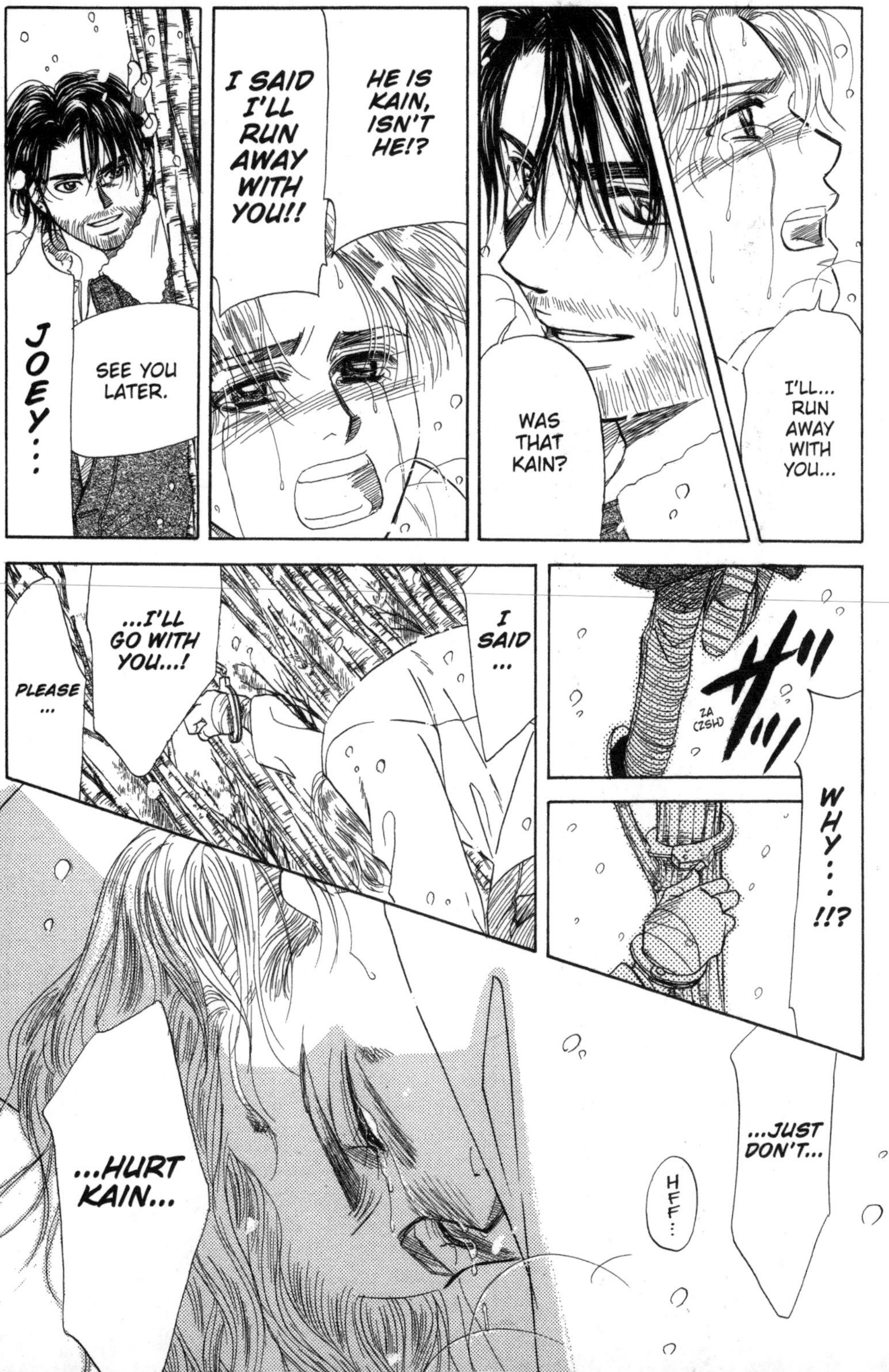
I'LL... RUN AWAY WITH YOU...
WAS THAT KAIN?
HE IS KAIN, ISN'T HE!?
I SAID I'LL RUN AWAY WITH YOU!!
SEE YOU LATER.
JOEY...
ZA (ZSH)
WHY...!!?
I SAID...
...I'LL GO WITH YOU...!
PLEASE...
...JUST DON'T...
HFF...
...HURT KAIN...

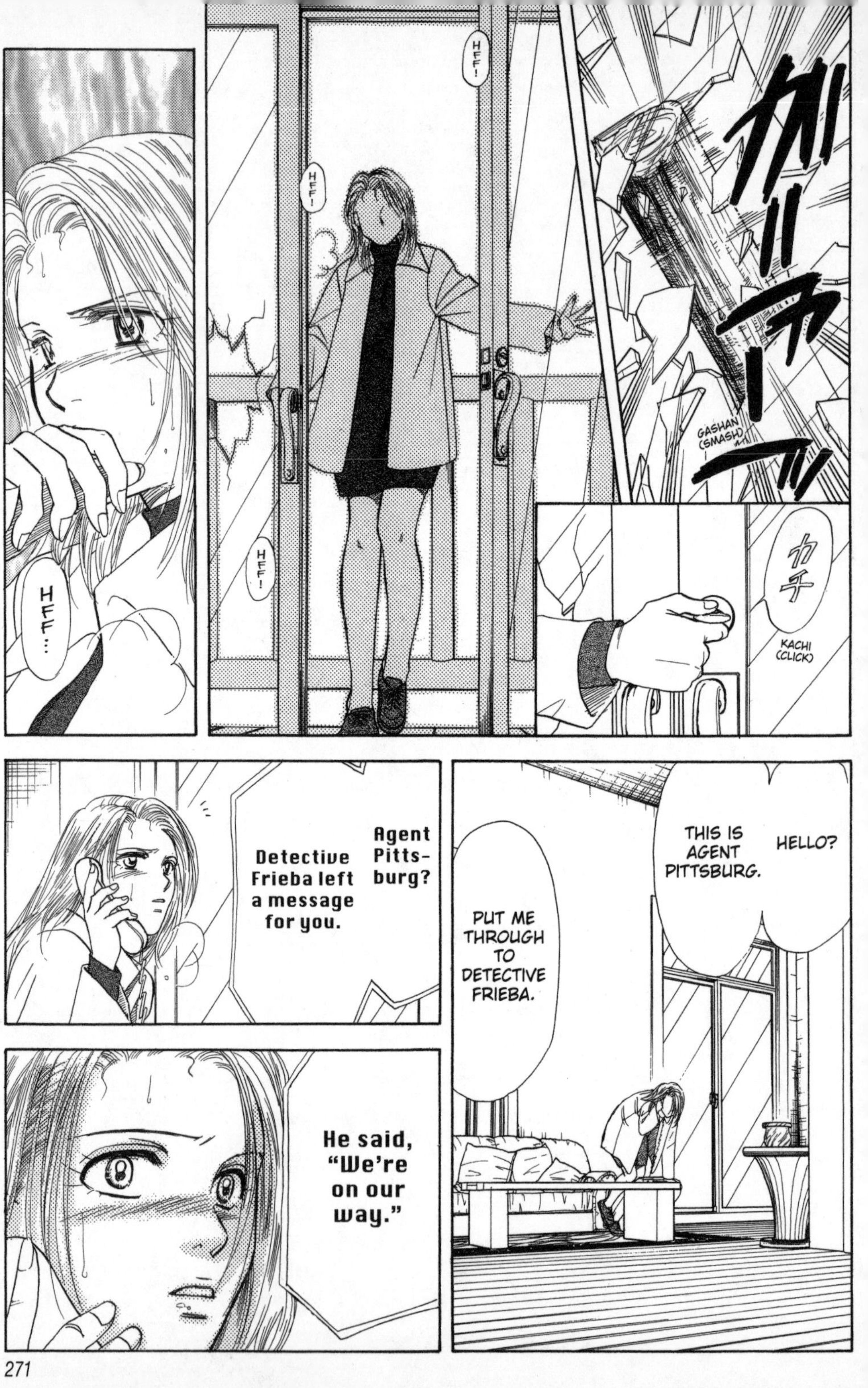
GASHAN (SMASH)
カチ
KACHI (CLICK)
HFF!
HFF!
HFF!
HFF...
HELLO?
THIS IS AGENT PITTSBURG.
PUT ME THROUGH TO DETECTIVE FRIEBA.
Agent Pittsburg?
Detective Frieba left a message for you.
He said, "We're on our way."

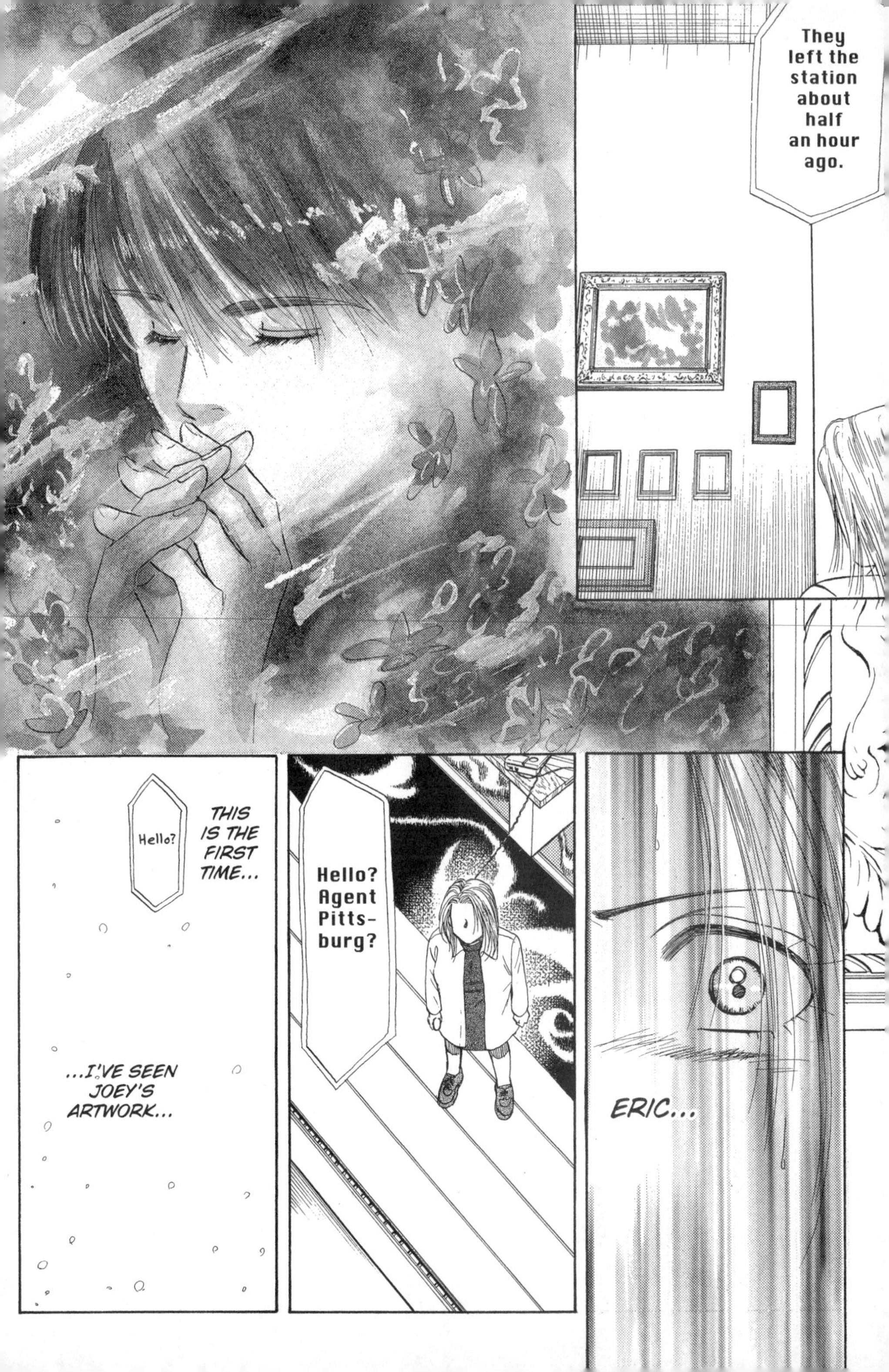
They left the station about half an hour ago.
ERIC...
Hello? Agent Pittsburg?
THIS IS THE FIRST TIME...
Hello?
...I'VE SEEN JOEY'S ARTWORK...

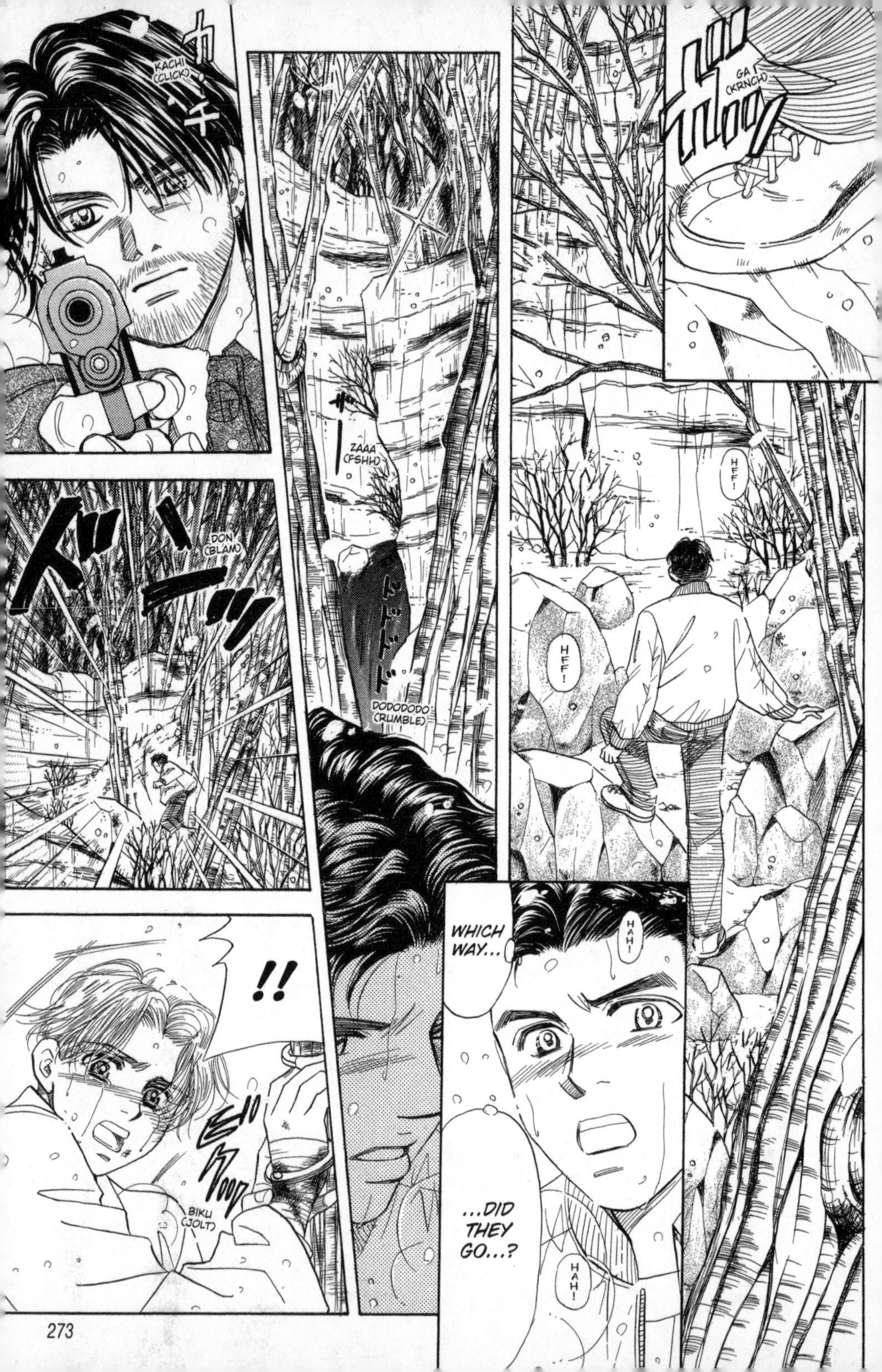
GA (KRNCH)
HFF!
HFF!
WHICH WAY...
HAH!
...DID THEY GO...?
HAH!
ZAAA (FSHH)
DODODODO (RUMBLE)
KACHI (CLICK)
DON (BLAM)
!!
BIKU (JOLT)

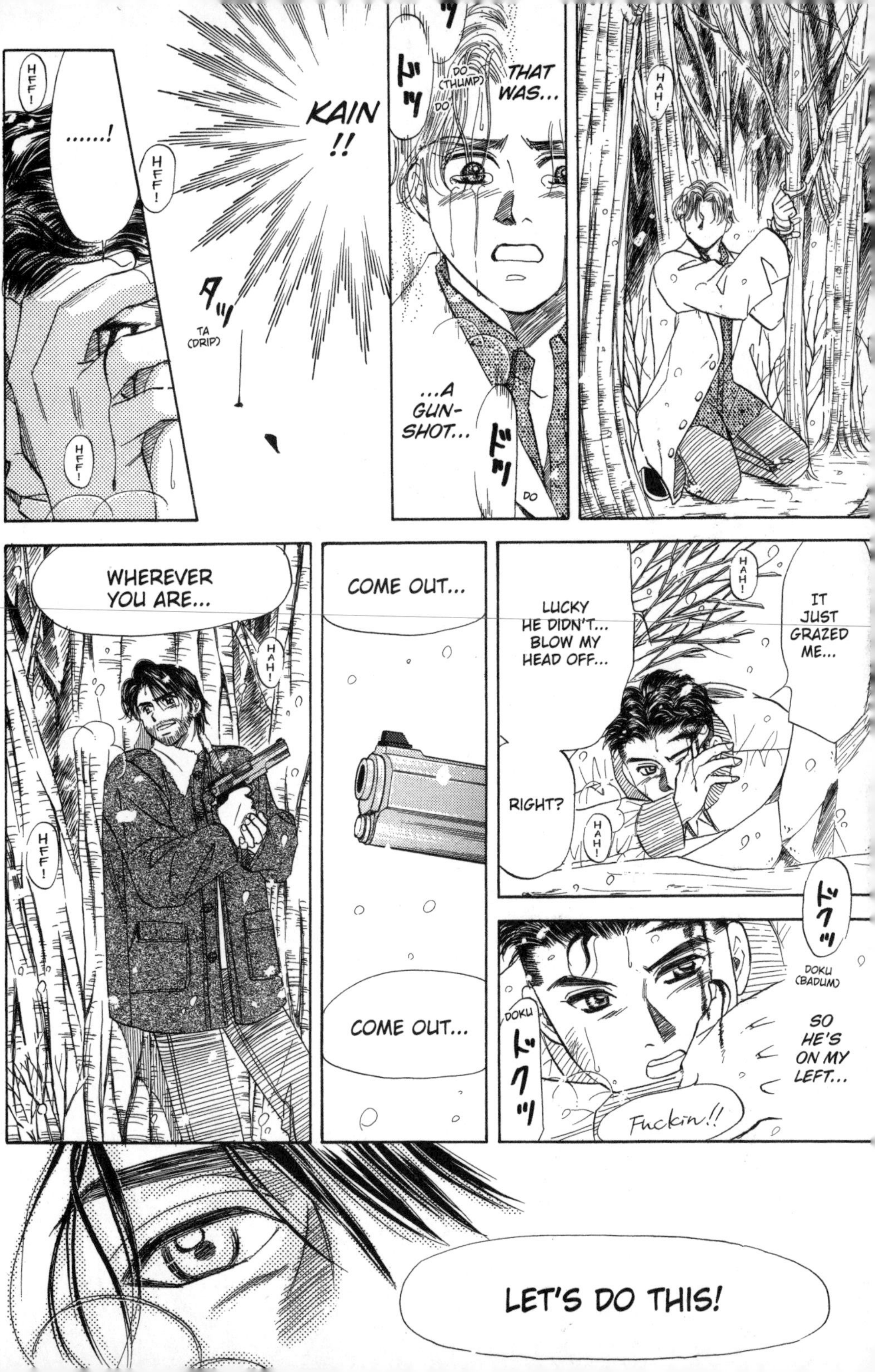
HAH!
ドッ
DO (THUMP)
DO
THAT WAS...
...A GUN-SHOT...
ドッ
DO
KAIN!!
HFF!
......!
HFF!
タッ
TA (DRIP)
HFF!
IT JUST GRAZED ME...
HAH!
LUCKY HE DIDN'T... BLOW MY HEAD OFF...
RIGHT?
HAH!
ドクッ
DOKU (BADUM)
SO HE'S ON MY LEFT...
DOKU
ドクッ
Fuckin!!
COME OUT...
COME OUT...
WHEREVER YOU ARE...
HAH!
HFF!
LET'S DO THIS!

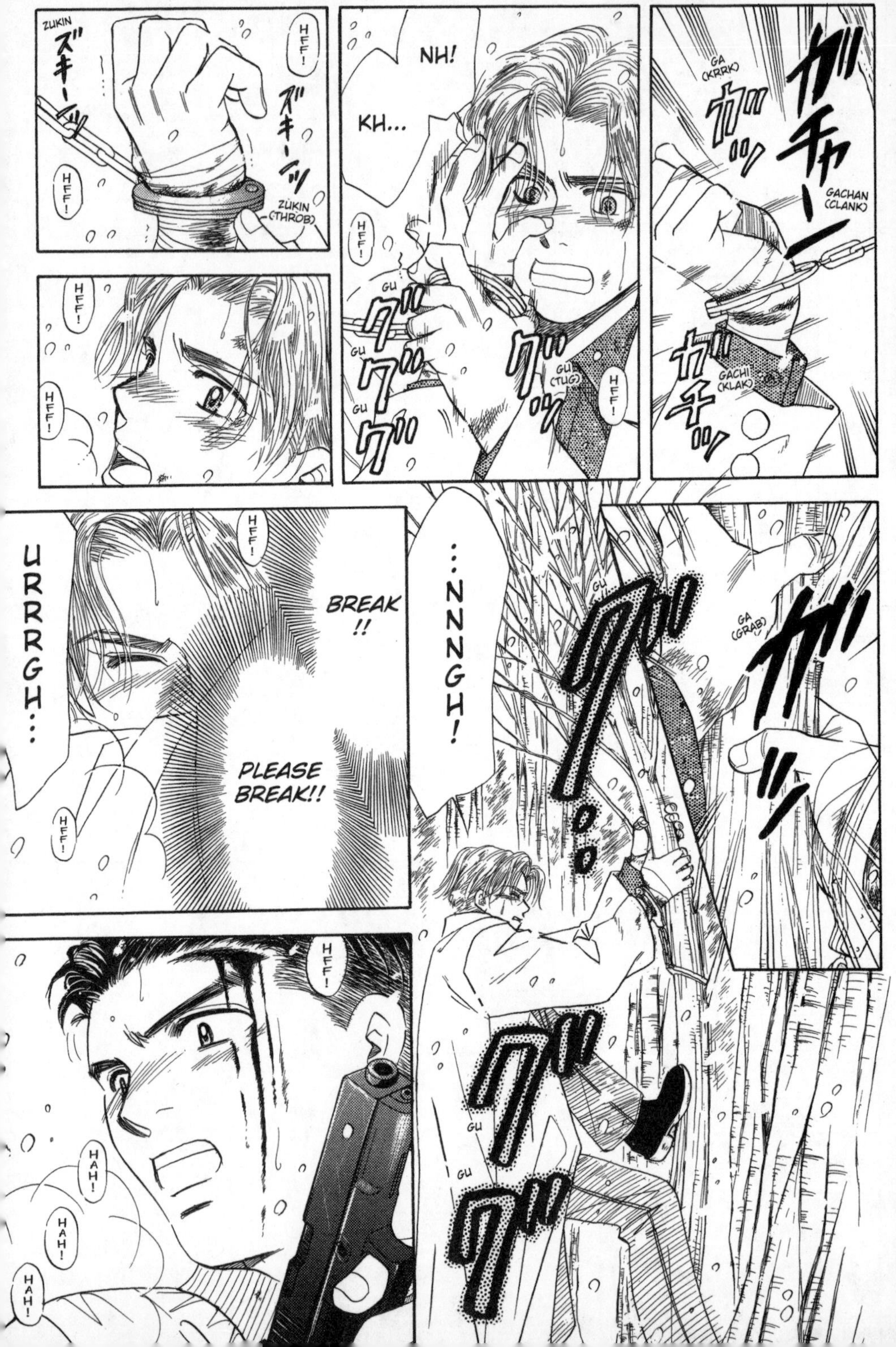
GA (KRRK)
ガッ
ガチャーン
GACHAN (CLANK)
GACHI (KLAK)
カチッ
NH!
KH...
HFF!
GU
GU
GU
グッ
グッ
グッ
GU (TUG)
グッ
HFF!
ZUKIN
ズキーンッ
HFF!
ズキーンッ
ZUKIN (THROB)
HFF!
HFF!
HFF!
GA (GRAB)
ガッ
...NNNGH!
GU
グッ
GU
GU
グッ
グッ
HFF!
URRRGH...
BREAK!!
PLEASE BREAK!!
HFF!
HFF!
HAH!
HAH!
HAH!

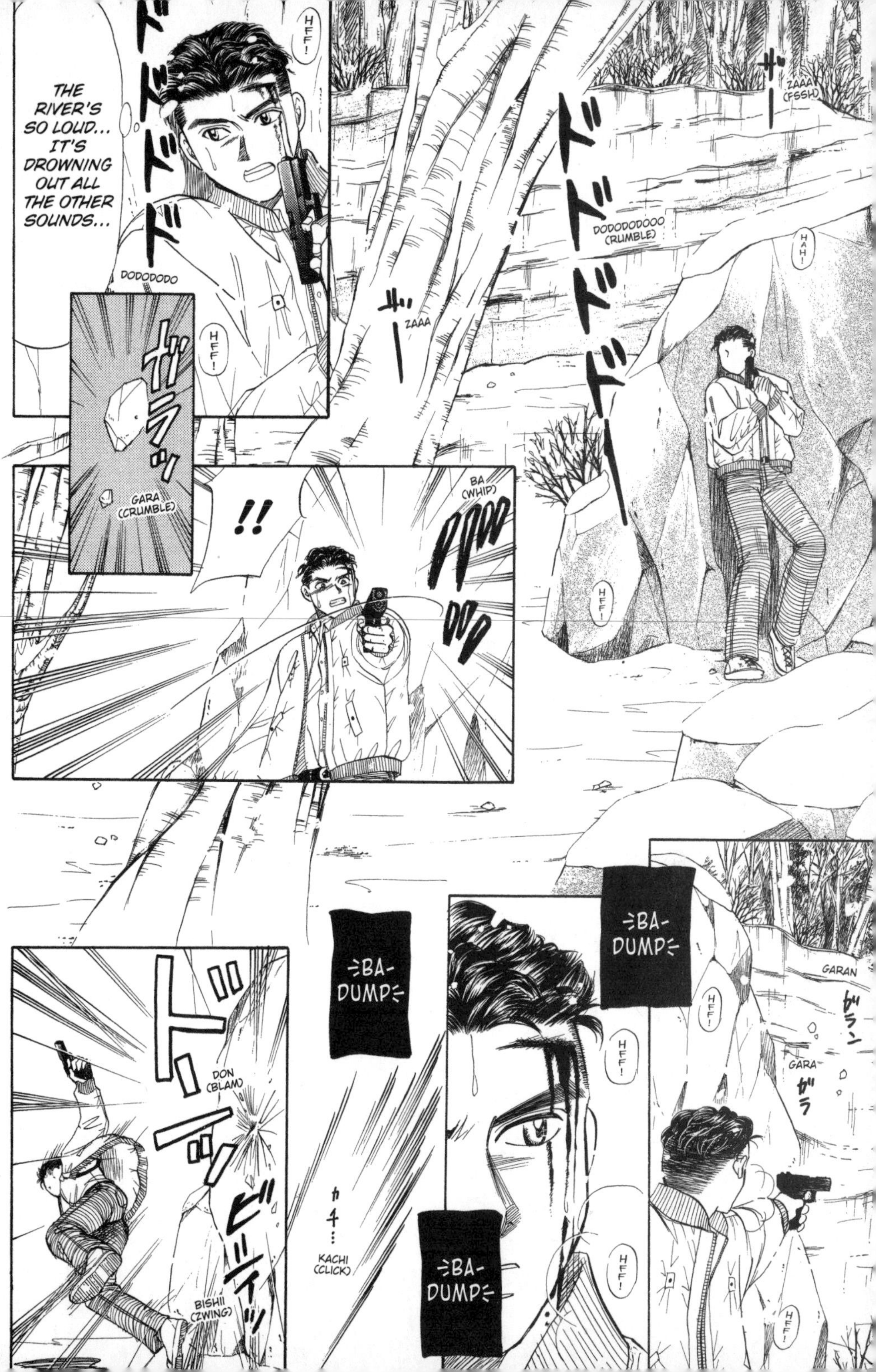
ZAAA (FSSH)
DODODODOOO (RUMBLE)
HAH!
HFF!
ZAAA
HFF!
THE RIVER'S SO LOUD... IT'S DROWNING OUT ALL THE OTHER SOUNDS...
DODODODO
HFF!
GARA (CRUMBLE)
BA (WHIP)
!!
GARAN
GARA
HFF!
HFF!
BA-DUMP
BA-DUMP
HFF!
HFF!
BA-DUMP
KACHI (CLICK)
BA-DUMP
DON (BLAM)
BISHII (ZWING)

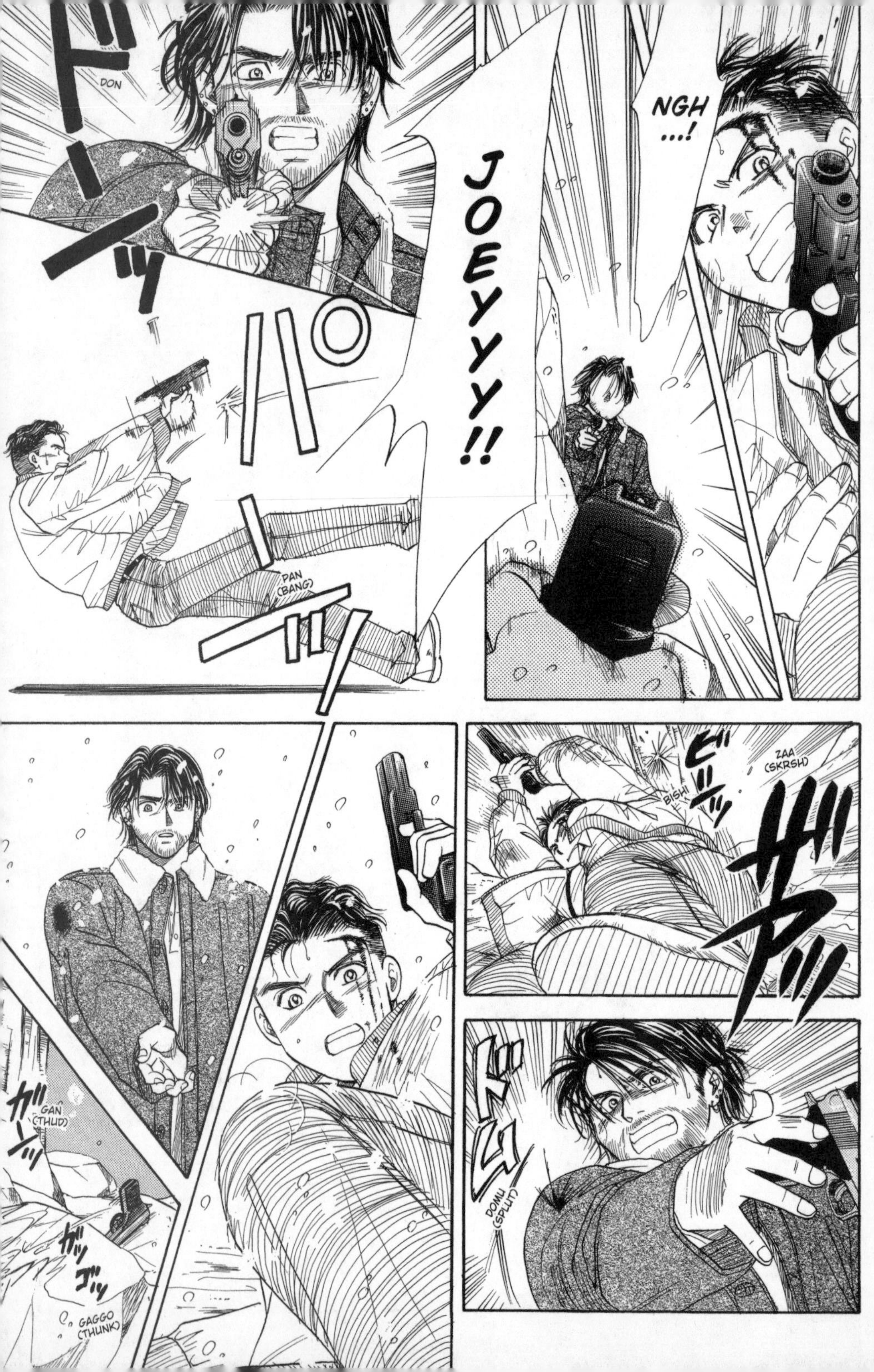
NGH ...!
JOEYYY!!
DON
PAN (BANG)
ZAA (SKRSH)
BISH!
DOMU (SPLUT)
GAN (THUD)
GAGGO (THUNK)

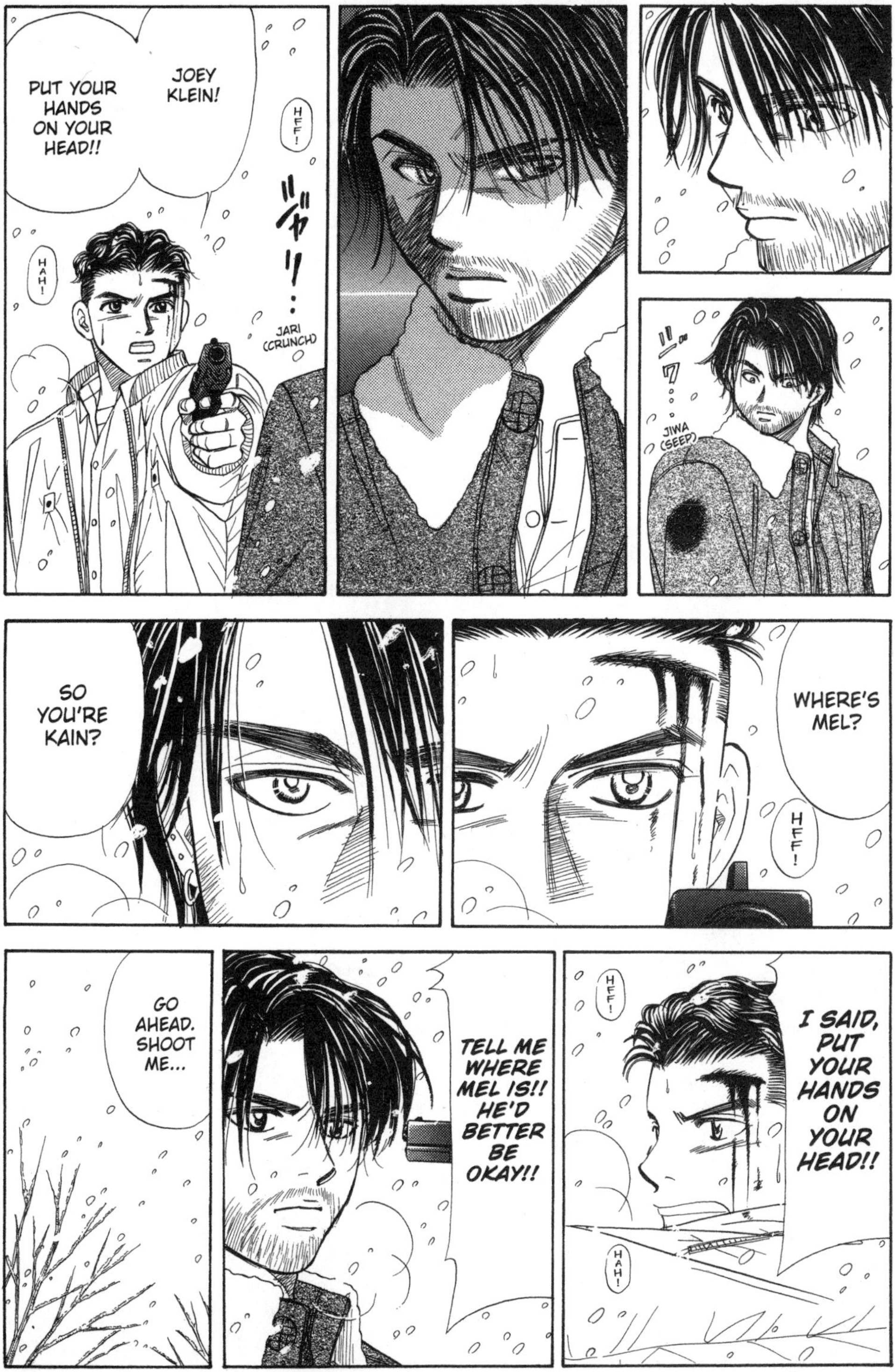
ジワ…
JIWA (SEEP)
JOEY KLEIN!
PUT YOUR HANDS ON YOUR HEAD!!
HFF!
ジャリ…
JARI (CRUNCH)
HAH!
WHERE'S MEL?
HFF!
SO YOU'RE KAIN?
HFF!
I SAID, PUT YOUR HANDS ON YOUR HEAD!!
HAH!
TELL ME WHERE MEL IS!! HE'D BETTER BE OKAY!!
GO AHEAD. SHOOT ME...

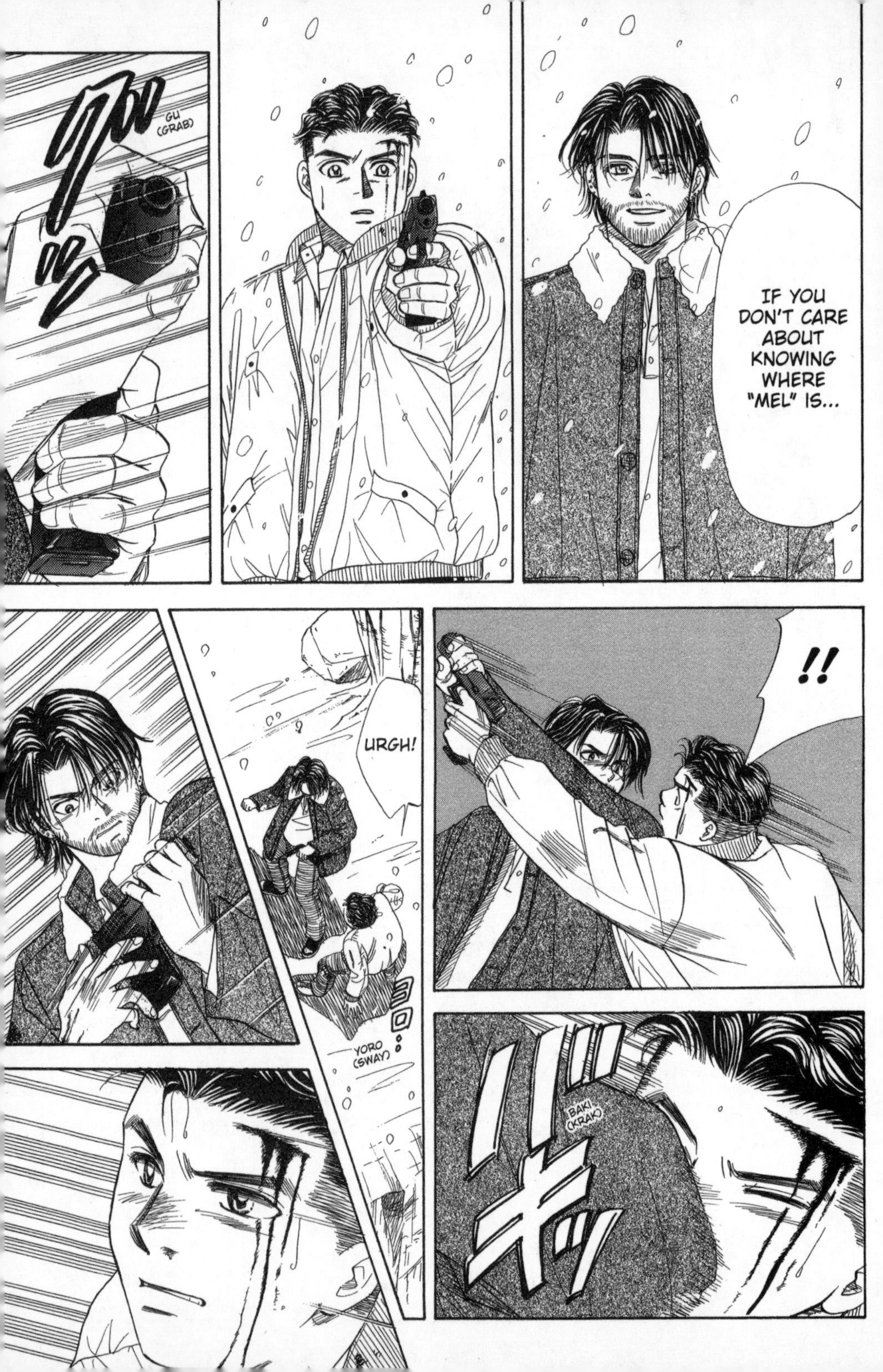
IF YOU DON'T CARE ABOUT KNOWING WHERE "MEL" IS...
GU (GRAB)
!!
URGH!
YORO (SWAY)
BAKI (KRAK)

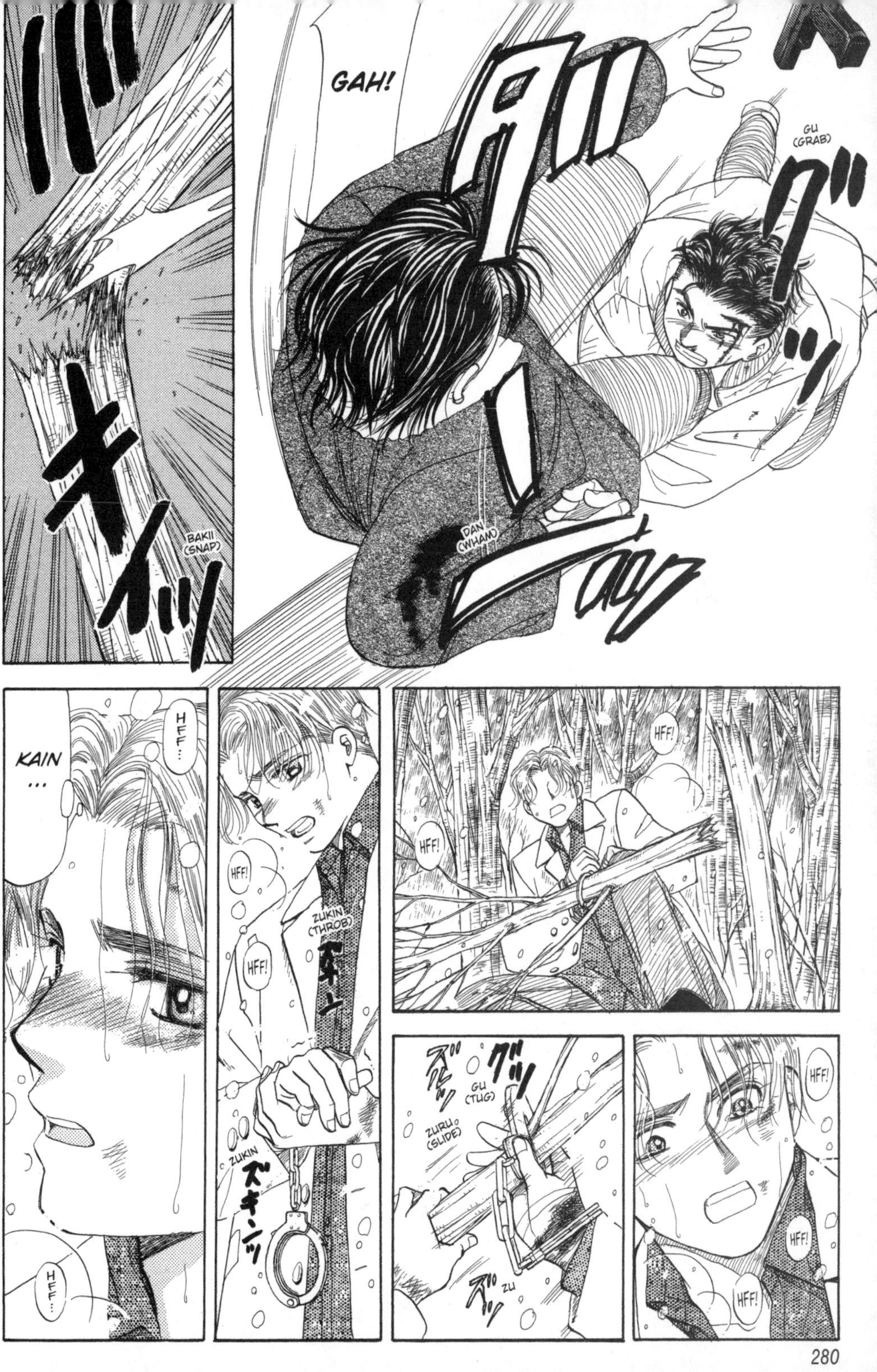
GU (GRAB)
GAH!
DAN (WHAM)
BAKII (SNAP)
HFF!
HFF!
HFF!
HFF!
HFF!
GU (TUG)
ZURU (SLIDE)
ZU
HFF!
ZUKIN (THROB)
HFF!
ZUKIN
HFF...
KAIN ...
HFF...

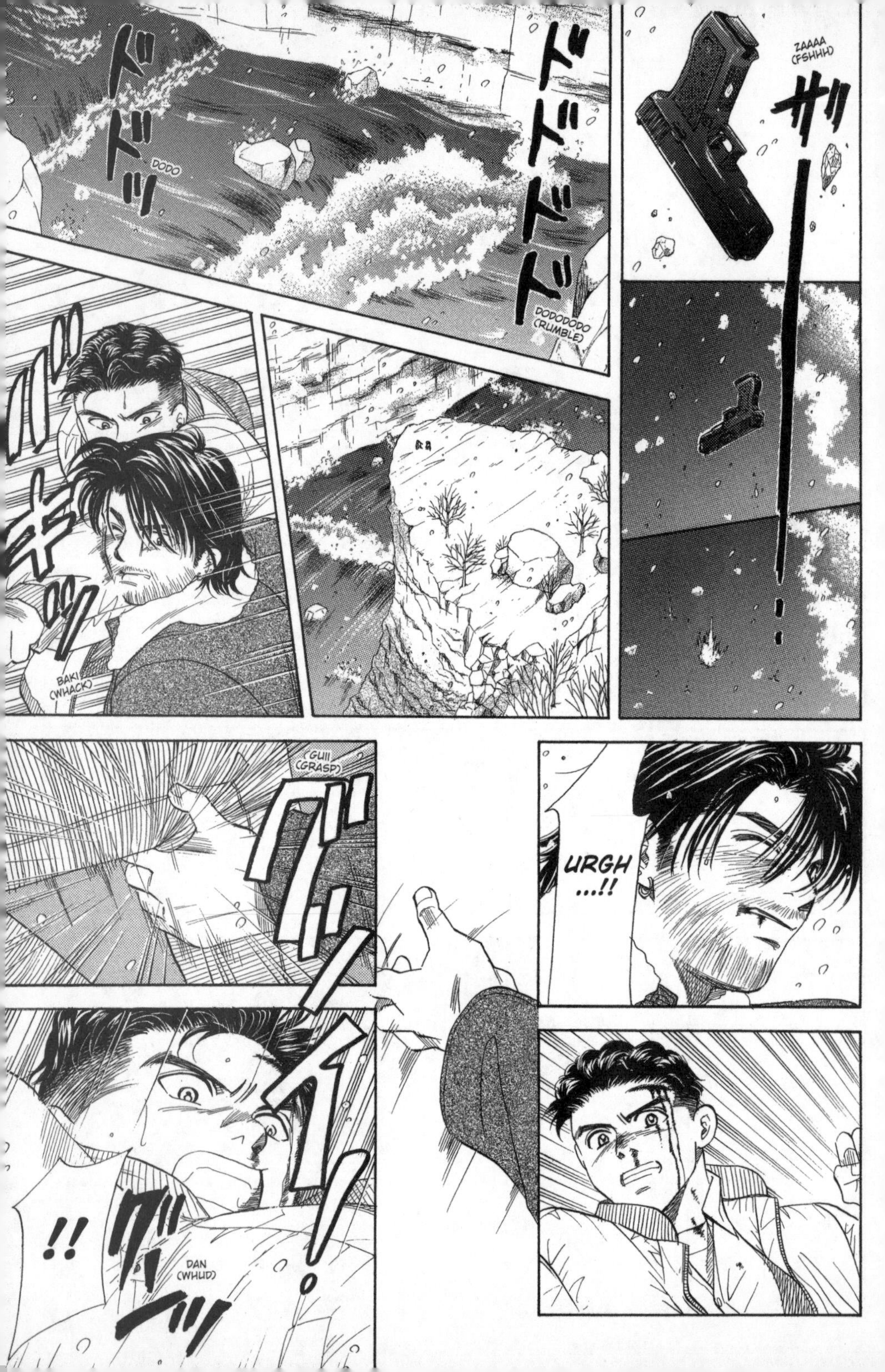
ZAAAA
(FSHHH)
DODODODO
(RUMBLE)
DODO
BAKI
(WHACK)
URGH
...!!
GUII
(GRASP)
!!
DAN
(WHUD)

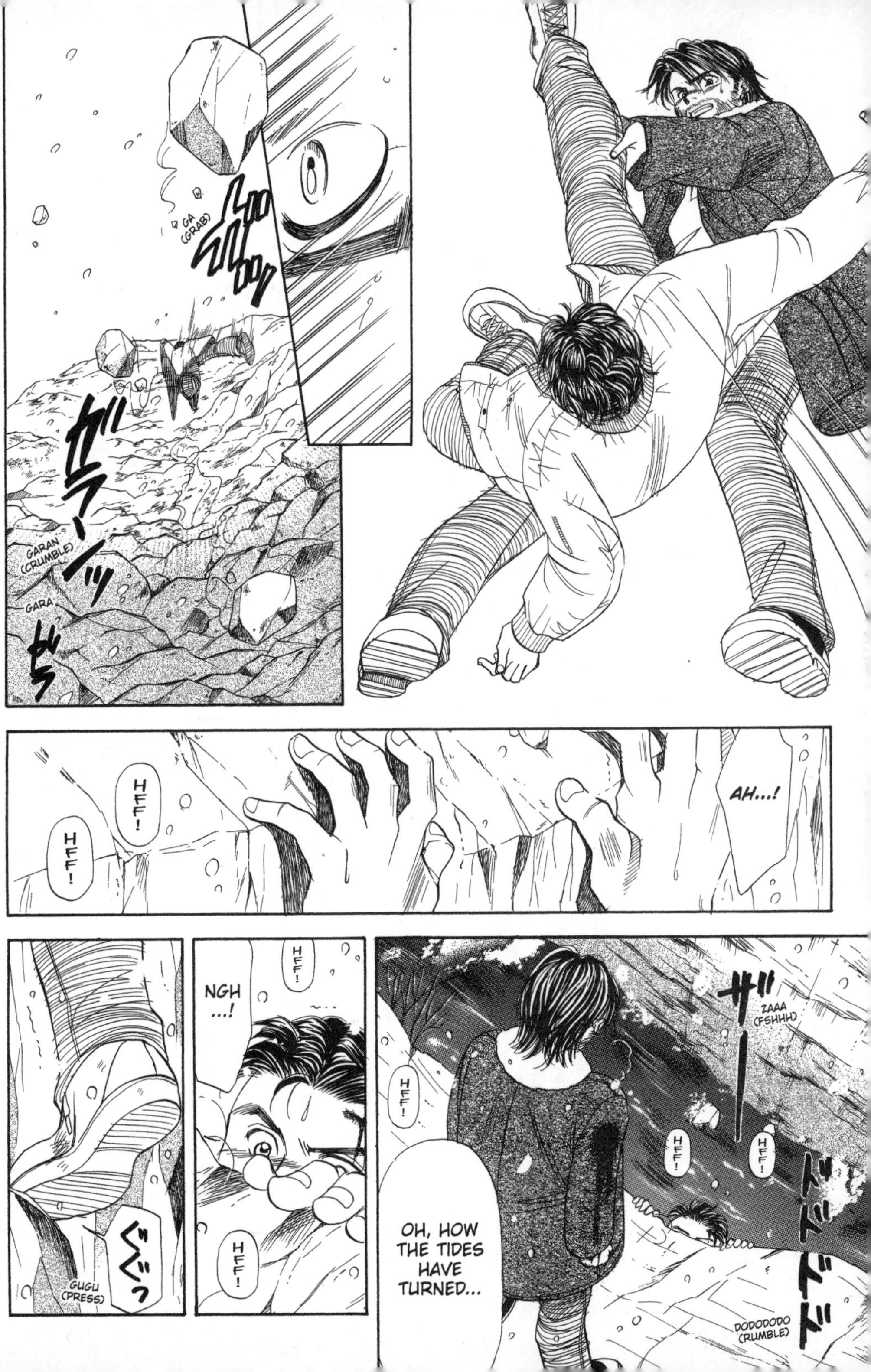
GA (GRAB)
GARAN (CRUMBLE)
GARA
AH...!
HFF!
HFF!
ZAAA (FSHHH)
HFF!
HFF!
HFF!
OH, HOW THE TIDES HAVE TURNED...
DODODODO (RUMBLE)
HFF!
NGH ...!
HFF!
GUGU (PRESS)

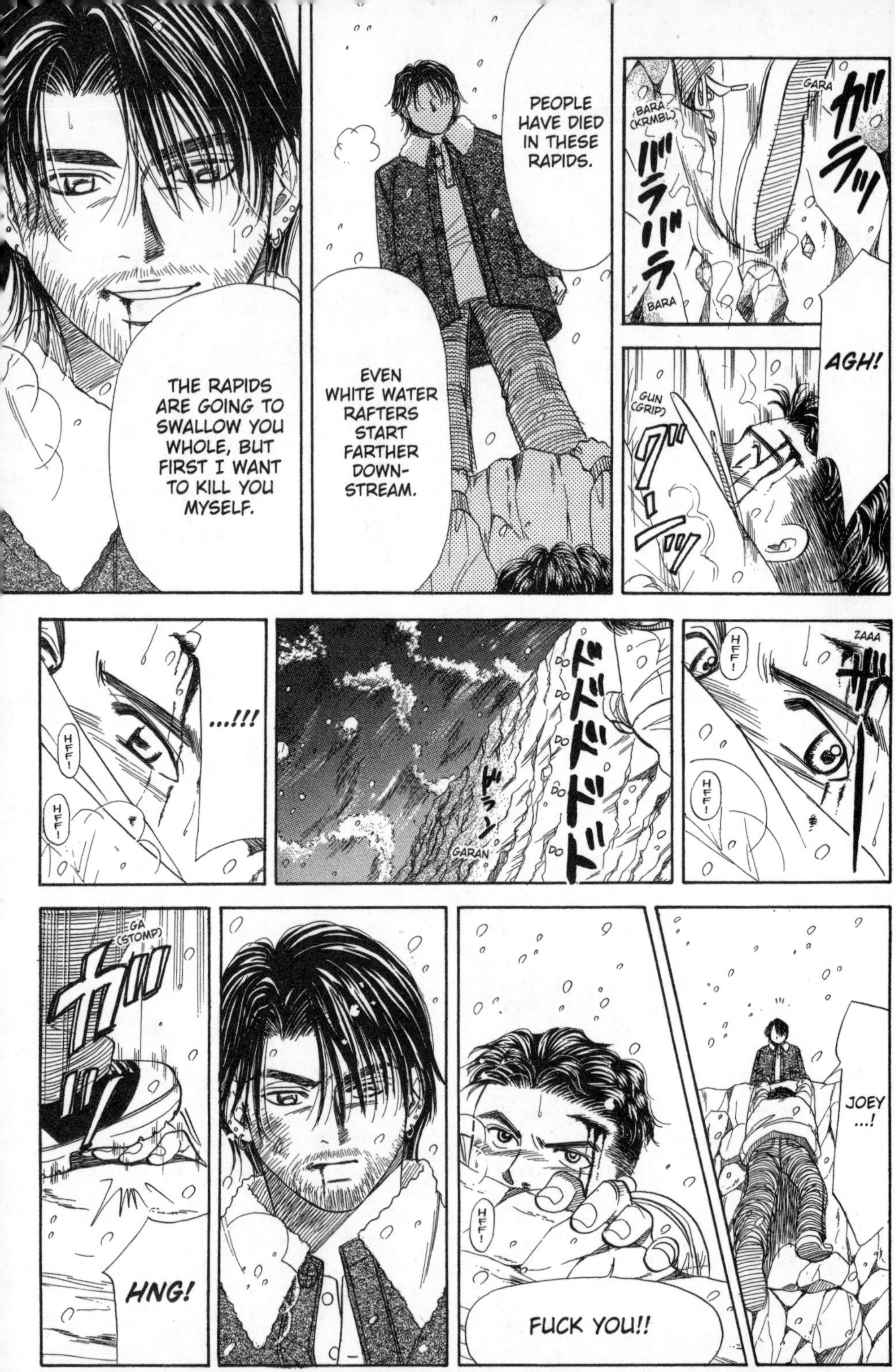
GARA
ガラッ
BARA (KRMBL)
バラバラ
BARA
AGH!
GUN (GRIP)
PEOPLE HAVE DIED IN THESE RAPIDS.
EVEN WHITE WATER RAFTERS START FARTHER DOWN-STREAM.
THE RAPIDS ARE GOING TO SWALLOW YOU WHOLE, BUT FIRST I WANT TO KILL YOU MYSELF.
ZAAA
ザッ
HFF!
HFF!
DO DO DO DO DO
ドドドドド
ガラン
GARAN
...!!!
HFF!
HFF!
JOEY ...!
HFF!
FUCK YOU!!
GA (STOMP)
ガッ
HNG!

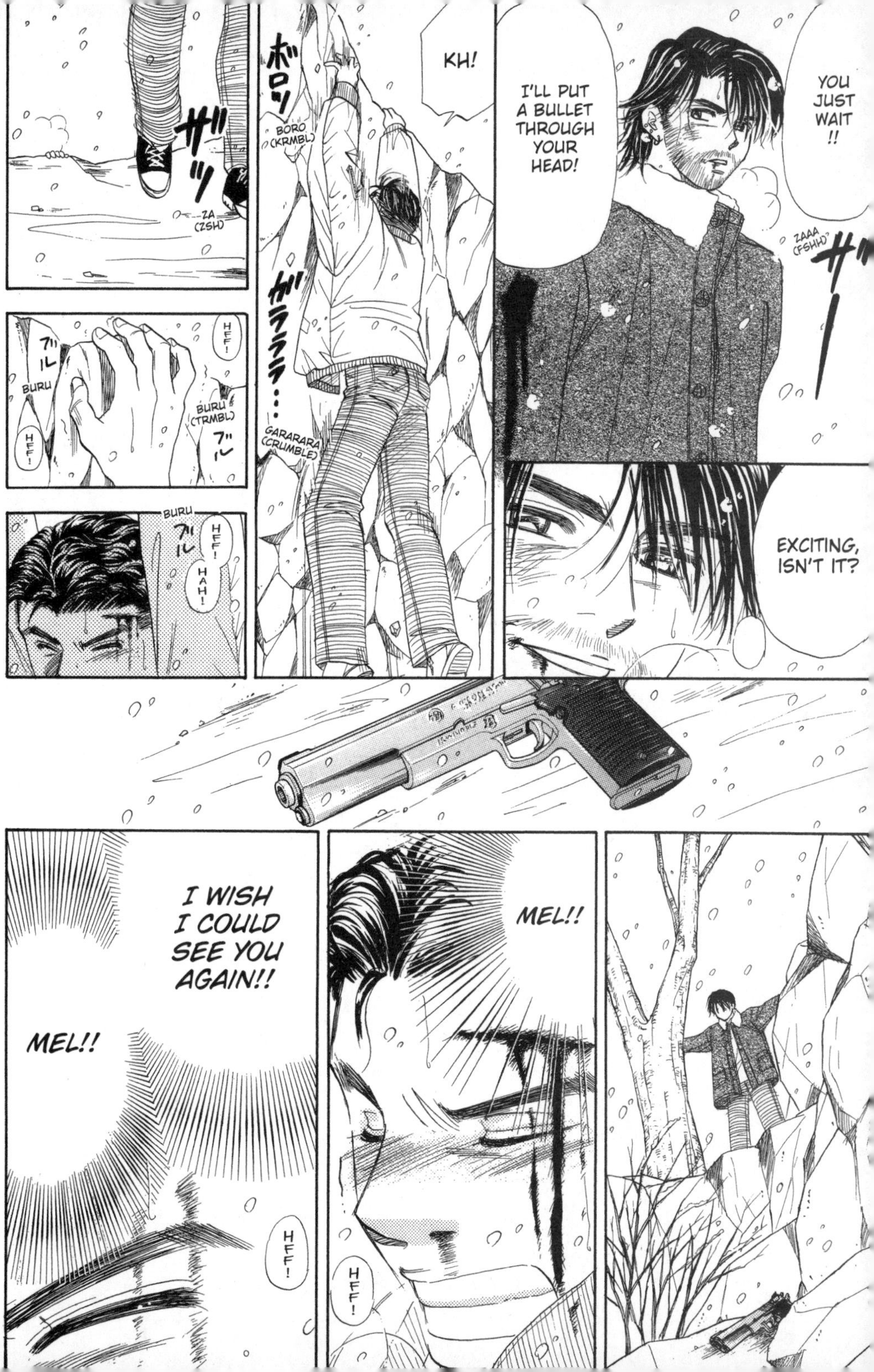
YOU JUST WAIT!!
I'LL PUT A BULLET THROUGH YOUR HEAD!
ザー
ZAAA (FSHH)
EXCITING, ISN'T IT?
KH!
ボロッ
BORO (KRMBL)
ガラララ…
GARARARA (CRUMBLE)
ザッ
ZA (ZSH)
HFF!
ブル
BURU (TRMBL)
ブル
BURU
HFF!
ブル
BURU
HFF!
HAH!
MEL!!
HFF!
HFF!
I WISH I COULD SEE YOU AGAIN!!
MEL!!

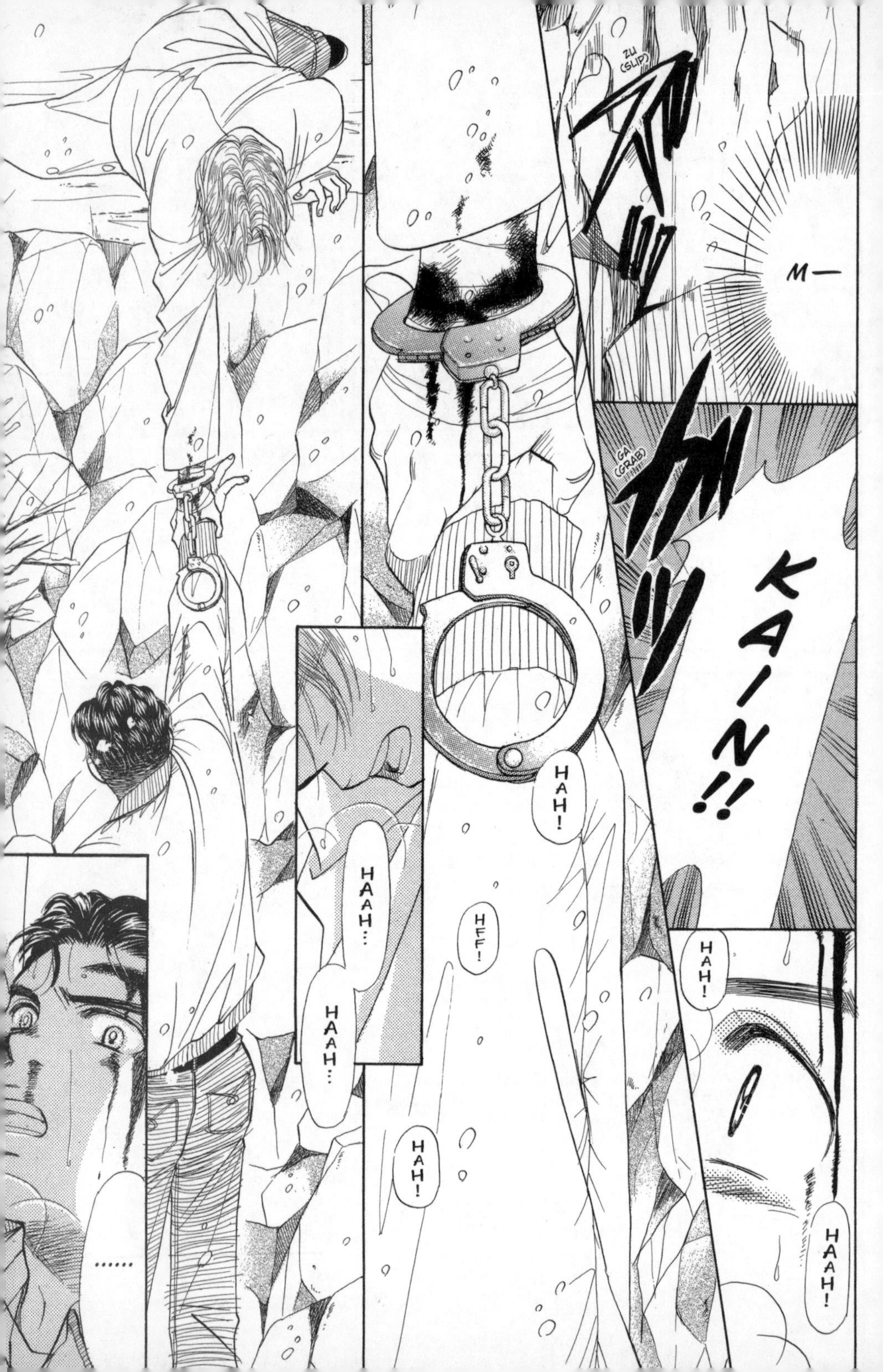
ZU (SLIP)
M—
GA (GRAB)
KAIN!!
HAH!
HAAAH!
HAH!
HFF!
HAH!
HAAAH...
HAAAH...
......

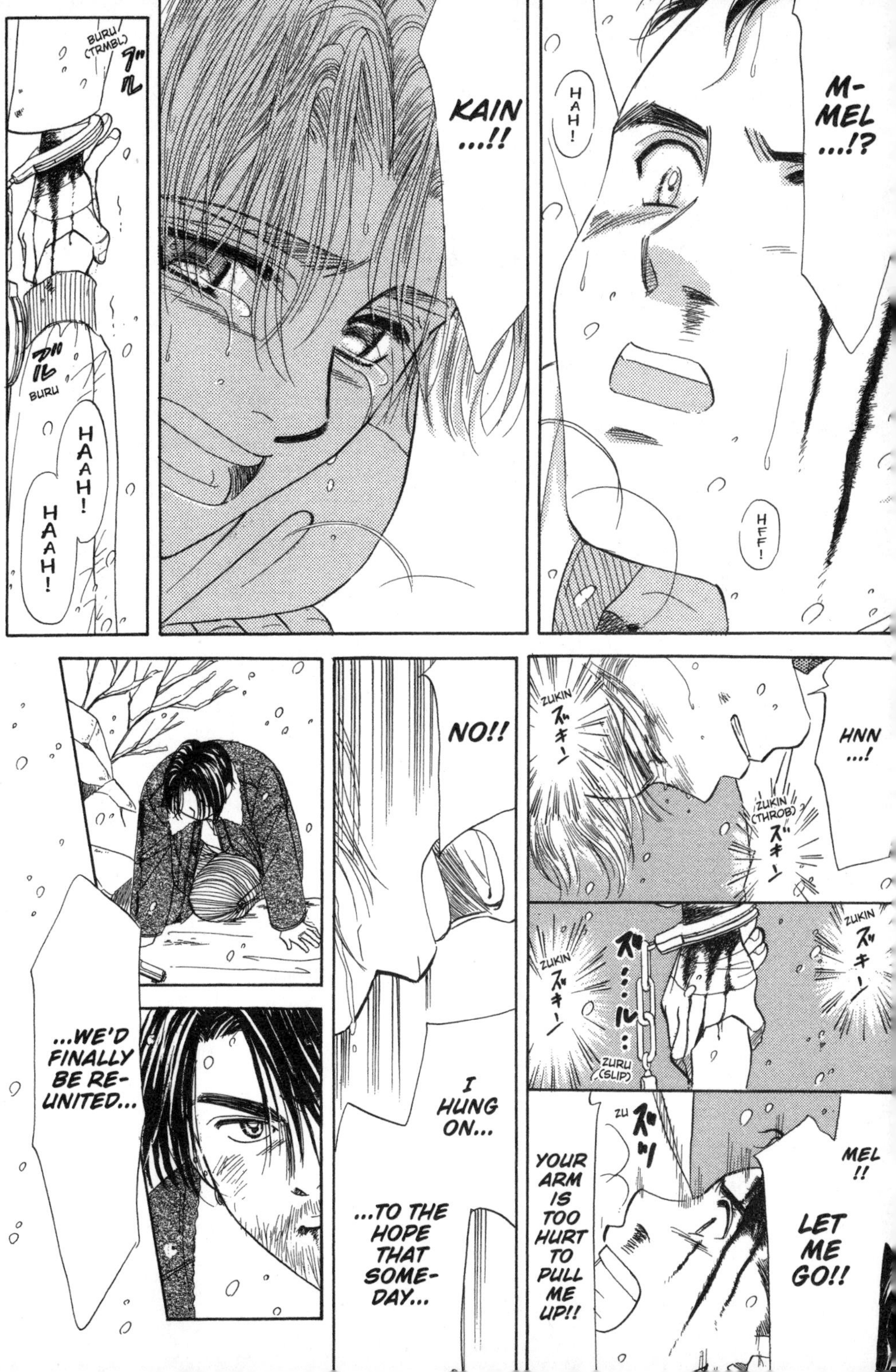
M-MEL ...!?
HAH!
HFF!
KAIN ...!!
BURU (TRMBL)
ブル
ブル
BURU
HAAAH!
HAAAH!
HNN ...!
ZUKIN (THROB)
ズキーン
ZUKIN
ズキーン
ZUKIN
ズキーン
ズ...ル...
ZURU (SLIP)
ZUKIN
ズキーン
MEL !!
LET ME GO!!
ZU
ズッ
YOUR ARM IS TOO HURT TO PULL ME UP!!
NO!!
I HUNG ON...
...TO THE HOPE THAT SOME-DAY...
...WE'D FINALLY BE RE-UNITED...

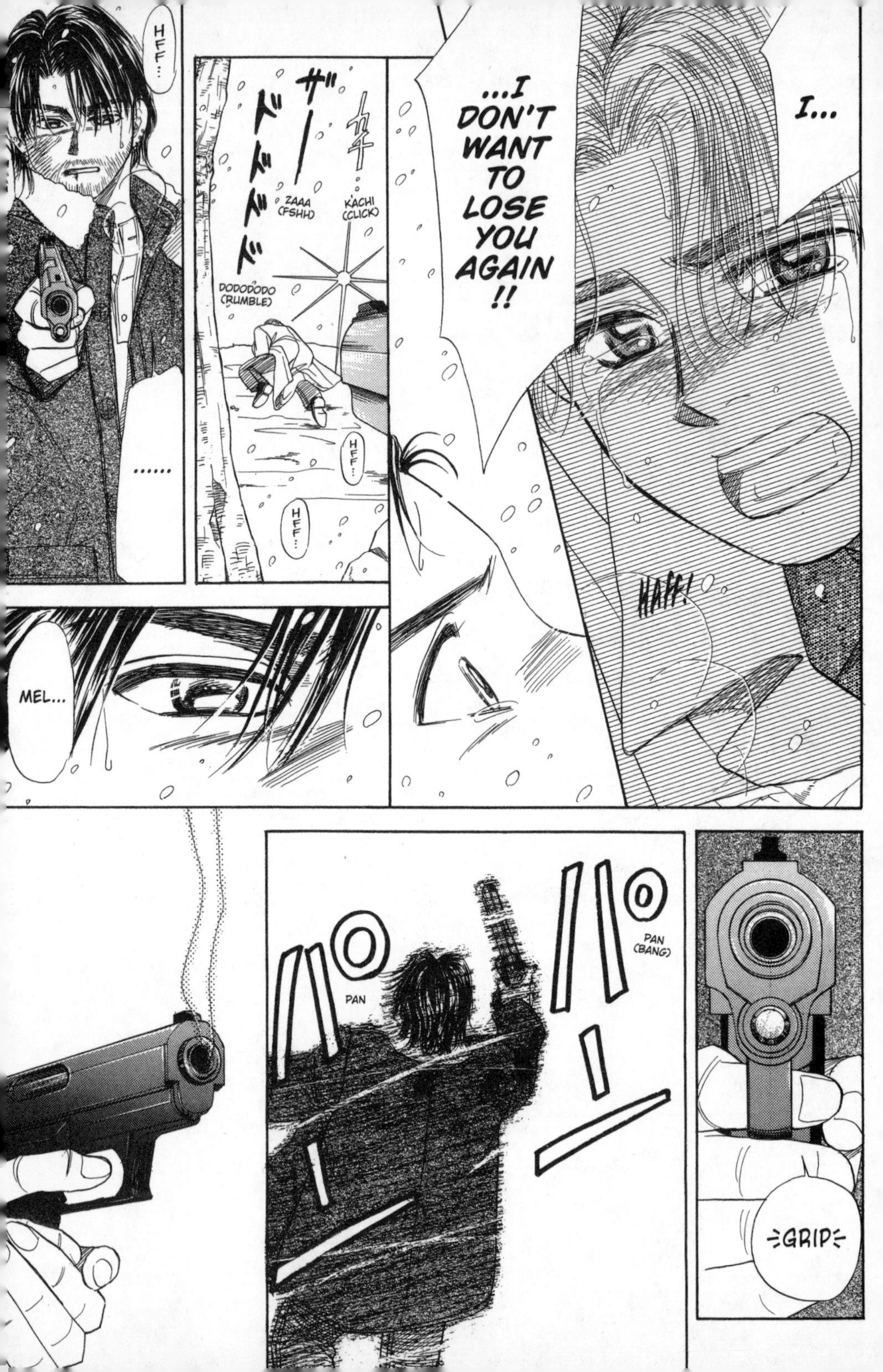
I...
...I DON'T WANT TO LOSE YOU AGAIN!!
HAFF!
カチ
KACHI (CLICK)
ザー
ZAAA (FSHH)
ドドドド
DODODODO (RUMBLE)
HFF...
HFF...
HFF...
......
MEL...
=GRIP=
パン
PAN (BANG)
パン
PAN

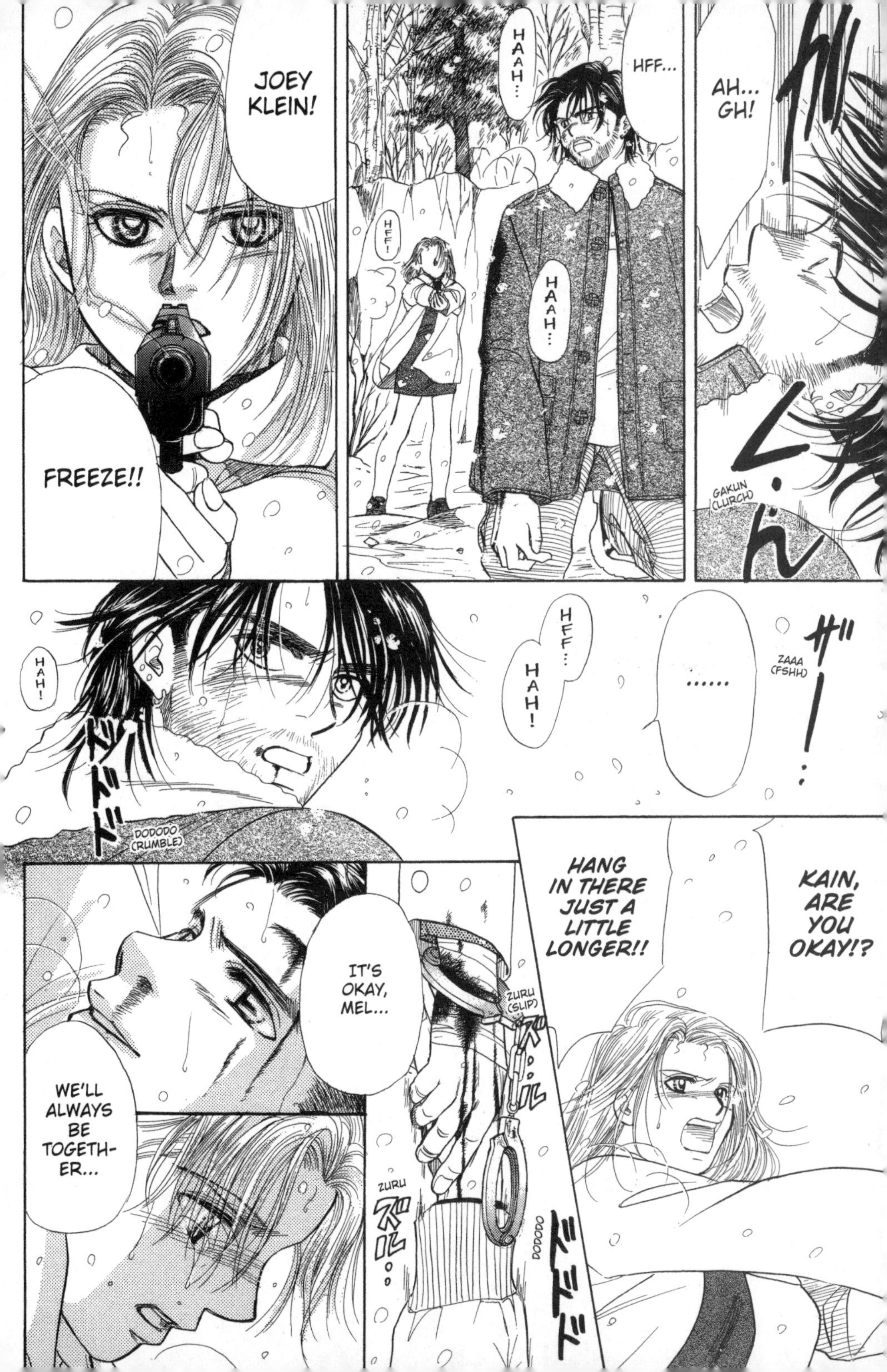
AH... GH!
GAKUN (LURCH)
HFF...
HAAAH...
HFF!
HAAAH...
JOEY KLEIN!
FREEZE!!
ZAAA (FSHH)
......
HFF... HAH!
HAH!
DODODO (RUMBLE)
KAIN, ARE YOU OKAY!?
HANG IN THERE JUST A LITTLE LONGER!!
DODODO
IT'S OKAY, MEL...
ZURU (SLIP)
WE'LL ALWAYS BE TOGETHER...
ZURU

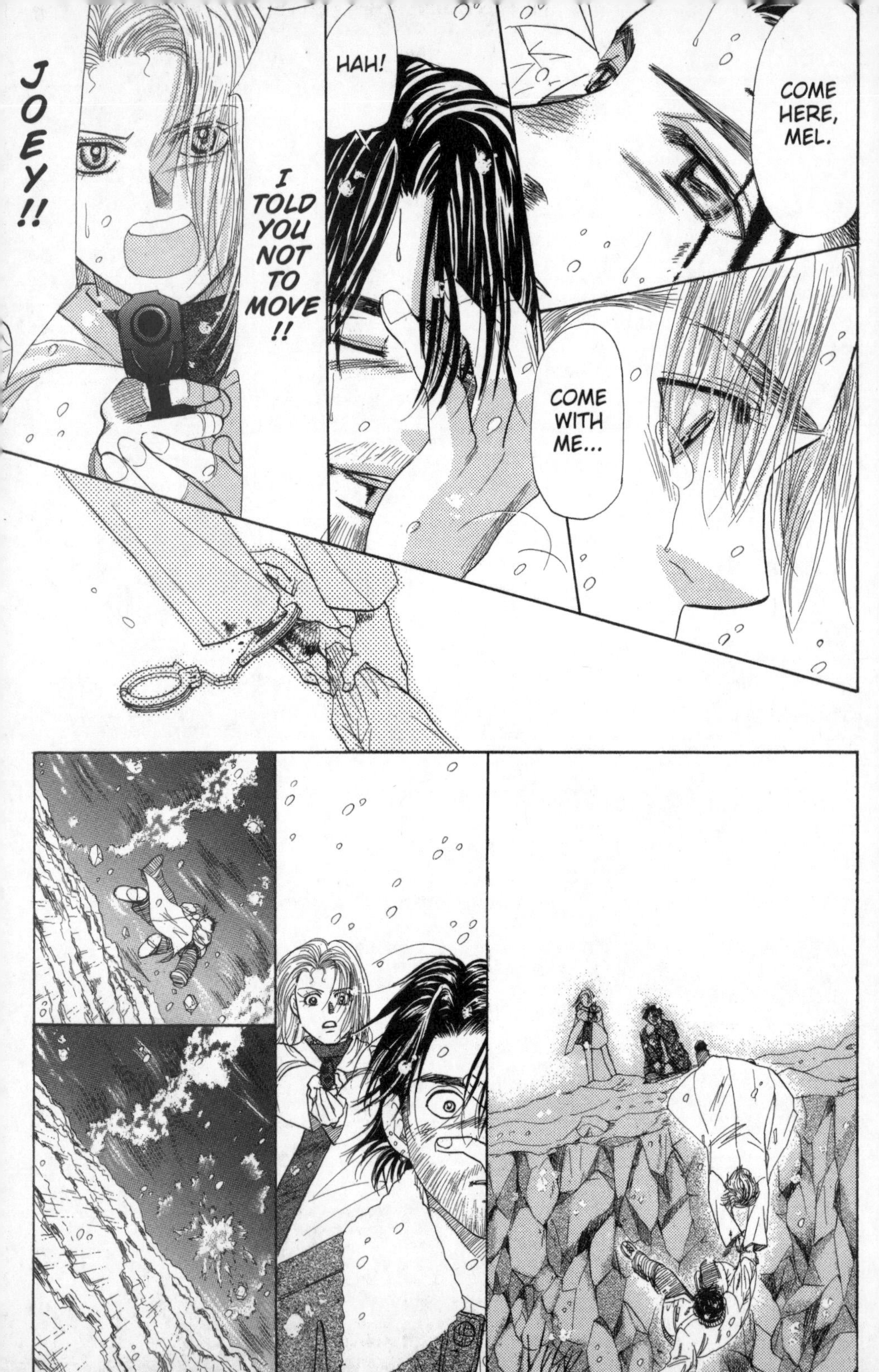
COME HERE, MEL.
COME WITH ME...
HAH!
I TOLD YOU NOT TO MOVE!!
JOEY!!

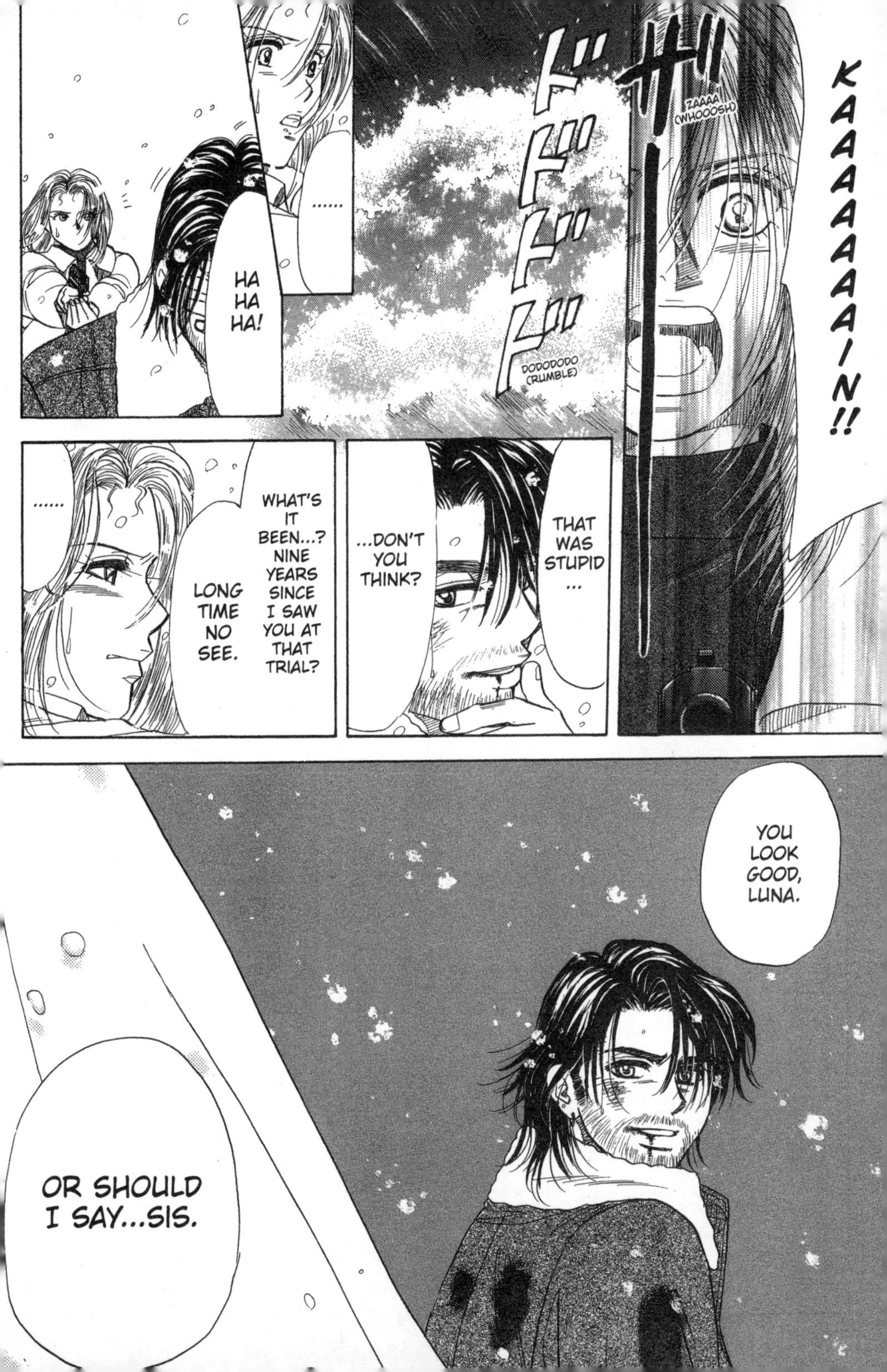
KAAAAAAAIN!!
ZAAAA (WHOOOSH)
DODODODO (RUMBLE)
......
HA HA HA!
THAT WAS STUPID...
...DON'T YOU THINK?
WHAT'S IT BEEN...? NINE YEARS SINCE I SAW YOU AT THAT TRIAL?
......
LONG TIME NO SEE.
YOU LOOK GOOD, LUNA.
OR SHOULD I SAY...SIS.

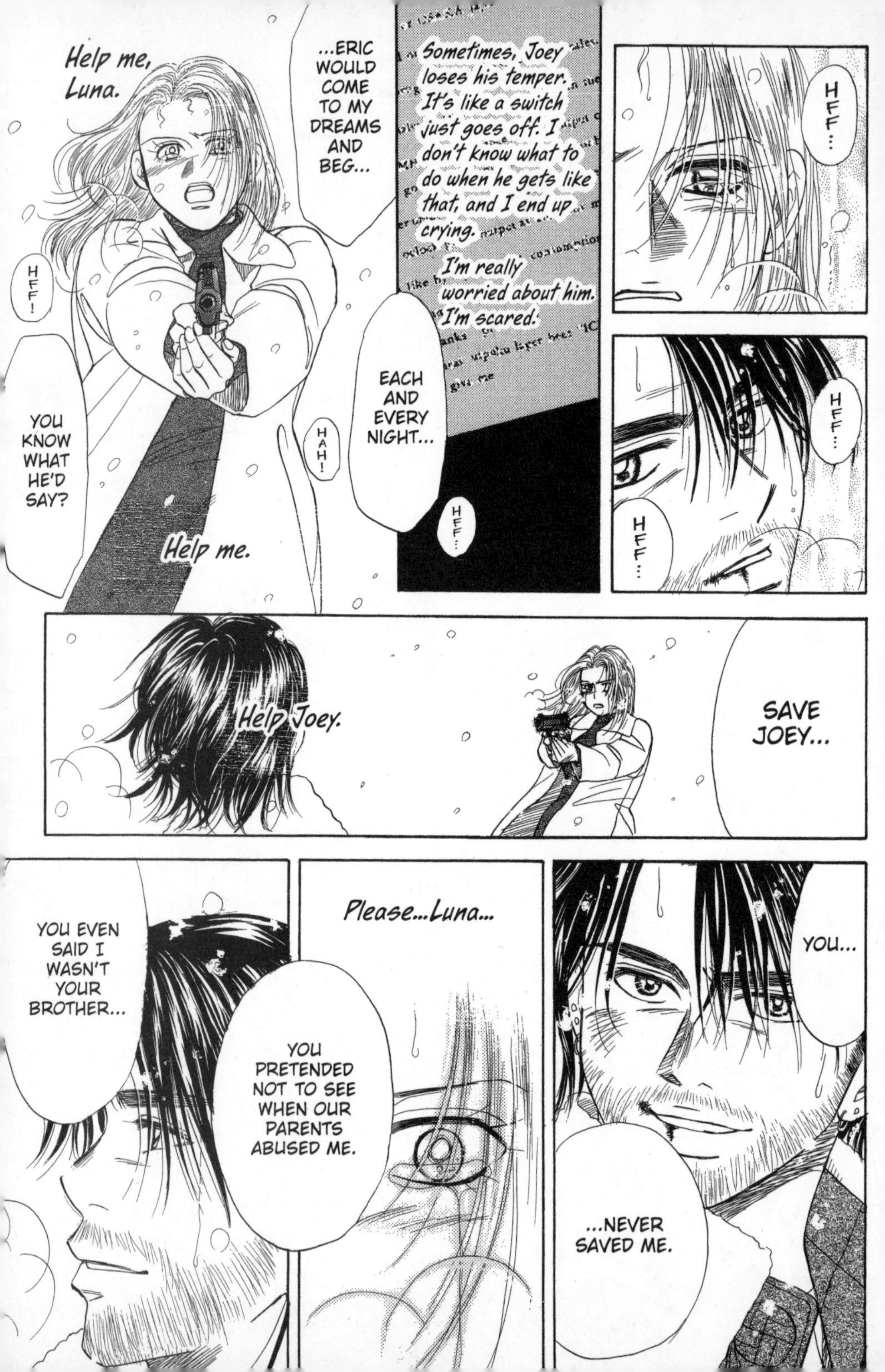
HFF...
HFF...
HFF...
Sometimes, Joey loses his temper. It's like a switch just goes off. I don't know what to do when he gets like that, and I end up crying.
I'm really worried about him. I'm scared.
EACH AND EVERY NIGHT...
HAH!
HFF...
...ERIC WOULD COME TO MY DREAMS AND BEG...
Help me, Luna.
HFF!
YOU KNOW WHAT HE'D SAY?
Help me.
SAVE JOEY...
Help Joey.
YOU...
...NEVER SAVED ME.
Please...Luna...
YOU PRETENDED NOT TO SEE WHEN OUR PARENTS ABUSED ME.
YOU EVEN SAID I WASN'T YOUR BROTHER...

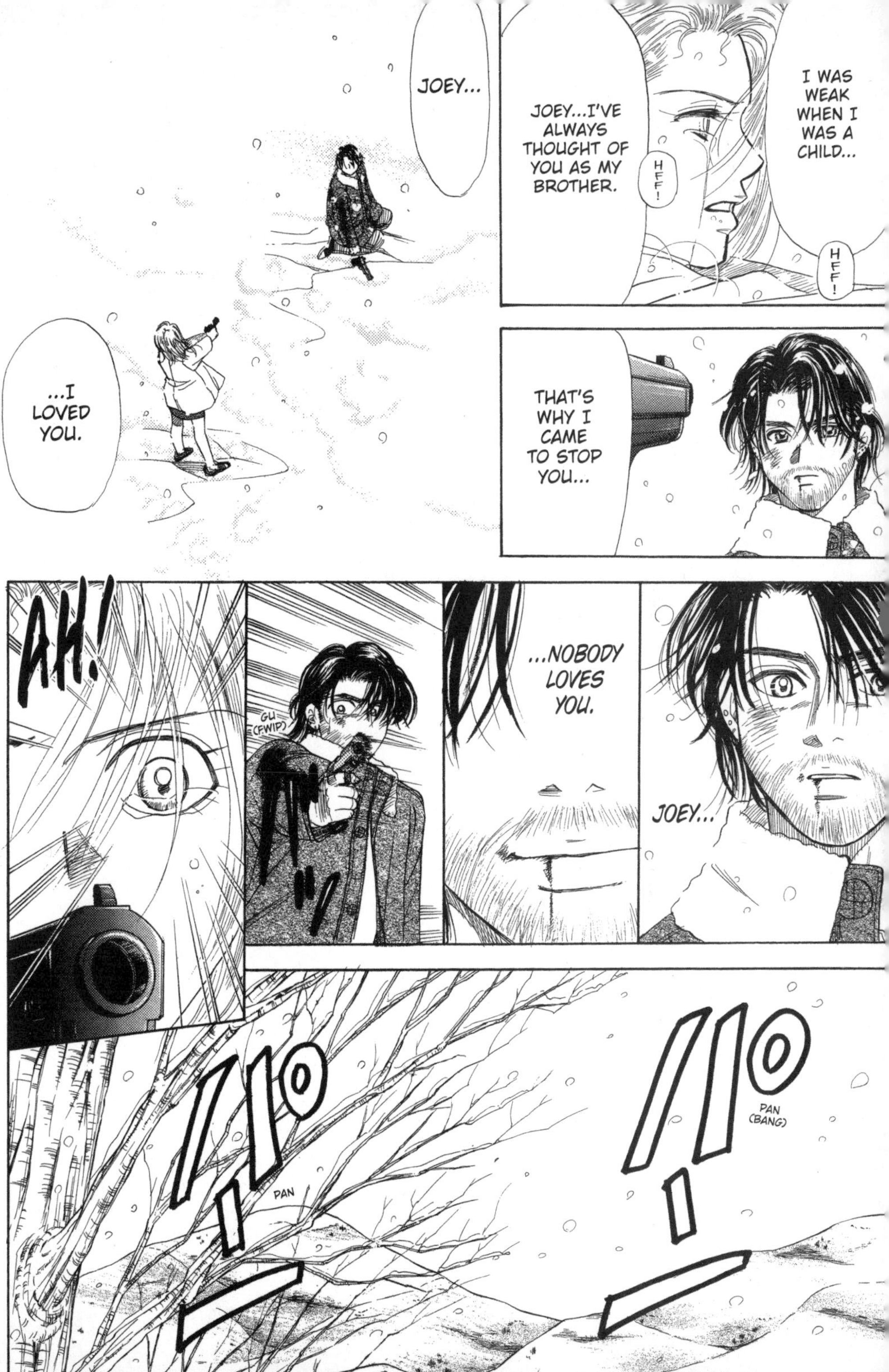

I WAS WEAK WHEN I WAS A CHILD...
HFF!
JOEY...I'VE ALWAYS THOUGHT OF YOU AS MY BROTHER.
HFF!
THAT'S WHY I CAME TO STOP YOU...
JOEY...
...I LOVED YOU.
JOEY...
...NOBODY LOVES YOU.
GU (FWIP)
AH!
PAN (BANG)
PAN

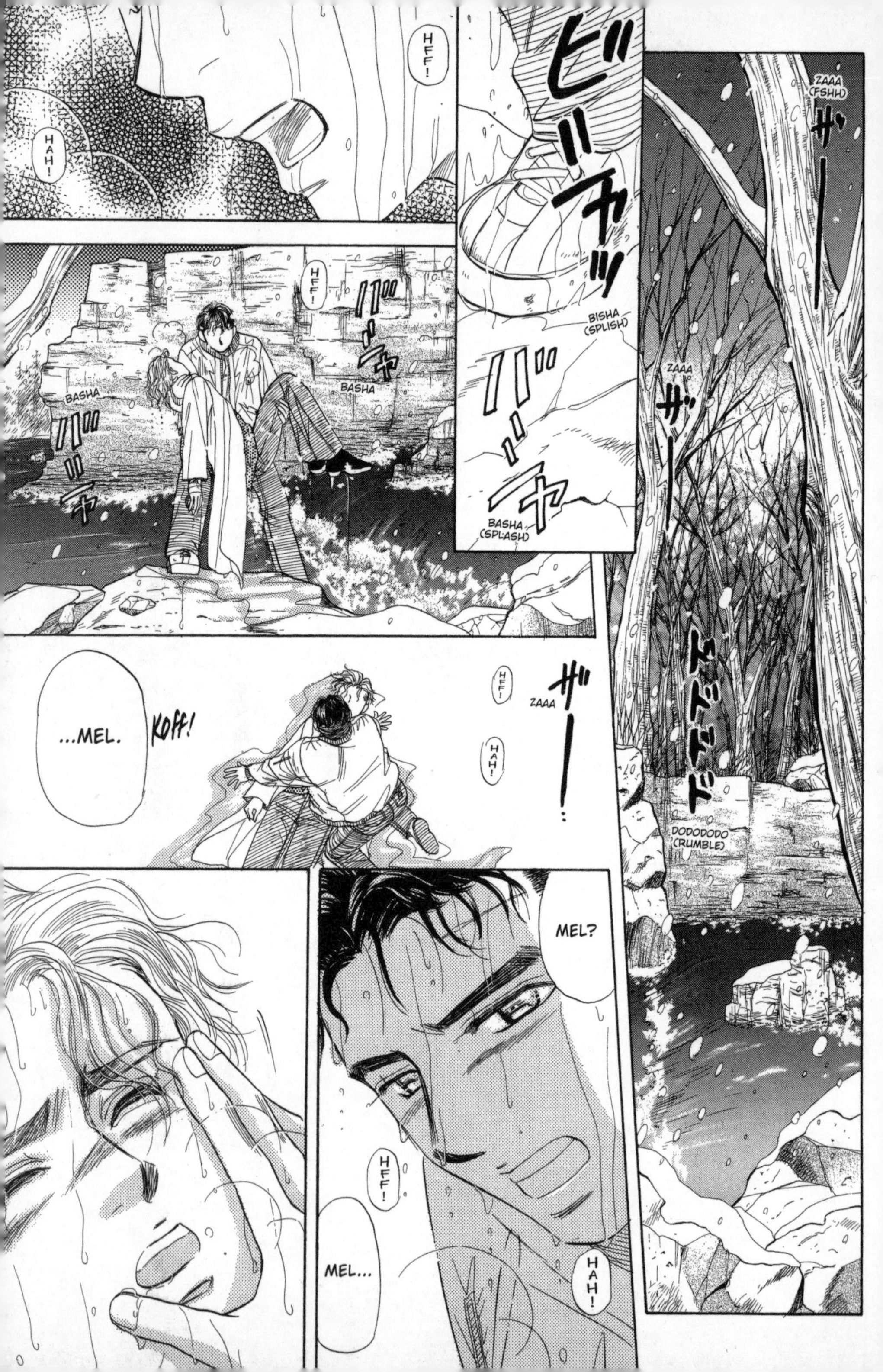
ザー
ZAAA (FSHH)
ザー
ZAAA
ドドドド
DODODODO (RUMBLE)
ビシャッ
BISHA (SPLISH)
バシャ
BASHA (SPLASH)
HFF!
HAH!
HFF!
バシャ
BASHA
バシャ
BASHA
ザー
ZAAA
HFF!
HAH!
KOFF!
...MEL.
MEL?
HFF!
HAH!
MEL...

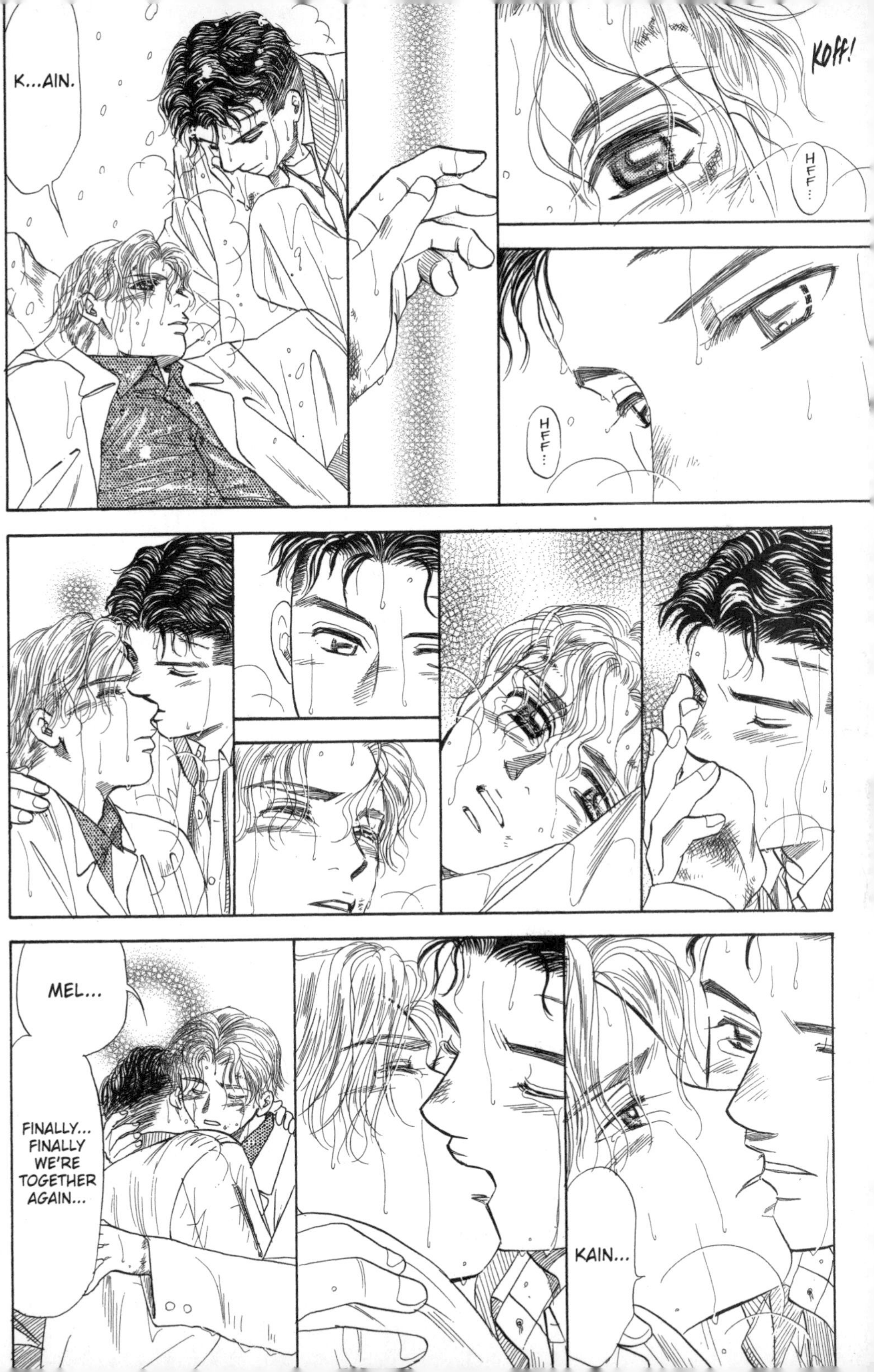
KOFF!
HFF...
HFF...
K...AIN.
KAIN...
MEL...
FINALLY... FINALLY WE'RE TOGETHER AGAIN...

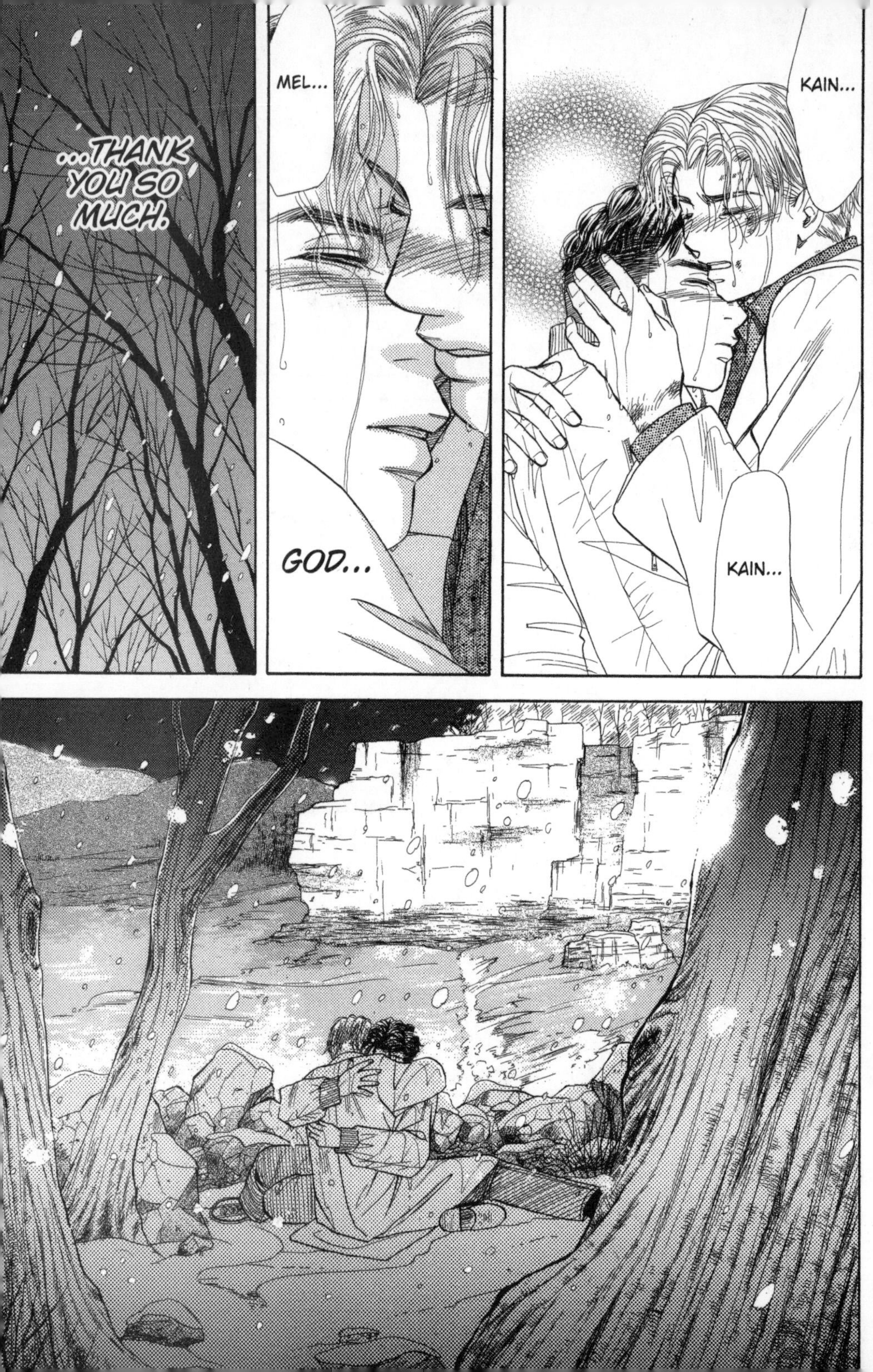
KAIN...
KAIN...
MEL...
GOD...
...THANK YOU SO MUCH.

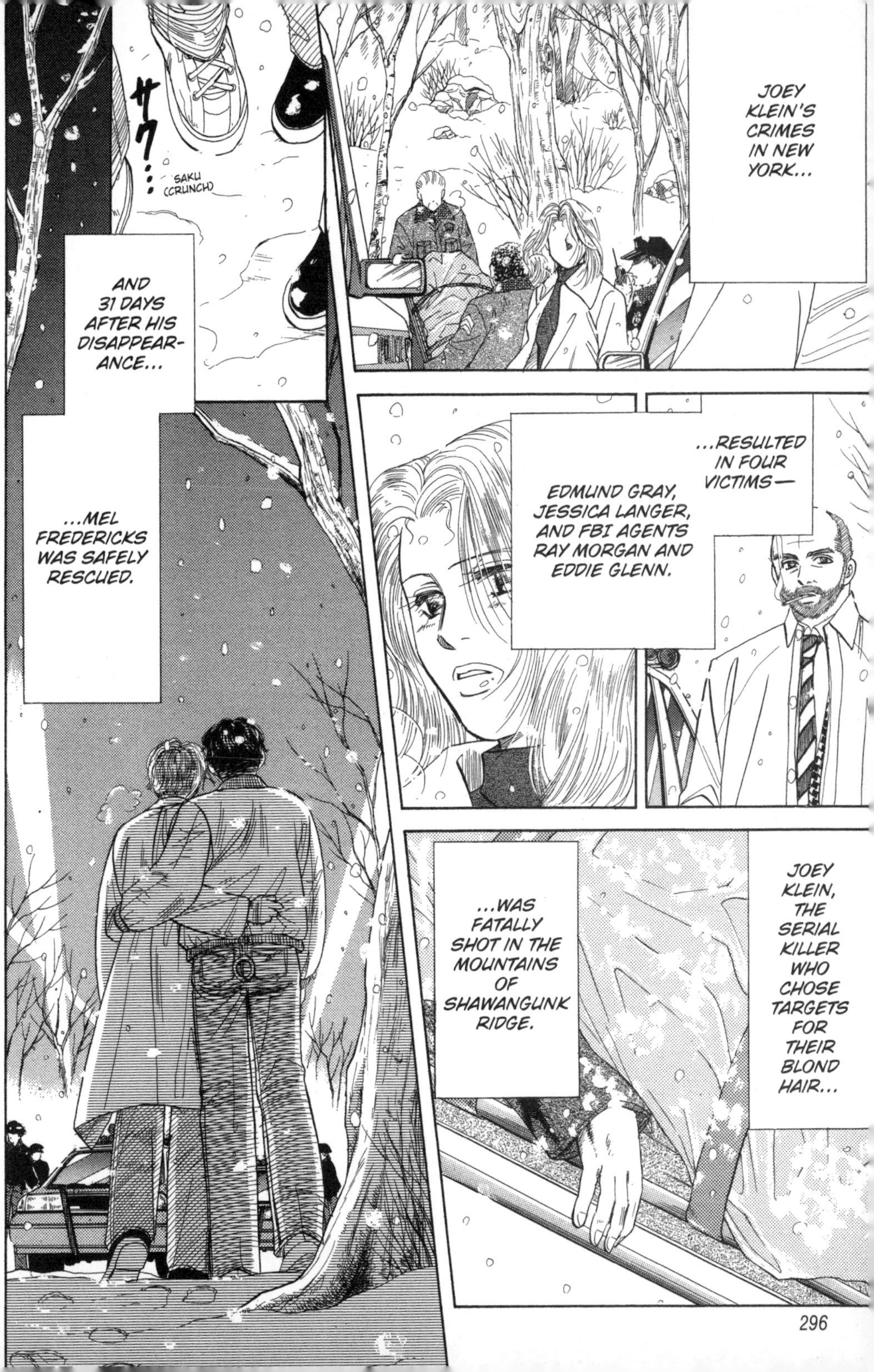
JOEY KLEIN'S CRIMES IN NEW YORK...
...RESULTED IN FOUR VICTIMS—
EDMUND GRAY, JESSICA LANGER, AND FBI AGENTS RAY MORGAN AND EDDIE GLENN.
JOEY KLEIN, THE SERIAL KILLER WHO CHOSE TARGETS FOR THEIR BLOND HAIR...
...WAS FATALLY SHOT IN THE MOUNTAINS OF SHAWANGUNK RIDGE.
サク...
SAKU (CRUNCH)
AND 31 DAYS AFTER HIS DISAPPEAR-ANCE...
...MEL FREDERICKS WAS SAFELY RESCUED.

EPISODE IV

SCENE 8

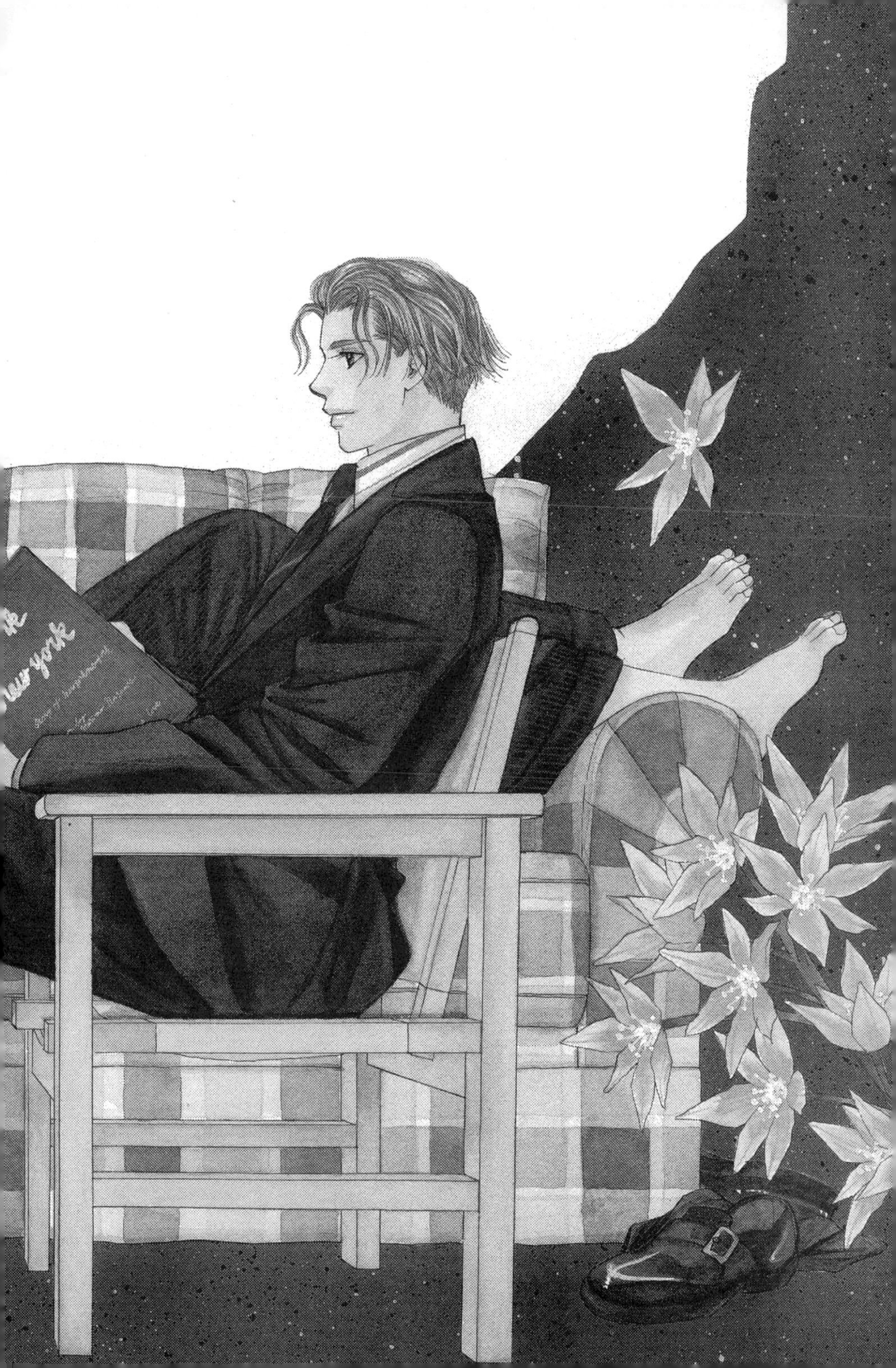

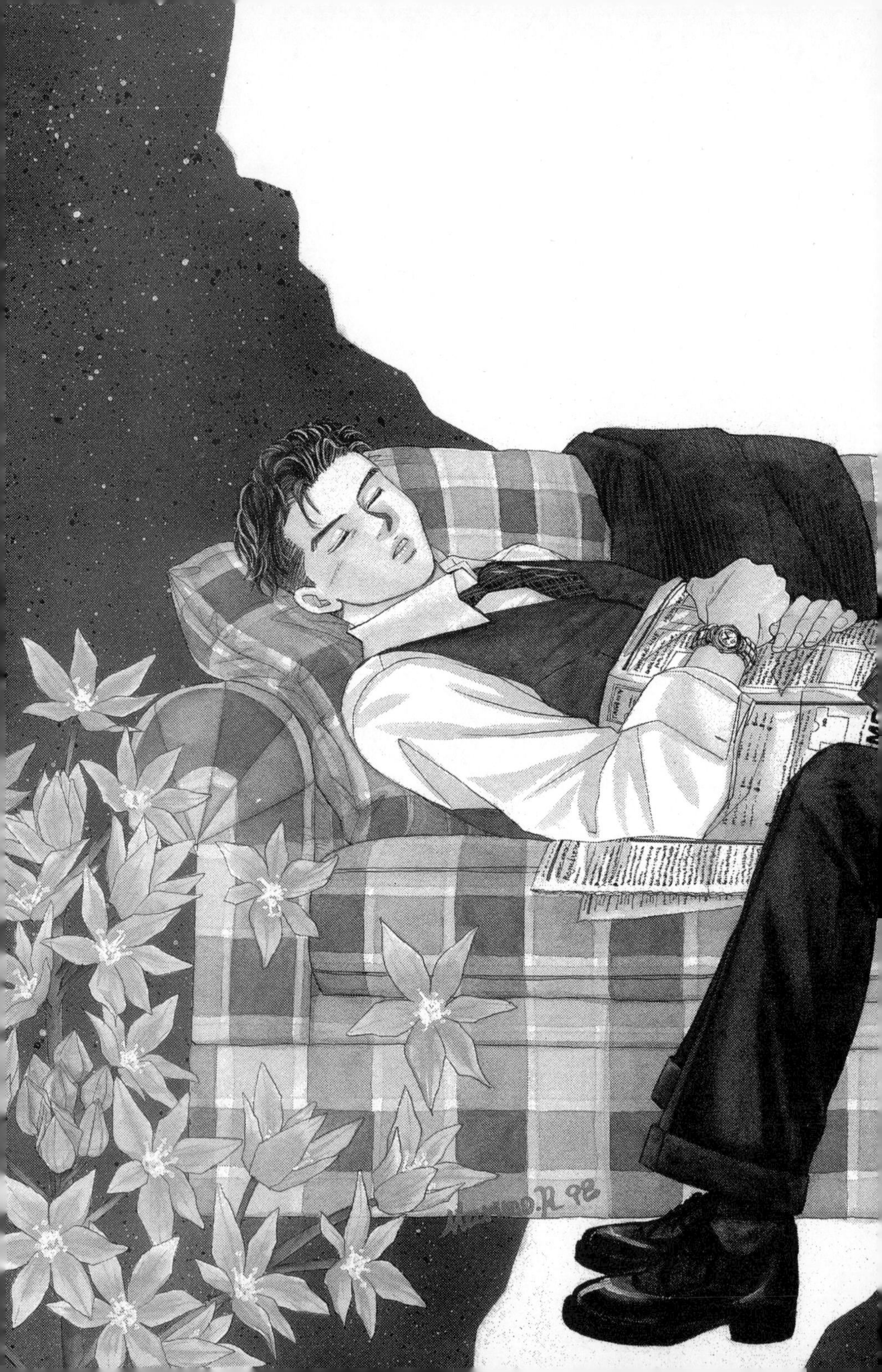

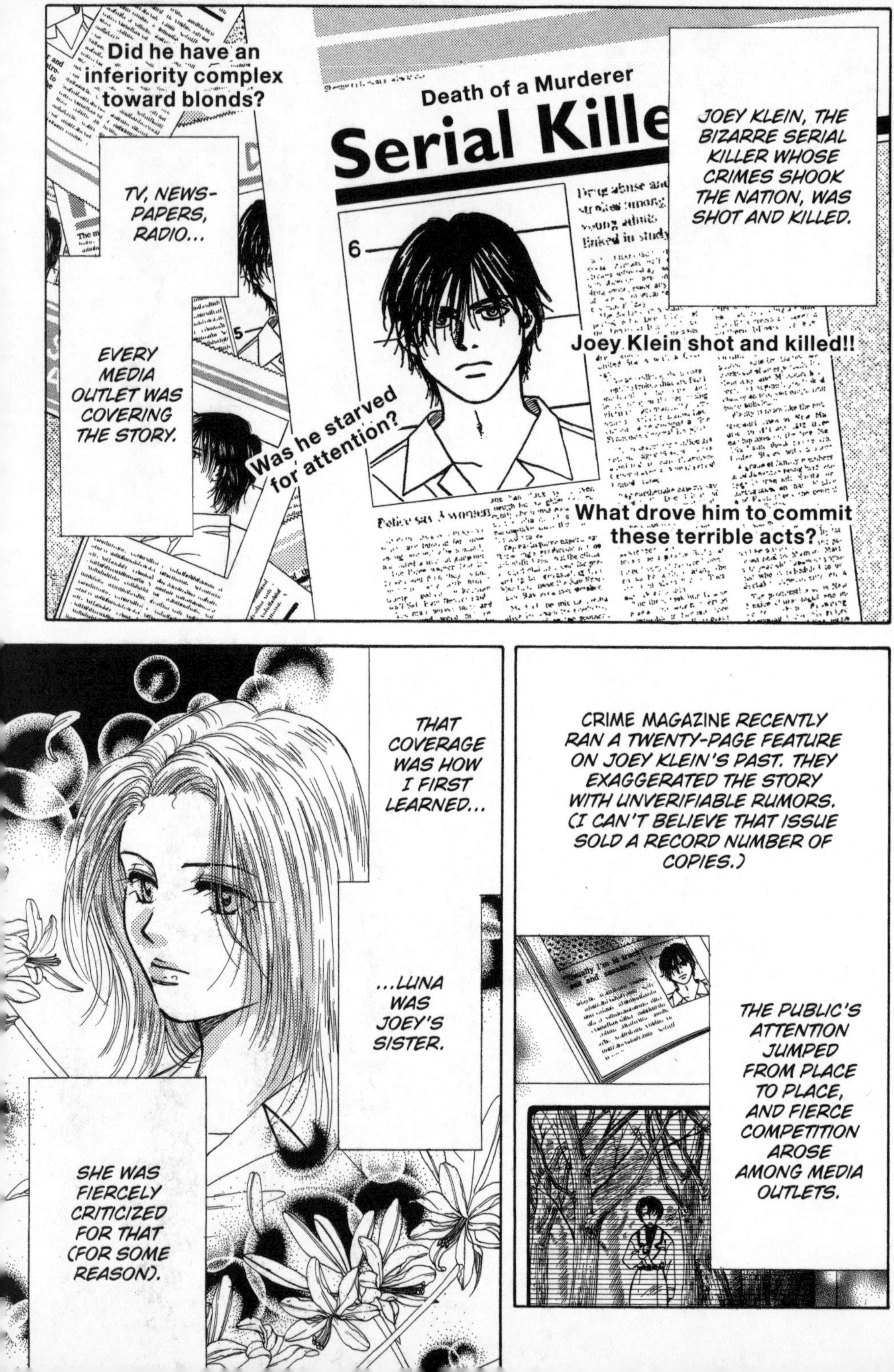
JOEY KLEIN, THE BIZARRE SERIAL KILLER WHOSE CRIMES SHOOK THE NATION, WAS SHOT AND KILLED.
Death of a Murderer
Serial Kille
Joey Klein shot and killed!!
What drove him to commit these terrible acts?
Did he have an inferiority complex toward blonds?
TV, NEWS-PAPERS, RADIO...
Was he starved for attention?
EVERY MEDIA OUTLET WAS COVERING THE STORY.
CRIME MAGAZINE RECENTLY RAN A TWENTY-PAGE FEATURE ON JOEY KLEIN'S PAST. THEY EXAGGERATED THE STORY WITH UNVERIFIABLE RUMORS. (I CAN'T BELIEVE THAT ISSUE SOLD A RECORD NUMBER OF COPIES.)
THE PUBLIC'S ATTENTION JUMPED FROM PLACE TO PLACE, AND FIERCE COMPETITION AROSE AMONG MEDIA OUTLETS.
THAT COVERAGE WAS HOW I FIRST LEARNED...
...LUNA WAS JOEY'S SISTER.
SHE WAS FIERCELY CRITICIZED FOR THAT (FOR SOME REASON).

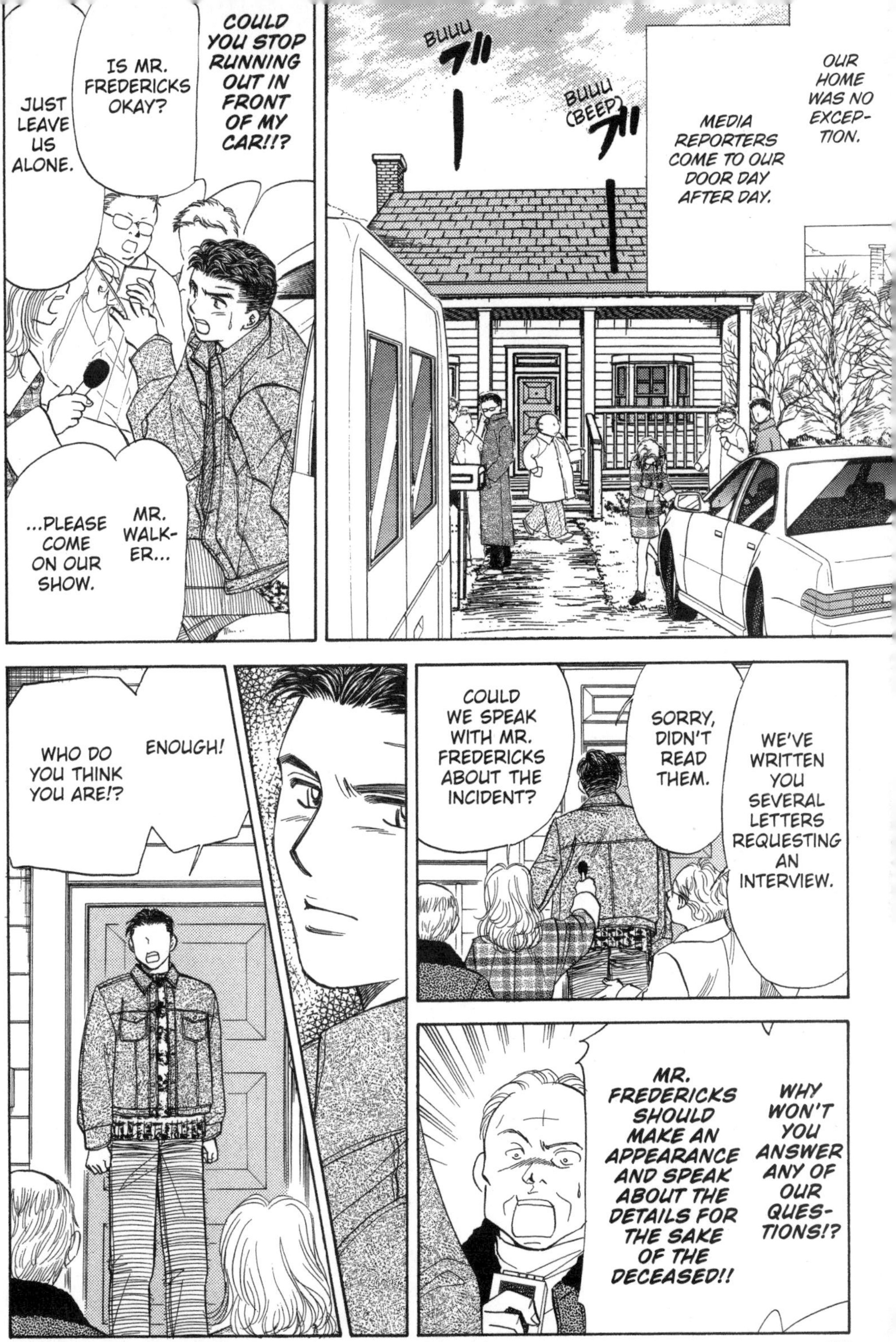

OUR HOME WAS NO EXCEPTION.
MEDIA REPORTERS COME TO OUR DOOR DAY AFTER DAY.
BUUU (BEEP)
BUUU
COULD YOU STOP RUNNING OUT IN FRONT OF MY CAR!!?
IS MR. FREDERICKS OKAY?
JUST LEAVE US ALONE.
MR. WALKER...
...PLEASE COME ON OUR SHOW.
WE'VE WRITTEN YOU SEVERAL LETTERS REQUESTING AN INTERVIEW.
SORRY, DIDN'T READ THEM.
COULD WE SPEAK WITH MR. FREDERICKS ABOUT THE INCIDENT?
WHY WON'T YOU ANSWER ANY OF OUR QUESTIONS!?
MR. FREDERICKS SHOULD MAKE AN APPEARANCE AND SPEAK ABOUT THE DETAILS FOR THE SAKE OF THE DECEASED!!
ENOUGH!
WHO DO YOU THINK YOU ARE!?

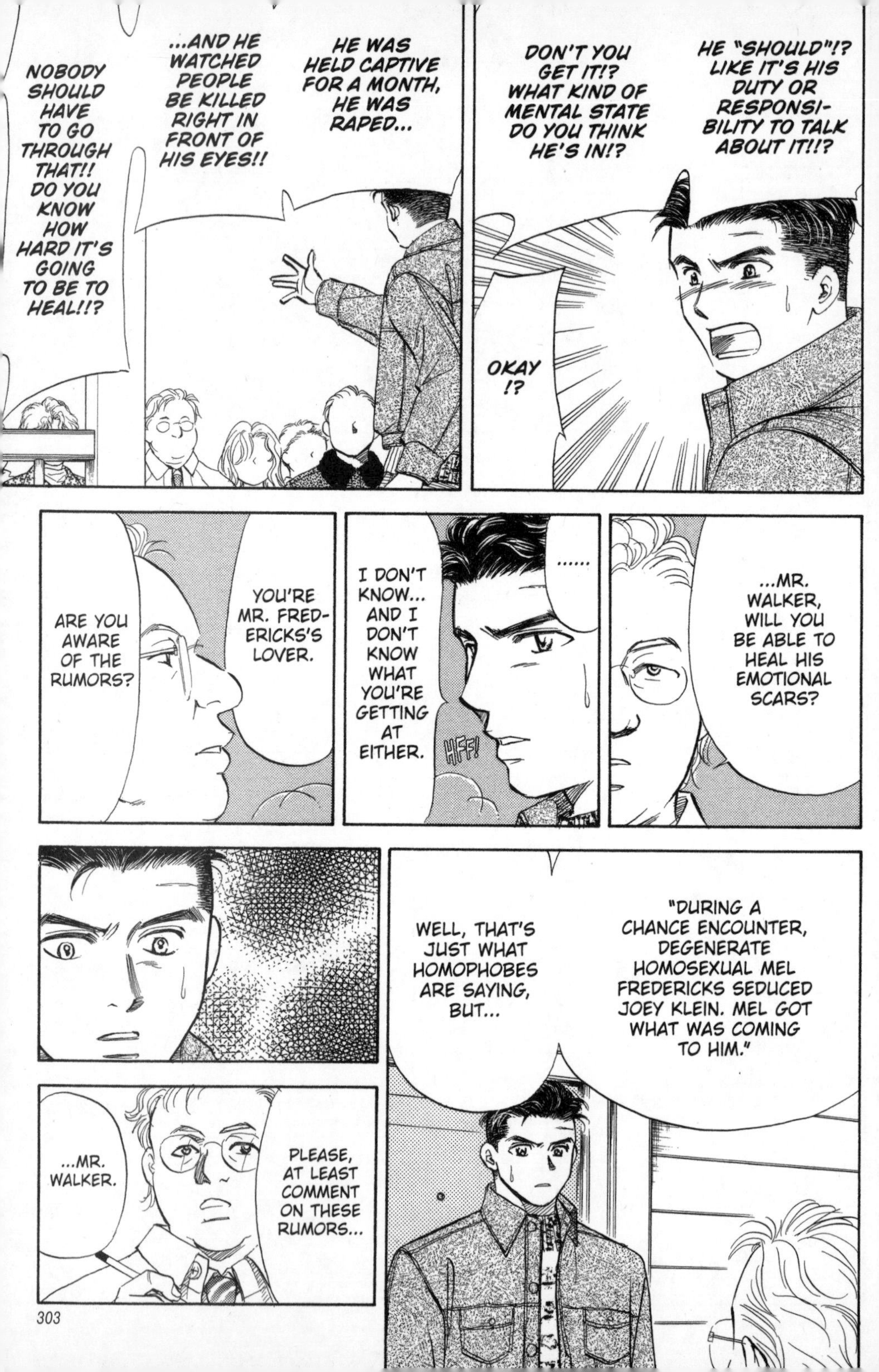

HE "SHOULD"!? LIKE IT'S HIS DUTY OR RESPONSI-BILITY TO TALK ABOUT IT!!?
DON'T YOU GET IT!? WHAT KIND OF MENTAL STATE DO YOU THINK HE'S IN!?
OKAY!?
HE WAS HELD CAPTIVE FOR A MONTH, HE WAS RAPED...
...AND HE WATCHED PEOPLE BE KILLED RIGHT IN FRONT OF HIS EYES!!
NOBODY SHOULD HAVE TO GO THROUGH THAT!! DO YOU KNOW HOW HARD IT'S GOING TO BE TO HEAL!!?
...MR. WALKER, WILL YOU BE ABLE TO HEAL HIS EMOTIONAL SCARS?
......
I DON'T KNOW... AND I DON'T KNOW WHAT YOU'RE GETTING AT EITHER.
HFF!
YOU'RE MR. FRED-ERICKS'S LOVER.
ARE YOU AWARE OF THE RUMORS?
"DURING A CHANCE ENCOUNTER, DEGENERATE HOMOSEXUAL MEL FREDERICKS SEDUCED JOEY KLEIN. MEL GOT WHAT WAS COMING TO HIM."
WELL, THAT'S JUST WHAT HOMOPHOBES ARE SAYING, BUT...
PLEASE, AT LEAST COMMENT ON THESE RUMORS...
...MR. WALKER.

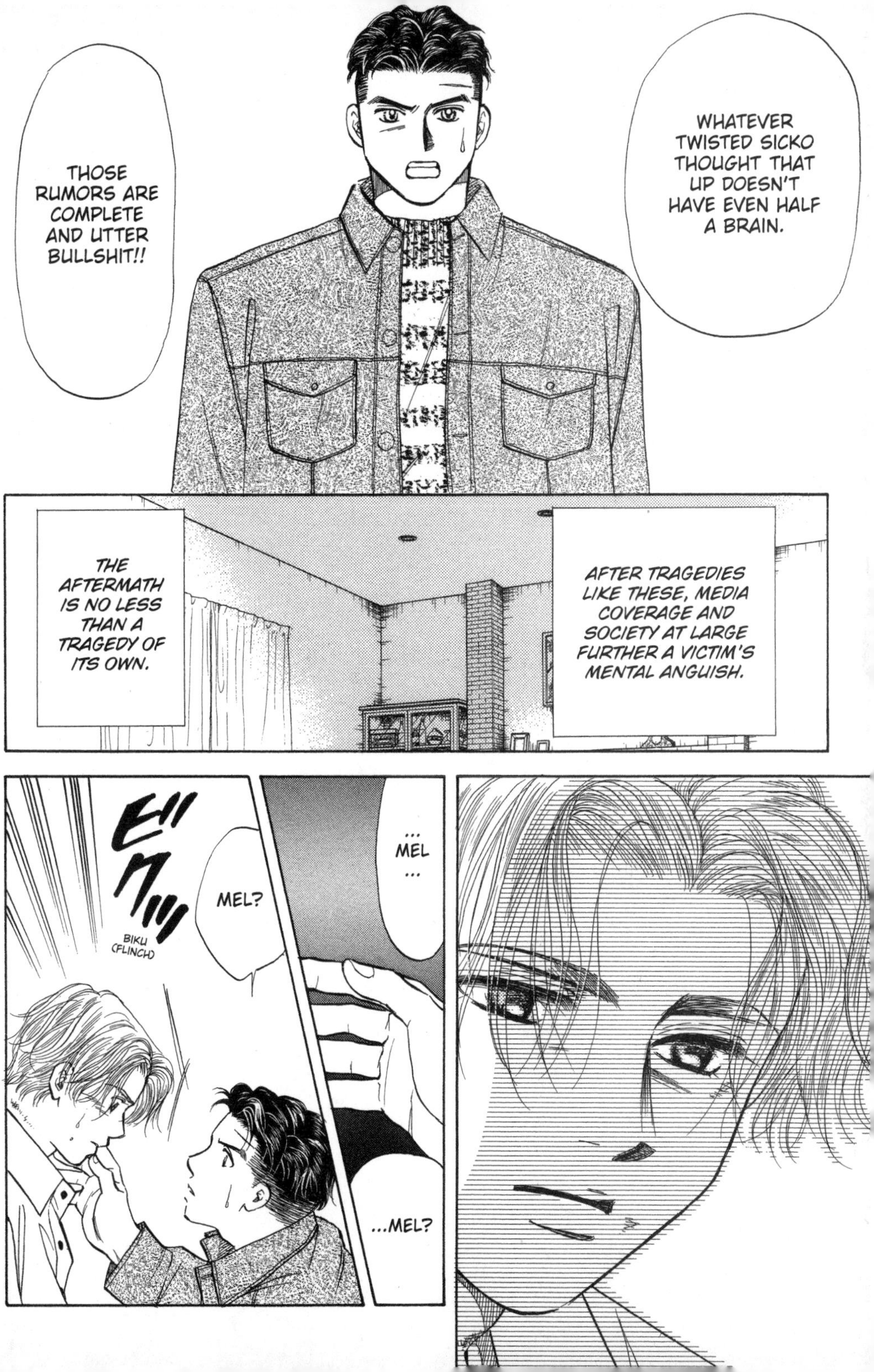
WHATEVER TWISTED SICKO THOUGHT THAT UP DOESN'T HAVE EVEN HALF A BRAIN.
THOSE RUMORS ARE COMPLETE AND UTTER BULLSHIT!!
AFTER TRAGEDIES LIKE THESE, MEDIA COVERAGE AND SOCIETY AT LARGE FURTHER A VICTIM'S MENTAL ANGUISH.
THE AFTERMATH IS NO LESS THAN A TRAGEDY OF ITS OWN.
... MEL ...
...MEL?
MEL?
BIKU (FLINCH)

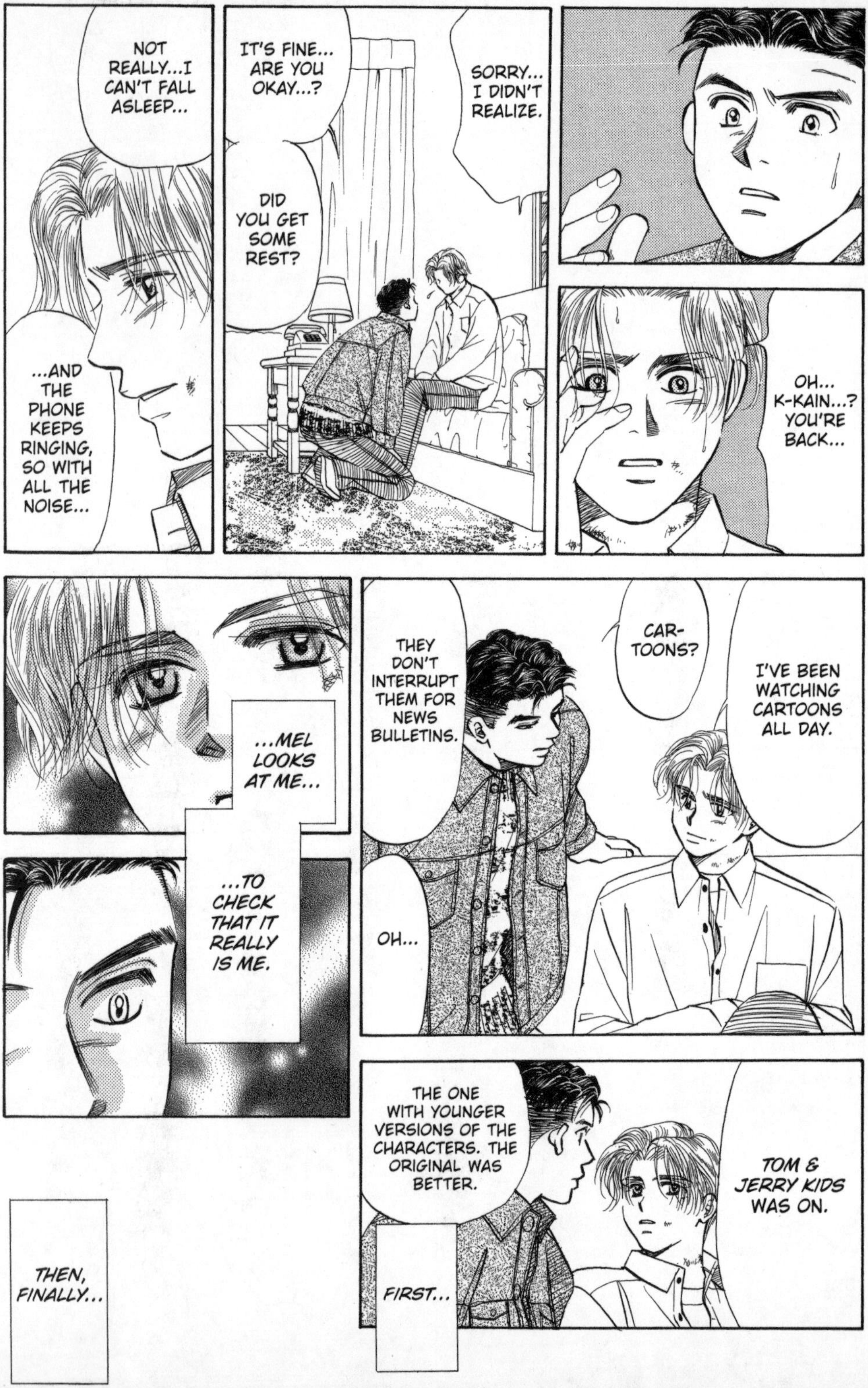
OH... K-KAIN...? YOU'RE BACK...
SORRY... I DIDN'T REALIZE.
IT'S FINE... ARE YOU OKAY...?
DID YOU GET SOME REST?
NOT REALLY...I CAN'T FALL ASLEEP...
...AND THE PHONE KEEPS RINGING, SO WITH ALL THE NOISE...
I'VE BEEN WATCHING CARTOONS ALL DAY.
CAR-TOONS?
THEY DON'T INTERRUPT THEM FOR NEWS BULLETINS.
OH...
...MEL LOOKS AT ME...
...TO CHECK THAT IT REALLY IS ME.
TOM & JERRY KIDS WAS ON.
THE ONE WITH YOUNGER VERSIONS OF THE CHARACTERS. THE ORIGINAL WAS BETTER.
FIRST...
THEN, FINALLY...

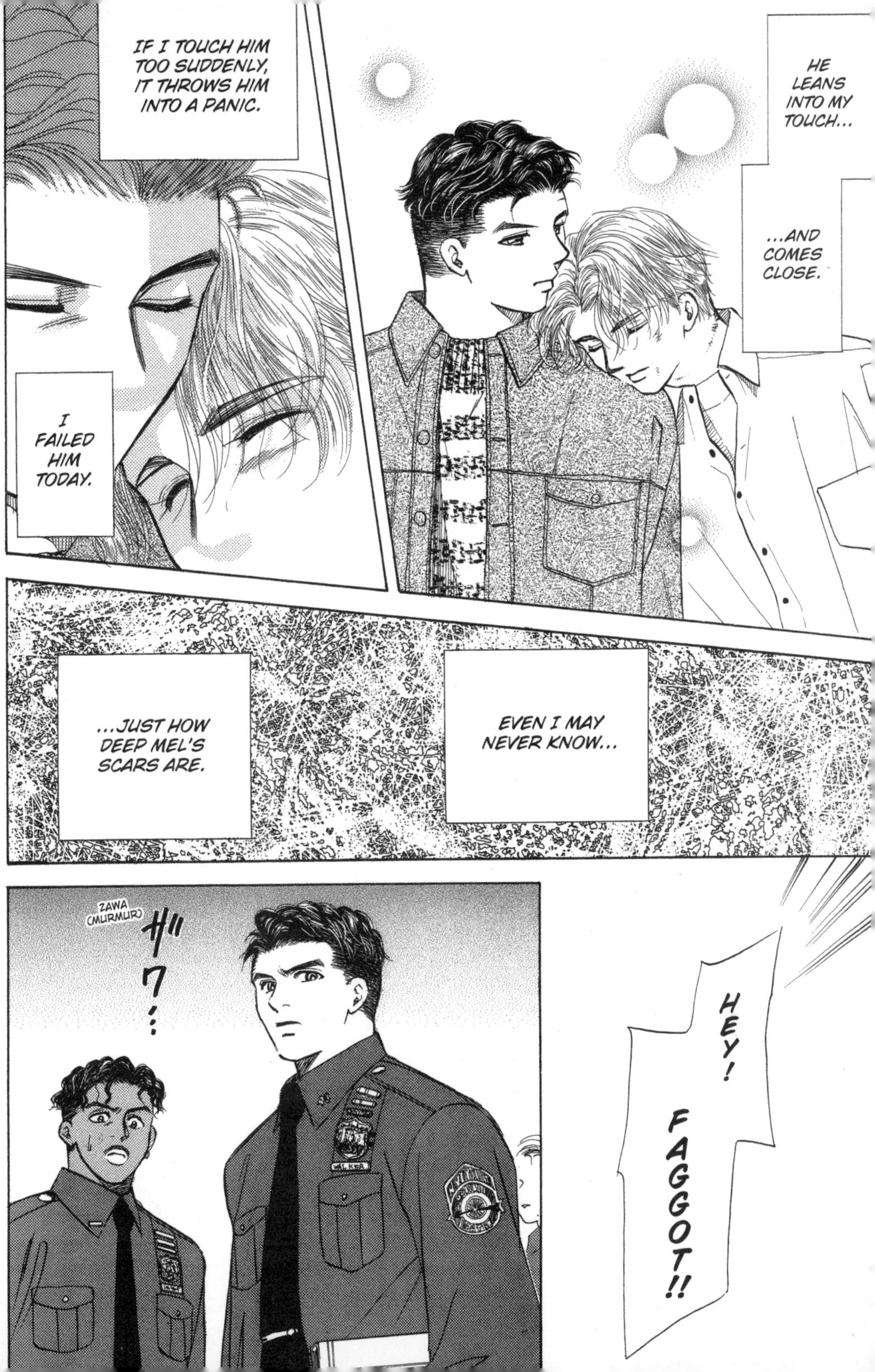
HE LEANS INTO MY TOUCH...
...AND COMES CLOSE.
IF I TOUCH HIM TOO SUDDENLY, IT THROWS HIM INTO A PANIC.
I FAILED HIM TODAY.
EVEN I MAY NEVER KNOW...
...JUST HOW DEEP MEL'S SCARS ARE.
HEY! FAGGOT!!
ザワ
ZAWA (MURMUR)
WALKER

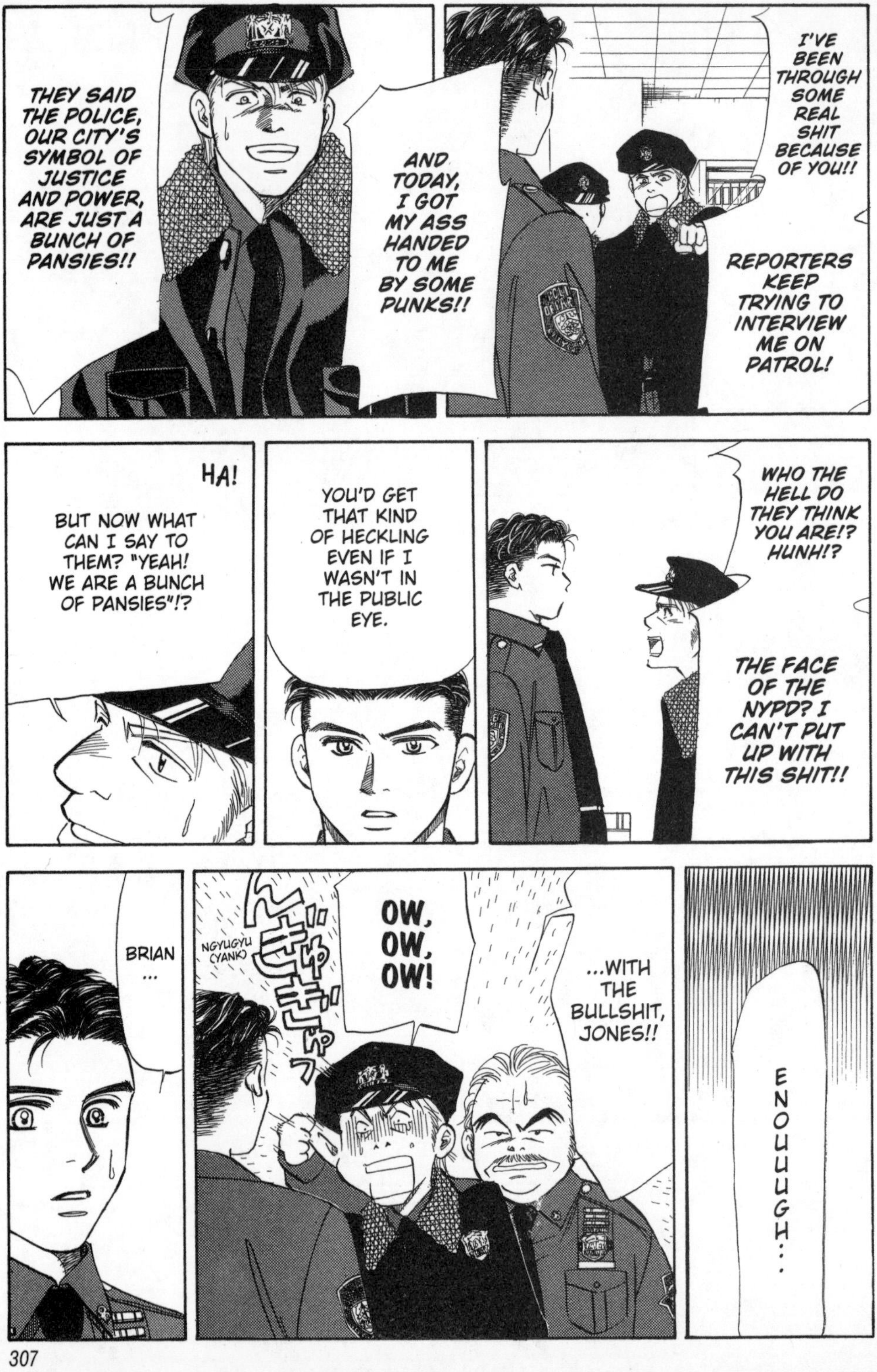
I'VE BEEN THROUGH SOME REAL SHIT BECAUSE OF YOU!!
REPORTERS KEEP TRYING TO INTERVIEW ME ON PATROL!
THEY SAID THE POLICE, OUR CITY'S SYMBOL OF JUSTICE AND POWER, ARE JUST A BUNCH OF PANSIES!!
AND TODAY, I GOT MY ASS HANDED TO ME BY SOME PUNKS!!
WHO THE HELL DO THEY THINK YOU ARE!? HUNH!?
THE FACE OF THE NYPD? I CAN'T PUT UP WITH THIS SHIT!!
YOU'D GET THAT KIND OF HECKLING EVEN IF I WASN'T IN THE PUBLIC EYE.
HA!
BUT NOW WHAT CAN I SAY TO THEM? "YEAH! WE ARE A BUNCH OF PANSIES"!?
ENOUUGH...
...WITH THE BULLSHIT, JONES!!
NGYUGYU (YANK)
OW, OW, OW!
BRIAN ...

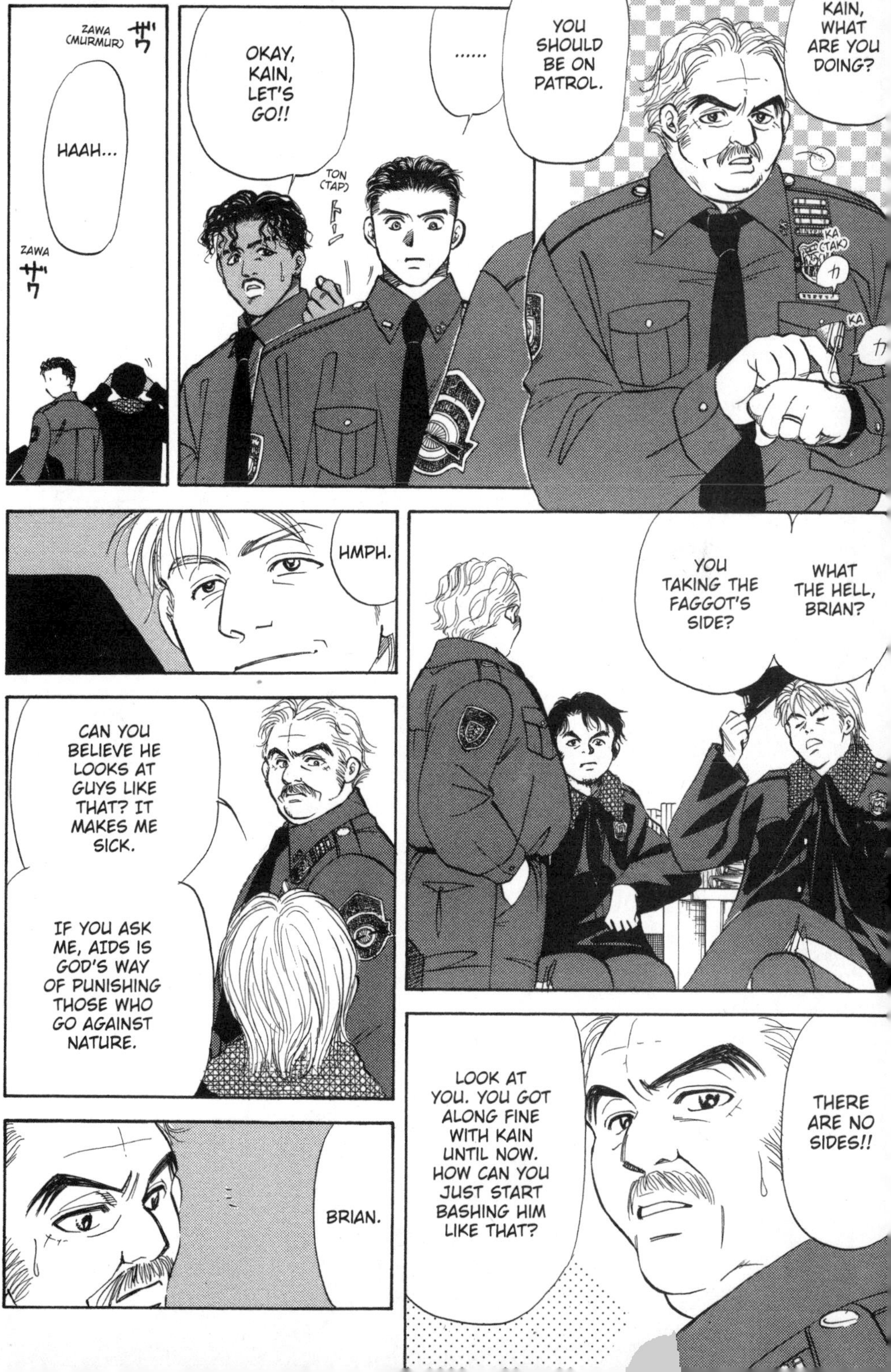
KAIN, WHAT ARE YOU DOING?
YOU SHOULD BE ON PATROL.
KA (TAK)
KA
......
OKAY, KAIN, LET'S GO!!
TON (TAP)
ZAWA (MURMUR)
HAAH...
ZAWA
WHAT THE HELL, BRIAN?
YOU TAKING THE FAGGOT'S SIDE?
HMPH.
CAN YOU BELIEVE HE LOOKS AT GUYS LIKE THAT? IT MAKES ME SICK.
IF YOU ASK ME, AIDS IS GOD'S WAY OF PUNISHING THOSE WHO GO AGAINST NATURE.
THERE ARE NO SIDES!!
LOOK AT YOU. YOU GOT ALONG FINE WITH KAIN UNTIL NOW. HOW CAN YOU JUST START BASHING HIM LIKE THAT?
BRIAN.

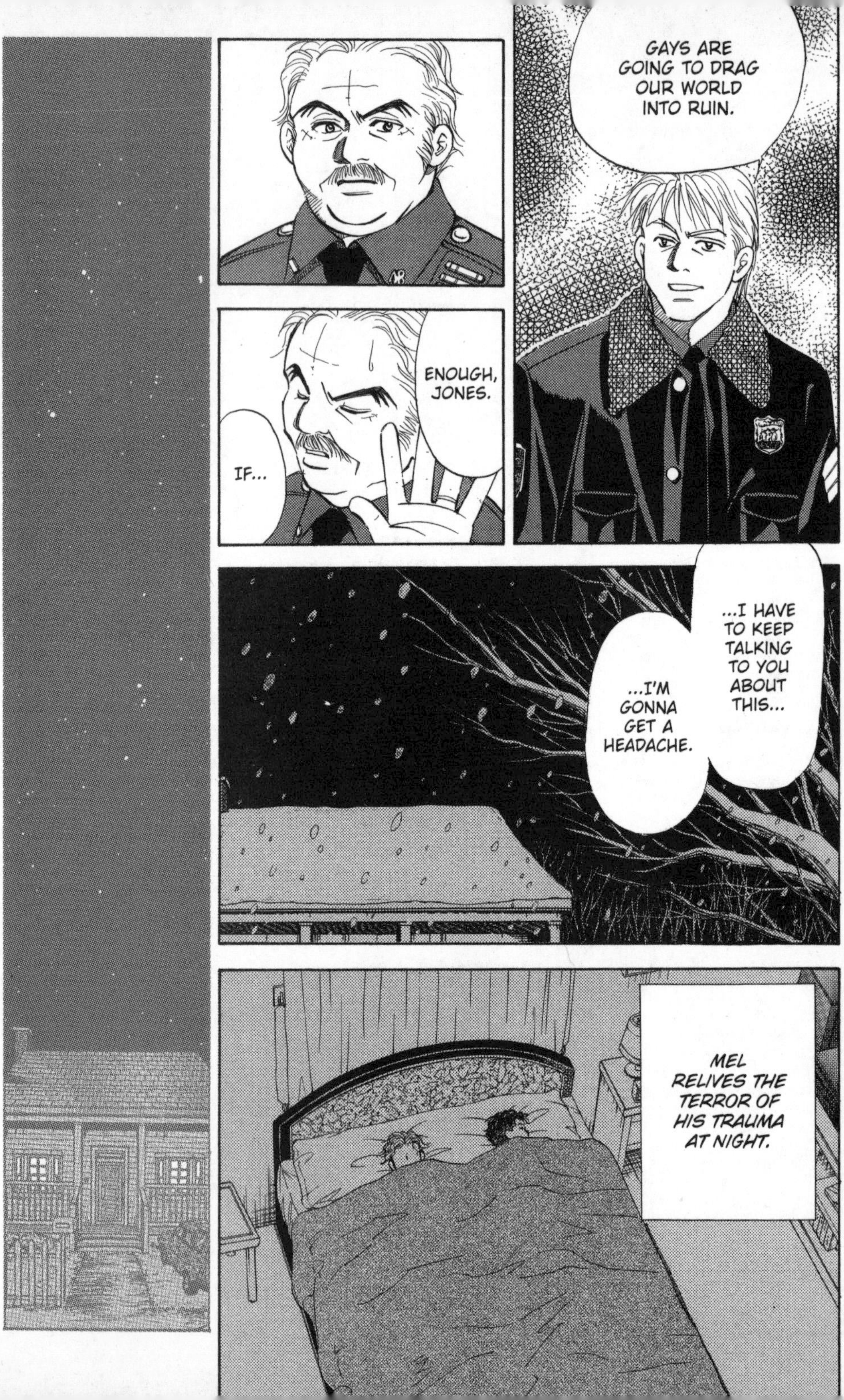
GAYS ARE GOING TO DRAG OUR WORLD INTO RUIN.
ENOUGH, JONES.
IF...
...I HAVE TO KEEP TALKING TO YOU ABOUT THIS...
...I'M GONNA GET A HEADACHE.
MEL RELIVES THE TERROR OF HIS TRAUMA AT NIGHT.

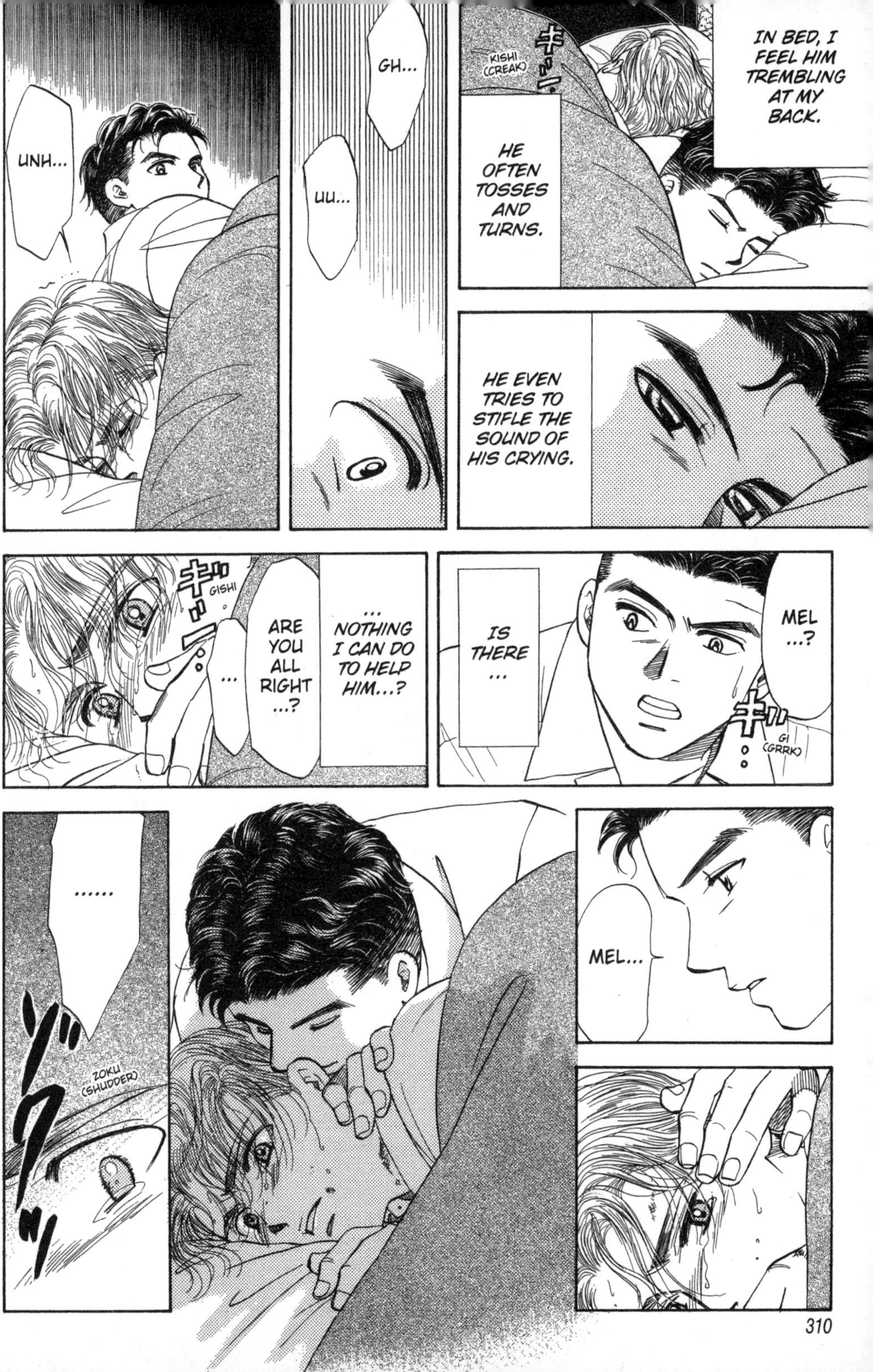
IN BED, I FEEL HIM TREMBLING AT MY BACK.
KISHI (CREAK)
HE OFTEN TOSSES AND TURNS.
HE EVEN TRIES TO STIFLE THE SOUND OF HIS CRYING.
GH...
UU...
UNH...
MEL ...?
GI (GRRK)
IS THERE ...
... NOTHING I CAN DO TO HELP HIM...?
ARE YOU ALL RIGHT ...?
...
GISHI
MEL...
......
ZOKU (SHUDDER)

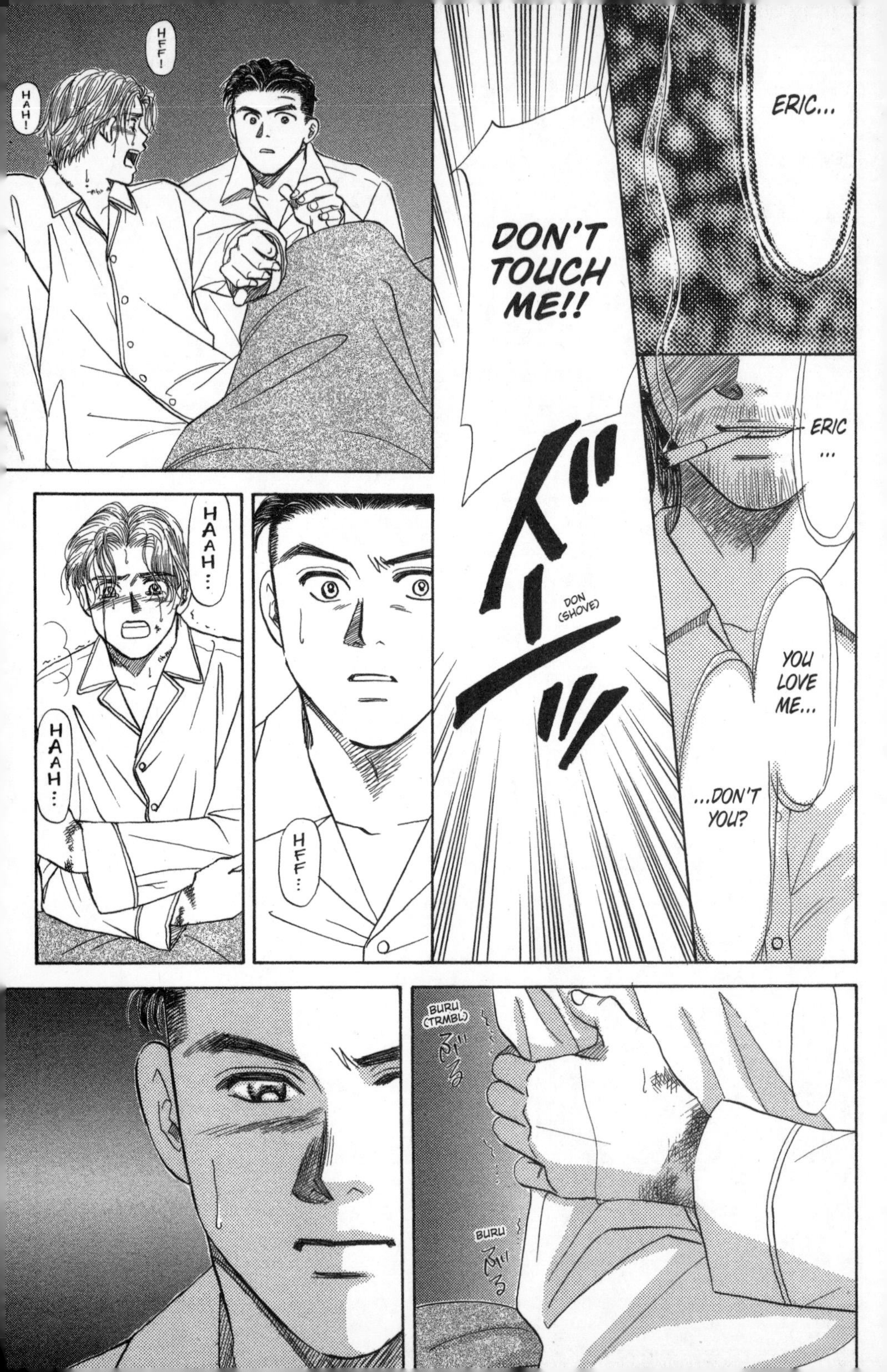
ERIC...
ERIC
...
YOU LOVE ME...
...DON'T YOU?
DON'T TOUCH ME!!
DON (SHOVE)
HFF!
HAH!
HFF...
HAAAH...
HAAAH...
BURU (TRMBL)
ぶる
BURU
ぶる

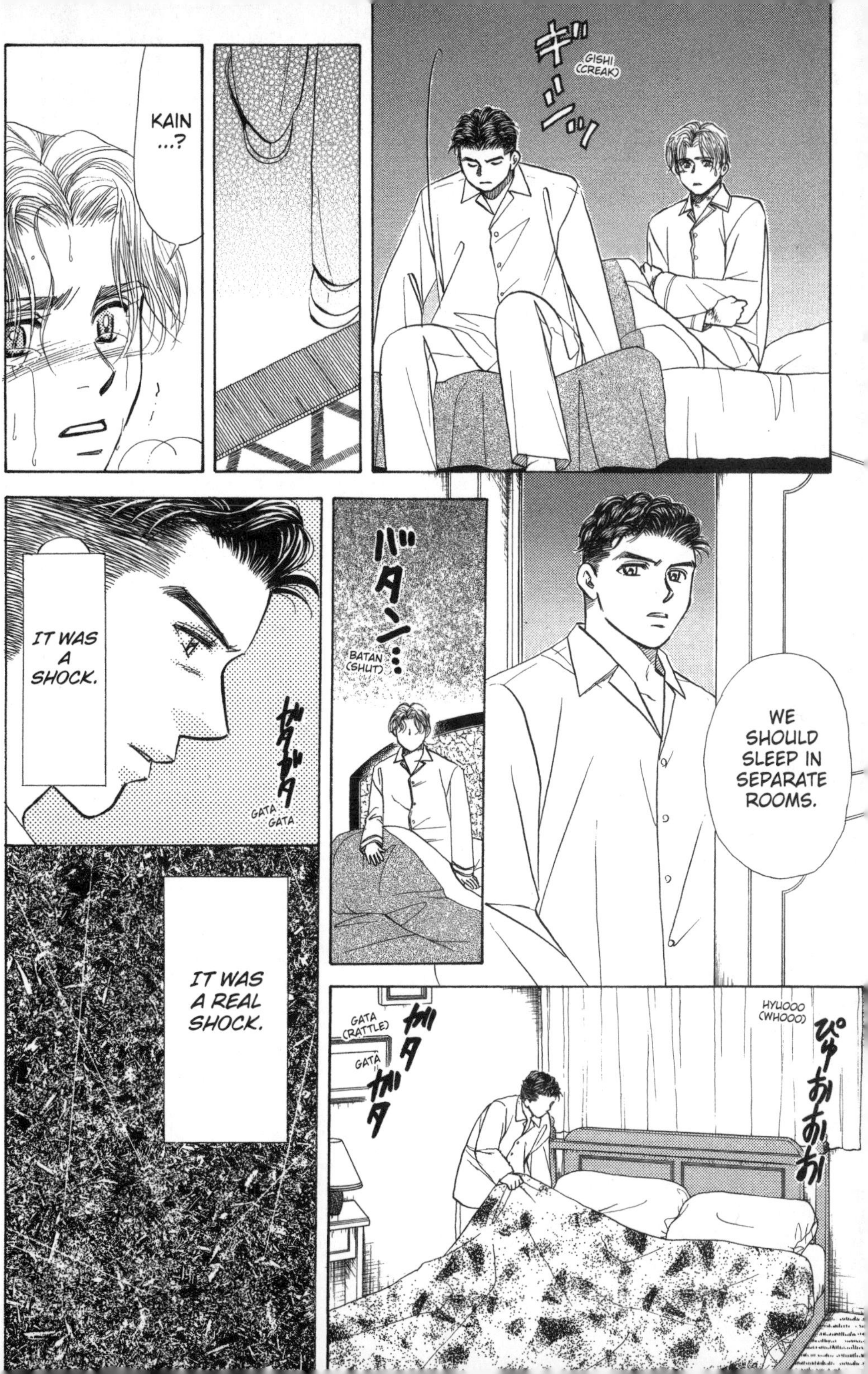
GISHI (CREAK)
KAIN ...?
WE SHOULD SLEEP IN SEPARATE ROOMS.
BATAN (SHUT)
IT WAS A SHOCK.
GATA GATA
HYUOOO (WHOOO)
GATA (RATTLE)
GATA
IT WAS A REAL SHOCK.

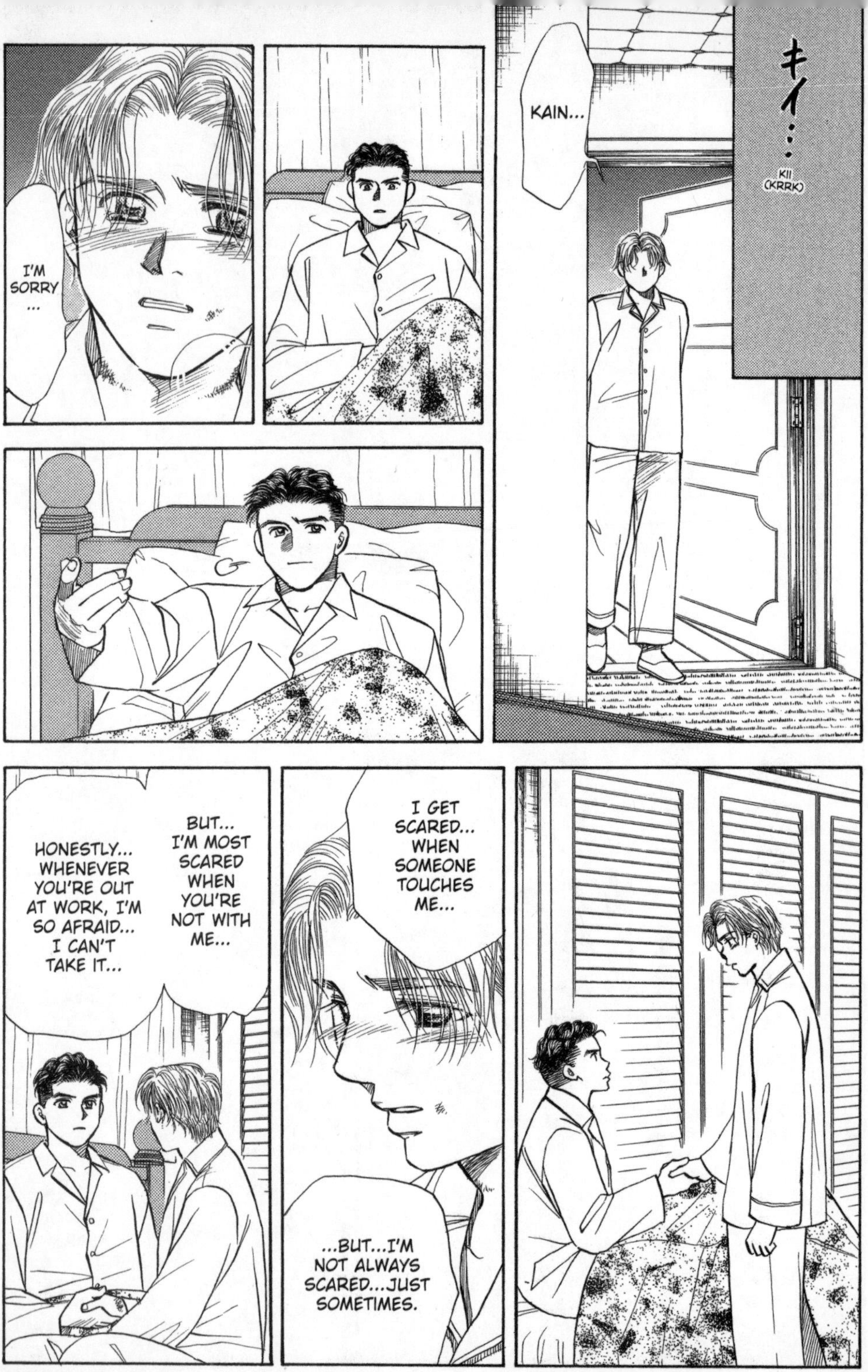
キイ・・
KII (KRRK)
KAIN...
I'M SORRY ...
BUT... I'M MOST SCARED WHEN YOU'RE NOT WITH ME...
HONESTLY... WHENEVER YOU'RE OUT AT WORK, I'M SO AFRAID... I CAN'T TAKE IT...
I GET SCARED... WHEN SOMEONE TOUCHES ME...
...BUT...I'M NOT ALWAYS SCARED...JUST SOMETIMES.

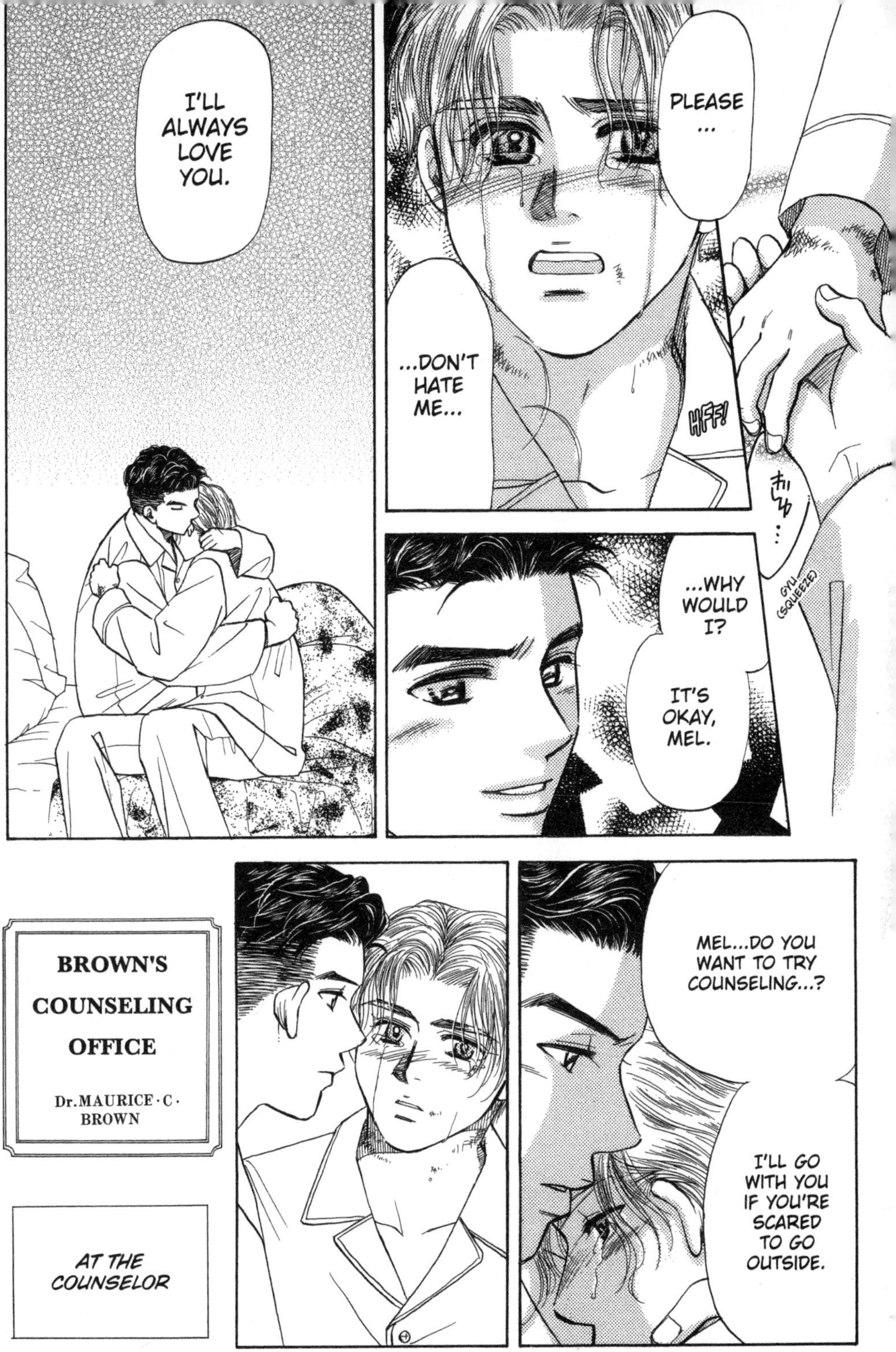
PLEASE ...
...DON'T HATE ME...
HFF!
GYU (SQUEEZE)
...WHY WOULD I?
IT'S OKAY, MEL.
I'LL ALWAYS LOVE YOU.
MEL...DO YOU WANT TO TRY COUNSELING...?
I'LL GO WITH YOU IF YOU'RE SCARED TO GO OUTSIDE.
BROWN'S COUNSELING OFFICE
Dr.MAURICE·C·BROWN
AT THE COUNSELOR

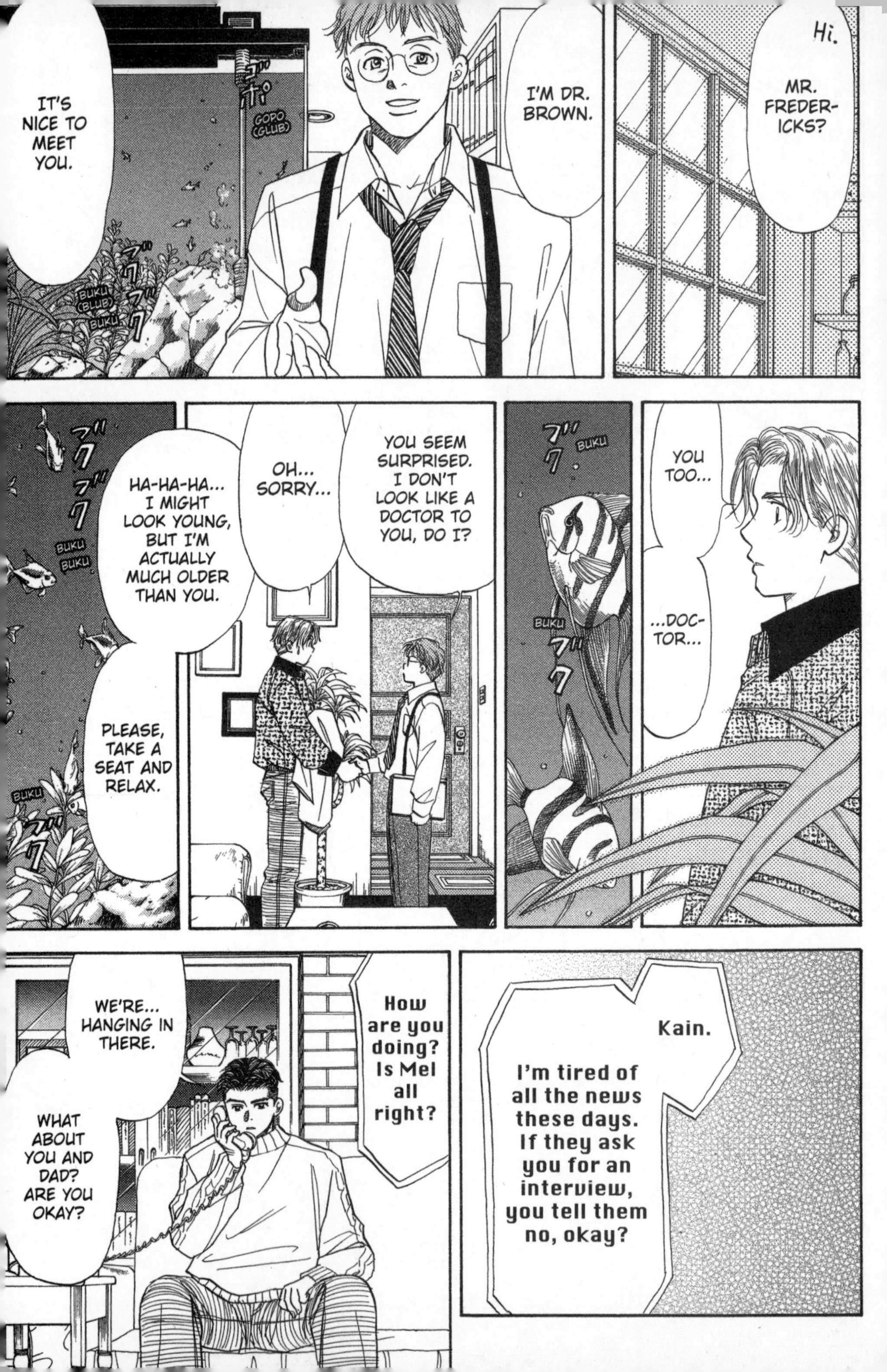
Hi.
MR. FREDER-ICKS?
I'M DR. BROWN.
IT'S NICE TO MEET YOU.
GOPO (GLUB)
BUKU (BLUB) BUKU
YOU TOO...
...DOC-TOR...
BUKU
BUKU
YOU SEEM SURPRISED. I DON'T LOOK LIKE A DOCTOR TO YOU, DO I?
OH... SORRY...
HA-HA-HA... I MIGHT LOOK YOUNG, BUT I'M ACTUALLY MUCH OLDER THAN YOU.
BUKU BUKU
PLEASE, TAKE A SEAT AND RELAX.
BUKU
Kain.
I'm tired of all the news these days. If they ask you for an interview, you tell them no, okay?
How are you doing? Is Mel all right?
WE'RE... HANGING IN THERE.
WHAT ABOUT YOU AND DAD? ARE YOU OKAY?

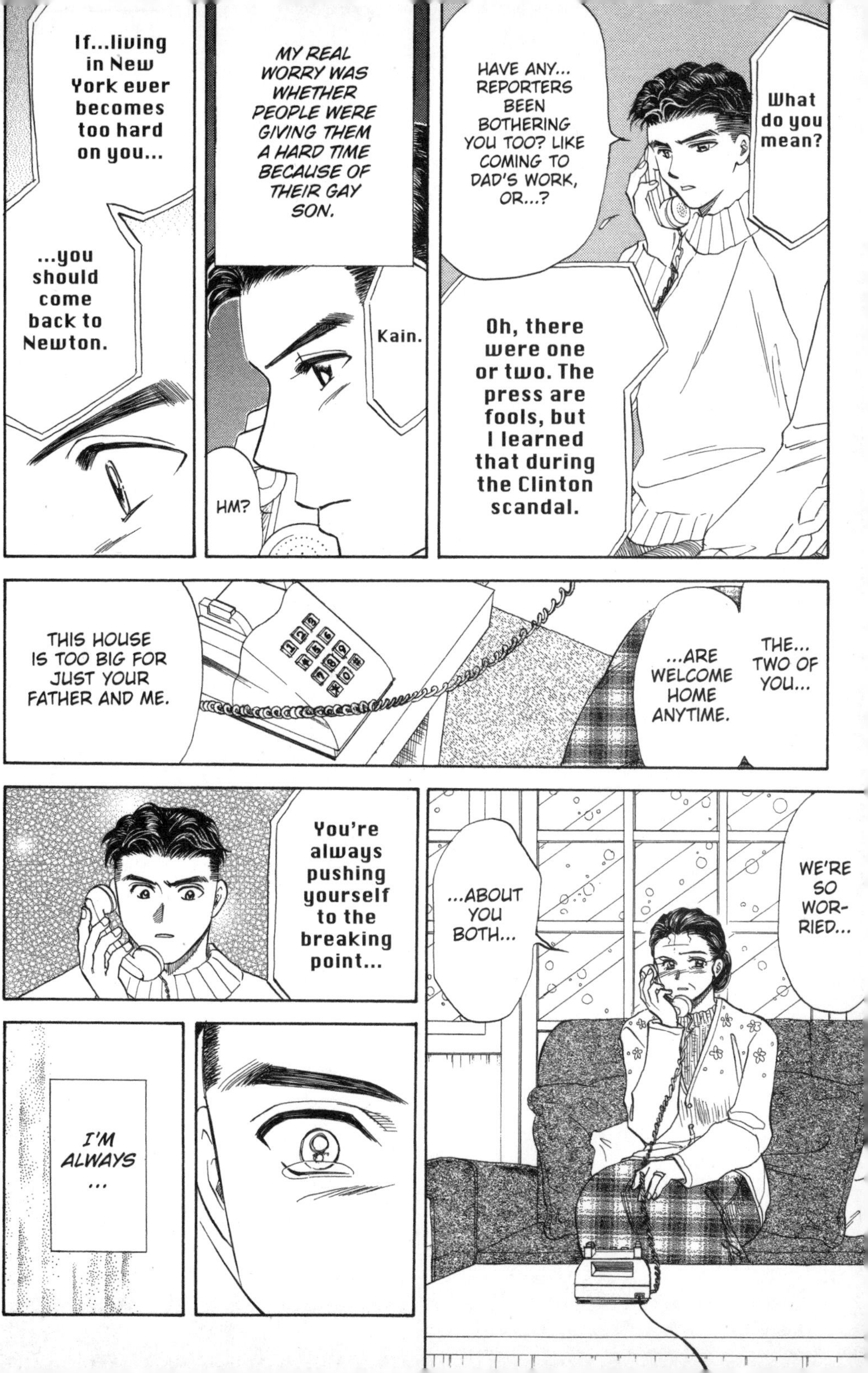
What do you mean?
HAVE ANY... REPORTERS BEEN BOTHERING YOU TOO? LIKE COMING TO DAD'S WORK, OR...?
Oh, there were one or two. The press are fools, but I learned that during the Clinton scandal.
MY REAL WORRY WAS WHETHER PEOPLE WERE GIVING THEM A HARD TIME BECAUSE OF THEIR GAY SON.
Kain.
HM?
If...living in New York ever becomes too hard on you...
...you should come back to Newton.
THE... TWO OF YOU...
...ARE WELCOME HOME ANYTIME.
THIS HOUSE IS TOO BIG FOR JUST YOUR FATHER AND ME.
WE'RE SO WOR-RIED...
...ABOUT YOU BOTH...
You're always pushing yourself to the breaking point...
I'M ALWAYS ...

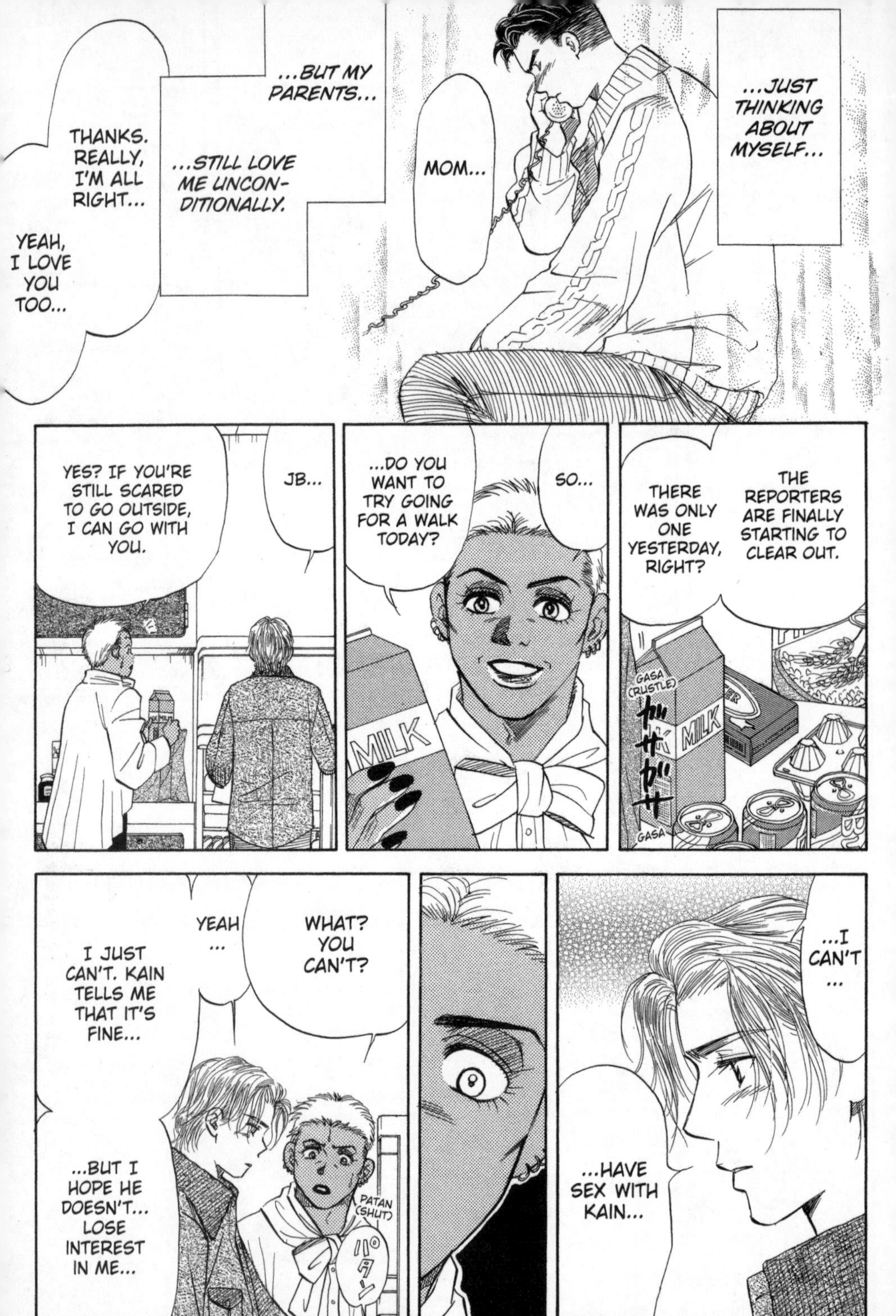
...JUST THINKING ABOUT MYSELF...
MOM...
...BUT MY PARENTS...
...STILL LOVE ME UNCONDITIONALLY.
THANKS. REALLY, I'M ALL RIGHT...
YEAH, I LOVE YOU TOO...
THE REPORTERS ARE FINALLY STARTING TO CLEAR OUT.
THERE WAS ONLY ONE YESTERDAY, RIGHT?
GASA (RUSTLE)
ガサガサ
GASA
MILK
SO...
...DO YOU WANT TO TRY GOING FOR A WALK TODAY?
MILK
JB...
YES? IF YOU'RE STILL SCARED TO GO OUTSIDE, I CAN GO WITH YOU.
...I CAN'T ...
...HAVE SEX WITH KAIN...
WHAT? YOU CAN'T?
YEAH ...
I JUST CAN'T. KAIN TELLS ME THAT IT'S FINE...
...BUT I HOPE HE DOESN'T... LOSE INTEREST IN ME...
PATAN (SHUT)
パタン

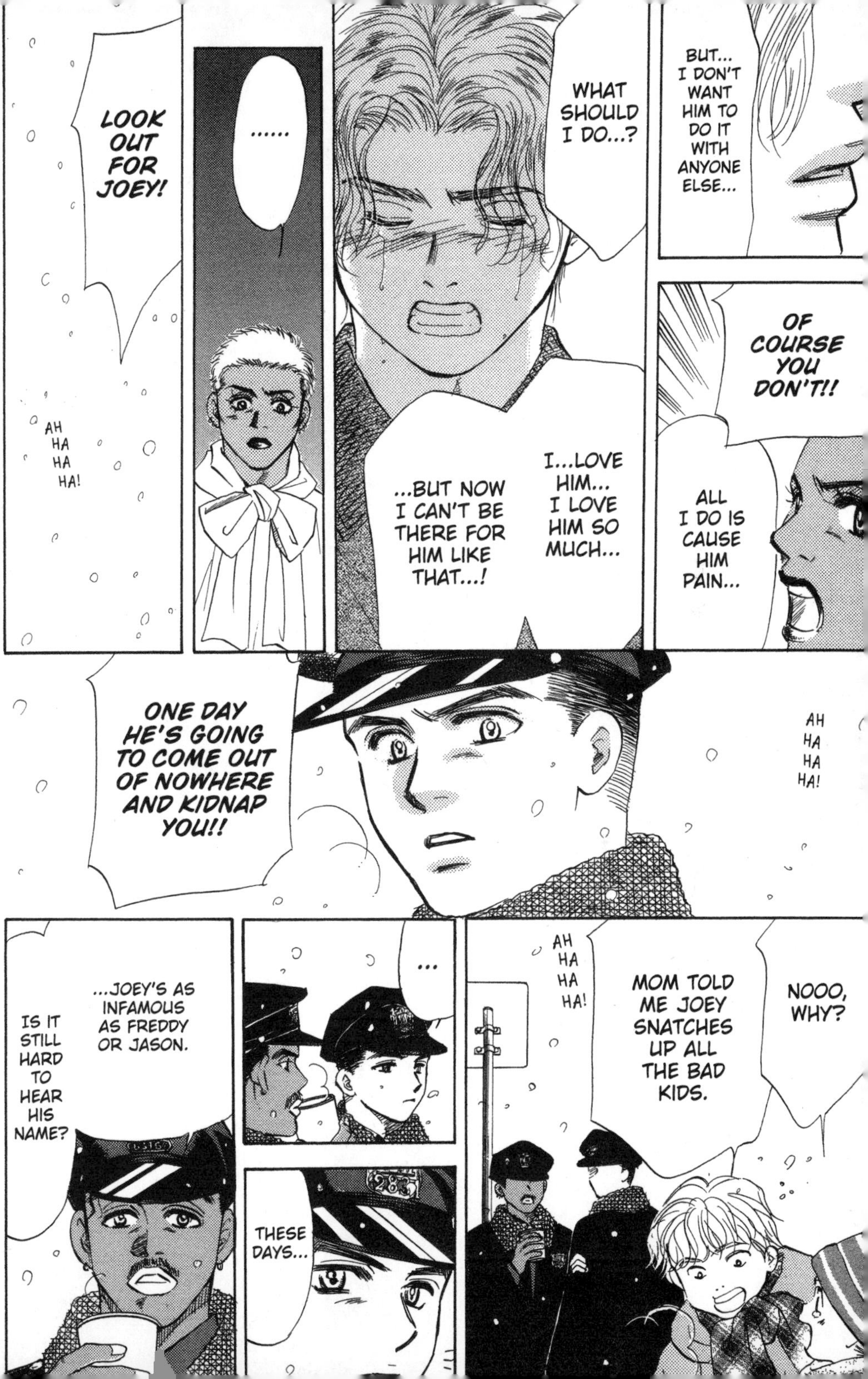
BUT... I DON'T WANT HIM TO DO IT WITH ANYONE ELSE...
OF COURSE YOU DON'T!!
ALL I DO IS CAUSE HIM PAIN...
WHAT SHOULD I DO...?
I...LOVE HIM... I LOVE HIM SO MUCH...
...BUT NOW I CAN'T BE THERE FOR HIM LIKE THAT...!
......
LOOK OUT FOR JOEY!
AH HA HA HA!
AH HA HA HA!
ONE DAY HE'S GOING TO COME OUT OF NOWHERE AND KIDNAP YOU!!
NOOO, WHY?
MOM TOLD ME JOEY SNATCHES UP ALL THE BAD KIDS.
AH HA HA HA!
...
THESE DAYS...
...JOEY'S AS INFAMOUS AS FREDDY OR JASON.
IS IT STILL HARD TO HEAR HIS NAME?

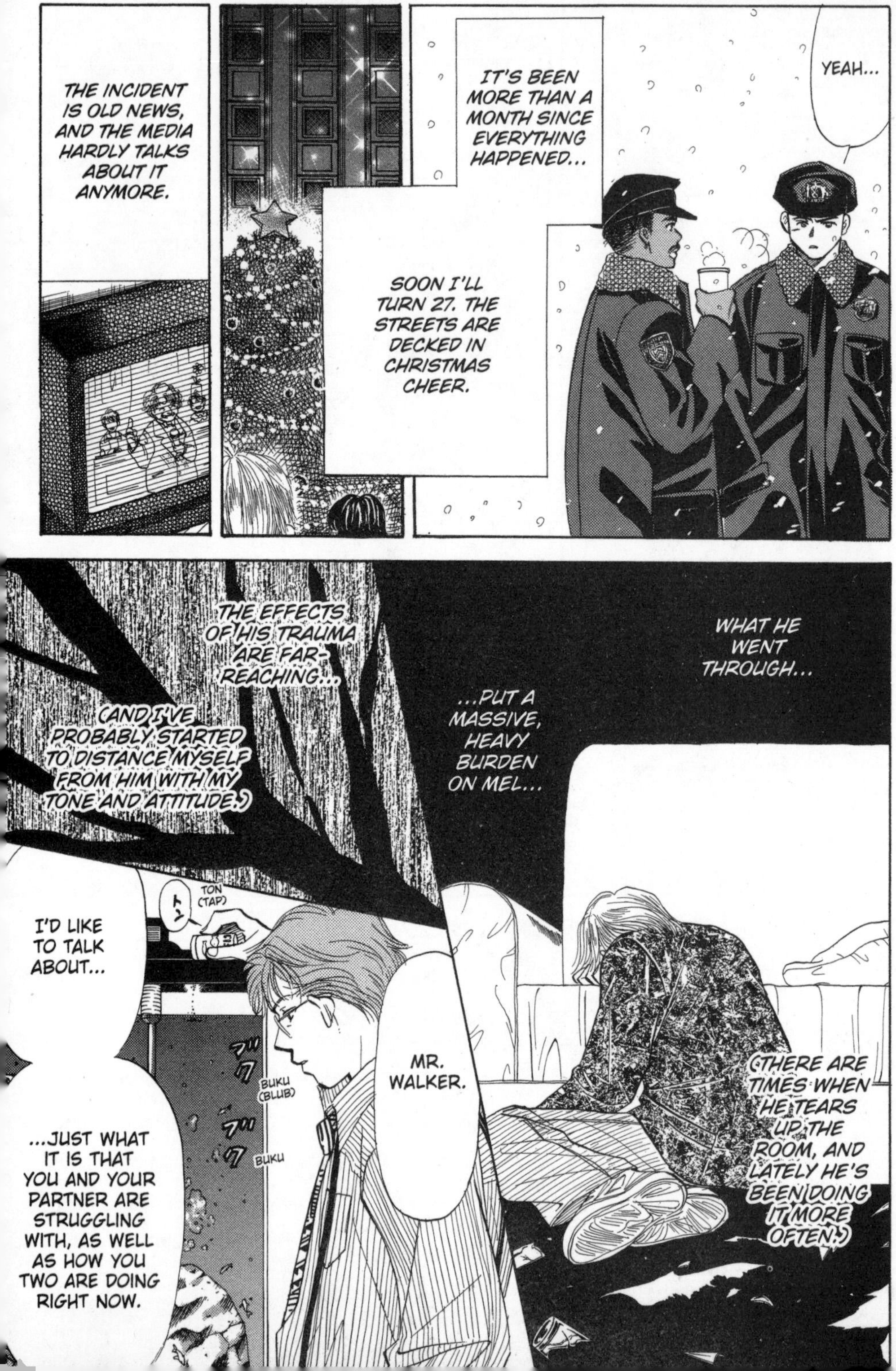
YEAH...
IT'S BEEN MORE THAN A MONTH SINCE EVERYTHING HAPPENED...
SOON I'LL TURN 27. THE STREETS ARE DECKED IN CHRISTMAS CHEER.
THE INCIDENT IS OLD NEWS, AND THE MEDIA HARDLY TALKS ABOUT IT ANYMORE.
WHAT HE WENT THROUGH...
...PUT A MASSIVE, HEAVY BURDEN ON MEL...
(THERE ARE TIMES WHEN HE TEARS UP THE ROOM, AND LATELY HE'S BEEN DOING IT MORE OFTEN.)
THE EFFECTS OF HIS TRAUMA ARE FAR-REACHING...
(AND I'VE PROBABLY STARTED TO DISTANCE MYSELF FROM HIM WITH MY TONE AND ATTITUDE.)
MR. WALKER.
トン
TON (TAP)
I'D LIKE TO TALK ABOUT...
...JUST WHAT IT IS THAT YOU AND YOUR PARTNER ARE STRUGGLING WITH, AS WELL AS HOW YOU TWO ARE DOING RIGHT NOW.
BUKU (BLUB)
BUKU

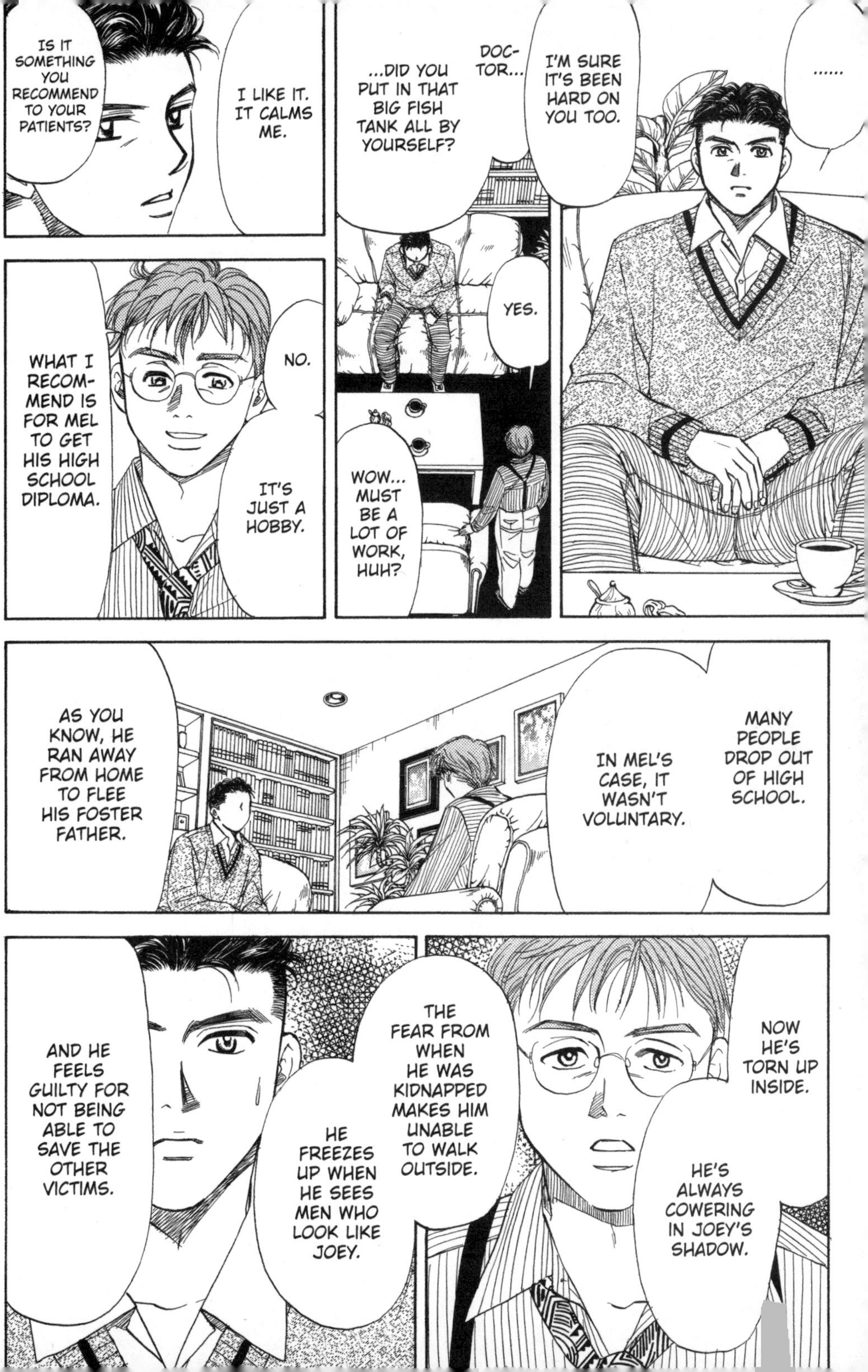
I'M SURE IT'S BEEN HARD ON YOU TOO.
......
DOC-TOR...
...DID YOU PUT IN THAT BIG FISH TANK ALL BY YOURSELF?
YES.
WOW... MUST BE A LOT OF WORK, HUH?
I LIKE IT. IT CALMS ME.
IS IT SOMETHING YOU RECOMMEND TO YOUR PATIENTS?
NO.
IT'S JUST A HOBBY.
WHAT I RECOM-MEND IS FOR MEL TO GET HIS HIGH SCHOOL DIPLOMA.
MANY PEOPLE DROP OUT OF HIGH SCHOOL.
IN MEL'S CASE, IT WASN'T VOLUNTARY.
AS YOU KNOW, HE RAN AWAY FROM HOME TO FLEE HIS FOSTER FATHER.
NOW HE'S TORN UP INSIDE.
HE'S ALWAYS COWERING IN JOEY'S SHADOW.
THE FEAR FROM WHEN HE WAS KIDNAPPED MAKES HIM UNABLE TO WALK OUTSIDE.
HE FREEZES UP WHEN HE SEES MEN WHO LOOK LIKE JOEY.
AND HE FEELS GUILTY FOR NOT BEING ABLE TO SAVE THE OTHER VICTIMS.

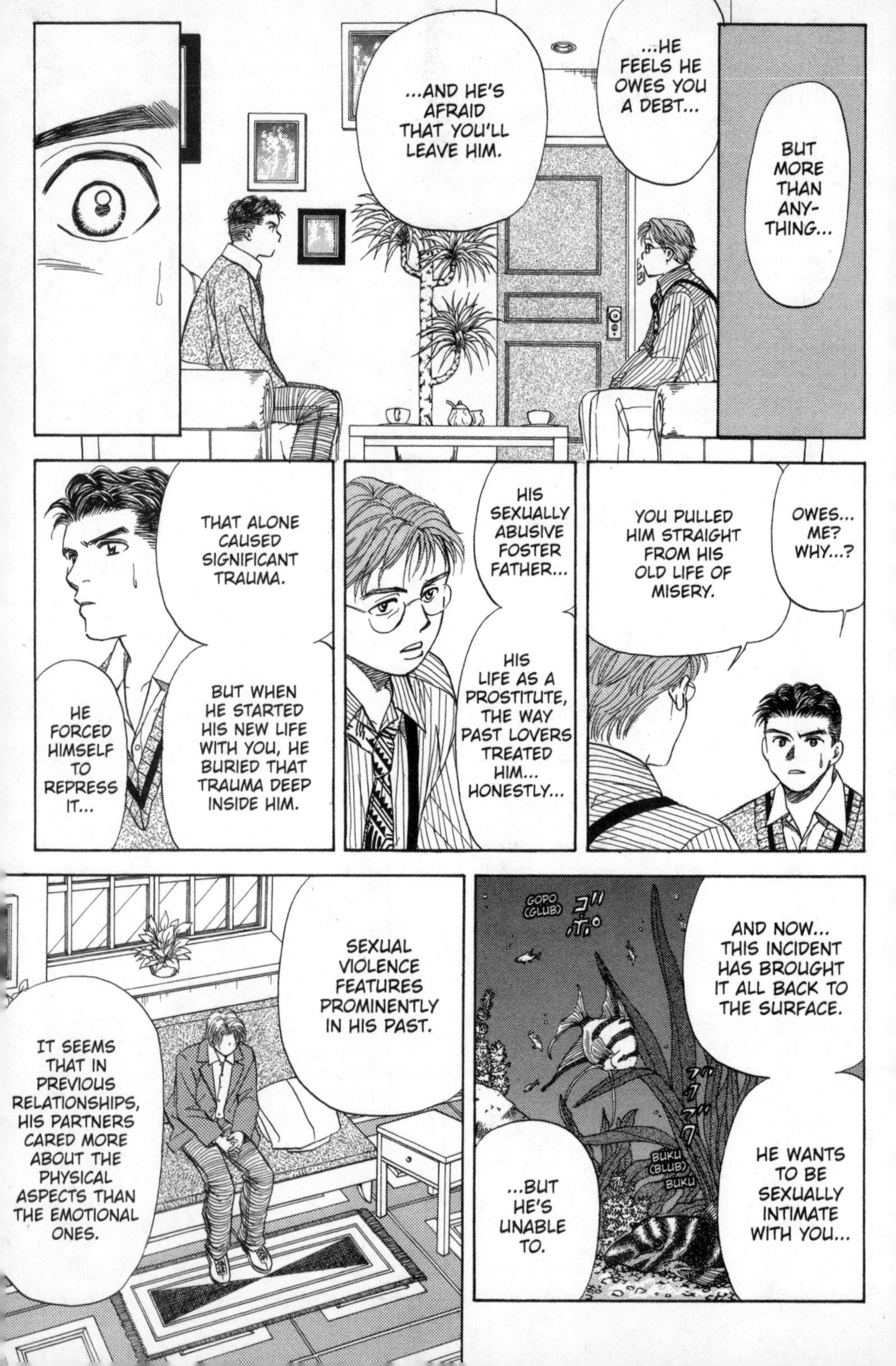
BUT MORE THAN ANYTHING...
...HE FEELS HE OWES YOU A DEBT...
...AND HE'S AFRAID THAT YOU'LL LEAVE HIM.
OWES... ME? WHY...?
YOU PULLED HIM STRAIGHT FROM HIS OLD LIFE OF MISERY.
HIS SEXUALLY ABUSIVE FOSTER FATHER...
HIS LIFE AS A PROSTITUTE, THE WAY PAST LOVERS TREATED HIM... HONESTLY...
THAT ALONE CAUSED SIGNIFICANT TRAUMA.
BUT WHEN HE STARTED HIS NEW LIFE WITH YOU, HE BURIED THAT TRAUMA DEEP INSIDE HIM.
HE FORCED HIMSELF TO REPRESS IT...
GOPO (GLUB)
AND NOW... THIS INCIDENT HAS BROUGHT IT ALL BACK TO THE SURFACE.
HE WANTS TO BE SEXUALLY INTIMATE WITH YOU...
BUKU (BLUB) BUKU
...BUT HE'S UNABLE TO.
SEXUAL VIOLENCE FEATURES PROMINENTLY IN HIS PAST.
IT SEEMS THAT IN PREVIOUS RELATIONSHIPS, HIS PARTNERS CARED MORE ABOUT THE PHYSICAL ASPECTS THAN THE EMOTIONAL ONES.

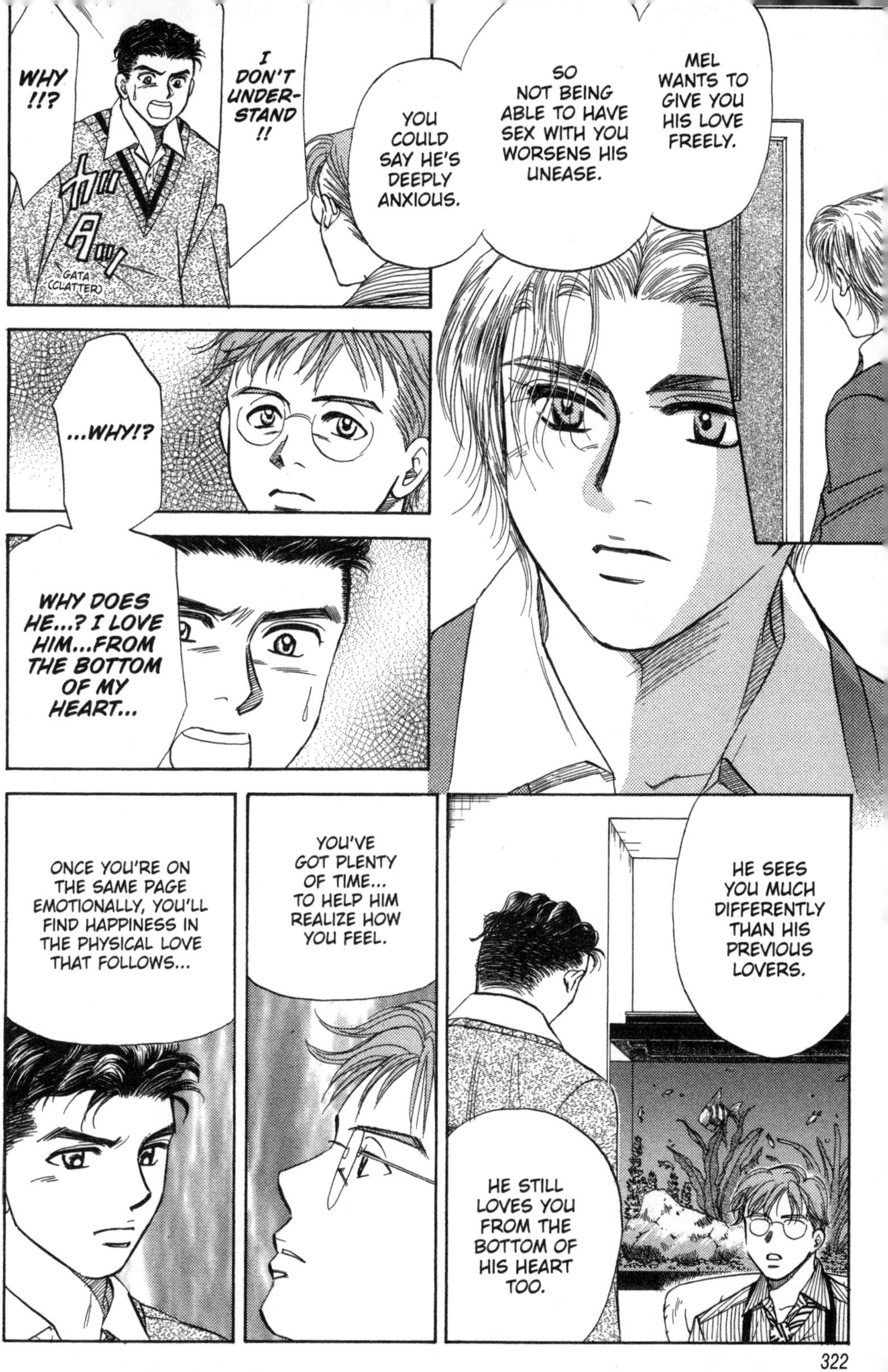
MEL WANTS TO GIVE YOU HIS LOVE FREELY.
SO NOT BEING ABLE TO HAVE SEX WITH YOU WORSENS HIS UNEASE.
YOU COULD SAY HE'S DEEPLY ANXIOUS.
I DON'T UNDER-STAND !!
WHY !!?
GATA (CLATTER)
...WHY!?
WHY DOES HE...? I LOVE HIM...FROM THE BOTTOM OF MY HEART...
HE SEES YOU MUCH DIFFERENTLY THAN HIS PREVIOUS LOVERS.
HE STILL LOVES YOU FROM THE BOTTOM OF HIS HEART TOO.
YOU'VE GOT PLENTY OF TIME... TO HELP HIM REALIZE HOW YOU FEEL.
ONCE YOU'RE ON THE SAME PAGE EMOTIONALLY, YOU'LL FIND HAPPINESS IN THE PHYSICAL LOVE THAT FOLLOWS...

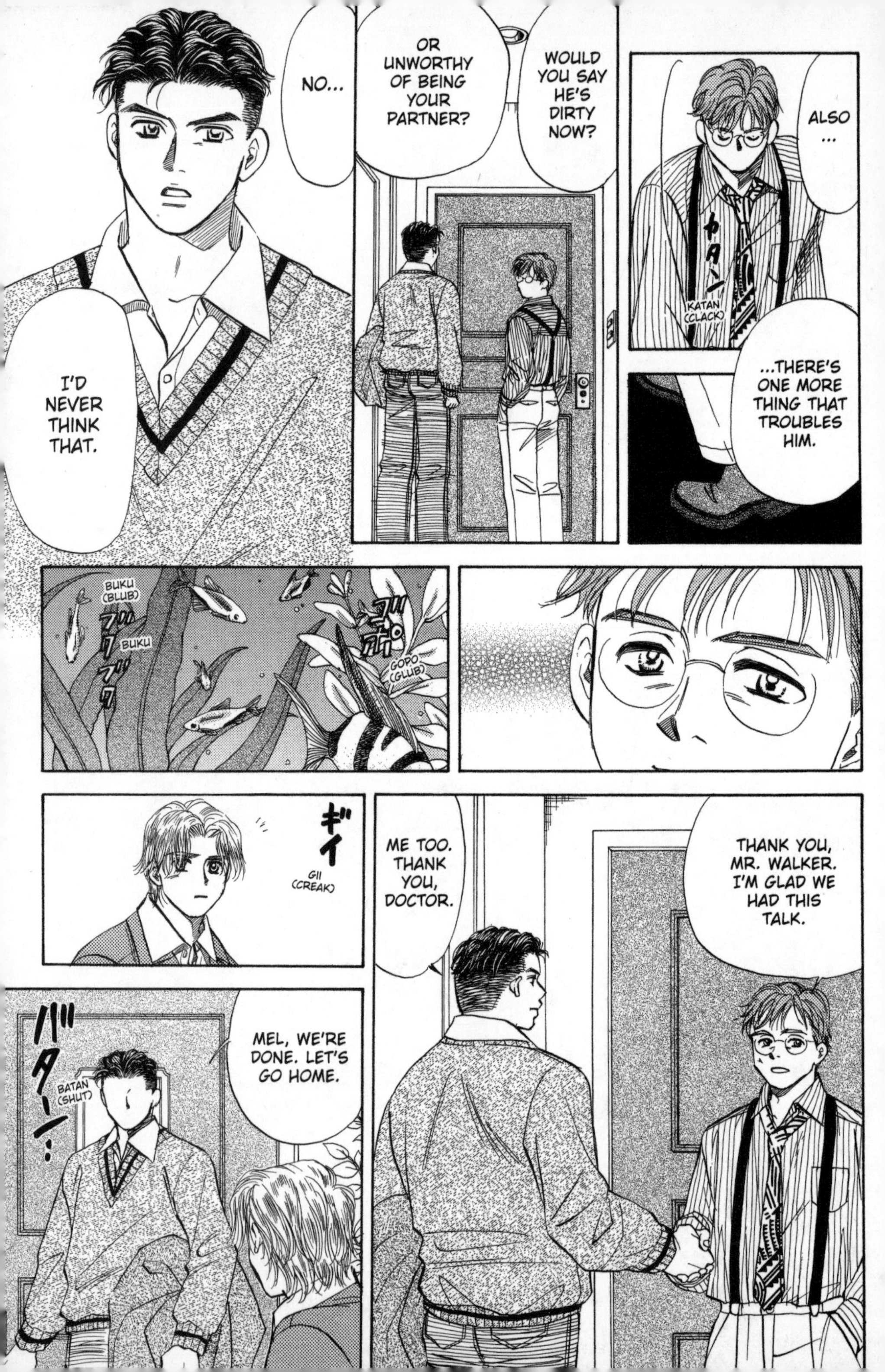
ALSO ...
KATAN (CLACK)
...THERE'S ONE MORE THING THAT TROUBLES HIM.
WOULD YOU SAY HE'S DIRTY NOW?
OR UNWORTHY OF BEING YOUR PARTNER?
NO...
I'D NEVER THINK THAT.
GOPO (GLUB)
BUKU (BLUB)
BUKU
THANK YOU, MR. WALKER. I'M GLAD WE HAD THIS TALK.
ME TOO. THANK YOU, DOCTOR.
ギイ
GII (CREAK)
MEL, WE'RE DONE. LET'S GO HOME.
BATAN (SHUT)

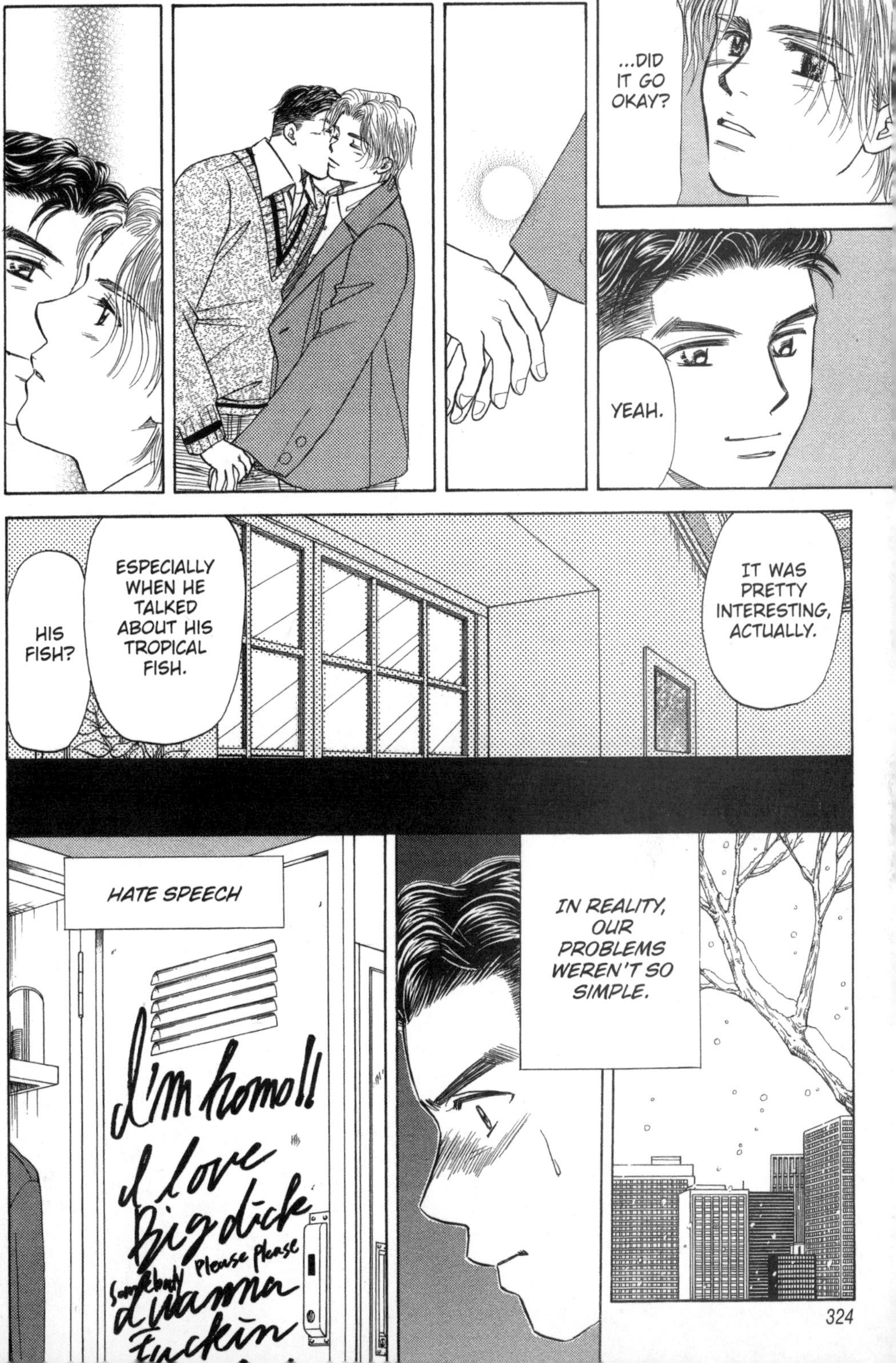
...DID IT GO OKAY?
YEAH.
IT WAS PRETTY INTERESTING, ACTUALLY.
ESPECIALLY WHEN HE TALKED ABOUT HIS TROPICAL FISH.
HIS FISH?
IN REALITY, OUR PROBLEMS WEREN'T SO SIMPLE.
HATE SPEECH
I'm homo!!
I love Big dick
Somebody Please please
I wanna
Fuckin

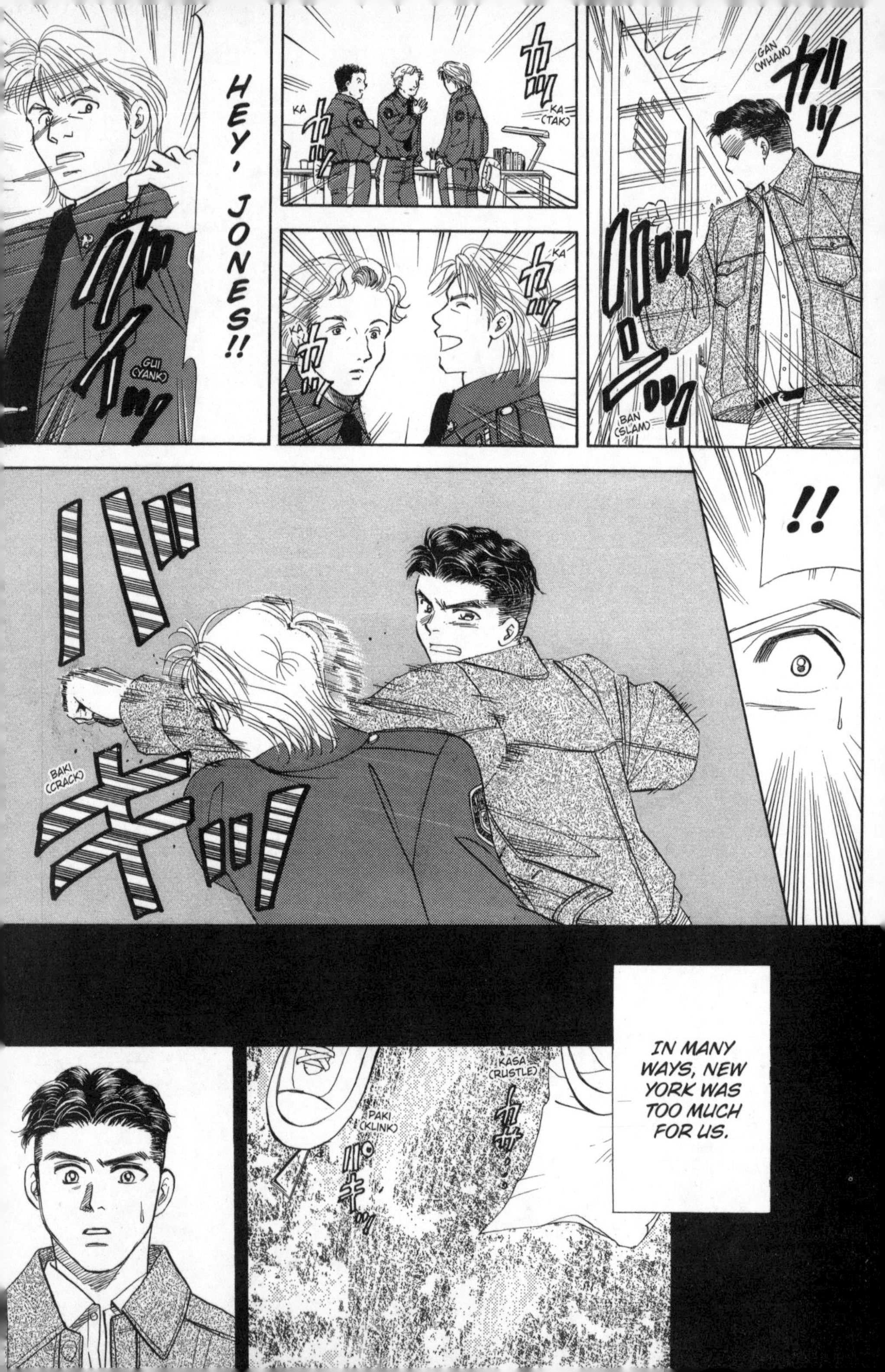
GAN (WHAM)
BAN (SLAM)
KA (TAK)
KA
KA
KA
HEY, JONES!!
GUI (YANK)
!!
BAKI (CRACK)
IN MANY WAYS, NEW YORK WAS TOO MUCH FOR US.
KASA (RUSTLE)
PAKI (KLINK)

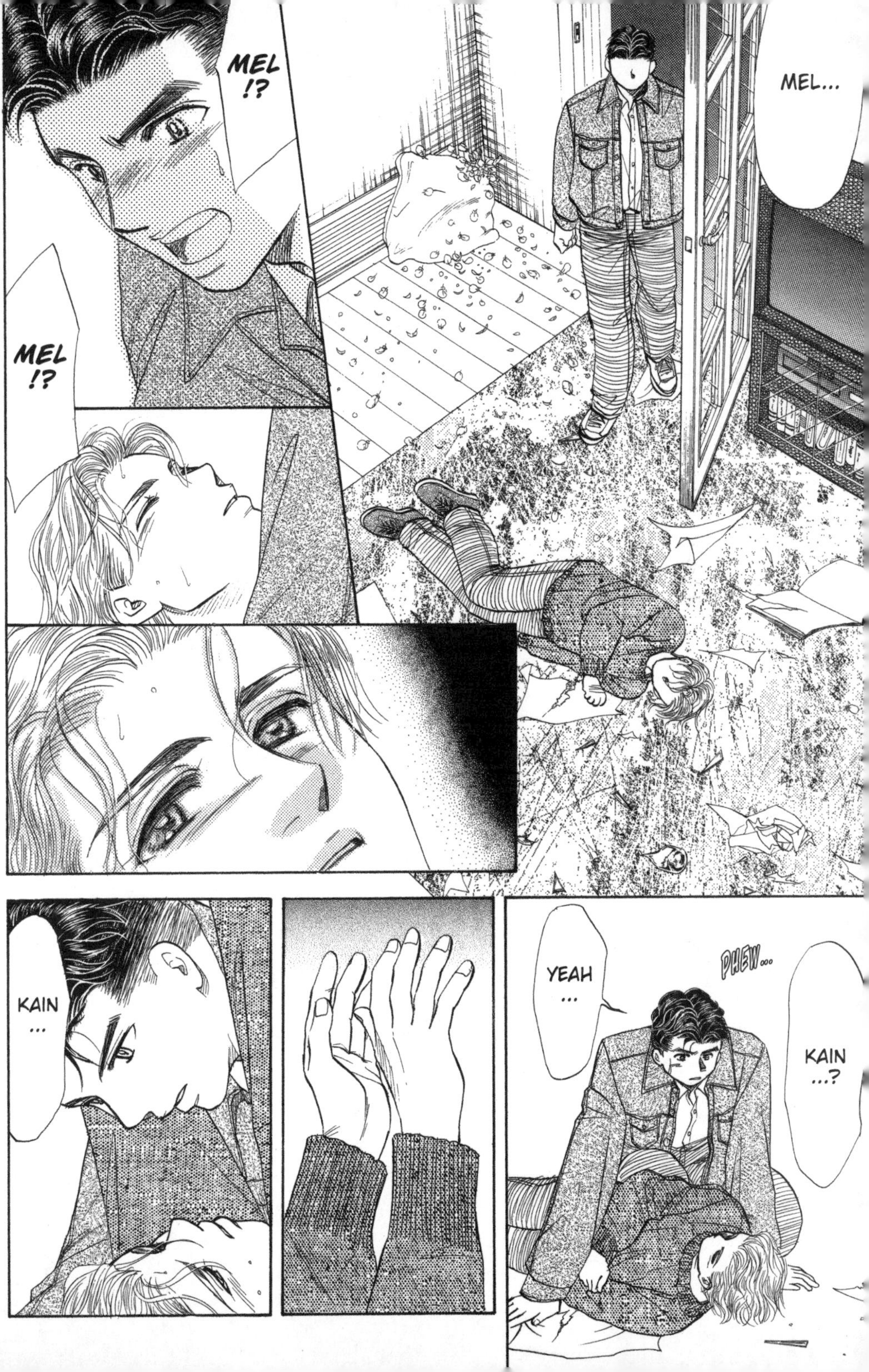
MEL...
MEL !?
MEL !?
KAIN ...?
PHEW...
YEAH ...
KAIN ...

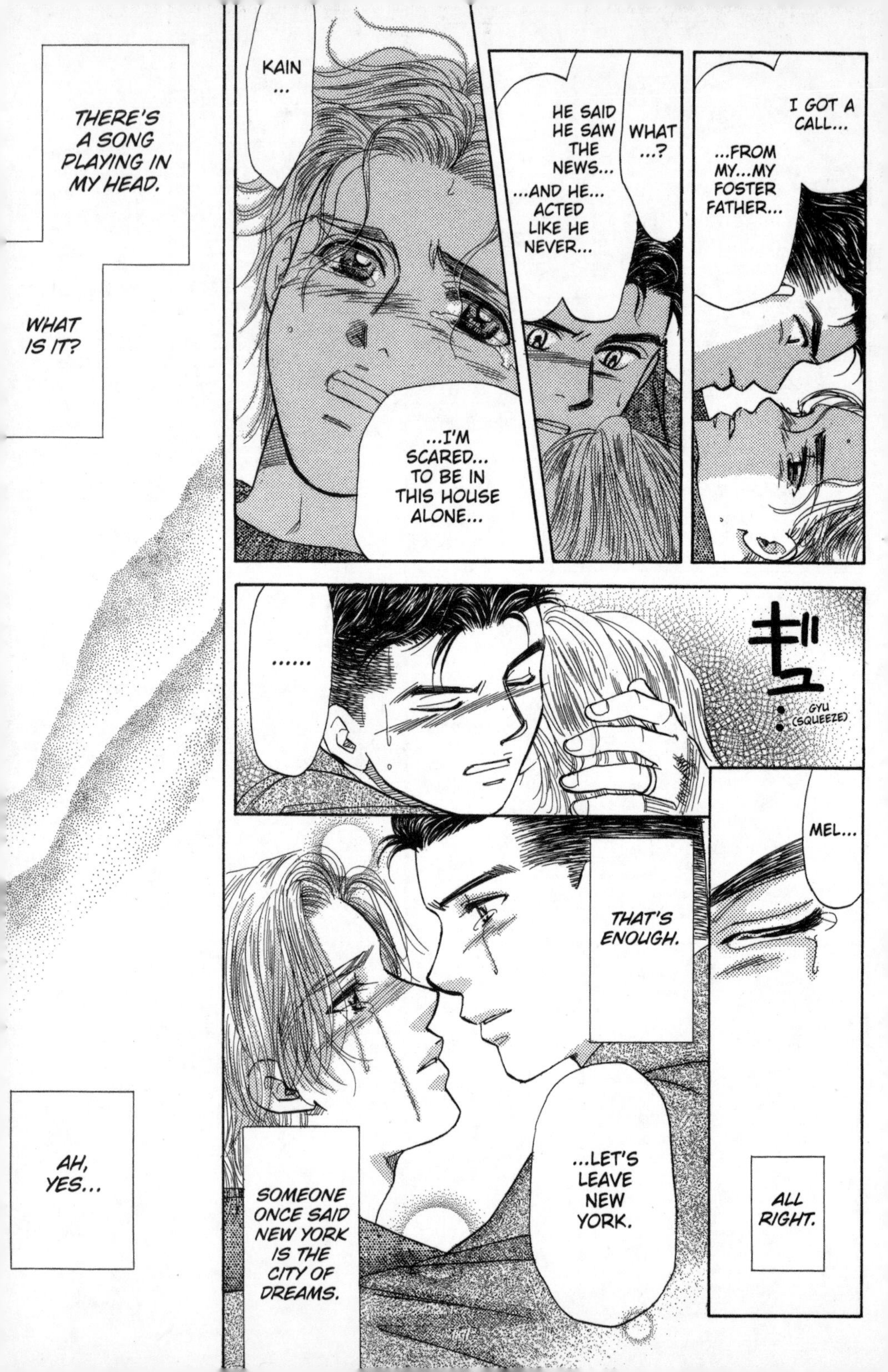
I GOT A CALL...
...FROM MY...MY FOSTER FATHER...
WHAT ...?
HE SAID HE SAW THE NEWS...
...AND HE... ACTED LIKE HE NEVER...
KAIN ...
...I'M SCARED... TO BE IN THIS HOUSE ALONE...
ぎュ
GYU (SQUEEZE)
......
MEL...
THAT'S ENOUGH.
...LET'S LEAVE NEW YORK.
ALL RIGHT.
SOMEONE ONCE SAID NEW YORK IS THE CITY OF DREAMS.
THERE'S A SONG PLAYING IN MY HEAD.
WHAT IS IT?
AH, YES...

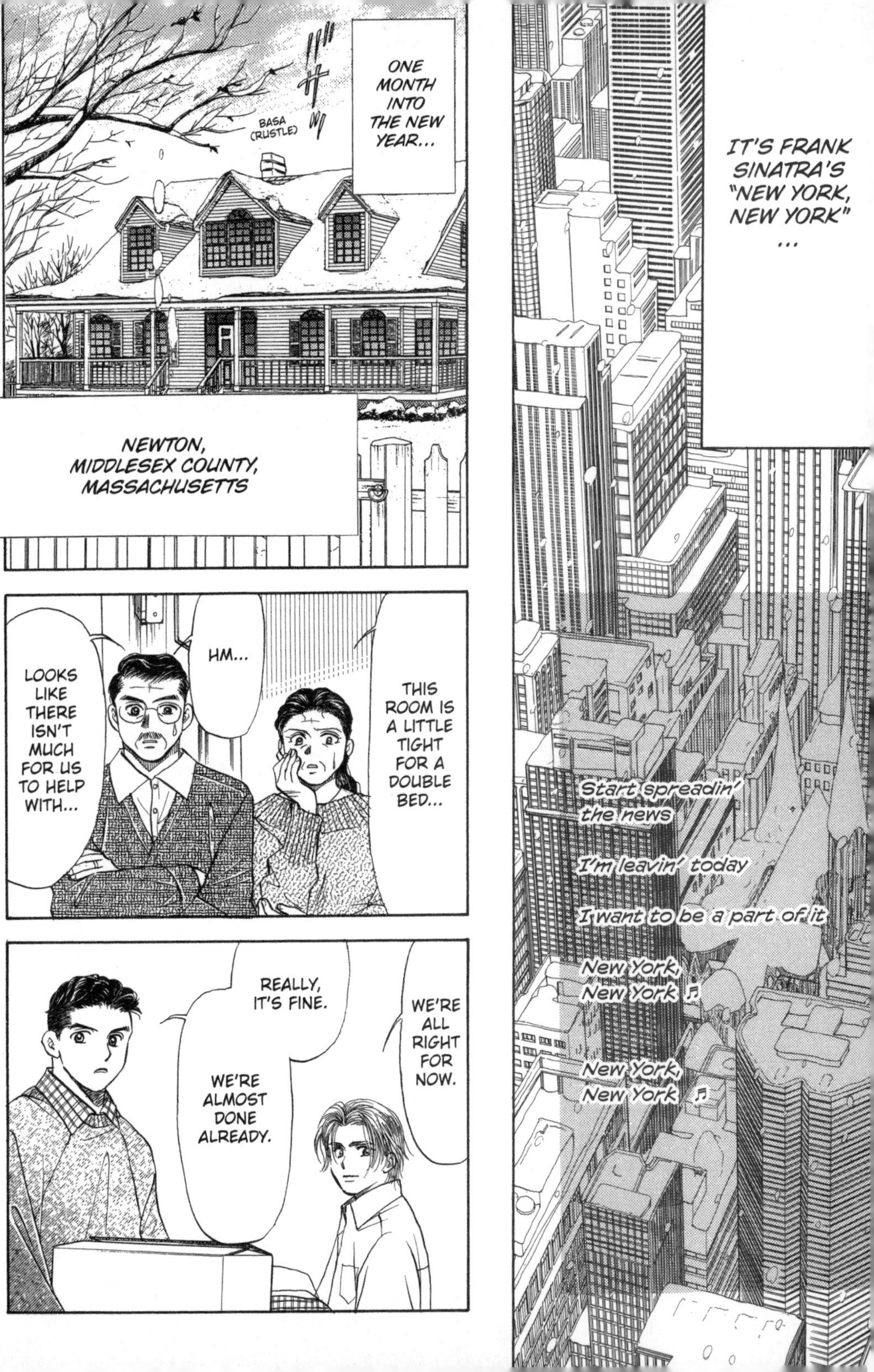
IT'S FRANK SINATRA'S "NEW YORK, NEW YORK" ...
Start spreadin' the news
I'm leavin' today
I want to be a part of it
New York, New York ♬
New York, New York ♬
ONE MONTH INTO THE NEW YEAR...
BASA (RUSTLE)
NEWTON, MIDDLESEX COUNTY, MASSACHUSETTS
THIS ROOM IS A LITTLE TIGHT FOR A DOUBLE BED...
HM...
LOOKS LIKE THERE ISN'T MUCH FOR US TO HELP WITH...
WE'RE ALL RIGHT FOR NOW.
REALLY, IT'S FINE.
WE'RE ALMOST DONE ALREADY.

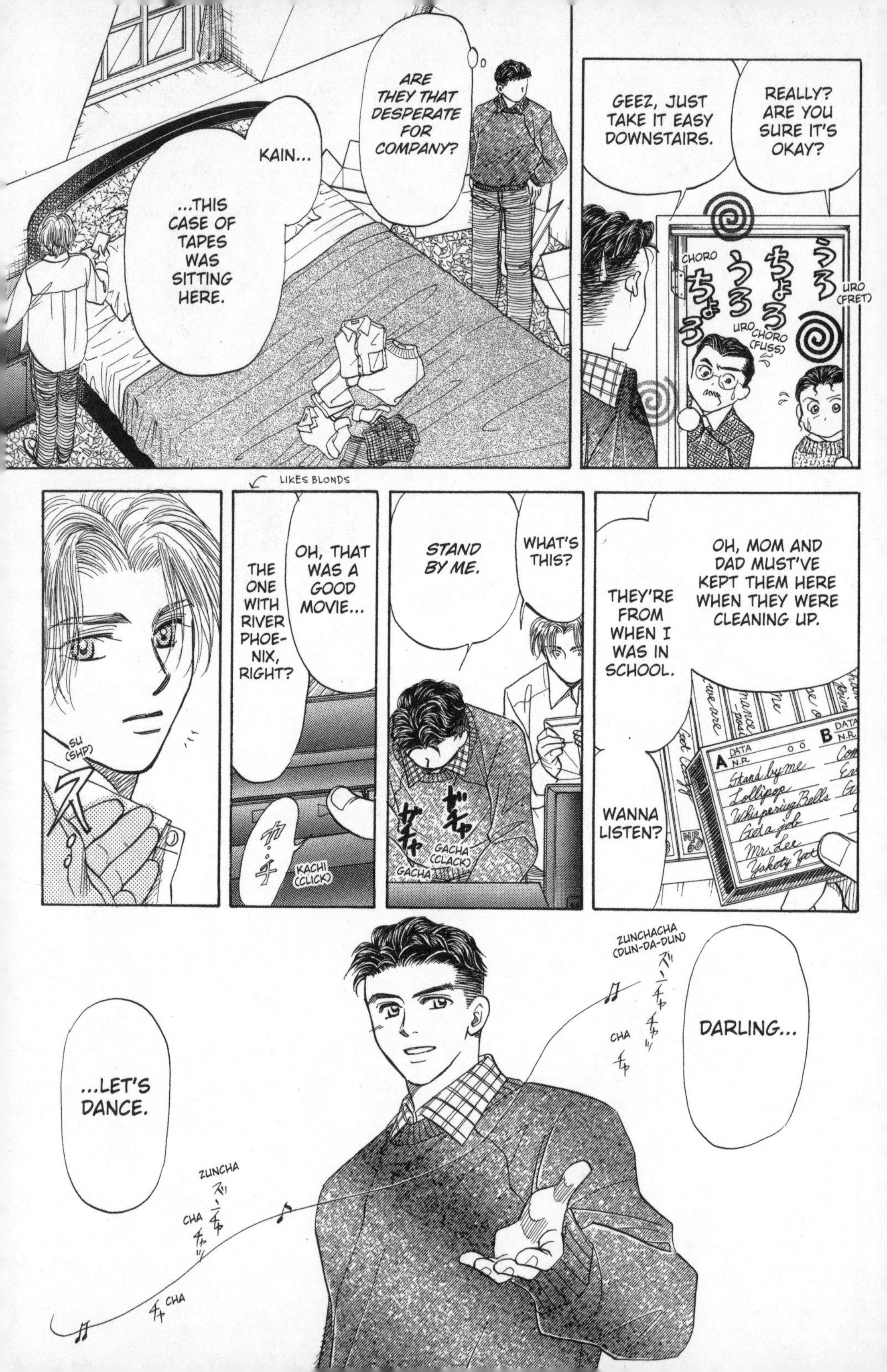
REALLY? ARE YOU SURE IT'S OKAY?
GEEZ, JUST TAKE IT EASY DOWNSTAIRS.
うろ URO (FRET)
ちょろ
うろ
ちょろ CHORO
URO CHORO (FUSS)
ARE THEY THAT DESPERATE FOR COMPANY?
KAIN...
...THIS CASE OF TAPES WAS SITTING HERE.
OH, MOM AND DAD MUST'VE KEPT THEM HERE WHEN THEY WERE CLEANING UP.
THEY'RE FROM WHEN I WAS IN SCHOOL.
WANNA LISTEN?
A DATA N.R.
Stand by me
Lollipop
Whispering Bells
Get a job
Mr. Lee
B DATA N.R.
WHAT'S THIS?
STAND BY ME.
GACHA (CLACK) GACHA
OH, THAT WAS A GOOD MOVIE...
THE ONE WITH RIVER PHOENIX, RIGHT?
KACHI (CLICK)
LIKES BLONDS
SU (SHP)
ZUNCHACHA (DUN-DA-DUND)
CHA
DARLING...
...LET'S DANCE.
ZUNCHA
CHA
CHA

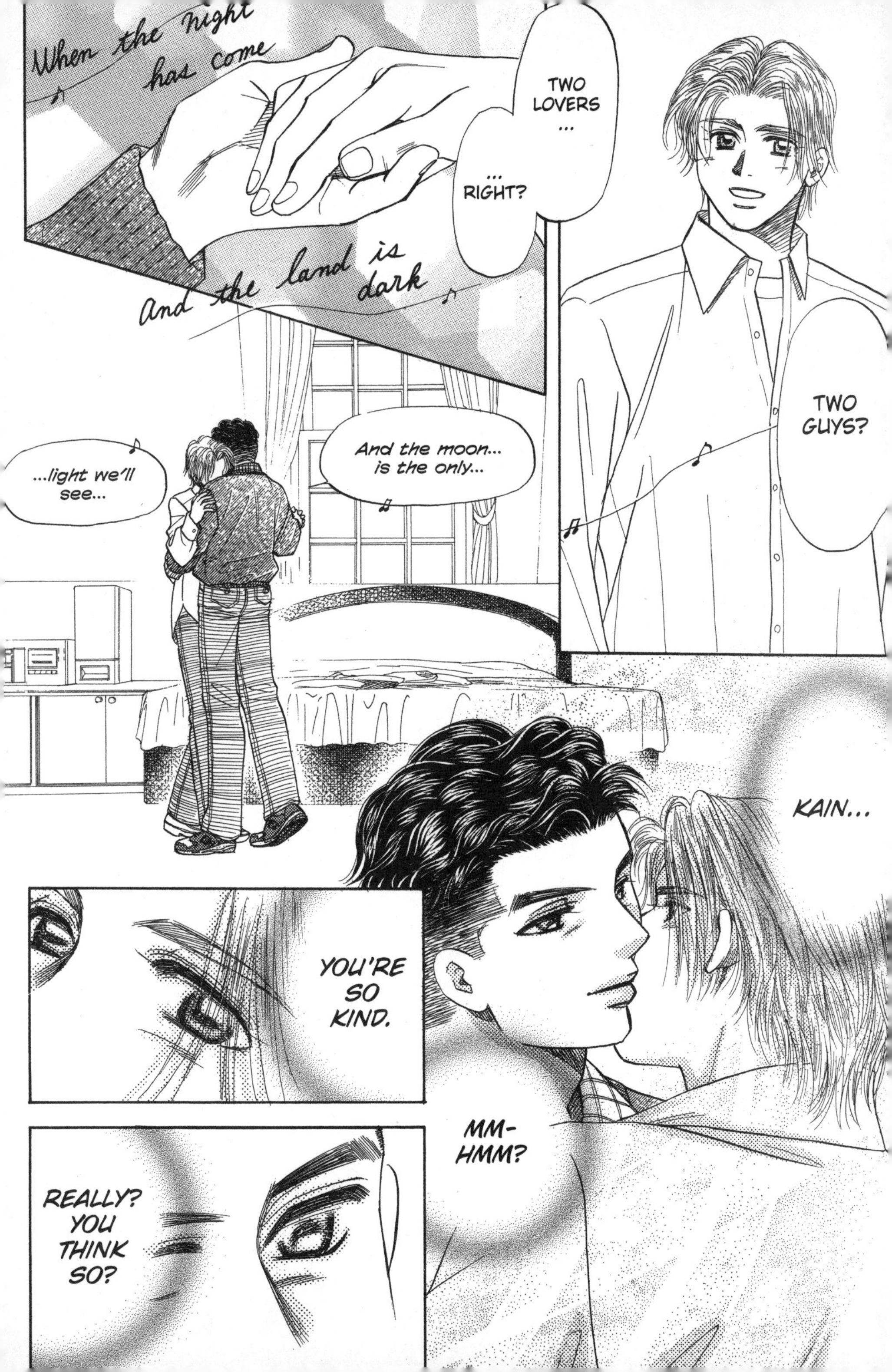

TWO LOVERS ...
... RIGHT?
TWO GUYS?
When the night has come
And the land is dark
And the moon... is the only...
...light we'll see...
KAIN...
MM-HMM?
YOU'RE SO KIND.
REALLY? YOU THINK SO?

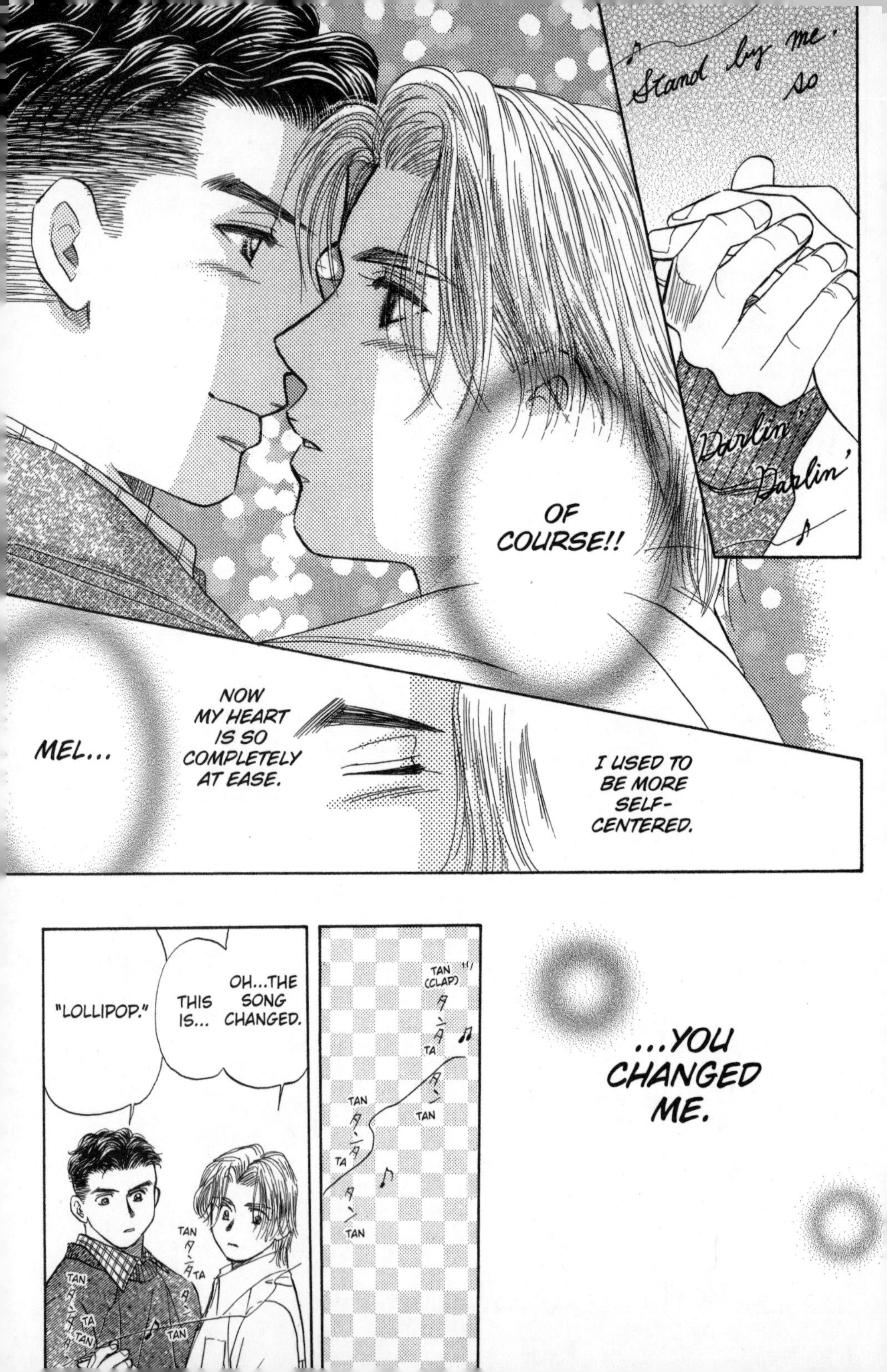
Stand by me, so
Darlin' Darlin'
OF COURSE!!
I USED TO BE MORE SELF-CENTERED.
NOW MY HEART IS SO COMPLETELY AT EASE.
MEL...
...YOU CHANGED ME.
TAN (CLAP)
TA
TAN
TAN
TA
TAN
OH...THE SONG CHANGED.
THIS IS...
"LOLLIPOP."
TAN
TA
TAN
TA
TAN
TAN

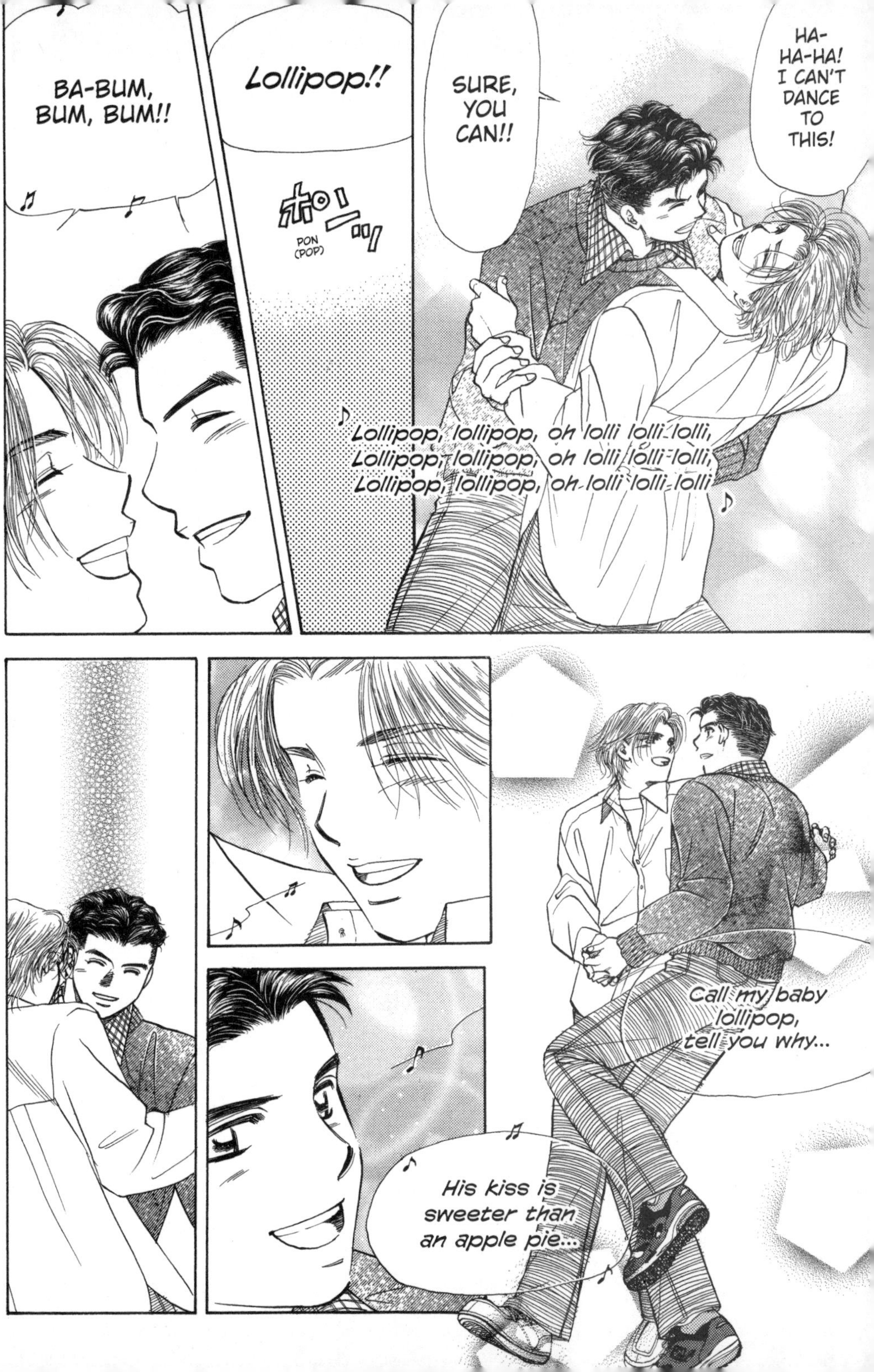
HA-HA-HA! I CAN'T DANCE TO THIS!
SURE, YOU CAN!!
Lollipop, lollipop, oh lolli lolli lolli,
Lollipop, lollipop, oh lolli lolli lolli,
Lollipop, lollipop, oh lolli lolli lolli
Lollipop!!
PON (POP)
BA-BUM, BUM, BUM!!
Call my baby lollipop, tell you why...
His kiss is sweeter than an apple pie...

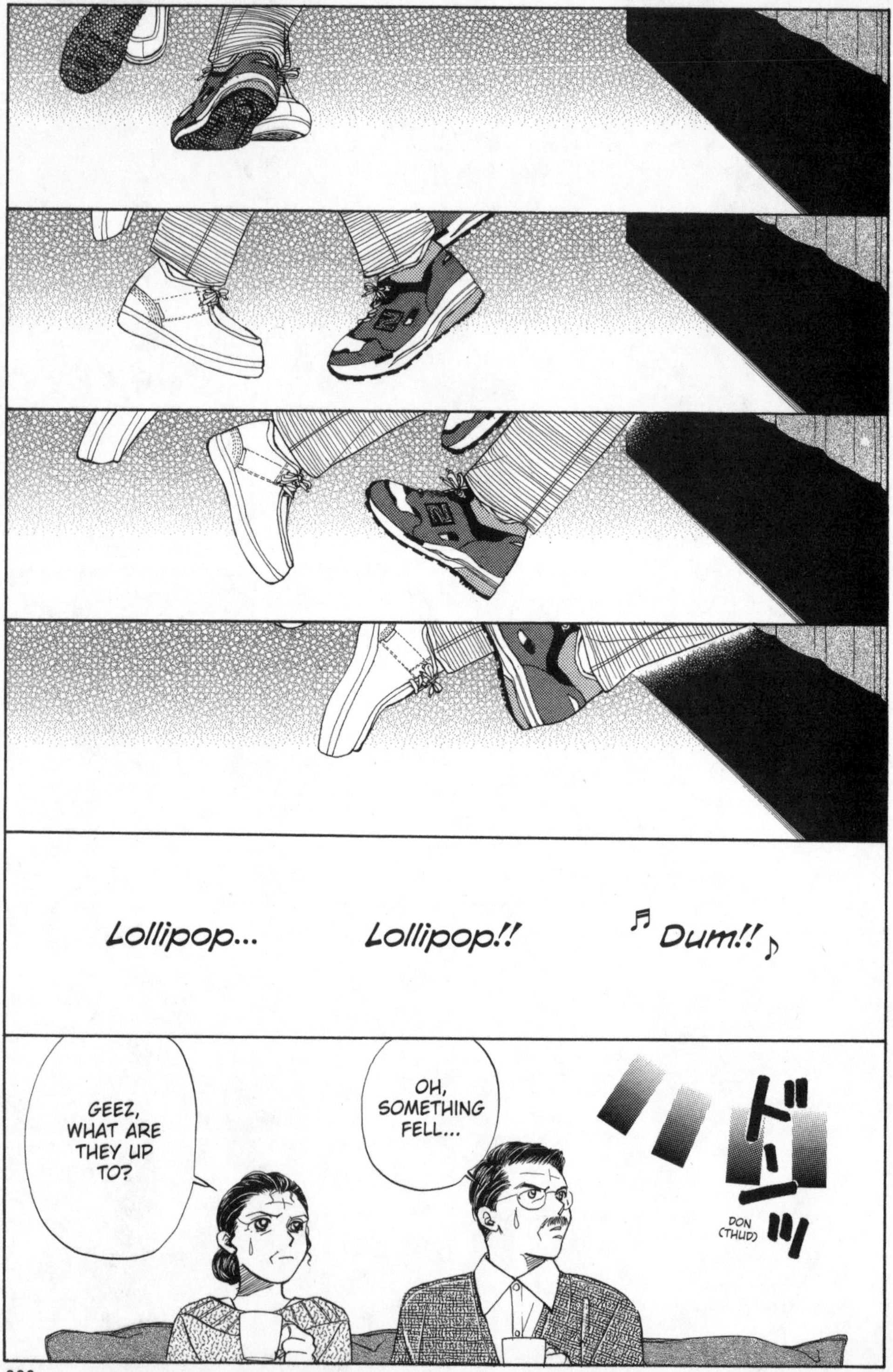
Lollipop... Lollipop!! ♬ Dum!! ♪
ドンッ
DON (THUD)
OH, SOMETHING FELL...
GEEZ, WHAT ARE THEY UP TO?

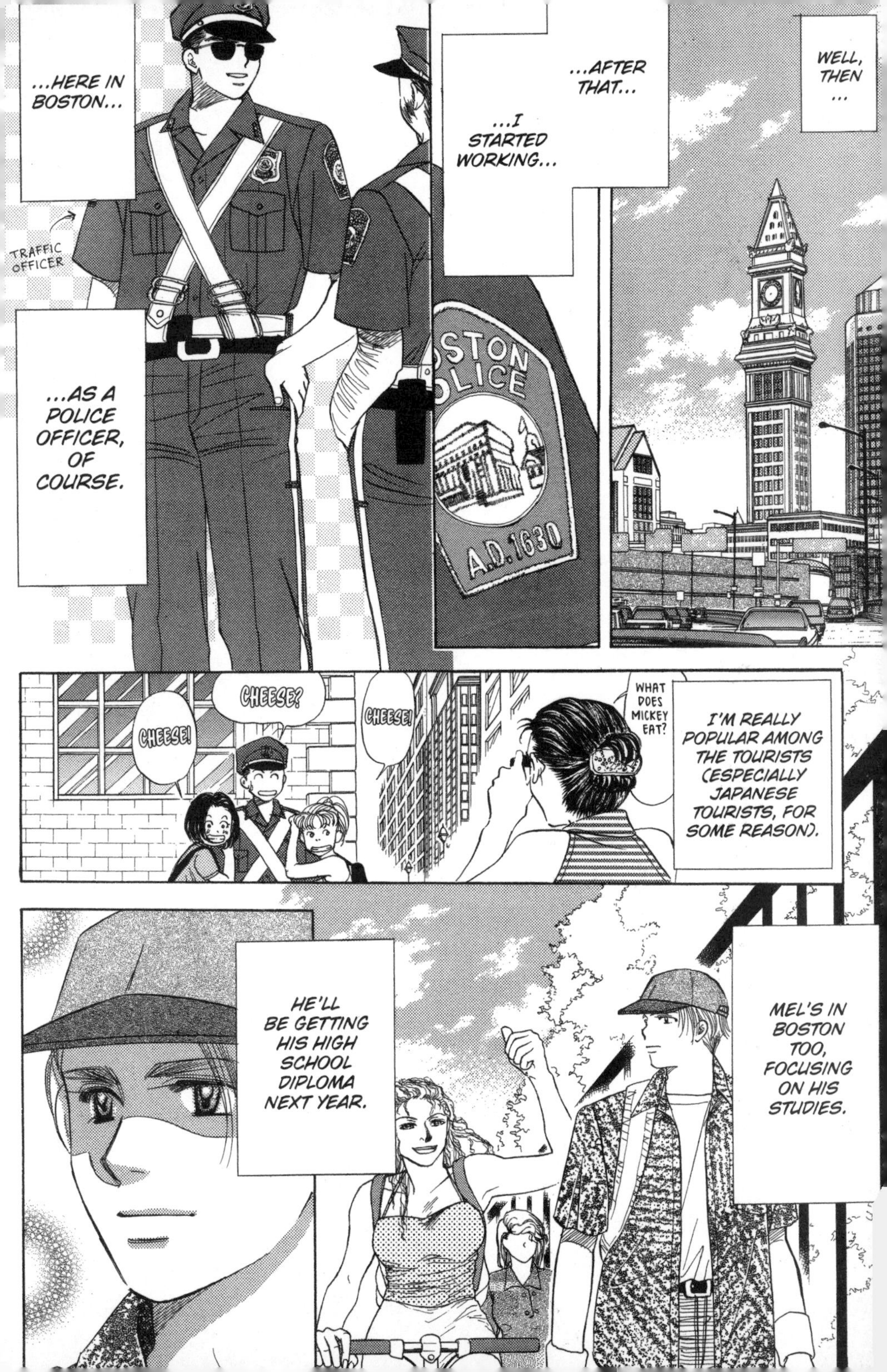
WELL, THEN ...
...AFTER THAT...
...I STARTED WORKING...
...HERE IN BOSTON...
TRAFFIC OFFICER
...AS A POLICE OFFICER, OF COURSE.
A.D.1630
I'M REALLY POPULAR AMONG THE TOURISTS (ESPECIALLY JAPANESE TOURISTS, FOR SOME REASON).
WHAT DOES MICKEY EAT?
CHEESE!
CHEESE?
CHEESE!
MEL'S IN BOSTON TOO, FOCUSING ON HIS STUDIES.
HE'LL BE GETTING HIS HIGH SCHOOL DIPLOMA NEXT YEAR.

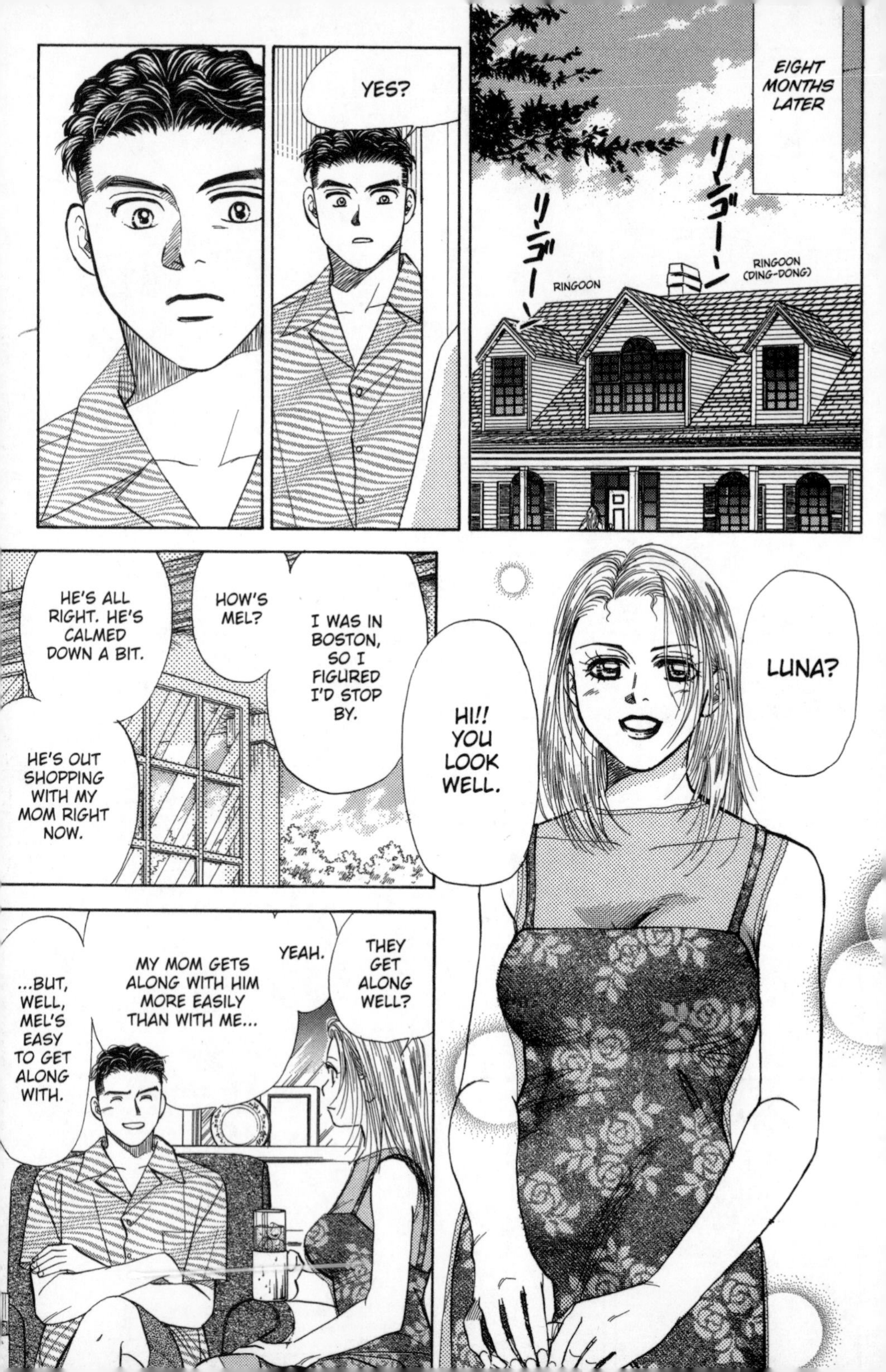
EIGHT MONTHS LATER
RINGOON (DING-DONG)
RINGOON
YES?
LUNA?
HI!! YOU LOOK WELL.
I WAS IN BOSTON, SO I FIGURED I'D STOP BY.
HOW'S MEL?
HE'S ALL RIGHT. HE'S CALMED DOWN A BIT.
HE'S OUT SHOPPING WITH MY MOM RIGHT NOW.
THEY GET ALONG WELL?
YEAH.
MY MOM GETS ALONG WITH HIM MORE EASILY THAN WITH ME...
...BUT, WELL, MEL'S EASY TO GET ALONG WITH.

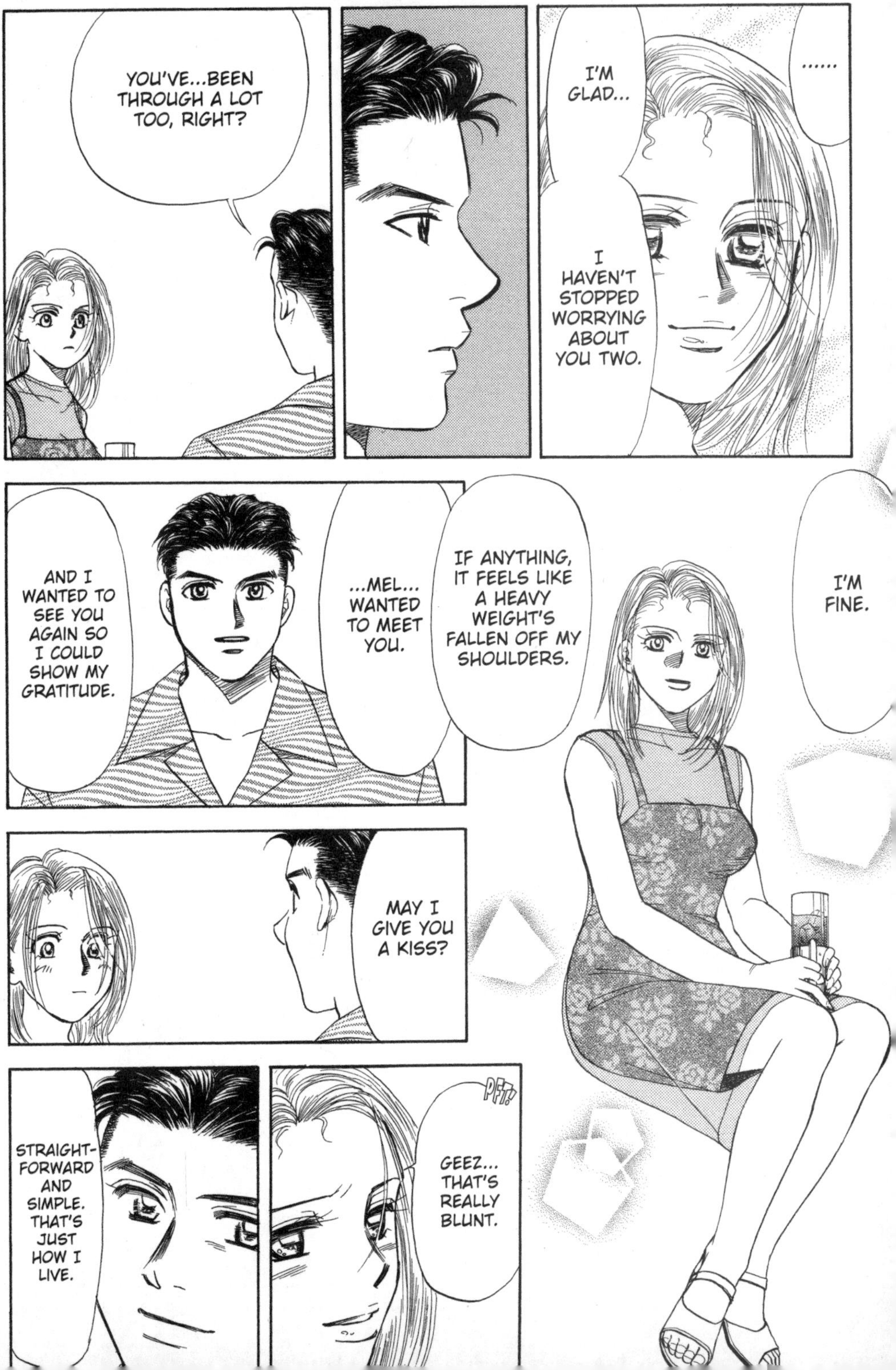
......
I'M GLAD...
I HAVEN'T STOPPED WORRYING ABOUT YOU TWO.
YOU'VE...BEEN THROUGH A LOT TOO, RIGHT?
I'M FINE.
IF ANYTHING, IT FEELS LIKE A HEAVY WEIGHT'S FALLEN OFF MY SHOULDERS.
...MEL... WANTED TO MEET YOU.
AND I WANTED TO SEE YOU AGAIN SO I COULD SHOW MY GRATITUDE.
MAY I GIVE YOU A KISS?
PFT!
GEEZ... THAT'S REALLY BLUNT.
STRAIGHT-FORWARD AND SIMPLE. THAT'S JUST HOW I LIVE.

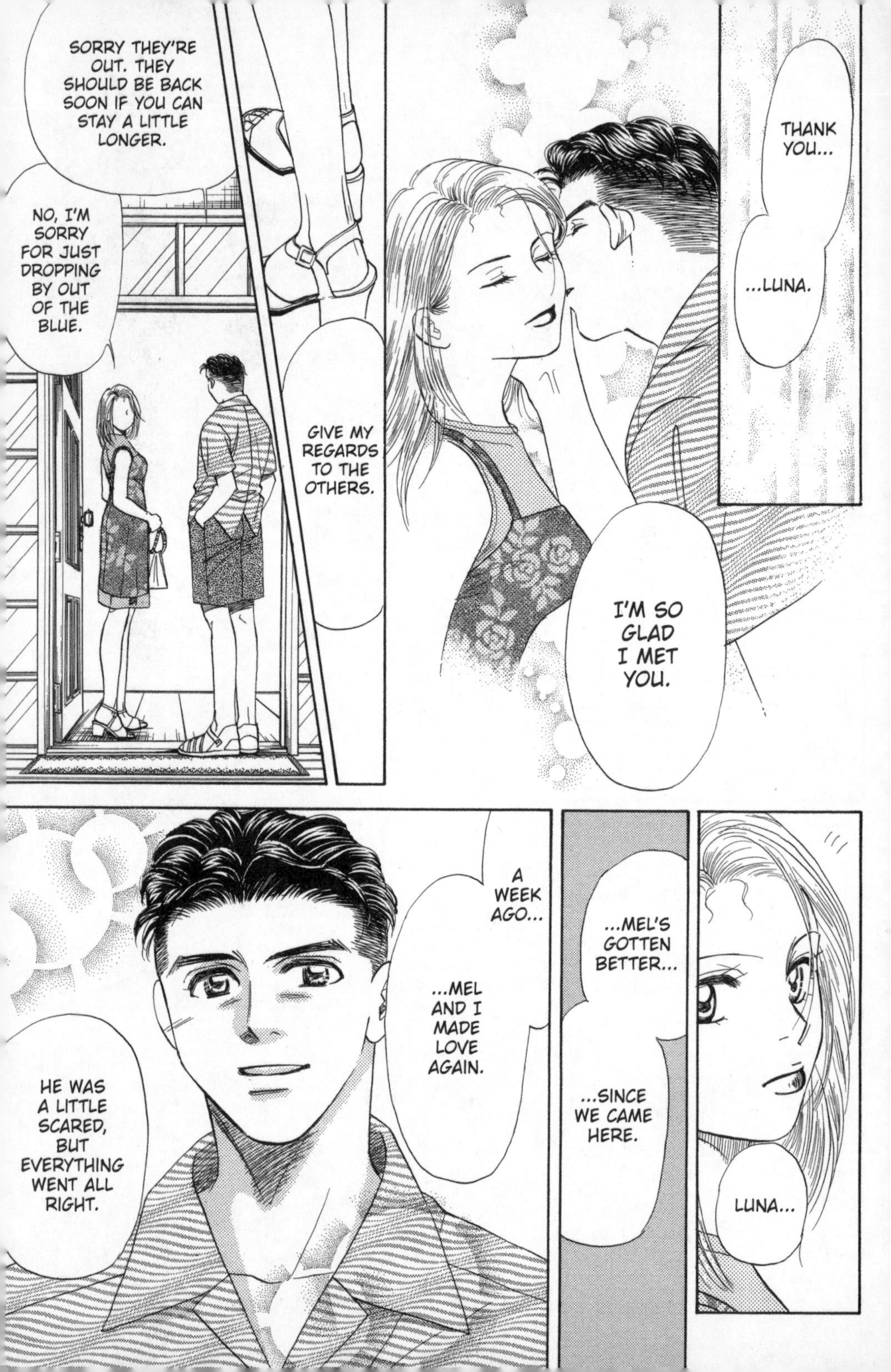
THANK YOU...
...LUNA.
I'M SO GLAD I MET YOU.
GIVE MY REGARDS TO THE OTHERS.
SORRY THEY'RE OUT. THEY SHOULD BE BACK SOON IF YOU CAN STAY A LITTLE LONGER.
NO, I'M SORRY FOR JUST DROPPING BY OUT OF THE BLUE.
LUNA...
...MEL'S GOTTEN BETTER...
...SINCE WE CAME HERE.
A WEEK AGO...
...MEL AND I MADE LOVE AGAIN.
HE WAS A LITTLE SCARED, BUT EVERYTHING WENT ALL RIGHT.

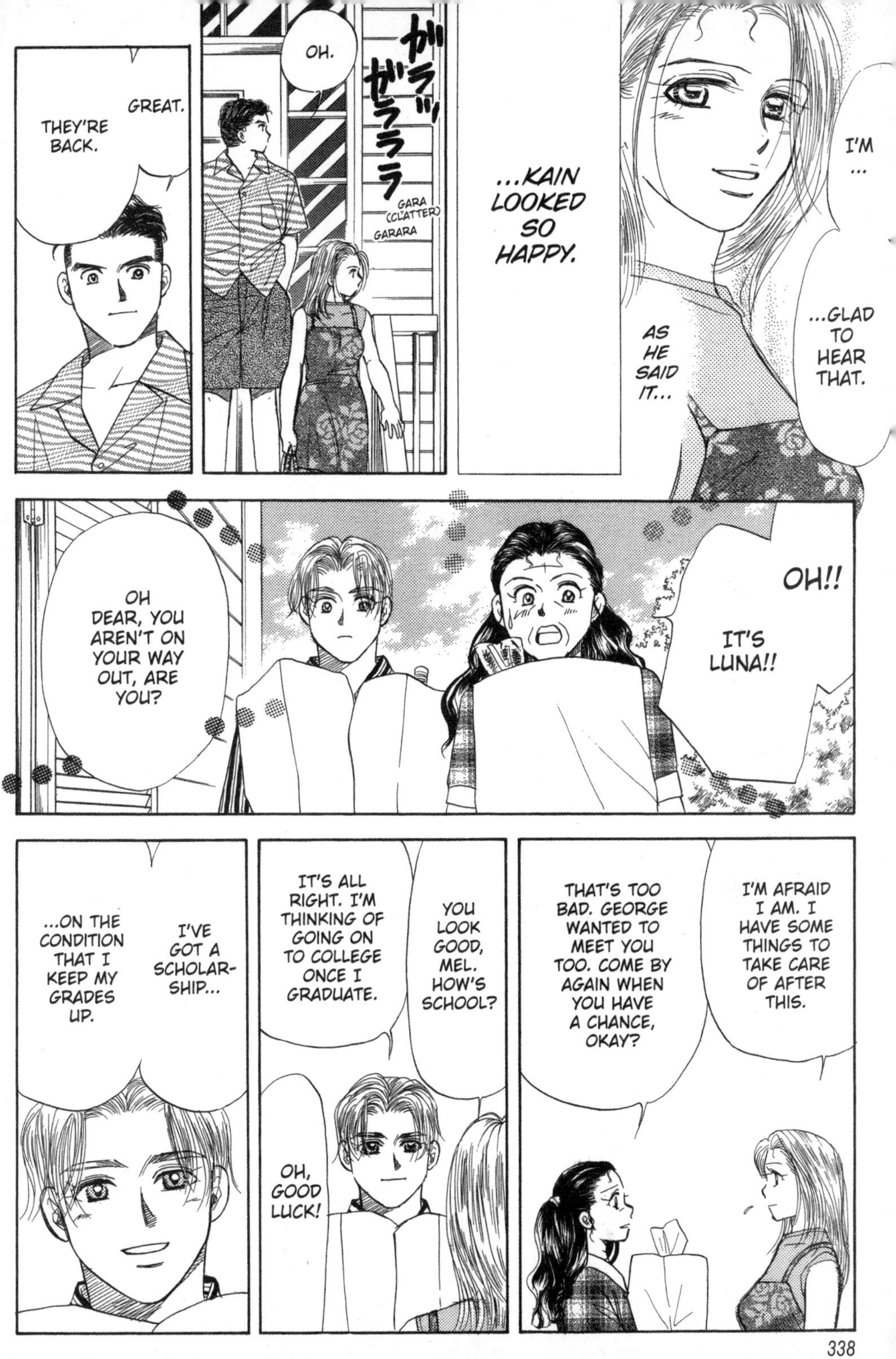
I'M ...
...GLAD TO HEAR THAT.
AS HE SAID IT...
...KAIN LOOKED SO HAPPY.
ガラッ ガララ
GARA (CLATTER) GARARA
OH.
GREAT.
THEY'RE BACK.
OH!!
IT'S LUNA!!
OH DEAR, YOU AREN'T ON YOUR WAY OUT, ARE YOU?
I'M AFRAID I AM. I HAVE SOME THINGS TO TAKE CARE OF AFTER THIS.
THAT'S TOO BAD. GEORGE WANTED TO MEET YOU TOO. COME BY AGAIN WHEN YOU HAVE A CHANCE, OKAY?
YOU LOOK GOOD, MEL. HOW'S SCHOOL?
IT'S ALL RIGHT. I'M THINKING OF GOING ON TO COLLEGE ONCE I GRADUATE.
OH, GOOD LUCK!
I'VE GOT A SCHOLAR-SHIP...
...ON THE CONDITION THAT I KEEP MY GRADES UP.

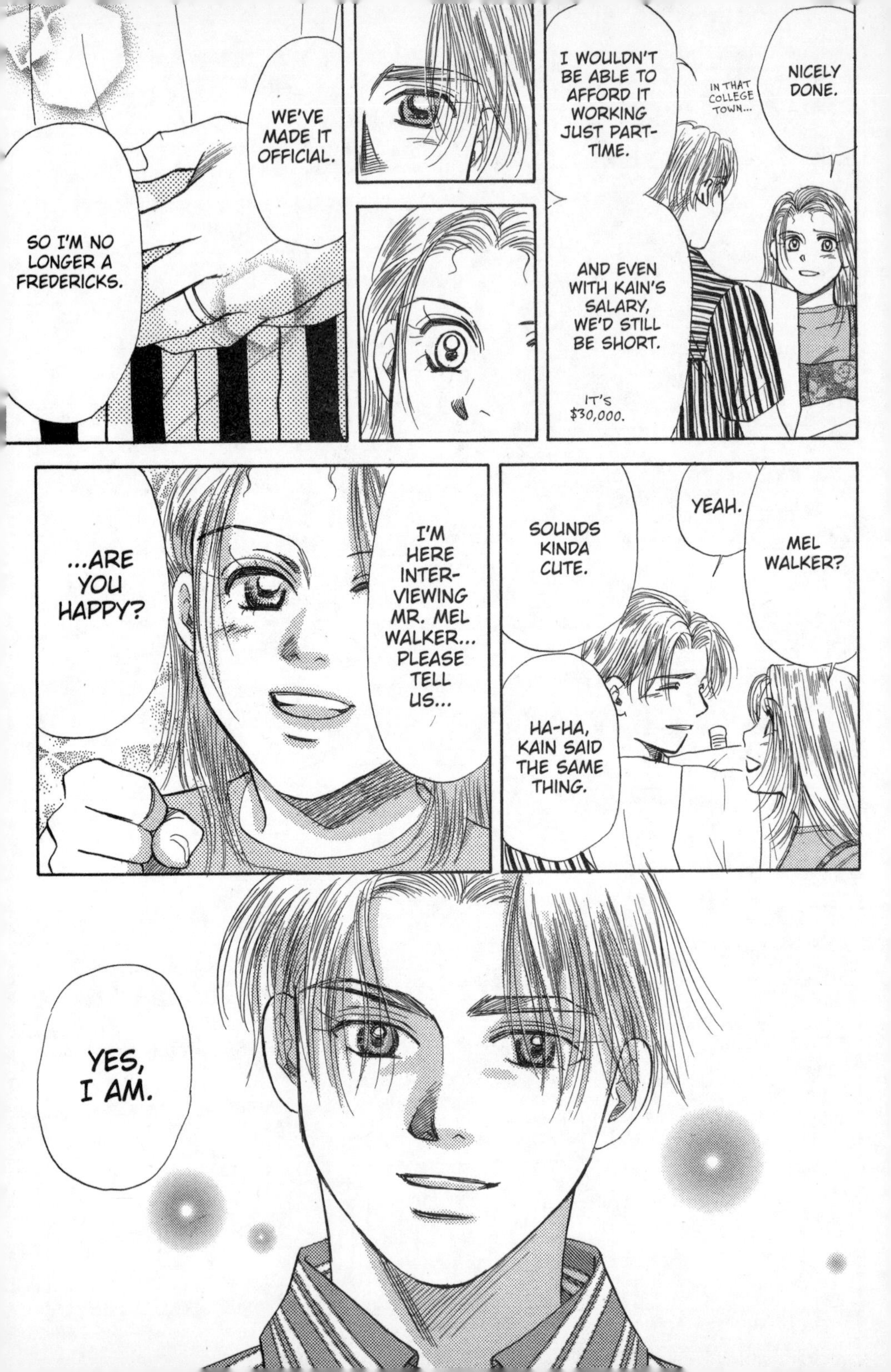
NICELY DONE.
IN THAT COLLEGE TOWN...
I WOULDN'T BE ABLE TO AFFORD IT WORKING JUST PART-TIME.
AND EVEN WITH KAIN'S SALARY, WE'D STILL BE SHORT.
IT'S $30,000.
WE'VE MADE IT OFFICIAL.
SO I'M NO LONGER A FREDERICKS.
MEL WALKER?
YEAH.
SOUNDS KINDA CUTE.
HA-HA, KAIN SAID THE SAME THING.
I'M HERE INTERVIEWING MR. MEL WALKER... PLEASE TELL US...
...ARE YOU HAPPY?
YES, I AM.

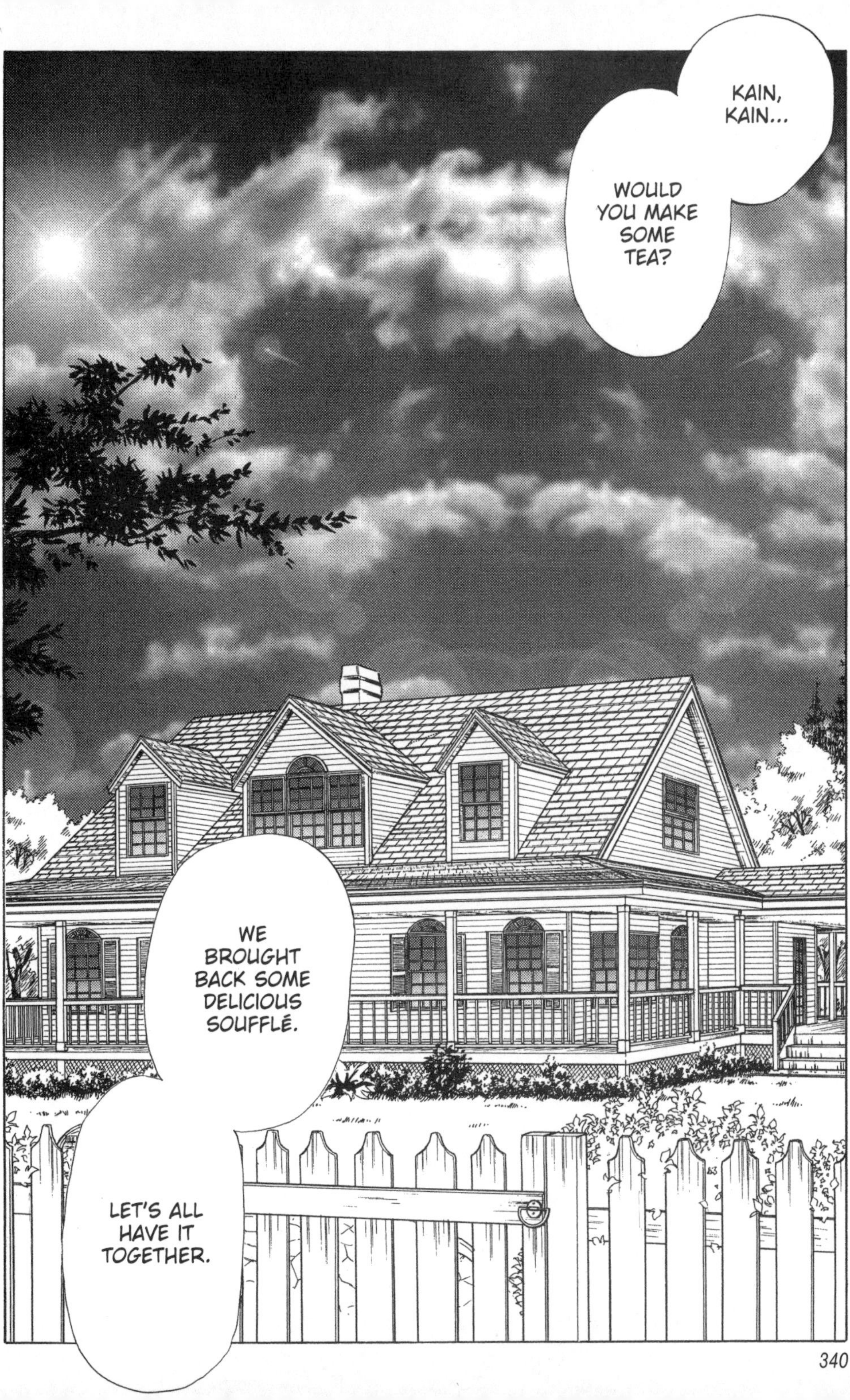
KAIN, KAIN...
WOULD YOU MAKE SOME TEA?
WE BROUGHT BACK SOME DELICIOUS SOUFFLÉ.
LET'S ALL HAVE IT TOGETHER.

EPISODE V

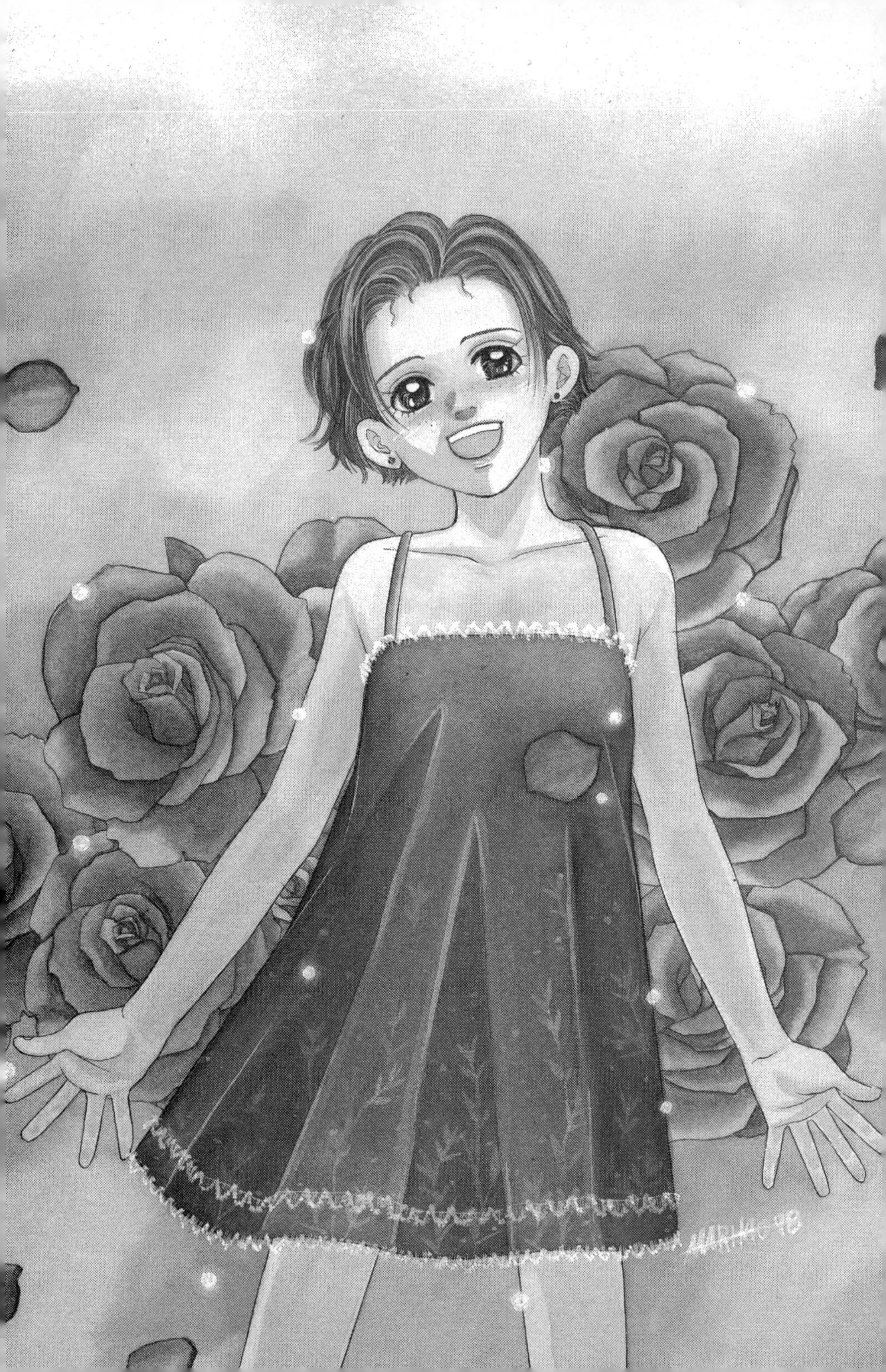

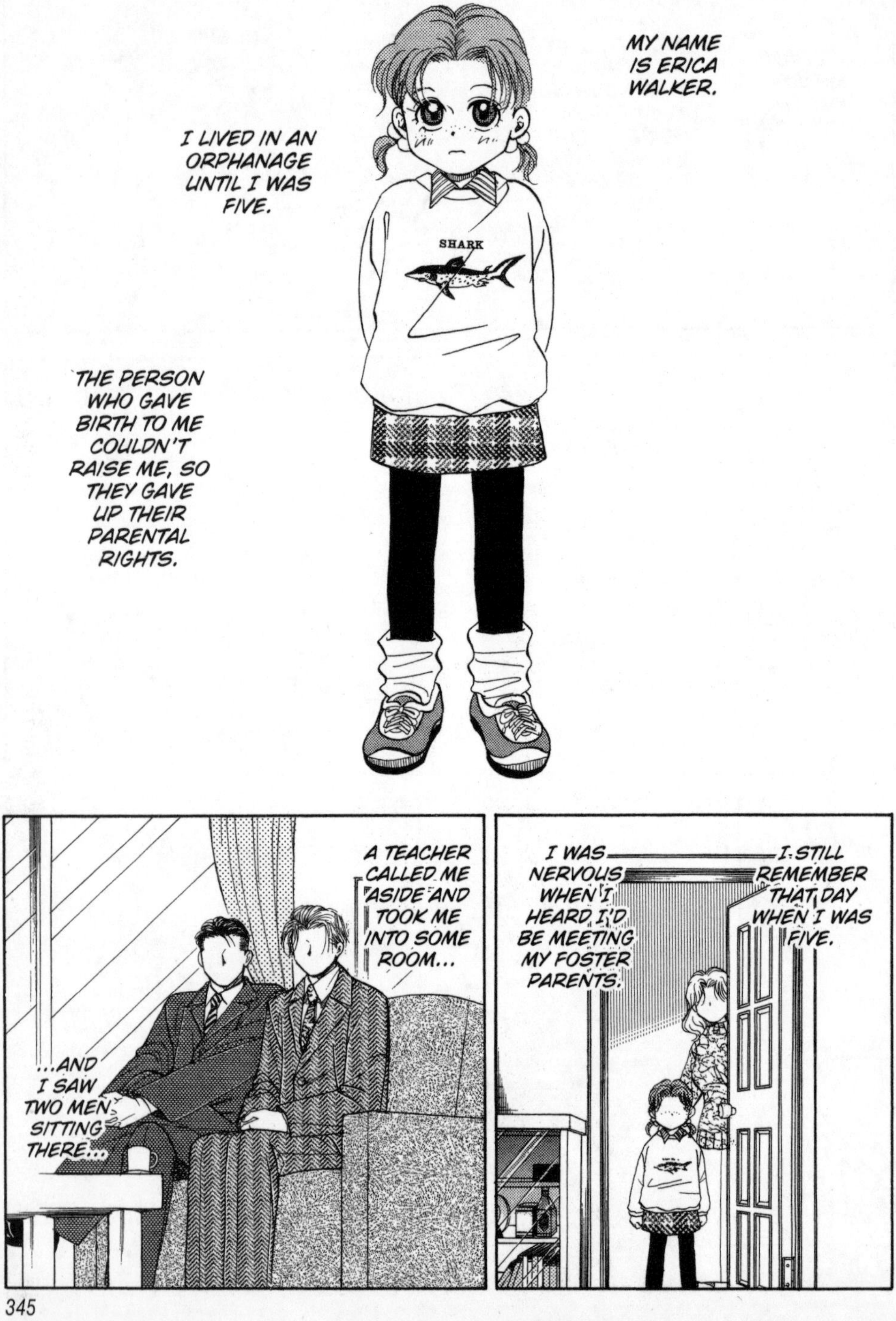
MY NAME IS ERICA WALKER.
I LIVED IN AN ORPHANAGE UNTIL I WAS FIVE.
THE PERSON WHO GAVE BIRTH TO ME COULDN'T RAISE ME, SO THEY GAVE UP THEIR PARENTAL RIGHTS.
I STILL REMEMBER THAT DAY WHEN I WAS FIVE.
I WAS NERVOUS WHEN I HEARD I'D BE MEETING MY FOSTER PARENTS.
A TEACHER CALLED ME ASIDE AND TOOK ME INTO SOME ROOM...
...AND I SAW TWO MEN SITTING THERE...
SHARK

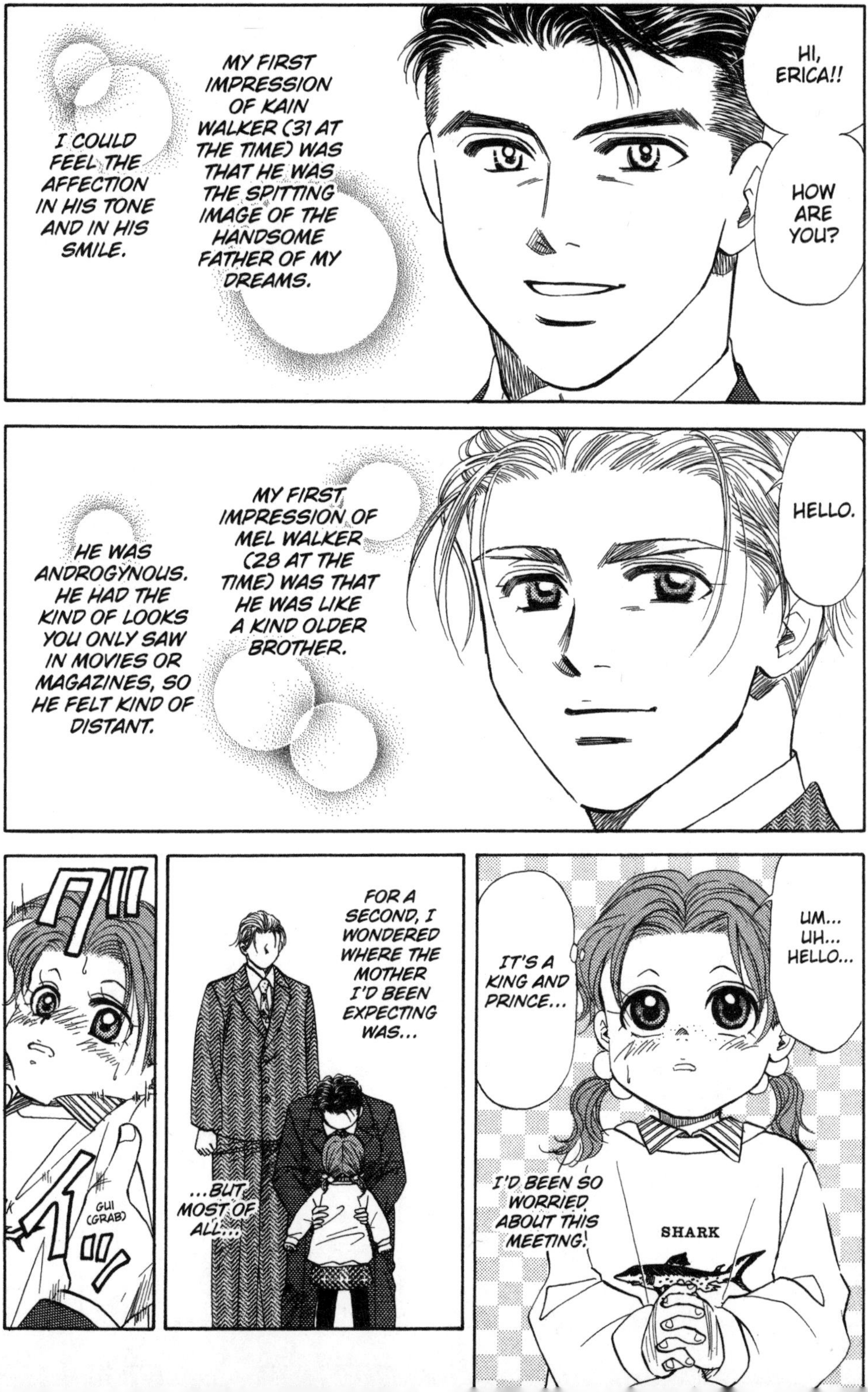
HI, ERICA!!
HOW ARE YOU?
MY FIRST IMPRESSION OF KAIN WALKER (31 AT THE TIME) WAS THAT HE WAS THE SPITTING IMAGE OF THE HANDSOME FATHER OF MY DREAMS.
I COULD FEEL THE AFFECTION IN HIS TONE AND IN HIS SMILE.
HELLO.
MY FIRST IMPRESSION OF MEL WALKER (28 AT THE TIME) WAS THAT HE WAS LIKE A KIND OLDER BROTHER.
HE WAS ANDROGYNOUS. HE HAD THE KIND OF LOOKS YOU ONLY SAW IN MOVIES OR MAGAZINES, SO HE FELT KIND OF DISTANT.
UM... UH... HELLO...
IT'S A KING AND PRINCE...
I'D BEEN SO WORRIED ABOUT THIS MEETING!
SHARK
FOR A SECOND, I WONDERED WHERE THE MOTHER I'D BEEN EXPECTING WAS...
...BUT MOST OF ALL...
GUI (GRAB)

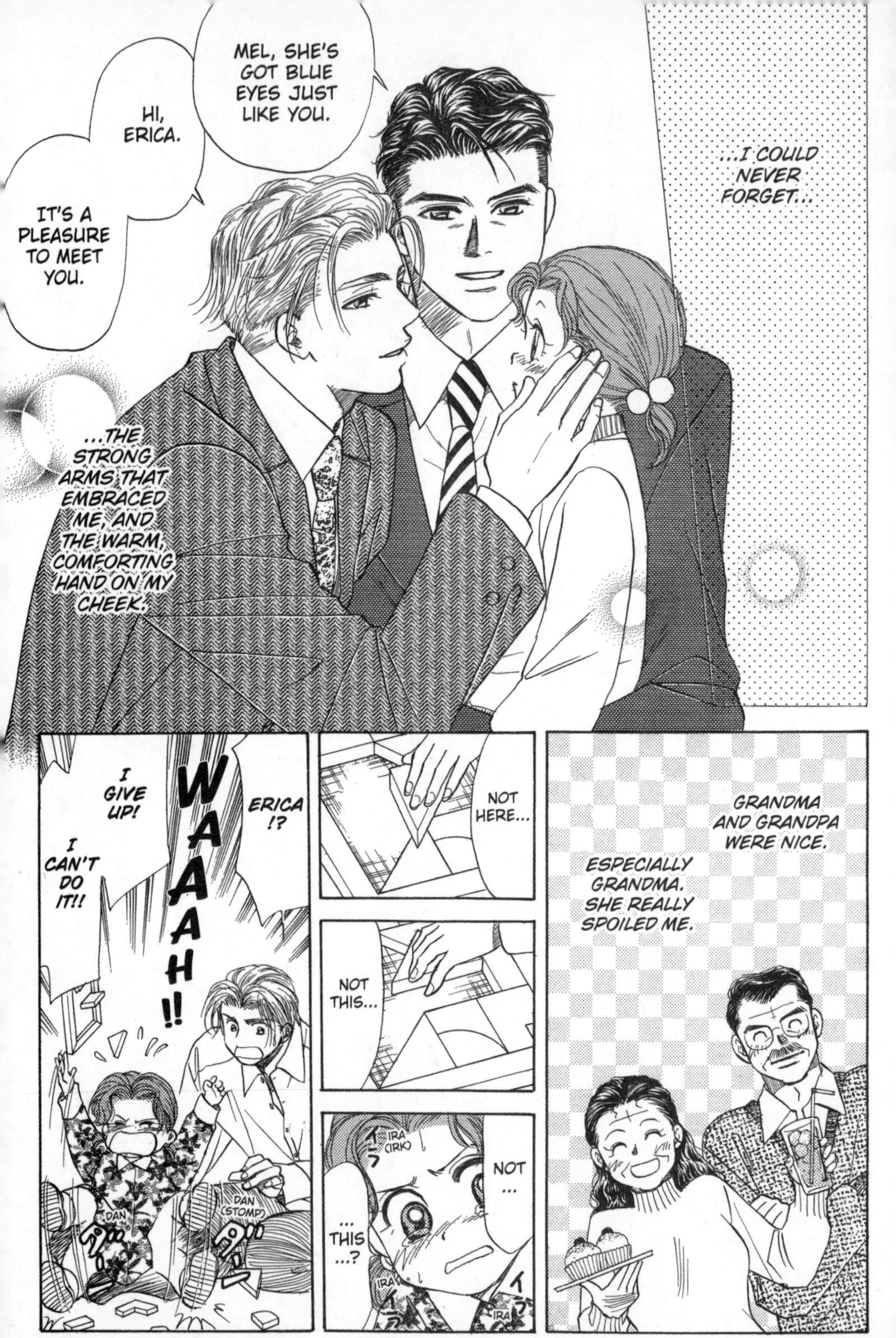
...I COULD NEVER FORGET...
MEL, SHE'S GOT BLUE EYES JUST LIKE YOU.
HI, ERICA.
IT'S A PLEASURE TO MEET YOU.
...THE STRONG ARMS THAT EMBRACED ME, AND THE WARM, COMFORTING HAND ON MY CHEEK.
GRANDMA AND GRANDPA WERE NICE.
ESPECIALLY GRANDMA. SHE REALLY SPOILED ME.
NOT HERE...
NOT THIS...
IRA (IRK)
NOT ...
... THIS ...?
IRA
IRA
ERICA !?
WAAAAH!!
I GIVE UP!
I CAN'T DO IT!!
DAN (STOMP)
DAN

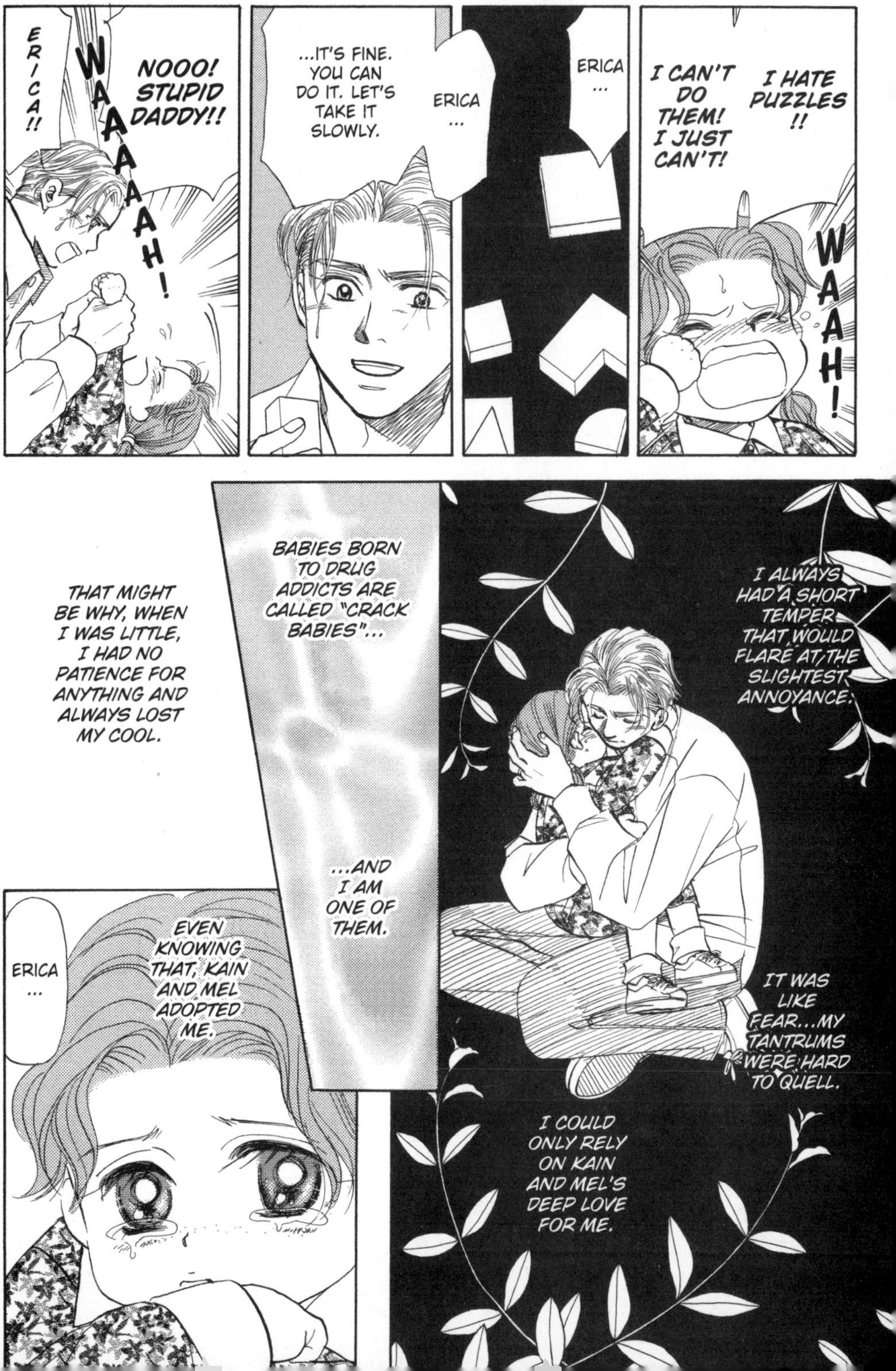
I HATE PUZZLES!!
I CAN'T DO THEM! I JUST CAN'T!
WAAH!
ERICA...
ERICA...
...IT'S FINE. YOU CAN DO IT. LET'S TAKE IT SLOWLY.
NOOO! STUPID DADDY!!
WAAAAAH!
ERICA!!
I ALWAYS HAD A SHORT TEMPER THAT WOULD FLARE AT THE SLIGHTEST ANNOYANCE.
IT WAS LIKE FEAR...MY TANTRUMS WERE HARD TO QUELL.
I COULD ONLY RELY ON KAIN AND MEL'S DEEP LOVE FOR ME.
BABIES BORN TO DRUG ADDICTS ARE CALLED "CRACK BABIES"...
...AND I AM ONE OF THEM.
THAT MIGHT BE WHY, WHEN I WAS LITTLE, I HAD NO PATIENCE FOR ANYTHING AND ALWAYS LOST MY COOL.
EVEN KNOWING THAT, KAIN AND MEL ADOPTED ME.
ERICA...

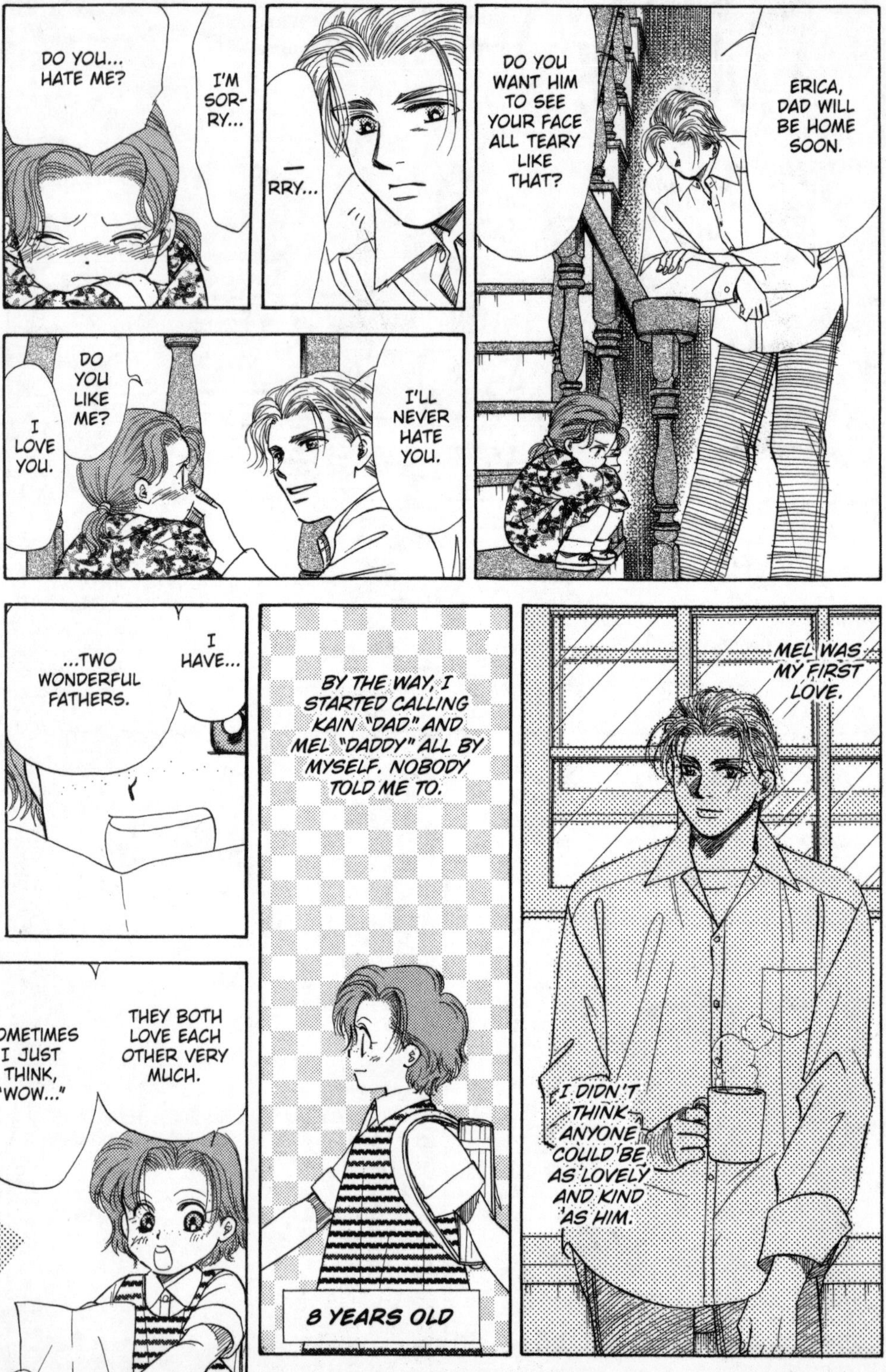
ERICA, DAD WILL BE HOME SOON.
DO YOU WANT HIM TO SEE YOUR FACE ALL TEARY LIKE THAT?
—RRY...
I'M SORRY...
DO YOU... HATE ME?
I'LL NEVER HATE YOU.
DO YOU LIKE ME?
I LOVE YOU.
MEL WAS MY FIRST LOVE.
I DIDN'T THINK ANYONE COULD BE AS LOVELY AND KIND AS HIM.
BY THE WAY, I STARTED CALLING KAIN "DAD" AND MEL "DADDY" ALL BY MYSELF. NOBODY TOLD ME TO.
8 YEARS OLD
I HAVE...
...TWO WONDERFUL FATHERS.
THEY BOTH LOVE EACH OTHER VERY MUCH.
SOMETIMES I JUST THINK, "WOW..."

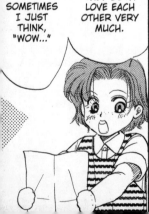

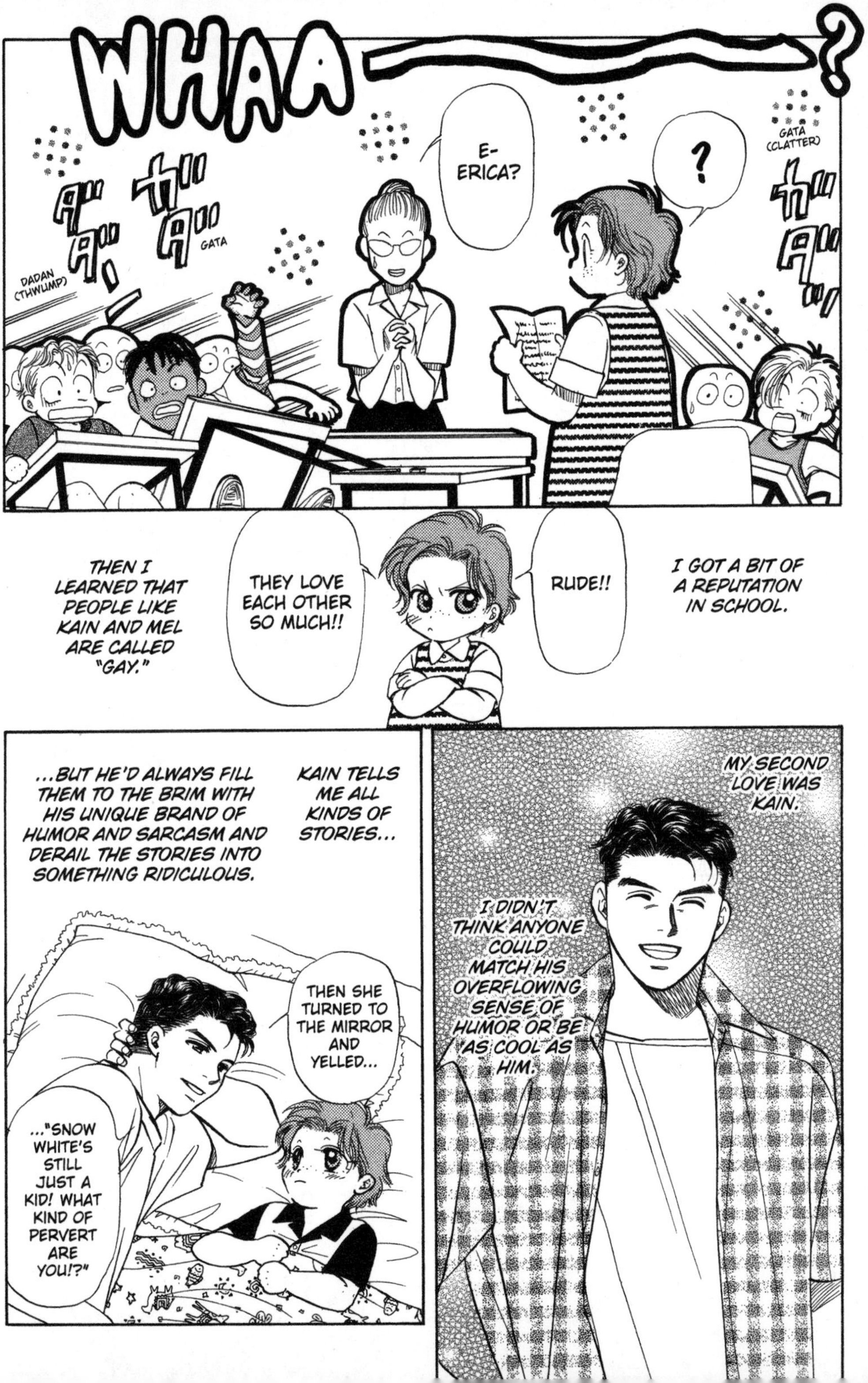
WHAA—?
GATA (CLATTER)
?
E- ERICA?
GATA
DADAN (THWUMP)
I GOT A BIT OF A REPUTATION IN SCHOOL.
RUDE!!
THEY LOVE EACH OTHER SO MUCH!!
THEN I LEARNED THAT PEOPLE LIKE KAIN AND MEL ARE CALLED "GAY."
MY SECOND LOVE WAS KAIN.
I DIDN'T THINK ANYONE COULD MATCH HIS OVERFLOWING SENSE OF HUMOR OR BE AS COOL AS HIM.
KAIN TELLS ME ALL KINDS OF STORIES...
...BUT HE'D ALWAYS FILL THEM TO THE BRIM WITH HIS UNIQUE BRAND OF HUMOR AND SARCASM AND DERAIL THE STORIES INTO SOMETHING RIDICULOUS.
THEN SHE TURNED TO THE MIRROR AND YELLED...
..."SNOW WHITE'S STILL JUST A KID! WHAT KIND OF PERVERT ARE YOU!?"

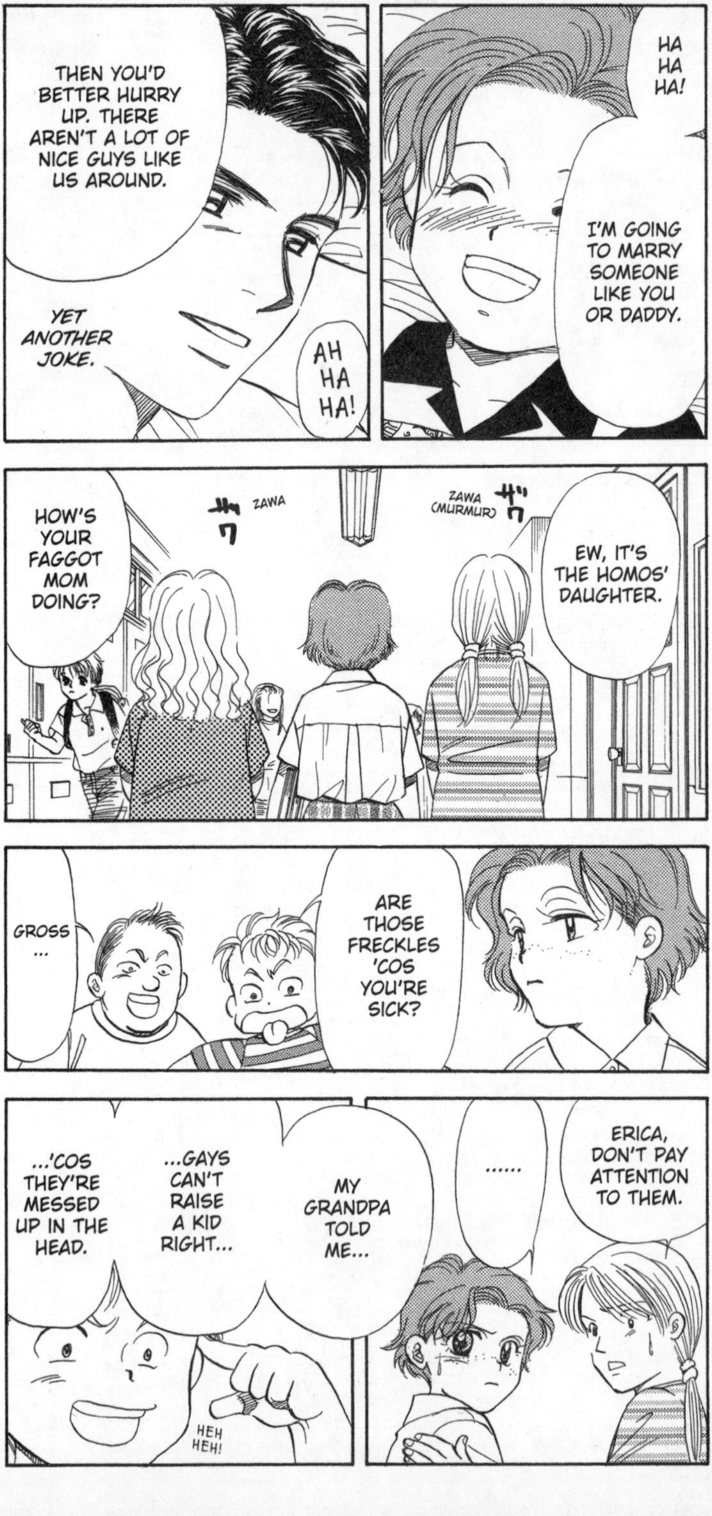
HA HA HA!
I'M GOING TO MARRY SOMEONE LIKE YOU OR DADDY.
THEN YOU'D BETTER HURRY UP. THERE AREN'T A LOT OF NICE GUYS LIKE US AROUND.
AH HA HA!
YET ANOTHER JOKE.
EW, IT'S THE HOMOS' DAUGHTER.
ザワ ZAWA (MURMUR)
ザワ ZAWA
HOW'S YOUR FAGGOT MOM DOING?
ARE THOSE FRECKLES 'COS YOU'RE SICK?
GROSS ...
ERICA, DON'T PAY ATTENTION TO THEM.
......
MY GRANDPA TOLD ME...
...GAYS CAN'T RAISE A KID RIGHT...
...'COS THEY'RE MESSED UP IN THE HEAD.
HEH HEH!

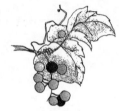

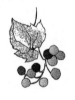

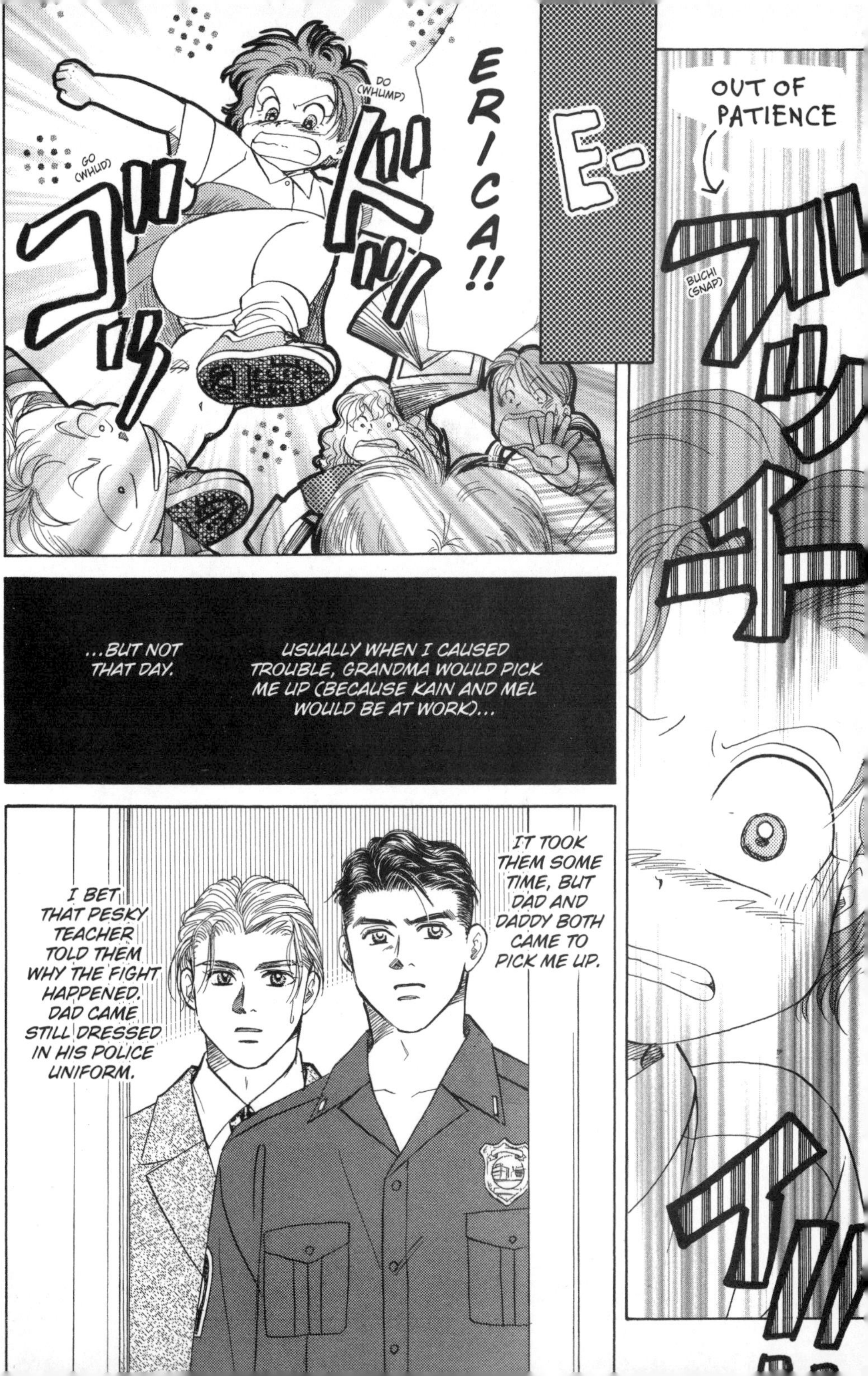
OUT OF PATIENCE
BUCHI (SNAP)
E-
DO (WHUMP)
ERICA!!
GO (WHUD)
USUALLY WHEN I CAUSED TROUBLE, GRANDMA WOULD PICK ME UP (BECAUSE KAIN AND MEL WOULD BE AT WORK)...
...BUT NOT THAT DAY.
IT TOOK THEM SOME TIME, BUT DAD AND DADDY BOTH CAME TO PICK ME UP.
I BET THAT PESKY TEACHER TOLD THEM WHY THE FIGHT HAPPENED. DAD CAME STILL DRESSED IN HIS POLICE UNIFORM.

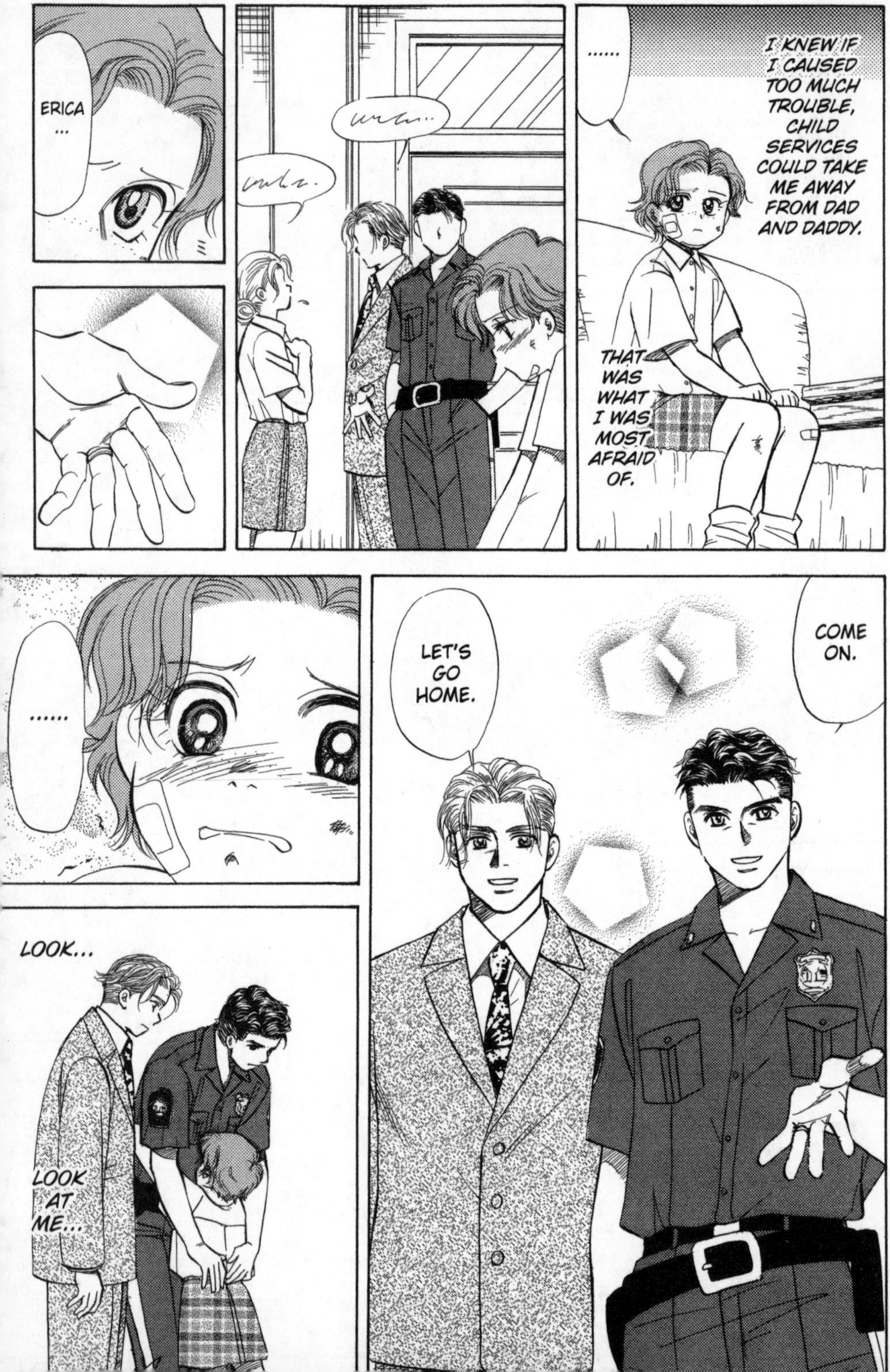
......
I KNEW IF I CAUSED TOO MUCH TROUBLE, CHILD SERVICES COULD TAKE ME AWAY FROM DAD AND DADDY.
THAT WAS WHAT I WAS MOST AFRAID OF.
ERICA ...
COME ON.
LET'S GO HOME.
......
LOOK...
LOOK AT ME...

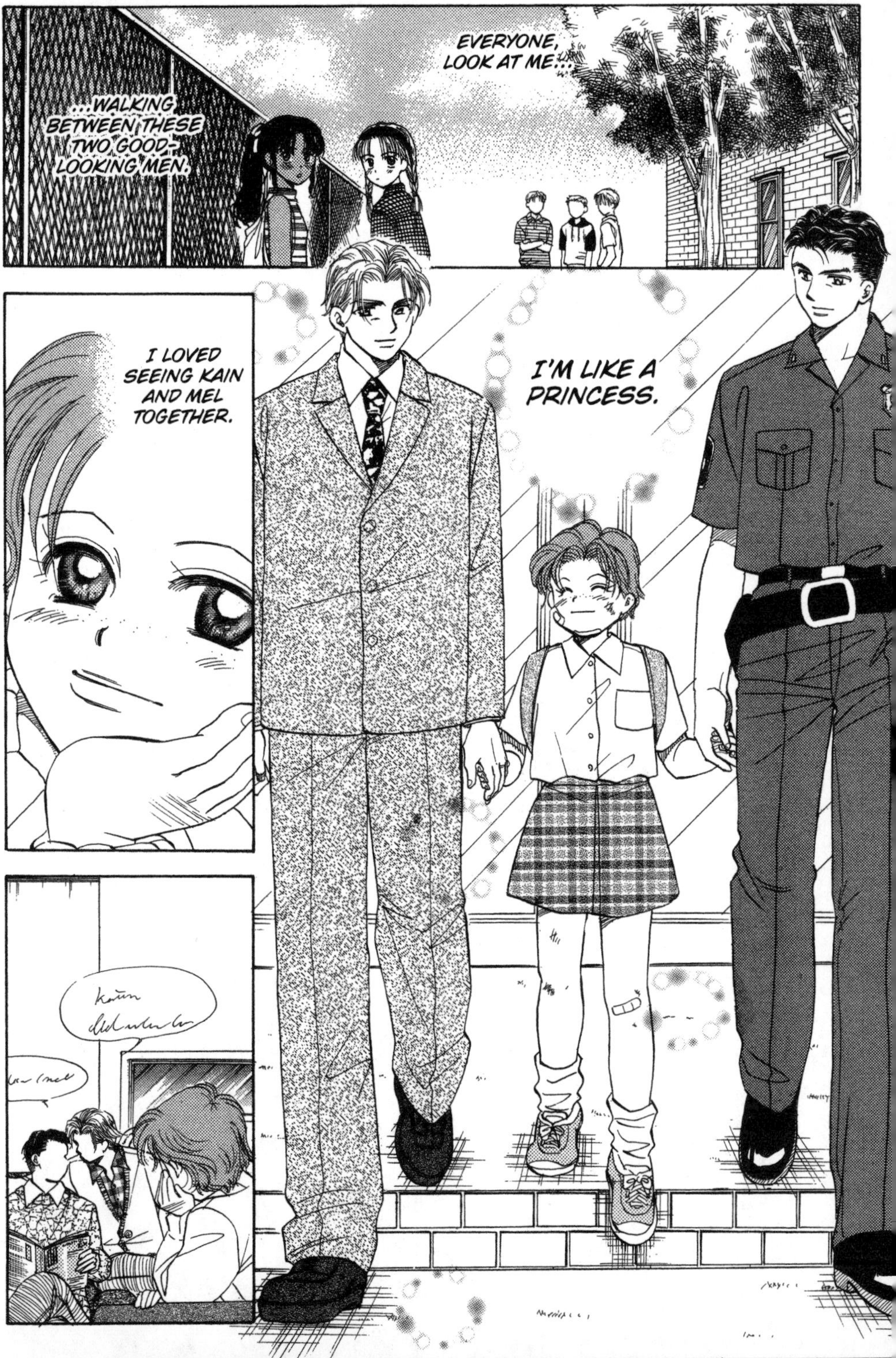
EVERYONE, LOOK AT ME...
...WALKING BETWEEN THESE TWO GOOD-LOOKING MEN.
I'M LIKE A PRINCESS.
I LOVED SEEING KAIN AND MEL TOGETHER.

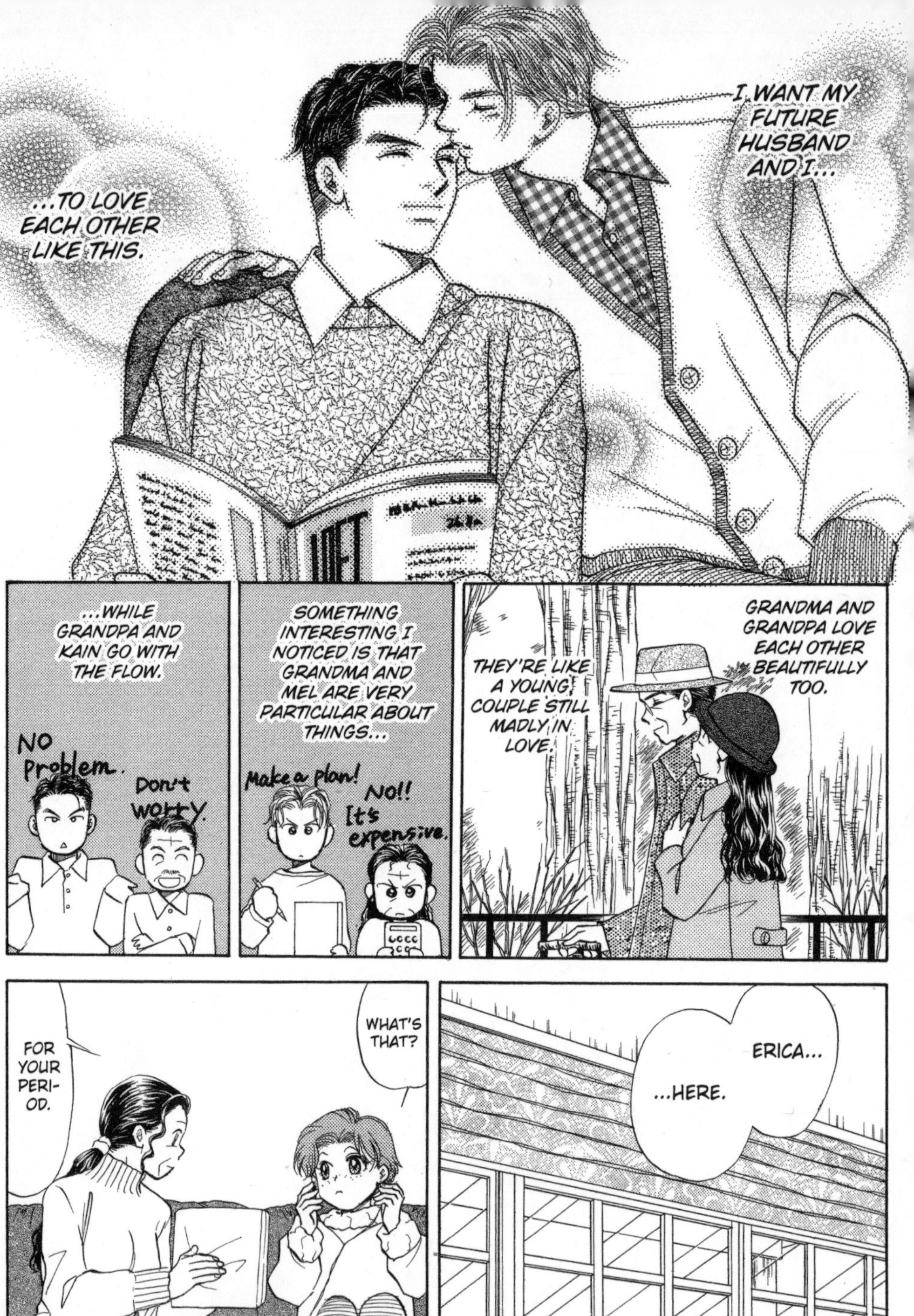
I WANT MY FUTURE HUSBAND AND I...
...TO LOVE EACH OTHER LIKE THIS.
GRANDMA AND GRANDPA LOVE EACH OTHER BEAUTIFULLY TOO.
THEY'RE LIKE A YOUNG COUPLE STILL MADLY IN LOVE.
SOMETHING INTERESTING I NOTICED IS THAT GRANDMA AND MEL ARE VERY PARTICULAR ABOUT THINGS...
Make a plan!
No!! It's expensive.
...WHILE GRANDPA AND KAIN GO WITH THE FLOW.
NO Problem.
Don't worry.
ERICA...
...HERE.
WHAT'S THAT?
FOR YOUR PERI-OD.

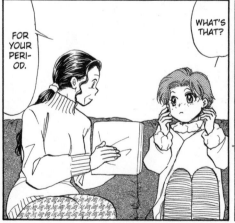

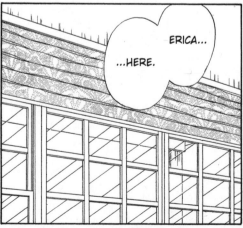

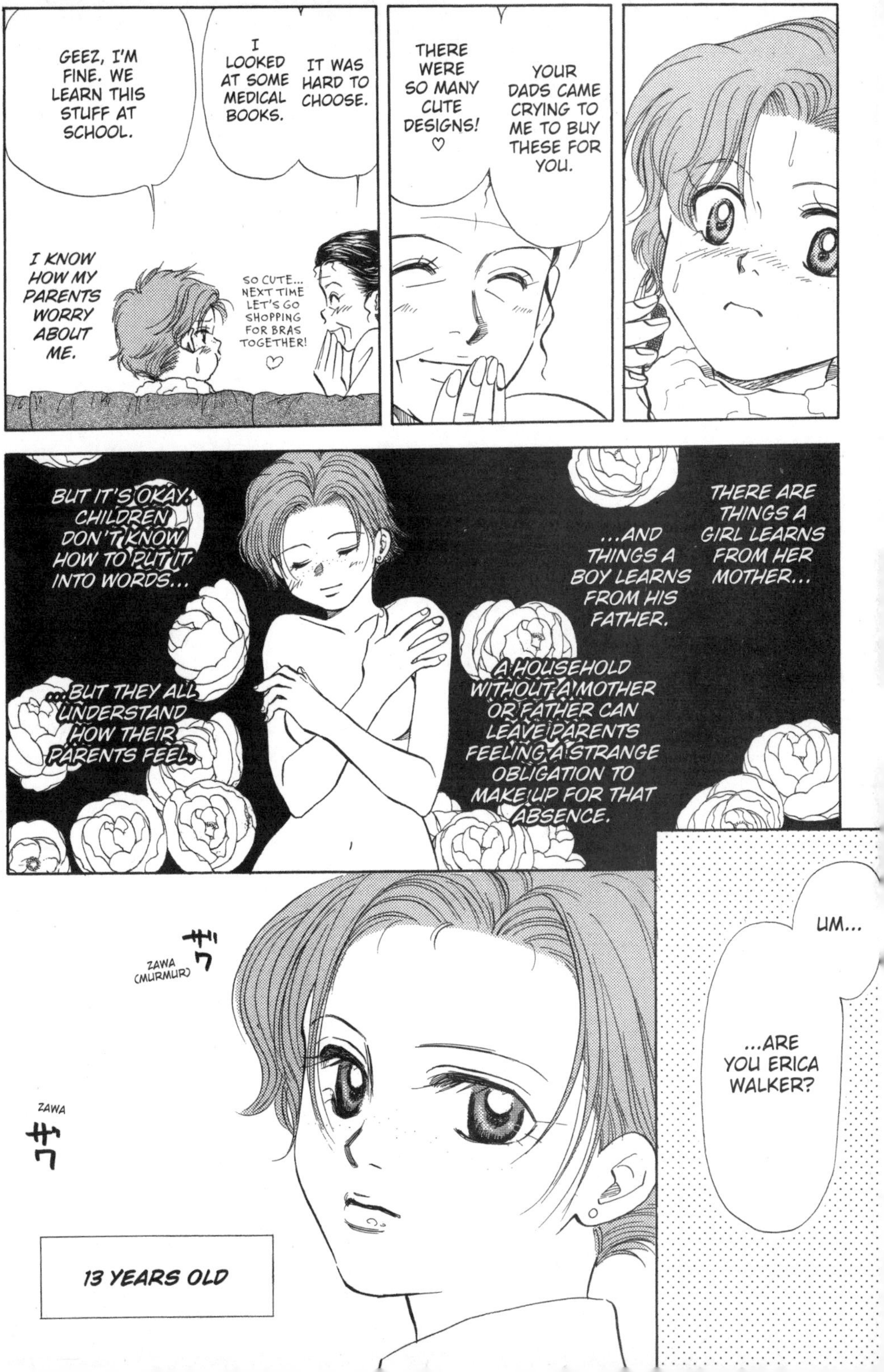
YOUR DADS CAME CRYING TO ME TO BUY THESE FOR YOU.
THERE WERE SO MANY CUTE DESIGNS! ♡
IT WAS HARD TO CHOOSE.
I LOOKED AT SOME MEDICAL BOOKS.
GEEZ, I'M FINE. WE LEARN THIS STUFF AT SCHOOL.
SO CUTE... NEXT TIME LET'S GO SHOPPING FOR BRAS TOGETHER! ♡
I KNOW HOW MY PARENTS WORRY ABOUT ME.
THERE ARE THINGS A GIRL LEARNS FROM HER MOTHER...
...AND THINGS A BOY LEARNS FROM HIS FATHER.
A HOUSEHOLD WITHOUT A MOTHER OR FATHER CAN LEAVE PARENTS FEELING A STRANGE OBLIGATION TO MAKE UP FOR THAT ABSENCE.
BUT IT'S OKAY. CHILDREN DON'T KNOW HOW TO PUT IT INTO WORDS...
...BUT THEY ALL UNDERSTAND HOW THEIR PARENTS FEEL.
UM...
...ARE YOU ERICA WALKER?
ザワ
ZAWA (MURMUR)
ザワ
ZAWA
13 YEARS OLD

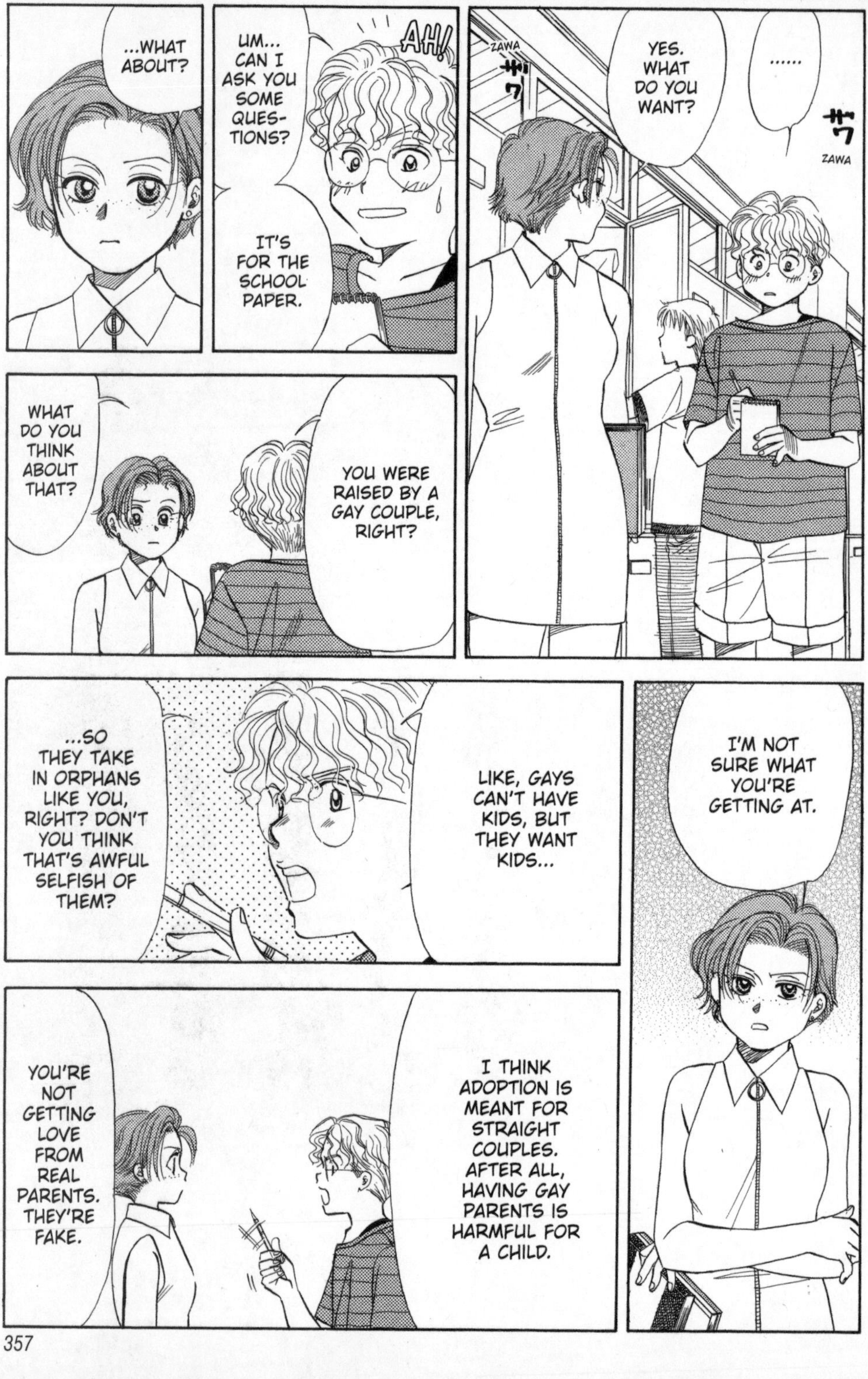
......
YES. WHAT DO YOU WANT?
ZAWA
ZAWA
AH!
UM... CAN I ASK YOU SOME QUES-TIONS?
IT'S FOR THE SCHOOL PAPER.
...WHAT ABOUT?
YOU WERE RAISED BY A GAY COUPLE, RIGHT?
WHAT DO YOU THINK ABOUT THAT?
I'M NOT SURE WHAT YOU'RE GETTING AT.
LIKE, GAYS CAN'T HAVE KIDS, BUT THEY WANT KIDS...
...SO THEY TAKE IN ORPHANS LIKE YOU, RIGHT? DON'T YOU THINK THAT'S AWFUL SELFISH OF THEM?
I THINK ADOPTION IS MEANT FOR STRAIGHT COUPLES. AFTER ALL, HAVING GAY PARENTS IS HARMFUL FOR A CHILD.
YOU'RE NOT GETTING LOVE FROM REAL PARENTS. THEY'RE FAKE.

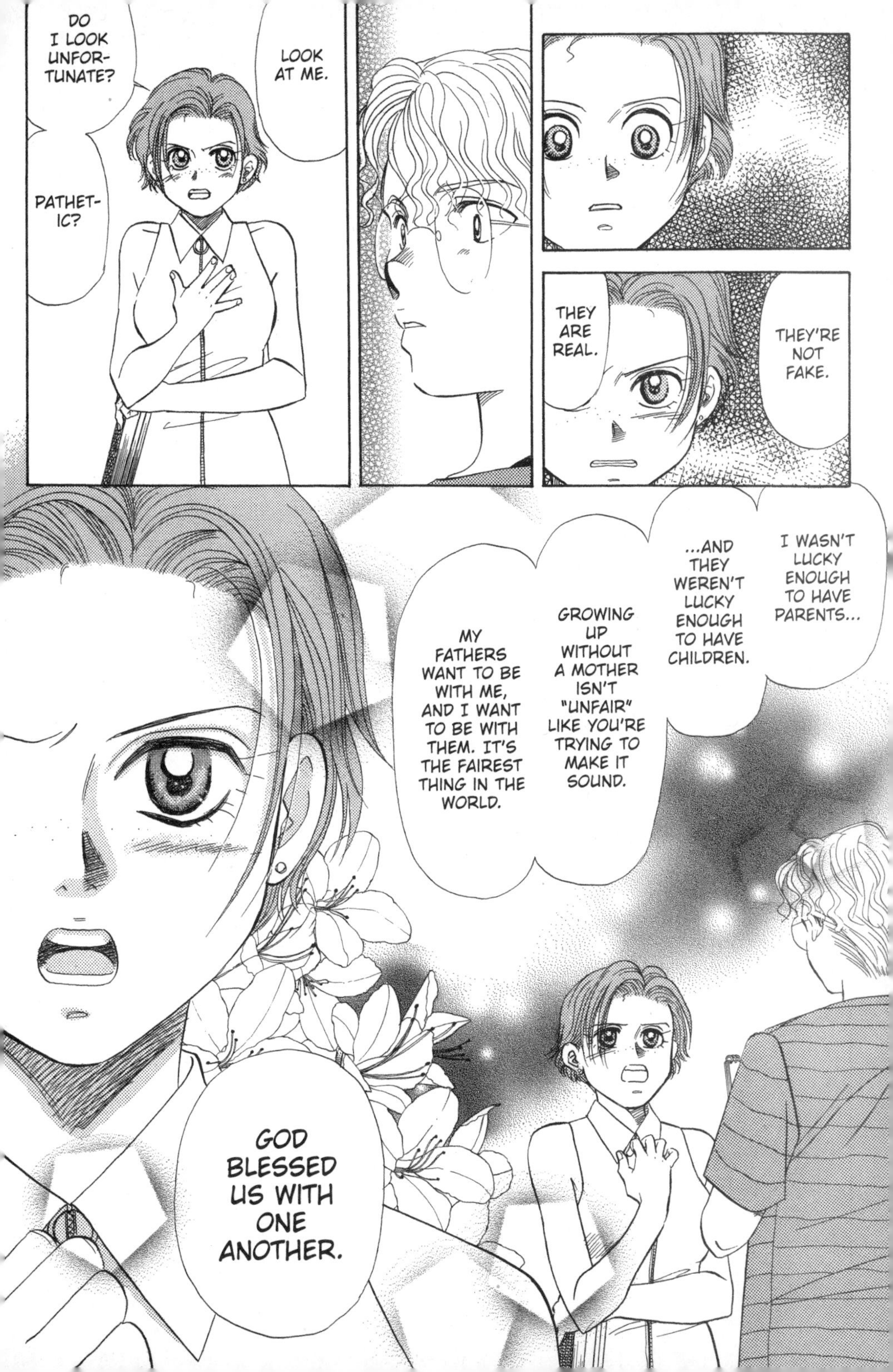
THEY'RE NOT FAKE.
THEY ARE REAL.
LOOK AT ME.
DO I LOOK UNFORTUNATE?
PATHETIC?
I WASN'T LUCKY ENOUGH TO HAVE PARENTS...
...AND THEY WEREN'T LUCKY ENOUGH TO HAVE CHILDREN.
GROWING UP WITHOUT A MOTHER ISN'T "UNFAIR" LIKE YOU'RE TRYING TO MAKE IT SOUND.
MY FATHERS WANT TO BE WITH ME, AND I WANT TO BE WITH THEM. IT'S THE FAIREST THING IN THE WORLD.
GOD BLESSED US WITH ONE ANOTHER.

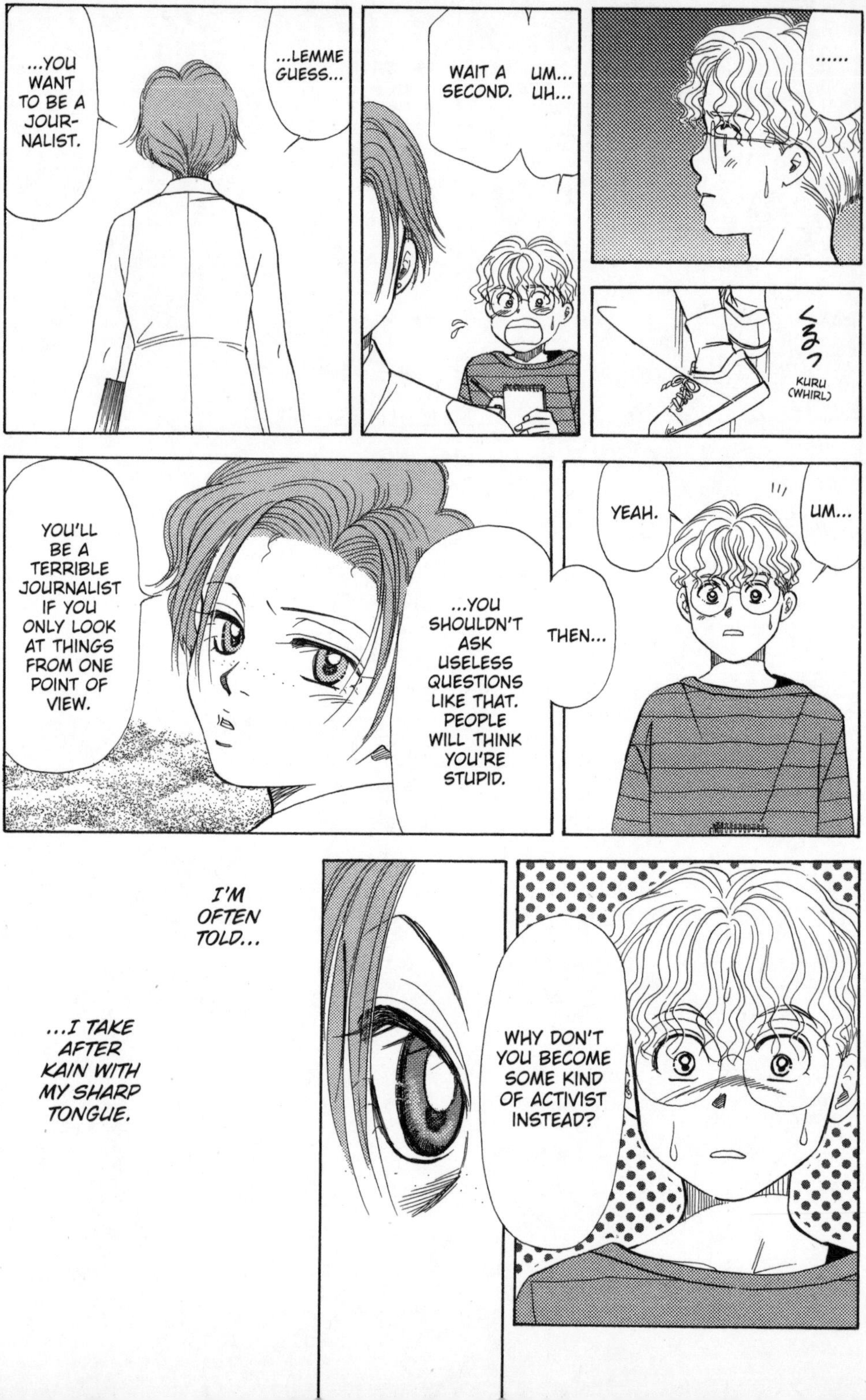
......
くるっ
KURU (WHIRL)
UM... UH...
WAIT A SECOND.
...LEMME GUESS...
...YOU WANT TO BE A JOURNALIST.
UM...
YEAH.
THEN...
...YOU SHOULDN'T ASK USELESS QUESTIONS LIKE THAT. PEOPLE WILL THINK YOU'RE STUPID.
YOU'LL BE A TERRIBLE JOURNALIST IF YOU ONLY LOOK AT THINGS FROM ONE POINT OF VIEW.
WHY DON'T YOU BECOME SOME KIND OF ACTIVIST INSTEAD?
I'M OFTEN TOLD...
...I TAKE AFTER KAIN WITH MY SHARP TONGUE.

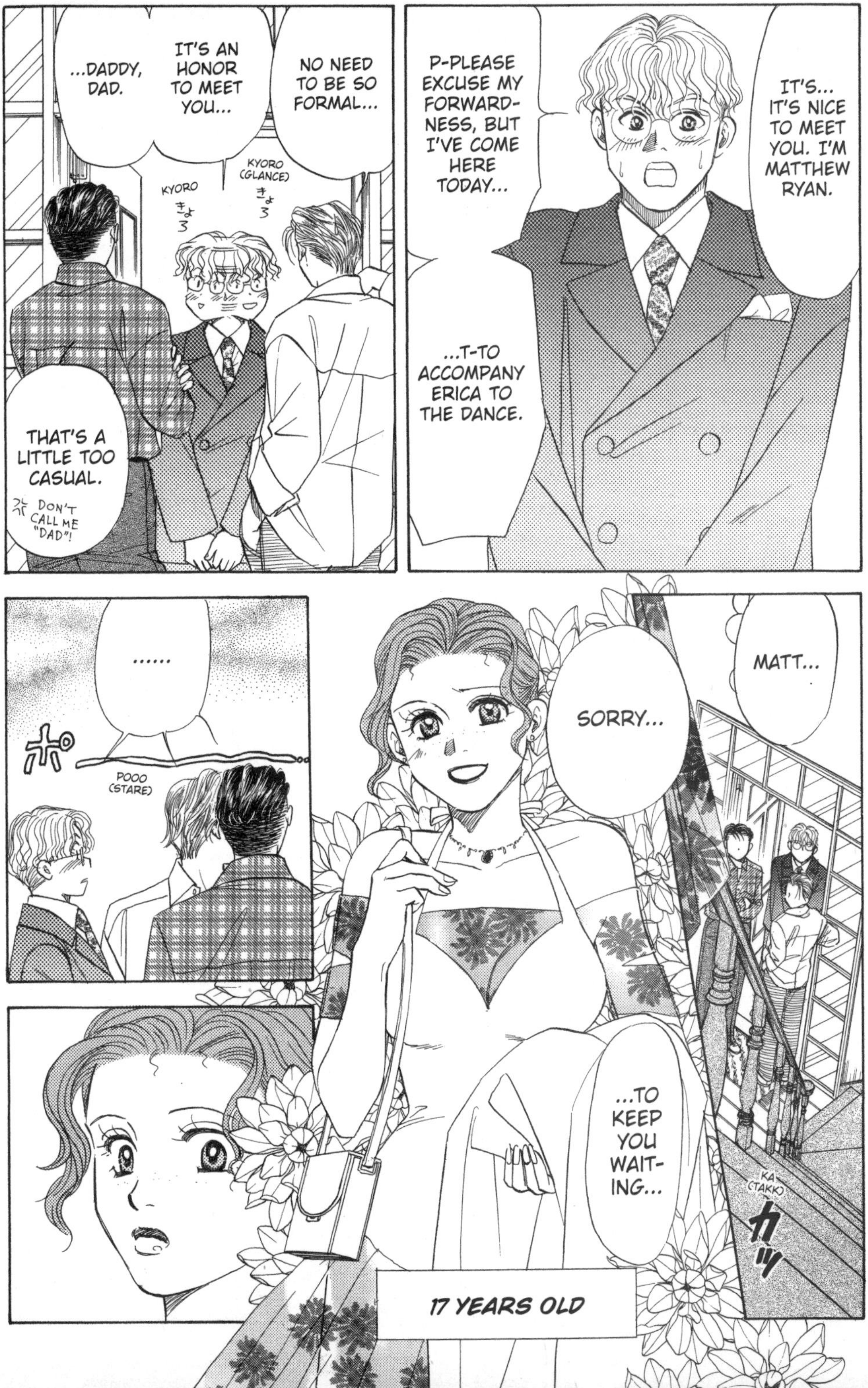
IT'S... IT'S NICE TO MEET YOU. I'M MATTHEW RYAN.
P-PLEASE EXCUSE MY FORWARDNESS, BUT I'VE COME HERE TODAY...
...T-TO ACCOMPANY ERICA TO THE DANCE.
NO NEED TO BE SO FORMAL...
IT'S AN HONOR TO MEET YOU...
...DADDY, DAD.
KYORO (GLANCE)
KYORO
THAT'S A LITTLE TOO CASUAL.
DON'T CALL ME "DAD"!
MATT...
SORRY...
...TO KEEP YOU WAITING...
KA (TAKK)
17 YEARS OLD
......
POOO (STARE)

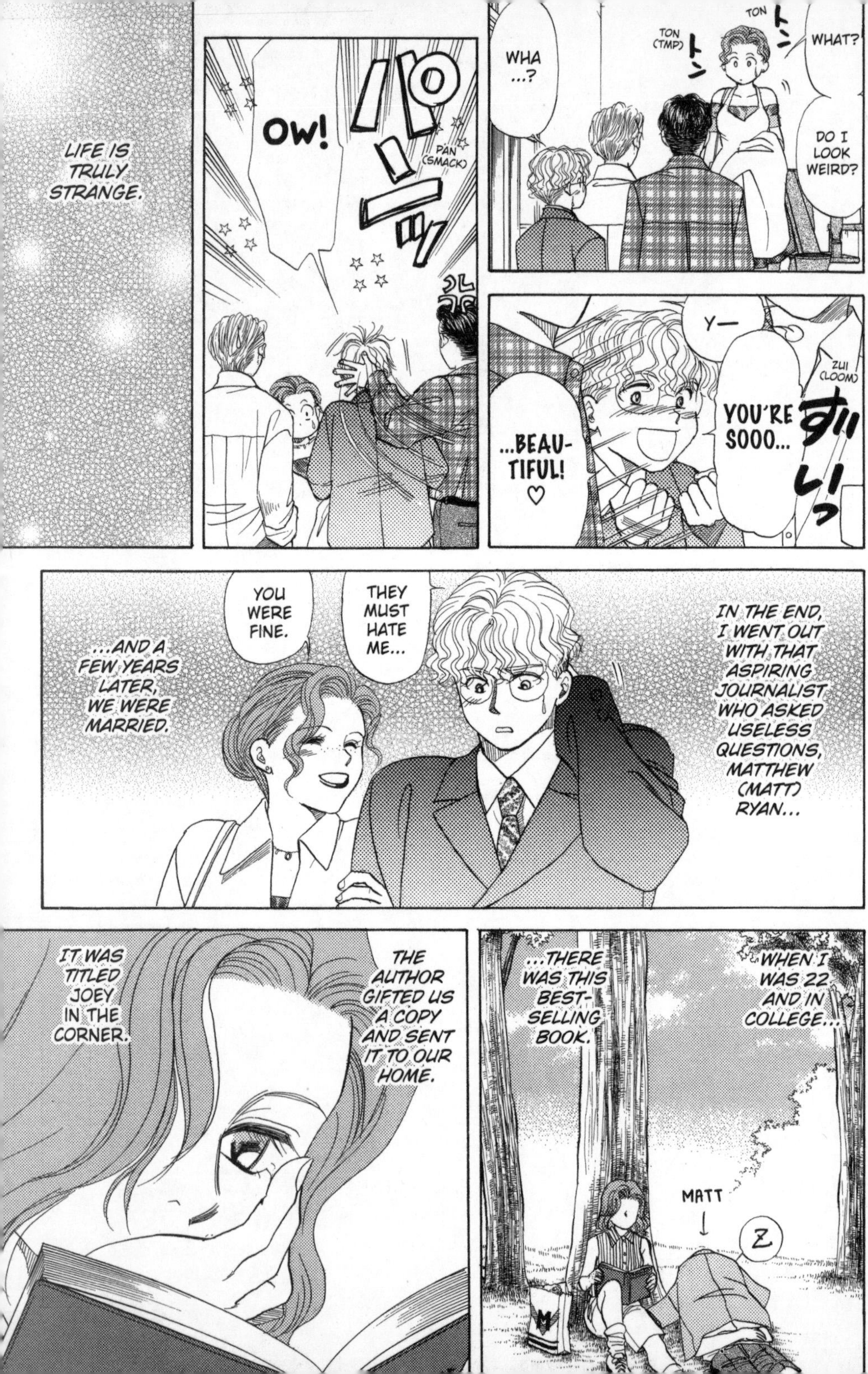
TON
WHAT?
TON (TMP)
DO I LOOK WEIRD?
WHA ...?
Y—
ZUI (LOOM)
YOU'RE SOOO...
...BEAU-TIFUL! ♡
OW!
PAN (SMACK)
LIFE IS TRULY STRANGE.
IN THE END, I WENT OUT WITH THAT ASPIRING JOURNALIST WHO ASKED USELESS QUESTIONS, MATTHEW (MATT) RYAN...
THEY MUST HATE ME...
YOU WERE FINE.
...AND A FEW YEARS LATER, WE WERE MARRIED.
WHEN I WAS 22 AND IN COLLEGE...
...THERE WAS THIS BEST-SELLING BOOK.
MATT
Z
THE AUTHOR GIFTED US A COPY AND SENT IT TO OUR HOME.
IT WAS TITLED JOEY IN THE CORNER.

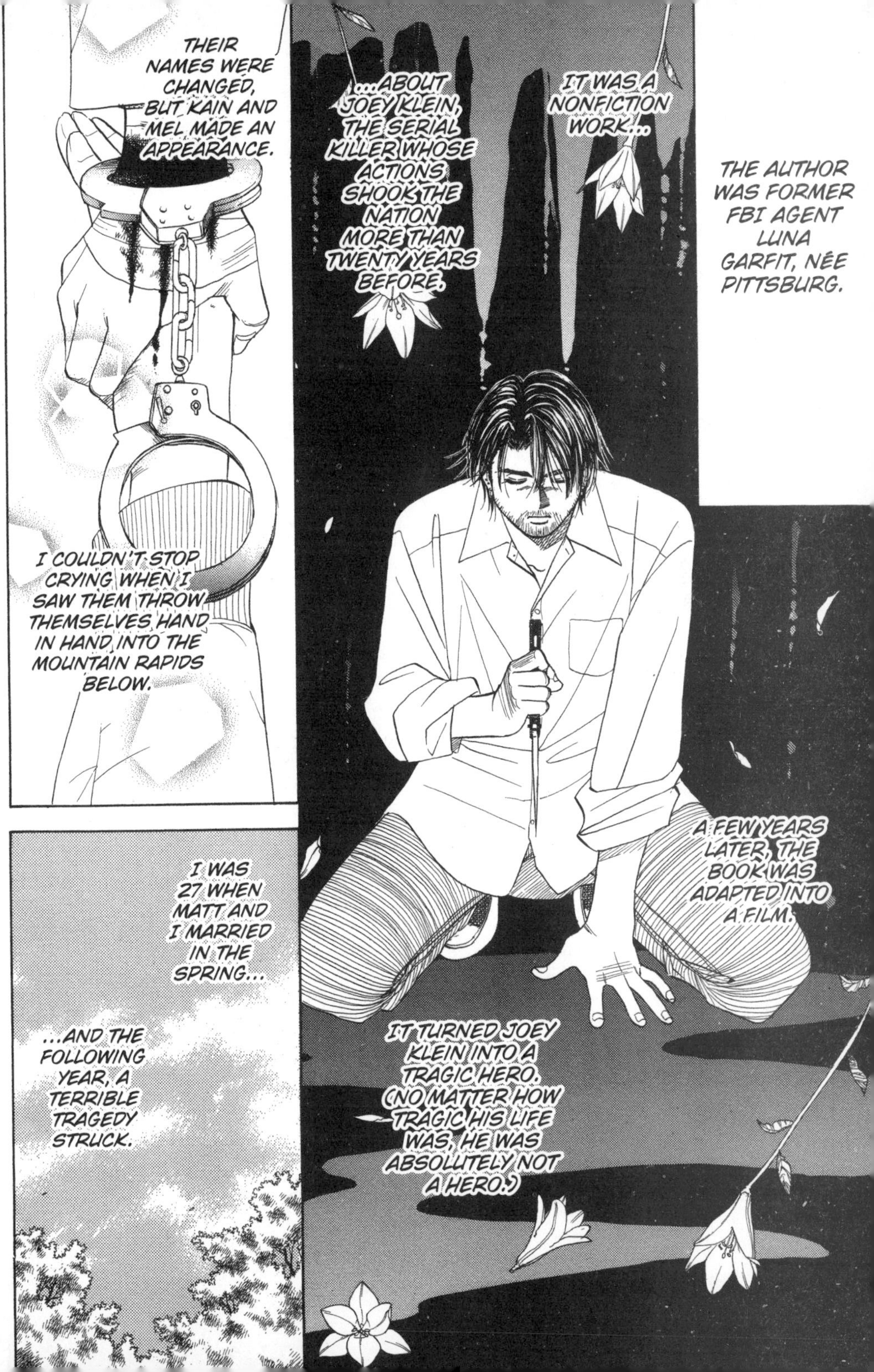
IT WAS A NONFICTION WORK...
...ABOUT JOEY KLEIN, THE SERIAL KILLER WHOSE ACTIONS SHOOK THE NATION MORE THAN TWENTY YEARS BEFORE.
THE AUTHOR WAS FORMER FBI AGENT LUNA GARFIT, NÉE PITTSBURG.
A FEW YEARS LATER, THE BOOK WAS ADAPTED INTO A FILM.
IT TURNED JOEY KLEIN INTO A TRAGIC HERO. (NO MATTER HOW TRAGIC HIS LIFE WAS, HE WAS ABSOLUTELY NOT A HERO.)
THEIR NAMES WERE CHANGED, BUT KAIN AND MEL MADE AN APPEARANCE.
I COULDN'T STOP CRYING WHEN I SAW THEM THROW THEMSELVES HAND IN HAND INTO THE MOUNTAIN RAPIDS BELOW.
I WAS 27 WHEN MATT AND I MARRIED IN THE SPRING...
...AND THE FOLLOWING YEAR, A TERRIBLE TRAGEDY STRUCK.

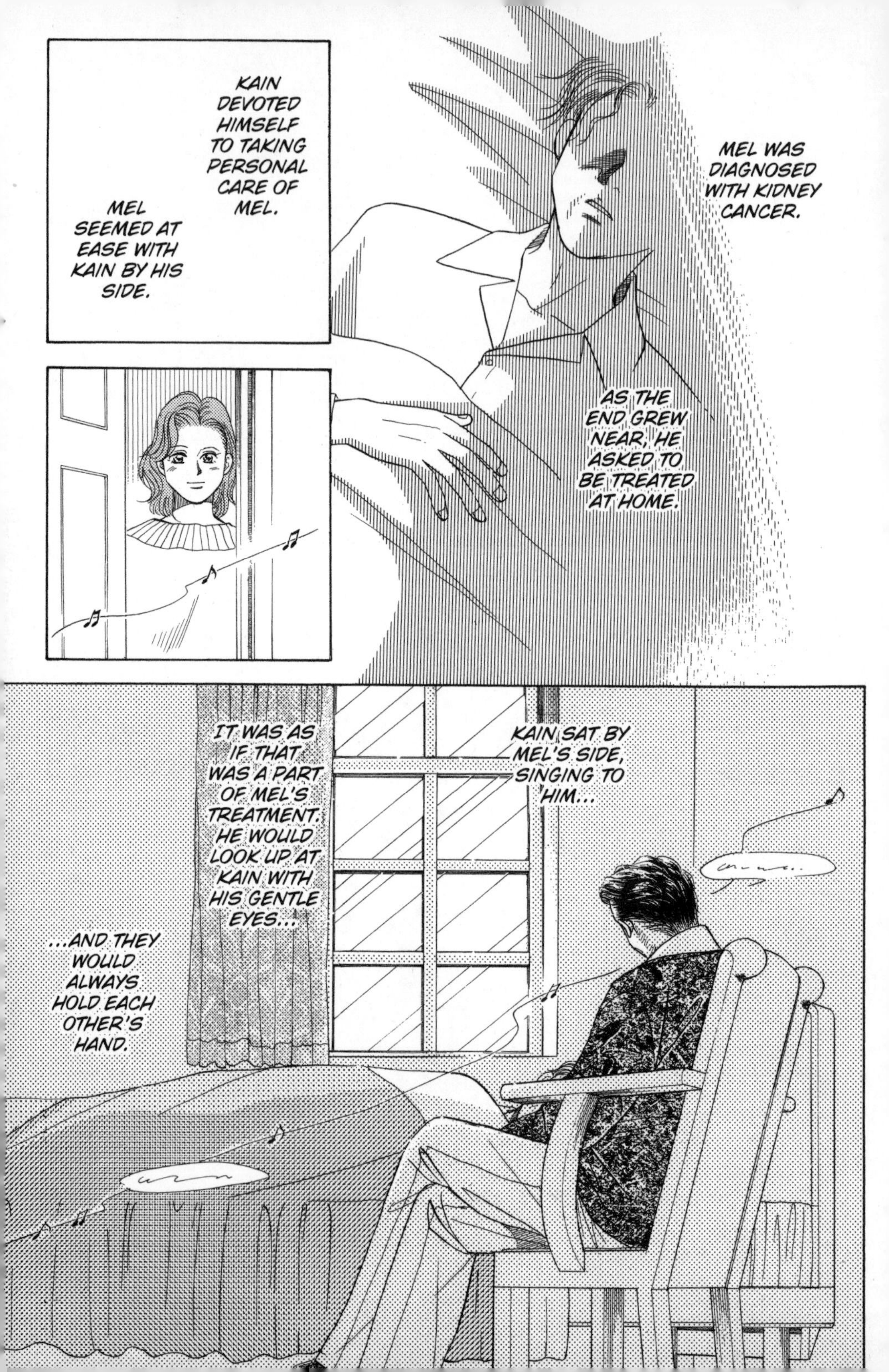
MEL WAS DIAGNOSED WITH KIDNEY CANCER.
AS THE END GREW NEAR, HE ASKED TO BE TREATED AT HOME.
KAIN DEVOTED HIMSELF TO TAKING PERSONAL CARE OF MEL.
MEL SEEMED AT EASE WITH KAIN BY HIS SIDE.
KAIN SAT BY MEL'S SIDE, SINGING TO HIM...
IT WAS AS IF THAT WAS A PART OF MEL'S TREATMENT. HE WOULD LOOK UP AT KAIN WITH HIS GENTLE EYES...
...AND THEY WOULD ALWAYS HOLD EACH OTHER'S HAND.

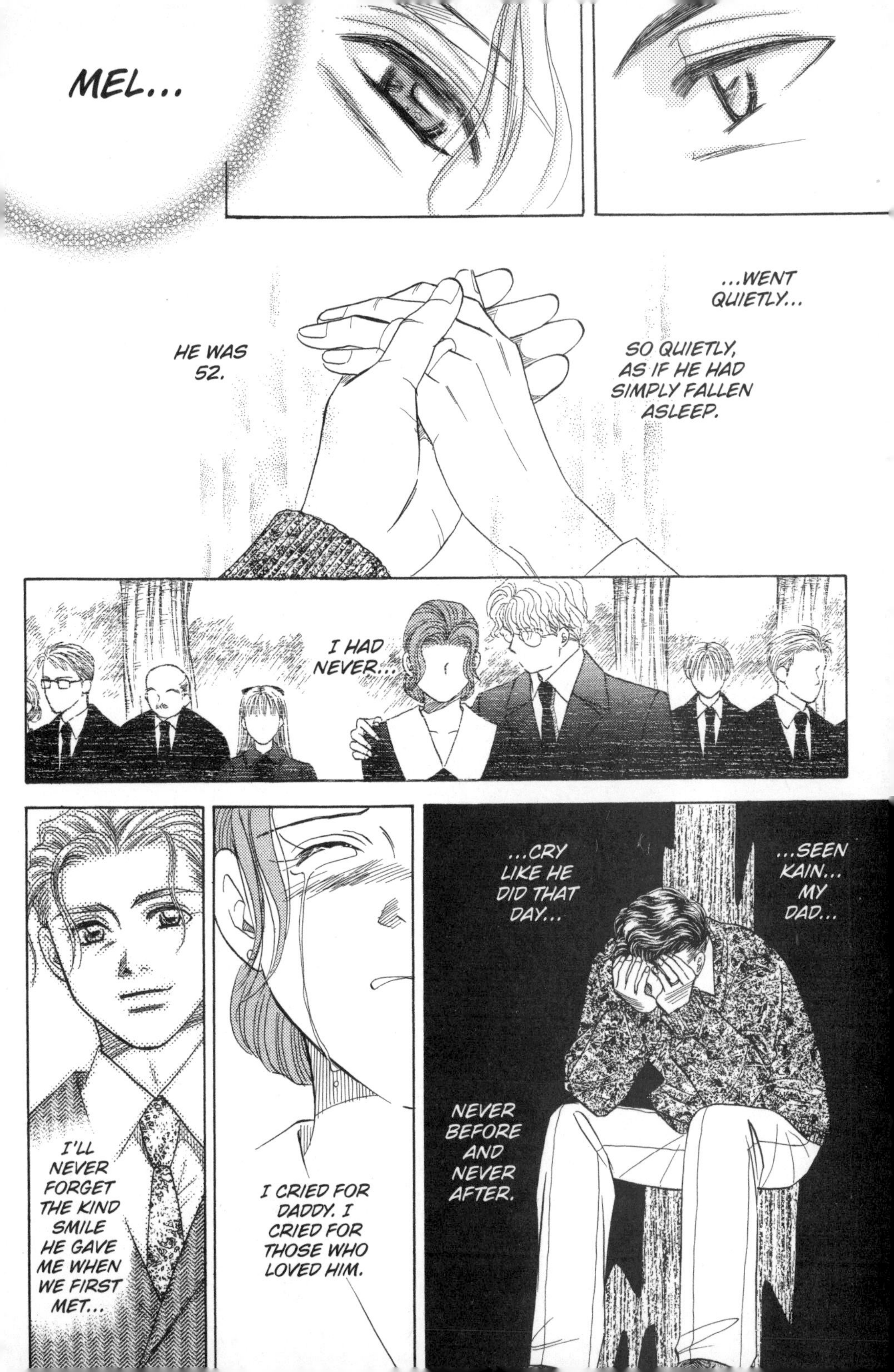
MEL...
...WENT QUIETLY...
SO QUIETLY, AS IF HE HAD SIMPLY FALLEN ASLEEP.
HE WAS 52.
I HAD NEVER...
...SEEN KAIN... MY DAD...
...CRY LIKE HE DID THAT DAY...
NEVER BEFORE AND NEVER AFTER.
I CRIED FOR DADDY. I CRIED FOR THOSE WHO LOVED HIM.
I'LL NEVER FORGET THE KIND SMILE HE GAVE ME WHEN WE FIRST MET...

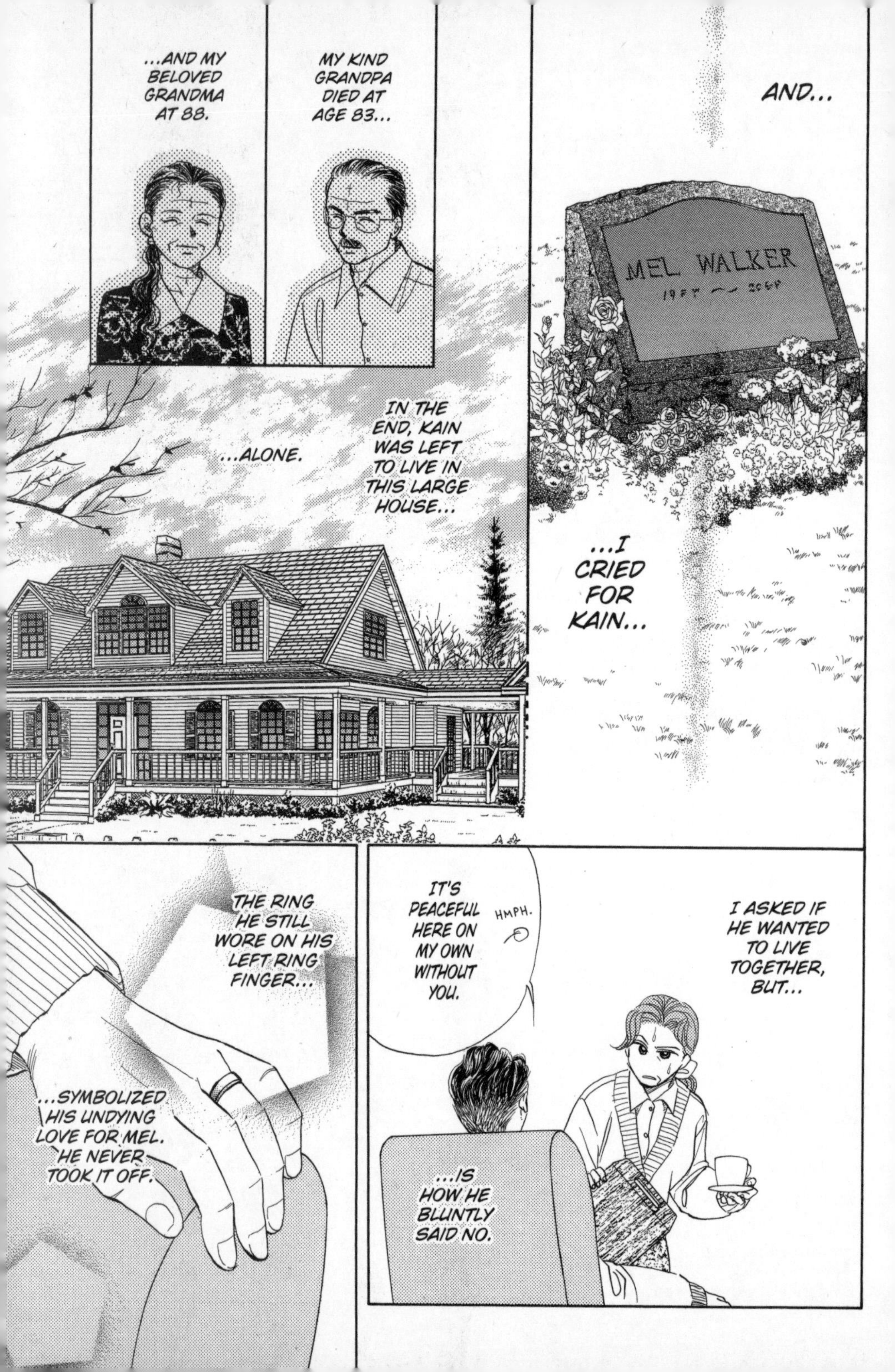
AND...
MEL WALKER
...I CRIED FOR KAIN...
MY KIND GRANDPA DIED AT AGE 83...
...AND MY BELOVED GRANDMA AT 88.
IN THE END, KAIN WAS LEFT TO LIVE IN THIS LARGE HOUSE...
...ALONE.
I ASKED IF HE WANTED TO LIVE TOGETHER, BUT...
IT'S PEACEFUL HERE ON MY OWN WITHOUT YOU.
HMPH.
...IS HOW HE BLUNTLY SAID NO.
THE RING HE STILL WORE ON HIS LEFT RING FINGER...
...SYMBOLIZED HIS UNDYING LOVE FOR MEL. HE NEVER TOOK IT OFF.

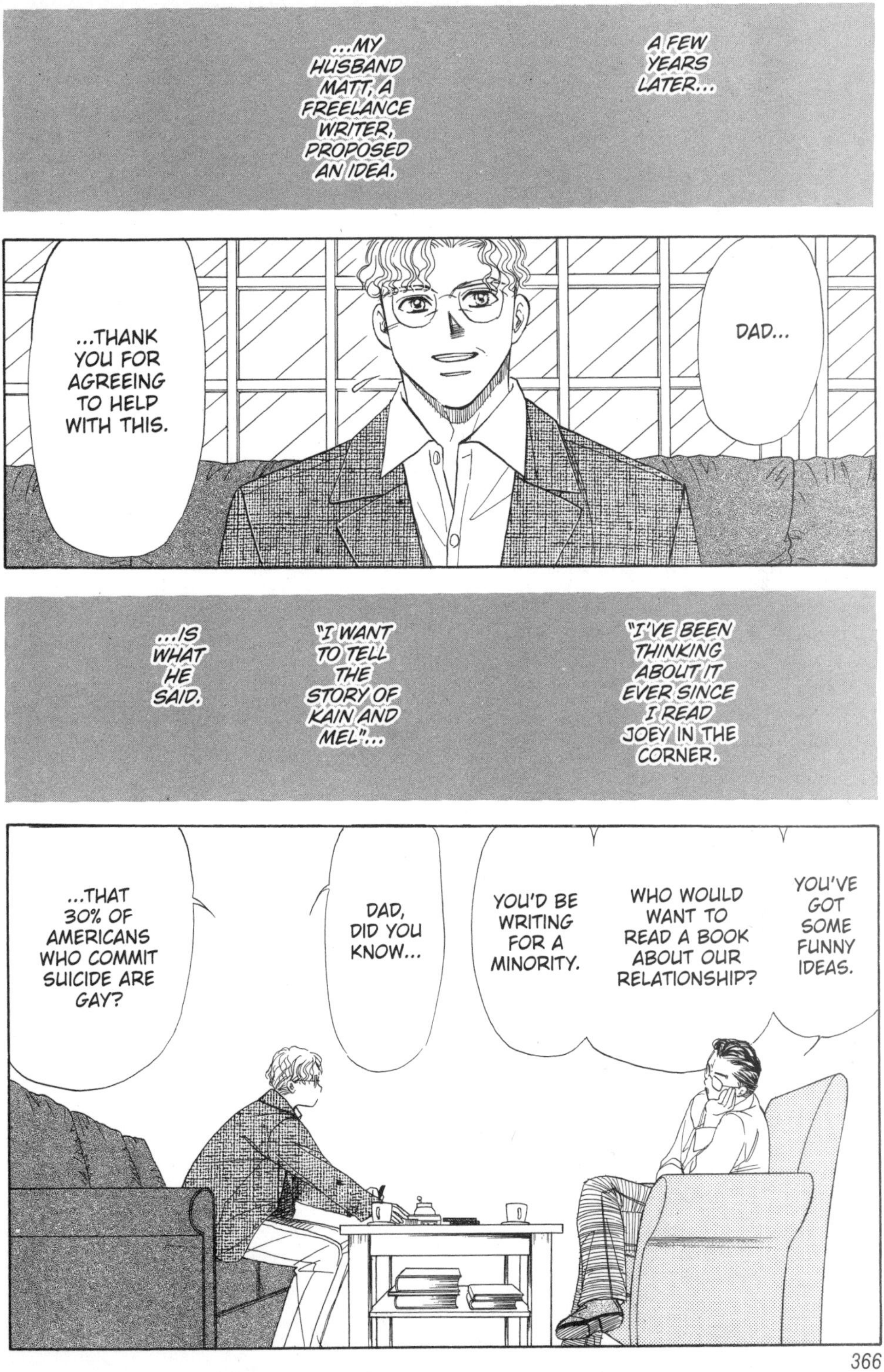
A FEW YEARS LATER...
...MY HUSBAND MATT, A FREELANCE WRITER, PROPOSED AN IDEA.
DAD...
...THANK YOU FOR AGREEING TO HELP WITH THIS.
"I'VE BEEN THINKING ABOUT IT EVER SINCE I READ JOEY IN THE CORNER.
"I WANT TO TELL THE STORY OF KAIN AND MEL"...
...IS WHAT HE SAID.
YOU'VE GOT SOME FUNNY IDEAS.
WHO WOULD WANT TO READ A BOOK ABOUT OUR RELATIONSHIP?
YOU'D BE WRITING FOR A MINORITY.
DAD, DID YOU KNOW...
...THAT 30% OF AMERICANS WHO COMMIT SUICIDE ARE GAY?

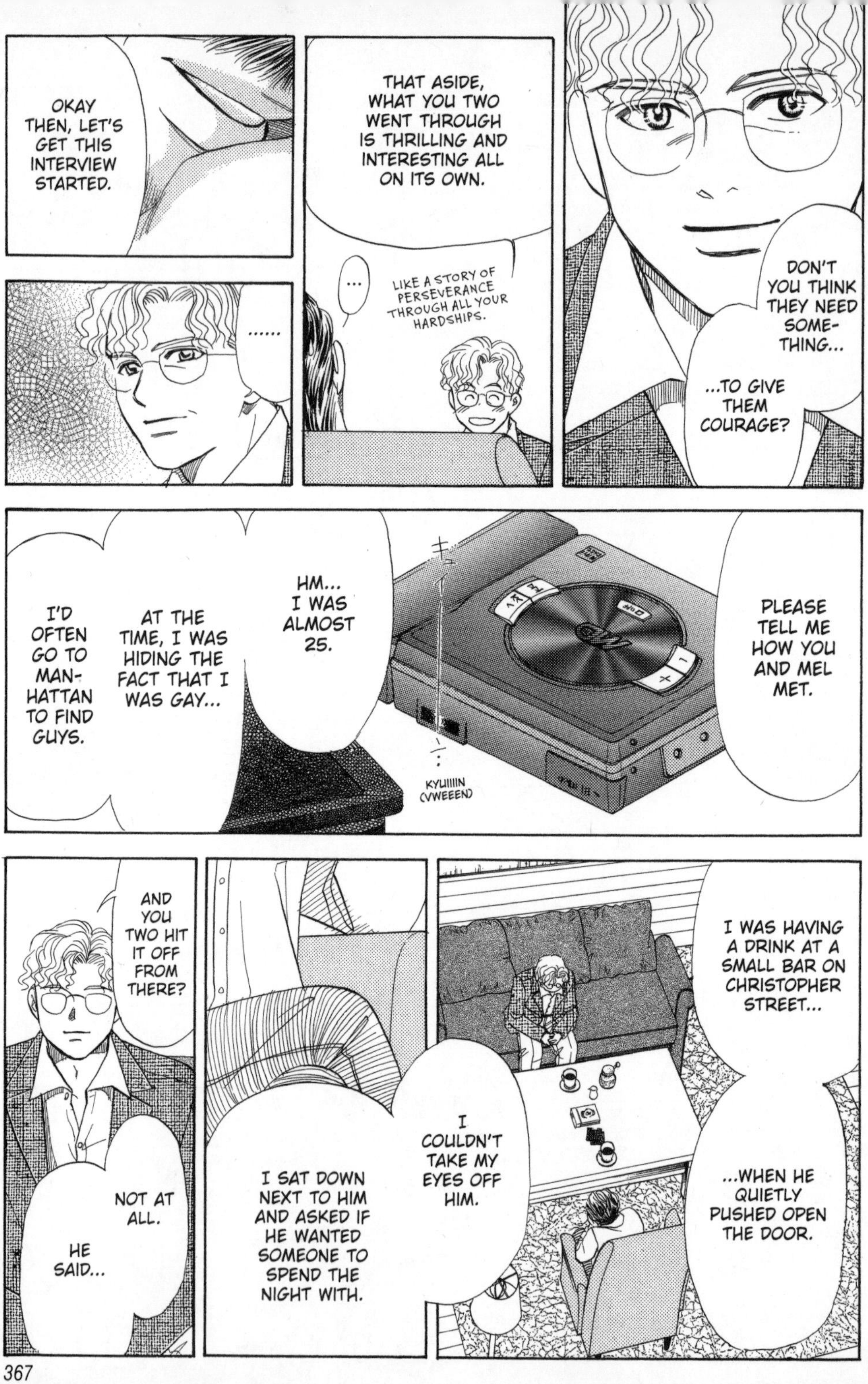
DON'T YOU THINK THEY NEED SOME-THING...
...TO GIVE THEM COURAGE?
THAT ASIDE, WHAT YOU TWO WENT THROUGH IS THRILLING AND INTERESTING ALL ON ITS OWN.
OKAY THEN, LET'S GET THIS INTERVIEW STARTED.
...
LIKE A STORY OF PERSEVERANCE THROUGH ALL YOUR HARDSHIPS.
......
PLEASE TELL ME HOW YOU AND MEL MET.
KYUIIIIN (VWEEEND)
HM... I WAS ALMOST 25.
AT THE TIME, I WAS HIDING THE FACT THAT I WAS GAY...
I'D OFTEN GO TO MAN-HATTAN TO FIND GUYS.
I WAS HAVING A DRINK AT A SMALL BAR ON CHRISTOPHER STREET...
...WHEN HE QUIETLY PUSHED OPEN THE DOOR.
I COULDN'T TAKE MY EYES OFF HIM.
I SAT DOWN NEXT TO HIM AND ASKED IF HE WANTED SOMEONE TO SPEND THE NIGHT WITH.
AND YOU TWO HIT IT OFF FROM THERE?
NOT AT ALL.
HE SAID...

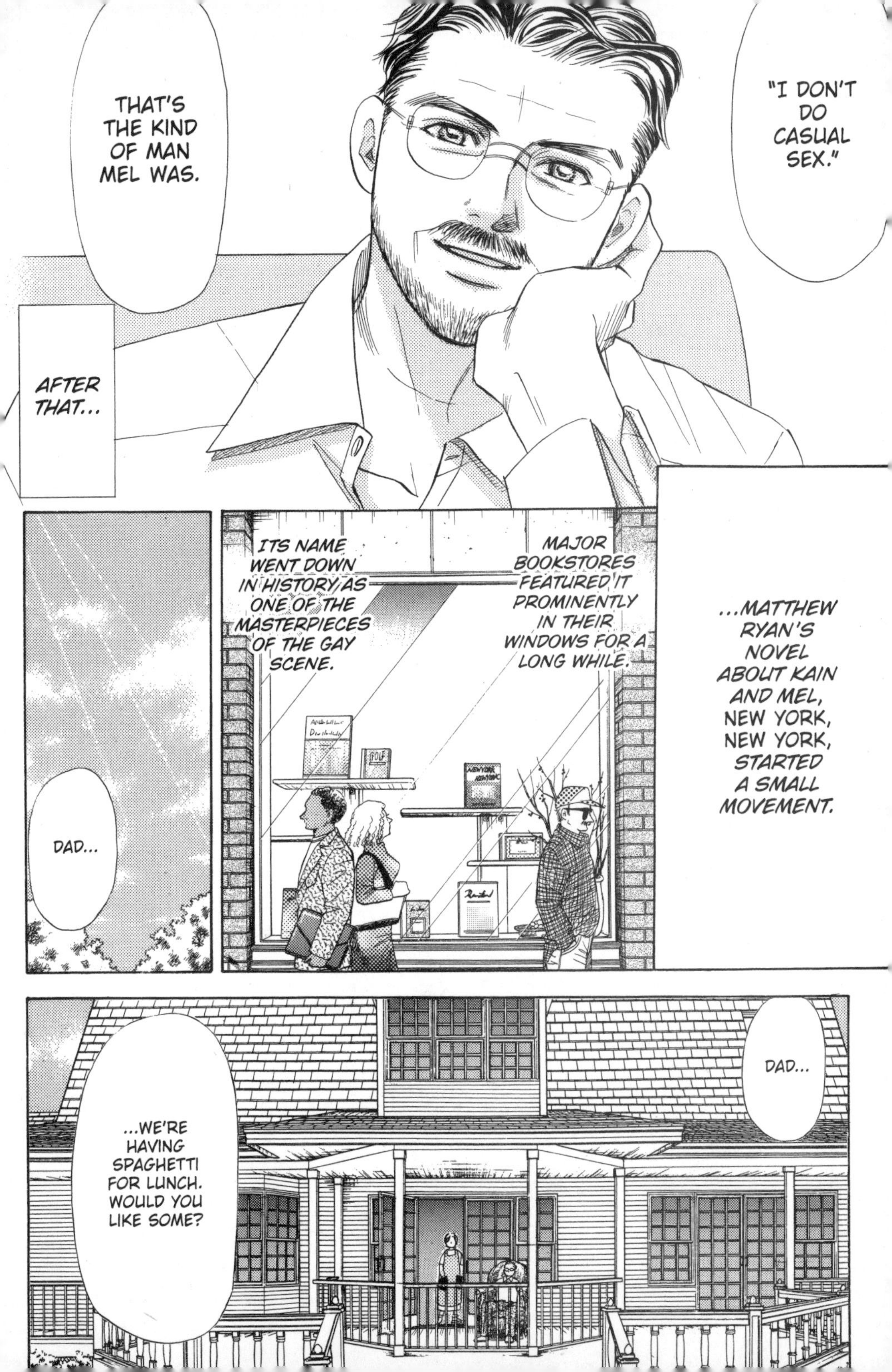
"I DON'T DO CASUAL SEX."
THAT'S THE KIND OF MAN MEL WAS.
AFTER THAT...
...MATTHEW RYAN'S NOVEL ABOUT KAIN AND MEL, NEW YORK, NEW YORK, STARTED A SMALL MOVEMENT.
MAJOR BOOKSTORES FEATURED IT PROMINENTLY IN THEIR WINDOWS FOR A LONG WHILE.
ITS NAME WENT DOWN IN HISTORY AS ONE OF THE MASTERPIECES OF THE GAY SCENE.
DAD...
DAD...
...WE'RE HAVING SPAGHETTI FOR LUNCH. WOULD YOU LIKE SOME?

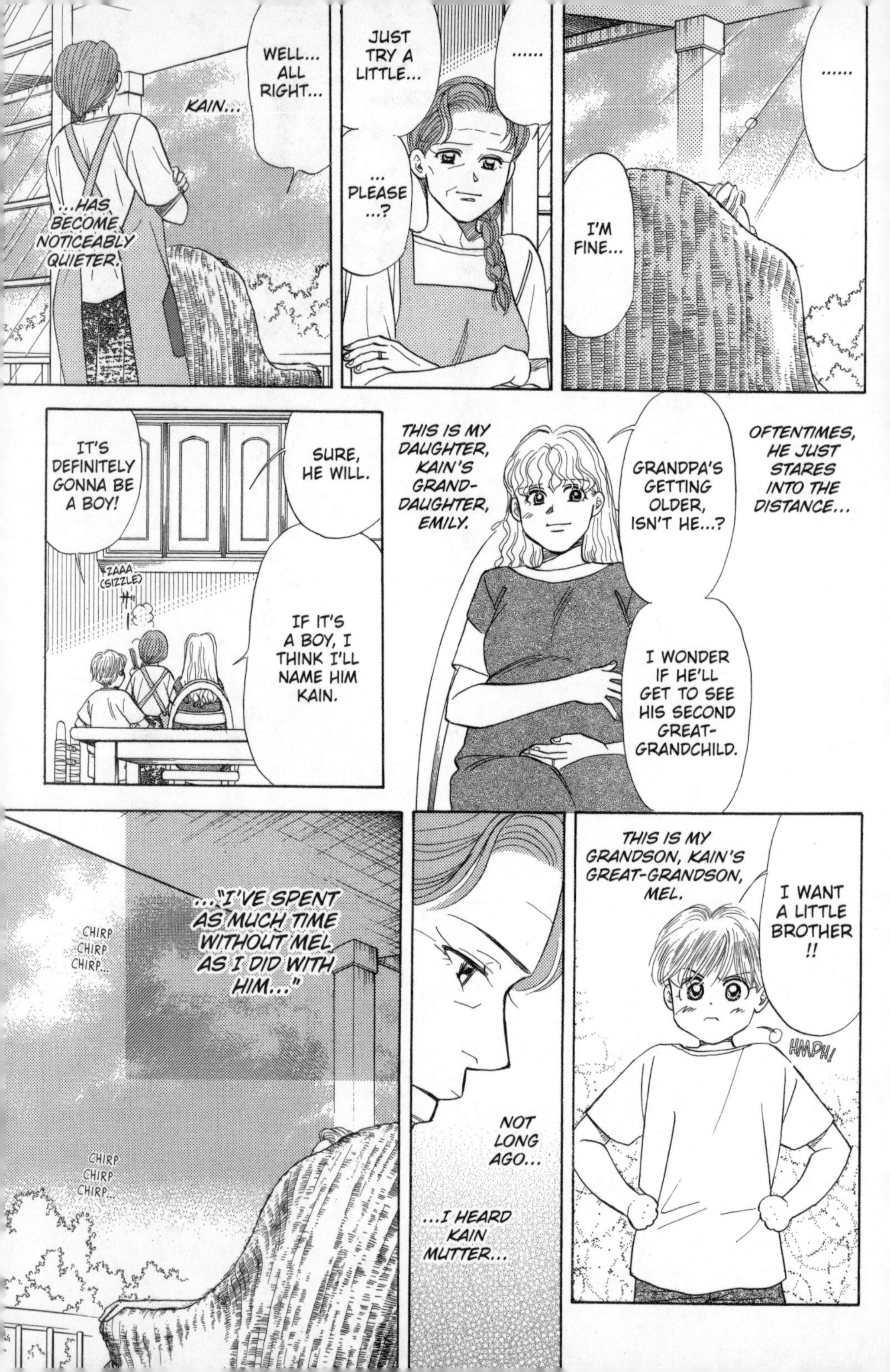
......
I'M FINE...
......
JUST TRY A LITTLE...
... PLEASE ...?
WELL... ALL RIGHT...
KAIN...
...HAS BECOME NOTICEABLY QUIETER.
OFTENTIMES, HE JUST STARES INTO THE DISTANCE...
GRANDPA'S GETTING OLDER, ISN'T HE...?
THIS IS MY DAUGHTER, KAIN'S GRAND-DAUGHTER, EMILY.
I WONDER IF HE'LL GET TO SEE HIS SECOND GREAT-GRANDCHILD.
SURE, HE WILL.
IT'S DEFINITELY GONNA BE A BOY!
IF IT'S A BOY, I THINK I'LL NAME HIM KAIN.
ZAAA (SIZZLE)
I WANT A LITTLE BROTHER !!
THIS IS MY GRANDSON, KAIN'S GREAT-GRANDSON, MEL.
HMPH!
NOT LONG AGO...
...I HEARD KAIN MUTTER...
..."I'VE SPENT AS MUCH TIME WITHOUT MEL AS I DID WITH HIM..."
CHIRP CHIRP CHIRP...
CHIRP CHIRP CHIRP...

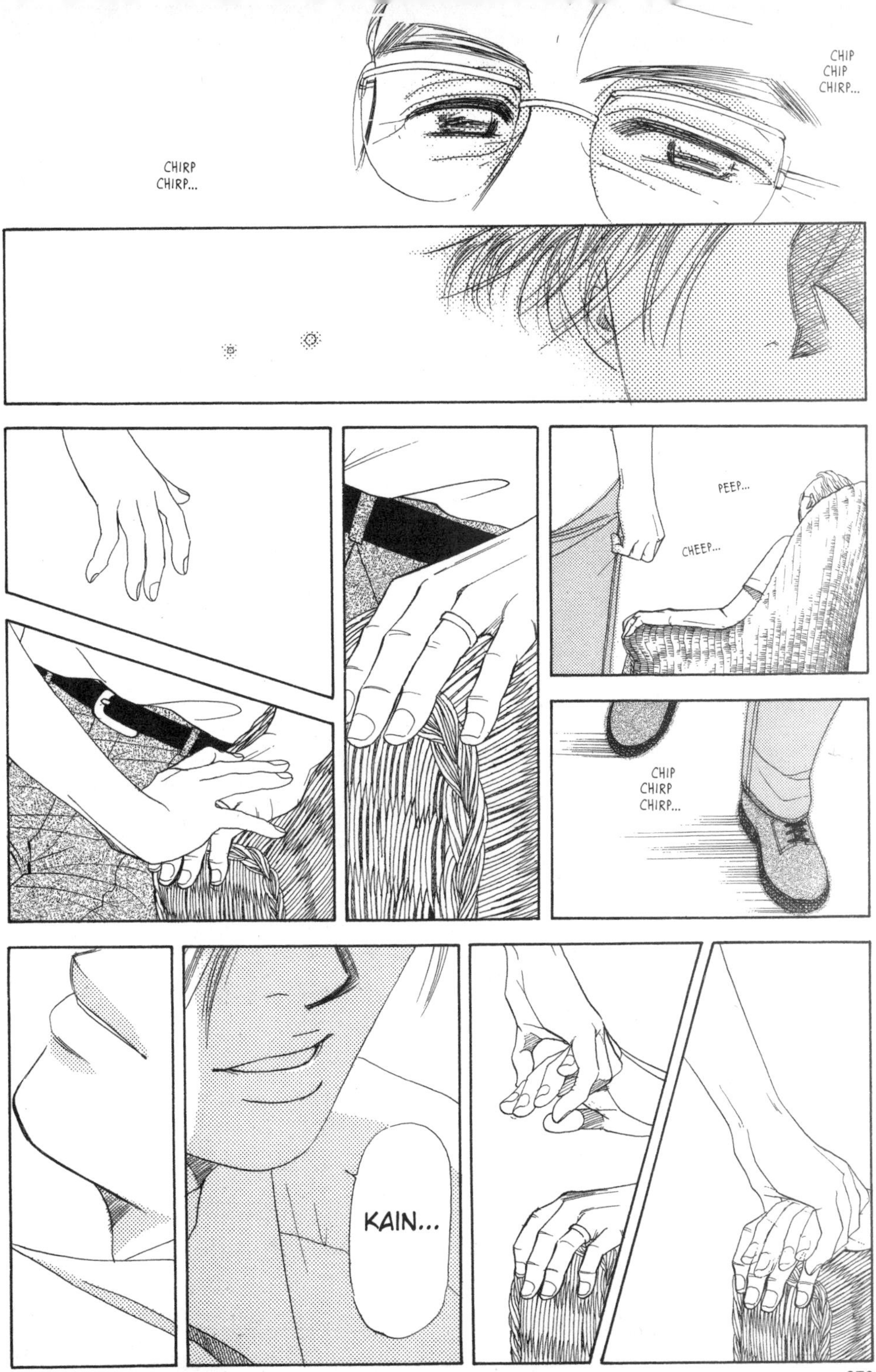
CHIP CHIP CHIRP...
CHIRP CHIRP...
PEEP...
CHEEP...
CHIP CHIRP CHIRP...
KAIN...

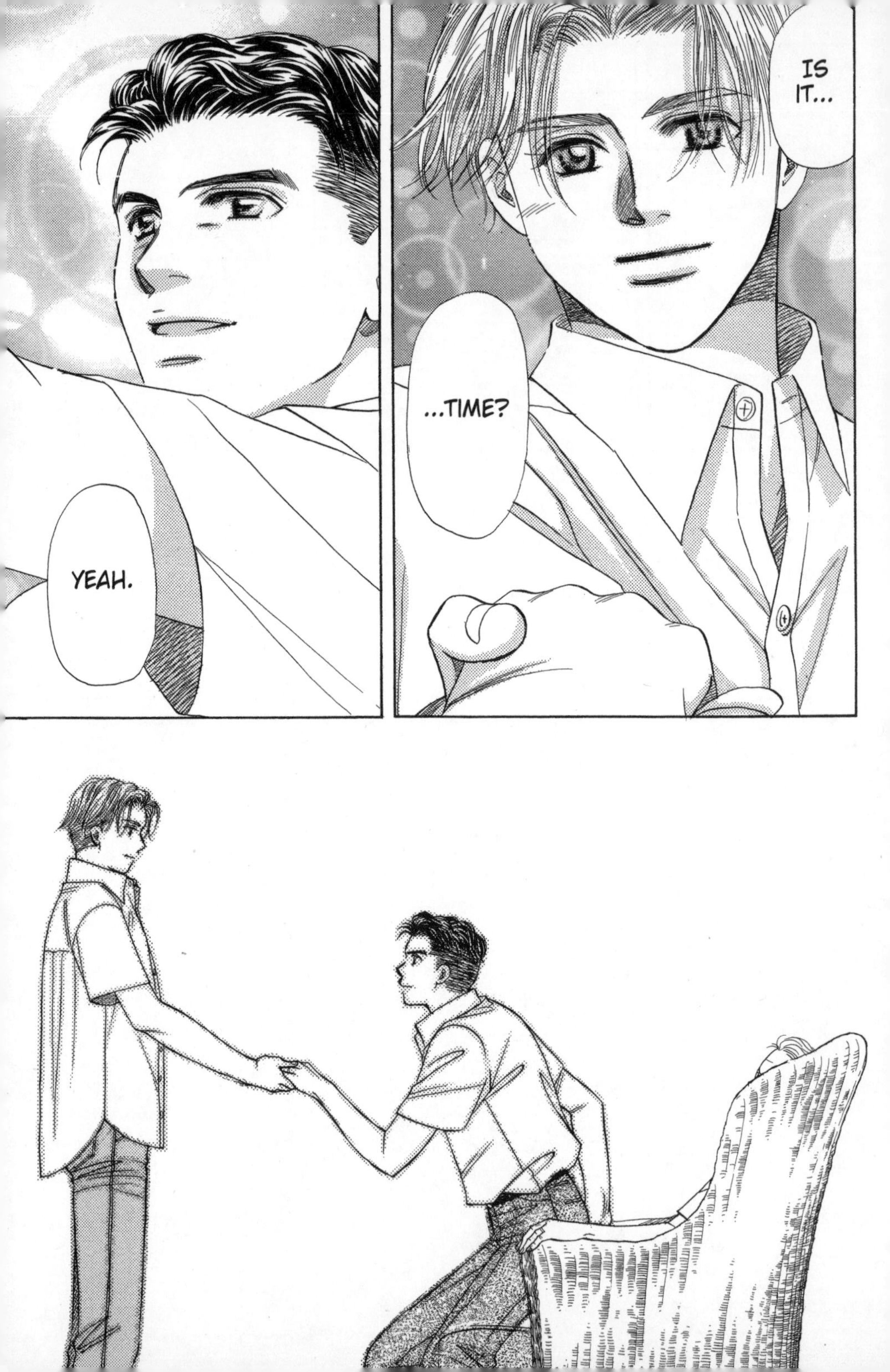
IS IT...
...TIME?
YEAH.

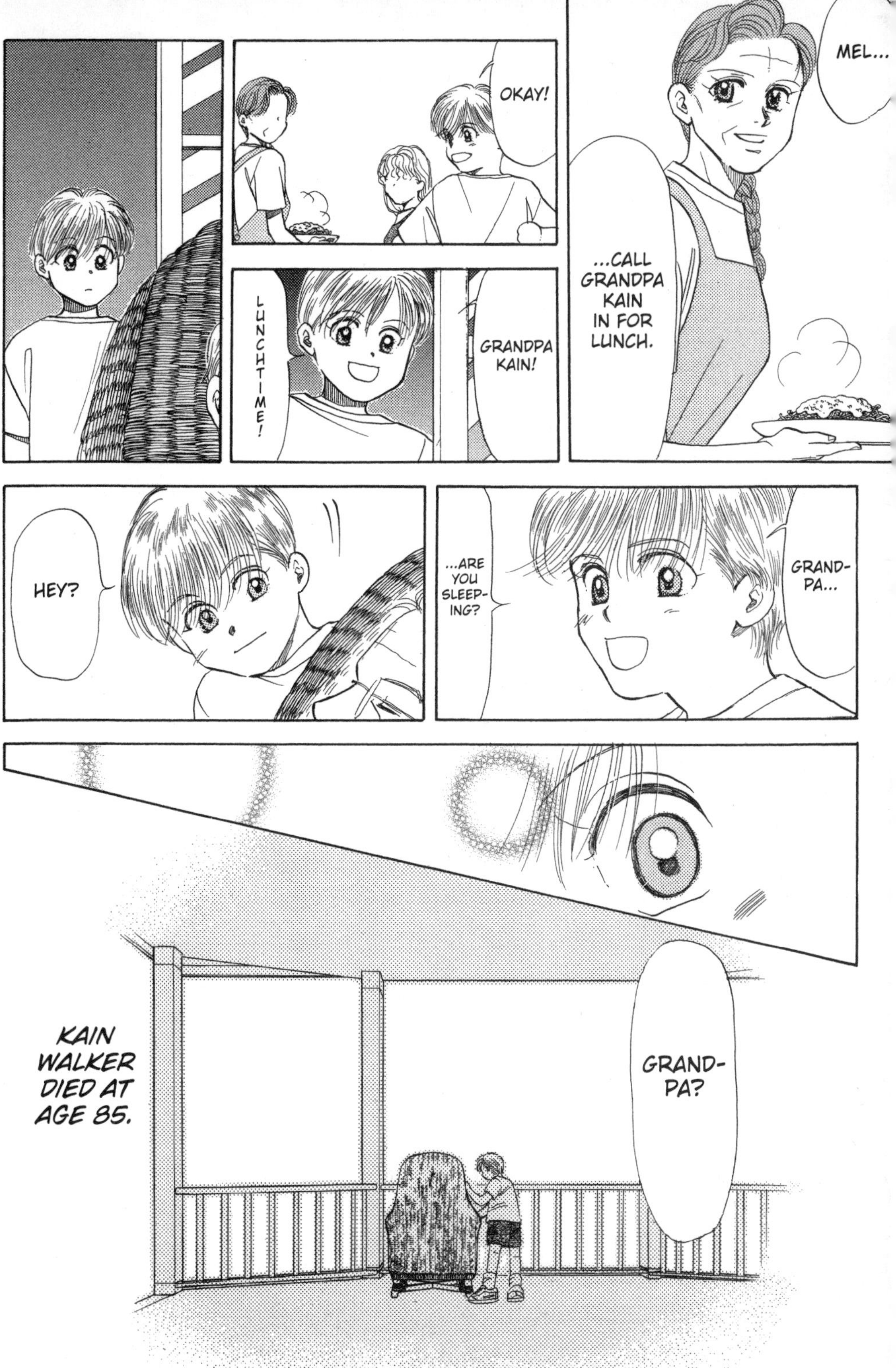
MEL...
...CALL GRANDPA KAIN IN FOR LUNCH.
OKAY!
GRANDPA KAIN!
LUNCHTIME!
GRAND-PA...
...ARE YOU SLEEPING?
HEY?
GRAND-PA?
KAIN WALKER DIED AT AGE 85.

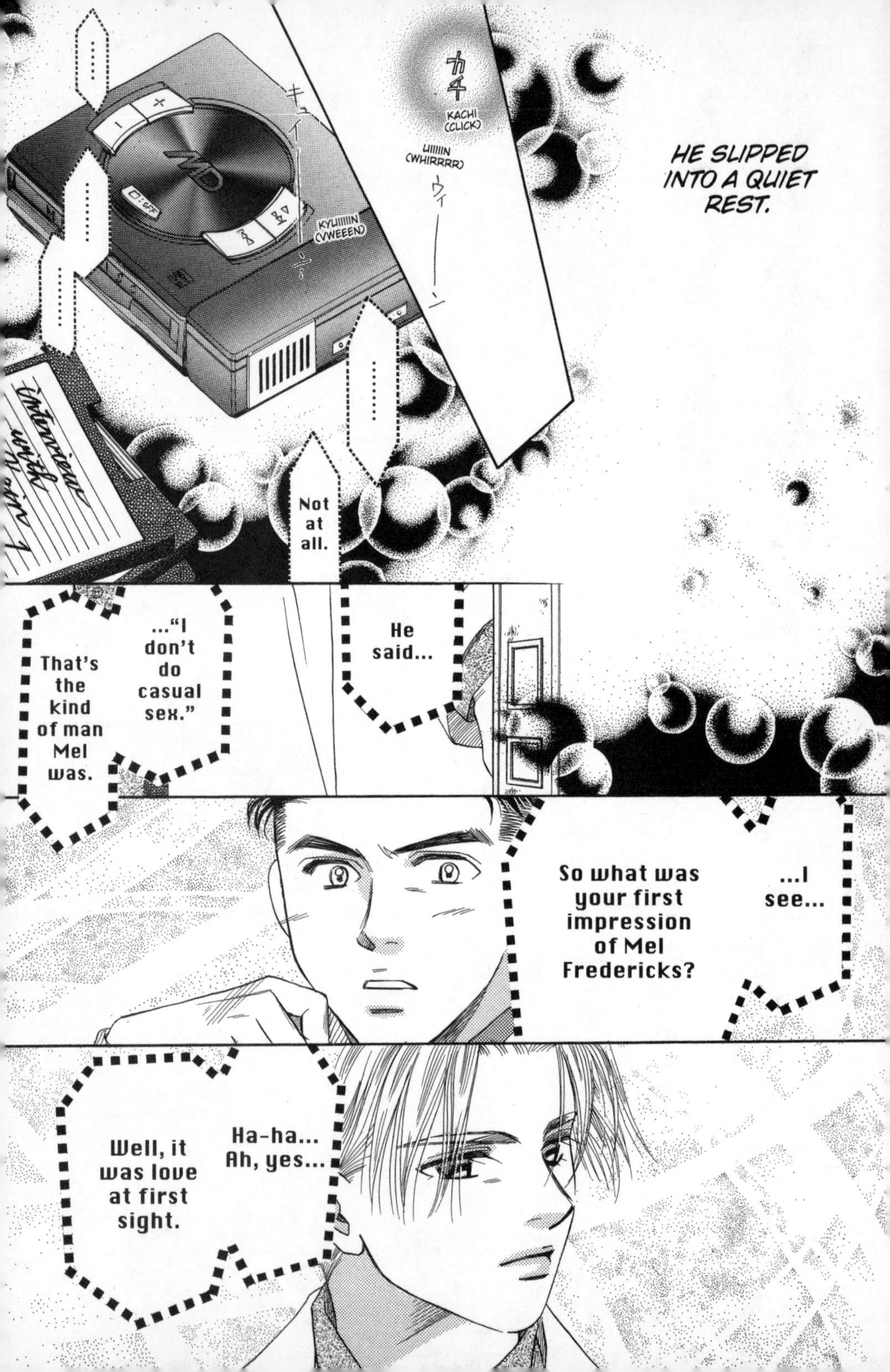
HE SLIPPED INTO A QUIET REST.
カチ
KACHI (CLICK)
ウィー
UIIIIN (WHIRRRR)
キュイーン
KYUIIIIN (VWEEEN)
......
Not at all.
......
......
......
He said...
..."I don't do casual sex."
That's the kind of man Mel was.
...I see...
So what was your first impression of Mel Fredericks?
Ha-ha... Ah, yes...
Well, it was love at first sight.

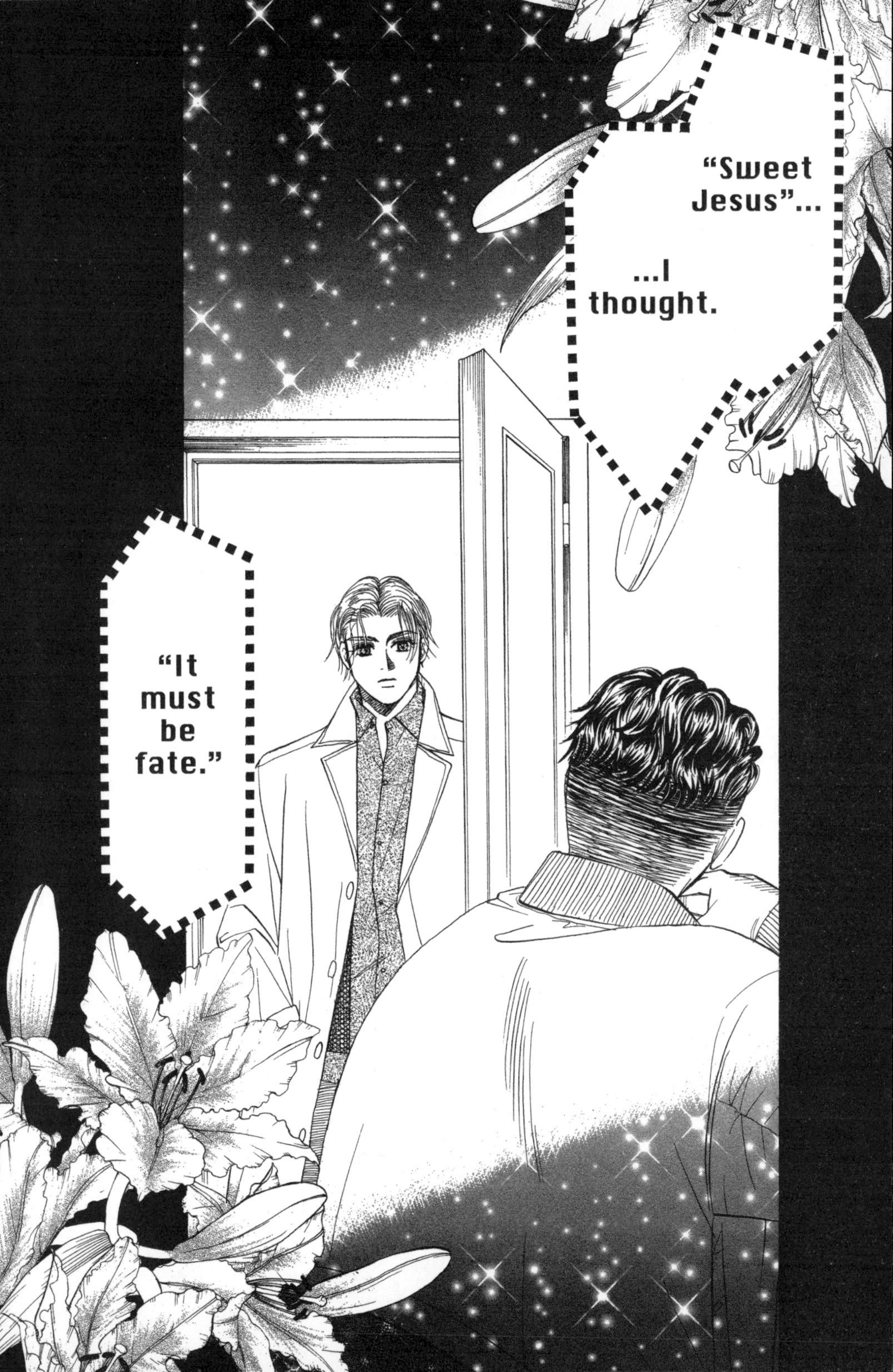
"Sweet Jesus"...
...I thought.
"It must be fate."

NEW YORK, NEW YORK 2 · END

NEW
YORK,
New York'

NEW
YORK,
New York'

**TURN TO THE
BACK OF THE BOOK TO
SEE EXTRAS FOR
NEW YORK, NEW YORK
FROM MARIMO RAGAWA**

NEW YORK, *New York,*

NEW YORK, New York' 2

Marimo Ragawa

Translation:
Preston Johnson-Chonkar

Retouch: Lys Blakeslee

Lettering: Abigail Blackman

Library of Congress Control Number: 2021943180

ISBNs: 978-1-9753-3814-5
(paperback)
978-1-9753-3815-2
(ebook)

10 9 8 7 6 5 4 3 2 1

WOR

Printed in the United States of America

NEW YORK, NEW YORK by Marimo Ragawa
©Marimo Ragawa 2003
All rights reserved.
First published in Japan in 2003 by HAKUSENSHA, INC., Tokyo.
English translation rights in U.S.A., Canada and U.K. arranged with HAKUSENSHA, INC., Tokyo through TUTTLE-MORI AGENCY, INC., Tokyo.

English translation © 2022 by Yen Press, LLC

Yen Press
150 West 30th Street, 19th Floor
New York, NY 10001

Visit us at yenpress.com
facebook.com/yenpress
twitter.com/yenpress
yenpress.tumblr.com
instagram.com/yenpress

First Yen Press Edition: July 2022
Edited by Yen Press Editorial: Carl Li
Designed by Yen Press Design: Andy Swist

LOVER	PAGE / PANEL	ACTION/DIALOGUE	NOTES
Mel's Third Lover Name, Age, Occupation: Unknown	Volume 1 Page 55 Panel 2	Mel talks about his previous relationships. "And there was one...that only lasted two weeks..."	Seems like they had a problem.
	Volume 1 Page 182 Panel 7	"You know how Mel doesn't like rough sex...? Well, he's kind of afraid of it."	IMPORTANT!! This has to do with why they broke up.

Marimo's Headcanon

His name is Alan. After Mel leaves Manhattan, he finds work at a jeans factory in the Bronx, which is where they meet. Alan falls in love with Mel at first sight, but it's completely one-sided. In the beginning, having just broken up with Youichi, Mel is still emotionally wounded, and he rebuffs Alan's advances. However, unlike Mel's exes, Alan is a passionate man who isn't afraid to be openly gay. He doesn't hesitate to confess his feelings to Mel or hug him in front of other people. Gradually, Mel yields to his affection and begins to open up. They break up two weeks after they become intimate due to sexual incompatibility. Alan is a sadist. He suppresses it at first, but eventually he can't hold himself back anymore. Given Mel's experiences with his foster father and as a male prostitute, he fears rough sex and has legitimate reasons for not wanting to be intimate with Alan like that. Alan pleads with Mel, begging him to try rough sex "just once." Seeing Alan's struggle, Mel agrees. But a few days later, Mel is shocked to find a leather suit in Alan's closet. The discovery suggests Alan must have stopped at one of *those stores* to buy it. The two of them get into an argument.

In Volume 1, page 293, panel 4, Alan is the one who says, "'Normally'!? What the hell is that supposed to mean!? You don't think it's normal for someone like me to do this?" With tears in his eyes, Mel starts to leave, but Alan, also crying, clings to him and says, "Please...I just want you. Not anyone else. You're the only one I love." Mel silently shakes his head and leaves. This is the first time Mel breaks off a relationship.

For whatever reason, it seems Mel is easily convinced to go along with what others want. He's a bit of a pushover...

Mel's Fourth Lover	You already know all about Josh, so I'll keep this brief.

Marimo's Headcanon

Josh Bronson, 26 at the time, is a model. Mel works part-time at a photo studio, and the two meet when Josh comes in for a shoot. Josh flirts with Mel, puts the moves on him, and makes Mel fall for him that same day. They move in together, but Josh is very unfaithful. He's generally easygoing, but there are times when he gets oversensitive. See Volume 1 for all the details!!

LOVER	PG. / PAN.	ACTION/DIALOGUE	NOTES
Mel's Second Lover Name, Age, Occupation: Unknown	Volume 1 Page 53	Kain returns to find Mel asleep, an origami crane on the table next to him. "...What's this? A bird?" "It's...a crane...I learned it from a Japanese guy..." "Another one of your exes...right?"	Jealous, Kain says this teasingly, but it's pretty cutting and is right on the money.
	Volume 1 Page 293 Panel 4	"You're just scared! Say it! Say, 'I'm gay!' Denying it only makes it hurt more."	**IMPORTANT!!** Mel's saying this to Kain.

Marimo's Headcanon

Youichi Iijima is a Japanese exchange student. He takes a part-time job at the restaurant where Mel is also working part-time, and that's how the two meet. At the time, Mel is 19 and Youichi is 21. Youichi is clumsy and often makes mistakes, leaving him discouraged. Mel covers for him, helps him out, and consoles him.

In the beginning, Youichi finds Mel's fair skin, blond hair, and blue eyes so beautiful that it makes him hesitate and draw back, but as time goes on, he gradually starts to open up. Youichi struggles with the pronunciations of r's and l's, b's and v's, and "th" sounds, and he learns English from Mel. Through all this, they become intimate and have sex. They start living together, but like Phil, Youichi doesn't want to admit that he's gay. Even during his parents' frequent calls from Japan, Youichi lies to them to keep up appearances. Mel begins mentally preparing himself to not have a future with Youichi. A few months later, they're forced to part ways. As Youichi feared, when he indirectly mentions Mel to his parents to test the waters, they demand that he return to Japan. Half-coerced, half-compliant, he obeys. Weak-willed, he believes his father when he says, "That man has seduced you. You're just sick."

"You can have all the stuff I'm leaving here. I'll let you know when things calm down," Youichi says, suitcase in hand, as he prepares to make his abrupt return to Japan. He and Mel argue on his way out. In the end, Youichi still chooses to go back to Japan, and Mel leaves all of Youichi's belongings in the room as he leaves their place behind him.

This part of his past is why Mel fears when people lie about their feelings or hide their lovers from their families. It's why he fears Kain's parents are going to hate him.

LOVER	PAGE / PANEL	ACTION/DIALOGUE	NOTES
Mel's First Lover Name: ? Age: 50s or 60s Occupation: college professor	Volume 1 Page 45	A chance encounter at the downtown bookstore.	His expression shows he hasn't seen Mel since the breakup.
	Volume 1 Page 46	"You haven't changed at all...All these books..." "That's because...these are my only joy in life."	Mel's a bookworm.
	Volume 1 Pages 47, 48	"I used to live without any regard for my own safety, and he saved me. So...I love him, but...it's not the kind of love you have for a partner...He has a wife and kids who he loves..." "When the time came for him to choose, he abandoned me without a second thought!"	**IMPORTANT!!** On page 186 of volume 1, Josh mentions Mel was a streetwalker, which is related to the note below. ↓
	Volume 1 Page 291 Panel 3	"Get out!! You filthy whore!! How could he have even called you his lover!?"	His wife is the woman who said this.

Marimo's Headcanon

Phil is a professor at a college in Manhattan, NY. He is not openly gay. One day, he buys Mel's services and finds himself falling in love with him. Incidentally, in Volume 1, page 293, panel 4, Phil is the one who says, "You can't go on like this. I want to help you...Isn't that what we call love?" and asks, "Want to move in together?" Phil has a wife, but he spends much of his time in his apartment on the west side of Manhattan that serves as his office-cum-library. He lets Mel live there. Their relationship was like that of student and teacher. More than "love," I think Mel felt a sense of "respect" for Phil. As you know, Mel's mother died in Central Park. After that, Mel couldn't even bear to go near the place, but Phil gives Mel the support he needs. The two go there together, and Mel faces his past head-on. He and Phil pass their days in their shared living space. Most of the time, Phil sits at his desk reading books, writing documents, and going through reports. Eventually, Phil's wife notices that Phil is spending a lot of time at his apartment, gets suspicious, and hires a private detective to investigate. Phil's relationship with his wife had been growing colder anyway, and when his wife finds out about Mel, she angrily bursts into the apartment, screaming and insulting Mel before slapping him in the face. She demands that Phil return to their home. Phil, his heart heavy, walks out the door, leaving Mel behind. All alone, Mel flees the apartment, and when Phil comes back the next day, Mel is nowhere to be seen. This is why on page 41 of Volume 1, Mel says, "A wife and kids? I hate when things are like that... Everyone gets hurt..." It's truly terrible.

NEW YORK, NEW YORK EXTRAS!!

SPECIAL BACKSTORY

"What kind of 'Special Backstory'?" you may wonder. Well, as I've brought the story to its conclusion, I think it's high time I shared the details of Mel's past lovers.

People have told me I should draw a manga about Mel's past. Unfortunately, his past is a series of tragedies, one after another. It would not be a fun manga to read, so I've decided to spill all the details like this instead. Some of it has been hinted at already, so we can use that as a jumping-off point.

I hope that when reading this, you'll think, "Oh, so that's why Mel said that." Or, "So that's what made him so timid." I hope this gives you a much deeper understanding of Mel's character.

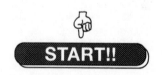

START!!

Mel's Past Lovers	Volume 1 Pages 54, 55	"I've had...five relationships...including you... But none ever lasted longer than two years..."

So, excluding Kain, four people.

NEW YORK, NEW YORK EXTRAS!!

MARIMO RAGAWA

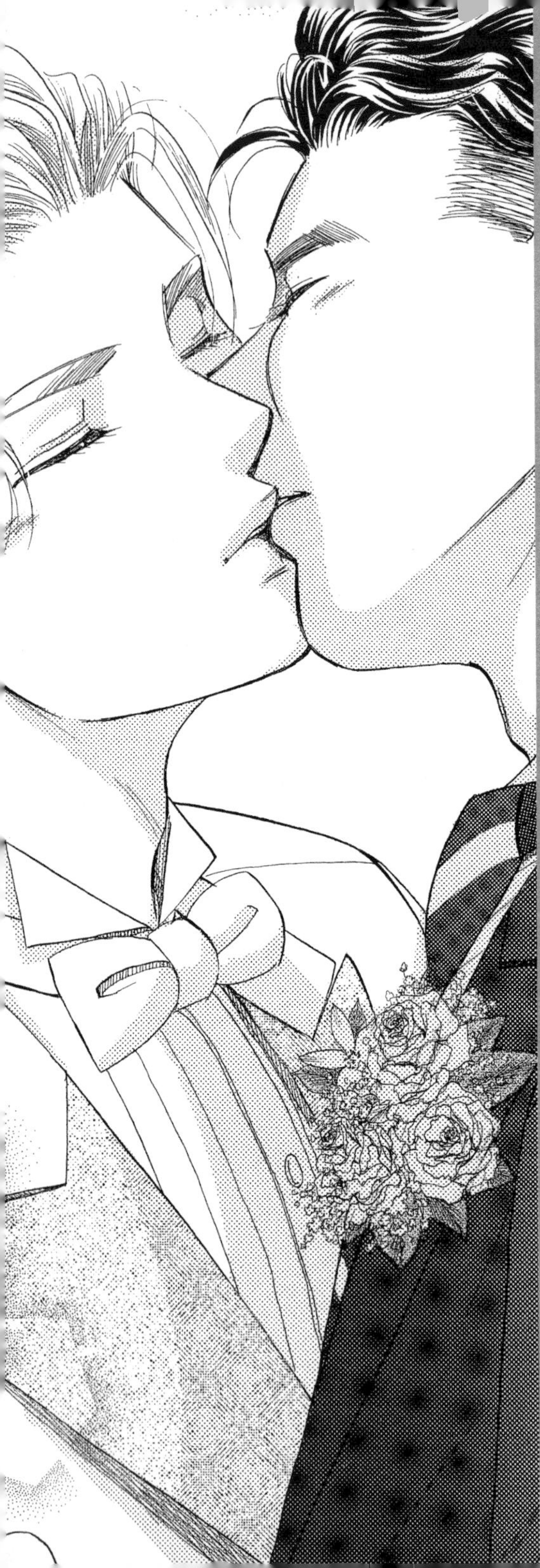

CONTENTS

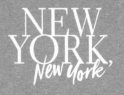

NEW YORK, New York

Marimo Ragawa

NEW YORK, *New York*

2/2

Marimo Ragawa